Also by Dan T. Carter

The Adaptable South (co-editor)
*When the War Was Over: The Failure of Self-Reconstruction in the South,
 1886–1867*
Southern Women in the Educational Movement of the South (co-editor)
Scottsboro: A Tragedy of the American South

The POLITICS of RAGE

GEORGE WALLACE, THE ORIGINS
OF THE NEW CONSERVATISM,
AND THE TRANSFORMATION OF
AMERICAN POLITICS

Dan T. Carter

SIMON & SCHUSTER
New York London Toronto Sydney Tokyo Singapore

SIMON & SCHUSTER
Rockefeller Center
1230 Avenue of the Americas
New York, NY 10020

SIMON & SCHUSTER and colophon are registered trademarks
of Simon & Schuster Inc.

Designed by Irving Perkins Associates

Manufactured in the United States of America

10 9 8 7 6 5 4 3 2 1

Library of Congress Cataloging-in-Publication Data

Carter, Dan T.
    The politics of rage : George Wallace, the origins of the new
conservatism, and the transformation of American politics / Dan T.
Carter.
        p.   cm.
    Includes bibliographical references and index.
    1. Wallace, George C. (George Corley), 1919–   . 2. Governors—
Alabama—Biography.   3. Alabama—Politics and government—1951—
4. Conservatism—United States—History—20th century.   5. United
States—Politics and government—1945–1989.   I. Title.
    F330.3.W3C37   1995
    976.106′092—dc20   95–31477
    [B]   CIP

ISBN 0-684-80916-8

To Jane

CONTENTS

PREFACE   9

Chapter 1   THE MUSE OF HISTORY   17

Chapter 2   STUDENT AND SOLDIER:
             "I'VE DONE MY PART"   45

Chapter 3   THE MORAL COMPASS OF AMBITION   68

Chapter 4   "THE THREADS RAN THROUGH":
             THE KENNEDYS FACE THE GOVERNOR   110

Chapter 5   "WE DARE DEFEND OUR RIGHTS":
             THE STAND IN THE SCHOOLHOUSE DOOR   133

Chapter 6   "ALL OF US ARE VICTIMS"   156

Chapter 7   A TREMOR, NOT AN EARTHQUAKE:
             GEORGE WALLACE AND THE PRESIDENTIAL CAMPAIGN OF 1964   195

Chapter 8   "ON WHAT MEAT DOTH THIS LITTLE CAESAR FEED?"   226

Chapter 9   "STAND UP FOR ALABAMA":
             THE QUEEN AND HER CONSORT IN A CAPTIVE STATE   264

Chapter 10   "STAND UP FOR AMERICA":
             THE POLITICS OF ALIENATION   294

Chapter 11   RICHARD NIXON, GEORGE WALLACE, AND THE
                SOUTHERNIZATION OF AMERICAN POLITICS   324

Chapter 12   THE WARS OF RICHARD NIXON:
                THE SURVIVAL OF GEORGE WALLACE, 1969–1970   371

Chapter 13   "SEND THEM A MESSAGE":
                VARIATIONS ON A THEME   415

                EPILOGUE: "Attention Must Be Paid":
                The Legacy of George Wallace   451
                NOTES   469
                BIBLIOGRAPHY   523
                ACKNOWLEDGMENTS   549
                INDEX   553

PREFACE

Monday, January 14, 1963: Inauguration Day, Montgomery, Alabama. George Corley Wallace had reached the goal he had dreamed about since he stood on the capitol portico in 1935 as a young legislative page. State employees hastily rounded up a handful of electric heaters for the parade review stand to ward off the bitter cold, while half-frozen technicians struggled with television cameras and microphones. In the nearby Montgomery armory, the inaugural ball committee checked the powerful spotlights which would follow the new governor and his wife, Lurleen, as they led the first official dance under a giant brace of flags: the Confederate Stars and Bars and a specially made white banner emblazoned with the slogan Wallace had adopted toward the end of his campaign: "Stand Up for Alabama."

Despite the coldest temperatures in nearly eighty years, huge crowds filled the city for a four-hour parade which snaked up and down the main streets and past the capitol reviewing stand. Only the out-of-town newsmen were tasteless enough to note the absence of the black bands and floats that had been part of the inauguration parade of former Governor James E. (Big Jim) Folsom, Wallace's political mentor. And neither the national nor the local press corps mentioned that blacks—who made up thirty percent of the state's population—had abandoned the streets to a sea of white spectators, many wearing white flowers as a symbol of their new governor's devotion to "Anglo-Saxon" supremacy. Alabama politics in 1963 was still the business of white folks.[1]

For weeks, Wallace had teased reporters with hints about his inaugural speech. His press secretary, Bill Jones, had talked with correspondents for the national media—the *New York Times,* the *Washington Post, Newsweek,* and *Time*—as well as with local reporters and stringers for the Associated Press and United Press International. He had made a special pitch to the three major networks in a successful effort to get them to send national correspondents rather than relying upon local feeds. Jones had promised a speech that would present the governor-elect's position in stark and uncompromising terms.

Members of the media were not disappointed.

Whenever Wallace had wanted to make a stir in his campaign for the governorship the previous year, he had turned to his favorite speechwriter, Asa (Ace) Carter, a onetime radio announcer, service station owner, and Ku Klux Klan organizer. "Ace," he would say, "write me something a little fiery."[2]

Throughout the week before the inaugural, Carter—chain-smoking one Lucky Strike after another—hacked away at an old Underwood typewriter as he sat in his cluttered room in the Jeff Davis Hotel. ("God, it was a pigsty," remembered one Wallace aide.) The governor-elect, as well as his advisers John Kohn and Grover Hall, offered suggestions, but some of the most memorable lines came directly from articles Carter had written in the mid-1950s for his race-baiting magazine, the *Southerner*. On the eve of the inauguration the speechwriter personally delivered a final version to Wallace. He proudly pointed a tobacco-stained finger to the middle of the fourth page. "Here's the lines that are gonna catch everybody," Carter said.[3]

The next morning Wallace, looking stiff and awkward in an unfamiliar morning coat, stood before his chilled audience. He began with the usual boilerplate rhetoric associated with inaugural addresses: a "sacred covenant" to avoid stealing and save the taxpayers money; a warning to the "big-wheeling cocktail-party boys . . . that their free whiskey and boat rides are over," promises to increase old-age pensions and to "invest in the future through education."[4]

But five minutes into his speech, Wallace's tone shifted. His voice took on a strident edge, halfway between a snarl and a defiant shout; his words refracted the resentments and rage he had sensed among white Alabamians as he campaigned across the state. He called forth the long, rancorous grievances of white southerners against the Yankee:

> *There were no government hand-outs [after the Civil War], no Marshall Plan aid, no coddling to make sure that* our *people would not suffer; instead the South was set upon by the vulturous carpetbagger and federal troops. . . . There was no money, no food, and no hope of either. But our grandfathers bent their knee only in church and bowed their head only to God.*

The Supreme Court's decisions outlawing segregation and forbidding school prayer, and President Kennedy's use of federal troops at Ole Miss the previous year were only the latest installment in the long tradition of Yankee oppression, now given a new and even more sinister twist as Communists in high places created a "basically ungodly government" which fed and encouraged everything "degenerate and base" in American society. If anyone missed the implications—the naked appeal to racial fear—the new governor reminded his listeners of the recent massacre of European settlers by African tribesmen. "The Belgian survivors of the Congo cannot present their case to the United Nations . . . nor [can] the citizens of Oxford, Mississippi!"

Through waves of applause, Wallace issued the call to arms.

> *Today I have stood, where once Jefferson Davis stood, and took an oath to my people. It is very appropriate then that from this Cradle of the Confederacy, this very Heart of the Great Anglo-Saxon Southland . . . we sound the drum for freedom. . . . In the name of the greatest people that have ever trod this earth, I draw the line in the dust and toss the gauntlet before the feet of tyranny . . . and I say . . . segregation now . . . segregation tomorrow . . . segregation forever.*[5]

Ace Carter had been right: "Segregation now . . . segregation tomorrow . . . segregation forever." That was the line everyone would remember. And it launched George Wallace into one of the most remarkable political careers of the twentieth century. Over the next twenty-five years, the Alabamian captured the governorship three more times—four, counting his wife's stand-in candidacy in 1966. Even more remarkably, his own shrewd political judgment and single-minded lust for power allowed him to step beyond the southern stage that had trapped most Dixie demagogues and to mount four whirlwind campaigns for the presidency, in 1964, 1968, 1972, and 1976.

White fear and hatred had never been the exclusive property of southerners. The mobbing of abolitionists in the Midwest in the 1830s and the New York City draft riots of 1863 were only part of the historical fabric of racial bigotry north of the old Confederacy. And as a trickle, then a flood, of southern blacks migrated and settled uneasily into the ethnic patchwork of the urban North, racial tensions exploded in dozens of race riots between 1916 and 1944. Whites outside the South came to reject the cruder trappings of white supremacy: the obsession with maintaining the racial purity of city buses and lunch counters and the denial of the vote to qualified citizens. But once past the racial boundaries of public accommodations and voting rights, whites North and South shared the same deep and visceral apprehensions. In the tight-knit ethnic and working-class neighborhoods of the inner cities and in the middle-class suburbs that ringed them lay the foundations for a white backlash.

Without using the cruder vocabulary of traditional racism, George Wallace began his national career by skillfully exploiting those fears and hatreds. For the age-old southern cry of "Nigger, nigger," he substituted the political equivalents of apple pie and motherhood: the rights to private property, community control, neighborhood schools, union seniority.

And as the civil rights movement expanded in the 1960s to inspire the women's rights movement, the antiwar movement, and the politics of sexual liberation, George Wallace adroitly broadened his message. Journalists might greet this growing counterculture with curiosity, even approval. But Wallace knew—instinctively, intuitively—that tens of millions of Americans despised the civil rights agitators, the antiwar demonstrators, the sexual exhibitionists as symbols of a fundamental decline in the traditional cultural compass of God, family, and country.

Barry Goldwater's conservative Republican candidacy in 1964 (and his landslide loss) marked the failure of a twenty-year effort by conservatives to roll back the hated New Deal of Franklin Roosevelt and to build a national majority on the twin shoulders of muscular anticommunism and hostility to the welfare state. George Wallace shared their obsessions with Communists, and he proved to be no slouch at fanning the flames of Americans' traditional uneasiness over taxes and welfare spending. But Goldwater and his generation of right-wing Republicans parroted the comfortable platitudes of the country club locker room. The genius of George Wallace lay in his ability to link traditional conservatism to an earthy language that voiced powerful cultural beliefs and symbols with a much broader appeal to millions of Americans: the sanctity of the traditional family, the centrality of overt religious beliefs, the importance of hard work and self-restraint, the celebration of the autonomy of the local community. On the flickering television screen and in giant political rallies, he evoked images of a nation in crisis, a country in which thugs roamed the streets with impunity, antiwar demonstrators embraced the hated Communist Vietcong, and brazen youth flaunted their taste for "dirty" books and movies. And while America disintegrated, cowardly politicians, bureaucrats, and distant federal judges capitulated to these loathsome forces.

George Wallace was not the first postwar political figure to call for a return to "traditional" American values. But the Alabama governor—more than any other political leader of his generation—was the alchemist of the new social conservatism as he compounded racial fear, anticommunism, cultural nostalgia, and traditional right-wing economics into a movement that laid the foundation for the conservative counterrevolution that reshaped American politics in the 1970s and 1980s.

IT is difficult to imagine what might have happened if Wallace had not been gunned down by Arthur Bremer in the spring of 1972. What seems clear is that his near martyrdom softened the hearts of all but his most unforgiving enemies. As the Catholic writer Michael Novak put it: "To all Governor Wallace's other accomplishments was added the symbol of his own blood: by it he was now purified."[6]

When the Alabamian finally left public life in 1986, he was deaf, riddled with arthritis, and tormented by never-ending pain. "Won't be long before I'm gone," he repeatedly whispered to visitors as he pled for understanding, for forgiveness. "Won't be long a'tall."[7]

John Cashin, a black politician who had run for the governorship against Wallace in 1970, never concealed his hatred for the man he believed had brought such suffering and pain to the black people of his state. "But then I saw him in a wheelchair," said Cashin. "It was like the hatred was just *gone*. How can you hate a man who's been brought so low?"[8]

As Wallace embraced black voters in the 1970s—whether from an authentic change of heart or for self-serving political reasons—and awkwardly apologized and acknowledged his remorse, the stage was set for a remarkable transformation.

For black Alabamians, his journey of supplication evoked the echoes of a thousand altar calls, a thousand hymns of decision, a thousand walks down the aisle:

There is a fountain filled with blood
Drawn from Emmanuel's veins
And sinners plunged beneath that flood
Lose all their guilty stains

The dying thief rejoiced to see
That fountain in his day;
And there may I, though vile as he,
Wash all my sins away. . . .[9]

Like Saul, said one Selma sharecropper who had marched with Martin Luther King, George Wallace "was struck down and then got up to do good."[10] One by one, the black men and women he had trampled on the way up reached out to grasp his hand as he tumbled downward.

In the flurry of television and news coverage that followed his retirement in 1986, the nation's newspaper of record, the *New York Times,* weighed the delicate balance of historical importance and moral memory. George Wallace had "sniffed out early the changes America came to know by many names: white backlash . . . the silent majority . . . the alienated voters . . . the emerging Republican majority." He had foreseen the tide on which Ronald Reagan sailed into the White House. The *Times*'s editorial represented the rough consensus among scholars and journalists about the Alabama governor's place in American politics. There had never been any likelihood that he would be elected President of the United States; he was too raw, too crude, too southern. But he had been one of the great transitional figures: poltergeist and weathervane in the America of the 1960s and 1970s.

The stain of race could not be washed completely away; the *Times* felt obliged to refer to Wallace's distasteful early career as the symbol of segregation. But that was not his final legacy, argued the editorial. "Years ago, he abandoned hateful race-baiting for racial harmony and black support in Alabama," with a precocious insight which offered a "nobler message" for the American people.[11] As one of the nation's newsmagazines had concluded four years earlier, the "tragedy of race was secondary in the drama of George Wallace." In the end, his career offered "forgiveness and redemptive possibilities" for America.[12]

"They rehabilitated Lyndon Johnson and he filibustered against civil rights," Wallace had once complained. "They rehabilitated Sam Ervin, and he said integration laws were unconstitutional. . . . Why won't they rehabilitate me?" His longing was reflected in his authorized biography, which begins and ends with an account of a visit from black civil rights activist and presidential candidate Jesse Jackson in July 1987.[13] As Wallace announced his retirement from politics, he seemed to have his wish.

Or did he?

In the fall of 1993, Wil Haygood, a young black reporter for the *Boston Globe* who had grown up in Birmingham, returned to his native state to write a gentle but probing profile, which captured the pathos of the aging Wallace. As he waited in the former governor's small Montgomery office, he glanced around the walls: "no photos of Bull Connor . . . , no photos of a bombed Birmingham church in which four black girls were killed. No photos of Wallace standing in the schoolhouse door to deny blacks the right to enter."[14] Haygood needed no photographs to jog his memory; neither do we.

As a historian, I have been drawn to the sheer incongruity of the story. How, in the end, could a man like George Wallace, provincial to the core, bereft of any of the traditional bases of national power, capture such a place in a time of change? My editor, Alice Mayhew, has constantly reminded me: this is not simply a biography, but a story of how one man's life illuminates what writer John Egerton so aptly called the "Americanization of Dixie and the Southernization of America."

In the six years since I began research, however, I have discovered that most people ask a quite different question: "Did he change?" Did the man who rose to power and national prominence on the wings of racial hatred in the 1950s and 1960s mean it when he grasped hands with black constituents and asked them to support him, to vote for him, to pray for him? George Wallace's success was possible only because he convinced his listeners that he would not stoop to the polite euphemisms of traditional politicians; he would tell the truth no matter what. Did he really mean it?

To the extent that I have wrestled with his motivation, I have been drawn to the cynically simple-minded explanation passed on to me when I first began this book.

"If George had parachuted into the Albanian countryside in the spring of 1962," said his former adviser John Kohn, "he would have been head of a collective farm by the fall, a member of the Communist Party by mid-winter, on his way to the district party meeting as a delegate by the following year, and a member of the Comintern in two or three years."

"Hell," he concluded, "George could believe whatever he needed to believe."[15]

But I have come to realize that the refrain, "Did he change," is more than simply a question about sincerity or authenticity. Evangelicals, particularly black evangelicals, were able to forgive George Wallace because the act of redemption sprang from the core faith of an oppressed people. For many of the rest of us, there is the promise: if George Wallace could wipe clean the slate of his past and reach across the divide of race, his is a story with an uplifting ending which offers hope for us all.

It is easy to tilt the scales from condemnation to forgiveness, particularly when we see in our mind's eye a broken and penitent George Wallace. After all, in succumbing to ambition, he was not alone. In the last angry days of segregation, southern politicians—as well as others threatened by the backlash of white racism—often confronted a choice somewhere between principled martyrdom and a surrender to demagoguery. If we refuse to distinguish among these choices, however, we dishonor those men and women who compromised and compromised again, and retreated from what they believed was right—until they reached a point at which they recoiled: "No more. This I will not do."

We can never weigh with certainty the mix of calculation and contrition that have marked the last years of George Wallace's life. "Men's hearts are concealed," the English biographer Boswell wrote to his friend Samuel Johnson. "But their actions are open to scrutiny."

Chapter 1

THE MUSE OF HISTORY

In the fall of 1916, Mozelle Smith stepped down onto the Clio, Alabama, railroad platform, prepared to begin her first teaching assignment in the nearby rural community of Blue Springs. A recent graduate of a Mobile preparatory school for young women, and a student of classical piano, the dark-eyed young woman had no college degree, or even teaching certificate. But she was intelligent, resourceful, and—despite her petite stature—commanding in presence. In any case, she did not plan to make a career as a spinster schoolteacher. Everyone in the small community understood that her appointment was temporary, arranged to allow a suitable period of courtship before her marriage to George Corley Wallace, the son of Clio's only doctor.

According to Wallace family lore, Mozelle Smith met her future husband in the Montgomery passenger depot as both changed trains on their way to college in the fall of 1915. She was nearly eighteen and beginning her two-year certificate course in music studies at the Judson Baptist Institute for Young Ladies in west central Alabama. He was six months younger, on his way to his second year at Southern University, a struggling Methodist institution for young men that was distinguished less for its academic reputation than for its faculty's insistence on religious orthodoxy and pietistic conformity.[1]

If George Wallace was something of a catch, the Black Belt hamlet of Clio was hardly a destination of choice. An itinerant violinist with a smattering of classical education, rejecting his own Greek goddess of dance, Terpsichore, for the more sonorous ring of Clio, muse of history, had christened the town in the 1850s, but more than two generations later, little in Clio seemed historic or grand. A handful of brick storefronts on the main street backed up to the railroad, while two hundred modest houses sprawled haphazardly onto a half-dozen side streets. Kerosene lamps glowed in businesses and homes alike, and a gasoline-operated Delco power generator furnished flickering illumination for evening events at the town school. In summer, horse-drawn buggies and wagons raised a pall of dust; in winter, they sank deep into the mud of the unpaved streets. Townspeople still drew their water from hand pumps or curbed wells. Over the years, cars and pickup trucks replaced the buggies and wagons; streets were paved, and many of the frame houses painted or replaced by square brick bungalows. But the rhythms of life in Clio seemed little changed. When Theodore White, chronicler of presidents and would-be presidents, made a cursory visit in the fall of 1968 he could not conceal his disdain for what he called a "seedy, mournful village" where local whites had nothing to do "except talk about crops, Negroes or politics."[2]

In later years, when her son became governor, Mozelle Smith Wallace was extraordinarily reticent in interviews with reporters. She always mentioned (tersely) that she had attended an Episcopal "private school" and had studied music at Judson College, but she turned away other questions about her childhood or family. Among many of her neighbors, among the media, and among Wallace's later biographers, there was always a vague sense that her engagement to George Wallace had been a step down the social scale. In a culture in which reminiscence provided a basic staple of conversation, she never talked about her childhood; her children and her friends came to understand the subject to be off limits. Only in later years did "Mother Mozelle" 's grandchildren realize that they knew nothing of their grandmother's past.

There were ample reasons for her reticence.

Mozelle Wallace was born in Ocala, Florida, in 1898, but her father, a railroad depot agent, transferred to Dozier, Alabama, just north of the Florida line, when she was two years old. Obediah Howard Smith never managed to accumulate enough capital to buy a house, not even in Dozier, where real estate was cheap. Still, after a few years he was promoted to telegraph operator and the family moved once again, this time to a respectable working-class district just south of Montgomery. Mozelle and the brothers and sisters that followed almost yearly became communicants in the city's Episcopal church.

Smith's death in 1905 ended that fragile security. Mozelle's mother, Kate, drifted back and forth with her six children—the youngest not quite a year old—among various members of her husband's family. She took in children in a "day nursery" in a house she rented in one of the poorest sections of Montgomery and worked briefly as a seamstress for a downtown Jewish department store, but she was forced to farm out her children to relatives while she struggled to make a living. At one point, Mozelle Smith's then-five-year-old sister, Gladys, was apparently cared for by a sixty-eight-year-old man and his common-law wife in a dilapidated boardinghouse in Birmingham.

Neighbors complained that Kate Smith neglected her children. Sometime in 1906, citing reports of her reputation as an unfit mother, the Episcopal bishop of northern Alabama dispatched three of the children—Mozelle, eight, Gladys, six, and two-year-old Wilford Thomas—to Wilmer Hall, the church's orphanage in Mobile.

Mozelle never returned to her mother's home, not even for holidays.

Despite the echoes of grandeur in its name, Wilmer Hall was a run-down, dimly lit compound in a poor and racially mixed neighborhood. Perpetually short of funds, the elderly unmarried women who ran the orphanage had to crowd as many as five or six infants, small children, and adolescents into each room of two old houses. For Mozelle, however, the grimness of Wilmer Hall was tempered by the chance to lose herself in music at nearby Barton Academy, which she attended as a "poor scholar" supported by the women's guild of Montgomery's Episcopal church. She practiced long hours at the piano, and the academy's music teacher, impressed by her talent, succeeded in persuading a local music club to sponsor her at Judson College.

By the time Mozelle entered Judson she had cultivated a studied refinement, a reserve, which others soon came to take for the quiet self-confidence of a comfortably middle-class upbringing. But the strain of the masquerade and the competition with other girls better prepared than she apparently proved overwhelming. After only three months she left Judson without taking her fall examinations.[3]

To Mozelle, George Wallace seemed a dashing young man with great prospects. His family had been pioneer settlers of Pike County and modest property owners before the war. But his grandfather—the first of four generations of George Wallaces—suffered serious wounds at the battle of Lookout Mountain during his service in the 57th Alabama Infantry. In 1869, the twenty-four-year-old ex-sergeant died, leaving a grieving widow, a one-year-old son, George Oscar, and a heavily mortgaged farm.[4] With the aid of family members, Mary Wallace managed to raise her son and to encourage his ambition. He worked his way through one of the state's normal colleges and then through the two-year course required for a degree at the Alabama Medical College in Mobile. Fresh from his medical apprenticeship and newly married, Dr. Wallace arrived in Clio in the spring of 1891. Only thirteen houses surrounded the six wooden-fronted stores stretched down one muddy street. There was no schoolhouse, and the land encircling the little settlement, he recalled, was a "primeval forest" of towering oaks, black gums, and pines.[5]

A two-year medical degree in an impoverished Deep South rural community was no guarantee of prosperity. Although his wife, Mary Elizabeth McEachern, came from one of Pike County's wealthier families, Doc Wallace, as he was always called, worked long hours at his "surgery" and his drugstore, frugally saving and investing until he owned his office and a home in Clio and three small tenant farms west of town. Revered for his Christian piety and his willingness to treat black and white for what they could afford to pay, he collapsed from overwork early in 1906, and family members feared for his life. But after a six-month cure at a mountain sanatorium, he returned to work, driving down the backcountry roads, a "short, stocky, distinguished gentleman . . . magnetic . . . talkative, always glad to see you."[6] His wife was not so lucky. Worn out after giving birth to seven children in sixteen years, she died in 1915, shortly after she delivered her eighth.[7]

While the old-timers of Clio revered their town doctor, they remembered his oldest son, George Corley, with more ambivalence. Young George was the "apple of Dr. Wallace's eye, no doubt about it," recalled a former patient. "Dr. Wallace indulged him in anything he wanted"—a politely Southern way of saying he was spoiled rotten.[8] At sixteen, an argument with his best friend, Shelly (J.S.) Jackson, had nearly ended in disaster when the two quarreled over a girl, then squared off in an empty lot behind the town privies. Jackson, who outweighed George by more than thirty pounds, had treated the argument as a joke, which seemed to enrage his opponent. After a few ineffectual swings, George Wallace whipped out a pocketknife, nicked Jackson across the face with one looping pass, and then made a deep, slashing cut across his schoolmate's arm. "I bled like a stuck pig," Jackson cheerfully recalled as, a half-century later, he exhibited the long vivid scar, irrefutable evidence that his old friend "was a scrapper, just like little George."[9]

Dr. Wallace hoped that Southern University, with its pious faculty and strict religious regimen, would tame the unruly instincts of his oldest son, but it served mainly as a finishing school for the slender, blue-eyed George. His quick wit, flair for conversation, and devil-may-care self-confidence captivated "Bitsy," the reserved young woman he had met while changing trains.[10] Through the fall of 1916 and the spring of 1917, Mozelle Smith lived in Clio and taught her music classes in nearby Blue Springs. She and George carried on a carefully supervised courtship on the weekends when her fiancé was able to make the four-hour train trip back to Clio from school.

As the war in Europe intensified, the Allies' demand for American goods pushed agricultural prices upward. Cotton jumped from thirteen to twenty cents, and then to twenty-eight cents by September of 1917. Beef cattle, which had sold for seven cents a pound on the hoof in 1913, climbed to ten cents, then to fourteen cents a pound.[11] Although he had shown little interest in his father's farms as an adolescent, George Corley Wallace was convinced that it made no sense to stay on at Southern, to struggle through algebra, composition, and twice-daily chapel for another two years, when there was a fortune to be made in farming.

He persuaded his father that they should raise beef cattle, not the scrubby animals that ranged the sagebrush pastures of South Alabama, but purebred Shorthorns—and made ambitious plans to expand the cotton fields, to purchase young mules, and to take on additional tenants. Dr. Wallace turned over management of his tenant farms to his oldest son and advanced him the money to go north to Tennessee to purchase his cattle.

In March of 1918 George and Mozelle married quietly at a small church near her mother's home on the outskirts of Birmingham and returned to their new home—a native-sawed pine shotgun house just off Clio's single main street. Doc Wallace had shared this grim four-room shanty with Mary Elizabeth before renting it out to a succession of tenants. The roof leaked incessantly; there was no electricity or running water; the only toilet was a ramshackle privy in the backyard. Their neighbors on one side, R.B. and Bertha Johnson, were black. In fact, sixteen of the forty-five families scattered up and down Louisville Road were black. "My mother was thrown into a totally different environment when she came to marry my father," said Mozelle Wallace's middle son, Gerald.[12] In that unpainted house on a stifling morning—August 25, 1919—Mozelle Smith Wallace gave birth to a healthy son. She and her husband named him George Corley Wallace, but both disliked the use of "Junior." He was always called George C. to distinguish him from his father, George, and his grandfather, Dr. Wallace.

Through the birth of three sons—George in 1919, Gerald in 1921, and Jack within another year—and daughter Marianne in 1930, Mozelle Smith Wallace stoically endured a regimen little changed from that of pioneer women in the early nineteenth century. Outside, in a cast-iron washpot, she boiled the clothes; meals were cooked over a wood stove and set out at "dinner" (noon) and supper. In the winter she bent over her treadle-powered Singer and sewed scratchy flour-sack underwear and sturdy shirts for the children and simple tailored clothes for herself. In the late spring, her husband plowed the garden plot out behind the house with a mule brought from the farm and laid off neat rows of field peas, pole beans, okra, corn, and tomatoes. From then until the first frosts of November, Mozelle worked in the garden or the kitchen every day—hoeing, picking beans and peas, shelling and canning vegetables for the long winter ahead. And when the first freeze came and the garden and the fields lay idle, she and the other womenfolk of the Wallace farms—black and white—rolled up their sleeves and joined the men of the farm in a frantic week of hog-killing.[13]

Her neighbors admired her stoicism in the face of adversity, her unfailing, ladylike dignity. The year her first son was born, she joined a dozen other women and formed a study group limited to fifteen members and devoted to the promotion of "intellectual culture" and "bettering general social conditions" in the little town.[14] She regularly attended women's missionary meetings as well as quilting bees, where the women could gossip and sew the hours away as they stitched their favorite patterns: "Ladies Fancy," "Crosstie," "The Magnolia," "Star in the East" and "The Fan."

And there was her music. At Judson she had studied classical piano; Beethoven, Chopin, and the American composer Edward MacDowell were her favorites. In Clio she sat patiently through long Saturday mornings as her young students struggled through the John Thompson graded piano books. Twice a year, proud parents and relatives gathered in the high school auditorium for painful recitals, followed by cookies and punch. On Sunday mornings and evenings, Mozelle took her place at the ancient upright of the Methodist church, coaxing the congregation through hymns that had echoed through the southern backcountry since John and Charles Wesley had evangelized in Georgia and the Carolinas one hundred fifty years earlier: "Marching Onward to Zion," "When I Survey the Wondrous Cross" . . . There was little demand for Beethoven or MacDowell in Clio.

Long before the children were grown, Mozelle Wallace had already come to see her husband's darker side, for marriage only marginally curtailed his explosive rages. After one bitter argument in the mid-1930s, Wallace pulled open his pocketknife and chased the chairman of the Barbour County Board of Revenue through the Clayton courthouse.[15] For the most part, the Wallaces remained publicly civil, if seldom affectionate. But not always. One fall noontime shortly after hog-killing, neighbors joined the family for dinner. After grace, George Senior looked out over the table, laden with vegetables, cornbread, turkey, and chicken, and demanded, "Bitsy, whur's the meat?"

Mozelle said nothing.

"I'm talking about hog meat," he said angrily. "What the hell do you think I killed them hogs for?"

His wife sat silently through the rest of the meal.

"She never would show any sign he could get her down," said the visitor who had watched the uncomfortable exchange, "leastwise not where there were other folks around."[16]

Summer and winter, she struggled with her husband over his drinking. In a culture which forbade the disclosure of unpleasant family secrets, the Wallace children seldom mentioned the tensions that ruled the household. Gerald circumspectly acknowledged that there was "some dissension between the two of them over drinking. My mother couldn't stand drinking, and my father was known to get his share."[17]

Sympathetic family members attributed George Senior's drinking and his dark moods to the pain he endured most of his life. By age twenty-five, he had only one good lung, a weak heart, and a deviated nasal septum which triggered week-long blinding headaches—headaches aggravated, recalled his friend Wallace (Buck) Mizell, by a fight in which a "feller hit him with some brass knucks or something right in the forehead." A primitive surgical procedure conducted in a Montgomery doctor's office under local anesthesia only seemed to intensify the pain. "He was just a little ole runty dried-up feller who was always freezin', even in the summertime," remembered one of his friends. On almost any day he could be found lying on one of the counters at Jackson's General Store in Clio, a cigarette in one hand and a Coke in the other, ready to chase another Goody's Headache Powder.[18]

Not surprisingly, his ambitious farming ventures failed. In 1924 he bought from his father (below market price) the 228 acres he had been supervising, and financed the purchase with one of what would be a series of increasing mortgages through the 1920s and 1930s. For the next thirteen years he struggled to wrest a living from the sandy soil of southwestern Barbour County. During the busy season—planting, cultivating, and harvesting—he worked side by side with three black tenant families. He raised cattle and hogs, grew corn and cotton, and experimented with peanuts; he even tried his hand as a jackleg veterinarian. Young George C. Wallace's first memory of his father remained his clearest one: "I couldn't have been more'n four or five," he recalled. "I had gone out in a field with my daddy to watch him plow behind a mule. I was sittin' on the ground in a hot sun, barefooted and watchin' him walk away from me, followin' that mule, going' away so far, so far, and I didn't think he was ever coming back."[19]

Gerald remembered a brief visit in late 1935 from his uncle Edwin. As fond of the bottle as his brother, but considerably more adept at living the good life, Edwin Wallace had managed to get a job in Washington as a filing clerk in the WPA. While on vacation, he had driven home to Clio late one evening and banged on the door until a sleepy George Senior came with a kerosene lantern. Clutching the doorframe for stability, Edwin explained that he needed a little loan so that he could "frolic" on down to Miami with a lady friend who was waiting in his yellow LaSalle convertible. "Daddy just slammed the door in his face," remembered Gerald. Earlier that day the power company had cut off the family's electricity.[20]

Whatever his own shortcomings, George Wallace, Sr., was also the victim of a generation-long agricultural depression. Historians would neatly bisect the second and third decades of the twentieth century as the Roaring Twenties and the Great Depression, but this division had little meaning for rural America, particularly in the South. Even though the First World War brought a brief taste of the good life for farmers, after 1921 the roller-coaster ride was all downhill. Cotton prices tumbled from thirty-seven cents a pound in 1919 to twenty-four cents in 1921 to twenty cents in 1927. By June 1932, the region's most important staple crop sold for 4.6 cents per pound on the New Orleans Cotton Exchange.[21]

What little the market left, the boll weevil finished. The Barbour County of George Wallace's childhood was a region of a privileged few and a desperately poor majority. A survey by the Alabama Department of Health in 1924 showed that eighty-five percent of all school children in the county suffered from hookworm. Pellagra, a disease caused by inadequate nutrition, had almost disappeared in the relatively prosperous war years, only to make a dramatic comeback. Most rural Alabamians had never seen a doctor or a dentist. While state public health programs brought some improvements in the late 1920s, the Depression ushered in a decade of economic deprivation so horrendous that even the most callous upper-class whites were moved to compassion by the suffering of the poor. By the mid-1930s, two thirds of all farmers in the state were tenants or sharecroppers; for blacks, the figure was over eighty percent.[22]

In a ratio little changed since the 1840s, six of every ten who lived in Barbour County on the eve of the Great Depression were black; forty percent of them could not even write their names. While such staggering figures for illiteracy were appalling, they were hardly surprising. If one-room schoolhouses for whites were still common in rural parts of the county, there was at least the skeleton of a primary education. When George Wallace enrolled in the fifth grade in 1930, the county allocated twenty-six dollars annually for educating each white boy or girl between the ages of six and fourteen, a respectable sum by the impoverished standards of Southern education. In contrast, the district spent less than four dollars for each black child who managed to enroll. There were no public schools for African Americans beyond the sixth grade; half attended classes for less than two years.[23]

As the cotton economy collapsed in the 1920s, the gradual depopulation of the countryside began, a movement led by young people in their teens, twenties, and early thirties. Despite the images of a region in which men and women put down their roots and cherished a sense of place, southerners had always been on the move. In the two decades after the Civil War, between ten percent and fifteen percent of the entire population of the state relocated. Most land-hungry tenants and restless sharecroppers followed the tide of the cotton culture and headed west to east Texas.[24] After the outbreak of World War I, the migration turned northward toward the industrial cities of the Northeast and Midwest. Black southerners journeyed north along the meridian, from the southeastern states to Washington and Philadelphia, then on to New York and Boston; from the old cotton states of the southwest—Alabama, Mississippi, Louisiana, and Georgia—the trains ran to Cleveland, Detroit, St. Louis, and Chicago.[25] Nearly a quarter million black men, women, and children left the dying farms and small towns of Alabama and joined the

great rural diaspora of modern America. On the eve of the civil rights revolution of the 1960s, more native-born black Alabamians lived in the urban
North than in the countryside of the state's old Black Belt.

While rural whites from Alabama kept pace with the black migration, they
were more likely to remain within the state when they abandoned the farm;
they settled into Montgomery, Birmingham, Huntsville, Mobile, and a dozen
other expanding mid-sized cities. Silently, this movement of people, black
and white, laid the foundation for an economic and racial revolution as, year
by year, Alabama and the rest of the Deep South became less black, more
urban.

But the implications of this demographic shift were scarcely visible during
the childhood of George Wallace. Because the rural Black Belt had one of
the highest birth rates in the nation, outmigration simply meant that the
number of people who lived in the county remained stable. Cousins, neph-
ews, nieces all pulled up stakes and moved, but Barbour County maintained
the illusion of stasis through the Great Depression. Individuals like George
Wallace's father stayed on, surviving, it sometimes seemed, on the capital
accumulated by an earlier generation. When George C. was thirteen, his
father inherited nearly three thousand dollars (a small fortune at the time)
from Mary McEachern Wallace's bachelor brother, William, who left an estate
with over $100,000 *cash*. George Wallace wanted to use the bequest to pay
off the mortgage on his farms, but for once Mozelle prevailed. In late 1932,
the family built a new home. Much of the heart pine wood was salvaged
from their old house, and initially there were only kerosene lanterns for light
and the same cast-iron wood stove in the kitchen. But the house was brick-
veneered and faced Main Street, across from the grocery store and town
shoe-repair shop. There was a cool, open front porch, a telephone, and
eventually (as Wallace said later) that "marvel of marvels, an indoor flush
toilet." After the Rural Electrification Administration brought in power
through the Pea River project, the family bought a radio and eventually a
washing machine. By the standards of middle-class America the Wallaces
were desperately poor in 1932; in Barbour County, Alabama, they were
better off than most whites and virtually all blacks.[26]

George Wallace would remember his father with sadness and his mother
with loyalty and admiration. She constantly struggled to introduce "refinement" into their rambunctious lives. There were books for Christmas—*Robinson Crusoe* and *Tom Swift*—and day in and day out she forced him to sit
at the bench of the family upright while his friends taunted him ("Aw, come
on, George—stop that sissy stuff and come out and play football!"). She
surrendered only when her son abruptly terminated his first recital by slamming his hands on the keys and stalking off the stage of the schoolhouse
auditorium in disgust.[27] What little energy survived the endless hours of

childcare, the constant chores, and the struggles with her cantankerous husband, Mozelle Wallace channeled into a fruitless effort to achieve control. For the Wallaces, as for most traditional rural households of the time, this meant strict adherence to the biblical admonition against sparing the rod and spoiling the child. Occasionally George Senior would bring out his broad leather razor strap; more often Mrs. Wallace would sternly send one of the boys into the yard with instructions to bring back a slender, supple peach branch. "She planted about twenty peach trees and she never got a peach off one of 'em. That's the damn truth," said Gerald Wallace. She "whipped the livin' shit out of us."[28]

Young George C.'s grandparents offered an emotional retreat. Dr. Wallace had remarried in 1920 and had moved eighteen miles away to the semi-rural community of Baker Hill. His second wife, Nora Mae Wyatt—Mother Mae—lavished undemanding affection on all her new grandchildren, but particularly on her husband's firstborn grandson. On long visits to Baker Hill, George C. would "get up early in the morning and come into our bedroom," said Mae Wyatt Wallace, and the little boy and her fifty-year-old husband "would have a romp in bed."[29]

In later years as he reminisced about his early years in rural Alabama, the governor's anecdotes were often stale and flat, recited mechanically out of the need to create an appealing biography of childhood and adolescence that would serve him politically. Reminding his listeners that he had been tested by the deprivations of poverty, he recalled the conventional pleasures of small-town life: Saturday afternoons in the old Clio Theater with Hoot Gibson, Tom Tyler, and Tom Mix; long afternoons picking blackberries along the roadsides; the integrated swimming hole outside Clio where he passed the stifling Alabama summers—a sort of Tom Sawyer–Huck Finn childhood.[30] Only when he spoke of accompanying his grandfather on house calls through the countryside in the doctor's Model T (the second car to appear on the streets of Clio), or of early mornings curled up in a warm featherbed between his grandparents, did he seem to speak with a genuine wistfulness for a lost time of childhood innocence and unconditional love.

Dr. Wallace, pious and devout, had hopes for the ministry for his grandson, but there is little evidence that daily family prayers and thrice-weekly church services transformed his boisterous nature. Stalking the banks of the Pea River searching for water moccasins, climbing the town water tower, endlessly quarreling and fighting, George and his two brothers seemed always to be reeling toward danger and involved in one fracas after another. Their father, no slouch at combat himself, encouraged his sons' aggressiveness.

Naturally athletic, well-coordinated, and "tough as a telephone pole," George Wallace made the high school football team as a 108-pound, five-foot-six-inch freshman. Three years later, he still weighed less than 120 pounds, but he guided his team to a seven-and-two record. He was the "smartest football quarterback I can recall in Clio," claimed one teammate. Even then he showed a blend of adolescent guile and imagination. In one of his last games, Clio faced a powerful team from nearby Troy, Alabama, a town of over ten thousand. Before the game, an indignant George Wallace gathered his outmatched team to read a letter—supposedly from one of the Troy players—that ridiculed the backwoods boys from Clio and threatened with teenage bravado to "run over" the small-town team. Only after the game, which Barbour County lost to the heavily favored Troy Wildcats by only six points, did his coach and team members learn that Wallace had written the letter.[31]

But it was boxing that marked him for life. The decades of the 1920s and 1930s were the heyday of boxing in America; Jack Dempsey rivaled Babe Ruth as a sports hero, and millions of American fans jammed auditoriums or outdoor arenas. Many of the brutal prizefights distilled the most elemental ethnic, racial, and nationalist tensions of America. Rural Americans—nowhere more than in the backcountry South—had celebrated the bare-knuckles brawler for generations. Preachers and respectable community leaders constantly emphasized piety, self-control, and hard work as the marks of respectability, but there was often a secret contempt for such marks of "effeminancy," and the most devastating epithet was "coward."[32]

Wallace remembered waiting on a cotton wagon in the line outside the gin house in the spring of 1931. His companion, a semiliterate tenant farmer who sharecropped for George Senior, was about twenty-five years old. "He had a pair of brogan shoes, no socks, and I know no underwear, and an old pair of overalls and a felt hat with sweat marks from top to bottom." As they lay there in the hot September sun, the young man filled a pipe from his can of Prince Albert, lit it, and turned to his twelve-year-old companion. "George C. . . . the United States is the strongest country in the world." You know, he continued, "we could whup ever' country in the world. We could whup 'em all put together or we could whup 'em one at the time."

The sharecropper's greatest pride—for himself and his country—was the ability to "whup somebody," said Wallace. He had "fought to live, he fought to eat, he fought to exist. . . . Southerners my age and a little younger, we were fighters because we went through a period of time when we fought to exist."[33]

In 1926 Wallace strained to hear through the static of a crystal radio the blow-by-blow description of the first epic match between Jack Dempsey and Gene Tunney. That same year, the *Chicago Tribune* sponsored the formation of Golden Gloves amateur bouts for young boys in the Windy City. The league soon spread across the nation in a network of elaborate competitions involving millions of boys between the ages of twelve and nineteen. In backyards and basements and in primitive neighborhood gyms, young men pummeled each other for hours in hopes of a chance to reach the Golden Gloves finals.

The summer George was ten, his father, returning from a trip to Columbus, Georgia, brought with him a pair of boxing gloves, and helped his three sons construct a ring from ropes strung from one two-by-four to another. Even when summer ended, the fighting simply moved indoors, where the living room became an improvised boxing ring. In the long winter evenings, the operator for the tiny Clio telephone exchange would look across the street into the Wallace living room, its bare light bulb hanging from the pine wooden ceiling. At a given signal he would ring the telephone to start and end the three-minute rounds and then would watch with amusement as the Wallace brothers and their friends flailed away.

"We fought all the time," said Gerald Wallace, but the end was inevitable: "He'd always whup me." George Wallace had found his calling; boxing became his passion. When the grocery boy from Baxter's IGA pedaled up to the house with his weekly delivery of staples, "George would stop him and make him spar," said Mozelle Wallace. Realizing that her protests were useless, she relented, though she never fully approved. Over the next five years, George relentlessly challenged a series of opponents from Clio and the surrounding countryside. By the time he was twelve, he and his friends were squaring off in a hastily improvised boxing ring during half-time at Barbour County High School basketball games. When elementary school classmates began to balk at contests with Wallace, he shamelessly pressured black boys off the streets of Clio to don gloves and climb into the ring with him. The diminutive George—always small for his age—appeared harmless enough, said one neighbor. But anyone who fought with him "was in a helluva fix." He'd "whale the hell out of them."[34]

George's first major test as an amateur came in the spring of 1935 when he entered the Bernard McFadden Golden Gloves Tournament, which brought boxers to Montgomery from all over southern Alabama. Wallace at fifteen was wiry, agile, and aggressive in the ring, but he faced Tommy Denton of Montgomery, an eighteen-year-old veteran of more than two dozen tournament bouts. Not surprisingly, the first round was a nightmare. For three minutes, the older boxer pounded the inexperienced Wallace, twice sending him to the canvas. "Denton smashed my face to a pulp," Wallace later admitted. But after each knockdown, George Wallace staggered to his feet, and by the beginning of the second round it was clear that Denton was exhausted. Wallace, who always prided himself on remaining in superb condition, jabbed and hooked for the next two rounds and won a unanimous decision. The next day, he was unrecognizable. His eyes narrow slits, his face swollen and purple, his ears still ringing from the pounding he had taken, he was ecstatic. Back in Clio he described each blow, each knock-down, and his comeback to awed friends and neighbors.

Three weeks later, bantamweight champion Aaron Franklin eliminated him in Alabama's Carnival of Champions in Birmingham. It was one of only four defeats he would ever suffer in competitive boxing. In 1936 and 1937 he won the bantamweight division of the Alabama Golden Gloves Championship and came within one bout of taking the 1936 Southern Golden Gloves Tournament in Nashville.[35]

Memories of Wallace were always filtered through the prism of his later prominence, but there was nevertheless a remarkable consistency in the way friends recalled him as a young man. Handsome like his father, he charmed the young women of Clio and surrounding neighborhoods. "Dances, any-where there'd be women and music, that's where you'd find George," re-membered one friend. "He was always around women. I mean, once he found out what they were, and what they were for, you couldn't beat him off with a stick." If no dances were scheduled, there were always the week-long revivals at churches in Clio and the nearby communities of Louisville, Blue Springs, and Elamville. Each night, said his brother Jack, George C. would ride the county schoolbus out to the revival site (Barbour County did not concern itself with the technical niceties of church-state relationships). He went "just to be there with the girls. He didn't care anything about the preaching."[36]

Unlike his father, he restricted fighting to the boxing ring or to scraps with his brothers—at least in high school. In the years when national reporters hustled to uncover the darker side of George Wallace, they could never find a classmate or teacher or boxing opponent who had anything to say that could not have been approved by the candidate's own press secretary. According to high school classmate Virgil Pelfrey, "Everybody liked George."

At the same time, those recollections had a curiously ambivalent edge. When Montgomery journalist Wayne Greenhaw questioned Wallace's contemporaries more closely, he was surprised to discover that none really described themselves as friends—surprised because, after all, Clio was a small, close-knit community, and in 1937 Wallace had only thirty-three fellow graduates. "George was really pretty much of an introvert around his classmates," said one high school acquaintance; he always maintained an invisible barrier. But when meeting older adults, he seemed to undergo a transformation. He would "go right up to some older person and grab their hand and shake it and start talking." Only in the world of adults—a world in which politics, the weather, and the crops dominated the conversation—was he at ease.[37]

George occasionally accompanied his father to late-night election counts in nearby Clayton. Sitting in the courthouse, he watched as election officials brought the boxes from across the county and hand-counted the ballots. "I wasn't but about ten years old, but I was fascinated," said Wallace. "Watchin' him count those votes was like watchin' somebody water-ski for the first time."[38] Four years later, thirteen-year-old George C. walked the side streets of Clio, passed out leaflets, and introduced himself importantly as a supporter of Fred Gibson, a candidate for secretary of state. (George Senior was Gibson's campaign manager for Barbour County.) Although Gibson lost decisively in the statewide primary that spring, he carried the village of Clio by eighty votes. Forty years later, George Wallace could still remember the tallies chalked up on the big board in the main courtroom.[39]

Young George may have been precocious, but he was hardly unusual in a county that had produced seven governors and generation after generation of representatives and senators who seemed to dominate state politics in Montgomery. His grandfather Dr. Wallace had served on the elected Clio school board before his election as probate judge from 1929 to 1934, and his father was absorbed in politics even before he returned from Southern University in 1917. "If he was asleep," said his friend Shelly Jackson, "you could wake him up by mentioning politics."[40] George Senior was a "yellow-dog Democrat" (so called because of a willingness to vote for *any* Democrat— even a yellow dog—in preference to a Republican). Even when his faith was most tested, in 1928, he had set aside his fear of priests and nuns in the White House and had campaigned for the Catholic New York Democrat Al Smith.

The Wallace family, like most poor and middle-class southerners, worshiped Franklin Roosevelt, but George Wallace, Sr., reserved his greatest passion for local politics. Before Roosevelt's New Deal, politicians, at least the politicians who counted, were those who served in Clayton or Montgomery. They alone could settle your lawsuit, raise or lower your tax assessment, and (after repeal of Prohibition in 1933) decide whether you would drink bonded whiskey or continue to rely upon the local bootlegger. George Senior ran his father's successful campaign for probate judge in 1928, served a term as elected chairman of the Barbour County Board of Revenue, and, even as his health deteriorated in the mid-1930s, talked incessantly of running his own campaign for probate judge.[41]

In January 1935, young George C. read in the *Clayton Record* that the Alabama Senate would appoint four pages for the summer term of the legislature. Ambitious young men across Alabama who dreamed of politics fought for the chance to serve as messengers for the senators. For up to two and a half months, pages lived with family friends or on their own in a series of boardinghouses scattered around the capitol square.[42] When the legislature convened, they scrambled through the Senate chamber, ready to respond to a raised hand, to carry a bill to the well, to retrieve a document from the library, and occasionally to pick up a bottle of whiskey from the bellboy in the nearby Exchange Hotel. In Depression Alabama, the two dollars a day they received was more than most grown men earned for a backbreaking ten hours of semiskilled labor.[43]

George Wallace immediately sat down and meticulously wrote each of the thirty-five state senators, introducing himself and soliciting their support for his appointment. When the legislature briefly convened in late January, his father drove him to Montgomery and gave him enough money to spend two nights in a cheap hotel. "Daddy just dumped him out in front of the capitol and told him to go to it," claimed his youngest brother, Jack. In George Wallace's more diplomatic memory, his father had "introduced me to the few Senators he knew . . . and then left me on my own to go around handshaking." For two days the wiry teenager wandered from one end of the capitol to the other, wearing his one good suit, his broad tie held firmly just below the knot with a narrow clip. "Hello, my name's George Wallace, I'm from Barbour County," he would begin, "and I sure would appreciate your vote for page." Senators nominated thirteen young men for the four positions. In later years Wallace remembered sitting in the gallery of the Senate, his stomach churning with fear until he realized that his intense lobbying had paid off.[44] In fact, he had easily won,[45] but he would repeat the pattern for the rest of his life: Anticipate the worst, never take victory for granted.

In late April, he made arrangements with his teachers at Barbour County High School to make up missed schoolwork, found a room at the Metcalf Boarding House on Catoma Street near the capitol, and settled in to share a roach-infested bathroom and a long trestle dining table with a half-dozen boarders, mostly railroad men. Within a week of his arrival, recalled one Montgomery lobbyist, Wallace was moving confidently around the Senate as though he were a senior lawmaker instead of a sixteen-year-old errand boy.[46] Intuitively, he grasped the difference between the influential solons who controlled and shaped legislation, and the powerless windbags. He shamelessly cultivated his sponsor, A. M. McDowell of Eufaula, and made it a point to get to know the even more important Barbour County representative in the lower house, Chauncey Sparks. Sparks, a taciturn Black Belt reactionary—"the Bourbon of Barbour County"—was at first bewildered and then amused by the ingratiating young man who always seemed to be at his side. Although the slender Wallace could scarcely see over the steering wheel of Sparks's Buick sedan, he was soon chauffeuring the senior lawmaker around town, offering to run personal errands, and getting an invaluable education in the workings of traditional southern politics.[47]

It was one of the happiest periods of his life. On the first day at the state capitol he stood on the bronze star where Jefferson Davis had taken the oath of office in 1861, and looked out across the city. "I knew I would return to that spot. I knew I would be governor."[48]

Despite the politicking, the social schedule, and a full menu of football and boxing, desperate economic conditions at home forced him to hold down a series of jobs through high school. During the summer of 1936, George pooled expenses with three other high school and college students, and, crammed into a Model T Ford, they traveled through Georgia, to North Carolina, then through Tennessee up into Kentucky and Indiana and as far north as Michigan, hustling subscriptions for the *Ladies' Home Journal,* the *Saturday Evening Post,* and *Collier's.* Elton Stephens, the Clio-born magazine distributor from Montgomery who first hired Wallace, was so impressed with his young salesman that he made him crew leader for the following summer. As Wallace rambled across the country with his friends, sometimes sleeping in the car, occasionally stopping at boardinghouses or threadbare tourist courts, he peddled his magazines with the same breathless, nonstop enthusiasm that he later would use to sell his political ideas.

"George was the best salesman they had," said one of the crew that traveled with him in 1937. "He was the biggest bullshooter ever born with those magazines." To the high-pressure ploys suggested by his Montgomery boss he added a few of his own. Away from the main roads in dilapidated shacks where the only reading material was the Bible, he would explain that the "federal government has passed a new law says you gotta have readin' material, and we're here to see what you'd like to pick out." If potential customers pled poverty, he would peer around the backyard, spy a few pullets, and strike a bargain. After a while, he and his crew traveled with a small chicken coop precariously tied to the rear of their Model T.[49]

Back in Clio by midsummer, he took a job vaccinating dogs for rabies with the state health department; he was paid fifty cents per dog. For a footloose young man who liked to meet people, the assignment was perfect. After paying for his transportation, serum, advertising, and other expenses, the enterprising Wallace cleared nearly three hundred dollars. What was more important, he met hundreds of rural voters, who would remember him a decade later when he returned from the war.[50]

THAT same summer of 1937—as George Wallace talked his way across middle America—Anne Kendrick Walker set out to write a history of Barbour County, Alabama. Miss Walker's father had once been a well-to-do Eufaula planter with a distinguished military record. He had fought at Cedar Creek, Second Manassas (or Bull Run), Chancellorsville, Sharpsburg, and Gettysburg, and he was one of the handful of officers chosen to accompany Lee to Appomattox Courthouse in 1865.[51] By the time he died in 1905, however, he had lost most of his plantation holdings along the Chattahoochee. What property remained went to two sons by an earlier marriage, and Anne Walker had to make her way in the world at a time when the only roles open to genteel southern white women seemed to be wife, mother, or dependent spinster aunt. A wealthy Eufaula widow gave her a parlor suite overlooking the town's Broad Street. For the rest of her life, Walker remained a familiar sight to strollers as she sat behind the clusters of japonica and oleander bushes on the colonnaded verandah of the old Kendall mansion, writing silently in her spiral notebooks with her carefully sharpened pencils. In 1934 she published her first book, *Tuskegee and the Black Belt—A Portrait of a Race.* Implicitly racist, sometimes condescending, it is nevertheless a surprisingly sympathetic treatment of the life and culture of the African Americans of the Black Belt. Over the next twenty years, Walker would complete a half-dozen books of local history and genealogy.[52]

That long hot summer of 1937 she traveled Barbour County on rickety local buses—a settled spinster lady in her mid-fifties, dressed in a veiled hat and white gloves—following the curve of the dusty roads westward from the river town of Eufaula through the little town of Clayton, and on to the "dreaming old hamlets" of Louisville and Clio, backtracking through Barbour County and collecting stories and documents for her latest book.

The geography of her day trips stretched across George Wallace's childhood and early political career. Eufaula, perched on the Chattahoochee River on the eastern edge of the county, had a population of ten thousand in 1920 and was the largest town as well as the center of economic and social life in the county. Though the distance from Eufaula westward to Clio was a journey of less than forty miles, these were separate worlds. Its shaded streets and grand mansions made Eufaula the South of Hollywood's imagination, a luxuriant creation of the brief golden age of Black Belt cotton culture from 1840 to 1880, when wagons loaded with cotton bales crowded the town streets on their way to warehouses and wharves. In the warm September nights, torches burned late into the night as black stevedores—slaves before the war, free men afterward—loaded shallow riverboats, the *Florence,* the *General Sumpter,* the *Oconee,* the *Barbara Hunt,* the *Versailles,* and the *Rebecca Everingham,* for the journey down the Chattahoochee to Apalachicola Bay and on to New Orleans. On the gallery of his Broad Street mansion, planter John Gill Shorter met with fellow secessionists throughout the late 1850s to plot the destruction of the Union. When word reached Eufaula in mid-December of 1860 that South Carolina had seceded and Alabama would soon follow, the town exploded in a gala celebration of passionate speeches and flag-waving parties. In the words of one reveler, the grand houses along Broad Street seemed "studded with diamonds in a glorious sun-light, so brilliant were the bonfires."[53] From Eufaula, John Shorter rode west to Montgomery to claim his seat as governor of the Confederate state of Alabama. Four and a half years later, at the Shorter plantation house just outside Eufaula, advance detachments of Union cavalry learned on April 28, 1865, that the war was over. Hours away from destruction, the beautiful river town was spared.

Eufaula experienced a brief economic rebirth in the 1870s and 1880s as tenancy and sharecropping replaced the old slave culture, and cotton resumed its journey through the crowded streets to the gins north of town and then down the Chattahoochee or, increasingly, onto the Central of Georgia Railroad for shipment to Mobile. As the cotton economy soured and new rail routes sprang up across southern Alabama, Eufaula drifted into the peaceful backwaters of a stagnant South. If the town fell upon harder times after 1890, it retained the gently decaying ambience of wealth, hard-won gentility, and self-confidence.[54]

Halfway between Eufaula and Clio stood the little town of Clayton, the county seat. Clayton's stuccoed courthouse with its four Doric columns pushed out over the narrow sidewalk and fronted on an unprepossessing square of lawyers' offices and brick and wood-frame stores that furnished dry goods, groceries, and farm supplies for the countryside. Clayton could not match the studied pretensions of Eufaula as a picturesque Old South stage set, but the cotton profits of the nineteenth century had made possible the construction of a pale facsimile. If the antebellum townhouses and Victorian cottages were scattered incongruously among dilapidated shacks and simple worker's cottages, they still gave the town a thin veneer of grace and beauty.

But Clio and the yeoman farms of western Barbour County were the South of George Wallace's childhood. More than a dozen years before the official expulsion of the Creek Indians in 1837, two dozen North Carolina migrants— all of them Scotch Presbyterians—illegally settled on a narrow creek just south of Clio and began clearing away the forests to plant their fields and build their church. Over the next hundred years, the cemetery next to the Pea River Presbyterian Church filled with crudely carved tombstones, the names on which spoke of a people far from the cool mountain lochs of Scotland: McNease, McBridge, McLeod, Campbell, McKenzie, McCall, and McGrigger. Though the parcels of land were poorer and smaller than in the eastern part of the county, and there were fewer slaves, the farmers of western Barbour County were drawn inexorably into the world of the Old South.

As Anne Walker made her slow journey through the countryside in the early summer of 1937, she recorded in her spiral notebook the sights she saw along the way: the alluvial soil of the rich cotton lands of the Black Belt from the Chattahoochee westward for twenty miles, gradually shifting to gently rolling stands of oak and pine, crisscrossed by scores of creeks, branches, and swamps, punctuated by smaller cotton and corn fields, their long furrows paced by tenants, black and white, and small landowners, overwhelmingly white.

Out of this prosaic landscape, from the documents she had collected and the stories she had heard, Anne Walker set to work to write her history of Barbour County. As a stylist, she never completely shed the ornate grace notes that she had acquired at Miss Crozier's School for Young Ladies; as a social observer, she generally ignored poorer whites, treated blacks with benevolent condescension, and identified unself-consciously with upper-class friends and acquaintances with whom she traveled and talked. But as she picked her way among the abandoned settlements, old churches, and cemeteries, through cut-over land, stubble, and briar, and even to the swampy edge of the Pea River where the Creek Indians had made their last stand in Alabama (two miles from Wallace's birthplace), she listened to the voices of the people she met. And layer by layer, she reconstructed her account of the past that shaped George Wallace.

The structure of Walker's book followed the contours of southern history: Indian removal and then agricultural settlement on the frontier, the coming of the cotton culture, secession, war, Reconstruction, and halting recovery. But Walker reached beyond these worn historical milestones as she recounted grisly stories of the extermination of Indians, of the deaths of whites at the hands of vengeful slaves, of constant duels among the gentry and less genteel forms of physical mayhem among the lower orders. As she herself acknowledged, she strayed far away from the "pleasant legends of a charming countryside." However romantic her prose, the theme remained the same: the hard-fought struggle between violence and gentility, order and disorder.

Actual events interwoven through the fabric of whites' historical memory presented a powerful series of object lessons which reinforced the notion of the importance of eternal vigilance against outside interference and black insubordination. And they steeled whites for the uncomfortable demands of maintaining absolute white supremacy in the years that followed the Civil War. In the months after Appomattox, the Republican Party moved beyond its wartime goals of defeating the Confederacy and abolishing slavery. Reluctantly, hesitantly, Republicans embraced the political enfranchisement of the South's former bondsmen. By 1868, southern whites were hardly powerless—they still held the reins of the economy—but they were enraged by the spectacle of their former bondsmen casting ballots in what had been so recently a slave society.

In Barbour County, the party of Lincoln, supported overwhelmingly by blacks but by only a few hundred whites, captured political control of the majority black county. Elias Kiels, a magnetic and handsome local white Republican, championed the racial and political revolution, but had no desire to maintain an all-black party. During his first term as judge of the City Court of Eufaula, he struggled unsuccessfully to persuade whites to cooperate, but most would have none of it. Planters and white lawyers particularly resented his dogged efforts to protect the rights of black defendants in his court. They effectively excommunicated him from respectable society.

As Alabama approached the crucial election of 1874, national Republican resolve weakened, white resistance to GOP state governments across the South grew stronger, and a blizzard of leaflets urged the white men of Barbour County to use the military skills they had acquired in "four years of patriotic struggle for Southern independence." One white man could "whip a hundred negroes if they would only stand up and do their shooting straight," said one prominent Eufaula lawyer in an angry stump speech.[55]

Before dawn on election day, November 3, 1874, more than a hundred white men crowded into second-story rooms overlooking Eufaula's main street. Black voters, warned of possible reprisals by whites, assembled in a nearby church and then began marching, to the spirited accompaniment of a drummer and a fife player, down Broad Street. As they neared the polling place, one marcher saw a man lean out into the street and fire a pistol into the air. Instantly the windows filled with gunmen; the shot had "fallen like hail," said one white bystander caught in the crossfire. A black voter who had stopped at the town well for a drink was hit five times before he managed to grab the bucket rope and lower himself into the water. Captain A. S. Daggett, commander of the small federal detachment stationed in the town, witnessed the massacre from his hotel window a block away. He estimated that the shooting was over in less than a minute. Over the next two hours, onlookers watched as drays of the wounded, dead, and dying were carried through the town. Nearly a hundred would-be black voters suffered gunshot wounds. No one would ever know the precise number killed; the estimates ranged from fifteen to forty.

Unaware of the Eufaula massacre, Elias Kiels and his son supervised the counting of ballots at a small country store in Spring Hill, several miles northwest of Eufaula. As dusk fell, nearly a hundred white Barbour County residents converged on a nearby general store, where they had secretly stored their weapons the night before, and awaited the orders of their commander, Wallace Comer. (Comer and his six brothers dominated Barbour County; all together they owned more than forty thousand acres in property spread across three counties.) Just after dark, as Kiels, his fifteen-year-old son, Willie, and two other election officials sat in the locked store counting the ballots, they heard a noise at the front door. Within seconds, the mob, led by Wallace Comer and his brother Braxton Bragg Comer, battered down the door of the country store and began firing at Kiels, who crouched with his son behind a wooden counter. When the gunfire stopped, Kiels called out to his son, but "he did not answer." A rifle ball had entered his lower bowel. While one of the gunmen held a lantern, Wallace Comer, gun drawn, walked carefully across the room and peered behind the counter, but could not bring himself to execute the unarmed Kiels and his dying son. Members of the mob quietly slipped away to their homes. Two days later, Willie Kiels died. None of the gunmen had worn masks; not one ever served a single day in jail. Three decades later Braxton Bragg Comer would become governor of Alabama.

Although Republican members of a special congressional committee condemned the murder of young Kiels and the massacre of black voters in Eufaula, southern Democrats on the committee faithfully endorsed the claim of local whites that the riot had begun when "blacks drew their weapons and commenced a general attack upon the whites," who "responded" and "only fought on the defensive." Elias Kiels, they concluded, had no one to blame for Willie's death but himself. He was a "pestiferous mischief-maker" whose encouragement of black insubordination had "inevitably led to race conflict." Warned by his friends that he would be assassinated if he remained in Barbour County, Kiels fled with his wife to Washington, where the Grant administration arranged a minor patronage appointment.

In the presidential election of 1876, only ten black Republicans went to the polls in Eufaula. Two years earlier, twelve hundred had voted. Within three months of the election, the last Republican governments of the South—riven by internal divisions and demoralized by the savage violence of their opponents—collapsed. Although sometimes incompetent and corrupt, these governments of freedmen and sympathetic whites in no way resembled the nightmarish scenarios of "Black Reconstruction" created—often out of whole cloth—by white southerners anxious to justify their resort to violence and terrorism.

The triumph of white supremacy came at great cost, not only to the defeated Republican Party, but to the very processes of government. Violence, already endemic in southern society, became institutionalized, and community leaders transformed the willful corruption and manipulation of elections into a patriotic virtue. And the one great lesson white southerners learned from the experience of Reconstruction—that all issues were subordinate to the need for white supremacy—became an invitation to corruption within the Democratic Party. As reactionaries tightened their grip on the political process, they used the one-party system to turn back all challenges. Whenever dissidents threatened, white conservatives issued the same stern warning: Division would lead to the return of the hated black Republicans. As the agricultural depression of the late 1880s and early 1890s deepened, however, even the imperatives of white supremacy could no longer silence the voice of angry protest.

Out of Barbour County the voice of Alabama populism emerged.

Reuben Kolb, a graduate of the University of North Carolina, enjoyed the privileged life of a wealthy Black Belt planter and merchant during the 1850s, but the Civil War transformed Kolb and his world. After Kolb, a decorated artillery commander, returned to Eufaula in 1865, he lost more than half his three thousand acres of land, and his once-prosperous mercantile store failed. For a while he scraped out a bare living managing Eufaula's down-at-the-heels "opera house," booking traveling theater companies and minstrel shows. In the 1870s and 1880s he achieved modest success as a truck farmer and developer of hybrid seed stock for southern farmers. Politically he remained a faithful and partisan Democrat who preached the gospel of white supremacy and modern agriculture to his struggling neighbors, and he easily won election as Alabama's first commissioner of agriculture in 1888.[56]

The 1890s brought the nation's first great industrial depression, but agriculture—particularly southern agriculture—had slipped into an economic abyss even before the crash of '93. The twin barometers of cotton prices and sharecropping moved in opposite lockstep through the late nineteenth century. For black southerners this meant further hardship; for marginal white farmers it often meant a retreat over the thin line that separated them from former slaves. Decaying farms, mountainous debts, and finally the loss of the bare means of existence brought a despair that mocked America's romantic notions of the sturdy independent yeoman. "No wonder Cain killed his brother," complained a bitter Mississippi farmer. "He was a tiller of the ground."[57]

As the devastating depression of the 1890s overwhelmed Kolb's efforts to bring agricultural prosperity through modernization and reform, the Civil War hero and former planter reluctantly turned to political revolt. In 1892, he embraced open political rebellion against the coalition of planters and emerging Birmingham industrialists that dominated the state Democratic Party, and declared himself the gubernatorial candidate of a third-party agricultural protest movement, which he called the "Jeffersonian Democrats."

Kolb and his followers emphasized fairer taxation within the state (including an income tax), improved educational opportunities for the impoverished white population, and protections for industrial workers in the expanding coal mines and steel mills of Birmingham. But the real force that drove them outside the vale of the one-party South, that moved them to try to join together disaffected landowners, marginal tenant farmers, and the coal miners and steel workers, was a bitter resentment against privilege and power. While the working people of Alabama struggled for daily bread, Kolb told one crowd of three thousand miners who gathered north of Birmingham in the summer of 1892, the "money kings, corporations and corrupt politicians ate at the table of plenty." Was it just and right that such men should use "foul and despicable means to accumulate their great wealth?"[58]

So desperate, so enraged were Kolb and the Jeffersonian Democrats that they risked the greatest gamble of all in late-nineteenth-century southern politics: an open appeal to black voters. Peyton Bowman, a radical Birmingham lawyer and close ally of Kolb, daringly assured a rally of African-American voters that he would rather see "the banks of every river and creek in Alabama lined with Federal bayonets and crimson with blood, than see you deprived of the privilege of voting."[59] The populist dream of black and white uniting against the old planter class and the emerging New South business elite seemed close to fruition.[60]

African Americans continued to vote in substantial numbers in the Deep South, and through the 1880s coalitions of predominantly black Republicans and renegade whites running under a variety of party labels polled from thirty-two percent to forty-nine percent of the vote in ten southern states. It was precisely the kind of political nightmare most feared by the men of property who controlled the Democrats—a class-based alliance of blacks and dissident whites.

As Kolb and his followers had anticipated, their support for black political participation gave Conservative Democrats a free hand to brandish the time-honored weapon of white supremacy; they demanded that the state legislature enact "such election laws as will better secure the government of the State in the hands of the intelligent and the virtuous." Across Alabama, newspapers—most of which opposed Kolb—warned that a vote for the Jeffersonian Democrats with their "radical social measures" would plunge the state into economic ruin and "raise the niggers to equality with the whites."[61]

When early returns from the 1892 gubernatorial race indicated a Kolb victory, ballots simply disappeared from the polling places as election officials manipulated the count. The Conservative Democratic machine—firmly in control of the election machinery in the Black Belt, where tens of thousands of black Alabamians still voted—used payoffs, intimidation, and ballot-box stuffing to make certain that most of those black votes were tallied for Kolb's opponent, Thomas Jones. That vote, coupled with those of white conservatives, gave Kolb a stinging defeat in Barbour County. Only in the poorer white communities did he fare well; Clio gave him a three-to-one edge.[62] Conservatives had voted "live negroes, dead negroes and dogs" to defeat the insurgent upstart, bragged one Eufaula Democrat. Black Belt planters and their business allies in Birmingham had thus "neutralized nigger supremacy with nigger votes[:] . . . the grandest political achievement of the century."[63]

Two years later, the party platform of the Jeffersonian Democrats made no mention of black rights—a telling reflection of the shallow commitment of Kolb and many of his followers to the notion of racial equality. After the party failed to win in 1896, Kolb confessed his apostasy and pathetically pleaded to be allowed to return to the party of white supremacy.[64]

Across the region, populist radicalism collapsed, a victim of racial division, shrewd maneuvering by conservative enemies, and the partial economic recovery of the twentieth century. The national Republican Party, convinced it could carry the national elections without the South, abandoned its former black supporters. The United States Supreme Court, in a series of rulings including the infamous "separate but equal" decision in *Plessy* v. *Ferguson* (1896), gave white southerners *carte blanche* to enact ever more flagrantly discriminatory laws.

In 1901 the Black Belt planter conservatives and north Alabama business interests—fully in control of the state political machinery—pushed through a new constitution, which not only completely disfranchised Alabama blacks but also reduced the number of poorer white voters, many of whom could neither pay the cumulative poll tax nor pass the newly established constitutional literacy and property requirements.[65] By the First World War, voter turnout for general elections across the region averaged less than twenty percent. The politics of Alabama, like those of the rest of the South, became Democratic Party politics, well-placed white folks' politics. Chroniclers of the state's history conveniently forgot the unseemly disputes of the 1890s, which had pitted white men against white men. In place of the overt struggles of class interests, economic conflicts became muted or obscure, filtered through the prism of race and the fires of a fierce localism. Voters generally supported local or regional candidates who in turn had to effect fragile coalitions with other parts of the state. The building blocks of these rickety alliances were those informal political units centered in the county seats and larger towns of the state which academics and sophisticated journalists glibly described as courthouse "gangs." The end result—a jerry-rigged southern version of Mad Ludwig's castle—was a political process seldom shaped by issues of public policy, but by informal relationships filtered through kin and class at the courthouse, the local cafe, the Masonic lodge, church suppers, and (in the more up-and-coming communities) in the Kiwanis or Rotary clubs.

Under the leadership of a handful of energetic and self-styled "progressive" governors, white voters in the 1920s and 1930s embraced a secular trinity as the road to prosperity: "Good Roads, Good Schools, and Good Government." But the old plantation regions stretching across south-central Alabama and the emerging industrial interests of the Birmingham coal and steel region continued to dominate the political process. Their common interests bound them together. Planters wanted to maintain control over their predominantly black labor force; the corporate interests of Birmingham (the Big Mules, as they came to be called) sought to check the potential power of their emerging industrial work force. Both groups favored low property taxes and limited government. Both fought tenaciously to limit the electorate; blacks were excluded on the basis of race and class, poorer whites on the grounds that their ignorance made them susceptible to the entreaties of "demagogues, [and] the so-cialistic and the communistic thinkers."[66]

In 1937, the year Anne Walker began work on her history of Barbour County, George Wallace left Clio for the University of Alabama. Less than six weeks after he arrived in Tuscaloosa, he received a telephone call in his boarding-house. His father was critically ill, not from one of the many ailments that had tortured him for most of his life, but from Brill's disease, a mild form of typhus spread by lice. The illness was seldom fatal, but George Senior was an old man, worn out at age forty. "I think he's gone this time," Dr. Wallace told his grandson. Two days later, black tenants on the Wallace farms filed through the small living room for a separate ceremonial viewing. White friends and neighbors followed. The women bought meat and covered cas-seroles, heaping bowls of vegetables, cakes and sweet pies. The men gath-ered in the side yard. And then they all shuffled quietly past the casket before following it on to the Methodist church and then to the Pea River Cemetery.

Most of the neighbors knew that the Wallace farms were hopelessly mort-gaged and run-down. A delegation of men offered to help supervise the properties, but Mrs. Wallace would take no charity. Buck Mizell, owner of Clio's Cash Drug Store, managed to save the family home on Main Street by selling off the farmland. By the time Mozelle Wallace had paid off the last mortgage, only a half-dozen mules and a handful of rusting plows and trace chains remained.[67]

Gerald, fifteen, Jack, fourteen, and four-year-old Marianne were still at home; Mrs. Wallace had no income beyond the pin money she earned giving music lessons. For a few days George wandered around the house in Clio and halfheartedly assured his mother he would drop out of school and stay on to help. No-nonsense as always, Mozelle Wallace told him to pack his clothes and go back to the university. "I could get along without him," Mrs. Wallace briskly explained. "I was probably right cruel about it, but I told him I could make out." Her relieved son returned to Tuscaloosa, where he plunged back into the race for president of the freshman class which his father's illness and death had interrupted. With the help of friends and family connections, his mother obtained an appointment as a sewing supervisor for young girls under a New Deal job-training program in Clio.[68]

Over the next five years, George Wallace would hitch a ride home a couple of times a year. Occasionally he brought a friend. Arriving without a suitcase and with only a toothbrush stuck in his shirt pocket, he scarcely paused to greet his family before he was "out on the streets, talking to people," said his sister, "talking to people on the street about just *anything*. He was always on the go!"[69]

On campus, too, he distanced himself from home and family. When Wal-

lace's first biographer, the *Newsweek* correspondent Marshall Frady, interviewed Mozelle Wallace in 1966, she frankly acknowledged her distant
relationship with all of her children. "My boys and I don't spend much time
together," she told Frady. "I hardly even talk to them on the telephone."[70] "It
struck us as kind of peculiar," one of his college classmates remembered. At
late-night bull sessions, at parties, or riding to football games, "we never
heard him mention his father or brothers or any other member of his family.
He could have been an orphan." It wasn't as though he was ashamed of his
background, said another college classmate. After all, the university was full
of impoverished students, and Wallace took a certain perverse pride in his
poor background. It was as though he had wiped away his past and started
all over again.[71]

YEARS later, George Wallace sat alone in his bedroom, reading and re-
reading the well-worn pages of *Backtracking in Barbour County*—his favorite book, said his daughter Peggy Sue. It was, of course, a tragically
incomplete chronicle. For the black men and women of Barbour County,
its themes were inversions of those Anne Walker played: the randomness
of terror; the need for careful attention to the mask of docility or, even
safer, the veil of invisibility.

The town bell on the lawn of the Clayton courthouse was a well-known
landmark until the 1930s, when it was moved to the nearby gardens of the
county judge and rehung in a bower of multiflora roses. "Its mellow tones,"
in Anne Walker's words, "once more rang out 'All's Well!' "[72] But African
Americans remembered it as the alarm summoning the "Slave Patrol," the
hated "patteroll" or white militia, a paramilitary force that recaptured run-
away slaves and ruthlessly enforced absolute white authority.[73] In 1940,
seventy-five years after the end of slavery, the black children still sang a song
whose upbeat tempo mocked the terror it described:

Run nigger run, the patter-o'll catch you,
Run nigger run, it's almost day,
Run nigger run, that patter-o'll get you,
Fer the patter-o'll says you can't get away.[74]

If the story Anne Walker told was incomplete, it was the story George
Wallace believed: the folk history of a people who struggled daily with the
cultural contradictions of a biracial society based upon the foundation of
unquestioning white supremacy. Over a century white folks' myths had
become white folks' wisdom. "My father used to tell me that poverty and
illiteracy in the South resulted from the way we were treated when the [Civil]
war was over," said George Wallace, "when they burned the schools down,

burned the railroads, just desecrated the South."[75] The world was a frightening place in which life was precarious and security a luxury found only in the hereafter. To the age-old burdens of sickness, poverty, and hunger were added the oppression of the Yankee and the incubus of race. For even though the African Americans with whom they worked side by side each day appeared docile, unambitious, and content, they were also seen as childlike, unstable, and easily misled. And there were always evil men—abolitionists, Yankee soldiers, carpetbaggers, unscrupulous southern white renegades— ready to channel that instability into a nightmare of black domination. Even when that danger was held at bay, southern whites were beset by other dimly seen enemies: men who would exploit them, would belittle and humiliate them. Little wonder that white southerners could seem unnervingly mercurial when they veered from a warm and effusive hospitality to an angry rage toward outsiders.

Throughout the 1920s, the Wallace family joined other Clio residents for the Old Soldiers' Reunion at nearby Blue Springs, where a dwindling band of aging veterans gathered for a weekend retreat. The United Daughters of the Confederacy organized dinner on the grounds and the program of fiddling, dancing, and speechmaking.[76] As a child, Wallace was part of that last generation with a direct link to firsthand accounts of the great war for southern independence; like many of his generation he spoke of the "War Between the States" with the familiarity of one whose youth had unfortunately barred him from service in the recent conflict. All his life, he loved to tell and retell the story of Jefferson Davis's capture and forced manacling by Union jailers. "He was sick and nearly dead," a stern-faced but proud Wallace would recount, but he told his Yankee captors that he had been the president of a country and he would not submit. "They grabbed him, and he started fightin'—that old man, weak as he was. It took a bunch of 'em to hold him long enough to get it done, and when they turned him loose again, he was still fightin'."[77]

In the years to come, national reporters who made the trek southward to understand George Wallace would summon visual echoes of the Lost Cause, like familiar backdrops in a musty schoolhouse auditorium: the polished bronze star on the capitol veranda where Jefferson Davis took his oath of office in 1861, the Confederate battle flag flying atop the state capitol (higher, it was always noted, than the United States flag), the ubiquitous soldier in granite gray on the Barbour County courthouse square, the small rectangular Confederate markers in the Pea River Cemetery where the Wallaces lay, the inevitable references to Wallace's great-grandfather wounded at the battle of Lookout Mountain. All were part of the notion of George Wallace as the personification of white southerners' obsession with foolhardy defiance and ultimate defeat.

Clayton's Confederate monument, the brightly polished brass star at the Alabama statehouse where Jefferson Davis launched the South's doomed cause, the family grave markers by the Pea River, the stories of Yankee persecution he had heard as a child: All were part of the history that made George Wallace. But so were the neglected tombstones of Willie Kiels and Reuben Kolb at the edge of the Eufaula cemetery. So were the unmarked graves of the black men who lost their lives in the Eufaula massacre of 1874. And so was the spirit that had ruthlessly swept away a two-thousand-year-old culture to make the land safe for the white man's cattle, for his cotton, and for his slaves.

Chapter 2

STUDENT AND SOLDIER

"I'VE DONE MY PART"

THE UNIVERSITY TO which George Wallace returned in the fall of 1937 teetered on the edge of economic and academic insolvency. In the century after its founding in 1834, the University of Alabama endured two disastrous fires (including one started by Federal troops in 1865), a student riot over bad food, and the great influenza pandemic of 1919. But it barely survived the slashing budgets imposed by the Alabama legislative sessions of 1932–1933 and 1934–1935. From 1929 to 1937, lawmakers steadily reduced appropriations until they were the lowest provided any major state-supported university in the nation. Library acquisitions shrank to one-fourth their pre-Depression level, the school's laboratories fell into disrepair, and university trustees increased teaching loads even as they slashed faculty salaries more than twenty percent. Football alone escaped unharmed. Buoyed by two Rose Bowl victories over much-vaunted "Yankee" teams, the athletic program saw its budget increase sixty percent between 1930 and 1936. Fittingly, the only major building constructed during these years was a new gymnasium.[1]

But to a country boy from Barbour County, Tuscaloosa's campus—however precarious its economic and academic status—was a place of perpetual excitement and adventure. Although young men and women from Alabama dominated the student body, nearly a third of the students in George Wallace's class came from north of the Mason-Dixon line, drawn by warm Alabama winters and low tuition ($120 a year)—and, some cynics argued, even lower academic expectations.[2]

Like most southern universities, the school was as much a haven for prolonged adolescence and a training ground for aspiring politicians as an institution of higher learning. Many of the sons and daughters of the state's middle and upper classes sandwiched obligatory classes between more important affairs: wangling an invitation to one of the better fraternities or sororities, attending cotillions, and religiously maintaining attendance at fall pep rallies and home football games. Politically ambitious students entered a world of feverishly conducted campus politics, friendships, and alliances, which would continue for the remainder of their lives. Many of the most powerful Alabama politicians of the 1930s and 1940s—Senator John Bankhead, U.S. Supreme Court Justice (and former senator) Hugo Black, Senators Lister Hill and John Sparkman, and Congressman Carl Elliott—began their careers with campaigns for campus office.

Most students at the university knew George Wallace because of his continued exploits in the boxing ring. University regulations barred pre-law students from taking part in athletics, but the law school's dean, Albert J. Farrah, was an avid boxing fan. Farrah, who had waited gloomily year after year for the emergence of a white man who could beat the Brown Bomber, Joe Louis, tacitly waived the restriction. Wallace fought a regular schedule of bouts, won election as captain of the school team, and finished his first year of college competition undefeated, with half of his victories technical knockouts, a rarity in the bantamweight class. Boxing coach Richard Brikates called him one of the "hardest-hitting little men in the South."[3]

But boxing, while a major sport in southern colleges and universities, lacked the glamour and prestige of football. By disposition and by necessity, Wallace remained an outsider. He had arrived on campus carrying a cardboard suitcase containing two shirts, a few changes of underwear and socks, the same suit he had worn as a page in the Alabama legislature, and one pair of dark-colored trousers so slick, said one friend, "you could see your reflection if you walked behind him on a sunny day."[4] He could not afford to join any of the fraternities on campus (even if he had been invited to pledge), and he defiantly described himself as a "G.D.I." ("The 'D.I.' stands for damned independent," explained one of his classmates. "You can figure out what the 'G.' stands for."[5]) A few faded photographs survive from his years at Tuscaloosa. In one group of snapshots taken at a football pep rally, Wallace and a half-dozen other underclassmen kneel on the platform in preparation for a pie-eating contest. While his sweatered classmates posture and laugh, Wallace—dressed in his too-tight suit with a vest that stops well short of his waist and pants two inches above his shoe-tops—stares pensively at the floor.[6]

Like many other Depression-era students, he could count on little help from his financially strapped family. He scraped by with a variety of part-time jobs, waiting tables at his boardinghouse in return for room and board and earning a little pocket money as a clerk in the registrar's office and as a fill-in taxicab driver.[7] On the relatively small campus, almost everyone soon knew the small, wiry, always smiling Wallace. Some of his more sophisticated classmates regarded his shiny pants, loud shirts, louder ties, and too-desperate attempts to win friends with amused condescension. Certainly few took seriously his oft-expressed boast that he would one day be governor of Alabama. He was, said one of his well-to-do classmates, "kind of like a pet or mascot type."[8]

Several northern students recalled him quite differently. They spoke of how warmly he had greeted them when they first arrived on campus, and of his lack of snobbery. Irvin Bergbauer, a Jewish pre-law major from St. Louis, was about the same size and weight as Wallace. Aware that his Barbour County friend had little more than the clothes on his back, he insisted that Wallace borrow his tuxedo for special occasions.[9]

But his closest friends were a handful of small-town and country boys like himself, drawn to the university as a way out of their hardscrabble childhood. In his first days at Tuscaloosa he struck up an inseparable relationship with Glen Curlee, a heavyset boy from Wetumpka, Alabama, whose rumpled suits and long trails of cigar ashes made Wallace seem a fashion plate by comparison. No one would ever accuse Curlee of being an intellectual heavyweight, admitted a classmate; he scraped through the university law school with a steady string of hard-won C's. But he was irrepressibly cheerful and unwaveringly loyal to his new friend from Clio. Others might make fun of George Wallace's desperate attempt to win friends and his naked political ambition, but not Glen Curlee. "You wait," he would often tell amused classmates, "you just wait: he's gonna be guvnah some day."[10]

During his last three years at Tuscaloosa, whenever friends could not locate Wallace at one of his ever-changing boardinghouse addresses, they could often find him on nearby Hackberry Lane at the tiny apartment of Ruth and Frank Johnson. As Curlee said, "We kind of made our headquarters there."[11] Ruth Johnson, beautiful and vivacious, was an even better student than her pre-law husband. Despite a part-time job, she graduated in three years with a double major in history and political science and turned down a graduate teaching fellowship. She had first seen George Wallace in the spring of 1940. He was "standing on a box, literally, in front of the [student] union making a speech."[12] Not for the last time, Wallace—skinny, eager, and shabbily dressed—touched a streak of maternal compassion. Later, when she invited him over for dinner, he wolfed down a home-cooked meal, and thereafter was a regular visitor to the Johnson table. In another photograph from his college years, Wallace poses with Curlee, their dates, and the Johnsons at the gym entrance to a cotillion. A half-smiling Wallace holds hands with both his date and the dark-haired Ruth.

Serious and reserved, the hardworking Frank Johnson seemed an odd addition to the Wallace-Curlee duo. Johnson was from Winston County, and he was a Republican. His politics, like those of his home county, fit squarely in the middle of a tradition of fierce dissent that stretched back into the early nineteenth century. The isolated yeoman farmers of the northern Alabama hill country had no more use for the plantation slavocracy than did the abolitionists of the North (though their hostility stemmed from different sources). As secession fever swept the South in late 1860 and 1861, Winston County voters persistently clung to the Union. Standing defiantly against ninety-one other delegates, Charles Sheats, the twenty-one-year-old school-master who served as the county's delegate to Alabama's 1861 secession convention, refused to sign the state's Ordinance of Secession.

Fewer than a hundred men from the county served in the Confederate army. More than twice that number—among them Frank Johnson's great-grandfather, James Johnson—enlisted in the 1st Alabama Cavalry Regiment of the Union army. Winston and the surrounding counties became the setting for burned homesteads, reprisals, and counterreprisals as Confederate authorities struggled unsuccessfully to dominate the troublesome hill country.[13]

After the war, many of these north Alabama whites put aside their racial fears and joined hands with the antislavery party of Abraham Lincoln. Down through the 1930s the Johnson family remained loyal to the GOP.[14] In a state that went for Franklin Roosevelt by a nine-to-one margin in 1936, Republi-canism was more than an anomaly; it was close to an absurdity.

Wallace and Curlee teased their north Alabama friend remorselessly over his political heresy; in one course, Wallace and Johnson good-naturedly exchanged barbs over Roosevelt's public power policies. Johnson dutifully upheld his party's position that public ownership of electric utilities violated the principles of free enterprise. Wallace gave no quarter as he defended the New Deal. He was a "genuine Franklin Roosevelt Socialist . . ." said Johnson. "I don't think he ever changed as far as his real feelings were concerned."[15]

"Why in hell do you want to be a Republican?" Curlee finally asked Johnson after a long night of serious dancing and moderate drinking. "The party's dead."

Deadpan, Johnson insisted there was a method to his apparent madness. There were "so few of us that one day I might be a federal judge." Wallace, recalled Curlee, mockingly replied: "Well, that'll be the day. I'll be governor by then."[16]

They seldom discussed race. To the extent that he had given the issue any thought, young George Wallace considered himself a humane segregation-ist. In later years, he described his views in the late 1930s as those of a paternalistic segregationist, and was prone to state, without embarrassment, how he "loved" a number of blacks with whom he had grown up. To Frank Johnson the issues of race that dominated the Black Belt of George Wallace's youth were as remote as questions about human rights in the Belgian Congo. Johnson's sister had grown up playing with two black girls whose father worked for the Illinois Central Railroad, but there had been only a handful of blacks in Winston County. "We didn't go to school together, we didn't socialize and it never occurred to me that that was good or bad. It was just there."[17]

Despite their political differences, the Johnsons found much in common with the young George Wallace. The part-time jobs, the constant economic struggles, and the crowded living conditions presented an exhilarating challenge. And they shared and admired Wallace's efforts to open up the smug and snobbish political system that shaped the university and the state. Well-to-do and socially connected students might look down on Wallace, but independents and outsiders in the student body saw him as "one of them," insisted Ruth Johnson. Her only uneasiness came when she saw that her friend took advantage of the young high school girls he dated. He was "always respectful to me," remembered Johnson, but he "treated them shabbily." Indeed, she recalled, he seemed to regard most women with thinly veiled contempt.[18]

Wallace advanced through the three-year pre-law curriculum and two years in the law school without (his friends claimed) ever buying a text. He became a master at borrowing books from friends, hurriedly scanning the material the night before examinations, and then sliding by with a B or a gentleman's C. In later life he never mentioned one book, one course, or one professor who had shaped his intellectual development at the university. What he could remember was the precise vote on each of the half-dozen student offices he had sought.

In his freshman year, before the fraternity leaders who dominated campus politics realized what was happening, Wallace mobilized a coalition of independents and unpledged freshmen and won election as class president. A year and a half later, he bluntly challenged the fraternities' sway over the campus when he announced his candidacy for presidency of the Cotillion Club.

Despite its innocuous name, the Cotillion Club was powerful: its officers arranged almost all social activities on campus and worked closely with the fraternities to control almost every honorary and elected student position. A loose coalition of fraternity leaders maintained a similar degree of control over the Campus Board of Publications.

On the eve of the spring election, the editor of the campus newspaper, himself a Sigma Chi, broke ranks with the clique that had selected him. Bob Collins's page-long editorial bitterly indicted a system ruled by provincialism and social snobbery. Northern students were barred from leadership roles; so were those who were Jewish, as well as independents like George Wallace. Had "anybody ever heard of a student who did not have a Greek letter behind his name holding an important position?"[19]

Despite Collins's eloquent indictment, the fraternity slate swept to an easy victory as it captured nearly sixty percent of the two thousand campus votes.[20] A year later, Wallace tried again and was trounced even more decisively. Outwardly he was a gracious loser. The candidate from Clio was "still able to smile, chew on his cigar and shake hands all around" after his second loss, reported the *Crimson-White*.[21] Privately, said one of his close friends, "he did not take defeat well."[22]

But each setback seemed only to heighten his driving ambition. In the spring of 1941, a Jasper, Alabama, lawyer and former university student body president returned to the campus to speak at a banquet of distinguished university alumni. Even though Carl Elliott had failed in his first race for political office the preceding year, he was widely regarded as a man on his way up: intelligent, charming, a great speaker with a knack for gaining the fanatical loyalty of his supporters. As Elliott and his wife left the banquet hall for the ninety-minute drive back to their home in north Alabama, they were approached by an "eager young man, an undergraduate student . . . , ambitious, and not one bit intimidated by this scene of Alabama statesmen all around him."

For a half-hour, the couple tried to get away while this "very intense young fellow . . . told me he knew all about me, told me how much he thought of me, of the career I'd had at the university and of the work I'd done since." Step by step the Elliotts retreated across the deserted parking lot while the young man continued his nonstop monologue on Alabama politics and the plans he had for the future. Finally, an annoyed Jane Elliott pulled her husband into the car. The young student was "still talking as we pulled away, telling me I was the greatest man that's ever been and maybe we'd cross paths again."

Relieved to be out on the highway and heading home, Mrs. Elliott asked, "Who was that?"

"Don't know him," replied her husband. "I think he said his name's George Wallace."[23]

Not content to buttonhole visiting politicians on the campus, Wallace repeatedly hitchhiked to Montgomery to keep alive the political contacts he had made as a young legislative page. In the spring of 1938 he worked as a volunteer in the unsuccessful gubernatorial campaign of his old Barbour County mentor, Chauncey Sparks. State senators and representatives grew accustomed to seeing the young student wandering around the lobby of their favorite haunt, the Exchange Hotel. To friends, Wallace confided his plans to run for the state legislature when he graduated.

The Japanese attack on Pearl Harbor reshuffled his ambitions. The campus soon echoed to the sound of marching cadences as Army and Navy Reserve Officer Training programs doubled, tripled, then quadrupled, and class schedules dissolved into chaos as twenty percent of the faculty left for military duty. More than 13,000 men in a dozen training programs soon crowded the university while regular enrollment dropped from 5,000 in the fall of 1941 to 1,850 by the spring of 1944.[24] A number of Wallace's friends (including Frank Johnson) joined the officer training program; he did not. He was allowed to graduate in June 1942, but knew it was a matter of time before he was drafted. Enrolling in the United States Army Air Force, he awaited his final induction notice and continued to cultivate his political connections.

While he waited, Chauncey Sparks moved to the front of a crowded field of gubernatorial candidates. The sixty-two-year-old lifelong bachelor proved an adaptable "born-aginner" candidate: against organized labor, against social welfare of any kind, against progressive taxation, against anything that smacked of the hated "collectivist" New Deal. The traditional Black Belt leadership, as well as Birmingham's Big Mules, rallied around Sparks in order to defeat Big Jim Folsom, the rustic north Alabama liberal who promised an Alabama version of Franklin Roosevelt's policies.[25]

Wallace might be a devoted follower of Roosevelt, but in Alabama politics, geography and friendship always proved thicker than ideology. Despite the pressure of law school classes and exams, he showed up in Montgomery in the final days of the 1942 primary campaign to run errands as he had done six years earlier. Sparks seemed amused by the hyperactive Wallace. After his election, the governor-elect wrote a letter to his young supporter, promising a job in state government when the war was over. Wallace carried that letter, creased and ragged from folding and refolding, with him across his half-dozen stateside postings and on to his ultimate assignment in the Pacific.[26]

HE had survived the last semester of law school waiting tables and washing dishes at his Tenth Street boardinghouse. Flat broke by the end of June 1942, he passed out a few cards announcing that he was practicing law with his slightly older friend Ralph Adams; without a law office or any connections in Tuscaloosa, the young attorney found that clients did not beat a path to his door.[27] But he managed to persuade a gullible highway department superintendent that he was a skilled dump-truck driver and was soon driving a state asphalt truck for the grand sum of thirty cents an hour.[28] With his first paycheck, he insisted on taking Ruth and Frank Johnson out to dinner.[29]

His financial problems temporarily solved, he was free to pursue a pretty, soft-spoken sixteen-year-old girl whom he had met in a Tuscaloosa dime store. "He always seemed to have very young high school girls with him," Ruth Johnson recalled. "I believe he sought [them] out . . . more for an adoring audience than for any romantic involvement."[30]

With Lurleen Burns, it was different from the start. To Wallace's first major biographer, the meeting between the young law school graduate and the high school senior was a scene out of a Tennessee Williams play. On that warm summer afternoon in 1942, wrote Marshall Frady, Wallace parked his asphalt truck at the curb outside Kresge's five-and-ten-cent store and "strolled up to Lurleen's counter—the still air filled with a sleepy whir of fans, the scent of popcorn heavy and delicious—and asked for a bottle of hair oil" ("Brilliantine," as Wallace recalled).[31] Smitten with the pretty young woman—she was just sixteen—he arranged a proper introduction through a mutual friend; on their first date, they shared a sandwich and Coke together at the nearby H. & W. Drug Store on Lurleen Burns's lunch break. He was soon pursuing her with the same intensity with which he had wooed potential campus voters. "She was all I could think about," Wallace recalled.[32]

Almost every evening after work, he boarded an aging city bus for the short trip across the Black Warrior River to Northport, where Lurleen lived with her older brother, Cecil, and her parents, Henry and Janie Estelle Burns. Occasionally, the two returned to Tuscaloosa for movies at the venerable Bama Theater. More often, given the state of his finances, they sat and talked through the evening in the parlor of the Burnses' small five-room bungalow on Eighth Street. More accurately: he talked, and she listened.

If George Wallace had grown up in a family that slipped from middle-class comfort to near poverty, Lurleen Burns was pure working class. Northport was a cheerless, run-down community. Many of its men worked in Tuscaloosa's B. F. Goodrich rubber plant or in the Gulf States Paper Mill, the Reichold Chemical Company, or the Central Foundry, which fouled the Black Warrior River. Some were strip coal miners. Still others worked on the loading docks along the river, which fed into the Tombigbee and ultimately into Mobile Bay. Henry Burns owned a small farm, but he spent most of his life working as a laborer—first as a bargeman on the river, and finally as a crane operator in the Mobile shipyards. Lurleen's mother, Janie Estelle, came from three generations of Alabama farmers. Both the Burnses were what middle-class contemporaries liked to describe approvingly as "good country people": soft-spoken, hardworking, law-abiding, churchgoing—and poor.[33]

At Tuscaloosa County High, which most of the country boys and girls attended (in contrast to the more upscale city high school), Lurleen Burns was an indifferent student. In later years teachers enthusiastically described her as someone who was "always sweet, gentle and thoughtful of other people. She was a very good girl."[34] Family friends remembered her as a confirmed tomboy, who often joined her much-loved brother, Cecil, on his fishing rambles along the banks of the Black Warrior.

At fourteen, her childish tow hair darkened, her figure filled out, and her flashing green eyes suddenly lighted on a new interest: boys. Often in hot water with her teachers for "cutting up" in classes, Lurleen, said her best friend, Lou Davis, was a "happy go lucky person, with more time for playing than for studying."[35] She was enthusiastic about her routines as high school majorette and followed sports avidly, but had little interest in books and—like most young southern women of her generation—absolutely none in the subject that obsessed her new boyfriend. "Politics," she explained, "was something Daddy discussed at our house with other people, not with me."[36] After graduation from high school, she talked about nursing school, a common aspiration for young women of her generation who grew up in working-class families. But she was too young for any of the programs in the state, and in any case her academic record was marginal. When Lurleen Burns met George Wallace that summer of 1942, she had begun typing and shorthand courses at a local business college.[37]

By the time her new boyfriend received his final induction notice in February 1943 and shipped out to south Florida for basic training, the two were spending almost every spare moment together. As with many wartime romances, crisis became the catalyst for marriage.

Shortly after he arrived at the Air Force Cadet Training Program in Arkadelphia, Arkansas, Wallace began complaining of fatigue and listlessness. On April 1, when he presented himself at the base hospital with a sore throat and a high fever, doctors quickly diagnosed spinal meningitis. For nearly a week, the young airman lay in a coma. Even following treatment with sulfadiazine, one of the first of the miracle drugs of the 1940s, he remained in critical condition for nearly three weeks. In mid-May 1943, doctors released him for a thirty-day medical leave. Frail and weak—his weight had dropped to 122 pounds—he took the first train to Tuscaloosa. "My reunion with Lurleen confirmed what both of us had long known," Wallace later recalled; "we were desperately in love." With surprising candor, he added, "We wanted each other so much that we decided on immediate marriage." At a time when religious and respectable families condemned premarital sex, even between engaged couples, marriage was the only acceptable route.[38]

Just after noon on May 21, Judge Adolph Forster pronounced them man and wife and they dutifully boarded the train to Montgomery so that Lurleen could meet her new mother-in-law for the first time.[39] Mozelle Wallace had sold the family home in Clio and had taken a secretarial job in the state health department; she shared a two-bedroom apartment with her daughter, Marianne. George Wallace and his new bride arrived unannounced. With considerable understatement, he later recalled that his mother was "shocked and surprised" at the marriage. She did not invite her son and daughter-in-law to stay overnight.[40]

The newlyweds took a cab to the same worn Catoma Street boardinghouse where George Wallace had lived as a Senate page eight years earlier.[41]

After breakfast they traveled to Clio, where they moved in with a friend of the Wallace family. For the rest of the week, Lurleen Wallace's new husband would leave after breakfast and spend the morning visiting with men along the main street of his hometown. After a quick lunch with his wife, he would return to the storefronts for an afternoon of more talking and politicking. Despite the fact that he was on his honeymoon, said one amused friend, he "wasn't real happy unless he was talkin' to the boys and shakin' somebody's hand, that's all."[42] If a wedding night in a boardinghouse and a week in a borrowed room in Clio fell short of the honeymoon most women dream about, Lurleen Burns Wallace never complained.[43]

The young bride who followed her new husband back to Arkansas was isolated and lonely until Wallace introduced her to the warmhearted Arkadelphia housewife and part-time office worker who had befriended him when he first arrived. Wynnie Sanders, or Mom Sanders as many of the Air Force cadets called her, had become an unofficial den mother to many of the homesick servicemen assigned to the training program. The small home that she and her husband had built in the 1930s was always crowded with airmen. They corresponded with her for years afterward.

Wynnie Sanders was always fond of her "young men," as she proudly called them, but she was particularly attached to George Wallace. And Lurleen "was truly a daughter to us in every sense," she remembered, the daughter she had never had. The gregarious Mrs. Sanders and the shy young woman from Alabama were soon inseparable. Lurleen accompanied her new friend to her job at a local lumber company and eagerly volunteered to do all the typing and to help keep the books. A rare week went by when the Sanderses did not have the couple over for dinner. On the weekends "Mom" Sanders gave tactful cooking lessons. "I also taught Lurleen how to can peaches, beans, pickles and things like that," recalled Wynnie Sanders. "She said she needed to learn because she expected to live in a small town all her life." On August 6, 1944, the last night before the young airman and his wife moved on to the next base assignment, she prepared all their favorite dishes: fried chicken, pole beans, collard greens, fresh corn on the cob, and apple cobbler.[44]

ALTHOUGH George Wallace had talked vaguely about becoming a pilot when he joined the air corps, his bout with spinal meningitis washed out any hope of completing the cadet program. And he turned down a chance to go to Officer Candidate School. "I sensed that if I got back to Alabama and into politics," he said, "there would be far more GIs among the electorate than officers."[45] Instead he was assigned to the fleet of long-range B-29 bombers intended for the last strike at the Japanese homeland.

Even before the outbreak of the war with Japan, American military planners realized that the vast distances of the Pacific required the development of a completely new long-range bomber if the United States was to have any offensive capability in the Far East; after Pearl Harbor, the project assumed the highest national priority. The Boeing Company, which eventually won the competition, settled on a daring and innovative design. Ninety-nine feet long, 138,500 pounds in weight when fully loaded, with a speed of 300 knots, the B-29 could fly nearly 4,000 miles at an altitude of 35,000 feet and deliver a 20,000-pound bomb load visually or with its onboard radar system. The new aircraft required a pilot, copilot, navigator, radar and radio operators, flight engineer, bombardier, three machine-gunners, and a gunnery fire-control officer who perched in a bubble atop the giant bomber. Air Force public-relations officers soon dubbed the craft the Superfortress because of its ability to absorb enormous amounts of damage and continue flying.

Despite its great promise, dozens of potentially fatal flaws in design and performance plagued the first generation of B-29s, rushed into service in late 1943 and early 1944. The powerful new engines repeatedly overheated and exploded in flames, and pilots soon learned the grim calculus of a "blowtorch": unless onboard foam extinguishers could put out the fire, the crew had less than two minutes to bail out before the wing's collapse sent the plane cartwheeling end over end. Only toward the end of 1944 did nearly a thousand design changes resolve some (though not all) of the most critical defects and allow the Air Force to begin shipping large numbers of the new aircraft to the Pacific.

In the twenty-two months between the end of his Arkadelphia training and his assignment to the Pacific, Wallace graduated from mechanics school to a training program as a flight engineer for the B-29. In early 1945, he received orders to report to Alamogordo, New Mexico. Richard Zind, a twenty-year-old newly married private from Chicago, was also posted to the base. Even before he unpacked, Zind's barracks sergeant sent him off to pick up a sidearm and armband in order to serve guard duty on the graveyard shift. As he strapped on his pistol Zind heard a "terrible row" in the next room and glimpsed a skinny (and slightly tipsy) airman standing inches away from a scowling military policemen. "I know my rights," the scrawny little airman kept yelling. "I'm a lawyer and you can't do this! I know my rights." When the eleven men assembled for the first time the following day, Zind realized that he had unknowingly observed the crew's flight engineer, George Wallace.[46]

At least three of the crew—Wallace, Zind, and Robert Bushouse—brought their wives to Alamogordo. Lurleen Wallace had shuttled back and forth for almost two years between temporary off-base quarters and her home in Alabama; she arrived in the early spring of 1945 with their new daughter, five-month-old Bobbi Jo. Wallace met them at the crowded train terminal with the embarrassed admission that he had made no arrangements for housing in the overcrowded base town. After spending one night in the March chill on a screened porch with the baby nestled between them, and another week in a single room, they snapped up a tiny two-room shanty which an enterprising local had converted from a chicken house. "It did have electricity and a kerosene stove," recalled a crew member, "but it was barely winterized and the floor was still dirt!"[47] (Actually, a thin layer of concrete topped the hard-packed ground.) Wallace had no apologies: "These were great accommodations in those days. . . . We were well off compared to some service families."[48]

Stretched between classes and training flights were long weekends. Alamogordo Air Base (now Holloman Air Force Base) lay in one of the most bleakly beautiful landscapes in North America, on the eastern edge of a desert, with the San Andres Mountains to the west and the Sacramento Mountains to the north. From the desert floor, where summertime daytime temperatures could soar above a hundred degrees, it was possible to stand on the main airfield and look northeast to the snow-covered twelve-thousand-foot Sierra Blanca Peak. In the foothills surrounding the mountain, in the heart of the Mescalero Apache Indian Reservation, the descendants of Geronimo still lived.

In their twelve weeks at Alamogordo, crew members got together for weekend parties and cookouts; in groups of three or four, they made long weekend drives north to Albuquerque and south through the Jarilla Mountains to Las Cruces and El Paso to explore the breathtaking and exotic landscape. All were young, and most partied with a frenetic gaiety. Several of the single men cherished hazy recollections of wild and raucous dancing parties, heavy drinking, and amorous escapades of a kind Havelock Ellis had never described. "A *wild party* in Victorville—girls—sex in a car—wild party after pickup in a bar . . . —sex in someone's house," reminisced tail gunner Art Feiner. "She wanted my wings for her collection—date with Indian girl in Alamogordo—sex in Ruidoso (a mountain village near Alamogordo)."[49]

Several members of the crew became inseparable, but George and Lurleen stayed aloof—in part because they were the only couple with a child; in part because of Lurleen's insecurity with the other more gregarious and sophisticated wives. At least twice, Wallace joined the crew for weekend picnics, but he did not bring his wife and baby. Lurleen Wallace spent her time in the small lean-to taking care of Bobbi Jo and preparing meals for her husband when he came home from the base. Despite the isolation, she loved being a mother, and she eagerly looked forward to her husband's evening return, to his intense conversations as he looked past the war to the future. Long into the night "he'd talk about what he was someday going to do, run for the legislature, build up a good record and maybe run for United States Congress," she remembered. "He couldn't wait to get back home and get started on his ambitions."[50]

During their three months at the New Mexico base, the eleven men attended long days of classes, practiced nerve-racking touch-and-go landings, and made high-altitude swings over the hundred-mile-long range for simulated bombing attacks. Missions as far west as California's Santa Catalina Island and eastward to a bombing range on the Isle of Pines off the coast of Cuba simulated the long flights they would take in the Pacific. Although Wallace and his new crew did not have to dodge Japanese fighters and anti-aircraft fire, they often seemed equally jeopardized by the casual maintenance of the planes they were flying. The best mechanics had been dispatched to the Pacific; the result was, at times, a kind of Russian roulette. During the last three months of 1944, more than a half-dozen B-29s stationed at Alamogordo went down because of mechanical failure, and few sorties returned to base without reporting an engine fire, a feathered engine, or other mechanical problems.[51] Nineteen-year-old gunner Johnny Petroff spent every spare moment sacked out—a defense against chronic depression and the tensions of training for combat.

On April 15, on a simulated high-altitude bombing mission, disaster threatened. Before dawn Captain Jack Ray and his crew, including flight engineer George Wallace, headed westward nearly eight hundred miles across Arizona to a drop zone over a gunnery and ordnance range just west of southern California's remote Chuckwalla Mountains. As they made their final run, bombardier George Harbinson opened the bay doors and began the countdown for releasing the plane's rack of hundred-pound practice bombs. But heavy cloud cover obscured the target area below, and Captain Ray, still unfamiliar with the plane's newly installed radar equipment, insisted on a visual drop. Reluctantly, he turned eastward to return to Alamogordo.

But the fore and aft electric bomb-bay doors refused to retract. No one wanted to land a B-29 with an open bomb bay: a hard bounce in landing could crush the open doors into the practice bombs, detonating them and scattering the aircraft across the California countryside.

Swearing with frustration, the intrepid Bushouse, the B-29's fire-control officer, hooked his parachute straps over a bar as a primitive safety strap, dropped down headfirst from the upper bomb racks—ten thousand feet above the hillsides of the Little San Bernardino Mountains—and tried without success to reach the lower racks to place disarming cotter pins in the practice bombs. George Leahy, radioman Dick Zind, and gunner Art Feiner held his feet.[52]

When Wallace tersely reported that one of the engines was out of control and overheating, Captain Ray began a rapid descent toward the nearest military airport. Unfortunately, Victorville had been designed for smaller single-engine and twin-engine planes; the runway was more than a thousand feet short of the recommended minimum length for a B-29. Ray gave permission for everyone to parachute to safety except the copilot and the flight engineer, Wallace, who was needed to monitor the engines. All elected to ride the plane down. The B-29, port engine ablaze, touched the ground so gently that several crew members realized they had landed only when they heard the brakes. As they screeched to a halt, co-pilot Jason Riley extinguished the fire.[53]

Less than two weeks after the harrowing landing in California, the eleven received their orders. With the war over in Europe they had been assigned to the Marianas for the last push before the scheduled fall invasion of the Japanese home islands. There was time for the long exhausting overland train trip back to Alabama and one last furlough. Years later, George Wallace remembered the continuous crying of Bobbi Jo and late-night curses from restless passengers as they made the two-day trip from Amarillo to Mobile, where Lurleen would live with her mother and father until the war was over.[54]

At Topeka, Kansas, Wallace rendezvoused with his crew to pick up one of the new B-29's ferried in almost every hour from Boeing's main assembly plant in nearby Wichita. Captain Ray asked for names for their new craft; when consensus proved impossible, he exercised his command prerogative and dubbed it the *Sentimental Journey* after the theme song of Les Brown's Band of Renown. Each man solemnly kicked in five dollars for the artist to inscribe the new logo, and on June 6, they lifted off the ground for a first test flight.[55] Ten days later, they were on their way to the war.

Robert Bushouse sat in his bubble atop the B-29 looking backward as they flew over the Golden Gate Bridge and watched the lights of San Francisco fade into the distance. "I thought to myself," he remembered, "I may never see this country again."[56] George Leahy had less dramatic feelings. In a typical military snafu, air force records had lost all his medical reports. Forced to retake eleven immunizations, he felt so sick he could only pray, "Let's get this over with."[57] Leahy, initially scheduled to ship out in February, had been reassigned after a bout of illness. Two weeks before their training ended, Leahy learned that the plane flown by his original team was "hit by flac [sic] and exploded over Tokyo."[58] The news sent him into a week-long depression. It unnerved George Wallace as well.

Even though the Air Forces tried to keep up morale, every airman knew the figures for flight losses in the Pacific. Through November and December 1944, on each mission, crews faced a 5.7 percent chance of being downed by Japanese air defenses or mechanical failure. With each flight, the odds against a safe return climbed; the chance of a crew completing its thirty-five missions was theoretically less than fifty percent. While aircraft losses declined through the spring of 1945, crew members were hardly encouraged by their last briefing in Sacramento.[59] As they prepared to head westward across the Pacific, Air Forces lawyers helped them prepare their wills.[60]

Three weeks earlier Wallace had spent his last day of leave strolling through the sun-filled streets of Mobile. Depressed and disconsolate, he repeatedly broke down and wept as he and Lurleen packed his bags. "I would look at her and she would look at me, and I thought my heart would break."[61] At the Mobile station, as "I walked down the steps with my flight bag, a feeling came over me that I might never see her again," he said. He had tried to put up a brave front, but he began weeping again as he reached the platform to board the train.[62]

Piloting their brand new B-29, Captain Ray and his green crew took off for the island of Tinian in the Marianas. During a stopover at Guam, Art Feiner acidly recalled, "some General . . . took our brand new ultra modern Sentimental Journey for himself . . . and gave us some beat up rinky dink '29 to take to Tinian."[63] Despite the loss of their plane, in later years the men always referred to themselves as crew members of the *Sentimental Journey,* perhaps because the substitute aircraft had the distinctly uneuphonious name of *Little Yutz.* They reached their new base on June 20, just as the air war over Japan reached a climax.

By the summer of 1945, the bleak coral island of Tinian had become home to thousands of airmen, soldiers, and sailors who lived in a sea of Quonset huts and tents surrounding the two runways. Most of the men and women stationed there minded the occasional Japanese soldiers still hiding in undiscovered caves less than they did the cold saltwater showers and miserable facilities.

While the capture of the Marianas in the fall of 1944 had made possible the first B-29 raids upon Japan, the initial bombing runs over major Japanese cities had resulted in heavy losses and minimal target damage. The huge B-29 Superfortresses could drop their 20,000-pound bomb loads from 31,000 feet, above the effective height of Japanese anti-aircraft ground fire (though not above the effective ceiling of Japanese fighters). But General Curtis LeMay, pioneer of nonevasive, straight-ahead bombing techniques in the European theater in 1943 and early 1944, soon became frustrated over the ineffectual results of these high-level daylight bombing missions.

Beginning in March 1945, the General launched a series of low-level nighttime incendiary attacks, which ignited huge firestorms in Japan's flimsily built wooden cities.[64] The Japanese called the first raid over Tokyo *himate,* "Raid of the Fire Wind." In that March 9 sortie, the fires that whipped through the city destroyed a quarter of a million buildings and killed more than 83,000 people, more than the well-known Allied raids on Dresden and Hamburg, more than the number immediately killed at Hiroshima. By June, fifty-seven square miles of Japan's capital lay in ashes and the city had ceased to exist as a military target. For the people below, said the usually prosaic LeMay, "it was as though Tokyo had dropped through the floor of the world and into the mouth of hell."[65]

Although Japan's depleted fighter command was almost totally ineffectual against the waves of American bombers, there were still formidable air defenses around the main Japanese cities, and mechanical failure forced dozens of B-29 crews to ditch their planes during the sixteen-hour-flight. The March 1945 invasion of Iwo Jima, halfway between Japan and the Marianas, provided an emergency landing site for crippled planes; by the time Wallace and his crew members arrived on Tinian, the number of planes on each mission had fallen from five percent to less than two percent. But Allied losses continued through the last spring and summer of the war in the Pacific. On a single May 25–26 mission over the industrial suburbs of Tokyo, 26 of 464 B29s went down.

George Wallace and his crew experienced heavy anti-aircraft fire for the first time in a July 9 night raid over the Japanese city of Sendai. By the time Captain Ray turned over command to bombardier Harbinson, the stench of the burning city filled the airplane. Crew members could clearly see the probing searchlights, the swirling columns of smoke rising through the darkness from red, orange, and yellow lakes of fire, and the tracer lines above the four-square-mile conflagration while bursts of exploding flak drowned the staccato din of voices from their radio headsets. Kevin Herbert, a B-29 tail gunner who flew out of the Marianas on many of the same missions, also remembered a low, keening sound that never seemed to stop, like the "cries of the living and the curses of the dead, from those falling out of the sky above and others pinned to the earth below."[66]

Isolated from the crew, his face covered by his oxygen mask, tail gunner Art Feiner was convinced that the other ten men on the plane could sense his absolute terror. "I knew I was supposed to be a man," said Feiner. But he was revolted at the idea of killing people, and—more than anything else—apprehensive that he might break down in front of his friends. By the time they had turned eastward toward the safety of the Pacific, his anxiety attack passed, but he never forgot the moment of sheer panic.[67]

Over the next five weeks, the men settled into the routine of their missions, all but one of which were nighttime incendiary attacks. After briefing, preflight checks, and takeoff between five and seven P.M., they took their place in the squadron formation for the long flight. Cruising the first four hours at one thousand feet to save fuel, they droned past the northern Marianas—Pagan, Asuncion, and Maug—and on to the Bonins. Over Iwo Jima, the halfway point, crew members heard the shifting pitch of the propellers as the lumbering B-29s slowly began their climb to bombing altitude, usually ten thousand to twelve thousand feet for night raids. Six to seven hours into the mission, they put on their oxygen masks in case a shell-burst depressurized the plane. Then they could only wait as the navigator brought them to their assembly point off the coast, ready to begin the terrifying twenty-minute run over their target.

On the long journey back, crew members—particularly the gunners—unwound while the pilot and copilot switched off flying time. But the nervous Wallace never relaxed. Every twenty to thirty minutes, he would instruct Bushouse, perched in the dome above the aircraft: "You watch those engines [for oil leaks], you heah?" His fellows sometimes laughed at Wallace for the way his southern accent deepened under stress, but they were secretly grateful for the neurotic attention he lavished upon his engines.[68] Back on Tinian after carefully going through their post-flight check and a quick debriefing, the eleven always gathered in their Quonset quarters as Captain Ray ceremoniously uncorked a fifth of whiskey and vigorously shook a large can of grapefruit juice. By the time bottle and chaser had made the circle once, both were gone. Then the men stumbled to their beds and awoke to the sound of crews going to chow at six P.M.

In early 1945, medical advisers to the Twentieth Air Force warned against the danger of combat fatigue; to maintain fitness and morale they recommended sixty flying hours per month. But LeMay never had enough men to enforce the guidelines. In late June, Captain Ray and his men, as well as the other B-29 crews, flirted with exhaustion as average monthly flight times reached as high as 130 hours.[69]

In many ways, the George Wallace who flew out of Tinian was unchanged from his years in Tuscaloosa. With his ever-present cigar and slicked-back hair, he looked like a "young raggedy Edward G. Robinson—tough," said Dick Zind. Others were quick to make the comparison with Robinson's most famous gangster character, Little Caesar. But the Alabamian was quick to greet other airmen with a smile and seemed as desperate as ever to be liked; "ingratiating" was the word one fellow airman used to describe him. After decking several opponents, Bushouse, an ex–amateur boxer, found it difficult to persuade fellow airmen to volunteer for a few rounds of sparring. Wallace offered to get in the ring with him. Bushouse, sizing up the thin, pale Wallace, demurred. "I told him I knew he was a good boxer and fast," said Bushouse, "but I was afraid I would hit him too hard and things might get out of hand and then we wouldn't be friends anymore." Wallace, who weighed 130 pounds to Bushouse's 180, seemed relieved.[70]

He quickly mastered the role of hillbilly innocent, as if to defend his own provincialism with self-deprecating humor. "A lot of those boys thought you were just ignorant 'cause you came from the South," he recalled. When an airman from Chicago mentioned the El train and then stopped to explain the abbreviation, Wallace—deadpan—insisted: "Ain't no trains that run up over the ground. We ain't so country we don't know there ain't no trains runnin' along on tracks up in the air with sticks. We ain't *that* country."[71] At Topeka, the base entertainment officer had told assembled airmen that they were trying to get a "big band"—perhaps even Glenn Miller's—for one of the service bashes. "Any other suggestions?" he had asked.

"Yes sir," replied a mock-serious Wallace: "I think Roy Acuff has a real good band."[72]

At times his companions glimpsed the intense feelings that lay under his easygoing demeanor. Almost all the crew had the same vivid memory of his political ambition: after a few drinks he would begin to insist, "I'm going to be governor of Alabama someday, you boys wait and see."

The response, recalled the jovial Bushouse, was usually the same: a round of laughter and then the inevitable rejoinder, "George, you are absolutely full of shit." The whole notion of George Wallace as governor of a state seemed absurd, said Bushouse. "He was just a skinny little country bumpkin. Just a country bumpkin."[73]

Less humorous were discussions of race. There were few blacks in the Air Forces, and even fewer on Tinian. Crew members, like all young men testing their mortality and manhood, teased and goaded each other with sarcastic comments that stopped just short of unacceptable. But race was one of those "touchy" subjects too volatile to be easily defused with humor, particularly since the group was divided almost fifty–fifty between southerners and northerners. Wallace, however, would launch into a lecture on the subject at a moment's notice. "You don't know what it's like living in Barbour County, Alabama," he would explain with quiet intensity. "I don't hate them. . . . The colored are fine in their place, don't get me wrong. But they're just like children, and it's not something that's going to change. It's written in stone. It's written in stone."[74]

"It was hard to tell if he was absolutely serious, or he was just practicing his debating skills," said Dick Zind, who liked Wallace but was sometimes unsettled by the Alabamian's passion on the subject of black inferiority. Crewmate Art Feiner, a passionate reader of Sean O'Casey and James Joyce who became a clinical psychologist after the war, held views on race 180 degrees away from George Wallace's. At an army dance in San Antonio, outraged by railroad ties separating blacks and whites, he had jumped over the barrier with his girl. (Military police ushered them back to the "white side of righteousness," recalled Feiner.) But the Bronx-born gunner took a more philosophical approach to Wallace: "It's just part of his culture. You can't expect him to change overnight."

Wallace seldom shared such talk with airmen outside his crew. Hawk Johnson, who bunked in an adjoining Quonset hut, remembered him as quiet, withdrawn, "hardly your typical 'grip and grin' politician." He seldom initiated conversation, certainly not on politics, said Johnson, and he seemed curiously passive.[75] During their days off, Wallace often disappeared for long hours. "It was funny, he just got up and left. He didn't socialize all that much with members of the crew." Dick Zind had the impression that he was out looking up fellow airmen from Alabama, but Wallace talked very little about his home or past (though they all knew he had gone to law school).

They did remember him hunched over one of the tables at the hastily assembled base post office, scribbling note after note to the voters of Barbour County. Wallace had begun this practice during his first days in the service; in Christmas of 1943 and 1944 he exercised his right as a member of the military to send mail postage-free. By the spring of 1945, he had mailed hundreds of cards to the folks back home, with a scrawled "Merry Christmas, your friend, George Wallace."

On July 19, 1945, with 126 other B-29s, Jack Ray's crew rendezvoused east of the coast for a night raid on Fukui, one of the most important industrial cities of Honshu. In this railroad center of almost 300,000 people, dozens of factories turned out aircraft parts, electrical equipment, machine tools, rubber goods, chemicals, and textiles. During a spring and summer when high winds and poor visibility had often hampered the missions over Japan, the nineteenth brought clear skies, relatively moderate winds, and only sporadic and ineffectual anti-aircraft fire. Shortly after one A.M., the first pathfinders marked the targets, and the B-29s, in a twenty-two-mile fan-shaped formation, rolled in over the city. By the time Captain Ray made his approach at 12,800 feet, the city was engulfed in flames (eighty-five percent of Fukui would burn that night), and he warned the crew that they were approaching a thermal rising from one of the fires set by the first wave of bombers. Everyone braced; within seconds after releasing their bombs, they hit the updraft. It was, Bushouse remembered, a "monster" current.

Freed from a seven-ton load of incendiary bombs, the plane shot upward. In the brightly illuminated night sky, the tail gunner saw a pursuing Japanese fighter tumbling end over end like a matchbox thrown into the air, while Wallace, facing backward in his engineer's chair, was convinced that the flexing wings would buckle under the strain. Ray and copilot Jason Riley watched helplessly as the altimeter spun frantically around to thirteen, fourteen, fifteen, sixteen, seventeen, and eighteen thousand feet. In a matter of seconds they reached nearly twenty thousand feet before the giant aircraft slipped off the thermal on its side and plunged downward toward the outskirts of Fukui.[76]

Bushouse, like the other gunners, lay trapped in his firing harness as the ground swept upward. "This is it, this is it, this is it," he repeated to himself.

Somehow, he said, the most unfair part seemed that it took so long to happen. "I had time to get out, but of course the force of the dive had me pressed up against the firing harness; I couldn't move."[77]

At four thousand feet Ray managed to level the plane out, only to discover they had lost two engines and were directly over a number of anti-aircraft guns firing from point-blank range. But their luck held. Wallace, working feverishly at his engineering panel, managed to restart both engines.

Miraculously, crew members suffered nothing except a few bangs and bruises, but they were, remembered Bushouse, a "stinking mess." In the radar room in the center section of the plane, the full five-gallon pail under the chemical toilet had spilled its contents, covering floor, walls, and ceilings. "It took us three hours to clean up that mess after we landed, but we didn't complain. We were just glad to be alive."[78]

At Okinawa, halfway home, the pilot and Wallace decided they had enough fuel to make it back to Tinian. "The sun was coming up and dead in our eyes, we were cruising at 6,000 feet on auto-pilot, we were all exhausted . . . ," recalled Jack Ray. "Watch it for a while, J.O.," he told his copilot, "I'm going to take a little nap." He climbed up, lay down on the flight deck, and was instantly asleep.

Two hours later, the sun high in the sky and shining in his face, Ray sat up with a start. His copilot was slumped in his seat, eyes closed; Wallace, too, "had his head on his console, asleep."

Clambering back into his seat, Ray began calling the roll. "There was not a soul awake" and they were 150 miles off course. For the next three hours, Wallace shifted his fuel load and adjusted his engines again and again to squeeze the last moment of flying time out of the dwindling fuel. When they touched down on the runway, the crew cheered. As they taxied back to their bay, the inboard engines cut off: the tanks were bone dry. They opened an extra fifth of whiskey for a postflight toast to the pilot and copilot and to George Wallace, who had managed to coax the plane's engines home.[79]

LeMay had hoped to launch a thousand planes on August 1, 1945, to celebrate Armed Forces Day. While the general had to content himself with putting 784 B-29s over Hachioji, Toyama, Nagaoka, and Mito, Japan, Wallace would always remember the silver Superfortresses in their tight V-shaped formations, "thousands of bombers"—or so it seemed in his memory—"glintin' in the sun as far as you could look in any direction."[80] A young bombardier who served with him remembered those last weeks on Tinian. "He was skinny as a rail, and nervous as hell. Just jumpy all the time."

In the late afternoon of August 5, the *Little Yutz* lifted off from Tinian on its ninth combat mission and rendezvoused with other squadrons from the 58th Wing for an incendiary raid over the city of Saga. Although pathfinder bombers had marked the target with incendiaries, dense cloud cover forced the attackers to rely entirely upon radar. None of the men saw any of Japan's handful of night fighters, and there was only listless anti-aircraft fire.[81]

An hour after daybreak over the Pacific, the plane's return flight path crossed that of the westbound *Enola Gay* as it droned toward the city of Hiroshima.[82]

When Captain Ray's crew checked in on Tinian, the debriefing was "peculiar," recalled Dick Zind. Instead of questions about their bombing mission, debriefers repeatedly asked about radio messages, "unusual sights and sounds," or anything out of the ordinary. And a surprise waited at their Quonset hut: orders to return to California for additional flight training. Because of their outstanding record, they had the dubious honor of having been selected as part of the elite group of flight crews chosen for lead bomber duty in the final assault upon Japan. Within hours, they were flown from Tinian to Guam, where they crowded aboard an air transport with more than 130 other crewmen being sent back to the United States, some for additional training, others because they had flown their thirty-five missions.

Somewhere between Guam and Hawaii, the copilot walked back into the cabin of the air transport and announced that the United States had dropped an "atomic bomb" on Hiroshima.

"What the hell is an atomic bomb?" asked one of the fliers.

"I don't know," the copilot replied; "some kind of superbomb."[83]

WALLACE stepped off the plane at Mather Air Field in California on August 9. Offered the chance to hitchhike on air transport back across the country, he chose instead a three-day train trip and returned to Mobile in time to be with Lurleen and Bobbi Jo on V-J Day, August 14. While joyous revelers filled the streets of the city and blocked traffic for hours, a spooked Wallace, exhausted and withdrawn, huddled inside his in-laws' home. "I had survived the war and I wasn't going to get run over in a victory celebration."[84]

Crew members were given a three-week furlough before reporting to California's Muroc (now Edwards) Air Base for training. All had assumed that, with the war effort winding down, their training would be canceled. When they reassembled on August 29, however, they discovered that in the inscrutable ways of the military, they were still assigned to high-risk training in preparation for missions that would never take place because of the Japanese surrender.

George Wallace refused.

In later years, he would justify his decision over and over. He had done his part. Day after day, he had pushed back his fear and willed himself to climb back into his engineer's chair. But even before his last mission, Wallace had neared the end of his mental reserve. After surviving months of dangerous air training and nine combat missions over Japan, he suddenly faced the prospect of slamming into a California hillside while training for a war that no longer existed. "Call it fear, call it anxiety coming to the surface, call it what you will—I decided I was through flying."[85]

There was an old saying in the Air Forces, said Wallace, that a "man can't be forced to fly if he doesn't want to, but he can certainly be made to wish he had wanted to." But he simply dug in his heels. Steadfast, he went up the chain of command with the same request: all he wanted, he stated, "was a clean record and an honorable discharge."

His wing commander brushed him aside. "I'm sorry, Sergeant, but the lead crew training program is still on," he told Wallace. "Your orders are to take part with your crew."

The base operations officer tried a different tactic: shame. "Sergeant, you are obviously a sick man—which is the kindest description I can make of you." When Wallace would not yield, he was ordered to the base hospital for evaluation.[86]

Fortunately for Wallace, with Japan's surrender, the pressure to keep men flying had lessened. A base medical officer confirmed that the young engineer was near collapse. His weight had slipped to 120 pounds, he was anemic and nervous, and he constantly fidgeted and stopped for long sighs. Wandering up and down the halls in his oversized bathrobe, he remained in the hospital for the next thirty days. Crew members who visited found him listless, depressed, and defensive. "I'm not unpatriotic," he kept insisting, "but I've done my share. I'm not going to fly any more."[87]

After several weeks of tests and evaluation, Air Forces physicians concluded that Wallace was unfit to fly. According to their diagnosis, the twenty-five-year-old airman was experiencing a chronic state of "severe anxiety," reflected in "anxiety attacks, anorexia and loss of weight." The examining officer recommended discharge, effective December 8, 1945. A Veterans Administration panel later granted a ten percent disability for "psychoneurosis" induced by combat duty.[88]

From San Francisco, Wallace wired Lurleen the news: he was coming home. As he left the base hospital, Wallace "had a lot of things that needed thinking out very carefully," and his week-long trip across America gave him ample time for reflection. In El Paso, just south of his old training base at Alamogordo, he picked up his mustering-out pay and pushed onto another crowded passenger train which snaked its way across the eight hundred miles of central Texas down through southern Louisiana, over the Mississippi into New Orleans, and finally toward Mobile.

Crewmates had greeted his release from duty with a touch of envy. When tail gunner George Leahy wrote his family that his crew had lost its engineer ("Georgie Wallace was nervous and underweight"), he added with a slight edge: "He expects to be sent to Santa Anna Army Air Force rest camp. . . . I wouldn't mind going there myself. Golfing, swimming, tennis, horseback riding, etc."[89] But neither Leahy nor the other members of his crew ever faulted Wallace for his decision. Most were as anxious as he to return to civilian life, and they had seen enough brave men break at some point to adopt an understanding attitude toward their friend's decision. In the years to come, several of the crew spoke with reporters about their wartime companion; none disclosed his decision to ground himself.

George Wallace always knew the value of flattery, but there was a special passion in his repeated insistence to the men of the *Sentimental Journey* that there were no connections in his long life—not in high school, not in college, not in years of politics—that compared with the bonds they had forged in months of training and combat.[90] Crew members faithfully exchanged letters every Christmas, and when they were finally reunited forty-five years later, "we took up immediately where we had left off," said Art Feiner.[91]

Wallace's comrades understood the pressures he had endured. But it required no great insight to see that, while military service was almost indispensable to election by a young man in post–World War II America, wartime heroism was even more advantageous. George Wallace's exemplary record had ended on a sour note. He dealt with this episode with relative candor, mentioning his flying career cursorily in campaign literature and seldom discussing his combat experiences except in the most self-deprecating way.

The war was over. It was time for the future.

Chapter 3

THE MORAL COMPASS OF AMBITION

===

TWO WEEKS BEFORE Christmas, 1945, Henry Burns dropped his son-in-law beside the road north of Mobile on old Highway 31. Wearing his World War II uniform with sergeant's stripes, George Wallace had no trouble hitchhiking the two hundred miles north to Montgomery.

By nine the following morning he was parked in the waiting room of Governor Chauncey Sparks, clutching the three-year-old letter promising him a postwar appointment. The taciturn Sparks was as good as his word; he told Wallace there was an opening in the attorney general's office for an assistant. Billy McQueen took one look at the twenty-six-year-old—skinny, pale, and almost cadaverous in the same baggy khaki pants and shirt he had worn to hitchhike. Assuring the candidate he would consider his application, the attorney general showed him the door.

With the same persistence that would mark his entire political career, Wallace walked back across the capitol grounds to the governor's office. "I couldn't understand why I wasn't hired on the spot, as the job was vacant and I was the only applicant," he complained to Sparks, who dutifully picked up the telephone and called McQueen. Four hours later, Wallace signed his personnel forms. He would begin work on December 16 at a salary of $175 a month.

Christmas dinner was a can of tomatoes and a box of saltine crackers, eaten at his desk as he prepared legal papers for state bond issues, and briefs for criminal cases under appeal, but he had no real interest in the work.

Within three months George Wallace requested a leave of absence. He was going to run for the legislature.

In California, a thirty-three-year-old ex–naval officer announced his candidacy for Congress; 2,500 miles to the east, a former PT-boat commander, the son of an ex-ambassador, began soliciting votes in Boston's Eleventh Congressional District. George Wallace, Richard Nixon, and John Kennedy were part of a postwar generation anxious to assume leadership as millions of returning GIs triggered a political revolution.

Americans faced skyrocketing inflation, widespread shortages, rising unemployment, and a wave of strikes from a labor movement intent on retaining gains made in the late 1930s and during the war. Fear of communism abroad and at home had already driven a nail in the coffin of the aggressive liberalism of Franklin Roosevelt's New Deal. After Ohio's Senator Robert Taft announced solemnly that the Democrats were "soft on communism," Republicans across the nation used the growing Red scare to link the Roosevelt-Truman policies with appeasement abroad and subversion at home.

The political battle in Alabama in 1946 was fought over the same terrain, but with surprising twists and turns. After eight years of reactionary political leadership under Frank Dixon and Chauncey Sparks, Big Jim Folsom—the self-proclaimed "little man's big friend"—would turn the state leftward against the tide of national politics. For more than a decade after the war, the colorful Folsom dominated the politics of his native state. If Chauncey Sparks had been George Wallace's first mentor, Folsom would become his master teacher.

Louisiana's Huey Long had given everyone a scare in the 1930s when he vaulted into national prominence and raised the specter of a home-grown American fascist movement. But Huey Long was, as his biographer T. Harry Williams said, sui generis. The more persistent image of Southern politicians was that of reckless demagogues whose harangues against blacks played on the emotions of simple, uneducated white farmers and blue-collar workers. Most fought their way into public office on a wave of soak-the-rich rhetoric. Once elected, they made their peace with powerful interest groups and offered their working-class supporters little more than a heavy dose of "nigger"-baiting. The first half of the twentieth century had seen a dreary succession of such unprincipled men: Mississippi's James K. Vardaman and Theodore Bilbo, South Carolina's Coley Blease and Ellison (Cotton Ed) Smith, and Georgia's Eugene Talmadge. Alabama had contributed Thomas (Tom-Tom) Heflin to this depressing rogues' gallery. For four decades as state legislator, then national congressman and senator, he had ranged up and down the state, rhetorical rope and faggot in hand, bellowing for the blood of African Americans and the scalp of that "dago Pope" in Rome.[1]

Heflin and his breed represented the dark side of the picture, but the media exploited a more benign image as well: that of the essentially harmless clown bringing a bit of entertainment to the dreary lives of backwoods folks.

Jim Folsom seemed born for that role.

Six feet eight inches tall and weighing 275 pounds, Big Jim towered over almost everyone around him. The north Alabama insurance salesman and former sailor in the merchant marine had made a habit of running for political office in the 1930s—and losing. When he declared for the governorship in 1946, pundits and editorial writers dismissed his chances. Alabamians, like most other southerners, considered religious piety a requisite for public office. Drinking, fornication, swearing, or gambling spelled political ruin, and Folsom was an acknowledged four-time loser. When chided, he assured followers that he was well aware of his shortcomings. Only recently, he told one rally, the pastor of his Cullman church had approached him about becoming a deacon. Big Jim demurred; perhaps he was not the "best caliber person" for that job. "I take a nip now and then and sometimes my language is not the best."

"That's all right, Jim," his pastor had responded reassuringly. "We want someone to represent the rougher element of the church."[2]

Folsom's roots lay deep in the dissenting tradition of the Alabama yeomanry. For a hundred years, these stubbornly independent upcountry farmers chafed under the dominance of the planter classes of the Black Belt and their post–Civil War allies—the Big Mules of industrializing Birmingham. The Great Depression, the New Deal, and the upheavals brought by World War II laid the foundation for a potential revolution.

In the 1920s, the powerful corporate structures of the metropolitan areas of the state—steel, mining, textile, and shipyard interests—successfully crushed those unions that had emerged in the late nineteenth and early twentieth century. Between 1933 and 1945, however, aided by the policies of Franklin Roosevelt's administration, membership in the state's labor unions tripled to nearly 200,000, to make Alabama the most unionized state in the Deep South. And most of these new members joined the Congress of Industrial Organizations (CIO) Unions, which were far more politically liberal than those of the American Federation of Labor (AFL).[3]

At the same time, the collapse of cotton tenancy pushed tens of thousands of black and white tenants off the land and into the cities of the South and the North. Voters protested the naked inequities of a political system in which sixteen hundred whites in Lowndes County, Alabama (none of the 23,000 blacks voted), exerted as much clout in the state senate as the nearly half-million residents of Birmingham and surrounding Jefferson County. And the 70,000 GIs who returned were anxious to make up for lost time and receptive to the voices of change.[4]

Franklin Roosevelt seldom directly challenged the all-important southern wing of the Democratic Party on racial issues, but many of his policies had unintended consequences. When southern congressmen and senators promoted federally subsidized power and cheap credit or voted for government programs that channeled federal spending into the region, they were primarily interested in making certain that federal largesse was distributed to their constituents. But their actions inevitably promoted the interests of a more dynamic, entrepreneurial generation of southerners less committed than their predecessors to maintaining racial and cultural traditions.

And Roosevelt did encourage what he called a "new generation of Southern political leadership." In the 1930s, Alabama's senators Hugo Black and Lister Hill unapologetically described themselves as "liberals" (at least on nonracial issues); they were joined in the 1940s by John Sparkman and the even more pro–New Deal congressman Carl Elliott. In contrast, the state remained comfortably under the control of politicians who often touted their "progressive" views, but who embraced policies that ran a narrow gamut from reactionary to cautiously conservative.

Folsom challenged that control as no politician had done since the nineteenth century. He bypassed the traditional conservative interest groups that dominated state politics: the powerful utility lobbies; the steel and mining interests operating through the state's chamber of commerce; the Black Belt planters with their operating arm, the Farm Bureau; and the highly politicized farm extension service (ironically, funded by federal dollars). Instead of meeting and soliciting endorsements from local courthouse officials and appointed community "leaders," Big Jim forged a direct personal link to the voters. A handful of leaflets, a small advertisement in the county weekly, and a few mailings to friends and supporters brought out the crowds in every crossroads, hamlet, and town. With no money and little organization, he traveled across the state in a raucous and joyous political medicine show, and reshaped the face of Alabama's politics.

By the time Folsom's caravan of a half-dozen cars, a sound van, and a flatbed truck had rolled into sight, anywhere from a hundred to a thousand voters—curious, hostile, or committed—would be on hand. Each rally began with a spirited concert by a country music band, the Strawberry Pickers. Folsom wandered through the crowd; few men (and "no damned women," complained an opponent) could resist his easygoing smile and seductive manner as he warmly greeted old friends and offered a bear hug or perhaps a chaste kiss on the cheek to his many female admirers. As the Strawberry Pickers ended their performance, he would clamber onto the back of the truck, run his hand through his tousled hair, nod to some of those in the crowd whom he had not yet greeted, and begin speaking in a low but powerful voice in a style akin to that of Will Rogers.[5]

While his rapt listeners leaned forward, he would hold up the kind of mop used by poor people to clean their worn wooden floors. "You see this corn shuck mop?" he would ask. "I'm going to take that mop and scour out the kitchen and open up the windows and let a green breeze out of the north . . . and you'll have the freshest, sweetest smell that you've seen in that old Alabama capitol since it was built." And then, because he was flat broke and his campaign had the support of none of the state's interest groups, he would pass his "suds bucket" through the crowd. With their hard-earned nickels, dimes, and quarters, voters joined his crusade to sweep the snooty rascals out of Montgomery.[6]

Underneath the hokum and hillbilly humor lay a voice of plainspoken eloquence. For James E. Folsom, the three pillars of a democratic society were the Bill of Rights, an activist and compassionate government, and an absolute, unqualified democracy. Andrew Jackson was his model; Franklin Roosevelt, his hero; his almost childlike faith in the people, the bedrock of his beliefs. "We've just finished fighting a war against hatred and violence," Folsom told his followers; but, he added, fearful voices were seeking to divide "race and race, class and class . . . religion and religion" by complaining of "radical" and "un-American" ideas.[7]

The democratic impulse could be heard in the words of Jesus as he "stood on the Mount of Olives and told us to love one another," Folsom told a meeting of North Carolina Young Democrats. They echoed through the writings of Tom Paine, in the eloquence of the Declaration of Independence, the Bill of Rights, and Lincoln's Gettysburg Address. "They are so simple," said Folsom, "that we often overlook them in our search for massive plans and world charters."

> We have got to give our fellow man the same rights and privileges which we ourselves expect to live by and enjoy. This means that every man and woman has a certain dignity which must be respected; that no man is to be enslaved by another; that every man has a voice in the choosing and operation of the government under which he lives; that he has one vote and the right to cast it; that he fears no reprisal for expressing his honest conviction.[8]

Folsom, like any successful politician, learned to trim his sails, but the core of his democratic faith remained intact. Nothing reflected that consistency more fully than his refusal to capitulate to the siren call of racism. Whenever he stepped down from the stump, recalled a political acolyte, "he immediately went to the first black person he could see and made it a point to shake hands with him and with everyone there."[9]

Most respectable whites were not threatened by this breach of racial decorum. Neither did they protest when Big Jim, in a statewide radio address, asked pointedly if Alabama's blacks, who made up thirty-five percent of the population, were "getting 35% of the fair share of living." Were they "provided with sufficient professional training which will produce their own doctors, professors, lawyers, clergymen, scientists—men and women who can pave the way for better health, greater earning powers, and a higher standard of living . . . ?" After all, within the framework of segregation, it was the duty of Christian white folks to hold out a helping hand to their colored brothers and sisters.

Had they listened more closely, they would have heard a more disturbing addendum to Folsom's plea for equal as well as separate educational and professional opportunity. "Are the Negroes being given their share of democracy, the same opportunity of having a voice in the government under which they live?" he asked. Folsom meant what he said when he talked about extending the franchise to *everyone,* black and white, rich and poor, by eliminating the poll tax and by ending the practice of automatically refusing to register black applicants. Race was a phony issue, a ploy used by the rich and powerful to divide poor people and blind them to their common interests.[10]

His opponent, Handy Ellis, warned that Folsom's election would lead to the "complete destruction of our segregation laws—laws which are best for the white man and the colored man—laws under which our white folks and colored folks here in Alabama and the South have lived in peace and harmony and friendly understanding."[11] When the political action committee of the Congress of Industrial Organizations—the CIO so hated by southern businessmen—endorsed Folsom, Ellis sharpened his attack. The "Communist left-wing C.I.O." and its head, Sidney Hillman ("a political agitator and rabble rouser . . . born and reared in Russia"), had set their cap on electing his opponent, he warned voters. When these "modern carpetbaggers" descended on the state, the sacred safeguards to the white ballot in Alabama would "vanish like tissue paper in a bonfire."

Red-baiting had worked for Richard Nixon, who in his first political campaign, that same year, had handily defeated Democratic liberal congressman Jerry Voorhis. Voorhis, Nixon charged, had consistently "voted the Moscow–[CIO]–PAC–Henry Wallace line." And Alabama seemed fertile ground for such arguments. Throughout the 1930s and 1940s, the state's most reactionary racial spokesmen had linked even the most timid black challenges to white supremacy with warnings of the growing Red menace, while Birmingham's business leadership bankrolled a flood of propaganda linking labor activism with Communist subversion.

Although Folsom had not publicly sought the support of the CIO, he refused to reject their backing and warned his followers of the real agenda of the "selfish interests" and greedy "got rocks" corporate leaders. They had a simple economic and political philosophy: "meager wages and keeping the people ill-informed."[12] "They are satisfied with things as they are. They are satisfied for Alabama to be way down at the bottom among the 48 states. They are satisfied for Alabama people to make less."[13]

In Black Belt Montgomery, where support for disfranchisement was strongest, Folsom pointed out that some people described as "black" were nearly as white as he was. "I want you to know that the sun didn't bleach 'em," he said sardonically. (In a later gubernatorial campaign he expressed bewilderment about why white folks were getting so worked up about the sacredness of segregation when it looked to him as though there was "a whole lot of integratin' goin' on at night.")[14]

Chagrined corporate leaders confided to one sympathetic newspaper editor that they were spending so much money trying to beat Folsom "they would be 18 months writing the expenditures off their books."[15] But they could only watch with frustration as Big Jim Folsom dismantled his hapless opponent. With his direct appeal to the voters, the little man's big friend had bypassed the traditional levers of political power and turned Alabama's political system upside down.

WHILE Folsom swept across the state, George Wallace practiced his own more modest version of people-to-people politics in his run for the legislature. Lurleen, still shy and embarrassed in the presence of strangers, typed away on a borrowed Underwood at the dining room table of the cramped apartment she and her husband had rented in Clayton. She responded to speaking invitations and wrote dozens of letters to friends and kin of the Wallace family, as well as congratulatory notes to new parents and letters of condolence to grieving relatives. Wallace left before seven A.M. and often did not return until nearly midnight. With no income except the few hundred dollars from his mustering-out pay and a thousand-dollar inheritance from a great-aunt, he could not afford a car. He hitched rides, and when there were no rides available, he walked the four or five miles between communities and stopped at farmhouses and fields along the way.

A woman who had known Wallace since high school watched with amusement as he scurried down the street buttonholing everyone who moved, sat, or breathed. "Oh, he was something, with those *awful* lime-green corduroy pants about two sizes too big," the seat worn until it was as slick as gabardine, she said affectionately. "Going from person to person, just like a little puppy dog. He was a sight. And those shirts. Oh my, those shirts." "George looked to me just like a, he was just like a little boy. Looked just like a little boy," recalled a political contemporary.[16]

Barbour County residents who had known Wallace as a rabies inspector for the health department often greeted his arrival with the gleeful announcement: "We're going to make a dogcatcher a legislator," an observation which said as much about their opinion of the Alabama legislature as it did about the candidate.[17]

One farmer recalled receiving Christmas notes in 1943 and 1944 from someone named "George C. Wallace." He "couldn't quite figger them out. . . . I wasn't quite sure I knew who this George C. Wallace was." And then, in April 1946, as he broke ground for the spring crop, the farmer saw a skinny young man striding down the road and then crossing the furrows, smiling, his hand outstretched, "and all of a sudden I knew why I'd been gettin' them nice cards every Christmas."[18]

The Air Force veteran overwhelmed a well-to-do Clayton businessman and attorney and an Army major still on active duty; of the 421 white voters in and around Clio, fewer than 70 voted for his two opponents.[19] Neighbors might joke about their "dogcatcher" representative, but it was clear that he had few enemies. Despite his poverty and his youth, Wallace had skillfully deployed his assets—a combat record, a name well-known in the county, a network of friends and relatives, and his own irrepressible energy—to forge those personal ties that were the glue of local politics. "Hell, George knew every voter, down to the chicken thieves," said McDowell Lee, the man who later replaced him in the legislature.[20]

Running in conservative Black Belt Barbour County, Wallace had conducted a cautious campaign. He supported Handy Ellis (though he seldom mentioned this on the stump, in order to avoid offending Folsom's backers), and he avoided controversial issues. But he soon found himself drawn to the towering Big Jim, whether because of Folsom's program of public services or his skills at attracting the adulation of voters; perhaps on account of both.

Folsom's smashing runoff victory in the June 1946 primary freed Wallace to become a born-again believer.

WHILE north Alabama towns like Huntsville, Gadsden, and Decatur had begun to spill over their prewar city limits, Montgomery slumbered on. Once a year, like little boys running away from their Baptist camp counselors, legislators abandoned wives and families for a few weeks of chaotic deliberations, punctuated by brief encounters with hardworking prostitutes and more leisurely conversations at well-known political watering holes like the Diplomat Lounge. As long as colleagues avoided breaching the etiquette of racial boundaries, there was considerable tolerance, even approval, of eccentricity. Still, there were limits. One state senator, reported a horrified legislator, had brought his *wife* to the legislative session.

The Folsom administration, bedeviled by unrelenting opposition from conservatives and hamstrung by the new governor's own miscalculations, sputtered along. Wallace had opened a small law office in Clayton above the town's drugstore (rent: $7.50 a month) and had secured a bare-bones apartment next door for his official "residence," but he had little interest in the practice of law. He much preferred the capitol, where, from early in the morning until late at night, he breathed the exhilarating air of his lifelong profession and his only unqualified love: politics. As a page, the young man from Clio had observed the delicate art of obfuscation. Amid the turmoil of the Folsom years, Wallace proved surprisingly adept at allying himself with the popular governor even as he maintained cordial ties with conservatives.

Ignoring the tacit understanding that freshman legislators were to be seen and not heard, Wallace passed on the word to the newly elected governor that he was "available" for the House speakership. (Folsom tactfully ignored the impolitic proposal.) Once in the House, Wallace proudly introduced fifty bills his first session, and quickly gained a reputation among parsimonious conservatives as a dangerous liberal. "He kept his desk so stuffed with that benevolent legislation that it lacked two feet of closing," claimed one veteran representative.[21] When a Montgomery legislative columnist reported that the newcomer intended to place 125 bills on the House calendar during his second term, the freshman issued a denial. "I've heard that rumor myself," he scoffed. "Hell, if people see that in print they'll think I'm going to rewrite the whole state code!" Actually, he said with modesty, "I'm going to introduce only 23 bills."[22]

His first bill in 1947 proposed a two percent tax on liquor sales, to be used to create several community-based, but state-funded, trade schools. With critical support from key legislators and from Folsom the measure won approval. (At Wallace's request, the state board of education named one of the five schools the George C. Wallace, Sr., Technical School.) It was the first of dozens of his proposals for the "furtherance of education, welfare and health."[23]

And he specifically asked for appointment to the board of trustees of all-black Tuskegee University. Wallace later tried to pass off this misstep with crude sexual jokes. "Well, you fellows are old nigger-haters, but I tell you one thing," one aide recalled him saying. "If you would have just spent one weekend with me and those little high-yellow majorettes over at the Tuskegee Institute you never would be against niggers."[24] In fact, he seems to have had a genuine, paternalistic interest in black education, and he may have wanted to keep his political options open in case the small number of black voters should increase in the 1950s. Whatever his motivations, Wallace proved to be an exemplary board member, attending all but one meeting during his tenure from 1950 to 1952.

His brother had returned from military service in the South Pacific with a case of tuberculosis which proved resistant to medication. With veterans' hospitals filled with wartime casualties, authorities sent Gerald to one of the dozens of county tuberculosis hospitals scattered across the state. Since the state paid less than a dollar a day to feed, medicate, and care for each patient, there was only skeleton staffing. On his first visit, George Wallace was appalled to find his brother in a noisy, smelly ward with ten beds. Stronger patients had to dress and bathe those too weak to help themselves. During his first year in office, Wallace traveled across the state, tirelessly promoting an increase in state funds for TB hospitals, and with the support of the Folsom administration, he attached an amendment to the appropriations bill doubling state payments.[25]

If he was a big spender, as conservative critics complained, he was also consistent in his efforts to shift the tax burden onto the shoulders of the wealthy. In 1951, when Folsom's successor, Gordon Persons, proposed an increase in the state's regressive sales tax, George Wallace eloquently denounced the measure. "What about taxes on corporations?" he demanded. "I think the pending bill should be called the 'sock the poor' act. This business of shackling the poor people is exactly what the Big Mules want."[26]

To doctrinaire fiscal conservatives like his old Barbour County friend McDowell Lee, "George Wallace was no more a 'conservative' than Lyndon Johnson. He was basically a big spender who made Folsom look like an amateur."[27] His political ideology, however, was only a faint echo of the earlier radicalism of Alabama populists. After all, Wallace himself always pointed to his successful support for recruitment of industry as his greatest achievement. State officials in a postwar South desperate to continue the economic upsurge of the war years had instituted a variety of industrial-promotion schemes. Some amounted to little more than glossy advertising campaigns enticing companies below the Mason-Dixon line to take advantage of the warm climate, low taxes, and cheap nonunion labor. In nine southern states, however, legislatures approved industrial bond programs, measures that allowed state governments to build plants and industrial parks with cheap, tax-free bonds, to rent them to businesses at nominal rates, and (since title to the property often remained in the hands of state or local government) to exempt them from all state and local taxes.[28]

The Wallace-Cater Act of 1951 (or the "Wallace Act," as he always called it) went one step further, authorizing *local* municipalities to enter directly into contracts with prospective industries and to finance new plants with tax-free municipal bonds. Learning of the measure, a first-term U.S. senator from Massachusetts warned that poor southern communities would end up paying the price for their reckless promotion of tax giveaways. "What happens," asked John Kennedy, "when their newfound [industrial] benefactors leave for another bargain elsewhere?"[29] (Kennedy was primarily interested in protecting his constituents from the industrial migration southward, but his criticism proved prescient. For many desperately poor and declining small Alabama communities, the legislation proved a recipe for disaster, as they built expensive facilities only to see their new industries quietly slip away once the tax advantages had expired.) Taken as a whole, Wallace's policies as state legislator and as governor remained squarely in the mainstream of the kind of "business progressivism" common since World War I. Good schools, good roads, and at least the promise of good government—with a dollop of class resentment thrown in for spice—were the mainstays of his appeal.

While the lifeblood of the profession is self-advancement, Wallace's inordinate ambition always made other politicians uneasy. Cynics like Congressman Carl Elliott acidly insisted that every action Wallace took was based on pure opportunism.[30] After Wallace quietly supported conservatives' efforts to limit the governor's executive powers, Folsom learned of his apostasy and never fully trusted the Barbour County representative; but whatever his private misgivings, he respected Wallace's energy and talents, and used him repeatedly in his legislative and political battles.[31]

By all the evidence, George Wallace was a remarkably appealing young man whose whirlwind energy led most fellow legislators to tolerate his single-minded ambition. As he scrambled to capture attention with the same eagerness that had marked his years on the Tuscaloosa campus, he gradually gained a reputation as a comer. Members of the press corps named him the session's "most promising young legislator." When Wallace ran unopposed for a third term in 1950, Eddie Reid, head of the Alabama League of Municipalities and the dean of the most powerful lobbyists in the state, predicted that George Wallace was "bound to go places in Alabama," perhaps, he said, all the way to the governor's mansion.[32]

ALABAMA law barred Big Jim Folsom from running for a second term in 1950. Frustrated by the studied contempt of Folsom's successor, Governor Persons, and generally ignored by the press, Wallace took the first of many gambles in his political career. An eighty-year-old circuit judge, J. Sterling Williams, decided to retire after serving nearly forty years in his Clayton courtroom. Wallace, just thirty-two, announced his candidacy.

Presiding over divorces, property disputes, hog rustling, and an occasional Saturday night murder seemed an unlikely venue for a high-voltage politician like George Wallace. Nor was his election a safe bet. When state senator Preston C. Clayton—a wealthy breeder of Arabian horses, decorated World War II veteran (a lieutenant colonel, no less), distinguished lawyer, and legislative floor leader for Governor Persons—announced for the post, most observers gave him the edge.

While Clayton made a few dignified forays through Barbour and Bullock counties, Wallace sallied forth every day at dawn, driving the green 1938 Chevrolet rattletrap he had inherited at his grandfather's death in 1948. At each stop, he promised a "fair and equitable enforcement of the laws" and reminded voters, many of whom were veterans, that he had been a sergeant. All the officers could vote for Clayton, he would announce with a mischievous grin; all the enlisted men could vote for him. Fifteen years later, a bitter Clayton still recalled the campaign. "He'd tell those country men that I was living out here in a mansion while he was living in a little house and paying twenty dollars a month rent, that I didn't *need* to be circuit judge." Besides, Clayton petulantly added, "he had all those rednecks."[33] Wallace swept the district with three-fourths of the vote.

No one was more relieved at his victory than Lurleen. The years from 1946 to 1953 had provided a sobering introduction to the realities of the life her husband had chosen. Each year she had shuttled back and forth between a variety of make-do quarters in Clayton and a tiny room in the Metcalf Boarding House on Catoma Street in Montgomery, where she lacked so much as a hot plate on which to cook her meals, and rinsed out their clothes in the shared bathroom down the hall.[34]

Pregnant for a second time, Lurleen remained in Clayton and gave birth to Peggy Sue in 1950. After a call from one of Lurleen's friends, Wallace drove the eighty miles to the Clayton Infirmary, inspected his new daughter, and then impatiently awaited the arrival of his mother-in-law so that he could hurry back to Montgomery. When George Junior was born eighteen months later, his father was at the capital making plans for his run for circuit judge; he once again arrived in Clayton too late to be with his wife at the birth.

By 1950, Wallace had become a well-known local figure in the county seat. He joined the Masons, attended the local Methodist church, won election to its Board of Stewards, and briefly served as Sunday school superintendent. He supplemented his rare legal fees by gaining appointment as Clayton's municipal attorney and joined former governor Chauncey Sparks in organizing a small life-insurance company. On paper a pillar of the community, in reality Wallace was nearly broke most of the time. He never made any significant money from his insurance venture; his retainer as city attorney was only a few hundred dollars a year; and the law practice he had opened in 1947 (and expanded to include his brother Gerald in 1949) was still a hand-to-mouth operation.

Gradually, Lurleen began to chafe at the careless way her husband treated his family obligations. He left early in the morning and often returned late at night. If he was not in his law office or away in Montgomery, he was out on the streets of Clayton talking politics. On Saturday, the one day of the week he might spend with her or the children, he played poker with his cronies until after midnight. Wallace acknowledged a few "minor squabbles" over family money spent on campaigning and politicking, but a friend of the family was far more caustic. "Hell, he'd dole out about $5 a week and expect her to buy groceries, and keep herself and the kids clothed and when she'd complain that it wasn't enough, he'd grump around for two or three days about how much money she was wasting."

In the summer of 1951, exhausted and pregnant with her third child, Lurleen finally confronted him. On a blistering hot Saturday he whiled away the morning talking to country folk who had come to town for market day, then drifted on down the street to begin an outdoor poker game. Driving a borrowed car, his wife roared up the drive next to the spreading shade tree where he sat with three friends. Her face a mask of fury, she plumped six-year-old Bobbi Jo into the lap of her embarrassed husband. "George, I can't wash and dry the clothes and take care of two children, all at the same time," she told him. Without waiting for a reply she stalked away.[35]

When Wallace won election to a six-year term as circuit judge at a salary of eight thousand a year, Lurleen put her foot down: they were not going to continue to live in boardinghouses and garage apartments. He made a small down payment on a forty-year-old frame house that backed up to the Clayton High School. The owner had rented out rooms, the roof and eaves were in disrepair, and the house had not been painted inside or out in fifteen years. But it was set in a large tree-shaded yard and had a big front porch with square wood pillars, nine-foot ceilings, and a wide hallway running through it from front to back. To Lurleen Wallace it seemed a palace.

The new home and job brought few changes in her husband's careless disregard for family life. "I'm sure it was hard on her," said Wallace's younger sister, Marianne, "because she had three small children to raise almost *alone*." He was "very *busy* all the time when I was a child—always on the go," remembered George Junior. As a twenty-four-year-old, Wallace's only son wrote a tortured account of his childhood, with earnest assertions of love and devotion to his father interwoven with painful recollections of a man who paid little attention to his family. Even the sweet pleasures of a childhood Christmas were marred by the memory of his father's lounging in bed until late in the morning, long after the presents were open and the wrapping paper scattered around the tree. "I used to nag him about coming out and playing more with me," said a wistful George Junior. "And yet I can't recall my dad ever explaining why he couldn't spend more time with me." Wallace's mind, explained his son, was always on his career.[36]

Lurleen began to make friends of her own. Catherine Steineker had known Wallace as a teenager and now she made a point of meeting his new wife. "She was the sweetest little thing—but really quite meek," recalled the outgoing Steineker. Mary Jo Ventress, who taught sewing, cooking, and "home management" courses at the high school, soon became Lurleen's closest confidante. Whenever Lurleen could arrange a baby-sitter, the two friends wandered down to the nearby Choctawhatchee River for a late afternoon of fishing. (Wallace could not abide long quiet hours sitting, watching a cork in the water.) In the mornings, when Mary Jo took her break, Lurleen would walk across the backyard to the high school, and they would sit in the tall-ceilinged teacher's lounge with cups of coffee and talk. Encouraged by her new friends, Lurleen brushed up her shorthand and typing and successfully applied for a job as part-time secretary to the county superintendent of education. She earned less than twenty-five dollars a week, but gained a sense of accomplishment and some degree of financial independence. For the first time, she even hired a black woman to help with the children and the chores.[37]

Despite his apparent exile in a backwater judicial circuit, her husband remained in the thick of state politics. In later years, Wallace would seek to minimize his close ties with the liberal Big Jim, but in 1953 he showed little hesitancy at broadcasting and exploiting those connections. When Folsom asked him to run his South Alabama campaign for the upcoming gubernatorial election, Wallace assured him that he was already "spreading the Folsom gospel in these parts."[38]

Although at the height of his popularity, Folsom remained vulnerable on two counts: whiskey and corruption. State newspapers—as well as political opponents—hammered away at the sorry record of petty (and not so petty) thievery that had marked his first administration and they reminded Alabamians of several bouts of public drunkenness as well as an arrest for driving under the influence during his first term.

But voters ignored the "lyin' newspapers," and readily accepted Folsom's good-natured dismissal of the charges. His mother had taught him how to handle such childish accusations when he was a boy: "If they throw mud at you," Folsom said, "don't try to wipe it off or it'll smear. Just wait until it dries and it'll fall off by itself."[39] Unspoken was a second maxim: go on the offensive and an opponent's charges are soon forgotten.

In four months of hard campaigning, Wallace learned the nuts and bolts of building a following. He saw how Folsom devoted as much attention to the ragged farmer as to the well-dressed businessman. When someone sent in five or ten or even two dollars, it was just as important to write a warm and personal response as to acknowledge the hundred-dollar- or two-hundred-dollar donor: each had the same number of family members and friends.[40] Above all, Folsom taught Wallace the role of spectacle and entertainment, the necessity to convince voters they were part of an important crusade. "Make no small plans," Folsom instructed, "they have no magic to stir men's blood."[41]

A few flickering films remain of the 1954 race. They show just how hard

Wallace tried to duplicate Big Jim's folksy platform rapport, a blend of exaggeration, hyperbole, ridicule, and a kind of "country sarcasm" that mocked his enemies. By nature combative and aggressive, Folsom's South Alabama campaign manager could never successfully mimic the relaxed style of the big man from north Alabama; when Folsom was taking the hide off an opponent, he managed to make it sound like a good-natured teasing over the backyard fence.

Still, even an awkward Wallace could bring a crowd to its feet. At a huge rally toward the end of the 1954 campaign he repeatedly mocked Folsom's opponents for their complaints that Big Jim was not "dignified and refined." In 1950, the "so-called 'decent and dignified' administration moved onto Capitol Hill," Wallace told his audience. "And let me tell you," he said, his arm waving in the air, "the first thing this so-called 'decent and dignified' administration did was to raise the taxes on the Little Folks." On May 4, Wallace told the cheering crowd, voters had the choice of turning to this "so-called 'decent and dignified' administration" or they could reelect Folsom. "I'll take Folsomism!" he shouted.[42]

He deftly positioned himself into the limelight. One of Folsom's television commercials led off with a plug for his political coordinator ("Original scrip [sic] by Judge George Wallace"). Wayne Greenhaw, who became a well-known Alabama journalist in the 1960s and 1970s, remembered sitting at his hometown barbershop with his father in the middle of the 1954 campaign when Wallace burst through the door. He talked and talked and talked and "mostly talked about himself," recalled Greenhaw. "He probably didn't say ten words about Jim Folsom." Back in their car, Greenhaw's father predicted, "That man's not going to stop until he's governor of Alabama."[43]

Surprisingly, Folsom's apostasy on race proved unimportant in the 1954 election, despite the fact that the campaign took place only weeks after the Supreme Court's *Brown v. Board of Education* decision called for the end of segregation in the public schools. But during the next two years, the crowds stopped laughing at Big Jim's jokes about "moonlight integration."

THE angry revolt of white southerners began in Mississippi. Within weeks after the court's decision in *Brown,* white business and civic leaders in the Delta town of Indianola ignited what would become an authentic grassroots uprising: the Southern White Citizens' Council movement. Community-based, but increasingly backed by a well-funded headquarters in Jackson, Mississippi, the anti-integration movement swept through the Delta and across the Black Belt, westward through Louisiana and into Texas, and eastward as far as the Tidewater of the Carolinas and Virginia. Its goal: "massive resistance" within the region to any changes in the "southern way of life." Citizens' Councils silenced the voice of moderate whites, coordinated the adoption of a wide range of state and local anti-integration legislation, and forced southern politicians to back away from even the most tepid support of peaceful compliance with the Supreme Court's decision.[44]

In Alabama the Citizens' Council movement initially had little support outside the handful of counties where blacks made up a substantial majority. The editor of the *Montgomery Advertiser* protested after Black Belt businessmen and landowners threatened to fire their black tenants and workers if they made any attempt to register to vote. The "manicured Kluxism of these White Citizens' Councils is rash, indecent and vicious," admonished Grover Hall, Jr. "The night-riding and lash of the 1920s have become an abomination in the eyes of public decorum. So the bigots have resorted to a more decorous, tidy and less conspicuous method—economic thuggery."[45]

After conservatives in the legislature called for a "school placement bill"—a tuition voucher system that would effectively cripple the public schools—newly elected Governor Folsom slyly turned it into a class issue. "I wouldn't want to sign a bill that would let rich folks send their kids all to one school and the poor folks to another school," he said. Unable to resist the temptation to tweak his foes, he added, "I just never did get all excited about our colored brothers. We have had them here for 300 years and we will have them for another 300 years. I have found them to be good citizens and if they had been making a living for me like they have for the Black Belt, I'd be proud of them instead of kicking them and cursing them all the time."[46] Fifteen months after the *Brown* decision, organizers had been able to form only five local Citizens' Councils.

But in August 1955, African Americans in seven Black Belt counties petitioned the Alabama State Department of Education to desegregate their county schools. Stunned whites insisted that it was a plot by the National Association for the Advancement of Colored People. In December, Martin Luther King, Jr., assumed the leadership of the Montgomery bus boycott. Graphic photographs of empty buses and packed civil rights rallies soon dominated state newspapers. And on Friday, February 3, 1956, by order of a federal court in Birmingham, a dignified young black woman named Autherine Lucy entered the University of Alabama. No longer an abstract threat, integration was a potential reality.

Folsom made no effort to challenge the court's decision ordering Lucy's admission; neither did he attempt to mobilize public opinion in favor of compliance. University officials, paralyzed by fears that forceful support of Lucy's admission would jeopardize their state funding, did little to prepare students for the racial integration of the campus. Emboldened by the passivity of state officials, students began a series of daily demonstrations, which culminated in a violent assault on Autherine Lucy. As she emerged from a Monday morning class, three thousand students and local thugs, shouting

"Nigger whore!" pelted the frightened young woman and her university escort with rocks, rotten eggs, and tomatoes before she fled, crouched face-down in the back of a speeding state police car. With Folsom away on a week-long drunk in Florida and the threat of violence increasing, the federal district judge who had ordered her admission acquiesced in her expulsion. Ellis Story, a member of the university's national championship debate team that year, watched officials cravenly give in, and recoiled in disgust. On the campus and throughout the state, he told a visiting newsman, "the mob is king."[47]

Between October and December 1955, membership in the Alabama Citizens' Councils grew from a few hundred to twenty thousand. After the mob forced Autherine Lucy off the campus, the number of "Councilers" doubled, then redoubled to eighty thousand by the spring of 1957 at a time when the winning candidate for governor might command fewer than 200,000 votes.

For Wallace, it was time to shift course.

As the mob gathered in Tuscaloosa for its final assault on Autherine Lucy, George Wallace called Associated Press correspondent Rex Thomas and issued an angry statement. The Federal Bureau of Investigation was collecting evidence in Cobb County, Georgia, to document the systematic exclusion of blacks from the county's grand juries, he announced. Any effort to determine the composition of the grand juries in *his* circuit would be a "gross violation of State Sovereignty, and illegal, and an open insult to the people of the counties of my district," he blustered. If any FBI agents employed their "gestapo methods," they would be "arrested and put in jail for contempt of court."

Thomas dutifully placed the item on the wires.[48]

A specially convened grand jury commended its circuit judge for his "desire to protect the integrity and sovereignty of state courts and grand juries against illegal and unwarranted investigations by the federal government."[49] A bewildered Justice Department official assured the Associated Press that, so far as he knew, there were no complaints about Judge Wallace's district. The department had no plans to send FBI agents to Barbour or Bullock County.[50]

There remained the embarrassment of Wallace's longtime ties with the once-popular Folsom. In addition to his silence on the Lucy case and distinct lack of enthusiasm for segregationist rhetoric, the genial Folsom had made a disastrous miscalculation that would haunt him for the rest of his political career. Harlem congressman Adam Clayton Powell had traveled to Alabama the previous fall to speak to Operation 5,000, a black grassroots movement created to register black voters in the city of Montgomery. Folsom had invited him for a drink in the governor's mansion. Afterward, the flamboyant

Powell told several local reporters that the two had enjoyed a warm visit over scotch and soda; Folsom, he claimed, had even endorsed an end to segregation.

Publicly, the governor tried to defuse the episode with humor. "Now you know that's a lie," he chided reporters, "Big Jim don't touch scotch."[51] Privately, he confided to advisers that "Powell was one son of a bitch I wish I'd never seen."[52]

In mid-February 1956, Wallace drove from Clayton to the capitol. Cigar ashes trailing down the front of his shirt, he buttonholed every legislator and lobbyist he could find, "cussin' [Jim] Folsom out so you could hear him at the other end of the building."[53] In the lobby of the Jefferson Davis Hotel, where legislators gathered around the overflowing ashtrays and yellowed palm trees, insiders listened while Wallace fumed. His old ally had "gone soft on the nigger question."[54] *Montgomery Advertiser* columnist Bob Ingram asked for confirmation of the stories sweeping the capital: Had Wallace decided to break with the governor over political, patronage, and racial issues? Shaking the ashes off his cigar, Wallace replied tersely, "From what you tell me you already know about the story, I'd say you had it just about right."[55]

Any doubts about his decision to abandon Folsom were dispelled a month later when 4,500 whites—the largest rally in the history of the county seat—filled Clayton's football stadium for the first public meeting of the newly created Barbour County White Citizens' Council. While Georgia's governor, Marvin Griffin, grinned at the catcalls directed at the missing Folsom ("Where's Big Jim? . . . He's with Lucy"), he praised the town's circuit judge for his "courage in informing the do-gooders and meddlers that he would put the [FBI] scalawags in jail."[56] Wallace basked in the applause of the cheering crowd and signed on as a regular speaker for the Citizens' Councils.[57]

Desperately, two of Folsom's men convened a peace parley at a crossroads cafe in Union Springs, halfway between Montgomery and Clayton. Wallace drank coffee and talked cordially, but he had made up his mind. Voters were "fed up with this entertainin' nigguhs in the mansion," he explained. "Something else they['re] fed up with too is the drinkin'. Naw, boys, I'm goin' all the way with it." To old friends who still stood by Folsom, his advice was even more stark: "Folsom's gonna gut you. Hit him. You better hit him now before it's too late."[58]

The governor tried his own hand at charming Wallace back into his camp. Sauntering up to his former campaign manager in the House chamber, he inquired, "How're you feeling, George? You ain't mad with me, are you?"

Wallace turned red and grinned with embarrassment.

"Then why don't you come to see me?" Folsom demanded in a booming voice that brought the crowded chambers to an awkward silence.

"I haven't been to see you because I've been so busy I haven't had time," Wallace blurted out.

The chambers rocked with laughter as Folsom sadly shook his head and ambled up the aisle.[59]

White supremacy had triumphed. In the nation's capital, over ninety percent of the region's congressmen and senators signed a "Southern Manifesto" drafted by die-hard Dixiecrat senator Strom Thurmond of South Carolina. Branding the high court's decision in the *Brown* case a substitution of "naked power for established law," the declaration called upon whites to unite in an unbroken phalanx of opposition to any changes in the South's racial system. Adlai Stevenson, who had staked his renomination for the presidency on the support of southern moderates, frantically dispatched one of his southern advisers, Harry Ashmore, in an effort to minimize the political fallout. Ashmore, an Arkansas newsman who would win a Pulitzer Prize in 1958 for his editorials during the Little Rock crisis, met with Thurmond's fellow Democratic senator from South Carolina, the more restrained Olin D. Johnston. "It's no use trying to talk to Strom," Ashmore recalled Johnston's response. "He *believes* that shit."[60]

Even when timid moderates managed to tone down the South Carolinian's bellicose rhetoric, the Southern Manifesto remained a reckless invitation to defiance. The entire Alabama congressional delegation, including "liberal" senators John Sparkman and Lister Hill, rushed to sign. Hill privately explained to his friend federal judge Richard Rives that although the document was bad constitutional law, which would exacerbate already inflamed public opinion, "changed political realities" forced their acquiescence.

"Well, Lister, I think I understand it now," responded Rives. "You fellas have just risen above principle."[61]

The editor of the *Richmond News Leader,* James J. Kilpatrick (later a syndicated columnist), sought to cloak the manifesto's defiant words with constitutional legitimacy. Conveniently forgetting the outcome of the Civil War, Kilpatrick insisted that the states had the constitutional authority to "interpose" themselves between the federal government and its citizens—a doctrine that sounded remarkably like the one sketched out by John C. Calhoun in the 1830s and 1840s. After *Brown,* Mississippi had been one of the first states to adopt a "Resolution of Interposition" asserting the power of state governments unilaterally to block any federal judicial decision (and by implication any federal law). Alabama lawmakers scrambled to follow suit. The Supreme Court's decision in *Brown v. Board of Education* was a "constitutional nullity," said the state's lawmakers in solemn and joint resolution.[62]

When the politicians start hollering "Whip the Nigger!" Folsom told dwindling crowds of supporters, "then you know damn well they are trying to cover up dirty tracks." He contemptuously dismissed the interposition resolution as so much "clap-trap . . . like a hound dog baying at the moon and claiming it's got the moon treed." And he refused to join the growing chorus of defiance against the decision in *Brown*. "You can call the Supreme Court justices s.o.b.'s if you want to, but that doesn't relieve Southern officials sworn to uphold the Constitution of their responsibility."[63]

After the state Senate passed a resolution calling upon the Congress to relocate southern blacks to the North where they were "needed and could be assimilated," Folsom could not resist one last taunt.[64] Most of the bill's sponsors made their living off the work of their black tenants and laborers, said Folsom. If all the Negroes were moved out of the Black Belt, "every last one of those folks who have been raising so much sand would starve to death."[65]

But Wallace had been right. Folsom was finished. Running for a seat as delegate to the Democratic national convention, he found himself branded the "host of the whiskey-drinking Negro congressman from Harlem" by his White Citizens' Council opponent, a little-known state representative from the Black Belt.[66] The once unbeatable Big Jim got less than twenty-five percent of the vote. With characteristic good humor he summed up the results. It was the most perfect race he had ever run. "I asked nobody to vote for me and nobody nearly 'bout did." If anyone "rumors we stole it," he told one of his cronies, "let's deny it to the bitter end."[67]

In the same May 1 primary, George Wallace was the top vote-getter in the state when he ran as a district delegate to the 1956 Democratic National Convention. He had gone far toward ridding himself of any connection with the Folsom administration, reported Bob Ingram, and in so doing had vaulted to the front of the list of possible candidates for governor in 1958.[68]

WALLACE's first brush with national politics had come when he won a seat as an alternate delegate to the tumultuous 1948 convention, which met in Philadelphia. His campaign ads, like those of his running mates, had pro-claimed in bold, underlined letters that he was *"unalterably* opposed to Nomination of Harry S. Truman and so-called 'Civil Rights Program.' "[69] As usual, he was broke and friends in Clayton and Clio passed the hat for money for a hotel room and meals. Another delegate who was driving to Philadelphia agreed to take Wallace along for gas money. He came to question his philanthropy more than once when his passenger kept up a nonstop filibuster during the twenty-two-hour drive.

The noisy hotel-lobby conferences, the feverish meetings in smoke-filled rooms, and the spinning of political wheels exhilarated the young represen-tative even though he and others from the region soon encountered an uninterrupted series of assaults on the "southern way of life." Humiliation began on opening night when—in the shocked words of one of Wallace's fellow Barbour County delegates—"a colored woman was allowed to sing the national anthem." It culminated with the adoption of the strongest civil rights plank by a major political party since the Reconstruction era.[70] Dozens of southerners, including half the Alabama delegation, walked out of the convention hall. With great fanfare, the ex-delegates—joined by a motley crowd of racial extremists, anti-Semites, and right-wing businessmen—re-convened in Birmingham to nominate South Carolina's J. Strom Thurmond as head of a new third party, the "Dixiecrats."

Wallace refused to join the walkout. In his official 1963 inauguration biography, he scrambled to obscure this unseemly defection from the cause of states' rights by insisting that his decision to remain within the national party was a tactical move to strengthen the region's position.[71] He had "challenged every proposal and bulldogged every asterisk of the infamous Civil Rights proposal," and had "forced recognition of the nomination of Senator Richard Russell, a loyal Southerner, for President." When he went down to defeat, said Wallace, he was on his feet again, "nominating Senator Richard Russell for vice-president."[72]

Even when judged by the elastic standards of political rhetoric, Wallace's account of his role in the Philadelphia convention bore only the most tangential connection to reality. He was a twenty-nine-year-old alternate delegate with one year of service in the state legislature. With the delegation evenly divided between national loyalists and hardcore racial reactionaries intent on walking out of the convention, Wallace tried hard—as he admitted to one friend—to "take advantage of the situation."[73] He attached himself to the head of the loyalists, Senator Lister Hill, who, like most mainline white southern politicians, elected to swallow the platform as meaningless blather. After all, Dixie's senators still had the filibuster to block Truman's civil rights legislation. And they had no intention of jeopardizing their links to the national party by joining the unruly mob of third-party Dixiecrats.

The young man from Barbour County was a segregationist in 1948, but he wasn't a *stupid* segregationist.

As a reward for his loyalty, Hill allowed Wallace to respond for Alabama when the roll call began on the vice-presidential nomination. In one sentence, Wallace called for Russell's nomination, but the Georgia senator refused to allow his name to be put forth. The *Birmingham News* mentioned Wallace's role in two sentences; other state newspapers ignored the story.[74]

But he had no need to exaggerate his role in the 1956 Democratic convention. Key leaders from the southern delegations had chosen the little-known thirty-seven-year-old Wallace as their chief spokesman to the platform committee. In the weeks leading up to the convention, he flirted with one faction that threatened a repeat of the 1948 walkout, and he talked vaguely of keeping northern Democrats "on the ropes and baffled because they don't know what the South is going to do."[75] But he also made clear to the more moderate Sparkman that his goal was to persuade the platform committee to "sugar the civil rights dose" by failing to spell out specific proposals for federal enforcement of voting rights or school desegregation.

The platform committee gave Wallace a forum for his views, but the real deal on civil rights was struck behind the scenes by nominee Adlai Stevenson, House Speaker Sam Rayburn, and other key Democratic party leaders. In the end, the platform committee, tightly controlled by Texan Rayburn, rejected measures which called for stiff antidiscrimination laws and pushed through a weak resolution endorsing an "end to all discrimination" without elaborating on how such a worthwhile goal might be accomplished.[76]

The most rabid southern segregationists regarded the platform as a defeat. "The people . . . don't want Alabama to yield to any man who believes Negroes were created equal to white men," warned Wallace's old college friend Glen Curlee. But Wallace, who was still trying to hew to a middle-of-the-road position in 1956, hailed the platform as a victory for the South.[77]

His delivery of a seconding speech to the presidential nomination of South Carolina's governor George Bell Timmerman demonstrated a masterful balance between caution and ambition. Vaguely alluding to the entrenched nature of the "customs of countless generations," Wallace promised that the South would respond to federal compulsion with firm resistance, but there was no blustering, no threat of retribution. "We are a law-abiding people," he assured his audience, in the only line which drew heavy applause, "and lawful ways will be found to preserve our social order." Only after he sat down did one of the South Carolina delegates realize that Wallace had talked at length about the greatness of his own state and his own unwavering devotion to constitutional principles, but had mentioned Timmerman only three times.[78]

When the convention adopted its cautious civil rights plank and nominated Stevenson and Estes Kefauver, Wallace zigged left and publicly endorsed the former Illinois governor as the "best the South could hope to get at this time." If he failed to campaign diligently, he nevertheless repeated his endorsement of the Democratic ticket in Alabama and made at least two speeches strongly attacking Eisenhower for his reactionary economic policies.[79]

Six months later when the U.S. House of Representatives held hearings on proposed civil rights legislation, he zagged right. Appearing in Washington before the committee chaired by Representative Emanuel Celler, Wallace was personally cordial, but would not yield an inch in his defense of segregation. Celler called his attention to the slogan—"White Supremacy"—that appeared on all primary ballots of the Alabama Democratic Party. Should Negro voters be forced to cast their ballot under this overt slogan of white supremacy? he asked.

"I approve of this ballot, Mr. Chairman," replied Wallace bluntly.[80]

Buoyed by his growing name recognition throughout the state, he had made his decision. He was going to grab for the prize he had sought since he stood on the steps of the capitol as a sixteen-year-old legislative page. But—for one of the few times in his life—George Wallace was about to make a critical political miscalculation. In Alabama in 1957, there was no tolerance for shifts left and right; there was no room for moderation.

WITH Folsom barred by law from succeeding himself and in disgrace over his racial views and the widespread corruption of his second term, the number of candidates for the governorship reached a baker's dozen by the March 1958 filing deadline. Three men quickly moved to the front of the pack: Wallace, south Alabama businessman and racial moderate Jimmy Faulkner, and state attorney general John Patterson. A month before the May 6 primary, the *Montgomery Advertiser* polled statewide political experts as well as local bookies. The consensus seemed clear: there would be a runoff between Wallace and Faulkner.

Despite his high name recognition and generally positive reputation among white voters in the state, Wallace had begun his campaign with little money for radio, television, or newspaper advertising. Most of the state's major newspapers had endorsed Faulkner, and Wallace had managed to assemble only the sketchiest statewide political network. At the last moment an old friend, McDowell Lee, agreed to serve as campaign finance chairman. Two Montgomery scrap metal dealers who backed him purchased 150 torpedo-shaped airplane fuel tanks at a government-surplus sale, painted the slogan "Win with Wallace" on them (flanking it with Confederate flags), and distributed them to key supporters, who mounted them on the roofs of their cars.

Copying the old master, Folsom, Wallace invited Grand Ole Opry comedienne Minnie Pearl to kick off his opening February rally at a high school stadium in nearby Dale County. When more than a thousand spectators showed up, he invited her back the following week. Only then did Lee learn that Wallace had made no arrangements to pay Pearl her usual fee of three thousand dollars per appearance, plus expenses. When his shaken finance chairman pulled Wallace aside and asked, "How are we going to pay?" the candidate shrugged and told him, "You take care of it."[81]

Lee, more accustomed to organizing $250 fish fry suppers, persuaded the board of directors of the People's Bank of Clio to cover a check for the Nashville entertainer. It was his baptism into a campaign characterized by improvisation.

Wallace had yet to develop the drawing power that Folsom had shown in the 1946 and 1954 campaigns. Voters seemed unenthusiastic about his sober defense of segregation and his promotion of "benevolent" programs. By March, his campaign was in quiet disarray. The used 1954 Ford he had driven over the state for two years was on its last rattling gasp; twice he missed a series of engagements because of a breakdown. Oscar Harper, a young businessman who aspired to improve his state contracting business, volunteered to drive the candidate. Even this generous gesture presented problems for the man who presented himself as the people's candidate: Harper owned a singularly gaudy, tail-finned new Cadillac.

At each country store or filling station, Wallace would loudly protest, "That's not my car, that's his car," and would ask with feigned bewilderment: "Now what kind of a car is that anyway . . . ? I got an old '54 Ford at home, all wore out, tires all wore out, and this man was nice enough to pick me up and ride me around. This is a nice car. But it isn't my car."[82]

He ran with the same reckless energy that had always propelled him through politics. Stopping at crossroads, speaking to service-club luncheons, walking the downtowns at a time when shopping malls had not yet stripped streets of pedestrians, and plunging on to often badly organized and poorly attended evening rallies, he seemed to survive on half-eaten hamburgers and Oreos. Wallace had always been a careless dresser. Now his handlers tried unsuccessfully to make him presentable. Driving toward Demopolis, Alabama, a disgusted Harper ordered his boss to take his old checkered blue shirt and "give it to some nigguh to burn."[83] By May, the candidate had lost twenty pounds. The suits Harper had bought for him hung loosely, and his eyes were surrounded by dark circles. Friends greeted him with worried concern: "George, you look bad."[84]

With frightening clarity, he realized he was losing—not to his much-heralded opponent, Jimmy Faulkner, but to the youthful, handsome Attorney General John Patterson.

Patterson had little political experience and background. He was an untested young lawyer, and voters had elected him to state office in 1954 on a wave of revulsion against the assassination of his father by small-town vice kings enraged over the senior Patterson's attempt to destroy their gambling operations in Phenix City, Alabama. His campaign received an additional boost from a luridly inaccurate but colorful B-grade movie, *The Phenix City Story*. In a move that foreshadowed the increasingly thin boundaries between television fantasy and political reality, Patterson ran clips from the fictional Hollywood film in his television commercials and played the role of the righteously vengeful son to perfection ("Whenever I take a law book off of my shelf, I get smut [soot] on my hands from where the gangsters tried to burn me and my Daddy out. . . .").[85]

"I'm running against a man whose father was assassinated. How'm I supposed to follow an act like that?" Wallace groused.

But Patterson's most effective weapon was his reputation as an effective foe of integration. By 1958, the political landscape of Alabama had been reshaped by widespread acceptance of the concept of massive resistance. Any flexibility, and, particularly, any capitulation in the face of black resistance—was perceived as a sign of weakness that would lead to the total collapse of segregation. A whole construct of rationalizations underlay the unspoken assumptions of white supremacy. Black assertiveness by its very existence became an illegitimate manifestation of the Communist conspiracy.

Shortly after the young attorney general had taken office, he called together a handful of the Deep South's best "constitutional lawyers" for a secret meeting in Birmingham. "It was very hush-hush. We didn't want anybody to know it," recalled Patterson. All agreed that while it was impossible to reverse the tide of the federal courts on racial issues, they could stage an aggressive delaying battle. "It became quite apparent to me," said Patterson, that the "prime mover in this thing was the NAACP."[86] Over the next four months, working with political officials in half a dozen southern states, he had coordinated a strategy designed to drive the nation's largest civil rights organization out of the region. By any definition of the law, it was a conspiracy to deprive black southerners of their civil rights.[87]

In the mid-1950s, an assistant state attorney in Louisiana had discovered a case in which New York successfully prosecuted the Ku Klux Klan for doing business in the state without properly registering as a "foreign" (out-of-state) corporation. The federal courts had upheld the New York decision.[88] The NAACP, like dozens of other national organizations, had long operated without registering with Alabama's secretary of state. Technically, however, it was in violation of the law. With great secrecy—and with great glee at the prospect of using a Yankee anti-Klan tactic to destroy the NAACP so hated by whites in Alabama—Patterson prepared an injunction enjoining the organization from operating within the state and presented it to Montgomery circuit judge Walter Jones. In a stunning abuse of judicial power, Jones signed the document without so much as a public hearing.

Early on the morning of June 2, 1956, the only paid staff member of the NAACP in Alabama was awakened by a telephone call from a sympathetic Associated Press reporter. Ruby Hurley had come to Birmingham five years earlier. During a time when women were often denied leadership roles, her dignity, organizational skills, and coolness under pressure had earned the respect of the state's often-fractured black leadership as she brokered peace between competing factions, encouraged (and sometimes cajoled) frightened local leaders, and methodically expanded the organization's strength. By the end of 1955, the association had forty-six local branches and more than ten thousand dues-paying members, making Alabama one of its strongest southern outposts.

Miss Hurley had grown up in Washington, D.C., a city as racially segregated as Richmond or Atlanta. But she found that she was unprepared for the casual brutality of black-white relations in Birmingham. After she supported the admission of Autherine Lucy to the University of Alabama, Hurley's life became almost unbearable. Night after night she picked up her telephone to hear a torrent of obscenities and promises of mutilation and death. Repeatedly she switched her unlisted number; repeatedly white telephone-company employees passed on her new listing to the men who tormented her. By the summer of 1956 she had lost twenty pounds; she was bone-weary, "sick of civil rights, and sick of fighting the white folks and sick of the South."[89]

As she talked with the AP reporter, she heard a firm knock at her front door. Opening it, she confronted two grinning deputy sheriffs, accompanied by reporters and photographers there to document the attorney general's legal and public relations coup. White southerners had mentally constructed an image of the NAACP as a lavishly funded juggernaut operating out of plush New York offices with dozens of paid agitators and lawyers poised to wreak havoc on an embattled white South. Instead, there was only an exhausted Ruby Hurley, her hair in curlers, clutching her robe. Such was the power of the paranoia that gripped white southerners in the mid-1950s.

Judge Jones, citing a variety of frivolous charges (including the baseless accusation that Autherine Lucy had been paid to file her desegregation lawsuit), enjoined the organization from operating in Alabama.[90] Equally devastating was his demand that Hurley hand over the names and addresses of every member of the NAACP within the state. Patterson was particularly anxious to "look at their membership [because] . . . there was a lot of white folks that were members of that thing." What his office would do with these names required no great imagination.[91]

After a hurried consultation with attorneys in New York, Hurley packed her bags, gathered the organization's records, and fled to the temporary safety of Atlanta. Pliant state courts next saddled the organization with fines totaling more than $100,000. Over the next four years, NAACP lawyers had to appeal to the Supreme Court not once, but twice, before the state courts reluctantly capitulated, withdrew the injunction, and vacated the fines. In the meantime, as Patterson had predicted, the hundreds of hours spent fighting the injunction drained resources from critical desegregation litigation.[92]

His success in crippling the NAACP and the mobilization of his father's memory became the cornerstones of the square-jawed John Patterson's campaign.[93] He mustered an army of clean-cut volunteers; away from the light of day, less savory supporters secretly printed thousands of handbills and leaflets attacking Wallace for being soft on segregation, but publicly attributed them to the third (and most racially moderate) candidate in the race, Jimmy Faulkner.

And Patterson's unscrupulous campaign manager, Charlie Meriwether, enlisted the support of what Montgomery's Grover Hall drolly called that "herd of albino swine"—the Ku Klux Klan.[94] To speak of the Klan in the singular was, of course, an error; nationally, the KKK existed as a shifting tide of splinter groups presided over by a motley collection of Grand Dragons, Imperial Wizards, and Kleagles of variously exalted ranks. Members, according to one undercover informer, exhibited only two body types: the "300 pound ones, with the beer gut, jowls and pig eyes," or the "raw-boned redneck types," who were "tall, skinny and long-faced and looked like they were born with a branding iron in one hand and a rope in the other."[95] Grand Dragon Robert (Bobby) Shelton fit the latter description. The dour former B. F. Goodrich tire worker briefly brought together most of the Klan fiefdoms under the banner of his Tuscaloosa-based "United Klans of America" in the summer of 1961, but his real power lay in his precarious control over the five thousand to seven thousand members of the Alabama Klan.[96]

The semiliterate Shelton's race-baiting ranged from old-timey, nineteenth-century folktales ("the full moon brings out their animal instincts") to anti-Semitism ("I don't hate niggers, but I hate the Jews") to occasional obsessive railing against fluoridation ("part of the Communist plan to take over the country"). He blandly assured listeners that the Klan was "against violence in any form whatsoever."[97]

Patterson—like many southern politicians of his generation—tended to characterize his Klan backers as slightly exaggerated versions of the characters Burt Reynolds later played in his "good ole boy" films of the 1960s and 1970s. "They'll work all night nailing up signs, putting out literature." And, he added with a grin, "they can also tear 'em [opponents' signs] down in one night. . . . I wasn't about to run 'em off." In fact, the Klan contained within its ranks thugs, pathetic misfits, drunks, and a terrifying minority of homicidal psychopaths.[98]

Twenty-four hours before the May 6 primary, newspapers acknowledged Faulkner's collapse as a serious candidate, but still predicted that the Barbour County circuit judge would lead the race going into the runoff.

Wallace knew better. Huddled with his closest advisers at Montgomery's Elite Cafe that night, he was depressed and bitter. "Every one of you has been sayin' I'll be at the head of the pack [tomorrow]," said Wallace, "and every one of you is wrong. Patterson's gonna run first."[99]

Two hours after the polls closed, his pessimistic prediction was realized. He had made the runoff, but trailed Patterson by nearly 35,000 votes. For the record, Wallace told supporters that he was encouraged by the results. "I hope none of you are concerned about my coming in second. We've come a long way from the beginning and we're going to win. . . ."[100] Privately, he confessed that it would take a miracle for him to overtake his opponent.

A week later, the *Montgomery Advertiser*'s lead story offered documented proof of what insiders had known for some time: Grand Dragon Shelton was an integral player in the attorney general's campaign. Patterson—using his official letterhead—had solicited the support of the state's most vociferous race-baiters and had sealed his bona fides by referring to their "mutual friend, Mr. R. M. (Bob) Shelton." Called for comment, he foolishly issued a denial. The next morning, side by side with his denial, the *Advertiser* produced copies of Patterson's letter, documentation of the Klan's role in fundraising, and a detailed account of Shelton's day-to-day involvement in the campaign.[101]

Charlie Meriwether carefully weighed the odds and decided that the Klan issue was not a serious liability. He ordered his candidate to make no further comment, dispatched the handsome Patterson to Hollywood to film a television show, *This Is Your Life,* and blanketed the state with a last-minute advertising blitz funded by large contributors who decided to leap on the winning bandwagon.

Facing almost certain defeat, Wallace gambled that voters, particularly those in north Alabama, would respond to a positive program emphasizing improved roads, better education, and industrial recruitment—along with a more dignified defense of segregation.[102] When the Klan publicly endorsed its candidate a week later, Wallace sharpened his attacks. "Patterson chatters about the gangster ghosts of Phenix City while he himself is rolling with the new wave of the Klan and its terrible tradition of lawlessness," he warned. There were a "lot of pistol-toters and toughs among Klansmen."[103]

But in the feverish climate of 1958, many respectable white southerners no longer regarded the Klan with horror. As one well-to-do north Alabama businessman explained (anonymously) to a Birmingham reporter, "Now I wouldn't think about joining the Klan myself [he was a member of the more respectable White Citizens' Council] and none of my friends would, but you know there are times when you need organizations like the Klan." He added with emphasis, "I'd rather have Attorney General Patterson attacking the Communists in the NAACP than running down an organization devoted to maintaining our way of life."[104]

In later years, Wallace and his supporters would downplay the importance of racial issues in the campaign, but Patterson never had any illusions. The "primary reason I beat him [Wallace] was because he was considered soft on the race question at the time. That's the primary reason."[105] From the outset, said Patterson, it was clear that white supremacy was the key issue. "It was political suicide to offer any moderate approach."[106]

On the evening of the runoff, June 9, faithful followers continued to chalk up the votes and shout, "Just wait till the next box comes in!" but George Wallace knew he was running a poor second. There were a few bright spots;

Mobile's all-black Ward Ten gave 1,346 votes to him and only 36 to Patterson.[107] But voters from the "progressive" north, urban counties, and most of the Black Belt turned out in record numbers to sweep Patterson into office. The prize Wallace had sought since he stood outside the legislature more than two decades earlier had slipped from his grasp.

He drove to a local television station for a short interview. Standing with his wife and children before the bright television lights, he refused to concede, but made no claims of pending victory. One of his advisers, Starr Smith, drove him back to the Greystone Hotel. Angered by the magnitude of the Patterson victory, Wallace silently smoked one of his ever-present cigars as the *Montgomery Advertiser*'s editor, Grover Hall, and Wallace's Barbour County friend Cecil Brown sat in the backseat and rehashed the election with campaign staffer Bill Jones. "We all agreed that Patterson had won because of his strong stand for segregation, the Klan support, and the adroit way . . . Charlie Meriwether . . . had orchestrated the black issue," recalled Smith. Finally Oscar Harper came out to plead with Wallace to go inside and make a concession speech: "People don't like a sore loser."[108] Reluctantly, Wallace opened the car door to go inside to greet his supporters. "Well, boys," he said tightly as he snuffed out his cigar, "no other son-of-a-bitch will ever out-nigger me again."*

By the mid-1950s, a reluctant Dwight Eisenhower and an equally cautious Democratic Senate majority leader, Lyndon Johnson, agreed that the federal government had to move to protect the most basic civil right of Americans, the right to vote. The Civil Rights Act of 1957 was, in the end, the product of Johnson's presidential ambitions. James Rowe, one of LBJ's staffers and a seasoned political pro whose experience went back to the Roosevelt years, urged his boss to push a limited measure. "Your friends and your enemies . . . are saying that you are trapped between your southern background and

---

*Marshall Frady used the "out-niggered" (or "out-nigguhed") quote in his 1968 biography of Wallace. The former governor's official biographer, Stephan Lesher, has supported Wallace's denial that he made the statement. This "harsh, cynical line, in one form or another, clung to Wallace like a sweat-soaked shirt throughout his career" despite the "inability of any other reporter to find a single credible source who could or would say that he heard Wallace make the remark," Lesher wrote. Although Bill Jones, Wallace's press aide, who was there that night, now says that "my memory fails me about the 'I won't be out-niggered again,' " Starr Smith, who was also present, emphatically recalls the exchange. Moreover, Seymore Trammell, a Patterson supporter who later became Wallace's top adviser, recalled that Wallace had returned to his Clayton office the morning after and glumly announced: "Well, Seymore, you all look like you outniggered me." Frady, *Wallace*, 127; Lesher, *George Wallace*, 129; Bill Jones to author, July 11, 1994; Starr Smith, author's interview; Starr Smith to author, June 1, 1994; Seymore Trammell, author's interview, November 28, 1989.

your desire to be a national leader," said Rowe. If Johnson was serious about a run for the presidency in 1960, he would have to "get all the credit for . . . a compromise [bill] . . . with the emphasis in the South on compromise, and emphasis in the North on getting a bill."[109]

Vice President Richard Nixon and Attorney General Herbert Brownell urged a stronger measure. Illinois's crusading civil rights senator, Paul Douglas, compared the bill that finally reached Eisenhower's desk in late August 1957 to a "soup made from the shadow of a crow which had starved to death." The Justice Department gained a civil rights division, and the newly created Civil Rights Commission could investigate voting rights abuses, but even in clear cases of discrimination by white southern officials, the commission had no coercive or punitive enforcement powers. If local officials ignored a request for access to voting records or continued to bar blacks from registering and voting, the commission's only recourse was time-consuming litigation through the federal courts. A Justice Department official accurately described the act as equivalent to "handing a policeman a gun without bullets."[110]

But the measure furnished enough gunpowder to revitalize George Wallace's career. Returning to Clayton as a lame-duck circuit judge in the fall of 1958, he discovered that the newly created United States Civil Rights Commission intended to investigate voting rights in three dozen counties of the Deep South. Included on the list were Barbour and Bullock, the two counties in Wallace's district. As the last six weeks of his judgeship ticked away, he summoned all the energy, imagination, and calculation that had propelled him upward through the ranks of Alabama politics. No one was more critical to his success than the circuit's solicitor, prosecuting attorney Seymore Trammell.

Trammell had grown up with seven brothers and sisters in the northern section of Barbour County; his father was the only white tenant on a five-thousand-acre plantation. "We were raised poor, I mean *poor,*" Trammell remembered. The work in the fields was backbreaking and school was a luxury that lay twenty-one miles away down a road dust-choked in the summer months and virtually impassable during winter rains.

For Trammell, as for many white southerners of his generation, Roosevelt's New Deal offered escape. During a stint in the Civilian Conservation Corps, the seventeen-year-old passed the open door of his work camp's small radio training center. "I saw this fellow working in the radio station in there using the Morse code, and he had on a tie, all dressed up. And I was out there with the rest of them planting kudzu. I said, 'Oh, my, this isn't for me.'" By the end of his tour, he had put on fifteen pounds and become radio training supervisor for the state.[111]

After three years in the Army, including service in the Far East, he came back to Alabama, cobbled together a list of courses he had taken in the service, persuaded the University of Alabama to admit him to law school, and, thanks to the G.I. Bill, whipped through the program in three years. The handsome redhead wore fifty-dollar sport coats and drove first an Oldsmobile convertible and then a Buick Roadmaster; his driving, drawling, singsong voice recalled his Black Belt roots. He seemed to spend much of his time on mysterious trips into the black communities of Tuscaloosa and nearby Birmingham. Students whispered that he was involved in the numbers racket; others thought he was tied in with black bootleggers. In fact, Trammell, a hustling entrepreneur all his life, managed the Harmony Jubilee Quartet, a popular black gospel group in central Alabama.[112] When talking with his friends, he was charming and jovial. But he could turn menacing and ruthless; in later years he cultivated his reputation as the "meanest son of a bitch in the Wallace Administration."[113]

By the time Wallace and Trammell ran for office in 1952, the sharecropper's son had become a wealthy man with widespread real estate interests. As district attorney, he had worked closely with Wallace, but the two men had never been personal friends or political allies. Known as a fair-minded prosecutor, on more than one occasion he had successfully prosecuted whites for physically attacking blacks. But he had no use for black political rights. His campaign literature always included a brace of Confederate flags with the words underneath: "I will dare defend against all forces calculated to destroy our Southern way of life."[114] During the 1958 governor's race, Trammell had remained publicly neutral. Privately, he had worked closely with Patterson and had even helped the attorney general's supporters put out an underground flyer accusing his opponent of tacitly condoning black voter registration in Barbour County.[115]

Back in Clayton, Wallace made his peace with Trammell. "Seymore," he said as they sat together in his office, "you know what defeated me for governor is the nigger question."

"It did, no question about it," Trammell agreed, as they reviewed the prospects for a run in 1962.[116] On the bedrock of racial politics, the two were reconciled as they hammered out plans for a Wallace comeback. On Wallace's instructions, Trammell persuaded friendly attorneys in the two counties to bring a frivolous complaint of unspecified voter fraud so that "Judge Wallace" could personally take charge of the counties' voting records. When Civil Rights Commission staffers subpoenaed county registrars from across the state, Wallace called a press conference to announce that he had control of the records in his circuit.[117] The stage was set for his first joust with federal authority. In an ironic twist of fate, the man he confronted was his old friend Frank Johnson.

The two had lost touch in the years since law school at Tuscaloosa. While

Wallace flew bombing missions in the Pacific, Johnson commanded a weapons platoon in Europe, and earned two Purple Hearts and a Bronze Star for heroism before coming back to Alabama to practice law. Despite his joking prediction a decade and a half earlier that he would be a federal judge, Johnson knew he had no guarantee of such an appointment. "You have to be where lightning strikes."[118]

In 1953, lightning struck. Eisenhower named the thirty-five-year-old Johnson federal district attorney for the Northern District of Alabama. (The appointee had headed "Alabama Veterans for Eisenhower" during the 1952 campaign.) When Johnson prosecuted a wealthy white landowner for holding his black laborers in peonage—and won a conviction before an all-white jury—he captured the admiration of high-ranking Justice Department officials. The President then nominated him for a federal judgeship in the Middle District of Alabama, a jurisdiction that included the counties over which Wallace presided.

Less than three months after taking office in 1955, Johnson joined a special federal panel to review the request of Montgomery bus boycotters for an injunction against segregated seating. In his first major case, he joined Circuit Court Judge Richard Rives in boldly expanding *Brown v. Board of Education* beyond the issue of public schools to all areas of public life. The implication of the *Brown* decision was clear, the two judges concluded: statutes and ordinances that required segregation on Montgomery city buses "violate the due process and equal protection clauses of the Fourteenth Amendment to the Constitution of the United States."[119]

On December 21, 1956, Martin Luther King, Jr., boarded the first integrated bus in Montgomery. That afternoon, the head of Alabama's White Citizens' Council called upon the white people of Alabama to remember the names of the "traitors" Richard Rives and Frank Johnson.[120] Within hours, Johnson began to receive a stream of angry letters and telephone calls, which would continue for the next twenty years.

They had little effect. Within weeks after he began presiding over the Middle District court in Birmingham he had acquired a fearsome reputation. Johnson's laserlike stare, delivered over half-moon reading glasses, was "terrifying for most lawyers, litigants and reporters," said a reporter who covered his courtroom. One Alabama assistant attorney general paid him a double-edged compliment: "He's fair—he treats all lawyers equally mean."[121] He was not a man to cross.

On January 9, 1959, at the request of the Justice Department, Johnson ordered his old law school friend to make the Barbour and Bullock County registration books available to staffers of the Civil Rights Commission. His statement was diplomatic, but clear: Wallace had four days in which to turn the records over to federal officials. The judge hinted that he would find

Wallace in contempt and jail him if he refused to comply with this order.

Two days earlier, George Wallace had stood before a jostling herd of newspaper reporters and television cameras and attacked the Civil Rights Commission's "Roman holiday investigation, held in a federal courtroom, surrounded by a circus atmosphere with television platforms and ladders, newsreel cameras and hired publicity agents." He intended to "stand up and defend the rights of the people of Alabama, regardless of the personal sacrifices."[122]

Glen Curlee watched the impending confrontation between his two old friends with increasing alarm. After Sunday church, he drove over to Clayton. "George, he can put your tail in jail," Curlee warned. "You've been doing all this bragging and talking and now the showdown's come, and in my judgment and opinion you're in trouble."

For the first time, Wallace seemed apprehensive. "You really think so?" he asked.

"I know so," said Curlee, who boldly proposed a meeting with the judge.

On Sunday evening, Frank Johnson had dined at the officers' club on Maxwell Air Force Base with his wife and son. The food was good, and an unpleasant run-in with local whites unlikely. On their return home, Johnson found Curlee waiting in his car.

"After Curlee came inside, he chewed around on his cigar awhile, and finally told me that little George—that's what we called him—wanted to talk to me."[123]

While a judge was not supposed to discuss a case with the parties involved, Johnson had no wish to let the crisis escalate into a courtroom clash in which he would be forced to jail a sitting state judge. And "George had been a friend in law school; even though we had lost touch with each other, he had sent a letter of support to President Eisenhower for my nomination as a federal judge." Johnson owed his old friend the favor of a meeting. "OK, I'll talk to him," he told Curlee.

Close to midnight, Wallace made the seventy-mile drive from Clayton to Montgomery. When Judge Johnson opened the door, his former classmate stood with coat collar turned up in the near-freezing night air.

"George, come on in," said Johnson. "It's too cold to be standing out there."

As they shook hands, Ruth Johnson, awakened by the doorbell, put on a robe and came out of the bedroom. She heard Wallace blurt out: "Judge, my ass is in a crack. I need some help." Discreetly, she returned to bed.

For two hours Wallace sat in Johnson's kitchen and, over one cup of black coffee after another, guilelessly explained his strategy. He wanted to run again for governor, he said, and had decided that defiance of the Civil Rights Commission would guarantee his election.

"George, you know I don't care about that," replied Johnson, wearily shaking his head.

"If you'll just give me ten or fifteen days [in jail]," Wallace pleaded. That would help politically.[124] But "if you send me for any length of time, it'll kill my mother; my wife won't care."[125]

"George, if you don't comply," warned Johnson, "I'll pop you hard."

Wallace knew that might mean six months in federal prison. There was a long pause in the conversation. "What if I turn 'em [the voting records] over to the grand jury in each county and let them turn 'em over to the Civil Rights Commission?" asked Wallace.

The judge shrugged. "That'll be OK. I don't care how you do it, just so you do it before the hearing."[126]

Shortly after two A.M., a groggy Seymore Trammell answered his telephone. A "very frightened, very shook" George Wallace blurted, "I have just left Frank Johnson's home where he threatened me."

"What kind of a threat are you talking about?" asked Trammell.

"Well, he told me that if I was doing this for political reasons to run for governor four years from now, that I was wasting my time because . . . if he put me in prison, I would still be in prison . . . if I ran for governor . . ."

Wallace, his voice trembling with fatigue and anxiety, told Trammell to meet him in his chambers at six A.M. Johnson, he claimed, had sketched out a plan to avoid a jail term for contempt. When Trammell walked into the Clayton office before dawn, Wallace had obviously been up all night. "He looked red-eyed, just trembling, he was a wreck."[127]

The plan required a delicate balance of face-saving resistance and private acquiescence. He would summon a special grand jury, issue a call of continued defiance against the Civil Rights Commission, turn the records over to the eighteen jurors, and then quietly encourage them to allow the commission access.

The following morning, the day of Judge Johnson's deadline, Wallace summoned a handpicked grand jury in a courthouse jammed—in Trammell's colorful phrase—"with rednecks, and nigger-haters, and footlog walkers, and possum hunters—and [they] all just spilled all out into the downstairs and out into the streets."[128] Wallace was at his belligerent best as he promised that he would hold the line against federal encroachment. He announced that he was turning the records over to the control of the most sacred instrument of the people's will: the grand jury. "I have kept them inviolate," he swore.

Later in the morning, he met with the press in his office. Chewing on a Tampa Nugget cigar, he played spin doctor, explaining how the lead should be pitched. "You've got the story of your lives, fellas," Wallace told reporters. "The most dramatic confrontation since the Civil War. A clear confrontation between a sovereign state judge and his court on one side, and the federal government and its court on the other."

Just before noon he returned to chambers and nodded to Trammell. "Well, let's go ahead and call the foreman up here and talk to him."

Wallace rambled on for twenty minutes; he explained the "problem" of a jail sentence. He argued that the damage would be minimal if the grand jury formed a small special committee of particularly trusted men and let the commission look at the records.

"Are you saying that you want us to do just the opposite of what you said in the courtroom?" asked jury foreman Wynn Martin.

"Naw, naw," insisted Wallace. "It's just a tough mess," but "you and me are in it together now." They had to do something to satisfy the commission and Frank Johnson. "I don't want all these folks [grand jurors] going to jail." On the other hand, he warned, "if your neighbors ever got the idea that you turned records over to the feds, your cattle'd be poisoned and your barn'd go up in smoke." Anything that was done would have to be done quietly.[129]

Outside Wallace's office, a troubled Martin asked Trammell again, "What in the world does George Wallace want us to do, Seymore?" Resigned, Martin sighed. "We'll do whatever he wants us to do."

Wallace closed the door to his office. "While you're down there with the grand jury," he told Trammell, "I'll type up a grand jury report."[130]

For the next two hours, he pounded away with two fingers on an old manual typewriter. The report expressed warm approval of Trammell and lavished praise on the circuit judge for his courage in placing official records in the control of the grand jury, "the sacred bastion of Anglo-Saxon liberty." "We commend the courageous action of the Honorable George C. Wallace," he typed, "who risked his very freedom in the federal courts in carrying out the duties and oath of office as a Circuit Judge. . . . The great need of the South today is for more men of the foresight and determination of Judge George C. Wallace."[131]

Just after eight P.M., Wallace called Maxwell Air Force base in Montgomery, where the director of the Civil Rights Commission's Office of Complaints was staying. As A. H. Rosenfeld would later swear under oath, a subdued George Wallace "said to me that if I would send two of my representatives . . . the next morning at nine thirty he believed we would see the records." Over the next two days, staff members of the commission went through the materials and compiled their findings for later action.[132]

The last hurdle was Judge Frank Johnson's threatened contempt citation. Before the bench on January 26, 1959, Wallace's attorney "lifted his arms grandly and intoned, 'We plead guilty. We plead guilty.' "

"I stared at him in disbelief," remembered Johnson. "I had already been told by the U.S. Civil Rights Commission that the voting records of Barbour and Bullock counties had finally been turned over to them by the grand juries."

Wallace stood before him, head down, fidgeting uneasily, clasping his hands first in front, then awkwardly behind.

Icily, the judge read aloud. For "some reason judicially unknown to this Court," Johnson told the packed courtroom, George Wallace had "attempted to give the impression that he was defying this Court's order by turning records over to hastily summoned grand juries." In fact, Wallace had arranged for access by federal officials. Despite the fact that "devious means" were used, said Johnson, "this court refuses to allow its authority and dignity to be bent or swayed by such politically generated whirlwinds." He concluded, "George Wallace is hereby found not guilty of contempt of this Court and stands discharged."[133]

Supporters erupted into applause. A grinning Wallace, Lurleen at his side, marched over to the Jefferson Davis Hotel for a press conference and victory celebration. Before a battery of television lights and nearly two dozen reporters, he triumphantly announced, "I was willing to risk my freedom" to fight the "evil Civil Rights Commission. . . . This 1959 attempt to have a second Sherman's March to the Sea has been stopped in the Cradle of the Confederacy."

What about Judge Johnson's accusation that he had secretly surrendered? asked an unsporting journalist.

"There is no testimony before the court on this subject either directly or indirectly," Wallace blandly insisted—an out-and-out lie.[134]

"The first inkling of the kind of politician George Wallace would be was shown to me during that case," Johnson recalled more than two decades later. "No matter how high up you threw him, he landed on his feet like a cat." From that moment on, said the still-bitter judge, "I would detest the way he would go about misleading the people of Alabama for the purpose of pursuing his political career."[135]

Wallace and Johnson never spoke privately again.

In the years to come, Wallace returned again and again to the standoff as though it were a sore that would not heal. In half a dozen state contests between 1958 and 1982, he would face nearly forty opponents. His political skirmishing, with one or two exceptions, seemed a form of grown-up fun and games; when the game was over he tended to be genial and gracious in victory. But the night after Johnson issued his findings from the bench, Wayne Greenhaw remembered Wallace was "tossing down whiskey right and left, hitting his head against the wall of the room and saying, 'He's a no-good goddamn lying son-of-bitching race-mixing-bastard.' "[136] Frank Johnson's decision "reflected on me and in effect made fun of me," an angry Wallace later recalled.[137]

Johnson "made fun of me": Wallace could stand abuse—he thrived on it—but his former friend's public dismissal of him as a liar and a poseur (a "fake," as Wallace angrily put it) was laced with the kind of mocking contempt that went to the very core of his insecurities.

BUOYED by his public confrontation with Johnson, Wallace unofficially launched his 1962 campaign for the governorship. With some of the proceeds left over from his unsuccessful effort in 1958, he bought a Chevrolet, the first new car the family had ever owned, and was soon on the road day and night, traveling across the state, speaking to Kiwanis clubs, chamber of commerce luncheons, Masonic lodges—any group that would invite him—with a desperate need to be reassured that next time, next time, there would be no defeat.

After his term as circuit judge expired late in January 1959, he spent more and more time in the state capital. His brother Gerald had opened a small law practice in Montgomery; George put his name on the door, but he was seldom in his office. Downtown regulars noticed him in the haunts of the city's politicians: the Capital City newsstand, the Elite Cafe, Turk's Cafe, the lobbies of the two main downtown hotels.

He began to down more than his single carefully husbanded drink. In comparison to his two-fisted colleagues, he was a model of sobriety, but it didn't take much to send him out of control. "One drink would set him off on a drunk," said one friend. And he "wasn't a very pleasant drunk, either. . . . He became belligerent, wanting to fight anything that moved."[138] Wallace, like his father before him, had let his temper run away with him before. While a student at the university, he had pulled a knife on an opponent ("I grabbed a butcher knife and jumped over the table and said I was going to cut his throat if he came any further," recalled Wallace), and as a young state legislator he had once broken his right arm in a brawl with an off-duty Alabama highway patrolman. (Wallace claimed the trooper was drunk and had slapped a woman.)[139]

More and more often there were indiscreet flings with women encountered on his nonstop campaign trail. "He liked to have them just before he left a town where he'd spoken, like it was a final conquest," one adviser told Wayne Greenhaw. And for some women in Montgomery, sleeping with Wallace seemed a "kind of merit badge. . . . They could wear it around the rest of their life and be proud."[140] Unlike the drinking, which was a temporary aberration, the womanizing was a persistent pattern, crudely—and devastatingly—summed up by Folsom: "George don't drink," Big Jim would explain with mock seriousness, "but he always was bad to fuck."[141]

If the years between the 1958 and 1962 campaigns were a purgatory for Wallace, they were a nightmare for his family. He moved Lurleen and the three children from Clayton into a tiny two-bedroom apartment in what the children always remembered as the "low-rent" section of Montgomery. The more outgoing Peggy Sue soon made friends, but "I was homesick and lonely," said George Junior.[142]

"The days were long," recalled Lurleen Wallace. "There was nothing to do. I mean, there was nothing exciting happening. I couldn't go fishing. I had very few friends in Montgomery. George was running from one end of the state to the other. I didn't know when he was coming home and when he'd be stuck with people."[143]

Relations between the two frayed to the breaking point as Lurleen Wallace bitterly complained about her husband's neglect of the marriage. "I tried to explain," Wallace recalled defensively, but he admitted that it was "really not explainable. . . . I kept going, going and going." After one angry confrontation, his wife took the children home to her parents, who had moved back to the old Burns home place in Greene County, Alabama. Unable to reach her husband at the Montgomery apartment or at his law office, she drove to the county seat and filed divorce proceedings.[144]

A divorce would have devastated Wallace's political career in Alabama. He pleaded with her to reconsider. Although one of his sidekicks admitted that it "got a little hairy for a while there," it seems unlikely that Lurleen was committed to divorce.[145] She had three children, no money, and little chance of making her way in the world. Wallace was not physically abusive and—by mid-twentieth-century Alabama standards, at least—did not appear especially neglectful.[146] In April 1961, his wife gave birth to their fourth child, Janie Lee (named for Robert E. Lee, the little girl was always called Lee). Increasingly, Lurleen seemed resigned to her husband's role as absentee father.

MINNIE Pearl returned to Alabama for the March 10 kickoff of the 1962 campaign, but the venue was no longer a run-down outdoor high school stadium. A three-man advance team had lavishly decorated Montgomery's city auditorium with bunting, balloons, and a giant banner hailing "Alabama's Fighting Judge." Viewers across the state watched on fourteen television stations as a half-dozen country music stars entertained the crowd while they waited for Wallace. At least token integration had occurred in every Southern state except Alabama, Mississippi, and South Carolina, but Wallace insisted that the cause of segregation was not lost. When forced to choose between sending the governor of a "sovereign state" to prison or retreating, the federal courts always backed down, said Wallace. And "when and if they say they didn't back down, they are integrating, scallawagging, carpetbagging liars!" If the federal government sought to integrate Alabama's schools, pledged Wallace, "I shall refuse to abide by any such illegal federal court order even to the point of standing at the schoolhouse door."[147]

The promise to "stand in the schoolhouse door" soon became one of his best applause lines.

Neal Davis, editor of a small but influential weekly published near the Auburn University campus, had listened the week before as the former Barbour County judge sneered at the "sissy britches in Alabama who say we've got to conform . . . to mixing the races in the schools."[148] But Davis was unprepared for the "frenetic, almost wild, pitch which Wallace reached in his campaign rally at Montgomery." Unfortunately, he added, the candidate had correctly read the pulse of the state's white voters when he chose to make Alabama's racial divisions the number one issue in his campaign.[149]

As the May 1 primary approached, endorsements came pouring in, while professionally produced ads blanketed the state and promised the usual good jobs, improved education, and highways from the Gulf to the Appalachians. Newspaper and print ads couched the issue in lofty terms; more ephemeral radio spots pulled no punches as a strident announcer called upon Alabama voters to "Vote right—vote white—vote for the Fighting Judge."[150] Seymore Trammell was well on his way to raising a third of a million dollars—a huge sum for a governor's race in Alabama in the early 1960s.

But two weeks into the campaign Wallace became obsessed with the notion that he was running out of money. His advisers became so concerned with his mental health that they checked him into a Montgomery hospital. "We slipped him down a back stairway after dark," said one aide. "The collar of his coat was turned up, and the brim of his hat was pulled down so nobody would recognize him. He looked like a Dead End kid," recalled Oscar Harper.[151] After a tip from an off-duty nurse, Montgomery reporter Bob Cohn went to St. Margaret's Hospital, where he talked his way past a "No Visitors Allowed" sign to find Wallace tired and drawn. Defensively, the gubernatorial candidate insisted that voters would "understand when you're sick."[152]

Marshall Frady later gave a colorful account of a psychological recovery plan engineered by one of Wallace's old friends, Billy Watson. Watson, said Frady, carried a bag filled with $20,000 to the hospital room, barged in, and "without a word, in a motion like a planter flinging out seed, threw the money across the bed."[153] "George got rejuvenated about as quick as I ever saw," remembered Oscar Harper.[154]

Back on the campaign trail, he whipped audiences to a frenzy with his attacks on the "lousy, federal court system," which was "destroying our schools, our government, our unions, our very way of life." Political observers inevitably compared his snappy, hard-hitting speeches with his relatively lackluster performance in 1958. Wallace's closest aides credited their new speechwriter, Asa Earl Carter.

A self-taught, earthy stylist, Carter had begun his public career in the early 1950s as a race-baiting pamphleteer and right-wing radio announcer who bitterly attacked blacks, Jews, Yankees, and all "lesser breeds" who challenged the divinely mandated supremacy of the Anglo-Saxon race. Through the decade he moved in and out of the public eye, first as an organizer for the Alabama Citizens' Council, then as the founder of his own Ku Klux Klan terrorist organization. In one eighteen-month period beginning in January 1956, his followers joined in the stoning of Autherine Lucy on the University of Alabama campus, assaulted black singer Nat King Cole on a Birmingham stage, beat Birmingham civil rights activist Fred Shuttlesworth and stabbed his wife, and, in what was billed as a warning to potential black "troublemakers," castrated a randomly chosen, slightly retarded thirty-three-year-old black handyman.[155] While the hard-drinking Carter often left the dirty work to his disciples, he had a fiery temper; in January of 1957, he had shot two followers who had the temerity to raise questions about his Klan's financial records.[156] Given his unsavory reputation, he kept out of sight in the 1962 campaign except to speak to Klan rallies. ("He'd get the crowds all churned up. He was really good at doing that," remembered Robert Shelton.[157])

Big Jim Folsom, discredited by charges of past corruption, excessive drinking, and insufficient devotion to the defense of white supremacy, returned to the fray in the hope of a third term. In a pathetic coda to his career, he lurched back and forth between pleas for racial tolerance and pledges to maintain segregation for the next four years.[158] He was erratic, poorly funded, and often drunk, but even a crippled Jim Folsom was a dangerous foe, particularly since he appealed to many of the rural and small-town voters Wallace saw as the core of his constituency. Folsom and his aides based their hopes on the kind of reluctant support reflected in the comment of a youthful Howell Heflin. Heflin, a racially moderate young politician who would eventually reach the United States Senate, told a representative of one civil rights organization that he had decided that it "might be better to be drunk on bourbon than drunk on defiance." As one north Alabama voter told the *Advertiser*'s chief correspondent, Bob Ingram: "The folks up here would rather face four years of stealing than four years of bloodshed."[159]

In thinly veiled attacks Wallace reminded voters of the corruption of the Folsom years. While his supporters distributed a heroic account of their candidate's life in comic book format—"The Fighting Judge from Alabama!"—a crude cartoon version of Folsom's career mysteriously appeared in rural letter boxes across north and south Alabama. In the final panel, Big Jim and a malevolent-looking Adam Clayton Powell were shown "sipping Scotch on the Governor's settee." When Wallace shouted, "I promise you I won't serve one drop of alcohol in the Governor's mansion!" voters understood that the pledge was about more than drinking liquor.[160]

On the night before the May 1 primary, the last serious obstacle between Wallace and the prize he sought vanished. Big Jim Folsom self-destructed before a statewide television audience in an episode which furnished grist for Alabama's conspiracy buffs for the next twenty years.

The two-term governor arrived at a Montgomery television studio on election eve to introduce a documentary film extolling his achievements. He had been drinking earlier in the day, but seemed clear-headed less than an hour before broadcast time, when his personal physician gave him a vitamin B_{12} shot. At the last moment, however, studio technicians discovered that the scheduled film had mysteriously disappeared, and Folsom had to go on the air for more than a token appearance.

The next morning's papers discreetly described the next thirty minutes as his "strange TV show." For most Alabamians, the episode would thereafter be known as Big Jim's "Tweety Bird speech." He tried to introduce his family but, confused and slightly out of focus, turned to one of his eight children and loudly asked, "Now which one are you?" He then launched into an attack on his opponents, who were "just a bunch of me-too candidates. Mee too! . . . Meetoo . . . Meetoo Meetoo meetoomeeetoo!"[161]

Angry partisans and members of the family were convinced that Folsom had been drugged, and no one ever satisfactorily explained the film's disappearance. But whatever happened that April evening, Folsom's career was finished. Back in Cullman the following night, he sat in his living room and watched the returns on television. A lifelong supporter came in before ten P.M. and told him matter-of-factly: "Well, it's all over." Wallace had swept the Black Belt and finished near the top in the supposedly more progressive north. After midnight, Folsom, quietly sobbing, walked down the steps of his white-columned home, ripped the "Win with Folsom" campaign stickers from his car, and drove off into the cool May night, heading toward Arkansas. His family did not see him again for two weeks.[162]

A month later, Wallace easily demolished Ryan deGraffenried, a handsome thirty-six-year-old lawyer from Tuscaloosa who had edged out Folsom for a runoff spot. And six months later, on January 14, 1963, as newly elected governor of Alabama, he stood before a cheering inaugural crowd to shout his defiance at the hated Kennedys.

Waves of applause punctuated a by now familiar litany of hate: "We will tolerate their boot in our face no longer"; [The federal] government has become our God"; "a system that . . . encourages everything degenerate and base"; "its pseudo-liberal spokesmen and some Harvard advocates"; "The Belgian survivors of the Congo cannot present their case . . . nor [can] the citizens of Oxford, Mississippi"; "No wonder communism is winning the world"; the "false doctrine of communistic amalgamation"; "segregation forever." Wallace concluded with one of the most incongruous perorations in the history of American political rhetoric: "And my prayer is that the Father who reigns above us will bless all the people of this great sovereign State and nation, both white and black."

Judged even by the standards of Deep South governors in the 1950s and 1960s, the 1963 inaugural address was a raw reflection of the depths of anger and paranoia that gripped whites in his region. Years later Wallace would defensively dismiss the speech as an overly zealous but principled brief for constitutional principles ("We were against big government. What we were really talking about was states' rights or state responsibilities, and so forth, and we never were against black people"[163]).

It was nothing of the kind. He had stepped past an invisible line of hyperbole and fallen down a dark hole of the bleakest demagoguery. When a longtime supporter confronted him about his capitulation to the politics of race, Wallace shrugged. "I started off talking about schools and highways and prisons and taxes—and I couldn't make them listen," he told Louis Eckl, editor of the *Florence Times*. "Then I began talking about niggers—and they stomped the floor."[164]

Asa Carter had been right. "Segregation now . . . segregation tomorrow . . . segregation forever": with this melodramatic rhetorical flourish Alabama's new governor had made himself the champion of embattled white southerners. No general ever succumbed to as many setbacks as George Wallace was to suffer in his battles against the forces of civil rights. But in some perverse violation of the laws that govern political combat, he gained strength as he retreated from each battlefield, somehow convincing his followers that every ignoble defeat was glorious triumph. Whites in the region had always been intoxicated by the power of words. Wallace promised them not only victory, but the balm of righteousness.

Chapter 4

"THE THREADS RAN THROUGH"

THE KENNEDYS FACE THE GOVERNOR

ON NOVEMBER 29, 1962, Burke Marshall, the Kennedy administration's assistant attorney general for civil rights, received a telephone call from the president of the University of Alabama. A federal court order mandating the desegregation of the campus was imminent, warned Frank Rose. Several black applicants looked promising, and the courts would likely order the integration of the university before the fall of 1963. The trustees would delay, but they would not defy the courts. The "problem," he gingerly explained, was Governor-elect George Wallace's promise to "stand in the schoolhouse door."[1]

A COLLISION with George Wallace was the last thing John Kennedy and his brother, Attorney General Robert Kennedy, sought in the fall of 1962. Only two months earlier, the administration had stumbled from embarrassment to disaster in managing the integration of the University of Mississippi. Long after it was obvious that Mississippi governor Ross Barnett could not be trusted to protect black applicant James Meredith, the President and his brother had desperately tried to work out a deal which would make it unnecessary to use federal force. When the riot broke out on September 30, a detachment of poorly trained federal marshals using only tear gas had struggled to defend themselves against an armed mob for more than five hours before federal troops arrived. The beleaguered men had suffered more than two dozen gunshot wounds and hundreds of contusions and cuts from flying debris; a bystander had been killed by a stray bullet; and unidentified members of the mob had coolly executed one foreign newsman.[2] Even in the midst of the riot the President worried over just what he was going to say at his first news conference.[3] As Robert Kennedy recalled, "We could just visualize another great disaster, like the Bay of Pigs, and a lot of marshals being killed or James Meredith being strung up."[4]

The Cuban missile crisis pushed coverage of the Ole Miss riots off the front pages and spared the Kennedys further embarrassment; buoyed by their patriotic enthusiasm for John Kennedy's successful stare-down of Castro and his Soviet allies, more than fifty percent of white southerners forgave the President his policy on racial issues and awarded him a good or excellent rating.[5] Determined to avoid the mistakes of Ole Miss, over the next seven months Burke Marshall spent hundreds of hours monitoring developments in Alabama, trying to anticipate and counter any moves Wallace might make. In February Marshall began to develop elaborate contingency plans—plans that included the possibility of committing federal troops to enforce the court decision. Although the Justice Department still hoped to avoid such a move, Deputy U. S. Attorney General Nicholas Katzenbach frankly acknowledged that the experience at Ole Miss had marked a "loss of virginity in a way, because after that it became easier to use troops if that's what had to be used."[6] Robert and his brother Jack agreed. This time there would be less concern about southern white sensibilities. Troops would be positioned nearby, and the Army ordered to prepare plans for a rapid deployment.

But the administration still hoped to avoid a confrontation. Initially, Marshall placed great reliance on the president of the University of Alabama. Rose, a handsome figure with a divinity degree and a penchant for well-tailored suits and soothing bromides, had assumed his post in 1958, the same year that Bear Bryant arrived to take charge of the school's failing football fortunes. Despite his limited academic background, he looked every inch a college president and had two additional assets: a close alliance with Bryant, and a resemblance to ex–Alabama football great Johnny Mack Brown, who had gone on from gridiron glory to become the star of dozens of B westerns. Youthful, dynamic, and self-confident, Rose captured the enthusiastic approval of university supporters, bruised by years of inadequate legislative support and the fallout from the Autherine Lucy case.

In conversations with Wallace, Rose assumed the role of the dutiful defender of segregation, harrassed by the implacable federal government and anxious to protect his beloved university from destruction. In encounters with the attorney general and other Justice Department officials, however, he became the reluctant foot soldier of the governor, an enthusiastic fifth columnist for the Kennedy administration, constrained only by the stifling conditions of Alabama politics. By the twenty-fifth anniversary of the stand in the schoolhouse door, Rose had managed to convince himself (and to assert publicly) that he had single-handedly persuaded the Kennedys, despite their misgivings, to press on with the integration of the University of Alabama.[7]

Considerably more circumspect in the late fall of 1962, the university president explained that he wanted to "keep in touch with the attorney general throughout and cooperate with him," but there was "this problem" with Governor-elect George Wallace. Contacts between his office and the Kennedy administration would have to remain secret so that the "governor didn't destroy the university."[8] Dutifully, Burke Marshall and Robert Kennedy took elaborate precautions to ensure that news of Rose's cooperation did not leak back to Alabama. Cryptic written communications, worthy of a James Bond film, passed between the attorney general's office and Rose's assistant, Jeff Bennett. Both parties reserved substantive discussions for furtive meetings held in Washington, often when the university president was in the capital on other business.[9]

Rose's fears of Wallace were not misplaced. Soon after his inauguration, the governor had met with the state's educational leaders and had issued a blunt warning. "If you agree to integrate your schools, there won't be enough state troopers to protect you," he had threatened, as he bluntly reminded them of the financial power he held over their institutions. ("I'm not going to ask the Alabama legislature for money to run an integrated school.") Throughout most of his blustery diatribe, Wallace had kept his eyes sternly fixed on Rose.[10] But the university president's cloak-and-dagger methods worked. Although the governor suspected there was contact with the Kennedys, he could not be certain of the extent of the relationship.[11]

The applications of several black students wound through the courts. In mid-March, 1963, Bennett called Marshall to report that Wallace had summoned the president and trustees of the university to a special executive session in Montgomery's Jefferson Davis Hotel. After two hours of delicately circling the main subject—his promise to block the scheduled June admission of black students to the Tuscaloosa campus—Wallace had confronted the issue head-on in rambling remarks that veered between belligerence and caution.

Although at least two board members told a Chattanooga reporter that their conference with the governor was a "stormy session," much of the meeting passed with the kind of bonhomie characteristic of southern political gatherings between friendly opponents. Wallace was cordial and reassuring, but he stood firm in his commitment to staging his political drama.[12]

If the federal government forced the desegregation of the university, he would fulfill his campaign pledge: he would stand in the schoolhouse door. He could not say for certain that he would not be forced to step aside. But he would not yield to the pressure of a paper order from a federal judge; he would force the Kennedy administration to use the Army to enforce its will.

He generously freed the trustees from any obligation to resist. "If the court orders admission the board must comply," he told the relieved assembly.[13] (Only in the months ahead did more politically astute board members see the reason behind Wallace's gesture of absolution: he was determined to stand alone at center stage as the heroic defender of the rights of oppressed whites.[14])

Despite the governor's assurances that he would avoid violence, Marshall and his boss knew that each confrontation between the federal government and southern advocates of resistance raised the stakes. The rebel yells and enthusiastic applause that had greeted Wallace's inaugural speech, his belligerent promise of "segregation forever," had escalated expectations.

Having sworn to prevent the desegregation of the university, Wallace could hardly surrender meekly to a federal court order. Orval Faubus, John Patterson, and Ross Barnett had remained intransigent until bayonet-wielding troops had forced them to back down. Could Wallace do less?

In the months between his election and his inauguration, he had suggested forming an irregular statewide "militia," arming and training them in "judo and other methods of self-defense." Unlike the National Guard, they could not be federalized, thus giving the state an armed force with which to resist federal desegregation orders.[15]

After several conservative followers recoiled at the prospect of a military face-off, the governor abandoned his plans, but his public statements remained truculent and threatening. When political columnist Drew Pearson talked with him by phone two weeks after his inauguration, Wallace ridiculed South Carolina governor Ernest (Fritz) Hollings, who had quietly accepted the court-ordered integration of Clemson University. Did Pearson know Alabama's state motto, "We dare defend our rights"? Alabama was "not going to retreat one inch. I don't care what the other states do. I have announced that I would draw a line in the dust. And I shall stand in the door to block the entry of federal troops or federal marshals or anyone else. They will have to arrest me before they integrate the University of Alabama."[16]

Although Wallace did not repeat this pledge to become "a states rights jail bird" (as a critic dubbed him), he continued to give trusted reporters "off the record" interviews in which he acknowledged that he might be overpowered by federal troops, but as soon as they withdrew, "I will tell the federal authorities . . . the negro students will come out of the school."[17]

To skirmishes with the Kennedys he brought the same mix of reckless bravado and careful political calculation that had always guided his career. George Wallace had no illusions about the likely outcome of a direct confrontation between the federal government and the state of Alabama. While bloodshed on the scale of the Ole Miss debacle would probably lead to his canonization among white Alabamians, it would also consign him to the ashbin of Dixie's gothic losers, faded symbols of fruitless defiance, briefly praised and soon forgotten.

His predecessor, John Patterson, gave him one piece of advice: Make no advance guarantees of law and order; keep the Kennedys guessing. Patterson's advice coincided with Wallace's own instincts. Beyond vague pledges to avoid violence, he committed himself to no set course of action. Indeed, he confided in no one, certainly not in Lurleen, not even in his closest aides, Bill Jones, Cecil Jackson, and Seymore Trammell.[18] Trammell, his most important adviser in the 1960s, had an uneasy relationship with the Alabama governor, but they had one thing in common: a shared reluctance to trust anyone. "I was always the kind of person that I'd never want anybody to get too close to me," said Trammell. "If you let them get too close to you, they recognize your weaknesses."[19] Wallace, too, listened, asked questions, and probed people around him for ideas. But in the end, he trusted his own instincts. When ready, he could act decisively, but "anyone who says they knew Wallace's plans [in advance] is a liar," said Trammell. "I'm not sure he knew himself what he was going to do from one day to the next."[20]

As the critical date drew near, Wallace rejected all Justice Department requests for consultation. Burke Marshall made repeated telephone calls to the governor's associates; all reported that the governor was keeping his own counsel. In contrast to their counterparts at Ole Miss, Frank Rose and Jeff Bennett maintained a steady flow of information to Robert Kennedy on what they surmised were Wallace's intentions, but Bennett frankly conceded these were little more than guesses.[21]

WHILE George Wallace taunted the Kennedy administration, the city of Birmingham erupted in the largest series of civil rights demonstrations in the nation's history. By the time the confrontation on the streets of Birmingham and the standoff between George Wallace and the federal government had reached an awkward resolution in early June 1963, all of the cautious assumptions that had guided the Kennedy administration in dealing with issues of race and politics had been swept aside. A year later, Burke Marshall sat and struggled to summarize the late-night conferences at the Justice Department and in the White House, the urgent telephone calls, the hurried flights back and forth to Alabama. If disorder ruled his memories, Marshall remained certain of one fact: there were "threads that ran through" the events that had unfolded in Tuscaloosa, Montgomery, and the chaos of Birmingham.[22]

Two years earlier, the *New York Times*'s Harrison Salisbury had visited Birmingham to prepare a profile of the state's largest city. "I had worked for years in Russia and behind the Iron Curtain," he recalled, but nothing had prepared him for the surreal atmosphere of this Deep South center of iron and steel production. Here in America he found a city in which decent, well-meaning, respectable citizens dismissed the most cautious criticisms of white oppression as evidence of "Communist sympathies," a city in which most whites supported or fastidiously turned their gaze away from a brutal system of absolute white supremacy maintained by "the whip, the razor, the gun, the bomb, the torch, the club, the knife, the mob, and police and many branches of the state's apparatus."[23]

There had been brief moments of hope for better days. Driven to desperation by the Depression, Birmingham's blue-collar coal, iron, and steel workers briefly forged alliances that cut across racial lines, but the faltering effort at biracial unionism collapsed after the war. When the last of the ore mines closed in the early 1950s, and U.S. Steel ended nearly a half-century of expansion, a coalition of local and absentee-owned corporations joined hands with an economically and racially threatened white lower middle class to create a political system personified by the fiery public safety commissioner, Eugene (Bull) Connor.

Connor and his lesser-known fellow city commissioners supported a political and economic system based on low wages (a race-discriminatory wage paid blacks even less than whites, and both were well below the national average), low taxes, and limited government services. Connor ran the police department like a plantation (he called his favorite cops "my nigguhs") and he tolerated blacks only if they were willing to grovel or to assume the role of "Sambos" and "Aunt Jemimas."[24]

Wartime labor shortages had forced steel plants and ore mills to hire black workers in slightly higher-paying jobs, and they began to look for housing outside Birmingham's compact and dilapidated African-American communities. In late 1946, a black forty-three-year-old drill operator at the Ishkooda ore mines used his life savings of $3,700 to purchase a frame house on the racial boundary line of the white working-class community of Fountain Heights. Local Klansmen gave Sam Matthews one warning: they painted a skull and crossbones on the front of the empty house. When he refused to abandon his plans, vigilantes broke into the vacant house and dynamited it on the night of August 18, 1947. No one could have anticipated that the destruction of Sam Matthews's home would be the first of more than fifty bombings directed against blacks over the next sixteen years. By the mid-1950s, people in Birmingham routinely referred to the Fountain Heights community as Dynamite Hill.[25]

From 1948 to 1965, blasts shattered more than two hundred black churches and homes, as well as synagogues, in the Deep South, but far more bombs exploded in Birmingham than in any other city. Dozens of men in the Steel City, as the Federal Bureau of Investigation soon discovered, were familiar with explosives and skilled in their illicit use.

City commissioners made it clear from the outset that the black victims, by directly or indirectly challenging the racial status quo, had no one to blame but themselves. When the Birmingham chapter of the NAACP complained to city officials in 1948 that Police Commissioner Connor had made little visible effort to investigate the explosions, Connor arrested the most recent victim and accused him of destroying his own home in order to help "those subversives who created this situation."[26]

What began as a violent tactic to prevent black neighborhood expansion soon became a favorite weapon to terrorize civil rights activists. And so long as the bombers directed their skills against bona fide integrationists—so long as the main effect was property damage and intimidation—civic élites made little effort to curb their police commissioner. Beginning in the 1920s and 1930s, middle- and upper-income whites had moved across Red Mountain into separate suburban municipalities: Mountain Brook, Homewood, and Vestavia Hills. After they rejected a proposed merger with Birmingham in 1958, white suburbanites hunkered down behind what one resident bluntly called their Maginot Line, safe from the uncomfortable dangers of school integration and economic competition. Geographically just over the mountain from Birmingham, they lived in a world a thousand miles distant from the back alleys and streets of the Steel City's black and white working-class communities.[27] In 1958, a black neighborhood watch apprehended three Klansmen seconds after they had bombed two homes on Dynamite Hill. One of the homeowners had actually seen the men lighting the fuse seconds before the blast; city police finally had terrorists—caught red-handed—in custody. But the *Birmingham News* dismissed the incidents as "harmless explosions" that were "probably" set by blacks in the neighborhood. The police, said the *News*, should be far more concerned about the Negroes who had "ganged up" on the white suspects. Connor refused to hold the three Klansmen.[28]

While the bombers plied their trade at night, scarcely a week went by without an account of the police shooting a black suspect, or a brief report, buried in the back pages of the *Birmingham News* or *Post-Herald*, on the death of a black person in custody. Inevitably, a perfunctory investigation would clear the gun-wielding police officer. Occasionally, community leaders murmured disapproval when police beat or abused a particularly inoffensive black man or woman. But most of the business and professional leaders who ruled Birmingham turned a blind eye to the excesses of Connor and his fellows, giving them a free hand to create one of the most brutal police forces in the nation. Fred Shuttlesworth did not exaggerate when he said that, for black people, Birmingham in the 1950s and early 1960s was "very close to hell itself; the Johannesburg of the South."[29]

Despite Connor's record, George Wallace never faltered in his support. In the spring of 1963, the Alabama governor went out of his way to encourage the police commissioner's hard-line response to civil rights demonstrations, and during Birmingham's critical mayoral election in March and April, he embraced Connor with unseemly enthusiasm. Even after Birmingham voters elected the more moderate Albert Boutwell as mayor, Wallace used the lame-duck Connor to try to sabotage any rapprochement between blacks and whites in the city. A quarter-century later, Wallace diffidently suggested to his official biographer that his "good friend Bull Connor was a little too abrasive," but that was as far as he could bring himself to go in criticizing his old ally.[30]

The prospect of storming Bull Connor's citadel seemed less daunting than outright suicidal to Martin Luther King's Southern Christian Leadership Conference (SCLC), still reeling from the embarrassment of its failed 1961–62 anti-segregation campaign in Albany, Georgia. If demonstrations mushroomed into widespread violence, they could easily destroy King as a national spokesman and deliver a devastating setback to a civil rights movement that had gained precarious national support only by shielding its defiance behind the public relations armor of nonviolence and martyrdom. Where there was danger, however, there was also opportunity. The fall of Birmingham would electrify the movement and rebuild the battered fortunes of the SCLC.

Civil rights leaders briefly delayed the beginning of demonstrations so as not to affect the outcome of an April 6 election in which a new city charter replaced the old mayor-commissioner government with a new mayor-council organization. The old mayor, hard-line racist Arthur Hanes, along with Bull Connor and his fellow commissioners, insisted that they should be allowed to serve out their terms. The newly elected Boutwell was forced to launch a court battle to assume office. In the meantime, Connor remained in control of the police. Whether Boutwell or Hanes was mayor seemed irrelevant to the movement's leaders; both were committed to maintaining the racial status quo. Within hours of the runoff election, sit-ins took place at half a dozen lunch counters; police arrested twenty-one demonstrators. The siege of Birmingham had begun.[31]

As the date for the integration of the University of Alabama grew nearer, the Kennedy administration found itself fighting a battle on two fronts. While Burke Marshall shuttled back and forth between Washington and Birmingham in the spring of 1963 in an effort to encourage negotiations between white community leaders and civil rights organizers, Robert Kennedy, fearful that the feverish climate of race relations might ignite a wildfire, sought to control the coming confrontation with George Wallace.

The attorney general was no virgin in dealing with Southern politicians; as his brother's campaign manager, he had courted the worst of the lot. Once

John Kennedy had won the White House, Mississippi senator James East-land, chairman of the powerful Senate Judiciary Committee, had introduced him to the hardball realities of racial politics. When the President nominated NAACP attorney Thurgood Marshall to the U.S. Court of Appeals, the senator held the nomination hostage while he maneuvered to gain the appointment of his old friend Harold Cox to the federal bench. (Cox, a vitriolic segrega-tionist, had once referred to blacks in his court as "baboons.") When he felt the Kennedys had squirmed long enough, Eastland offered the attorney general a deal: "Tell your brother that if he will give me Cox I will give him the nigger."[32]

Kennedy appointed Cox to the federal bench; Eastland allowed the Mar-shall nomination to come to a vote.

Although civil rights activists regularly criticized the President's brother for foot-dragging, Robert Kennedy knew that the political climate in the Deep South required elected officials to demonstrate their devotion to segregation. Perhaps if he could talk personally with Wallace, he might establish a face-saving understanding which would permit a graceful retreat. But the gover-nor of Alabama, like most white southerners, had convinced himself that the younger Kennedy was nothing more than a yes-man for the hated Martin Luther King. He ignored the request for a meeting.

With increasing apprehension, Robert Kennedy sought southern political allies who might serve as intermediaries, and Wallace courteously returned calls from several, including Alabama's senators, John Sparkman and Lister Hill. Both frankly admitted they had no influence over the governor of their state. On the contrary, concluded Robert Kennedy, it was "Wallace [who] had them over the barrel." When Burke Marshall tried to approach the governor through state attorney general Richmond Flowers, who had staked out a more moderate position in the 1962 campaign, Wallace's response was equally unyielding. "Dammit," he told Flowers, "send the Justice Depart-ment word, I ain't compromising with anybody. I'm gonna *make 'em* bring troops into this state."[33]

Finally Robert Kennedy reached down into his list of Alabama contacts and called Edward Reid, executive director of the Alabama League of Mu-nicipalities and one of the few political figures in the state who had managed to maintain cordial relations with both the federal administration and the Wallace regime.

Eddie Reid did not fit the profile of a self-effacing lobbyist. A diminutive five feet, two inches, with mesh two-tone shoes, a double-breasted suit, a garish tie, and a trim Panama hat, he looked like a Chicago gangster who had gone to the best haberdasher in south Miami. He had become a key lobbyist in Washington and Montgomery in the 1940s and 1950s, his politics shaped by his "yellow dog" Democratic background and by his worship of Franklin

D. Roosevelt. To paraphrase Will Rogers, he never met a federal program he didn't like (particularly if it held a potential grant for one of his municipal clients). Jack Kennedy, then still a senator from Massachusetts, had met him on a trip to Birmingham in 1957.

Reid's close associations with national Democratic leaders aroused the suspicions of his fellow southerners, but he managed to disarm them with an endless supply of hilarious political anecdotes, delivered with an unerring mimicry of the voice and gestures of Alabama politicians (including "Little George"). More important, Reid had been a Wallace fund-raiser in the 1958 and 1962 campaigns. The dapper little "Mr. Fixit" seemed an ideal choice to serve as intermediary.[34]

Wallace finally agreed to a meeting, but only if the attorney general formally—and in writing—requested it. On Reid's instructions, Kennedy telegraphed the governor and told him he would be in Montgomery on April 24 and 25. "I . . . would be pleased to pay you a visit if it would be convenient for you." Stiffly, Wallace agreed.[35] He emphasized to Montgomery reporters that he had not requested the meeting, but had decided to "grant an audience" to Kennedy in order to "let him know how strongly we resent in Alabama the concerted efforts on the part of the central government in Washington to take over local government and destroy our cherished traditions."[36]

Omens for the late April trip could not have been more unpromising. The tempo of events in Birmingham had temporarily slowed, but the city remained a tinderbox. And Wallace's actions gave chilling evidence of his willingness to endanger the public safety for his own political advancement. Even as he spurned the attorney general, the governor doggedly undercut every effort to negotiate a compromise between King's demonstrators and increasingly uneasy whites. When Palm Sunday demonstrations led to the arrest of King and dozens of other activists, and to the first use of police dogs in Birmingham, Wallace dispatched his hated state troopers. (They were soon withdrawn after King's arrest failed to trigger large-scale demonstrations.) When he heard rumors that business leaders were planning secret negotiations with the movement's leaders, the governor publicly denounced them as "white renegades."[37]

Robert Kennedy, Burke Marshall, and Justice Department press secretary Edwin Guthman arrived in Montgomery on the evening of April 24, 1963. A burly state trooper met them at Maxwell Air Force Base and grimly announced that he would be in charge of security. Instinctively, Kennedy reached out to shake hands. The trooper crossed his arms, glowered, and turned his back.[38]

From his room in the officers' club of Maxwell Air Force Base, the attorney general called Frank Johnson and invited him to a breakfast meeting. Kennedy had carefully cultivated the friendship; in March he had arranged a private social meeting in the Oval Office between the President, Judge Johnson, and the judge's son, Johnny. John Kennedy had spoken with the boy for nearly half an hour, with a graciousness that clearly touched the stern federal judge. Over bacon and eggs, the attorney general asked Johnson's advice for dealing with Wallace. Nothing positive would come from the meeting, the judge told Kennedy. "Governor Wallace is making as much political hay out of this as he can. I know you know that," said Johnson. "You should proceed on the basis that anything you say which might be construed by Wallace as helping him, will be used by him for that purpose."[39]

On the short drive from Maxwell to the capitol Kennedy noted more than two dozen chanting picketers carrying hand-lettered signs: "Kosher Team—Kennedy/Kastro/Kruschev [*sic*]"; "Christians Wake Up"; "Mississippi Murderer"; "No Kennedy Congo Here." Although the demonstration appeared to be spontaneous, Asa Carter had engineered it, and it had the desired effect. The attorney general turned to Burke Marshall with a kind of awe: "It's like a foreign country."[40]

As Kennedy, Marshall, and Eddie Reid walked up the steps and onto the portico of the capitol, a delegation from a group called Women for Constitutional Government placed a large wreath of red and white carnations over the brass six-pointed star that marked the spot where Jefferson Davis had taken the oath of office as president of the Confederacy. It was "put there to keep the enemy off sacred ground," explained a stern-faced Montgomery matron. The card on the arrangement was signed "Unreconstructed."[41]

Inside, a handful of young women, squealing with excitement and waving, began "acting like Kennedy was a crooner," said one disgusted state policeman. The President's brother walked over toward them, but stopped short when one of his state-supplied bodyguards ("the biggest state troopers you ever saw," remembered Kennedy) placed his nightstick against the stomach of the attorney general of the United States and gave it an emphatic shove. Kennedy was stunned. The message was unmistakable: "[My] life was in danger in coming to Alabama because people hated me so much."[42]

As he walked into the governor's spacious office, the attorney general saw on the desk a large microphone and an oversized reel-to-reel recorder. During the Ole Miss crisis, the Kennedys had recorded their telephone conversations with Ross Barnett, then had leaked them to the press to show that they had been double-crossed. Wallace did not plan to make the same mistake; the obvious placement of the tape recorder on his desk was a studied insult.[43]

Kennedy remembered Judge Johnson's breakfast warning: "You should proceed on the basis that anything you say which might be construed by Wallace as helping him, will be used by him for that purpose." There would be no private understanding, no face-saving deal. Their meeting was a political soapbox, a discouraged Kennedy decided, and he was resolved. "I couldn't let anything he'd say go by . . . unanswered."[44]

The governor puffed silently on his cigar as Kennedy began almost apologetically, "Well, I just thought I would perhaps just explain our position, I would hope that these problems could be worked out at the local level by state officials and . . ."

Wallace cleared his throat and spat noisily into a handkerchief, an unnerving habit he had developed as a young man. Kennedy, looking down at the governor's desk, plunged doggedly on.

"I have a responsibility that goes beyond integration or segregation to enforce the law of the land, and to insure that court orders are obeyed. . . . I think if you were in my position that you would do no less."

But Wallace would have none of it: "Nobody knows what the law is anymore with the present court system we have got, because they write the law as they go along."

The issues had been settled by the United States Supreme Court, insisted Kennedy, attempting to placate his host. "If the orders of the court can be disobeyed by you, Governor . . . , then they can be disobeyed by anybody throughout the United States who does not happen to think that the particular law of the federal court applies to them." The end result, said Kennedy, would be "complete havoc and lawlessness."

Wallace lunged for the opening. There was more "law and order in Alabama in one minute than you have in an entire year in Washington, D.C.," he informed Kennedy. "I can go right now myself into any colored section of this town, people speak to me, 'Hello Governor,' . . . but you can't do that in Washington. You can't do that in Chicago or Philadelphia." If there weren't so many "colored voters that vote in blocs like they do in certain sections," he sarcastically added, "why, I doubt if there would be so much interest evidenced in their so-called civil rights."

He tried to shift the focus of the discussion. "[The] NAACP and all these groups feel that you people are almost gods, and I believe you could exert some influence on them" to stop their litigation and agitation, said Wallace.

Blacks were denied their most basic democratic rights in Alabama, Kennedy responded. "We have had instances where individuals, Negroes who were college professors . . . would go in and attempt to register, and would be denied the right to register on the grounds they were illiterate,"— sometimes by a white registrar, he bitterly added, "who could hardly write his own name."

For the first time in their meeting Wallace went on the defensive. It was a state matter, he said, but "I think people ought to be allowed to vote if they are qualified to vote."

Sensing an opening, Kennedy pressed his advantage, and Wallace feebly counterattacked. You could find "discrimination in every county in America. In other words—"

"We do not find that in every county in America," interrupted Kennedy. "We do find it in the state of Alabama."

Seymore Trammell had sat quietly through the first forty-five minutes of the meeting, but he was increasingly unhappy with its direction. Wallace, he thought, was doing precisely what his chief aide had feared: he was allowing Kennedy to set the agenda and force him into making impolitic statements.

Local officials should be allowed time before being pressed on these issues, interrupted Trammell: "Maybe a year, maybe five years, maybe ten years."

Kennedy sat bolt upright: "What? To permit somebody to register to vote?" he asked sharply.

Just use your persuasive powers to stop the lawsuits, Trammell told him. "This thing can't be overcome overnight."

Wallace suddenly saw the snare—a call for delay rather than defiance. He interrupted: "Let us get it straight now, because I am not for using persuasive powers on us to persuade us to integrate."

In other words, said Kennedy cuttingly, "just use the persuasive powers on the other side."

"That's right," responded Wallace, oblivious to Kennedy's acerbic tone. Integration was "bad"; law and order would always break down "when you try to mix races here in our part of the country." "I have nothing against people of opposite color," he insisted, as though he were trying to explain a local custom to a slightly dim foreign visitor. "I got colored people—I have lived around them all of my life . . . my children right now are being nursed by colored folks. . . . I just don't believe in social and educational mixing."

An hour into the meeting, it was obvious that the discussion was going nowhere. As aides began rustling around the room, a resigned Kennedy turned to the governor. "I hope you will see the President when he comes down."

Once again Wallace was the gracious host. "We are happy to have any high-level government official visit our state. This is the courtesy capital . . . of the South." Wallace's press secretary, Bill Jones, and Kennedy's aide Ed Guthman came into the room and reminded the four men that reporters were waiting outside. "Do y'all want to issue a joint statement?" asked Jones.

The nub of the issue seemed pretty clear, said the governor; the attorney general had promised to "enforce integration orders, and I . . . said I am going to resist integration orders." According to "y'all's attitude," Wallace said, turning toward Robert Kennedy, "you . . . say we may have to send troops and jail you as a governor of a state."

Kennedy interrupted: "If you put my words accurately, it was that we

would enforce the orders of the court and the laws of the United States. . . .
I have no plan or idea of using troops."

The situation at Tuscaloosa "had nothing to do with segregation," said
Marshall; he and the attorney general were simply acting as officers of the
court.

Trammell, that "awful man" as Kennedy later described him, had a temper
to match his fiery red hair. "Of course we all know that that is what it *does*
have to do with," he said. "If it was not for the segregation and integration
issue we would not be here talking. . . . I would like to know if you are
[going to use troops]," Trammell said belligerently.

Everyone always complained about civil rights abuses, chimed in Wallace,
but no one in Washington seemed the least concerned about the "shooting
of students and the gassing of students" at Ole Miss. Federal troops had
abused people, searched automobiles that came on campus, "opened people's suitcases, belongings, had colored troops stopping white women and
searching their belongings." And Wallace expected nothing better for his
state: "I know you are going to use all of the force of the federal government.
In fact, that is what you are telling me today, if it is necessary you are going
to bring troops into Alabama."

With bitter exasperation, Kennedy repeated: "I have no plans to use
troops. You seem to want me to say I am going to use troops."

As Kennedy turned to leave, Wallace lunged one last time. They could
solve this problem, he said, "if you talked to these people who are trying to
get into the schools here at the University of Alabama, and ask them to
withdraw their applications." The mask of politeness dropped. Martin Luther
King, Jr., was a "phony," a "fraud," he said angrily. ("It's nothing more than
a commercial enterprise," interjected Trammell). The federal government
was always talking about the need for obeying the law, but President
Kennedy was constantly on the telephone with Martin Luther King, "solicitous of him, and *he* is the man advocating the lawlessness."

For the first time in the hour-and-twenty-minute conversation, Robert
Kennedy seemed on the edge of losing his composure. "I didn't come to see
Martin Luther King. I came to see you . . . for the purpose of paying a
courtesy call," he said brusquely. The tape recorder on Wallace's desk hissed
softly as the men trooped out of the office.

Glumly, Kennedy rode to the airport. "I suppose I can understand the
governor's position politically," he confided to Marshall and an accompanying newsman. "But that Trammell is a son of a bitch. He wants somebody
killed."[45]

Back in his Washington office, he scribbled a two-line note to Frank
Johnson: "You were right. There wasn't much accomplished at the meeting."[46]

*   *   *

WITH negotiations with Wallace at a dead end, the administration faced renewed crisis in Birmingham. After nearly a month of sporadic and ineffectual demonstrations, King and his followers decided to risk tragedy to force concession. On May 2, an army of more than two thousand demonstrators, most of them black schoolchildren and some as young as eight or nine years old, poured out of Birmingham's Sixteenth Street Baptist Church. "We want to go to jail," one group of preteen girls in starched dresses told a policemen who stood silently as the throngs moved past him.

"Jail's that way," he said, pointing southward toward the center of Birmingham, and watched as they ran, gleefully shouting, "We're going to jail!" across the park toward the commercial district.[47]

By noon the children's crusade had overwhelmed the city's police forces. The entire business district had come to a standstill.

While children filled the streets—and the city's jails—a blustering Wallace went before the state legislature. Repeating his pledge to stand in the schoolhouse door, he promised to stamp out the revolutionaries who were paralyzing the city of Birmingham. Everyone knew that the demonstrations were Communist-inspired and Communist-led, Wallace told his listeners, who interrupted him twenty-one times with tumultuous applause. He dismissed civic leaders trying to negotiate a compromise settlement and warned that, should deaths occur, King and his associates would be "guilty of the highest crimes, including murder, and the Jefferson [County] grand jury in my judgment should so indict." Bitterly attacking the "agitators, integrationists and others" who had set out to "destroy the freedom and liberty of Americans everywhere," he announced his decision to return 250 state troopers to the troubled city.[48]

As the demonstrations intensified, one of Bull Connor's patrol leaders could see the police commissioner's self-restraint unravel. "He was just desperate. 'What the hell do I do?' "[49] On May 3, as a new wave of marching children, adults, and teenagers filled the streets, Connor gave the fateful order to bring in the K-9 units and turn on the fire hoses. For much of the next week, he stormed up and down the streets, urging his army of policemen, state troopers, and hastily deputized "irregular" forces to "get the niggers off the streets." When a high-pressure hose slammed movement leader Fred Shuttlesworth up against the wall of the Sixteenth Street Baptist Church and sent him to Holy Family Hospital for Negroes, Connor fumed over his poor timing. "I waited a week to see Shuttlesworth get hit with a hose," he told a Birmingham reporter. "I'm sorry I missed it. I wish they'd carried him away in a hearse."[50]

But Connor's tactics backfired. For weeks, a small minority of white businessmen had tried to reach an agreement with civil rights leaders, but they had repeatedly been undercut by the intransigence of the lame-duck mayor and commission as well as the unwillingness of the men who controlled the real power to support even the most cosmetic concessions. They had survived on a kind of gallows humor: "Why is everybody running down Birmingham?" asked one wag. "We're the only city in the United States with two mayors, a King, and a parade every day!"

On May 7, the "Senior Citizens Committee"—Birmingham's top seventy corporate and business leaders—gathered in the chamber of commerce's paneled conference room under the watchful eye of the President's representative, Burke Marshall, to negotiate a truce.

In the dispirited meeting that followed—a meeting punctuated by the sound of fire engines and police sirens racing through the streets below— there were no righteous declamations, no discussions of the morality of the conflict. It was, said Sid Smyer, who had worked for months to pull off a settlement, simply a "dollar-and-cents thing."[51] With business at a standstill downtown and Birmingham an object of international opprobrium, the economic costs of maintaining the status quo had begun to outweigh the psychic benefits of Jim Crow. Birmingham's "Big Mules" reluctantly endorsed the agreement to hire a token number of black clerks, to desegregate downtown lunch counters and department store dressing rooms over the next ninety days, and to pressure city officials to lower bail on the eight hundred demonstrators still jailed in the area. Civil rights and business leaders announced the accord in separate but equal press conferences on May 10.[52]

During most of the month-long protest, state troopers had worked side by side with city police, but within hours after business and civil rights leaders announced the accord, the head of the state's police forces ordered troopers back to their home stations.

When George Wallace became governor in 1963, he had recruited Albert J. Lingo to head the Alabama Highway Patrol, despite his limited experience in law enforcement (Lingo had served a brief stint as a state highway patrolman during the 1930s.) Although the former Barbour County businessman lacked experience, he had a reputation indispensable for Wallace in the early 1960s: He was known as "hell on niggers" and a man who seemed to relish confrontation. At Lingo's suggestion, one of Wallace's first acts was to rename the Alabama Highway Patrol the "Alabama State Troopers" and order Confederate battle flags bolted onto the front bumper of each car. While Lingo directed his often uncontrollable temper against those blacks he considered "insubordinate," his own recruits learned to stay out of his path; he was a dangerously unstable man whose mercurial moods were seldom improved by his tendency to use tranquilizers (by the "handful," said one state investigator).[53]

Lingo's decision to withdraw his men from the streets alarmed Ben Allen, a longtime state investigator. "I had information that the Gaston Motel in Birmingham [where King was staying] was gonna be dynamited."[54] Laurie Pritchett, the Albany, Georgia, police chief, who had traveled to Birmingham to offer advice on handling the demonstrations, also cautioned the public safety commissioner: "Bull, you got the Ku Klux Klan just over the mountain here holding a meeting. They're going to blow King up. And if anything ever happens to him, wherever he's at, the city's going to burn. Cities all over this United States are going to burn."

Earlier that day, Connor had refused Police Chief Jamie Moore's request to guard King (that "nigger son of a bitch") and he was in no mood to listen to the Georgia policeman. "Let them blow him up," Connor told Pritchett. "I ain't going to protect him."[55]

He was as good as his word. Just after midnight on May 12, two powerful bombs exploded: one outside the home of King's brother and another at the black motel where civil rights leaders maintained their command post. The Gaston Motel bomb was placed against the back wall of the room directly below King's usual accommodation (the bombers did not know that the civil rights leader was out of town). The blasts came within minutes after the half-dozen black bars in the neighborhood had closed for the Sunday curfew; hundreds of angry Saturday-night drinkers took to the streets. More than two thousand neighborhood residents—mostly young black men in their teens and twenties—ignored the pleas of civil rights leaders and began to throw rocks as police arrived on the scene. Measured by the standards of the major race riots of the 1960s the final damage was relatively minor: six businesses, three houses, and a two-story apartment gutted by fire, nine police and state patrol cars damaged, and several hundred windows broken. To white Alabamians it was the Apocalypse.

Just as the concerted efforts of city police, Jefferson County deputies, and civil rights leaders seemed to bring disorder under control, Al Lingo returned to Birmingham with the first of more than 250 state troopers, supplemented by a ragtag group of about a hundred Dallas County civilians. Governor Wallace had personally awakened Sheriff Jim Clark in the Black Belt city of Selma and requested the irregulars. Although the state troopers carried semi-automatic shotguns and lead-filled billy clubs, Clark's force was armed with hunting rifles totally inappropriate for urban riot control.[56]

"Will you please leave," pleaded Birmingham police chief Jamie Moore. "We don't need anybody down here."[57]

Furiously chewing on a cigar and wielding a repeating shotgun, the commander of state troopers pushed Moore aside. "I'm here on personal orders of Governor Wallace," Lingo shouted above the noise of the sirens and racing engines.

Chief Moore knew that Birmingham blacks hated the troopers even more than they did local policemen (they called the troopers "Colonel Lingo's head-beaters"). "Will you please put that up?" he plaintively asked. "You all might get somebody killed."

"You're damned right it'll kill somebody," retorted Lingo as he cleared the chamber of his shotgun, turned his back on Moore, and ordered his men to sweep the area.[58] A reporter stationed across the street from the bomb-shattered Gaston Motel could hear the screams and the "thonk" of wood and metal against bone and flesh as the Dallas County irregulars ranged up and down the compound.[59]

While Mayor-elect Boutwell nervously tried to salvage the fragile racial accord by balancing attacks on the mob with condemnations of the bombing, Mayor Art Hanes laid the ultimate responsibility for the riots on the white businessmen who had met with black community leaders ("a bunch of quisling, gutless traitors") and on Attorney General Robert Kennedy ("I hope that every drop of blood that's spilled, he tastes in his throat, and I hope he chokes on it.")[60]

Wallace agreed. When this "so-called biracial negotiating group of appeasers" signed an agreement with "mobsters" like Martin Luther King they had made the "task of maintaining peace and order doubly difficult," he lectured. And "high officialdom in Washington" had given "sympathy and tacit approval" to the "Negro mobs." As for the specific culprits in the bombing, there had been "sufficient activity in Alabama by outside subversives to strongly indicate their involvement in the bombing incident."[61]

Wallace had "virtually taken over the city," Robert Kennedy reported to his brother. Burke Marshall bitterly accused the governor of working with the outgoing city government to "make that agreement blow up"; the highway patrolmen were "deliberately being awfully tough to provoke incidents on the theory that the more incidents they can provoke, the more repressive means they can use in the city and the more scared everyone gets including the white businessmen."[62]

The events of May 12 showed Wallace at his most reckless and irresponsible, but he was right on one point: the Kennedy administration was indeed responding again and again to political pressure from King and the civil rights movement. The necessity to strengthen King's influence against what he considered to be more radical and dangerous elements within the black community was the only substantive justification Robert Kennedy could offer for intervening in what was essentially a local dispute.

Ultimately, neither Al Lingo's troopers nor the President's threat to send troops brought peace to Birmingham. Tirelessly, King and other civil rights leaders walked the streets of the tense city and pleaded with young men to avoid confrontations with the police. The accord, however limited, had to be maintained. By nightfall on Sunday, May 12, 1963, quiet prevailed and the tenuous agreement between the movement and white community leaders held.

A WEEK after the Birmingham riots, President Kennedy arranged a one-day tour of the Tennessee Valley Authority facilities on the thirtieth anniversary of the TVA's creation. His inspection concluded with a quick helicopter trip from Muscle Shoals to Huntsville, Alabama—all part of his effort to refurbish his tattered image. At Muscle Shoals, he spoke before a generally enthusiastic crowd of eight thousand to ten thousand, and—as if to prove that he was still popular in the region—plunged into the crowd for ten minutes to shake hands. Afterwards, with Governor Wallace, Alabama senator Lister Hill, and local Scottsboro congressman Bob Jones, he boarded the presidential helicopter.

Wallace was partially deaf, but he had little difficulty following Kennedy's pointed criticism. In the fifty-minute flight, Kennedy never mentioned the upcoming Tuscaloosa standoff; he was still preoccupied with the intransigent resistance of Wallace and other political leaders to any change—even cosmetic changes—in race relations. Why, he asked, did Birmingham's businessmen refuse to hire Negroes as salesclerks in downtown stores? The very people who were resisting change "had Negroes serving their tables at their homes."

"I have no objections to the businessmen hiring who they want," the governor replied, "What I do object to is the government telling a businessman what he should do or should not do." The "vast majority" of blacks in Birmingham had "behaved themselves very well during the recent trouble." The big problem was the activities of outside agitators, particularly that "faker" Martin Luther King. King and the Reverend Shuttlesworth had no interest in solving Birmingham's problems, complained Wallace. They spent most of their time competing to see "who could go to bed with the most nigger women." And "white and red women too." Nor was that all, he added bitterly, they "ride around town in big Cadillacs smoking expensive cigars."[63]

Given John Kennedy's presidential Cadillac, his taste for good cigars, and his sexual athleticism, it is difficult to imagine that he was swayed by Wallace's argument. In any case, Kennedy was fixed on the political, not ethical, problems. As he later confided to his press secretary, Pierre Salinger, the governor's views on King might be "outrageous," but "we still have to solve the Alabama problem."[64]

When they landed and greeted well-wishers thirty minutes later at the Redstone Arsenal at Huntsville, the President smiled stiffly, but—as one member of the platform observed—made it clear that he "did not wish to be photographed or anything with him [Wallace]."[65]

The governor reported to a packed news conference that he and the

President had "discussed the situation in Birmingham briefly," but he politely deflected all questions with the statement (repeated twenty-five times, according to one newsman) that the President was a "refined courteous person."[66]

By mid-March of 1963, Burke Marshall had established close personal (and confidential) connections with editors and publishers of half a dozen of the state's newspapers, as well as with ministers and business and community leaders. Fifteen to twenty times a day he took calls from prominent people anxious to avoid a repetition of the violence at Ole Miss.[67] Alabama, unlike Mississippi in 1962, had dozens of civil leaders willing to counsel dignified retreat.

A special Justice Department task force methodically prepared a list of the officers and directors of 375 businesses operating in Alabama. Copies of that memo were distributed to members of the President's cabinet, the Securities and Exchange Commission, the Federal Communications Commission, the Federal Aviation Administration, and the head of the National Aeronautic and Space Administration, which had extensive facilities in Huntsville, Alabama. By May 29, cabinet officials and high-level appointees had contacted ninety-four business leaders in the state, fifty-seven of whom agreed to urge Wallace to accept the integration of the University of Alabama.[68]

The Justice Department task force had hoped to use the administration's leverage with out-of-state corporations like U.S. Steel, which employed over thirty thousand workers in Birmingham. But company president Robert M. Blough went out of his way to announce that any attempt to use his company's position in Birmingham to pressure local whites was "repugnant to me personally" and "repugnant to my fellow officers at U.S. Steel."[69] Out-of-state corporations "were the worst, the *absolute worst*," said Winton (Red) Blount, an Alabama businessman who had reluctantly accepted desegregation. The executives assigned to Alabama seemed terrified of antagonizing their white workers; the only thing they cared about was "getting through Birmingham or Montgomery or Gadsden and back to their national headquarters with the least headaches."[70]

The real heroes among white businessmen were those like Tuscaloosa's George LeMaistre. A bank president and former law professor, he had wrestled for years with the moral implications of white southerners' feverish defense of the racial status quo. The devastating economic decline in Arkansas that following the Little Rock imbroglio had given LeMaistre the argument he lacked. In private conversations, he had tried to convince fellow businessmen that fanatical resistance to *Brown v. Board of Education* would be disastrous for the state.[71]

The Ole Miss crisis and George Wallace's promise to stand in the schoolhouse door made George LeMaistre go public. He was a handsome, articulate man, a devout Presbyterian layman and pillar of the community, but most of his public statements seemed patterned after the annual reports he gave to the local bank board. "I think he took public-speaking lessons from Calvin Coolidge," a close friend said with a laugh.

As LeMaistre stood before the Tuscaloosa Civitan Club in November 1962, however, he spoke with passion and conviction.

Alabamians must stop sitting quietly, cravenly, on the sidelines. "For too long now, rabble-rousing hate groups and loud-mouthed politicians have undertaken to state the Southern viewpoint on matters which affect our lives." Economic issues were of course at stake, he admitted, but "I feel just as strongly the legal, moral and political issues that are involved."

Agree or not, like it or not, the Supreme Court was the "final interpreter of the Constitution." No state official, he continued, "has the right to put himself above the law. . . ." He paused a moment for effect, looked around the silent dining room, and added in a voice edging toward anger: "And that includes a governor or a governor-elect."

There was an audible gasp of shock and then an astonishing response: almost everyone in the crowded room stood and applauded.[72]

Accompanied by two small-town newspaper editors and Mobile lawyer John McConnell, LeMaistre confronted the governor in his office. Wallace dominated the conversation, but LeMaistre kept hammering away at his main point, the same point Robert Kennedy had stressed in his interview: the U.S. Supreme Court was the final arbiter of the law, and outright defiance of the court led to a broader disrespect for law.

With an irritated wave of his cigar, Wallace contemptuously dismissed the argument. A Supreme Court decision was *not* the law of the land, he said, it was simply the judgment of nine men. When LeMaistre stubbornly refused to retreat, Wallace exploded. "Law and order is a communist term," he said angrily. "Every time the communists take over, they clamp down with law and order."

As the urbane Tuscaloosa lawyer-banker later acknowledged, he "lost it." Leaning forward, inches from Wallace, he angrily responded: "George, that's bullshit! That's bullshit!"

As they left the capitol, a shaken McConnell confessed, "I never heard anybody talk like that to the governor."

Well, replied an unrepentant LeMaistre, "maybe that's what he needs."[73]

Wallace staked his final hopes for forestalling the scheduled June 11 integration of the university on an intensive background investigation of the two black applicants, Vivian Malone and Jimmy Hood. In the mid-1950s, University of Alabama trustees had hired private detectives to discredit Autherine Lucy. Though ugly, the practice had become institutionalized. When university officials received applications from African Americans, they furnished the candidates' names to the state law enforcement division, and state investigators then launched a far-reaching background check to uncover information that could be used to disqualify the applicants or blackmail them into withdrawing.

The system had usually worked. In one case, state investigators discovered that a prospective student's father had a criminal record; another applicant had been convicted of bigamy in a nearby state. Few of these episodes were more unsavory than the university's treatment of Joseph Epps, an academically talented young man from northwestern Birmingham who had completed two years of pre-med at Atlanta's prestigious Morehouse College. Because of Epps's outstanding record, university officials realized they would be hard pressed to reject his application. Sam Christian, a Birmingham private detective, quickly discovered Epps's vulnerability. His mother ("an 'Aunt Jemima' type," said Christian) who suffered from hallucinations and recurrent episodes of paranoia, was under the treatment of James Sussex, chief of psychiatry at University Hospital in Birmingham. Seventy-two hours after receiving the report, a school official reviewed the medical records and enlisted Sussex to call in mother and son for a meeting. Alone with Epps, the psychiatrist repeatedly warned that "his admission might put [his] mother in [the state mental] asylum." Joseph Epps returned to Morehouse College.[74]

When Frank Rose dutifully passed on the applications of Vivian Malone and James Hood to the governor's office, Wallace called Al Lingo and issued his instructions: "Do what y'all did with Autherine Lucy."[75]

Lingo assigned Willie Painter and Ben Allen, two veteran plainclothes officers with long experience in state law enforcement and in background investigations of black applicants. The two lawmen hit a dead end in their search for salacious or derogatory information. Admired by whites and blacks, the Malones were respected members of the northeast Alabama community of Gadsden where Vivian had grown up. The daughter's application had angered "violent elements" in the community, the two investigators warned; they could not guarantee protection from reprisals.[76] The hardboiled Allen later claimed that he was taken with the self-possessed and attractive Vivian Malone. She had applied to the university only because Alabama A & M, the state's impoverished black university, did not have an accredited accounting program. She had made good grades and she "wasn't the type to try to lord it over people, so to speak." Her family were "good people," he concluded, and there was nothing in her background to bar her as a student.[77]

Hood's character, too, seemed unimpeachable.

Their reports ignited a tirade from Lingo, which Allen later refused to recount because it "wouldn't be fit to print." The "governor's going to have my ass if those boys don't find something on those two niggers," Lingo told his assistant as he stomped up and down his office. "He's going to have mine, and I'm going to have theirs."

Wallace's rage matched Lingo's: "If you can't get something on them, dig up something on their daddies and mamas," he ordered. A renewed investigation brought forth no new evidence. "I had a gut feeling," said Allen, that Vivian Malone was going to "break the color barrier in the state of Alabama."[78]

Chapter 5

"WE DARE DEFEND OUR RIGHTS"

THE STAND IN THE SCHOOLHOUSE DOOR

Just before four p.m. on May 29, John Kennedy hurried to the White House basement to take a call on the White House scramblerphone. When he stepped off the elevator, however, aide McGeorge Bundy led him past the Situation Room and into the White House mess, decorated with bunting and balloons to celebrate the President's forty-sixth birthday. Press Secretary Pierre Salinger, master of ceremonies for the occasion, welcomed him with a spoof of Lincoln's Gettysburg Address ("Twoscore and six years ago there was brought forth at Brookline, Mass. . . .") and then presented the official gifts: a model space capsule to be passed on to Republican rival Barry Goldwater (the card read: "Hope you have a good trip, Barry") and a pair of boxing gloves to equip Kennedy for his upcoming bout with George Wallace.[1] The party lasted less than thirty minutes; the President was soon back at work.

Three days later, he convened a rare Saturday night work session at the White House, the third meeting dealing with civil rights in less than two weeks.[2] He was determined to regain the initiative by introducing civil rights legislation, but how far could he go? Should he concentrate on extending the ballot, a move that would arouse resistance only in the Deep South? Or should he take on the thorny issue of public accommodations, strike at the heart of legal segregation, and risk the political fallout that would come from antagonizing the southern wing of the Democratic Party? Vice-President Lyndon Johnson seemed unwilling to take a firm position; he warned that any public accommodations measure would face difficulty in the Senate.

But John Kennedy's brother dominated the discussion.

"Most people acquire certainties as they grow older," writer Anthony Lewis later said of his friend, Robert; "he *lost* his. He changed—he grew—more than anyone I have known."[3] Robert Kennedy was the only person in the room who argued for a strong civil rights measure, but if he had modified his position, he was frustrated and off-balance over his inability to control events in Alabama. Most of his anger seemed directed against the movement rather than Alabama's governor and the segregationists. Wallace he could understand. But the civil rights activists were impossible.

"Ninety percent of the [black] people who were demonstrating [in Birmingham] certainly didn't know what they were demonstrating about. And none of the white community knew what they were demonstrating about." Negroes, he said gloomily, "are getting mad for no reason at all[;] . . . they want to fight and they want to fight with white people . . . the big problem area . . . it's going to be the northern cities. . . . Like one of them [a black person] said yesterday, 'We've got them scared, now let's make them run.' . . . They [blacks] are all nationalists . . . you can't get a reasonable Negro leadership because . . . they're competing with one another. . . ."[4]

Burke Marshall remembered the President's reaction to the turbulence of the civil rights movement. "He didn't like it at all. It was politically unpleasant for him."[5] Unpleasant: the word was not simply the understated description of the phlegmatic Marshall; it accurately captured the tepid and calculating response of John Kennedy. But for once, his cool, detached style was preferable. He went to the heart of the matter: "The problem is today there is no other remedy. . . . We can't be [going] around saying 'you can't demonstrate' and at the same time not have them have some means of getting . . . justice in the matter. They can't demonstrate. They can't get a solution. I think we can't duck this one."[6]

Robert Kennedy, confident of his brother's ability to persuade the American people, wanted him to go on national television to outline his civil rights legislation, but even he realized it was prudent to wait and see how the situation in Alabama played out. Southern scenarios, the administration had learned, had a way of getting out of hand. "We didn't know," the attorney general confessed, "whether, in the . . . end, like the University of Mississippi, the president would have to go on [the air] and announce the use of troops . . . or the occupation of Tuscaloosa, or the arrest of the governor."[7] He wanted no repetition of the Ole Miss fiasco in which John Kennedy—on national television—had praised white southerners for their compliance even as the riot had begun.[8] For the moment, they would have to let the Tuscaloosa crisis unwind, and live with the uncomfortable reality that, within limits, Wallace was calling the shots.

TWELVE hours after the White House meeting broke up, George Wallace was on the attack. Lawrence Spivak, producer of television's most important news interview show, *Meet the Press,* had invited the Alabama governor to face a grilling by a panel composed of Spivak, Anthony Lewis of the *New York Times,* Frank McGee of NBC News, and Vermont Royster of the *Wall Street Journal.*

Wallace flew to New York with his on-again, off-again sponsor and patron, Grover Hall, Jr., editor of the *Montgomery Advertiser.* Hall had first encountered the awkward Wallace in 1945, sitting at the lunch counter of Montgomery's Cloverdale Grill, still wearing his baggy Air Force uniform and discussing politics nonstop with anyone within earshot. When they attended the Democratic convention in Philadelphia in 1948, Hall had taken the young legislator under his wing, and he had continued as confidant and adviser in the 1958 and 1962 gubernatorial campaigns.

Hall's father, editor of the *Advertiser* for more than thirty years, had won a Pulitzer Prize in 1928 for his scalding attacks on the Ku Klux Klan, though at times it seemed difficult to tell if he found the Klansmen's penchant for violence or their lack of breeding more offensive. Grover Junior had inherited many of his father's prejudices against the excesses of the rabble. A flamboyant dresser given to flowing silk handkerchiefs, brightly colored (but tasteful) silk ties, and custom-tailored sport coats, he never appeared in public without a fresh rosebud in his lapel. The Saturday morning stag brunches at his house in the genteel Cloverdale section of Montgomery were as much theatrical performances as social occasions. After a drink, more often after *several* stiff drinks, he loosed his mynah birds from their cages, then watched with detached amusement the reactions of his guests to his pets' exquisitely articulated Middle English poetry or Anglo-Saxon obscenities.[9]

Hall confided to a cousin during the 1958 campaign; "George has many weaknesses"; he had been careful "not to present him as a man of stature or statesmanship."[10] But in the years that followed, his admiration overrode any misgivings, and he remained a devoted acolyte throughout the 1960s. A passionate attachment to the conservative values of white southern society underlay his cynical exterior. While he might treat Wallace with the faintly patronizing contempt planters once reserved for their favorite "darkies," Hall recognized that in the twentieth century he was an anachronism. Wallace was something else, explained Wayne Greenhaw, "emotional, energetic, single-minded, rough-hewn, strong and appealing to the masses," a kind of redneck Ivanhoe "astride a great white charger," doing battle for the white people of Alabama and the South.[11]

Hall encouraged and soothed his friend (who had traveled under an assumed name) as they checked into the hotel and settled in for the night. When the time came to leave for the NBC studios at Rockefeller Center the following morning, however, George Wallace suddenly developed a first-class case of stage fright. "For God's sake, Grover, what about my foreign policy?" he demanded. "If I'm going to run for President next year, I've got to have a foreign policy!"

After several unsuccessful attempts at reassurance, Hall finally ripped out an analytical piece on East-West relations which had appeared the previous day in the *Wall Street Journal.* Here, George, he said soothingly, "That's a perfect foreign policy." His charge frantically read and reread the *Journal* story even as nine plainclothes detectives whisked him through a crowd of five hundred chanting anti-Wallace demonstrators. In the heaviest security alert around the NBC studios since Nikita Khrushchev had appeared on *Meet the Press,* the New York City police department stationed dozens of officers in the corridors of the building as well as on the street and had ready an ambulance and medic on Fiftieth Street, near the skating rink.

As he went downstairs to watch the program on a studio monitor, Grover Hall whispered his last advice: "Hold your temper, even if they spit on you."[12] After a quick visit to makeup, the governor sat and waited for the live show to begin, nervously shifting in his chair, drumming his fingers on the table and clenching one fist and then the other.

Once the lights came on, Wallace was the complete professional. Jules Loh, the Associated Press national correspondent who covered the Alabama governor during his early career, was amazed at the transformation. Seconds before going onstage he had observed Wallace muttering to himself, twisting nervously, breathing in short gasps. Then, like an actor standing in the wings just before his cue, the governor took a deep breath: "At that moment the tremble left his hands and the quaver left his voice and George C. Wallace Jr. was in total command of himself and at least partial command of his audience."[13]

In the years to come, the American people would come to know a surly Wallace—his head cocked to one side, his lips twisted into a pouting sneer as he mouthed invective which veered between scorn and semi-libelous abuse. On June 2, 1963, viewers saw another Wallace: smiling, good-humored but serious, totally at ease as he deflected the most cunningly contrived questions. Conservative editor and columnist James J. Kilpatrick would later describe his style with a flurry of vivid metaphors. The Alabama governor had "refined the base-stealer's art of sliding through an infielder's leg.... Cornering Wallace is like cornering a colt in an open field.... His one rule of political combat is that the best defense is a good offense. He never stops throwing punches."[14]

Exactly what was he going to do at the University of Alabama on June 11? demanded Spivak.

"I shall stand at the door as I stated in my campaign for Governor," Wallace smoothly replied, then hastily added: "The confrontation will be handled peacefully and without violence." He would challenge the Kennedy Justice Department in order to "raise constitutional questions that can then be adjudicated by the courts." The issue was far greater than the integration or segregation of the University of Alabama; the question was whether the American people could halt the "march of centralized government that is going to destroy the rights and freedom and liberty of the people of this country."

No one on the panel had prepared for the interview more intensely than Tony Lewis. A former Harvard classmate and close friend of Bobby Kennedy, a veteran and sympathetic reporter of the civil rights movement, he was hardly a disinterested journalist (a fact that had caused some apprehension among his editors at the *Times*). Hadn't the issue been settled by the courts already? asked Lewis, an edge to his voice. Less than a week earlier the Supreme Court had unanimously brushed aside one of Wallace's lawsuits challenging the Kennedy administration. Wasn't the schoolhouse-door promise a "political gesture to try to arouse violence?"

Not at all, replied Wallace in a tone which managed to convey both exasperation and reasonableness. For more than half a century, the federal courts had embraced the doctrine of separate but equal; there was still time for a return to sanity in court decisions. In any case, there was going to be no violent resistance. "If I am ever arrested by the federal government, I will go peacefully. There has never been any intention to resist and to fight the federal forces . . . with bottles and rocks and guns. I am against that as much as anyone else."

Had he not attacked the rulings of the Supreme Court as "lousy" and "irresponsible"? asked Frank McGee of NBC News.

"That is correct," replied Wallace, pausing for a moment to pull a note card from his pocket and to put on his reading glasses. The Supreme Court, he read, has "improperly set itself up as a third house of Congress, a superlegislature . . . reading into the Constitution words and implications which were never there." The South's difficulty with the court today, he told the panel, "arises not from the Court as an institution but from human beings within it." That was the position of Franklin Roosevelt in 1937, said Wallace as he folded his glasses. "I concur in it."

The *Wall Street Journal*'s Vermont Royster began, "I believe you are very active in the Baptist Church—"

"No," interrupted Wallace, "the Methodist Church." But, he continued with the little-boy grin he used when he was trying to be most ingratiating, "I have no objection to the Baptist Church. I married a Baptist."

Awkwardly, Royster continued, with a summary of the history of educational and religious discrimination in Alabama. His was less a question than a moral indictment, the kind of indictment that, in future years, would arouse Wallace to a rage against "Northern hypocrisy and self-righteousness." But he replied to Royster in a tone of injured innocence. There was "nothing immoral or sinful or irreligious about separate churches and separate school facilities"; they were the choice of the white and Negro citizens of Alabama.

Somehow the governor even managed to avoid his usually offensive pronunciation "Nigra," and to come up with something approximating the more respectable "Knee-grow." Despite this newfound sensitivity, he blandly denied that blacks suffered discrimination in voting in Alabama and, when asked about racial violence in his home state, responded as always by going on the offense ("You can't even walk in Central Park at night without fear of being raped or mugged or shot"). Anthony Lewis knew that schools for white students in Alabama had received from three to five times the funds allotted to blacks for most of the twentieth century. When he pointed out to Wallace that Alabama—like other southern states—had begun to equalize school facilities only when faced with the threat of integration in the 1940s and 1950s, Wallace earnestly insisted there was no difference in the support, both black and white schools had been equally poverty-stricken because the South had been "discriminated against for a hundred years."

Spivak, McGee and Royster all weighed in with a final round of increasingly accusatory questions. Wallace—confident that he had held his own— seemed at ease. He was going to stand in the schoolhouse door, but there was "going to be a peaceful solution. We are not going to have any violence."[15]

As the lights went down, the guest accepted rueful congratulations from the panelists and cheerfully scurried around the studio shaking hands with technicians and cameramen. Ten minutes later he walked downstairs and greeted Hall. Lighting up his cigar, Wallace pulled the crumpled *Wall Street Journal* article from his pocket and handed it to his friend. "I don't need a foreign policy," he told Hall with an impish grin. "All they wanted to know about was niggers," he said, "and I'm the expert."[16]

FORTY-eight hours after Wallace flew back to Alabama, federal judge Seybourn H. Lynne granted the Justice Department's request for an injunction against the Alabama governor. Although he declined to bar Wallace from the campus, Judge Lynne prohibited his interference in the admission of James Hood and Vivian Malone on June 11. If the governor ignored the injunction, the judge would hold him in contempt of court, subject to jail and fines. In an emotional departure from his usual detachment, Lynne—a graduate of the university and its law school—appealed to other natives of his home state. "I love the people of Alabama. I know that many of both races are troubled and, like Jonah of old, are 'angry even unto death.' " But the concept of law, the very essence of a republican form of government, rested upon the notion that, once the judicial process had reached a final judgment, "all persons affected thereby are obliged to obey it." The Supreme Court of the United States had rejected the doctrine of interposition, said Lynne. The governor no longer had any valid constitutional grounds "to obstruct or prevent the execution of the lawful orders of a court of the United States."[17]

Through dozens of indirect communications, word reached the attorney general that even if the governor had not formulated a precise plan, he intended to avoid violence. Bill Jones, Wallace's press aide, talked with Ed Guthman, his counterpart in the Justice Department, and gave him vague reassurances that Tuscaloosa would not be a repetition of Ole Miss. Senator John Sparkman had passed the word to the White House the previous fall that Wallace had confided that he simply wanted to get his message across. Responding to Judge Lynne's injunction in a statewide television address, the governor reaffirmed his plans to block the admission of Hood and Malone, but he called Senator Lister Hill (no close ally) and asked him to notify the White House that there would be no violence. Wallace wanted to make certain, Hill thought, that the Kennedys would not press for a jail sentence for him.[18]

On June 5, informants within the Klan passed on encouraging news to their FBI handlers. Al Lingo, chief of Alabama's state police, had telephoned the Grand Dragon of the Marion, Alabama, Klan and warned him that any known Klansmen in Tuscaloosa would be arrested. Two days later, Wallace ally Bull Connor spoke to a White Citizens' Council meeting in Tuscaloosa; afterward Connor met privately with Klan members to relay the word that the governor wanted private citizens to stay away from the university town. Presumably Wallace had no trouble establishing communication with Alabama's two most prominent Klansmen—Asa Carter and Robert Shelton— since they were, for all intents and purposes, on his payroll.[19] Carter, closeted in the basement of the capitol writing the statement Wallace would read at the university, took time out to visit Edward R. Fields, head of the National States' Rights Party, a group described as neo-Nazi, headquartered in Alabama. The speechwriter "requested that we not go down to Tuscaloosa and hold any type of demonstration," said Fields. "He said that it would be best for us to leave the entire event strictly to the Governor."[20]

But how much control did Wallace really wield over the violent men who had rallied to his call for resistance? Carter and Shelton had made careers of publicly giving lip service to law and order while privately inciting—in some cases orchestrating—acts of violence and terrorism against civil rights workers. And members of Shelton's group, the United Klans of America, could hardly be described as disciplined soldiers. Many Klaverns were little more than drinking clubs, which offered alienated working-class whites a politically acceptable rationale for abandoning their wives and families to spend their evenings carousing and ineffectually cursing blacks and "nigger-loving whites." The far more dangerous independent Klans answered to no one; such Klaverns as the infamous Cahaba River Group, the Eastview Klavern No. 13, and internal cells such as Unit 900 were responsible for dozens of bombings and several murders.[21]

In late May, a young man from Birmingham had appeared on the Tuscaloosa campus, soliciting students for donations to buy a rifle with telescopic sight, to be used in "taking care of Vivian Malone and Jimmy Hood," President Rose told Robert Kennedy.[22] While a public announcement of intent hardly seemed the mark of a professional assassin, it reflected exactly the kind of irrational act that was beyond the control of Shelton—even had he wished to exercise control.

The worst apprehensions of Frank Rose and the Kennedy administration seemed to receive chilling support in the last days before the scheduled June 11 integration of the university. On Saturday afternoon, June 8, Gary Rowe, a member of Birmingham's notorious Eastview Klavern, and a longtime FBI informant, received a call from one of his Klavern's leaders. His assignment (Rowe later claimed), was to go to Tuscaloosa and "tear the school apart." Rowe loaded into the trunk of his car five carbines, four twelve-gauge pump shotguns, five boxes of double-ought buckshot, four bayonets, fragmentation hand grenades, tear gas grenades, a .45 caliber machine gun, and a dozen dynamite sticks and caps. (At the insistence of his FBI control, he left behind the Klan-owned antitank bazooka.) From his home in Birmingham, he drove to Butch Bell's Barbecue outside Tuscaloosa and picked up Exalted Cyclops Herbert E. (Gene) Reeves and four other Klansmen.[23] In two cars, they moved out toward the campus.

As a covert operation, the operation lacked subtlety. Reeves and one of his sidekicks wore steel-toed jackboots and white jumpsuits with the insignia "KKK" boldly embroidered on the chests. Both of the vehicles sported Klan bumper stickers and conspicuous whip aerials for their police-style radios.[24]

Just outside the city limits, the six men encountered a roadblock manned by a half-dozen heavily armed state troopers tipped off by the FBI. With considerable reluctance, they arrested the Klansmen. "Jesus Christ," one officer exclaimed, "we sure hate to bust you when you come down here to help us keep the goddamn niggers away from the school!" But Lingo had been emphatic.[25]

Within hours the Klansmen were released, and by morning they had recovered all their weapons. Bobby Shelton insisted that the six were part of a security detail assigned to protect a Klan rally north of the city.[26] (He may well have been telling the truth; Rowe was generally considered a notoriously unreliable informant.) But news of the heavily armed Klan foray unnerved the federal officials in Tuscaloosa.[27]

Meanwhile, *New York Times* reporter Claude Sitton relayed word to a friend in the Justice Department that Wallace had told him in an "off the record" interview that, when he was pushed aside, he intended to "pull out the highway patrol" and let the handful of federal marshals worry about law and order, a scenario that bore alarming similarity to the events that had led to disaster at Ole Miss.[28] Whether Wallace's resistance would be "symbolic or serious," Deputy Attorney General Katzenbach concluded, would probably not be settled until the morning of the confrontation. The dilemma remained: "[If we] move too quickly with too much force, we will be subject to criticism; if we fail to do so we run a greater risk of genuine resistance and mob violence."[29]

As Rowe loaded his Klan arsenal, Attorney General Kennedy made one last effort to come up with a firm script for the Tuesday confrontation. He placed a late-afternoon call to the governor's office.

The conversation began badly. Wallace, fearful of a last-minute ambush, refused to talk. Instead he listened over an extension as his legal assistant, Cecil Jackson, and his special counsel, John Kohn, explained that the governor was "unavailable."

What he wanted to do, said Kennedy, was to "find out from the Governor what he is going to do on Tuesday and find out specifically what his course of action is going to be."

John Kohn despised both Kennedys, particularly the President's younger brother. He disliked his politics ("evil and dangerous"), his manner ("ruthless"), and even his sharp New England accent ("Bobby has a voice that would irritate the Angel Gabriel.").[30] With the phone connected to the office tape recorder and a nervous Wallace secretly listening on an extension phone, Kohn took the receiver and gave no ground. "Well, Mr. Kennedy, I think that's a prerogative exclusively within the governor's mind . . . and the details of it will have to depend upon the circumstances."

"Looks as though I can't find out. Is that right?" asked Kennedy. He asked to speak to Jackson. "I thought we were going to handle it as civilized people . . . but I can't get that, obviously."

Jackson bridled. "Well now, Mr. Kennedy, I think you know that we are civilized people. . . . I think the Governor would be willing to talk to you if you are interested in discussing ways and means by which these . . . Negroes withdraw their efforts to go to the University of Alabama. . . ."

"There is nothing to be negotiated," Kennedy told Jackson coldly. Hood and Malone were "going to be attending the University of Alabama."[31]

Only twenty-four hours before the scheduled confrontation in Tuscaloosa, the President delivered one of his most memorable foreign-policy addresses. Speaking on June 10 at the American University commencement exercises, the cold warrior Kennedy eloquently spoke for an America at the crossroads. It was time, he told his listeners, to turn away from the weary recriminations of the postwar era. Although the Soviets held a distorted view of America's goals and policies, that very gulf of misunderstanding should be a "warning to the American people not to fall into the same trap as the other side." History taught that enmities between nations did not last forever, he reminded his audience, and if the two nations could not yet resolve their differences, "at least we can help make the world safe for diversity. For, in the final analysis, our most basic common link is the fact that we all inhabit this planet. We all breathe the same air. We all cherish our children's future. And we are all mortal."[32]

The American University speech was the culmination of a remarkable political comeback for Kennedy, who had been humiliated in the Bay of Pigs débacle during the first months of his administration. His adept handling of the Cuban missile crisis in late 1962 and his bold plans for tax cuts to stimulate the economy in early 1963 had earned him growing respect and, not incidentally, a strong rebound in the polls.

Now the President of the United States, Robert Kennedy's brother and boss, who held in his hand the power of war or peace, was having to preoccupy himself with a sleazy, strutting Alabama redneck. It was undignified. The Marquis of Queensberry's Rules were no longer appropriate.

By Monday evening, June 10, more than four hundred raucous, elbowing newsmen had gathered in the little college town of Tuscaloosa to watch Wallace's long-promised stand in the schoolhouse door. *Newsday* correspondent Michael Dorman had retreated to his motel room, where he received a telephone call from a man he would later identify only as a "high-ranking Justice Department official who had been sent to Tuscaloosa to help enforce the court order." Dorman, a former Associated Press reporter, had covered a variety of Washington stories. His work on organized crime and the labor movement had brought him to the attention of Robert Kennedy; he was an ideal choice for leaking confidential information.

Wallace, the caller confided, had a documented history of "mental illness." The governor's official biography had described the severe case of spinal meningitis he had contracted in 1943 while in the Air Force. What it did not mention was his nervous breakdown in the early fall of 1945 when he refused to fly. He had been treated and released—and, according to Dorman's informant, was still receiving a ten percent disability check from the Veterans Administration for "nervous disability."

Dorman found himself unexpectedly invited into the crowded room of

Nick Katzenbach, who had set up his headquarters at Tuscaloosa's Hotel Stafford. The assistant attorney general, flanked by two aides, confirmed the details of Wallace's military health records. The reporter had more than a passing suspicion that Katzenbach was well aware of the leak. Unable to reach Bill Jones, Wallace's press aide, for a comment, Dorman called Grover Hall at the *Advertiser*. "There's nothing to the story," said Hall, but he promised to check with Wallace.

Thirty minutes later, Hall was back on the phone with Dorman. The governor had acknowledged, said the editor, that he had been grounded after returning from the Pacific for "flight fatigue, anxiety state," and that he had been getting a ten percent disability check.

Did he have any other comment? asked Dorman.

Yes, said Hall, Wallace sent word that "this gives me a perfect defense in any contempt-of-court case—insanity."[33]

When Katzenbach learned that the governor had admitted to having a nervous breakdown, he jumped up from his chair in excitement and grabbed a drink. National circulation of the story would surely throw Wallace off his stride and raise questions about his mental stability in this moment of contrived crisis. But Dorman's editors at *Newsday* refused to run the story; in the context of the more restrained journalism of the early 1960s, it was off limits and potentially libelous. Katzenbach, a former law professor, reminded Dorman that "so far as libel is concerned, truth is a perfect defense." The *Newsday* editors would not be persuaded.[34]

The possibility of violence added the only suspense to what was increasingly becoming a theatrical event staged at the insistence of, and for the benefit of, George Wallace. A researcher for independent filmmaker Robert Drew had approached Robert Kennedy in mid-May with a proposal to do an inside cinema verité account of a crisis in the making: the stand in the schoolhouse door. Drew, one of the most innovative documentarians of the early 1960s, had already produced a highly flattering portrait of the President in *Primary,* which chronicled Kennedy's campaign (and victory) in Wisconsin's Democratic primary. A year later, Drew had completed a second film (*Adventures on the New Frontier*), which was even more of a "puff piece," focusing on the informal and "personal" attractiveness of Kennedy as decisive president and doting father. Fluid camera angles, obviously unrehearsed dialogue, and occasionally poor technical quality gave viewers a sense that they were watching the raw materials of history. In reality, of course, such films were carefully crafted and edited, with the story line that viewers were increasingly coming to expect in documentaries as in their feature films. After checking with the White House and reviewing one of Drew's more recent films, Bobby Kennedy agreed.[35]

Although Wallace knew nothing of the Drew-Kennedy relationship, his natural suspicion of "Yankee" newsmen and his still-uncertain attitude toward television made him hesitate. "I know what they'll do," he told aide Earl Morgan: "They'll have Bobby Kennedy looking like a' eloquent statesman, and they'll have me picking my nose." (They did "leave out the nose-pickin,' " Morgan later chuckled; they just settled for shots of Wallace "slurping his food.")[36]

Early Monday morning, June 10, cameramen recorded the attorney general at his Virginia house as he telephoned instructions to Katzenbach, surrounded by his exuberant children and his even more irrepressible black Labrador, Brumus. Drew had promised the Kennedys the right to review the film before its airing, but they had no worries. They were clearly the heroes of the story.

The attorney general unexpectedly invited Drew's team to join the President and his staff for a Monday afternoon update on the Tuscaloosa crisis. While John Kennedy had approved the decision to allow the filming, he was clearly on guard during much of the meeting. While Robert Kennedy and Burke Marshall reviewed the plans for the next day, the President sat in his rocking chair, eyes slightly hooded, listening carefully, saying little.

In an earlier meeting, Katzenbach had toyed with the idea of using federal marshals to push the governor aside. It "might not hurt to have him look somewhat ridiculous," one Justice Department attorney had suggested. General Creighton Abrams, commander of the federal troops waiting near Tuscaloosa, had two of his best (and burliest) men practice a maneuver in which they would seize the five-foot, seven-inch Wallace by the wrists with one hand, under the arms with another, and then would forcibly carry him to the side.[37]

But when his brother brought up the exasperated Katzenbach's longing to shoulder the governor aside by "pushing a little bit," John Kennedy spoke for the first time. "Try to walk around him," he insisted.

Another film crew trooped into the Alabama governor's mansion. In years to come, George Wallace would become comfortable in the presence of the camera, but he came across poorly in the Drew documentary. He briefly picked up his daughter, but little Lee squirmed to return to the arms of her black nanny. Intent on projecting a heroic mode in keeping with what he called this "solemn occasion," the governor positioned himself reverently before a portrait of Alabama's most recalcitrant secessionist, William Lowndes Yancey. "I'd rather live a short life of standing for principle than live a long life of compromise," he said, quoting Yancey and gazing awkwardly into the camera. "Of course that may not mean much to you folks."

On the way to the airport for the short flight to Tuscaloosa, Wallace seemed even more ill at ease. "Separation has been good for the Nigra citizen and for the white citizen," he said as he glowered into the camera, then stared sullenly out the window.[38] Aboard the governor's plane, it was clear to John Kohn that Wallace was experiencing of one of his typical pre-performance anxiety attacks. Despite the public self-confidence he projected, the constant stream of attacks from within the state had left him rattled and fearful that he might have overplayed his hand. Even his beloved stepgrandmother, Mother Mae, had confided to Lurleen Wallace that she was "upset" over her grandson's decision to stand in the schoolhouse door.[39] As Wallace talked, nervously shredding a piece of paper, his mood abruptly switched. If Katzenbach used physical force to remove him from the door, "I'm going to hit him."

Kohn looked at him with a shocked expression.

"Why not?" asked Wallace belligerently.

"Because your political career will be ruined," Kohn explained patiently. And, as one member of the Kohn family recalled his saying, because "the Kennedys will put you in jail with two hundred niggers."[40]

The governor reviewed Judge Lynne's injunction once more before going off to an early supper with President Rose. Overcome by another attack of the jitters, he fretted to executive secretary Earl Morgan, "What if they take me to jail? Y'all will have to bring my shaving kit, toothbrush, and razor." By the time he arrived for his eight P.M. meeting with the board of trustees, he appeared almost out of control, according to Rose and several trustees. During the two-hour session, said board member Red Blount, Wallace "acted as though he were on amphetamines."

But he was not so nervous that he neglected the political dimensions of the meeting. In order to protect himself from the charges of "moderates" within the state who attacked him for intervening at Tuscaloosa, he presented for ratification a one-page statement of unconditional surrender. The document, prepared by Cecil Jackson, unequivocally endorsed his presence on the campus: "Be it resolved by the Trustees . . . that the said presence of Gov. Wallace is necessary to preserve peace and order."

A handful of board members ever so gently raised a few questions and managed to insert a fig leaf; the final version of the statement included the vague explanation that Wallace's presence was necessary "under the circumstances to preserve peace and order." These "circumstances" were, of course, the insistence of the governor that he stage his confrontation, and the possibility that events would spin out of control if he did not have his moment in the limelight.[41]

While Wallace met with the trustees, Bobby Kennedy and a handful of advisers once again convened in the attorney general's office. Over a speaker phone Kennedy and Marshall deliberated issues of protocol: Should the assistant attorney general shake hands with Wallace? Who would accompany him to Foster Auditorium, the university's official registration site, for the standoff? Would the black students sit in the car or walk beside Katzenbach?

Once again, Katzenbach proposed decisive action. Why not just bypass the sham confrontation at the auditorium? With the cooperation of the university, the students had, in fact, already pre-registered at the Birmingham courthouse earlier that morning; they had selected all their courses and filled out all their forms. The assistant attorney general had even obtained keys to the dormitory rooms for Malone and Hood. Why not simply put the students in their rooms and then send them on to their classes on the twelfth? "Why don't we just let him stand up there by himself?"

In the middle of their telephone conference, Robert Kennedy's secretary interrupted with a call. President Rose's assistant Jeff Bennett had slipped away from the meeting with Red Blount; they had gone to a downtown pay telephone to give the attorney general their last-minute assessment of the governor's plans. ("We weren't sure the phones weren't tapped at the University," Blount later recalled.) They surmised that Wallace would capitulate to federal troops, though not to a court order from Katzenbach.[42]

Bennett and Blount's description of the agitated Wallace seemed to reinforce the attorney general's caution. "You'd better give him his show," Robert Kennedy told Katzenbach, "because I'm concerned if he doesn't have it . . . that God knows what could happen by way of violence."[43]

Katzenbach spent a sleepless night; Wallace—alternately jovial and uneasy—settled into his suite at Tuscaloosa's Stafford Hotel. Shortly after eight A.M. on Tuesday, June 11, surrounded by friends and hangers-on, he summoned two of his favorite Alabama reporters, Bob Ingram of the *Advertiser* and Rex Thomas of the Associated Press, for an exclusive interview. Ingram could not refrain from good-naturedly teasing Wallace about his ungubernatorial appearance. (He had borrowed a faded pair of short pajamas from the taller Seymore Trammell, since he had forgotten to pack his.) But such in-house humor was more than matched by the gravity of the occasion. John Kohn was all solemnity. "You have divine blessing today," he told Wallace as he put his arm around the governor. "Good luck and may God bless you." Outside the entrance to the hotel, when the cameras from Drew's film crew began rolling, Kohn dutifully repeated his good wishes to a chorus of "God bless you—God bless you" from admirers who had gathered. Both Ingram and Thomas reported to their readers that the governor was visibly moved.[44]

Ninety miles away, Lurleen Wallace and the three youngest children—Lee, two, George, Junior, eleven, and Peggy Sue, thirteen—gathered before a television set at their modest summer house on Lake Martin to watch the confrontation. Peggy Sue was bursting with pride in her father, the "bravest man alive," she thought. Only later did she remember her mother: pale, drawn, smoking one cigarette after another as she paced back and forth between the living room and the front porch.[45]

Bill Jones prepared the stage. A university janitor borrowed a slender podium from a nearby classroom and placed it six feet in front of the double swinging doors that marked the entrance to Foster Auditorium, site of the official registration. Another aide checked and double-checked the microphone the governor would wear. While reporters and pooled television cameras jockeyed for viewing positions behind a chalk circle laid off by Jones, sharpshooters climbed to the roofs of nearby buildings and waited in the growing June heat.

The governor walked across the campus with his entourage of security men and aides; he greeted students, but his smile seemed forced. Even in the midst of the most important moment of his political career, he could not forget the grievances still rankling from his impoverished days on the campus. When they passed the Phi Delta Theta fraternity house, he turned to John Kohn. "That's where you were," Wallace growled, "while I stayed in the barracks."[46] As he stepped with state police investigator Ben Allen into a small air-conditioned anteroom, the mask of self-confidence slipped away. "Ben," he asked anxiously, "do you think they'll actually arrest me?"[47]

The attorney general and his staff had made their last critical decisions. The administration would federalize those units of the Alabama National Guard already placed on standby by the governor. (After federal troops were used to quell the anti-integration riots at Ole Miss the previous fall, southern segregationists had repeatedly compared their intervention with the hated "Yankee" occupying forces of the Reconstruction era. Using Alabama National Guardsmen allowed the administration to minimize the visible presence of the federal government.)

The action would proceed in two stages; first, Katzenbach would confront the governor, and then, after nationalization of the guard unit, its commander would ask Wallace to step aside. Presumably at that point he would capitulate.

Almost as an afterthought, Katzenbach, Burke Marshall, and their boss agreed to leave Hood and Malone waiting in the car while Katzenbach led the entourage and demanded the applicants' admission. "I don't want to put the students through that indignity. I don't want the man [Wallace] to stand there and say things to them," Kennedy told his assistants. "They've had a hard enough life being black."

Katzenbach agreed: "I didn't want that picture on national television, his turning down two black students." It was much better for the confrontation to be between "federal and state authority, not the racial one."[48]

While Kennedy and Katzenbach's concern for the applicants may have been a factor, leaving Malone and Hood in the car, Kennedy later confided, "permitted us not to charge him [Wallace] with contempt, because the students weren't [physically] there yet."[49] Thus, it was possible to sustain

Wallace's fiction that he was challenging the constitutional validity of a federal order, not blocking the integration of the university.

However appropriate this decision might have seemed at the time, it could not have been better scripted by Wallace. Alabama's governor was given the freedom to act like a particularly disgraceful alley cat prancing back and forth in front of a firmly chained pit bull. And the very notion of couching the confrontation as a constitutional issue was *precisely* in keeping with Wallace's strategy: an abstract struggle between "states' rights" and the "central government." In the short run, it would not have hurt him—it would have helped him—to stand in the door of Foster Auditorium and physically spurn two qualified black students. But it would have presented a visual image that he could never have escaped and thus would have destroyed the carefully constructed illusion that the issue had nothing to do with race. For quite different reasons, Wallace and the Kennedys wanted to avoid the rawness of that confrontation, but Seymore Trammell had been right when he angrily faced Robert Kennedy in Wallace's office in April:

This had everything to do with race.

NICK Katzenbach had not slept in thirty-six hours. By the time the federal motorcade pulled up in front of Foster Auditorium shortly before eleven A.M., the temperature had reached ninety-five degrees; in his non-air-conditioned government sedan, the assistant attorney general felt he was riding in a steam bath. As Kennedy's deputy got out of his car, Seymore Trammell took his hat off to signal the governor. Wallace stepped out of the building and up to the podium. U.S. Attorney Macon Weaver and federal marshal Peyton Norville, both graduates of the university law school, accompanied Katzenbach as he walked from his car up the brick steps of the building.

From his vantage point at the front of the crowd, Claude Sitton of the *New York Times* could see Katzenbach's hands trembling. The assistant attorney general was not (as several newsmen thought) so much unnerved as he was exhausted and furious. White lines "like stage instructions" showed "everyone where to stand in the production," said Katzenbach, who mistakenly blamed Rose for the layout. And his mark had been painted nearly twenty feet away from Wallace's podium. "He was standing in the shade and he wanted me in the sun. . . . I was sweating enough as it was."[50]

Katzenbach walked to within four feet of the podium.

Wallace sternly raised one hand, like a bailiff swearing in an unruly witness.

"I have here President Kennedy's proclamation," Katzenbach began. "I have come to ask you for unequivocal assurance that you or anyone under your control will not bar these students." He paused awkwardly, and then began again. "I have come here to ask now for unequivocal assurance that you will permit these students who, after all, merely want an education in the great University—"

Wallace interrupted with what he intended to be a firm command, but it sounded more like a snarl: "Now you make your statement, but we don't need a speech."[51]

"I am making my statement, Governor," replied a visibly angry Katzenbach. He asked Wallace once again to assure him that he would not interfere with the two students.

His adversary pulled out the four-page "statement and proclamation" which Asa Carter and John Kohn had prepared for him. By Wallace standards it was fairly tame: an appeal to the rights of the "sovereignty of the states," a swipe at the "illegal usurpation of power by the Central Government," a series of turgid "whereas"es. It concluded with the peroration that would end up on the television screens of all major networks: as governor, "mindful of my duties and responsibilities under the Constitution of the United States, the Constitution of the state of Alabama, and seeking to preserve and maintain the peace and dignity of this State, and the individual freedoms of the citizens thereof, [I] do hereby denounce and forbid this illegal and unwarranted action by the Central Government."

Katzenbach, who had stood, arms folded across his chest, throughout the seven-minute declamation, looked as though he had just stepped, fully clothed, out of a summer rainstorm. He was soaked in sweat, his pants were wrinkled, and his right coat pocket bulged with his walkie-talkie. But he had fully recovered from his inarticulate beginning.

The attorney general's last call to Katzenbach that morning had advised, "Make him look ridiculous. That's what the President wants you to do." Wallace was "really a second-rate character to you," Kennedy had coached. "He's wasting your time. He's wasting the students' time."[52]

His deputy gamely tried to follow instructions.

"I'm not interested in this show," he said sarcastically, waving his hand vaguely at the cameras and newsmen. "From the outset, Governor, all of us have known that the final chapter of this history will be the admission of these students." James Hood and Vivian Malone would "remain on this campus. They will register today. They will go to school tomorrow," Katzenbach said emphatically.

Wallace stared straight ahead, jaw lifted, mouth pursed. For nearly a minute, the only sound from the hundreds of officials and newsmen was the rapid clicking of dozens of cameras. When the governor refused to respond, Katzenbach returned to his car. Vivian Malone joined him, and they walked to her dorm across the parking lot. Other Justice Department officials drove Hood to his dormitory across the campus. Wallace stepped back into the air-conditioning of Foster Auditorium to await the next phase of the showdown.

The house mother warmly greeted Vivian Malone and invited her to lunch in the dorm dining room. Calling from his office, Frank Rose lost the veneer of control that had marked his relations with the press. "There's gonna be a riot if you do this," he warned her, but Katzenbach was brusquely unsympathetic. "Look," he responded sharply, still angry over what he felt was Rose's cooperation with Wallace. "She's gonna be eating in that dormitory, she might as well start with lunch." Vivian Malone walked through the cafeteria line and seated herself alone; a half-dozen smiling young coeds came over to her table with their trays, sat down, and introduced themselves.[53]

National Guard general Henry V. Graham, a Birmingham real estate man, had been summoned by helicopter from his summer training camp and ordered to take command of the guard units which had been federalized within minutes of Wallace's refusal to yield to Katzenbach. Between one and two P.M., after Graham arrived in Tuscaloosa, Taylor Hardin, who had vetted the final version of Wallace's speech, called to arrange a brief meeting. If the general would allow the governor one last statement, he would then step aside and end the standoff, promised Hardin.

Graham forwarded the message to General Creighton Abrams. Though it was a "rather sticky situation for all of us," said Graham, who was sensitive to the political dimensions, it did represent a "way out." Robert Kennedy, anxious to have the episode ended, agreed.[54]

A relieved Wallace wolfed a steak, hash brown potatoes, and fried onion rings, all doused with ketchup and washed down with three glasses of iced tea and a glass of milk. There remained only a final late-afternoon coda for the benefit of cameras and journalists.

Once again, the governor stepped out of the doorway and up to the podium. Graham, his starched uniform freshly pressed, a small Confederate battle flag stitched on his breast pocket, marched to the same spot where Katzenbach had stood. He paused for a moment and then saluted. "It is my sad duty to ask you to step aside, on order of the President of the United States."

"But for the unwarranted federalization of the National Guard, I would be your commander-in-chief. It is a bitter pill to swallow," Wallace intoned. Even though the "trend toward military dictatorship continues," he sternly told the television cameras and newsmen, there must be no violence. "Alabama is winning this fight against Federal interference because we are awakening the people to the trend toward military dictatorship in this country." The attorney general, listening to Wallace's speech on the radio in his Washington office, flashed a quick, tight smile of disbelief. But it was worth the wait for the last line of cautious capitulation.

"I am returning to Montgomery to continue working for constitutional government to benefit all Alabamians—black and white." Despite the governor's repeated campaign promises that he would hold the line and maintain racial segregation in Alabama, Vivian Malone and Jimmy Hood were officially students of the University of Alabama. Putting the best possible construction on the situation, Wallace was abandoning Richmond and falling back toward Petersburg.[55] As he rode back to the airport, accompanied by the Drew Associates cameraman, his mood appeared to waver between relief and belligerence. He was still uncertain over just how the episode had played for the cameras.

In Tuscaloosa, Katzenbach and Ed Guthman returned to their hotel room and quietly celebrated with a stiff drink, confident that they had not only integrated the university but also forced Wallace into a position where he "looked ridiculous," said Guthman.[56]

In Washington, the President agreed. Just before one P.M., with Vice President Lyndon Johnson at his side, Kennedy had welcomed Senator Everett Dirksen and Representative Charles Halleck into the Cabinet Room near his office to tell them that he had decided to introduce a strong civil rights bill in the Congress. The Tuscaloosa standoff had confirmed that racial conflict would accelerate in the South unless blacks were assured the basic rights guaranteed in his proposed legislation, he told the two Republican leaders. He badly needed their support to break an anticipated filibuster by southern Democrats.[57]

Halfway through their meeting, secretary Evelyn Woods had summoned Kennedy to his office to take a call from his brother. Robert Kennedy had passed on the details of the last-minute deal with Wallace. By the time Dirksen and Halleck left the White House at one-forty-five P.M., the networks had rushed film to Birmingham, interrupted regularly scheduled programming, and begun a delayed telecast of the Wallace-Katzenbach confrontation. As the President sat down in his secretary's office to catch the replay, his brother called from the Justice Department, where he, too, had tuned in. Together they watched the first installment of the stand in the schoolhouse door.

Buoyed by the news that Wallace had agreed to back down, John Kennedy confided that he had decided to make a televised address that evening unveiling the outlines of his proposed civil rights bill.[58] Just that morning, the *New York Times* had reprinted excerpts from a Sunday news show in which Martin Luther King had scolded the President for his timid leadership.[59] Kennedy had decided to use the successful resolution of the Tuscaloosa episode to demonstrate his commitment.

Burke Marshall, watching the news coverage with the attorney general, was stunned. "How could he possibly do that?" he asked himself. There simply wasn't time.[60]

Speechwriter Ted Sorensen, along with staff aides, had begun planning for a presidential address, but they had never anticipated going on the air with less than six hours' advance notice. Minutes before eight P.M., Kennedy's speech consisted of a jumble of retyped pages, fragments, and notes inserted crazily up and down the margins; some sections would have to be delivered extemporaneously. Robert Kennedy, who was "not bothered by many things, was shaken by the president not having his prepared text," said Burke Marshall.[61]

Fifteen seconds before the red light flashed on the television camera, Kennedy scribbled a last reminder and self-consciously brushed his hand over his head to make sure his hair was in place. Then he began:

"Good evening, my fellow citizens. This afternoon, following a series of threats and defiant statements, the presence of Alabama National Guardsmen was required on the University of Alabama [campus] to carry out the final and unequivocal order of the United States District Court. . . ."

The confrontation had ended peacefully, Kennedy continued, but it seemed an appropriate time to reflect upon the events of the last twenty-four hours. "I hope that every American, regardless of where he lives, will stop and examine his conscience. . . ."

The harried last-minute preparations showed. The President appeared awkward and stiff as he occasionally groped for the next sentence and once repeated a phrase.

"Today we are committed to a worldwide struggle to promote and protect the rights of all who wish to be free. And when Americans are sent to Vietnam or West Berlin we do not ask for whites only," said Kennedy. It ought to be possible, therefore, for American students of "any color to attend any public institution they select without having to be backed up by troops." And it ought to be possible for them to receive "equal service in places of public accommodation," to "register and to vote in a free election without interference or fear of reprisal."

Three minutes into his remarks, the President's tone shifted, becoming more personal and more impassioned.

> *The Negro baby born in America today . . . has about one-half as much chance of completing a high school education as a white baby born in the same place on the same day; one-third as much chance of completing college; one-third as much chance of becoming a professional man; twice as much chance of becoming unemployed; about one-seventh as much chance of earning $10,000 a year; a life expectancy which is seven years shorter. . . .*

Kennedy's voice rose with an unaccustomed intensity. The nation, he said, was "confronted primarily with a moral issue" as "old as the Scriptures and as clear as the American Constitution . . . : whether we are going to treat our fellow Americans as we want to be treated." If a black American were barred from all the rights of a "full and free life" then "who among us would be content to have the color of his skin changed and stand in his place?" And who, he added, would be "content with the counsels of patience and delay[?] One hundred years of delay have passed since President Lincoln freed the slaves, yet their heirs, their grandsons, are not fully free. . . . And this nation for all its boasts, will not be fully free until all its citizens are free."

Across the nation, said Kennedy, "the fires of frustration and discord are busy in every city. Redress is sought in the street." The only way to end these potentially violent civil rights confrontations was to deal with the source of the conflict. "I am therefore asking the Congress to enact legislation giving all Americans the right to be served in facilities which are open to the public—hotels, restaurants, theaters, retail stores and similar establishments." It seemed, said Kennedy, "an elementary right. Its denial is an arbitrary indignity that no American in 1963 should have to endure."

As recently as mid-April, the consensus in the administration had been clear: a civil rights bill with a public-accommodations section would never make it out of committee in Congress. The events of May and early June toppled these assumptions. Although White House and Justice Department aides had been reviewing a range of civil rights legislation, the President's speech marked his first explicit public commitment to a civil rights act which would end segregation in private as well as public facilities.

The last part of his remarks seemed to drift as Kennedy improvised. He ended with an evenhanded lecture to blacks to be "responsible" and "uphold the law" and a reminder to whites that blacks had the "right to expect the law will be fair," an admonition that seemed to suggest that the criminal and the victim were equally responsible for breaches of public order.[62] Nevertheless, his insistence that the struggle for legal equality was a moral question marked a decisive break from his earlier neutral position on civil rights.

EVEN as the President spoke, a fanatical white fertilizer salesman from Mississippi crouched in a matted clump of honeysuckle vines on a littered empty lot in the black section of Jackson. Shortly after midnight, Byron de la Beckwith watched Medgar Evers, veteran of the Normandy invasion and longtime NAACP organizer in Mississippi, get out of his station wagon after a long and wearying strategy meeting. His wife and children, excited and moved by Kennedy's speech, were waiting to give him the good news. Beckwith peered through the scope of his 30.06 bolt-action Winchester; Evers's white shirt offered a perfect target in the harsh light of the carport's naked bulb. As Evers reached for the handle of the kitchen door, the steel-jacketed bullet ripped through his back between the tenth and eleventh rib; exiting, it left a massive hole just below the sternum. He died within the hour.

Afterward, Beckwith told a group of Klansmen at a training session in Mississippi: "Killing that nigger gave me no more inner discomfort than our wives endure when they give birth to our children. We ask them to do that for us. We should do just as much."[63]

Across much of the deep South, condemnations of the Evers assassination were muted. Far more common were bitter complaints that the Kennedys had insisted upon burying a civil rights agitator at Arlington Cemetery with full military honors. The President's eloquent rhetoric fell upon deaf ears.

In the weeks after the integration of the university, an avalanche of supporting telegrams and letters—most from outside the state—poured into the governor's office, urging him to stand up to the Kennedy administration. Wallace dispatched to the President a series of surly and ill-tempered telegrams (all of which he released to the media). He attacked Kennedy for his continuing "unwarranted and illegal" occupation of the campus by "military forces of the central government." Washing his hands of responsibility for public security, he warned ominously that when federal troops were ultimately withdrawn, "Alabama cannot insure absolutely the personal safety of the individual [Negro] students." When the President urged him to assume responsibility for maintaining order and thus allow the federalized guardsmen to go home, the governor replied with a vituperative telegram (again released to the press) which crossed the line of civil language. "You cannot usurp the powers reserved to the State of Alabama and then place the burdens thereby created on my shoulders," he lectured. "I will not be intimidated by your calculated attempt to pass to me the responsibility for the duration of duty of the National Guard." He pointedly omitted his customary salutation, "Respectfully," and simply signed his name.[64]

Before a hysterical White Citizens' Council rally in Jackson, Mississippi, Wallace, joined by Ross Barnett, charged that activation of the Alabama National Guard in Tuscaloosa made possible a "military dictatorship in the United States at any time any president chooses to invoke this concept of executive power." The proposed civil rights measure demonstrated that the federal government was "well on its way to 'land-reform' legislation under which people will be called upon to redistribute the real estate which they have labored so hard to accumulate."[65]

By the end of 1962, John Kennedy had faced growing opposition from whites in the Deep South, but during the spring and summer of 1963 his support steadily eroded among border state voters as well. After the Tuscaloosa standoff, reported pollster George Gallup, the number of white southerners who thought the President was pushing integration "too fast" went from fifty-nine percent to seventy-seven percent while the number who supported him fell from sixty-four percent to thirty-five percent.[66]

The confrontation, warned Don Jones, Burke Marshall's closest link to

Alabama affairs, had strengthened Wallace. "For one reason or another, the people seem in great numbers to have concluded that he 'succeeded' at Tuscaloosa, despite the Negro students' entry."[67]

THE handling of the stand in the schoolhouse door—the careful operational planning and close attention to political detail, topped off by a nationwide television address that showcased an eloquent, uplifting, and quietly self-confident President—had shown the Kennedys at their best. It was fitting that his speech on civil rights came only thirty-six hours after his most revolutionary and ambitious address on foreign policy: the famous American University commencement speech. At home and abroad, the way was difficult but the course of action was clear. "We shall pay any price, bear any burden, meet any hardship, support any friend, oppose any foe to assure the survival and the success of liberty," Kennedy had announced at his inauguration.[68] Identify the problem, order the tangled threads of history, and lay out the solution: it was the measure of a President and a generation challenged, but still self-confident.

A hundred years earlier, another president had confronted equally intractable problems with considerably less bravado. "I claim not to have controlled events," Abraham Lincoln had written an admiring newspaper editor in the spring of 1864, "but confess plainly that events have controlled me."[69] It was an acknowledgment of limitations a century away in time and sentiment from the can-do world of John and Robert Kennedy. In such a universe of eloquent words and noble deeds, the strutting little Wallace seemed a pathetic footnote to history as he rode away from Foster Auditorium, muttering inanely to the hundreds of reporters, "Make sure y'all come back to Alabama, you heah!"

Chapter 6

"ALL OF US ARE VICTIMS"[1]

"WALLACEISM IS BIGGER than Wallace," Martin Luther King, Jr., warned CBS television correspondent Dan Rather after the stand in the schoolhouse door. Before Tuscaloosa, Americans outside the South perceived the governor—in the newsman's cutting phrase—as a "corn-pone redneck big-man-in-Alabama but nowhere else." But King saw in Wallace an enemy far more dangerous than Strom Thurmond or Ross Barnett. The civil rights leader believed that Wallace was "perhaps the most dangerous racist in America today. . . . I am not sure that he believes all the poison he preaches, but he is artful enough to convince others that he does." He "is smart enough so that he only gives three, maybe four speeches," King observed to Rather. "He just has four, but he works on them and hones them, so that they are little minor classics."[2]

In his own brief public career, King had become a master in shifting rhetorical gears; he could rouse a black working-class congregation to joyous celebration with his jazzlike improvisations and then address a group of white Presbyterians with the sober demeanor of an academic theologian. In his grudging tribute to Wallace's skills, Martin Luther King proved far more prescient than most of his contemporaries.

George Wallace had spent most of his life giving speeches, but his performance in Tuscaloosa propelled him from small-town civic clubs and flatbed trucks to the exhilarating arena of network television, national conventions, congressional committees, and packed college lecture halls. His appearances on national television in May and June had hinted at the resourcefulness that would carry him to the center of American politics. During the summer after the Tuscaloosa standoff, he seized his brief moment in the limelight to make himself the spokesman for the white South.

*   *   *

When a half-dozen of the nation's governors gathered in Gettysburg, Pennsylvania, in early July for the hundredth anniversary of the decisive battle of the Civil War, Wallace was the center of attention. Charming and generous in his praise of the bravery of northern heroes, he was surrounded by television and radio interviewers as well as reporters from all the major newspapers, including the *New York Times*, the *Baltimore Sun,* and the *Washington Post.* "He was good copy on the stump; he was good copy when you interviewed him," said Jack Nelson, the *Los Angeles Times* reporter who covered Wallace for most of the Alabama governor's career.[3] At the end of the two-day commemoration, the local Harrisburg paper carried a half-page feature on the Alabama governor, the "favorite with the Centennial crowds."[4]

In mid-July 1963, the Senate Commerce Committee opened hearings on President Kennedy's proposed civil rights legislation, and Wallace led off a parade of Southern politicians anxious to dramatize their opposition to the bill. Over two days of testimony and questioning from senators who drifted in and out of the committee room, he dominated the discussion by refusing to become bogged down in a defense of race relations in Alabama and the South. As always, for Wallace, the best defense was a good offense, and he hammered away at the bill's ideology ("part of the drift toward centralized socialist control and away from the free enterprise system") and at what he called the cynical political motives that prompted the proposed legislation. The President of the United States, said a disgusted Wallace, was so caught up in the "mad scramble for the minority bloc vote" that he was willing to sacrifice private property rights and to invite racial strife and turmoil by telling blacks "if you don't get what you want, you should continue rioting in the streets."

The people of the South ("the Confederate States," he called them in one overexuberant statement) would not tolerate the passage of the civil rights bill. If the Congress passed this revolutionary bill, warned Wallace, "you should make preparations to withdraw all our troops from Berlin, Vietnam and the rest of the world, because . . . they will be needed to police America."

"Some of my best friends are Negroes," he said self-righteously, then blushed slightly as the chairman gaveled the laughing audience to silence. He wanted to assure the members of the Senate and a watching nation that southern Negroes had been peaceful and contented before vote-hungry politicians and civil rights leaders had beguiled them with "false promises of a utopia."[5]

If the President was simply following his misguided political instincts, far more sinister forces were at work within the "so-called civil rights leadership," warned Wallace. "I personally resent the actions of the Federal Government . . . fawning and pawing over such people as Martin Luther King and his pro-Communist friends and associates." King's "top lieutenant in Alabama, Fred L. Shuttlesworth, a self-styled 'Reverend,' " was president of the Southern Conference Educational Fund, a New Orleans–based organization founded to "promote communism throughout the South."

Ross Barnett had tried his hand at Red-baiting in his brief appearance before the committee, but, where the Mississippi governor had seemed confused and unsure of his facts, Wallace spoke with a crisp authority. He held up a large photograph of King at what he derisively called the "Highlander [Tennessee] Folk School for Communist Training."

Myles Horton, a homegrown white southern radical and a student of the eminent theologian Reinhold Niebuhr, had founded Highlander Folk School in 1935, in the same East Tennessee Cumberland mountains that had served as a center of Unionist resistance during the Civil War. During the first two decades of the school's existence, Horton and his staff ran workshops and training programs for labor organizers and rank-and-file unionists. After the *Brown* decision, Highlander's educational mission shifted from labor organizing to promoting interracial cooperation and an end to segregation. In the summer of 1955, less than six months before she challenged the city's bus segregation ordinance, Montgomery seamstress and NAACP activist Rosa Parks had attended one of the center's biracial workshops and had found a haven from the racial tensions that surrounded life in Alabama. "I was forty-two years old," she later recalled, "and it was one of the few times in my life . . . when I did not feel any hostility from white people."[6]

It was true that a handful of Communists had been among the thousands of political activists who attended the school's conferences over the years; Horton fiercely maintained an open-door policy throughout the history of the institution. But only in the lurid setting of the 1950s Red scare could Highlander be labeled a "Communist training school." Hatred for Horton's beleaguered dream stemmed less from its "Bolshevik ideology" than from the spectacle of black and white Southerners living, studying, working, and eating together.

Wallace continued to lecture his audience. In the row in front of King, he pointed out, was "Abner W. Berry, a Negro member of the Central Committee of the Communist Party." By 1963, the infamous "King at Communist Training School" photograph had already been plastered nationwide across hundreds of billboards, courtesy of the John Birch Society. An undercover agent from the Georgia attorney general's office had attended a Highlander meeting in 1957 and had carefully framed the photograph to include Berry, a minor party functionary who had been a passive spectator at the conference.

As spectators and senators craned for a better view, Wallace pointed to a slender, bespectacled white man seated next to Martin Luther King in the

Highlander photograph. Aubrey Williams, Wallace told the committee with a scowl, was a well-known Montgomery radical. He quoted from a "congressional committee" report in which Williams was "identified by a witness as one who had been a member of the Communist Party." Of course Williams had denied this, Wallace said, "but he admitted that he had been connected with a number of Communist-front organizations." The existence of men like Williams was the reason the South was being torn apart by conflict.

In a different era, Williams would have been revered as one of Alabama's most distinguished sons. As an innovative and courageous administrator for Franklin Roosevelt in the 1930s, he was known for his leadership in work relief efforts and for his role as head of the New Deal's program of assistance for young people, the National Youth Administration. Williams played an equally important role as one of the southern liberals who, with the encouragement of Eleanor Roosevelt, pushed federal strategies that might end the region's crippling legacy of racism and poverty. His persistent challenges to racial discrimination in the federal programs he administered ultimately proved his undoing. When Roosevelt nominated him to head the Rural Electrification Administration in 1945, southern senators successfully blocked his confirmation.[7]

After the war he returned to Alabama and worked in a number of civil rights organizations. His influence had steadily waned, particularly after Mississippi's virulently anticommunist Senator James Eastland subpoenaed him before the House Un-American Activities Committee in the mid-1950s and pilloried him before klieg lights in a New Orleans hearing that amounted to a show trial. "Aubrey hates Communists like the devil hates holy water," a friend had pointed out, but facts had never gotten in the way of Eastland or any white southerner desperate to find links between Communism and the hated integrationists.[8]

In his testimony before the Senate Commerce Committee, Wallace gave the impression that Williams remained in Montgomery, where he presumably continued to operate his diabolical Communist cell. In fact, the seventy-two-year-old former New Dealer, dying of cancer, had fled to Washington in mid-May after he became convinced that the new Alabama governor would have him dragged before some kind of state anticommunist investigating committee. In his weakened condition he felt that he "just couldn't take it." The attack by Wallace—duly reported in all of the Alabama newspapers—was mean-spirited and gratuitous.[9]

Read in the cold light of day a generation later, Wallace's uninhibited Red-baiting of King, Shuttlesworth, and Williams seems astonishing. In the context of a decade and a half of anticommunist hysteria led by the FBI's J. Edgar Hoover, it nestled comfortably in a public rhetoric that accepted careless public slander and guilt by association. After all, within less than six months, Attorney General Robert Kennedy would authorize, albeit with some reluctance, extensive wiretapping of Martin Luther King in order to discover what Hoover believed were the civil rights leader's connections to the Communist Party. No wonder a healthy minority of white Americans, north and south, believed that the Communist Party played a major role in fomenting civil rights disturbances.

Two senators mildly took exception to Wallace's characterization of the civil rights movement as a hotbed of Communism. Perhaps, New Hampshire Republican senator Norris Cotton gently suggested, the Alabama governor's protestations of justice for black citizens might be more convincing if they had been accompanied by a willingness to enforce the voting rights of his state's "Negro citizens." But no one contradicted Wallace's matter-of-fact description of Highlander as a Communist training school. Nor did anyone rise to defend Aubrey Williams. Senator Warren Magnuson, chairman of the committee, assured Wallace that his charges would be turned over to Mississippi's senator James Eastland for investigation by his Internal Security Subcommittee, an assurance that understandably drew the governor's support ("I think that would be splendid"): Eastland's committee had been the source of most of the slanders he cited.

While Wallace paused at the back of the Senate Caucus Room to shake hands with admirers, the next witness before the committee, Arkansas attorney general Bruce Bennett, leaned into the microphone and began a review of race relations in his state, beginning with the Little Rock crisis of 1957. The "racial unrest in Arkansas was deliberately planned by the Communist Party as a part of the directive handed down by Moscow in 1928," said Bennett as Wallace moved out into the hall to meet waiting reporters.[10]

It was heady stuff for a first-term southern governor who had just retreated from his first showdown with the Kennedy administration. The *New York Times* ran long excerpts from Wallace's opening statement; the *Washington Post* gave him page one billing for three days; and the three major networks featured him as the voice of southern opposition to the President's civil rights bill. "Senators Admire Spunky Governor," headlined the *Birmingham News* back home. "Even if you don't agree with him," the Alabama newspapers quoted Clair Engle, the liberal Democrat from California, "you have to admire the way he presents his case. He's smart."[11]

Wallace constantly improvised as he abandoned old rhetorical strategies and adopted new ones, but his goal was always the same: to command a more visible political stage. That meant walking a tightrope between defending racial segregation aggressively but with dignity, and catering to the powerful impulses of raw racism which the civil rights movement had flushed into the open. His testimony before the Senate Commerce Committee showed his fine ear for tailoring the message to his audience. Before national reporters and television cameras, he was feisty and argumentative but careful to couch his message in the more congenial terrain of economic conservatism, states' rights, anticommunism, and the public's fear of social disorder.

But in the midst of his testimony, Wallace readjusted his rhetorical sights. He flew south on an overnight trip to speak to the annual convention of the South Carolina Broadcasters Association; away from the spotlight of the national media, he returned to the visceral battle cries of race. The "Negro has not received any ill-treatment in the South," he told his all-white audience. But now the Kennedy administration proposed a civil rights bill which would "take our property away in order to appease Negroes who would still be in Africa in the brush if the white people of this country had not raised their standards and helped them progress in an atmosphere of peace and harmony." "The Negro shows his sense of responsibility by flaunting [sic] law and order throughout this country," he continued. He "no longer wants mere equal treatment, he expects and apparently intends to bludgeon the majority of this country's citizens into giving him preferential treatment." The "safety of our wives and children" hung in the balance. Washington, D.C., was the nightmare that waited: a city where "you and your family cannot walk the streets . . . without fear of mugging, raping, killing or other physical assault."[12]

Newspapers in South Carolina reprinted highlights of the governor's speech, and the right-wing *Charleston News and Courier* gave it extensive coverage. But even though he had addressed an audience of dozens of broadcasters, there was no reporting of his remarks in the national press. For the time being, Wallace's identification as a spokesman for the segregationist South meant that his racial comments were of no interest unless he stepped over the shaky line into overt race-baiting.

Intoxicated by the adulation of southern audiences during a summer of speechmaking, Wallace honed his arguments in the earthy language that he would come to make his own. "I've had enough of Kennedy," he told one White Citizens' Council rally in north Louisiana. The president "encourages a wave of mass demonstrations accompanied by sit-ins, stomp-downs, kneel-ins, lie-ins, shout-and-sing ins . . . and assaults with deadly weapons on officers of the law whose only offense was undertaking to maintain order, protect human lives and private property." Kennedy and "little Bobby" denied that Communists controlled the integration movement, "but when, in history, have the commies ever ascended to power as 'Communists'?" The media pundits and public officials who exonerated King and his "pro-communist friends and associates" were "the same people who told us that Castro was a 'good Democratic soul,' that Mao Tse Tung was only an 'Agrarian Reformer'."

The Supreme Court's May decision in the case of *School District of Abington Township v. Schempp,* barring devotional Bible reading and state-sponsored prayers in the nation's classrooms, added a new arrow to Wallace's rhetorical quiver. The nation's high court had already shown its true colors, he said. The "chief, if not the only, beneficiaries of the present court's Constitutional rulings have been duly and lawfully convicted criminals, communists, atheists and clients of the NAACP." And now, "we find the court ruling against God."[13]

IN mid-August a homegrown crisis forced Wallace to curtail his southern speaking tour. After years of delays the federal courts had ordered the integration of public schools in Black Belt Macon County and the cities of Birmingham, Huntsville, Tuscaloosa, and Mobile. Local community leaders reluctantly acquiesced; the governor's retreat at Tuscaloosa had already broken the color barrier in the state. The Macon County seat, Tuskegee, home of Booker T. Washington's famous black university, would be the site of the first integration of public schools in Alabama. The county school superintendent, C. A. (Hardboy) Pruitt, a lifelong resident of the community, initially opposed the admission of black pupils, but once the federal district court issued its final order, he worked day and night to mobilize religious and civic support for a peaceful transition to integrated schools. Despite continuing opposition among die-hard whites, Pruitt and other community leaders believed they had convinced a majority of residents to accept without violence the admission of thirteen black students to Tuskegee's all-white high school.[14]

Birmingham's political leadership had also decided to face up to the inevitable. Albert Boutwell, the cautious moderate who had assumed the post of mayor in the wake of the Bull Connor regime, announced that the city would support the school board in its decision to keep schools open. In early August he assembled a task force headed by the chief of police and the county sheriff and ordered them to begin preparing plans to prevent the outbreak of violence when the schools opened in early September. School boards in Tuscaloosa, Huntsville, and Mobile reached the same conclusion: it was no longer possible to maintain absolute racial segregation in the public schools of Alabama.

While few whites in the Deep South were pleased at the prospect of even limited desegregation, most had little stomach for another trip to the barricades. In Alabama, the White Citizens' Council movement was a pale shadow of its former strength. Only splintered Klan and extremist groups continued to organize for all-out resistance.

But with the roar of the crowd still echoing through the state, George Wallace could hardly counsel compliance with the decisions of the federal court. Somehow, under far more difficult circumstances, he had to stage-manage a confrontation that would establish him as an unyielding defender of the cause but would avoid violence. While many in the nation tuned in to the massive and peaceful March on Washington on August 28, Wallace made a point of announcing to reporters that he had better things to do than "waste my time" watching a march led by "communists and sex perverts"; a week after King's "I have a dream" speech, the governor moved boldly to renew his opposition to the Kennedy administration and the federal courts.[15] Having exhausted all constitutional rationales for resistance, he turned to one final argument: the integration of the public schools was so repugnant to the white people of Alabama that it would inevitably lead to a bloody confrontation.

The argument was as tattered and indefensible as the doctrine of interposition. As far back as 1932, the U.S. Supreme Court had made it clear that state executives, confronted by a crisis in which a mob threatened the constitutional rights of its citizens, did not have the right to "assist in carrying out the unlawful purposes of those who created the disorders . . . by suppressing rights which it is the duty of the state to defend." If state officials disregarded the rights of its citizens "in order to pacify a mob," a lower federal court pointed out in 1936, their actions inevitably encouraged violence.[16] When Arkansas governor Orval Faubus had justified his defiance of federal-court-ordered integration in 1957 on the grounds that he was acting "to maintain or restore order and to protect the lives and property of citizens," the federal courts—including the Supreme Court—had brushed aside his argument without comment.[17]

Despite the weakness of his constitutional position, Wallace moved forward with his plan. As the September integration of public schools drew near, he embarked on a round of speechmaking throughout Alabama which repeated one refrain: "We will never surrender!"[18] Asked at each stop about the scheduled integration, he always responded elliptically: he would announce his actions in "due course." On one point he was unequivocal: the Kennedys would bear the responsibility for any violence that might come in integration's wake.[19]

George Wallace was riding a tiger, with no way to get off. Having staked his political future on all-out opposition to integration, he could hardly counsel his followers to surrender. But if he urged open resistance and the result was widespread bloodshed, all hope of appealing to a national audience would be lost. The trick was to insist that disorder stemmed from one source alone: the efforts of civil rights "agitators" to end segregation.

Few pieces of legislation more aptly captured the topsy-turvy moral ground of segregation than Title 14, Section 407 of the Alabama Code, enacted in 1962. In order to bar civil rights demonstrations, state legislators had made it a criminal offense to commit any "acts or make gestures or communications which are calculated to, or will probably so outrage the sense of decency and morals or so violate or transgress the customs, patterns of life and habits of the people of Alabama as to be likely to cause a riot or breach of the peace."[20] By the reasoning that ruled the political universe of Alabama in the dying days of segregation, individuals who were assaulted as they sought to change the "customs, patterns of life and habits of the people of Alabama" had no one to blame but themselves.

As a growing chorus of critics in the state pointed out, however, it was the governor who seemed to be courting violence. George Wallace "talks about 'fighting' and at the same time says he wants no violence," said the editor of Tuscaloosa's afternoon newspaper. "What kind of fighting does he mean?"[21] Still, Wallace was right on one point: the ingredients for violence were near the surface, particularly in the city of Birmingham.

AFTER years of shadowing civil rights organizations, Birmingham's police department had begun to expand its surveillance to include ultra-right hate groups. As tensions rose in the summer and fall of 1963, they increasingly focused their investigative efforts on a neofascist splinter organization which called itself the National States' Rights Party. Even within the context of the zany bestiary of racist right-wing politics that characterized much of Alabama's political culture, this Dixie version of the Hitlerjugend careened over the edge. The party had been formed in 1958 in Jefferson, Indiana, from an amalgam of anti-Semitic, anti-Catholic, and anti-black fringe groups. It achieved immediate notoriety when four of its members used twenty-eight sticks of dynamite to devastate Atlanta's largest synagogue, Temple Beth-El, in 1958. Drifting from Jefferson to Louisville to Atlanta, the NSRP found a more congenial climate in Birmingham in 1961.[22]

J. B. Stoner and Edward Fields, two Atlanta "nutcases" (as one Birmingham detective called them), engineered the move. Purchasing a ramshackle frame house in the working-class suburb of Bessemer, they set up a "white man's bookstore" in the crowded front room, and from this dilapidated command center, launched their mission to "save Alabama and the nation from Jew Communists and their nigger allies."[23]

Stoner, the organizer of half a dozen different anti-Semitic and Klan groups, continued to support his personal Klavern, the Christian Knights of the Ku Klux Klan, and retained close ties with the most violent of the independent Klan factions through the 1950s and into the 1960s. FBI officials strongly suspected that, between court appearances defending his various rabble-rousing clients, the forty-year-old Atlanta attorney was involved in dynamiting at least a dozen synagogues (including the one in Atlanta) and black churches across the South. However, it took twenty-two years to gather conclusive evidence to move forward against and convict Stoner, and they did so in only one case: the bombing of Fred Shuttlesworth's Birmingham church in 1958. (They were equally certain that Bull Connor had protected Stoner.[24]) In a not-for-attribution interview, Atlanta's police chief, Herbert Jenkins, told an investigative reporter that Stoner had "probably been involved in more bombings than any one individual in the South. . . . Invariably the bastard is in the general area when a bomb goes off."[25]

Police believed that Stoner was no longer building or transporting explosive devices by the early 1960s. His distinct limp (he had suffered polio as a child) made him too easy to identify. But they also suspected that, as he curtailed his personal involvement, he became a kind of "honest broker," who lined up professional bombers for disgruntled local whites lacking appropriate skills and raw materials.[26] His standard operating procedure, recalled one policeman who had shadowed him for nearly a decade, was to move into a community filled with racial tension and to identify the "hard core of nuts in that community." Once he identified the most violent, Stoner would make his pitch: "OK, you fellas have got trouble here with these niggers and their friends, the Communistic Jew S.O.B.'s. You've got to *do* something. . . . If I were you people, I'd put a bomb down someplace."[27] His role as legal counsel and adviser for the National States' Rights Party provided a convenient cover as he shuttled back and forth between Atlanta and Birmingham.

Edward Fields, a handsome thirty-year-old chiropractor from Atlanta, valued Stoner for his links to the Klan tradition, but found his associate hopelessly naïve in his intellectual understanding of the "menace of Communist Jewry." Fields, the "national information director" for the NSRP, wearily endured the problems of working with the unsophisticated race-baiters attracted to his movement. He himself had studied long and hard and knew his spiritual ancestors. Publicly, Fields credited Georgia's race-baiting governor, Eugene Talmadge, as his main inspiration.[28] When speaking with fellow believers, he made it clear that his hero was Julius Streicher, the editor of the Nazi periodical *Der Stürmer.*

From his Birmingham headquarters, Fields published forty thousand to fifty thousand monthly copies of the *Thunderbolt* (a symbol taken from the Hitler's Waffen SS). He distributed some twenty-five percent of them in the state, the rest throughout the country. In lurid illustrations, some lifted directly from pre–World War II German Nazi propaganda, he combined traditional anti-Semitic cant with pieces that seemed to challenge the boundaries of the First Amendment; in a 1963 editorial, for instance, Fields called for the execution of the members of the Supreme Court.[29] In other pieces he outlined what he called the "ultimate solution" to America's racial problems: the expulsion of all Jews to Madagascar (as Hitler had proposed in *Mein Kampf*) and blacks to Africa. Only then could America become a true "Nordic" nation.

The NSRP occasionally exhibited a surrealism bewildering to the stolid Birmingham police, accustomed to dealing with the race question within the narrow focus of traditional southern race-baiting. Long after the incident took place, detectives smirked over Fields's importation of a Bakersfield, California, States' Rights Party organizer to boost morale. While the police department's undercover agent sat slack-jawed along with another thirty-five Birmingham blue-collar workers, a tall and effeminate "Captain X" pranced around the living room of the Bessemer headquarters. Dressed in a theatrically fitted Nazi riding uniform, polished jackboots with stiletto heels, and sunglasses (though it was dark), the Californian periodically slashed a riding crop against the leg of his jodhpurs. "P.S.," added the agent in his report, "he was wearing rouge and mascara."[30]

When the Alabama Supreme Court ordered Bull Connor and his fellow commissioners to give way to the newly elected mayor and council in May 1963, Klan groups lost a powerful ally. But individual Klansmen retained close connections with sympathetic members of the police department. The States' Rights Party—many of whose members were Yankees, to boot— became fair game, and Fields complained that his organization had become a scapegoat. His contention was not without merit; Birmingham police officials spent a disproportionate amount of their time and energy monitoring the "States' Rights' crowd," as they contemptuously called them, while ignoring equally dangerous Klan cells.

As they increased their surveillance, however, police detectives assigned to shadow the NSRP discovered that Fields and his men had support in high places. The governor of Alabama and the head of his state troopers, Al Lingo, had enlisted the Dixie fascists as allies.

Six weeks before the fall opening of schools in Alabama, Edward Fields addressed a small rally liberally sprinkled with Klansmen outside Anniston, site of an infamous 1961 attack on Freedom Riders. (When black and white civil rights activists boarded Greyhound buses and traveled south in May of 1961 challenging segregated terminal facilities, white mobs—often with the cooperation of local police—savagely beat integrated riders in Anniston, Birmingham, and Montgomery; in Anniston, they burned the bus, and riders narrowly escaped with their lives.) When he stepped down from the back of the truck that had served as his speaking platform, a plainclothes member of the Alabama State Patrol quietly asked him to follow him to a nearby motel room.

There, Fields and his fellow States' Rights organizer James Warner found Al Lingo sitting at a small table. As Fields later recounted, "Col. Lingo told me that if we waged a boisterous campaign against the integration of the schools

and petitioned the Governor for the closing of such schools and held demonstrations in front of those schools on opening day, that this would give
Governor Wallace reason enough to close mixed schools."[31]

Fields needed little encouragement.

On Saturday, August 31, with Tuskegee's school desegregation scheduled
for Tuesday, September 3, and Birmingham's for the following day, Fields
led an NSRP caravan of nearly a hundred cars and small trucks from Birmingham to Montgomery to present a petition. The document called upon
the governor to close all public schools scheduled for integration. Wallace,
committed to speak at one of his daily rallies, wrote Fields a long and
remarkably warm letter. "I want to assure you," he said, "that my not being
here is because of a previous engagement of longstanding." He promised to
have his "personal representatives" present to meet with the group and
accept their petition.[32]

Shortly after two P.M., Fields led his motorcade around the state office
buildings and then delivered a speech from the capitol steps. After praising
Wallace, he accused the Kennedys and "Martin Luther Koon" of promoting
the "mongrelization" of the races: "It boils down to blood, the blood of a
white man." Inside the state capitol, Fields and two of his top aides privately
met for nearly an hour with Cecil Jackson, Seymore Trammell, Al Lingo, and
the governor's executive secretary, Earl Morgan.[33]

THAT same weekend, a Birmingham Klansman named Ross Keith took his
girlfriend for a ride on his Harley-Davidson. Stopping at a small frame house
in Bessemer, he invited Yvonne Fike in to meet his friends, Robert and Flora
Lee (Tee) Chambliss. Chambliss and Keith left the two women alone in the
kitchen. After a few minutes, Yvonne Fike asked to use the bathroom; Mrs.
Chambliss pointed vaguely down the hallway. Opening a door, Fike surprised Chambliss and Keith, who knelt in front of a box on the floor in a
small room. Inside were three or four bundles that looked like "oversized
firecrackers," "tied with a cord like you would fix a package to mail with."

Chambliss was furious; the "door was supposed to have been locked," he
angrily told Keith. When Keith and Fike left, Chambliss was still ranting and
raving.[34]

SIX weeks earlier Robert Chambliss, Klansman Robert Shelton, and National
States' Rights Party organizer Jerry Dutton had disrupted a public meeting
called to mobilize support for the peaceful integration of Birmingham's
schools.[35] Plainclothes detective Thomas Cook noted the presence of "Dynamite Bob" Chambliss, a fifty-nine-year-old battle-scarred veteran in the
underground war for white supremacy and member of Birmingham's Robert
E. Lee Klan Klavern. When a black insurance salesman moved into a house

on the edge of an all-white community in late 1948, Chambliss had publicly—and repeatedly—threatened to level the house with dynamite. City officials had briefly suspended him from his city job as an auto mechanic, but he was soon back at work. As Chambliss had bluntly told FBI agents who questioned him some years later, "he had only been doing what he was told to do by Bull Connor." In a word, he was one of Connor's "boys."[36]

But the Klansman eventually proved so unstable that even Connor publicly distanced himself from his former protégé. In early 1959 the public safety commissioner suspected Dynamite Bob of involvement in the bombing of several black churches. Fred Shuttlesworth and his ilk were fair game, but these churches had not endorsed civil rights activities. Connor had his men bring Chambliss in for questioning in the middle of the night.

Released from city jail next day, the angry Klansman broke into a meeting of the State Democratic Party executive committee to confront his old friend. "You drug me out of bed at 3 A.M. and threw me in old sol [solitary confinement]," screamed Chambliss. "You treated me worse than a G—— D—— Nigger."

It was all a misunderstanding, said an embarrassed Connor.

"You're a nigger lover and a liar," Chambliss accused as a city policeman led him outside.[37] Having cultivated the psychopathic Klansman for his own purposes, Connor learned that he had little control over Dynamite Bob.

ON Sunday, the first day of September, with integration only three days away, Albert Boutwell went before the people of Birmingham to defend his decision to accept limited integration in three city schools. As a candidate for mayor in the spring of 1963, he reminded them, he had come out "squarely for keeping the schools open. . . . My opponent [Bull Connor], on the contrary, was a vocal advocate of closing the schools." His victory, Boutwell said, was a mandate for keeping the schools open. "If we close the schools, we close the doors to higher education to all except the children of the well-to-do . . . we would be closing the doors to jobs for our local young people."[38]

Back in Birmingham after their petition-bearing trip to Wallace's headquarters in Montgomery, Fields, Stoner, and other NSRP leaders shuttled back and forth between their Bessemer headquarters and a "command suite" in the Redmont Hotel, only a few blocks away from schools scheduled to be integrated. On a dozen tables they spread out Nazi literature for the young white men who wandered in and out of the rooms. (Thousands of leaflets had been distributed in the white working-class districts of Birmingham.) Frantically, police dispatched informants to try to get some fix on the group's plans.

One of their agents learned that Fields and his men were detailing squadrons to move from school to school and "close them down." But specifics were frustratingly absent; NSRP organizers told their followers they would receive instructions at the last moment. According to the report of an informant which came too late to help police, Fields had directed supporters to "break through the police lines" and turn the school buildings into a shambles.[39]

JUST after midnight on the night of September 1, black Birmingham Civil Defense captain James Edward Lay walked his rounds through the heart of Birmingham's downtown African-American community; westward down Fifth Avenue North, the parade route for the spring demonstrations; past the front of the A. G. Gaston Motel, which had been bombed earlier that year; then northward up Sixteenth Street and past Kelly Ingram Park, made immortal by the May television footage of fire hoses, demonstrators, and snarling police dogs. As he reached the Sixteenth Street Baptist Church, the staging ground for the spring demonstrations, Lay spied a white man carrying a package emerge from a 1957 Ford and walk toward the west side of the huge church. When Lay called out, the man stopped, then calmly walked back to the car and opened the door. Illuminated in the dome light, Lay saw a second white man. Wizened and in his late fifties or early sixties, he was wearing a short-sleeved shirt. Lay would later identify him as Robert Chambliss.[40]

The car sped off into the darkness.

AT seven-thirty the next evening, twelve hours away from the opening of integrated schools in Tuskegee and thirty-six hours away from integration day in Birmingham, a crowd of nearly ten thousand whites gathered in Ensley Park, a tired city facility in the middle of Birmingham's blue-collar district, to cheer a half-dozen politicians and anti-integration leaders. When police detective Marcus Jones arrived, he found the park "full of Klansmen" and observed Bull Connor huddled with Fields and several States' Rights organizers. To his surprise, Connor and George Wallace invited Fields onto the hastily constructed speaker's platform.

At the conclusion of the recently ousted police commissioner's diatribe against the city's "lying foreign-owned newspapers" and the infamous "Bobbysox Kennedy," Wallace took his place behind the microphones. Alternating between an appeal to the crowd to "let law and order handle the situation in Birmingham" and assurances that "as governor of this sovereign state" he would take "whatever action is necessary to maintain segregation," he promised his listeners that he had a few "secrets for Birmingham and other places." "I'm not going to tell any of my plans up here, but I've got plans. We've always got plans in Montgomery." Marcus Jones thought it was a "curious" talk. He thought it even more curious that the governor of Alabama would share a platform with Edward Fields.[41]

As dawn broke in Tuskegee, Alabama, the next morning, Macon County superintendent Pruitt woke to the sound of a state trooper pounding on his front door and discovered Wallace's "secret": an executive order announcing the closing of Tuskegee High School to "preserve the peace, maintain domestic tranquility and to protect the lives and property of all citizens of the State of Alabama."

It was clear that the governor planned to block integration in Birmingham, Huntsville, and Mobile as well as Tuskegee. It was equally clear that he had not anticipated the angry opposition of the growing number of white Alabamians who had decided that the time had come for an orderly retreat. The governor "talks about letting local people solve their problems," said Macon County's young prosecuting attorney, Broward Segrest, "but then violates these principles."[42] If it wasn't "evident to all the world that the executive head of our government is a sick man," said Huntsville's police chief, Chris Spurlock, "then by God, none of us are discerning enough to read the facts."[43]

As radio and television announcers broke into regular programming to describe the angry accusations of white community leaders, Wallace suddenly found himself, in the words of the *Montgomery Advertiser,* "sitting on the hot seat," and he scrambled to deflect the attacks. Albert Boutwell answered the telephone shortly after ten A.M. to confront a determined and "inflamed" governor. Bluntly, Wallace demanded that the mayor and city officials take the lead and close the public schools. To avert massive violence, efforts to integrate the public schools must be abandoned. To ensure peace in the meantime, Wallace told Boutwell that he intended to deploy several hundred state troopers under the direction of Al Lingo.

Having watched the state troopers rampage through the streets of Birmingham in May, the last thing the mayor wanted was their return. Perhaps the troopers could wait on a "standby basis," a nervous Boutwell suggested. Police Chief Jamie Moore had assured him that his men could maintain law and order.

"That is what you thought when the [spring] demonstrations occurred," snapped Wallace, and it was "almost too late when our men got there. What is your objection to state forces? When I shake hands with the police officers, they say they would like our help." The best thing for the mayor and city council to do would be to delay the opening of the schools "on the grounds that violence might erupt. . . . I made my promise to fight for segregation in my campaign and I am still fighting for what I said." It was time for Birmingham's political leadership to go the "last mile" against the federal government.

Plaintively, Boutwell insisted, "I am going [the] last mile. I am as strong for segregation as I have been." When faced with the choice of closing the public schools or allowing a few black students to enter, however, he had decided to accept limited integration.

It was the "idea, not the number of Negroes entering school," Wallace lectured Boutwell. Whether it was one hundred or three, four or five, "it inflames me," he said, and warned again of the likelihood of violence.

"I hope and pray there will not be—" began Boutwell.

"Albert, you can hope and pray," interrupted Wallace, but "what about dynamiting, blowing up?" It had happened before, and the people who planted these bombs—"Negroes or maybe Communists"—could strike again.

Boutwell hardly needed to be reminded of Birmingham's history of racially inspired bombings. In the four months since the spring settlement between city businessmen and civil rights demonstrators, six blasts had rocked the homes of civil rights leaders; the mayor had spent those four months frantically trying to salvage the city's image.[44] Desperately, Boutwell pleaded with Wallace to stay out of the city. He finally offered a fig-leaf promise to look into the possibility of requesting a postponement from the federal district court. As Wallace feared, the mayor did nothing.[45]

National States' Rights Party leaders dispatched 150 members to Graymont Elementary School the following morning. Screaming "Hang Albert Boutwell!" they marched toward a wall of city policemen and sheriff's deputies. Batons swung, and the battle ended in a decisive rout. Angry demonstrators, their numbers reduced to less than sixty by the disturbing realization that the police were, in the enraged cry of one mob member, "on the side of the niggers," retreated to their cars and sped on to nearby Ramsey High School. There, hardcore believers, throwing bricks and swinging wooden-staved placards, again charged police lines. Outside the police perimeter, several demonstrators disarmed a motorcycle patrolman and kicked and beat him for several minutes before he was rescued by fellow officers. But the attempt to overwhelm police at the city's largest high school proved equally unsuccessful. Police bloodied several of the most aggressive demonstrators and arrested three men who seemed to be coordinating the assault. Surrounded by dozens of armed policemen and sheriff's deputies, two of the five black children scheduled to enter the three city schools spent a quiet day at their desks; the other three waited for tensions to subside before joining them in their classes. Police Chief Moore issued warrants for the arrest of the key rioters and reported confidently that the "States' Rights crowd" was under control.[46]

ALTHOUGH Robert Chambliss had joined in the mini-riots at the two schools, he seemed to hang back during the assaults on the police lines. He was not arrested. That same afternoon, he visited the construction-supply house of a fellow Klansman, Leon Negron, and purchased the better part of a case of dynamite. "If you're going to blow up some niggers, I will throw in a few extra sticks," Negron cheerfully told Chambliss.[47]

BACK at their Redmont Hotel headquarters, the beleaguered remnants of the self-proclaimed Dixie fascists gathered to protest (without any apparent sense of irony) the "gestapo tactics" of "Boutwell's Storm Troops." They were heartened by the support of Imperial Wizard Robert Shelton, who announced that his Klans were "compiling reports from various areas of . . . police brutality." This "brutality . . . against women and children . . . ," he warned, "will not be tolerated by the citizens of Alabama."[48]

One of Detective Marcus Jones's informants secretly tape-recorded Field's aide, Edward Ramage, as he confided that he had "talked to Governor Wallace just before the meeting" and "the Governor had promised that Al Lingo would have the State Troopers at the schools in the morning to see that the people were not manhandled by the Police."[49]

Arthur Shores, a black Birmingham attorney who lived near the scene of the early-morning demonstrations, settled into an easy chair to watch the ten P.M. news. As he watched, he learned that city officials had issued a statement condemning the rioters, but Wallace indignantly insisted to reporters that the demonstrators at Ramsey and Graymont were "not thugs—they are good working people who get mad when they see something like this happen. It takes courage to stand up to tear gas and bayonets."[50]

Shores's home had been dynamited two weeks earlier in retaliation for his role in the lawsuit to integrate the city schools; one end of the house was still boarded up from the blast. He told his wife that "the old saying that lightning doesn't strike twice in the same place may be all right, but I'm gonna sit out on the porch a little while with my double-barreled shotgun and kinda watch out." As he walked toward the cabinet where he kept his shotgun, an estimated four sticks of dynamite blew the front door off its hinges, knocked him to the floor, and shattered windows for half a block. "If I had stepped a step closer it [the door] would have caught me full in the face."[51]

The bombing of Shores's home and the demonstrations outside the city schools gave George Wallace all the ammunition he needed to put the city on a war footing. Lingo and the governor's legal counsel, Cecil Jackson, called Chief Moore and demanded that he close the schools and call in the state troopers. Stubbornly, Moore refused: "I informed them [the governor's office] that after checking with the superior officers at the scene I did not think that their assistance was necessary."[52] Moore's obstinacy enraged Wallace. He called Birmingham school board attorney Henry Stimson and issued a blunt ultimatum: Either they could close the schools or he would. City officials quietly folded. Police arriving to protect newly integrated schools the next morning found them closed and ringed by state troopers in full battle gear. A contemptuous Lingo had not bothered to inform Moore that he was no longer in charge of public safety in the city of Birmingham.[53]

Wallace was now set for a reprise of the role he had played so well at Tuscaloosa: David standing against the Goliath of a federal government callously willing to endanger the lives of innocent schoolchildren.

Although Fred Shuttlesworth warned the Kennedy administration that they were making a mistake in playing "cat and mouse with George Wallace," the Justice Department once again assembled a command center to deal with Alabama's governor. During the week of September 9, Wallace mobilized the National Guard; the President federalized the guardsmen and ordered them to stand down; the governor filed suit in federal court to stay the integration orders; the Justice Department countered with a legal brief insisting that integration go forward.[54]

Each feint and parry placed Wallace in the limelight as the heroic rear-guard defender of segregation. In one bizarre motion filed in federal court in Birmingham, he demanded that his old nemesis Judge Frank Johnson recuse himself from the integration cases. Given his repeated attacks on the judge, said Wallace, Johnson would inevitably be subject to "personal bias and prejudice."

"If statements made by a defendant against a judge could constitute a legal basis for asking a judge to disqualify himself," Johnson icily retorted, "then any defendant could at his own will render the judge disqualified by making [negative] public statements about him." In fact, he drolly observed, the governor could simply disqualify *all* federal judges by criticizing them in the press.[55]

In the face of federal court orders and with growing opposition from the city's white leadership, Wallace slowly retreated. "I can't fight federal bayonets with my bare hands," he said petulantly. (It was much the same statement he had issued after his standoff and retreat in Tuscaloosa.) A week after he bullied Birmingham officials into closing the schools, they reopened with only minimal disturbances from a handful of States' Rights Party pickets.

But Wallace continued to endorse the "no surrender" policy of the right-wing extremists. On the night of September 7, he spoke to an anti-integration fund-raiser at Birmingham's Thomas Jefferson Hotel. Just before the dinner, said Edward Fields, one of Colonel Lingo's assistants "phoned me and said that there would be a reserved table for us at this dinner." When the young chiropractor and his aides arrived at the Jefferson, they found that their table had been placed directly below the speaker's platform. Wallace repeatedly praised the men for their struggles against the integration of the schools.[56]

Within the week, Fields and his assistants would be questioned and then indicted by a federal grand jury for conspiracy, but to the Alabama governor they were heroes.[57] "At the end of his speech, Gov. Wallace walked down the steps to our table and shook hands with all four of us," said Fields. "We considered that to be our reward for helping him in the struggle against the integration of the Birmingham public school system." During the Tuscaloosa stand-in-the-schoolhouse-door crisis, said Fields, they had stayed away, on Wallace's orders. In Birmingham in the fall of 1963, "we operated at the request of the Governor himself."[58] Several weeks after the grand jury returned the indictments, District Attorney Macon Weaver quietly dropped the cases.

George Wallace would always insist that his words and actions were designed to take the issue from the streets to the courts by serving as a safe and nonviolent legal outlet for white southern resistance.[59] His longtime press secretary, Bill Jones, made the most cogent summary of this argument. The "people of Alabama and to a great degree the people of the South felt that George Wallace was doing everything that could be done to prevent the integration of the schools." As the "only figure of any consequence that was fighting that thing in the courts . . . he kept it [the battle] out of the streets."[60] In Tuscaloosa, Wallace often reminded newsmen, there had been no repetition of the debacle at Ole Miss.

But events in Birmingham in that September of 1963 tell a different story. The evidence is persuasive that George Wallace deliberately encouraged the NSRP extremists in order to give credence to his claims that integration inevitably led to public disorder. It is probably true that his goal was disorder, not bloodshed. But Alabama and other states in the Deep South in the late 1950s and early 1960s harbored a small minority of mentally unstable whites anxious to exact revenge against blacks, Jews, and "nigger-loving" whites. Having recklessly incited the hate-mongers, the governor of Alabama soon learned that he could no longer control the unfolding events.

"The society is coming apart at the seams," he told one newspaper reporter the day after he had ordered Birmingham officials to close the city's integrated schools. "What good is it doing to force these situations when white people nowhere in the South want integration? What this country needs is a few first-class funerals," he said bitterly, "and some political funerals, too."[61] His offhanded comment was made in the heat of rhetorical combat. Refracted through the tragic events that followed, it became a horrific monument to George Wallace's insensitivity to the implications of his words and deeds.

ON Saturday morning, September 14, Elizabeth Hood, the twenty-three-year-old niece of Flora Lee Chambliss, visited her aunt and her uncle Robert in their Bessemer home. On the afternoon before, one of Elizabeth Hood's friends had been sitting in a van at a traffic light when a young black man reached in through the window and sliced her arm with a pocket knife. Friday afternoon's newspaper had described the assault and the story seemed to ignite Chambliss's rage. If he had been there, he growled, "that nigger wouldn't have gotten away." George Wallace, he complained, was a "coward, or he could have stopped all this."

He had been "fighting a one-man war since 1942," his niece recalled him saying. If only his fellow Klansmen had backed him up, "they wouldn't have the nigger problems on their hands." But he was not going to give up, he said. And he added ominously, he had "enough stuff put away to flatten half of Birmingham."

Elizabeth Hood said she pleaded with him not to do anything foolish. What good would any of "that" do?

Chambliss looked at her grimly. "You just wait until after Sunday morning and they will beg us to let them segregate."[62]

JUST after one-thirty A.M. on Sunday, September 15, Birmingham police officer Earnest Cantrell received a call from the city dispatcher. An anonymous tipster claimed that a bomb had been placed at the Holiday Inn on the edge of Cantrell's patrol area. With most of the city's squad cars tied up in monitoring a Klan auto caravan cruising noisily through the downtown business district, Cantrell responded with two other squad cars and began searching the motel.[63]

At about two A.M., Gertrude (Kirthus) Glenn, a young black woman from Detroit visiting in Birmingham, returned to the apartment where she was staying, just across the street from the Sixteenth Street Baptist Church. She passed a late-model white-and-turquoise Chevrolet parked a block away. Although it was dark, the car's dome light was on and she could see three white men. She gave the vehicle a careful once-over; this was, after all, a virtually all-black community. But she went on to bed. In a later interview, FBI agents showed Glenn thirty-four pictures of Klan members in the Birmingham area. She identified only one person: Robert Chambliss.[64]

MINUTES later, one of the three men placed a box under the Sixteenth Street side steps of the church up against the two-and-a-half-foot-thick stone and masonry wall of the basement. Just inside that wall was one of the women's rest rooms. In the container were between ten and twenty sticks of dynamite with a chemically operated fuse. The timing system was ingenious, but simple: a fishing bob floating in a bucket of water with a small hole in the bottom. When most of the water had leaked out, long after the bombers had vanished, the line attached to the floating cork would trigger the explosion.[65]

*   *   *

JUST after three-thirty A.M., Cantrell and his fellow officers returned to their regular patrol. Too late, he would realize that the Klan motorcade and the false Holiday Inn bombing report had been a carefully timed ruse.

Even before Chambliss and his accomplices had placed their explosive device under the steps, a young woman who worked as a snitch for Jefferson County deputy sheriff James Hancock woke him at his home late Saturday. A bomb would be planted or had already been planted at the Sixteenth Street Baptist Church, she told him. The informant, code-named "Dale Tarrant" because she often met with Hancock in the industrial Birmingham suburb of Tarrant City, was a friend of Robert Chambliss's wife, Flora Lee. In fact, investigators later came to believe that the tip on the bomb came directly from Flora Lee.[66] Tarrant was hardly an uncertain source; she had been furnishing information to the deputy sheriff for more than a year. The young Birmingham woman had even planted a listening device in the Chambliss home at his request. But Hancock did not report the call to his superiors. By his own account, he rolled over and went back to sleep. There were "false alarms every time I turned around," he later explained defensively. "If I checked them all out, I've have done nothing else."[67]

Mid-September could be as brutal as August in the Deep South, but the heat of the past week had broken. The Sabbath air was hazy with clouds, the temperature a cool sixty-one degrees. When Hancock woke up, he called Dale Tarrant to arrange an early-morning meeting at their usual rendezvous. Once again, she repeated her story: she had reason to believe that a bomb had been planted at the church. And once again, Hancock made no move to call in the report. It was a "personal thing," he later told investigators. They surmised that he had been sexually intimate with Tarrant during the early morning hours and thus was distracted from filing a report.[68]

But Dale Tarrant later denied any such relationship with Hancock. She insisted to her friend, Elizabeth Hood (Chambliss's niece), that, when Hancock had met her that Sunday morning, he drove around aimlessly for several hours. While he asked dozens of questions (and "teased her," she said) he did nothing to follow up on her frantic warnings. As a result, in Elizabeth Hood's words, he had "effectively kept Dale isolated so that she could not give her information to anyone else."[69] By Hancock's own account, sometime after ten A.M., he finally left his undercover contact at their Tarrant City rendezvous and began driving back toward Birmingham.

Sunday school classes at the Sixteenth Street Baptist Church were in full swing. But five eleven- to fourteen-year-old girls, all dressed in white, had found various excuses to gather in the women's lounge. Cynthia Wesley, Addie Mae Collins and her younger sister Sarah, Denise McNair, and Carole Robertson chatted excitedly as they anticipated the special young people's service, which was to begin at eleven A.M. Addie Mae would serve as one of the junior ushers; two other girls prepared to put on their choir robes. At 10:22 A.M., Sarah Collins had just turned on the water to wash her hands; her sister Addie retied the bow on her friend Denise's dress.[70]

Deputy Sheriff Hancock was nearly two miles from the downtown church when he heard the distinctive *whomp* that the people of Birmingham had come to know all too well. John McCormick, an FBI explosives expert sent to Birmingham to investigate the Shores bombing, felt the windows shake throughout the Bankhead Hotel, where he sat reading in his room more than six blocks away.[71] He knew instantly that it was a major explosion. When he arrived at the church minutes later, he found cars parked along the street crumpled, windows a block away shattered, and glass littering the sidewalks. But the greatest devastation was inside: dynamite tore a six-foot-by-eight-foot hole in the thirty-inch granite wall and showered the women's restroom and adjacent hall with a lethal combination of brick, masonry, stone, wood, and plaster.

The force of the blast threw people to the floor and blew out stained-glass windows in the sanctuary seventy-five feet away. "It sounded like the whole world was shaking," said the church pastor, John Haywood Cross. Dust and soot made it impossible to identify people five feet away.[72] Only the massive stone-and-brick construction of the old church prevented the deaths of dozens of worshipers.

Frantically, Cross—his dark suit covered in dirt and plaster—urged everyone out of the building; he feared a second explosion. As members of the congregation staggered into the street, they were joined by neighborhood crowds. "In church!" wept one woman. "My God, you're not even safe in church."[73] Cross borrowed a portable megaphone from the first firemen who had arrived on the street. The lesson, he told the angry crowd, "was about a love that forgives and we should be forgiving, as Christ was forgiving." Even as Christ hung from the cross, the pastor reminded them, he said, "Father, forgive them, because they know not what they do."[74]

Only after the crowd seemed calmer did the minister lead a team of white firemen and young men from the church down to the ground floor, where the greatest devastation had occurred. They began to clear the rubble near the women's lounge. After "digging a foot and a half, or two feet, someone said, 'I feel something soft,'" remembered Cross.[75] One by one, they removed the crushed bodies of Cynthia Wesley, Carole Robertson, Denise McNair, and Addie Mae Collins. Sarah Collins, protected by a partition, was still alive, although badly injured. (She lost one eye and had to undergo repeated plastic surgery in the years that followed.)

As news spread of the deaths of the four girls, shock gave way to anger. For Denise McNair's grandfather, M. W. Pippen, there was only rage. "My grandbaby was killed," he sobbed as he wandered through the rubble. "You know how I feel? I feel like blowing the whole town up!" A reporter arriving on the scene saw a slender young man, incoherent with frustration, screaming over and over: "Let me at the bastards. I'll kill them! I'll kill them!"[76] Within minutes, an unidentified black man had smashed the window of a parked car near the church and set fire to the vehicle; several blocks away a black teenager hurled a brick and fractured the skull of a sixteen-year-old white boy returning from work at the downtown farmers' market.[77]

The violence rippled outward from the center of the city. At a huge early-afternoon anti-integration rally in the blue-collar Birmingham suburb of Midfield, Jefferson County sheriff's deputies successfully pleaded with the organizers to cancel a thousand-car motorcade into Birmingham's downtown. Larry Joe Sims, a sixteen-year-old Eagle Scout, and his best friend, Michael Farley, had planned to ride in the cavalcade on the back of Farley's motor scooter. Angry over the integration of Phillips High, the boys were looking for trouble; three days earlier they had purchased a .22 caliber pistol from another teenager for fifteen dollars.[78]

The cancellation of the rally and motorcade added to their frustration, and the two boys rode to the headquarters of the States' Rights Party on nearby Bessemer Road, where they found a half-dozen fellow students from Phillips manning a table. Sims and Farley purchased a Confederate battle flag for forty cents, attached it to the back of the motor scooter, and began riding toward a nearby black neighborhood. They soon met two black teenagers out for a Sunday afternoon bicycle ride. James Ware and his thirteen-year-old brother, Virgil, ignored the noisy scooter, but as the two white teenagers approached the bicycle, Farley handed Sims the pistol. Sims pulled the trigger twice. Virgil Ware tumbled from the handlebars. "Jim, I'm shot," he cried, and died in his brother's arms.[79]

An hour later—just after four P.M.—a caravan of white youths ignored police orders to cancel the motorcade into the downtown. Their cars decorated with Confederate flags, they cruised through the streets surrounding the Sixteenth Street Baptist Church. Loud blasts from their horns celebrated the bombing. When neighborhood boys and young men began throwing rocks at the cars, police opened fire. One shotgun blast hit a sixteen-year-old black teenager in the back as he fled the scene; he died instantly. By dusk, fires burned at three locations while sporadic gunfire could be heard crackling through the streets of downtown Birmingham. For a moment it seemed that the bombing might ignite a full-scale racial war.[80]

That evening, Martin Luther King wired President Kennedy that only decisive federal intervention could prevent the "worst racial holocaust this nation has ever seen."[81] The President had already dispatched Burke Marshall to Birmingham, but FBI and local officials, well aware that hundreds of blacks had armed themselves to form a loose-knit defense force, refused to drive the assistant attorney general of the United States to King's command center at a private home in a black neighborhood. Black activists put Marshall, face down, in the back of an automobile and smuggled him past dozens of gun-toting neighborhood guards into the King compound. The experience of being driven through an American city by black self-defense forces armed to the teeth seemed to unnerve the phlegmatic Marshall. The situation was "much worse than last May," he advised the attorney general the next day in a report which alternated between alarm and despair.[82]

The mayor, city officials, and civil rights leaders went on television to plead for calm. In reality, the violence of September 15 played itself out well before the arrival of state troopers and national guardsmen. Black residents of Birmingham were "sick, frightened, angry, disappointed, [and] disillusioned," said the president of a local black college. And they were almost desperate to find some shred of meaning in the martyrdom of their children.[83]

"They did not die in vain," insisted Martin Luther King in his funeral sermon four days later. The "innocent blood of these little girls may serve as a redemptive force that will bring new life to this dark city," he said consolingly as he pleaded with blacks to control their rage and avoid the temptation to return racial hatred for racial hatred. "At times, life is hard, as hard as crucible steel," he told an overflow congregation of eight thousand mourners. "In spite of the darkness of this hour, we must not lose faith in our white brothers."[84]

THE governor of Alabama became the lightning rod for that anger and the symbol of a people who would never say they were sorry. *Time* magazine's cover story for the week featured a haunting photograph of the shattered stained-glass window above the altar of the Sixteenth Street Baptist Church. With surgical precision, the explosion had blown out the face of Jesus as he stood surrounded by little children. Over that evocative image, editors superimposed a stern-faced three-quarter profile of George Wallace. But *Time*'s implicit censure was tame compared with that of liberal editorial cartoonists, who outdid themselves in their efforts to capture the governor's moral irresponsibility. The Nashville *Tennessean*'s Tom Little lacked the biting edge of the usual political cartoonist; objects of his gentle attacks were more likely to ask for the original drawing than to react with rage.[85] But the morning after the bombing he presented this sketch to the editorial board of his newspaper: George Wallace stood at the entrance of the church. His mouth twisted in a scowl; his arms, gorillalike, dripping with blood and gore, hung by his sides.

"I told you I'd stand in the door for you," read the caption.[86]

Robert Kennedy had always regarded Wallace as a troublemaker, but his anger was often mixed with a kind of grudging respect for the governor's political adroitness. In the wake of the Birmingham bombing, he had only contempt and disgust. The Klansmen might have planted the dynamite, said Kennedy, but the ultimate responsibility rested upon "Governor Barnett and . . . George Wallace and political and business leaders and newspapers." The bombing forced the attorney general to reexamine his own history of working with more "moderate" southern leaders. In spite of their "smiles and all the graciousness of [senators] Dick Russell and Herman Talmadge and Jim Eastland and George Smathers and [Spessard] Holland . . . none of them made any effort to counter this."[87]

But these were private musings. President John Kennedy chose his words carefully when he issued a press release the following day. It was "regrettable that public disparagement of law and order has encouraged violence which has fallen on the innocent." When a reporter asked if the President was referring directly to the governor of Alabama, press secretary Pierre Salinger replied that the statement "speaks for itself and is very clear."[88]

Most whites in Birmingham experienced a kaleidoscope of emotions which shifted inexorably from compassion to self-pitying anger. Only a particularly callous individual would not recoil at the prospect of four innocent children, even black children, murdered in their best Sunday school dresses. When the pastor of a downtown white Methodist church announced the horrifying news in the middle of the church service, dozens of the dignified middle-class church members spontaneously dropped to their knees. And on the day after the bombing, as local newspapers carried details of the blast, silent whites began arriving at the homes of the four little girls with plates of covered food and awkward condolences. One black hospital worker would always remember the next morning when she went into a downtown drugstore to pick up a bottle of aspirin. The white clerk looked up and in a strangled voice began, "I'm so sorry," then wept in a convulsion of empathy and guilt: "I'm so sorry, I'm so sorry."

Monday at noon, Birmingham attorney Charles Morgan spoke to the monthly luncheon of the city's Young Men's Business Club. The thirty-three-year-old Morgan was one of the infamous "Gang of Five": young attorneys who had worked to bring social and racial change to Birmingham in the late 1950s and early 1960s. Where his friends had quietly worked from within, Morgan had become increasingly outspoken as he watched lawyers and judges cynically transform Alabama's legal system into a mockery of justice. By the fall of 1963, he was one of a handful of white lawyers in the state willing to represent civil rights activists.

On the night of the bombing he had watched the pastor of the city's largest Baptist church join the mayor, sheriff, and police chief on television to call for prayer and to urge listeners to avoid violence because of the damage it would do to the city's reputation. "All of us are victims," said Mayor Boutwell, "and most of us are innocent victims."[89] As Morgan had listened to official after official lament the city's tattered image or insist defensively that the bombing was the "act of a lone person," he became almost sick with rage. Four children were dead, yet officials and civic leaders seemed obsessed only by the fact that Birmingham had suffered another public relations disaster. He told his wife that the moment for weighing words had ended.[90]

Everyone was asking, "Who did it?" said Charles Morgan as he looked out over his audience. "The answer should be, 'We all did it.' " The "who" was everyone who "talks about the 'niggers' and spreads the seeds of his hate to his neighbor and his son." It was everyone who had ever said, "They ought to kill that nigger." The "who" was "every Governor who ever shouted for lawlessness and became a law violator." Politicians, the business and professional community, newspaper editors: all had abdicated any moral leadership. And the preachers of Birmingham's white community, the one group that should stand for what was right, "call for prayer at high noon in a city of lawlessness and, in the same breath, speak of our city's 'image,' " said Morgan. He spat out the word "image" as though it were a kind of obscenity.

Birmingham was a city where "four little Negro girls can be born into a second-class school system, live a segregated life, ghettoed into their own little neighborhoods, restricted to Negro churches, destined to ride in Negro ambulances to Negro wards of hospitals, and from there to a Negro cemetery." Birmingham was not a dying city, Morgan said: "It is dead."[91]

There was no applause as the heavyset attorney walked back to his seat at the head table. Several in the audience seemed angry; others, deeply moved. One of Morgan's friends stood. "I move that we admit . . ." He stopped and started again. "I make a motion that we admit Negro members into Birmingham's Young Men's Business Club." The seconds ticked away. It was probably less than half a minute, but it seemed far longer before the club's president broke the awkward silence and announced that, in the absence of a second, the motion had died. Club members straggled out into the bright sun of the mid-September day; a handful stayed behind quietly to congratulate Morgan. He did not ask why no one had been willing to offer a second to his friend's motion.[92]

Alabama's attorney general, Richmond Flowers, had already charted a separate course. The death of the four children left him distraught and more than a little guilty at what he candidly described as his own failure to speak out in defense of the rule of law. Speaking to a Birmingham civic club in the wake of the blast, he joined the national chorus of attacks on Governor Wallace in an indirect but unmistakable rebuke. "In their way," said an emotional Flowers, "the individuals who bombed the 16th Street Church . . . were standing in the schoolhouse door."[93]

But few public figures in Alabama risked joining Morgan or Flowers in accepting blame or in laying responsibility squarely on the shoulders of the white community. Indeed, when Washington journalists called the offices of United States senators and representatives from the region, only J. William Fulbright of Arkansas and Atlanta congressman Charles Weltner condemned the murders. As waves of abuse poured in from the rest of the nation, momentary spasms of guilt and compassion were overwhelmed by the traditional reflexive indignation with which southern whites always greeted criticism from "outsiders."

Charles Morgan's indictment of Birmingham stung the pride of the city's whites and reinforced their sense of persecution, particularly after portions of his speech were reprinted in the *New York Times* and *Life* magazine. George Wallace dismissed the attorney as a spokesman for "a few left-wingers and 'sissy breeches' who would like to see Birmingham dead." "He represents the NAACP, as you know," he glibly assured a supporter. "It is people like him who have helped bring about the trouble—his agitation and asinine statements."[94]

Within hours after the blast, state senator Walter Givhan, former president of Alabama's White Citizens' Council, told reporters that the bombing was "done strictly by a Negro in an attempt to further their cause."[95] During the first few days after the bombing, a handful of Birmingham whites wrote letters to the *Birmingham News* and *Post-Herald* pleading for an end to hatred and mistrust, but the tide soon shifted as letters-to-the-editor columns alternated between angry denials of white responsibility and endorsements of Givhan's accusation. While Wallace received several hundred hostile letters and telegrams from outside the state, most of the mail from Alabama correspondents mirrored the accusations of the newspaper columns.[96] Even if it was a white man, complained the usually urbane Grover Hall, Jr., Wallace had no need to apologize for his actions. It was John Kennedy who had "inflamed the Negroes during the recent trouble by rehearsing their historic grievances. He may also have inflamed him who finally planted the dynamite at the church."[97]

Although no one ever conducted a scientific survey of white Alabamians on the question of the perpetrator, a substantial minority—probably a majority—believed the bombing to have been a tragic miscalculation by civil rights "fanatics" who had set the device to go off earlier (or later) when the church was empty in order to drum up support for a faltering campaign. Noted William Spencer, one of the city's most prominent businessmen, in a "position paper" presented to Mayor Boutwell, with the "unfortunate exception" of the Sixteenth Street blast, no blacks had been killed by the recent bombings. Could it be, asked Spencer, because the bombs were set by "sleek, fat [civil rights] agitators" who only wanted to create "mobs of negroes"?[98]

However bizarre such explanations might seem, they were part and parcel of a decade-long tradition of blaming the victim which had its origin in the Birmingham bombings of the late 1940s and 1950s. Nor was such a mentality restricted to Birmingham. During the Montgomery bus boycott, when terrorists planted bombs in a half-dozen churches and homes in that city (including the home of Martin Luther King and the church of the Reverend Ralph David Abernathy), it became an article of faith among Citizens' Council members and many other conservative whites that blacks were responsible.[99]

Six days after the blast at the Sixteenth Street Baptist Church, Robert Chambliss and his niece Elizabeth sat in his Bessemer home and watched a report of the latest developments in the Birmingham bombing on the Saturday evening news. The local anchorman reported widespread rumors that an arrest would soon be made and the perpetrators charged with murder.

Chambliss leaned forward and spoke intently as though he were talking directly to the television announcer. It "wasn't meant to hurt anybody. It didn't go off when it was supposed to."[100]

On September 23 Birmingham mayoral assistant William Hamilton led a five-man delegation to Washington for a conference with the President. Kennedy had met with Martin Luther King and a half-dozen black Birmingham leaders four days earlier, and he had continued to counsel patience and nonviolent resistance. "We can't do very much unless we keep the support of the white people in the country," Kennedy had argued. But he was still smarting from the pained response of a black Birmingham college president: "Well, what about those four Negro children?"[101]

He opened his meeting by urging at least a few token gestures to ease tensions: hiring black salesclerks (as businessmen had promised in the May settlement) and appointing a black policeman. But the President's suggestions indicated to the group how little he understood the realities of race relations in Birmingham. One by one, they argued against Kennedy's pleas. The Reverend Dr. Landon Miller, president of the Birmingham Council of Ministers, explained that their hands were tied. "We're already branded as liberals," he told the President sorrowfully. And Hamilton was particularly adamant that the city could not hire a black policeman. "[If] a third of our police force at this particular moment were forced to share a uniform with a Negro and all that stands for, they would walk out on us."

Kennedy turned to Frank Newton, president of Southern Bell Telephone and Telegraph, the kind of man with whom one could reason: president of the Birmingham chamber of commerce in 1962, active in community affairs, Birmingham's Man of the Year in 1963.

"Is there anything that you can do now?"

Newton insisted there was no problem which could not be solved if the President would get all the "outside agitators" out of the city so that "we could sit down and talk with our colored citizens and work these matters out."

"There seems to be a belief on the part of you people," Kennedy snapped, "that we can move these people in and out. I am just telling you flatly that we cannot."

If Kennedy thought he was going to intimidate Newton, he was wrong. The Alabama executive paused for a moment and then firmly told the President that he wanted to give him a respectful answer, but a "straightforward answer." Any concessions to blacks in the city would "only encourage those people." And he added sadly, "a lot of people . . . think you've been giving those people encouragement." It was precisely the line that George Wallace had been peddling since May, and it seems to have angered the usually dispassionate Kennedy.

"Let me make it clear," he responded frostily. Even though he had not encouraged street demonstrators in Birmingham, he supported many of their goals. "I regard getting a[n] [integrated] police force as legitimate," he said. "And I regard [black] people working as clerks in the stores as legitimate." If the armed forces could place black and white southerners in the same units where they could live together, eat together, and "use the same john," then integrating lunch counters and motels was the least that could be expected.

"I think your public accommodations, your proposal for public accommodations goes a lot further than that," responded Newton.

"Public accommodations is nothing!" exploded Kennedy with unconcealed exasperation. Blacks faced massive unemployment, whites were fleeing cities ("just running out of Washington"), while the gap between blacks and whites widened. "My God," he repeated, "public accommodations is nothing . . . !"

In the silence that followed his outburst, Reverend Miller made an effort to find common ground by turning the conversation toward what he called "our mutual problem, George Wallace," but before Kennedy could respond, Newton once again warned the President that he had to get King and Shuttlesworth out of Birmingham.

For both the President and Burke Marshall, it seemed to be the last straw. King and Shuttlesworth did not set the bomb at the Sixteenth Street Baptist Church, nor at any of the other locations around Birmingham, Marshall said coldly. King and Shuttlesworth, in fact, had calmed the situation and prevented what could have been a bloodbath.

The meeting sputtered to a close. Kennedy told his visitors he had decided to send a "fact-finding" team to Birmingham: ex–secretary of the Army Kenneth Royall and former West Point football coach Earl Blaik. The flat voice with which he made his announcement seemed to suggest that he did not expect much to come from their visit. Nothing did.[102]

Back home, the President's visitors confided to friends their worst fears. John F. Kennedy had no understanding of the pressures they faced. Why couldn't he see that his support of black troublemakers like Shuttlesworth and King inevitably incited violence by unstable white people? Hamilton, Newton, Miller—all "moderate" men of goodwill—saw themselves only as victims, whipsawed between "radical extremists" like Martin Luther King and angry rednecks who wanted blacks put back in their proper place in the old order.

Underlying that sense of victimization was the unspoken frustration of a powerful elite forced to relinquish absolute authority. When Martin Luther King led his nonviolent army into the streets in April he had obtained only minimal concessions (on which whites had almost immediately reneged). But he had fundamentally rearranged the political process as it had existed throughout the ninety-year history of Birmingham. Whites accustomed to unchallenged authority found the very notion of "concessions" obscene. No wonder they longed for the old days when they could meet quietly with a handful of conservative black "leaders" and make vague promises of indeterminate action at some indefinite time in the future.

For his part, Kennedy was simply baffled. The people who sat in his office in their well-tailored suits were not threatened steelworkers or marginal white-collar southerners on the brink of poverty; they were wealthy, educated, cosmopolitan. Yet they could not grasp the moral bankruptcy of a community that blandly dismissed any responsibility for a climate which (Kennedy was convinced) had led to the death of four little black girls. Instead, they insisted that the real problem was that the President of the United States had supported "outside agitators" who demanded little more than the right to buy a hot dog at a seedy lunch counter or to apply for a job as a salesclerk. The outspoken Frank Newton seemed to have become a symbol of that bizarre outlook in Kennedy's mind. Afterward, he never referred to Newton by name; he simply pointed to the end of the couch where the Alabama telephone executive had sat and identified him with mocking sarcasm as "that son-of-a-bitch who sat there."[103]

SECURE in the growing support of his constituents, George Wallace went on the offensive. In a blitz of news conferences and press releases he accused the national media of deliberately misleading the American people about the state of affairs in Birmingham and Alabama. With the same show-and-tell techniques he had used in congressional testimony against the civil rights bill, Wallace appeared on NBC's *Today* show on September 27 for a twenty-minute interview with newsman Martin Agronsky.

Agronsky proved no more successful at controlling the Alabama governor than had his fellows on the spring *Meet the Press* program. Wallace brushed aside the reporter's careful questions ("It has been suggested that there is a complete breakdown of communications between the races in Alabama. . . .") and took control of the interview. There had been "no breakdown of communications between the Negroes and whites," he snapped. The real story—the story of the ruthless efforts of the Communists to foment disorder and chaos in Birmingham—had gone unreported. Wallace held up the copy of the *Time* magazine cover superimposing his stern visage on the shattered stained-glass window of the Sixteenth Street Baptist Church. This was a typical example of the way in which the media engaged in "defamation by photography." Fortified with surveillance photographs taken by state police, Wallace whisked half a dozen pictures of "known subversives" in front of the television camera. All were self-avowed white radicals; all had been accused at some time or another of "pro-Communist" affiliations. In reality, all were on the periphery of events in the Steel City, but Wallace assured his audience that these people had a "direct hand in planning Negro demonstrations in Birmingham."[104]

If he drew back from explicitly charging that the bombs had been planted by civil rights activists, he made clear who bore the onus for the murders. The "Supreme Court, the Kennedy administration and the civil rights agitators are more to blame for this dastardly crime than anyone else," he told television viewers.[105]

Despite the city government's efforts to shore up its image, Mayor Boutwell refused to parrot Wallace's bizarre contention that the bombers might be blacks, Communists, or civil rights workers. Nor did Police Chief Jamie Moore and Sheriff Mel Bailey adopt Bull Connor's usual methods of malevolent misdirection. Instead, city detectives and sheriff's deputies began working around the clock in an attempt to solve the Sixteenth Street Church bombing. Maurice House and Marcus Jones, considered "experts" on the racial tensions within the city, headed up the investigation.

Jones, like his partner, had worked his way up the ranks from beat patrolman to detective. Beginning with his surveillance of Fred Shuttlesworth in the mid-1950s, he had become a regular fixture in the back rows and balconies of black churches. As he quietly slipped into place on the first hymn, it was hard to miss his pink complexion, close-cropped gray hair, jug ears, and bifocals, which he moved absentmindedly from face to mouth and back again. Night after night, he drew quick sideways glances as he dutifully took out his stubby pencil and steno pad and painstakingly recorded the names (and automobile license plate numbers) of prominent black figures and white visitors. Over the years, with a diligence which surpassed the energy of the most dedicated church secretary, Jones and his fellow officers recorded every announcement, every hymn and freedom song, every sermon riff. "I would hate to go to meet God and have to explain to Him what I was doing in His house with a pistol on my hip," said one Birmingham black minister as he glowered at his unwelcome visitor.[106] But Fred Shuttlesworth seemed to delight in teasing Jones and his colleagues. At the beginning of one long service, he welcomed his white police visitors to the Bethel Church balcony with the playful observation that they had "come to church so much that they should have religion by now."[107]

By 1963, Marcus Jones was intimately familiar with the black congregations he had visited for half a decade, as well as with the secret cadres of white men who made up the Klan and other hate groups. Ever the cynic, he continued to hold open the possibility that *some* of the bombs had been planted by civil rights agitators who wanted to capitalize on the ensuing publicity. But he knew that the men who had killed the four little girls were the white terrorists who had turned Birmingham into the bombing capital of the world.

Although FBI forensic crews painstakingly combed through the wreckage of the church, the only physical evidence ever recovered was a misshapen fishing bob attached to a wire cord, which had been blown free of the blast. (Experts speculated that the object's light weight had prevented it from being destroyed in the explosion.[108]) Federal agents and local police had to build their case through a compilation of tedious details. Ironically, their task was made more difficult by the vast, but crude, intelligence network established in the early 1960s.

Informants of varying reliability furnished dozens of potential suspects with names that bore, at times, the comic overtones of a Dixie version of Damon Runyon: "the Bowling Boys" (two brothers from Atlanta); a strong-arm Klansman with the unlikely nickname of "Nigger" Hall; "Lucky," a.k.a. "Daddy," Collins; Lewandoski "the Polack"; "Sister" White; and, of course, Dynamite Bob Chambliss. Some specialized in booby traps (for protecting arms caches). Others were "nigger-knockers," who assaulted blacks. And some were "powder men," whose expertise in dynamite had earned the respect and fear of their comrades.

Further complicating the case was the notorious reluctance of the FBI to share information with state police in high-profile cases like the Birmingham bombing. Since Wallace maintained overt ties with top Klansmen like Robert Shelton, the FBI was adamant that there be no cooperation with Al Lingo's state troopers. It seemed advisable, as well, to remain at arm's length from a local police department with suspected ties with the Klan. Still, agents needed the cooperation and inside knowledge of men like Detective Jones and Jefferson County deputy sheriff James Hancock. Cautiously, gingerly, local authorities and federal agents began selectively to share information. Two names—J. B. Stoner and Robert Chambliss—topped both lists.

Within a week after the bombing, both the Bureau and local police investigators were convinced that the murderers belonged to the deadly Cahaba River Group, a small breakaway faction from Robert Shelton's Eastview Klavern No. 13. The FBI had learned "who bought the dynamite, who made the bomb, who placed it there, and who engineered the crime," said Birmingham's federal district attorney, Macon Weaver.[109] But they lacked enough hard evidence to obtain a conviction. Agents placed Chambliss, Stoner, and a half-dozen other men under round-the-clock surveillance, settled down to the long process of accumulating evidence, and hoped for a lead that would allow them to make an arrest.

Despite (or perhaps because of) Deputy Sheriff Hancock's failure to follow up on the tip from his lover and informant, Dale Tarrant, he seemed obsessed with breaking the case. He soon felt he had a clear fix on the major figures involved in making and planting the bomb. With the help of Tarrant and (FBI officials were convinced) Chambliss's wife, Flora Lee, he planted a voice-activated microphone in the Chambliss kitchen. As Chambliss and his fellow Klansmen sat around the table, "some of the conversations they had would curl your hair," said Hancock. One of Chambliss's cronies—the suspected driver on the night the bomb was hidden at the church—boasted that someday he would "go to Fort McClellan and get a .45 machine gun and step inside the door of the church and show you how to kill some 'niggers.'" Chambliss chimed in with enthusiasm. "We're going to have to kill a bunch of them sons of bitches before we bring them to their knees."[110]

If the relentless investigative pressure caught white terrorists in the city off-guard, they were not ready to back off. As Robert Chambliss would later boast to an investigator in the case: "I ain't never run from a fight."[111]

On Monday, September 23, Detective Jones received a telephone call from a contact in the Atlanta police department. Detectives shadowing J. B. Stoner and the Bowling Boys reported that the three men had left the city in separate cars heading westward on Highway 78 toward Birmingham. Jones quickly picked up their trail at the Chambliss home and stepped up surveillance of the National States' Rights party headquarters in Bessemer. But phone taps picked up little information beyond the fact that party leaders were infuriated by FBI harassment. Frustrated, but still convinced that Stoner and Chambliss were up to something, Jones filed his report with Chief Moore on Tuesday morning and went to bed.[112]

In the predawn hours of Wednesday, September 25, a late-model car with out-of-state plates quietly slipped into a black neighborhood on the south side of Birmingham. Chief Moore had placed his officers on twelve-hour shifts and had doubled patrols around black churches and throughout Dynamite Hill. But the south side was well away from the black communities that had suffered most of the violence of the previous decade, and it was not under special surveillance. The bombers placed an explosive device in the middle of a side street. Ninety feet away, just back from the edge of a weed-filled empty lot, they concealed a five-gallon paint can containing two sticks of dynamite covered with thirty pounds of nails, hammer claws, bolts, rusty pieces of metal, and the jagged clutch plate of an old Hudson. They carefully set the fuse on this second bomb to go off fifteen to twenty minutes after the first explosion.

At 2:21 A.M., the first blast gouged a hole in the pavement one and a half feet deep and three feet wide, sheared off a nearby utility pole, and plunged the street into darkness. Dozens of black residents swamped the police switchboard with their calls, but the nearly thirty police cars that responded converged on the wrong street, two blocks away from the explosion. At 2:34 A.M., when the second bomb went off, a lethal spray of jagged metal slashed through the weeds and bushes of the vacant lot like an unsharpened scythe.

As shaken police extracted rusty chunks of metal from nearby automobiles and the walls of houses over a half-block radius, they concluded that the two-bomb sequence was not just "to scare niggers." The bombs could well have been designed to lure black residents out of their homes and into a lethal killing field, but Birmingham policemen drew (to them) more unnerving conclusions. "It was meant for us," said one patrolman. "It was set to allow just enough time for us to get there. If we had found the [first] bomb, maybe fifty officers would have lost their lives or been mangled."[113]

Pundits would later depict the Birmingham church bombing as a "turning point" in the history of race relations in the city. The real shift came in the way that the city's police department began to deal with white terrorists. Klansmen and States' Rights Party fanatics were not immediately abandoned by all of their police friends—party officials constantly bragged over the phone that they had spies in both the uniformed and detective divisions and in the city council as well. Moreover, city detectives continued their harassment of civil rights figures, and police brutality against blacks remained an ugly reality of life in the Steel City. But in the aftermath of the explosion of the brutal shrapnel bomb in the predawn hours of September 25, Birmingham ceased to be a safe haven for the men with the bombs.

GEORGE Wallace had promised the national audience of the *Today* show that the state would soon apprehend the guilty parties. On September 29, four days after the south-side blast and just two days after his television interview, Wallace's office issued a brief and unexpected announcement. "State investigators expect to break the Birmingham-church case within the next few hours."[114]

Three hours later, Chambliss and fellow Klansman Charles Cagle quietly surrendered to state officials, and the governor's office issued a second statement announcing their arrest. Bill Jones told a hastily called news conference that state police had acted independently from FBI and local investigations because "we wanted to make sure those responsible for the bombings are apprehended."[115] Over the next three days, the arrest of Chambliss and Cagle made front-page headlines across the nation.

FBI agents and Birmingham city detectives learned the news along with the rest of the country; Al Lingo's state police had not consulted with city or federal officials. Privately, the announcement stunned and infuriated Bureau and local police. They had scarcely begun to accumulate the growing mountain of circumstantial evidence linking Chambliss to the church bombing, although Deputy Sheriff Hancock had persuaded two of the prime suspects to come in for questioning without a lawyer, and one of Chambliss's closest buddies had foolishly agreed to take a lie detector test (he failed). Hancock and Jefferson County sheriff Mel Bailey were certain that paranoia among the men would eventually lead one of them to turn himself in. Bailey was so enraged at what he regarded as Lingo's grandstanding that he refused to allow the suspects to be placed in the county jail; city officials reluctantly agreed to house the two men while state plainclothes investigators questioned them.

The federal task force assembled in Birmingham knew that Al Lingo and the state patrol were running a separate investigation. But they were baffled by the decision of Lingo and his men to jail Chambliss and his cronies. They knew that state investigators lacked sufficient evidence. Lingo's men had only one hope for solving the case: the remote chance that Chambliss and his fellow conspirators might break down under interrogation. But even that possibility quickly vanished. Within less than an hour after they were arrested, Matt Murphy, a well-known Klan lawyer, appeared at the city jail. He instructed his clients to remain silent.[116]

Local FBI agents were already suspicious about the motivation of Wallace's state police investigators. They reported to Washington with dismay that Klan leader Robert Shelton had been seen riding around with state investigators as they carried out their investigation. In his report to Attorney General Robert Kennedy, FBI director J. Edgar Hoover concluded that Wallace's men had "certainly 'flushed' the case and I doubt that they will be able to hold these two men." Once Chambliss and Cagle learned they were prime suspects, he warned, the task of making a case would be far more difficult.[117]

Chambliss's niece, Elizabeth Hood, also doubted Lingo's commitment to solving the case. On the night her uncle surrendered to authorities, a state

investigator, accompanied by Don Luna, a well-known Klansman, had arrived at the Chambliss house, she recalled. According to Hood, Luna assured
Robert that "they"—presumably the Klan—would "get him out of it."[118]
Fifteen years later, while doing research at the Birmingham Public Library,
Hood (now married, and Elizabeth Hood Cobbs) found an unsigned document in a cache of abandoned city police surveillance records. According to
the unsigned, typewritten report, Lingo and one of his top aides met with a
half-dozen Klansmen (including Robert Shelton) early the same night of the
arrest of Chambliss and his fellow Klansmen. The last sentence of the document ended with a chilling phrase: "Don Luna accompanied state investigator Posey, and these two men knocked on Robert Chambliss's front door
on the evening in a joint operation."[119] A joint operation. To Cobbs, the
evidence was overwhelming: Lingo and his men had never had any intention
of seriously making a case against Chambliss and his accomplices.

But Wallace captured all the headlines. "We certainly beat the Kennedy
crowd to the punch," he bragged to journalists in Montgomery. "Lingo's men
pulled something of a coup . . . by making the first arrests in the case,"
agreed the *Advertiser*.[120] Three days later, John Herbers of the *New York
Times* played the role of doubting Thomas. FBI officials, he noted, were
"surprised" by Lingo's arrests. An agent had told Herbers that the arrest of
Chambliss and Cagle had "possibly hampered or prevented a solution to the
case."[121] But most newspapers, including the *Washington Post* and the *Los
Angeles Times*, as well as UPI and AP reporters in Birmingham, played the
story as a serious attempt to catch the bombers; there was no hint that Lingo's
strategy might be a charade.[122]

On October 8, eight days after their arrest, Chambliss, Cagle, and a third
Klansman linked to the bombing went on trial in Birmingham City Court.
They pleaded guilty, not to murder, but to a misdemeanor which one observer sardonically noted was as "common in Birmingham as jaywalking in
many a U.S. City": possession of a box of 122 sticks of dynamite without a
permit. The Klansmen received a hundred-dollar fine and a six-month jail
sentence. News cameramen photographed a grinning Chambliss as he
walked from the courtroom, and city recorder Langner emphasized that the
trial showed no connection between the defendants and the Sixteenth Street
bombing. Even the jail term was suspended by Langner after Chambliss and
his friends filed notice of an appeal.[123]

A little more than a year after the bombing, Burke Marshall and Robert
Kennedy sat in the attorney general's Virginia home and confided to interviewer Anthony Lewis their belief that Wallace and Lingo had deliberately
sabotaged the investigation. The Klan bombers had "got themselves arrested, really, by the state highway patrol, and charged with illegal possession of dynamite" in order to head off murder charges, said Marshall. A

shocked Lewis recoiled from the idea. "Is it conceivable that George Wallace thinks people should be allowed to bomb churches and kill little girls? I mean, is he . . ."

Kennedy took one small step back. "I don't think he's had, has to face it in that context."

"I don't know," echoed Marshall. "But he certainly . . . must have known that they blew a chance."[124]

George Wallace's quick-witted resilience had never been shown to better advantage. His announcement of the arrest of the suspected bombers commanded national media attention; the denouement received only brief coverage. *Time* and *Newsweek* quoted Fred Shuttlesworth's acrid assessment of the Wallace-ordered arrests ("It was a farce"), but the conviction of Chambliss and two accomplices on minor charges was almost ignored. The October 9 issue of the *New York Times* mentioned the misdemeanor conviction and release of Chambliss and his cronies in a brief news item on page 28.[125] There would be no full-scale trial to draw the scrutiny of the national press and highlight the governor's ties with Bull Connor, Robert Shelton, and Asa Carter and, through them, the most unsavory elements of the southern white resistance movement. Television and print journalists moved on to other stories. As Claude Sitton, one of the two *New York Times* reporters in the region, recalled, there was a "new fire breaking out every day all over the South."[126]

The *Birmingham News* and the *Post-Herald* alone had the resources and the rationale for digging deeply into the full implications of George Wallace's recklessness. Both newspapers had journalists with contacts in the city's police department and Jefferson County sheriff's department who were bitter (and willing to talk) about what they regarded as the cynical sabotaging of the case by Wallace and Lingo. But the local press had never had the stomach for exposing the raw sores of that city's troubled racial history. They were not about to take on the popular governor with an investigation that would have accused him of cynically playing politics with the murder of four black children.

Although the investigating officers in the Birmingham police department and the Jefferson County sheriff's department continued to try to break the case, Birmingham's politicians, for obvious reasons, were happy to place the entire episode behind them. The FBI had mounted a massive investigation of the bombing and eventually assembled an unbroken chain of evidence linking Chambliss to the murders. Despite Lingo's botched handling of the case, by December the Birmingham field office of the FBI had accumulated sufficient evidence to go forward with a prosecution of Chambliss. But J. Edgar Hoover told Justice Department officials he doubted that white southerners would ever convict the bombers on the basis of circumstantial evidence, and he refused to allow his Birmingham office to brief prosecutor Macon Weaver. He did not tell his Justice Department superiors about his second concern: that a full-scale trial would disclose the embarrassing fact that Robert Chambliss had been a paid informer for the Bureau.[127] While the FBI's investigation plodded on for another six years, Hoover returned to the more agreeable task of trying to prove that Martin Luther King was a sexual degenerate and a tool of the Soviet empire.[128]

There were soon other crises, other more pressing and urgent civil rights issues. Faced with a demoralized and bitterly divided black community, King sensed that to harp on the unsolved murders simply exposed the movement's impotence. Fred Shuttlesworth continued to voice dark suspicions of a cover-up, but decided that he had struggled long enough in Birmingham; he accepted a pastorate in Cincinnati. When King hinted at the need for additional street demonstrations, the city's wealthiest and most conservative black leaders (both bombing victims), Arthur Shores and A. G. Gaston, rejected the veiled threat of renewed protests. There was "no need for any additional outside help at this time." White political and civic leaders effusively praised their "good judgment," and Birmingham's newspapers gave their brief statement front-page coverage.[129]

THE governor of Alabama had not, as Burke Marshall seemed to suggest, deliberately sabotaged the effort to arrest and convict the authors of one of the great crimes of the civil rights era. He had not really cared one way or the other. As always, he kept his finely tuned political ear to the ground. If whites in Alabama had decided in their sovereign wisdom that the bomb had been planted by Communist civil rights agitators (with the encouragement of the Kennedys), who was he to challenge the voice of his people? Three and a half months after the bombing, retired admiral Lawton Ford, a conservative Louisiana supporter, asked the governor to clarify his views on the events in Birmingham. Wallace assured Ford that he was "shocked at the tragedy which occurred in Birmingham when some demented person or persons bombed the Negro Church." But, he added, he was "not sure this was the work of white persons. It could very easily have been done by Communists or other negroes who had a lot to gain by the ensuing publicity."[130]

A sequel is seldom as successful as the original. Farce in Tuscaloosa had become tragedy in Birmingham. But Frank Johnson had it right the first time: "No matter how high up you threw him [Wallace], he landed on his feet, like a cat."[131] With a few mirrors and an endless supply of smoke, he had managed to mystify and confuse his audience.

In early October George Wallace announced his decision to launch a northern speaking tour. He told newsmen that he was seriously considering a plan to enter a number of Democratic primaries in 1964. There is a "lot of

Southern sympathy in all the states," said Wallace. Ohio, Michigan, Wisconsin, Maryland—even a ten percent vote in one of those states would amount to a "moral victory over the Kennedys. You don't have to win a majority of votes to win."[132]

CODA

The night of the Birmingham bombing, a young law student from the Wiregrass region of Alabama sat in his fraternity house in Tuscaloosa. While friends chattered about the Crimson Tide's upcoming football game with the University of Georgia, William J. Baxley could think of nothing except the four girls dead in their white Sunday school dresses only sixty miles away. I felt "sick to my stomach," said Baxley. "I promised, I told one of my friends that evening, some day, *some day*, I'm going to do something about it." A little over a decade later, Bill Baxley would win election as attorney general of Alabama. On the long-distance phone card he constantly used when he was on the road, he wrote the names of the four bombing victims so that every time he picked up the phone, he reminded himself of the promise he had made as a twenty-five-year-old law student.[133] In 1977, he brought Robert Chambliss back to a Birmingham courtroom where a racially mixed jury convicted him of the murder of the four girls. Chambliss could have shortened his sentence by turning state's evidence against his Klan accomplices and telling for the first time the full story of the events leading up to the night of September 15. But he would not violate his Klan oath of secrecy. On October 29, 1985, he died in an Alabama prison.[134]

The trial brought a brief resurgence of interest in the case, but, with the exception of the *New York Times*'s Howell Raines, a native of Birmingham, the reporters who covered the case seemed interested only in the guilt or innocence of the defendant. There was little attempt to unravel the tangled web that linked the choices of community leaders, violent Klansmen, policemen, and self-serving politicians with the lives and the deaths of Cynthia Wesley, Carole Robertson, Denise McNair, and Addie Mae Collins. That was old news: old, complicated, and painful.

Chapter 7

A TREMOR, NOT AN EARTHQUAKE

GEORGE WALLACE AND THE PRESIDENTIAL CAMPAIGN OF 1964

THERE WAS SOMETHING SAD, almost pathetic, about the way white southerners so desperately longed for approval from those they professed to despise. In early September of 1963, George Wallace made an appearance at a University of Alabama pep rally. After an obligatory nod to the football fortunes of the Crimson Tide, he announced with great fanfare: "I want y'all to be the first to know that your governor has been invited by Harvard University to come up there and tell them how we do things here in Alabama . . . ! So this is a great night for Alabama!"[1]

The decision to stage a northern speaking tour had evolved in the weeks following Wallace's June stand in the schoolhouse door and his successful appearance on NBC's *Face the Nation*. Dozens of invitations poured in from around the country. Most came from segregationist and politically right-wing organizations, but a surprising number of mainline political groups seemed anxious to hear the Alabama governor. Nowhere was interest greater than on the nation's college and university campuses.

The great cultural upheavals of the decade remained just over the horizon, but student organizations—particularly at the nation's more prestigious schools—had begun to assert their independence by inviting controversial speakers to the campus, often to the displeasure of administrators who feared embarrassment or disorder. Since he asked for neither honorarium nor expenses (state taxpayers picked up his expenses), the controversial Alabama governor proved an irresistible attraction.

And George Wallace had nothing to lose. If listeners responded rudely or shouted him down, it would only reinforce his support at home and build sympathy for him among the great majority of middle Americans whose awe of the Ivy League was mixed with a healthy dose of contempt. If he fared well, university approval would enhance his respectability, rescue him from his role as a marginal regional demagogue, and lay the groundwork for his presidential plans. And in what better place to open than the alma mater of the hated Kennedys?

Wallace became part of a long tradition of southern emissaries seeking an audience for the gospel of the peculiar region. Slavery defender George Fitzhugh had debated abolitionist spokesman Wendell Phillips in Boston (without much success), and during the 1890s, South Carolina senator "Pitchfork" Ben Tillman had earned a lucrative income on the Chautauqua circuit as he lectured sober-minded Yankees on the bestiality of southern blacks.[2] But Dixie's politicians, like southern sweet corn, had traveled badly in the 1950s and early 1960s. Ross Barnett's limited mental faculties had become the stuff of legend. It was said that at Barnett's first press appearance as governor in 1960, a newsman interrupted his meandering discussion of executive appointments to ask, "What do you think of Ma-tsu and Quemoy?" (The two Taiwanese islands were front-page news because of their daily bombardment by mainland China.) After floundering for a moment, Barnett righted himself and explained earnestly that both were "good men, and I'm sure I can find a place for them in Fish and Game." The story is, alas, apocryphal, but like many tales of southern politics, it captures a larger truth. As the *Nation*'s Robert Sherrill concluded, this man was "bone dumb."[3] In a half-dozen speeches on northern college campuses after the 1962 Ole Miss debacle, Barnett lived up to his reputation, and students greeted his litany of nineteenth-century racism with contemptuous hilarity rather than anger. But Wallace, it soon became clear, was no Ross Barnett.

ON November 4, 1963, the sons and daughters of Harvard and Radcliffe gathered to hear George Wallace in much the same spirit of festivity that had guided those Union spectators who rode south from Washington in the summer of 1861 to watch the Federal army rout the rebels at a little creek named Bull Run. When the governor walked onto the stage of Sanders Theater, a packed crowd of twelve hundred greeted him with a mixed chorus of polite applause and sustained hisses.

Wallace had arrived in Boston with a curiously bifurcated speech written by Asa Carter and John Kohn.[4] In language borrowed directly from Carter's racist writings of the 1950s, the first portion of the text blamed the existence of the South's mixed-race population on the promiscuity of Union soldiers in the Reconstruction era and warned of the frightening consequence of racial amalgamation.[5]

But Kohn's second half was low-key and thoughtful. In addition to the obligatory quotes from *The Federalist,* the speech included a discussion of the limited juridical background of Supreme Court appointees and a shrewd analysis of the methodological weaknesses of Kenneth Clark's celebrated "dolls" experiment, which the NAACP had used in its brief against school segregation in *Brown v. Board of Education.*

With that sense of rhetorical pitch that seldom failed him, the Alabama governor blue-penciled all racist references and stuck to the high road of constitutional analysis.[6] At the same time, he proved to be an ingratiating guest. When a heckler in the balcony interrupted, Wallace grinned and retorted, "You cut that out fella, you made me lose my place." Pausing to drink from a glass on the podium, he good-naturedly begged listeners not to spread any rumors, since "I've taken the [temperance] oath to the folks back home."[7]

By the time he began to take questions from the floor, his audience's mood had shifted. Students came down the aisle to the microphone to "pose a stumper," said a correspondent for the college alumni bulletin, "and walked away chagrined."[8] With a humorous aside or with what appeared to be disarming honesty, Wallace deflected controversial queries. ("Should Negroes be allowed to vote in Alabama?" "Of course, if they're qualified"; "Do you think Negroes are biologically inferior to whites?" "I don't know, I'm not an anthropologist.") When Gordon O. DuBois II, a grandson of famed black historian and civil rights leader W. E. B. DuBois, attempted to goad the southerner by declaring his intention eventually to run for President, Wallace simply smiled and offered encouragement. "Between you and me both, we might kick out that crowd down in Washington," he said, and then paused for dramatic emphasis: "Maybe we should run on the same ticket." The audience roared.[9]

Halfway through the question-and-answer period, a young white man walked to the microphone. "How do you square what you say about civil rights with your police brutality—" the questioner began in a soft southern accent.

"Oh, I know you," interrupted Wallace, "you're Bob Zellner and you are a renowned Alabamian. In fact, you have been in a number of jails in Alabama. . . ."[10]

Over whistles, shouts, and applause, Harvard law professor Arthur Sutherland scolded Zellner for posing a "Have you stopped beating your wife?" question, but the governor quickly recovered his composure. With that deft selection of facts that would become his specialty, he quoted (out of context) one of President Kennedy's statements praising Alabama state and local law enforcement officers and begged the students not to believe everything they read in the national press. Two Alabama newsmen who covered the speech reported to readers that Wallace had received a "standing ovation";

a writer from the *Harvard Crimson* insisted the audience had applauded Zellner.[11]

Irwin Hyatt, an Atlanta-born Harvard graduate student, sensed little passion or commitment for or against the governor. Instead, as Wallace jousted with hecklers and critics, most members of his audience found themselves caught up in the performance. Surprised to find the Alabamian amusing, quick-witted, and clever, they saluted a master showman.[12] Wallace certainly felt he got the best of the exchanges; in later years he claimed with mock seriousness that the next day students flocked to Cambridge barbershops to have their long hair trimmed.[13]

Just after ten P.M., a smiling Wallace, surrounded by a half-dozen Cambridge policemen, slipped out a back exit. At the main entrance to the theater, an angry crowd of three hundred civil rights activists vented their frustration by slashing the tires of the limousine loaned by Massachusetts governor Endicott Peabody. Inside, however, the men and women of Harvard and Radcliffe seemed pleased with their broad-mindedness. The vast majority of students might disagree with the Alabama governor, but his talk had been "fascinating," said Burt Ross, president of the Harvard Young Democrats, which had sponsored the event. The "overwhelming support of the Governor's right to talk is a glowing testimony to our University and to the fact that our motto—*Veritas*—lives on."[14]

From Harvard, on to Dartmouth, Smith, and Brown, the tour that followed was a great success, at least as measured by the volumes of print in Alabama's newspapers. There were a few boos, and Wallace occasionally overstepped in his defense of southern racial customs. During his one-week foray, however, he spoke to thousands, and reached much of the New England public in two dozen radio and television interviews.

Equally important, the venture gave him status and legitimacy. As an adviser recalled with wonder, "We thought those [northern newspaper] reporters and students and college professors up there were smart." But "they were really pretty dumb." After the first couple days on the road, Bill Jones catalogued a list of potential questions, and he and Wallace reviewed a range of answers. In press conferences and interviews, they were never surprised.[15]

"Wallace Wins Harvard!" headlined the *Birmingham News*.[16] "Ivy League Tour a Triumph for Alabama Governor," declared the usually critical *Huntsville Times*.[17] William Bradford Huie, a north Alabama writer and longtime Wallace foe, raged in frustration. He could understand well-to-do Yankees' secret support: "They think he knows how to get the votes of poor white men and then rig tax structures against them." He could accept the racist response of working-class people of Eastern European background, who feared blacks would steal their jobs and their homes. What he could never forget or forgive was the sight of the well-bred, "supposedly intelligent" sons and daughters of Harvard University and Radcliffe College laughing and applauding the cleverness of George Wallace.[18]

On the morning of November 22, 1963, the governor flew to northwest Alabama to dedicate a new high school. As the chairman of the Haleyville school board finished his introduction, a radio announcer who had rigged up local coverage of the event blurted out, "We have just had a bulletin from Dallas that President Kennedy has been shot and is seriously injured." Wallace, his complexion gray, his chin thrust out awkwardly, his hands clenching and unclenching, first stood and then sat back down. After the music director of Haleyville's First Baptist Church broke the awkward silence by standing and singing the "Lord's Prayer," the governor walked to the podium.

"What are we coming to when a president cannot ride down a street of an American city without being shot . . . down in gangster fashion while riding the streets of an American city," he fumbled, then returned to his seat. A reporter from the *Birmingham News* who had covered the feisty Alabamian for several years had never seen him so inarticulate. "Literally, the attack on the President left Wallace speechless."[19]

If the murders of Cynthia Wesley, Carole Robertson, Denise McNair, and Addie Mae Collins had little effect on the governor, the assassination of John Kennedy left him uneasy and deeply disturbed; despite his political hostility, he had secretly admired the handsome and graceful Kennedy. In contrast to his perfunctory statement of regret after the Sixteenth Street Baptist Church tragedy, Wallace spoke passionately and repeatedly of his personal regard for the slain President. He ordered the state's flag lowered to half-staff, announced a thirty-day period of mourning, and wrote an effusive note of sympathy to Jacqueline Kennedy. At the funeral in Washington, reporters found him subdued and withdrawn. He could not help but draw unsettling comparisons to his own vulnerability. "I think he thought to himself: 'This could happen to me,'" said Earl Morgan. "You know, people loved him. But just like Kennedy, there were some people that hated him an awful lot."[20]

E. L. Holland, the editor of the *Birmingham News,* confided to one of Robert Kennedy's aides that "Gov. Wallace was very deeply shocked . . . he is indeed doing a lot of thinking." While he wanted to avoid false hopes, Holland said, it was important to remember that Wallace "once was a liberal young Alabamian, and that he artificially, in my opinion, put himself in the [race-baiting] position he did, explicitly in order to be elected." The federal government, Holland advised, should avoid placing the governor in "any corner so that he would have to resume a fighting stance."[21]

The notion that he might reverse direction and accept a rapprochement with Washington was an astonishing misreading of George Wallace's political bloodlines; he was never more comfortable than when he was on the attack. A second lecture tour in December and January across the Midwest, the Rocky Mountains, and the West Coast proved a success far beyond the most optimistic projections of the southerner and his staff. Halfway through the trip, Alabama reporters accompanying the governor did a quick calculation of his West Coast media exposure: three hours and fifteen minutes on commercial television special shows, an hour and thirty-nine minutes of spot news coverage, nearly three hours on educational television, and dozens of newspaper and magazine articles generated by the 370 reporters who had appeared at scheduled news conferences.[22] "To buy that much TV time in Los Angeles alone would probably take the entire State General Fund," said one awed Montgomery columnist. "Wallace got it for nothing."[23] By mid-February, he had spoken at more than twenty of the top schools in the country. Only Yale, at the insistence of Provost Kingman Brewster, had publicly spurned him.

He took pains to avoid any serious gaffes or embarrassing confrontations. When civil rights activists turned out to challenge him, he was unfailingly courteous, disarming, and amusing. More often than not, audiences turned on the hecklers and applauded the speaker. "Governor George C. Wallace of Alabama came to town yesterday," editorialized the *Tacoma Tribune*. He was not the "rabble-rousing, Negro-hating zealot with horns that many people expected." The people of Seattle had instead found him to be a "mild-mannered person with a sense of humor and a message. His message is mainly a firm belief in states' rights."[24] Aides made certain that copies of the favorable coverage reached Alabama's newspapers and television stations, and newspapers across the state reprinted admiring editorials that had appeared in a half-dozen smaller West Coast and Rocky Mountain newspapers.

Wallace's almost uniformly good press back home quickly wiped out sour memories of his September antics. When the governor had blocked the integration of Huntsville's schools, he was at the "bottom of the totem pole in popularity," said one north Alabama opponent. But by mid-November there was a complete turnabout. The trip to New England was the primary factor. "People may not say it," said a county commissioner in Huntsville, but "a lot of Alabamians have resented the fact that they and their state were sneered at by outsiders." Their governor, with his "sensible, intelligent and legal manner" had "wiped some of those sneers off the face of easterners."[25]

Wallace dropped vague hints to journalists covering his West Coast tour that he might enter the presidential primaries the following year. The prospect of a meaningful challenge—particularly one led by a segregationist southern governor with a national reputation for inciting mayhem—seemed so farfetched that the national media ignored his trial balloons. In the months after Kennedy's assassination, President Lyndon Johnson rode a wave of national popularity that made him not only the overwhelming choice for the Democratic nomination, but the odds-on favorite for victory in November 1964.

However, Johnson insisted—until opening day of the Democratic convention—that he was undecided about running for reelection. He declined to enter any of the spring Democratic primaries. While his pretended indecision allowed him to avoid the trench warfare of an intra-party fight, it left him vulnerable to the rogue challenge of the Alabamian.

Two days before his January 1963 inaugural, Governor-elect George Wallace had discreetly invited right-wing Virginia columnist John Synon and seven politicians and activists from across the South to a meeting in his hotel suite. Fresh from the Ole Miss debacle, Ross Barnett was poised to launch a nationwide speaking tour to alert northern whites to the perils of racial mongrelization and a Kennedy political takeover of local government. Wealthy Louisiana oil man and politician Leander Perez had begun his career as one of Huey Long's parish bosses; newspaper readers across the nation remembered his furious exhortations to whites to resist the church's decision to integrate its Louisiana schools ("Don't wait for your daughters to be raped by these Congolese," Perez had told a White Citizens' Council rally in New Orleans), and his equally noisy excommunication from the Catholic church. Unbowed, Judge Perez continued to rail against his church and the "Zionist-Jews" who had used their "Congolese burr-heads" to integrate New Orleans parochial schools.[26]

Five lesser-known figures joined Wallace, Synon, Barnett, and Perez at the Jefferson Davis Hotel: James Gray and Roy Harris of Georgia; South Carolinian Farley Smith; Mississippi's Judge Russell Moore; and Louisiana's wily architect of massive resistance, Willie Rainach. All were closely associated with the White Citizens' Council movement; all were fanatical white supremacists. It seemed an unlikely brain trust for a man with secret national political aspirations.

Synon, a business and political lobbyist in the 1940s, had proved a master at Red-baiting when he was hired by the California oil industry to discredit California's liberal Republican governor, Earl Warren. A decade later he had returned to suburban Washington, D.C., where he helped to form a new right-wing business lobbying group, the Americans for Constitutional Action, and had developed the famous ACA voting index, a supposedly nonpartisan measurement of the true "constitutional conservatism" of the nation's lawmakers.[27] By the 1960s Synon had drifted from the edge of political respectability toward the seedier fringes of the White Citizens' Council movement. Founding the Patrick Henry Press, he began publishing such titles as *Breeding Down*, a lurid account of dangers whites faced from "mongrelization" with a "Negro race" "less advanced in an evolutionary sense than is the white race by perhaps 200,000 years."[28]

Synon labored tirelessly throughout the South to foster an "independent elector" movement. In 1964, he argued, Dixie's voters would face the choice of voting for Kennedy or a "liberal" like Nelson Rockefeller. By running slates of independent third-party electors, headed in each southern state by popular "favorite-son segregationists," the region could assemble a voting bloc that would deadlock the electoral college and force concessions from national candidates.[29]

Flushed with the enthusiasm surrounding Wallace's inauguration—an enthusiasm supplemented by a well-stocked bar—the eight men agreed to draw up plans for 1964. Without debate, they appointed Synon "executive secretary" of the as-yet-unnamed organization, which promptly sank into oblivion.

If the Synon plan had planted the seed of a presidential run in Wallace's mind, the response to his stand in the schoolhouse door and his northern lecture tour in early November had opened more audacious possibilities. Synon thought purely in terms of a kind of southern veto on national politics. What if there was a substantial audience beyond the region for the politics of race?

ON February 19, 1964, only nine days after the House of Representatives passed the Kennedy-Johnson civil rights bill and sent it on to the Senate for consideration, Wallace arrived on the Madison campus of the University of Wisconsin. Although Wisconsin had been home to Senator Joseph McCarthy, America's most influential right-wing anticommunist during the postwar era, the Madison campus boasted the largest collection of left-wing political activists in the Midwest. At the entrance to the lakefront student union, protesters waved their signs—"We Shall Overcome"; "End Racism in Alabama"—while a raucous band of demonstrators inside sang freedom songs.

Wallace, by this time totally at ease with hostile student audiences, mockingly expressed gratitude for the opportunity to "see new beard styles" and soon disarmed hecklers. "Southern charm oozed out," complained one student. Prepared for a vicious race-baiting demagogue, his listeners seemed bewildered over how to respond to a hillbilly humorist. By the end of the talk, wrote the editor of the campus newspaper, his jokes had the audience in "perplexed convulsions."[30]

That night, Oscar Harper, Ralph Adams, and Billy Watson, three of Wallace's traveling buddies, celebrated by sampling some of Wisconsin's famous local brews in their lakeside hotel room. When the phone rang, Harper answered. The caller identified himself as a public relations specialist from Oshkosh, Wisconsin, and asked to speak with the Alabama governor.

Harper covered the telephone receiver. "This is some damn fool wanting George to run for president in Wisconsin," he said to Ralph Adams. "You talk to him."[31]

Lloyd Herbstreith and his wife, Dolores, had driven over a hundred miles on two-lane roads in a steady snowfall to hear Wallace speak. His success in taming the unruly students and his skill at pitching the issue in "constitutional" rhetoric confirmed the Herbstreiths' belief that this conservative southerner was the man who could save the nation. Thousands of angry and discontented voters were willing to give Wallace a fair hearing, explained Lloyd Herbstreith, and the state primary was easy to enter. Presidential primary candidates had only to present a slate of certified delegates to the Wisconsin secretary of state by the March 6 deadline. He and his wife would take care of that part of the paperwork. Intrigued, Adams arranged a meeting.

The next morning the Alabama entourage awakened and looked out over Lake Mendota. Angry students had mixed up a solution of red Kool-Aid and had spelled out FUCK WALLACE in huge letters on the frozen lake.[32] But the Herbstreiths were uninterested in obscene college pranks. While Wallace spoke to a downtown press conference, they gave Adams, Watson, and Harper a forty-minute crash course in Wisconsin politics.

Newsmen usually described Herbstreith as a conservative businessman turned political organizer, but he was hardly a political novice. He had supported Joe McCarthy in the early 1950s and then had turned to other right-wing causes after the Wisconsin senator faded from public view. By 1963, he and the articulate Dolores were devoting hundreds of hours to the passage of the so-called Liberty Amendment, a constitutional measure designed to "destroy the welfare state" by abolishing the federal income tax. The campaign was funded primarily by California right-wing businessmen. Repeal of the Sixteenth Amendment had actually won approval in five Deep South states.[33] (Six months after the Wisconsin primary, Wallace legislative floor leaders gaveled it through the Alabama legislature on a surprise voice vote.)[34]

To the Wallace staff, the University of Wisconsin seemed only one degree to the right of Moscow State. The notion that their governor might find support in this liberal midwestern state initially seemed preposterous. African Americans made up a small minority, and outside the city of Milwaukee most whites seldom saw a black face except on television. But the Herbstreiths insisted on the possibility of a strong showing against Governor John Reynolds, scheduled to run as a favorite son stand-in for Lyndon Johnson. Reynolds's support for higher taxes had soured rural voters, while his unsuccessful efforts to pass a strong open-housing law had made him unpopular among "ethnic" groups and suburbanites in Milwaukee. Moreover, in the absence of a contested GOP primary, conservative Republicans who had made up the core of support for the late Joseph McCarthy would respond to Wallace's anticommunist–states' rights–limited government rhetoric. In Wisconsin's wide-open primary system, they were free to cross over and cast a protest vote against their hated Democratic governor and President.

Operating out of the Herbstreiths' kitchen, the impromptu Wallace for President committee worked day and night. While her husband furnished names and suggestions, Dolores Herbstreith recruited a slate of sixty convention delegates, organized a complex system of car couriers to distribute and round up the notarized filing forms, laid the foundations for a statewide campaign, and proudly reported to a Wallace aide that her committee had raised almost two thousand dollars.[35]

On March 6, the deadline for filing, George Wallace again landed in Madison. His plane, a small Lockheed Lodestar prop plane, was normally decorated with a brace of Confederate flags and the slogan: "Stand Up for Alabama." A sharp-eyed reporter noticed that an artist had substituted an American flag for one of the Confederate flags. The retooled slogan read: "Stand Up for America."[36]

"Underwhelmed" is the best way to describe the response to Wallace's presidential announcement. The *New York Times* buried the story in a brief Associated Press dispatch on page 76. None of the networks mentioned it; even the Alabama press gave the news modest play. Although Governor Reynolds canceled plans to lead a trade delegation to Europe and stayed home to campaign, an early public opinion poll showed that the southerner had the support of less than five percent of Wisconsin's Democratic voters.[37]

To arouse his constituents and to raise the stakes for Wallace, Reynolds warned that the Alabamian might get as many as 100,000 votes if the total turnout in the primary reached three-quarters of a million.[38] That level of support would be a "catastrophe." "Churches were bombed and children killed in his state," he reminded television viewers as he expressed confidence that the people of Wisconsin would join him in a "moral crusade" to repudiate the Alabama governor and "all he stands for." Privately, Reynolds estimated his opponent would win fewer than fifty thousand votes (a figure the challenger himself considered reasonable). Dolores Herbstreith confidently predicted that her candidate would draw as much as a third of the vote.[39]

Wallace opened his campaign, at the suggestion of the Herbstreiths, in Appleton, hometown of Joseph McCarthy. The Alabama governor praised the former Wisconsin senator as a man who was "just a little ahead of his time," but he seemed ill at ease as he read from a text devoted to treason in the State Department and the giveaway at Yalta—subjects likely to strike a responsive chord among old Red-baiters, but never central to his own passions.[40]

After his kickoff address and press conference, Wallace's customary remarks shifted to the more comfortable terrain of civil rights. Before small-business owners and service clubs he spoke of the "destruction of property rights" and of the "unnatural and unhealthy accumulation of power in the hands of an all-powerful central bureaucracy." He cautioned blue-collar workers about the devastating impact of the Kennedy-Johnson civil rights bill on the hallowed union traditions of seniority, and reminded suburbanites in the handful of Wisconsin cities with a sizable black population of the likelihood of future open-housing measures. And he warned audiences of Eastern European extraction of ominous links between the Soviet Union and supporters of the civil rights measure. For the most part, he avoided verbal pyrotechnics and remained even-tempered and good-humored. Out on the streets of Appleton in nine-degree weather, he assured Wisconsin voters that if the "War Between the States had been fought in Wisconsin instead of Virginia, you would have won in a week."[41]

Wisconsin's political and civic leaders took no chances. To their four hundred union affiliates, AFL-CIO leaders sent a letter branding Wallace a "carpetbagger, a bigot, a racist, and one of the strongest anti-labor spokesmen in America."[42] A coalition of Catholic, Jewish, and Protestant church officials abandoned a long tradition of nonpartisanship and urged followers to repudiate the racist southerner who posed a "threat to the moral quality of our nation and to the basic freedom which every American is entitled to enjoy." State Democratic officials published a pamphlet picturing Governor Reynolds and the still-popular Lyndon Johnson on one page and police dogs attacking blacks on another. Wisconsin's governor even revived the tactics of the "bloody shirt," which had served northern politicians so well after the Civil War. Before voters pulled the lever for Wallace, said Reynolds, they should go to "Vicksburg in Mississippi and visit the cemetery there and visit the graves of Wisconsin men who gave their lives to destroy the institution of slavery."[43]

As the attacks mounted, Wallace embraced the role of the injured victim of slander and misrepresentation. "I have tried to speak the truth, nothing more," he told a Milwaukee rally as election day drew near. In so doing, he had brought down upon himself the hatred of liberals, who had engaged in an "express train of rhetorical abuse." This "emotional wave of propaganda serves the purpose of silencing opposition and of creating such an atmosphere of charged emotionalism that factual knowledge goes by the board."[44]

Reporters who traveled with the Wallace caravan across Wisconsin during that blustery March could never quite pinpoint the moment when his campaign began to take off. The first sign was the uniformly favorable response at small-town luncheons and service clubs where businessmen and professionals warmly applauded his complaints concerning red tape, high taxes, and an overbearing federal government. To Wallace, the turning point came with his April 1 visit to Milwaukee's south side. Bronko Gruber, an ex-Marine Milwaukee tavern owner with strong ties throughout the community, had called Bill Jones and volunteered to arrange a rally at Serb Memorial Hall, a rather grand appellation for a worn, low-ceilinged community center operated by St. Sava Serbian Orthodox church. John Kennedy had packed the place in the Wisconsin primary of 1960; women in babushkas had screamed with excitement as working-class Polish-Americans and Serbian-Americans surged forward to touch the handsome young candidate.[45]

But Kennedy was a northern Irish Catholic. Would anyone show up for Wallace? advisers wondered. And if they did, how could a Deep South segregationist relate to a group of Polish-Americans and Serbian-Americans? Jones argued that to make a dent in the vote-rich "ethnic" precincts of Milwaukee they must take the gamble.

Forty-five minutes before the scheduled speech, only a handful of supporters were in the hall (which seated six hundred), while nearly seventy-five civil rights picketers circled the church parking lot. By seven-thirty, however, more than seven hundred people jammed the stifling hall; another three hundred milled around outside. As Wallace strode into the room, a local band struck up "Way Down upon the Swanee River," then "Dixie." The exuberant audience stumbled through the song in a mixture of Polish and English.

This was Wallace country. Scattered through the south side of Milwaukee were neat single-family houses in blue-collar neighborhoods, proudly insular and intensely patriotic, but still bound by ties of emotion and blood to Poland, Czechoslovakia, Hungary, and Yugoslavia. In the late 1950s and early 1960s, adjoining black neighborhoods had expanded, pushing against the boundaries of the old Eastern European wards. Governor Reynolds's support for a tough new open-housing law had aroused bitter, almost unanimous hostility in the community.

Racial tensions escalated during the first twenty minutes of the rally. Three black Milwaukee civil rights activists who had braved the overwhelmingly white crowd to confront Wallace refused to stand during the national anthem. And as the governor waited in the background to be introduced, one of them, the Reverend Leo Champion, taunted: "Get your dogs out!" The mood turned from threatening to near-homicidal.

Bronko Gruber grabbed the podium microphone. "I'll tell you something about your dogs, padre!" he shouted. "I live on Walnut Street [a main residential thoroughfare on the south side of Milwaukee] and three weeks ago tonight a friend of mine was assaulted by three of your countrymen or whatever you want to call them. . . ." Thunderous applause drowned the rest of his sentence. Gruber, fists clenched, barged ahead. "They beat up old ladies 83-years-old, rape our womenfolk. They mug people. They won't work. They are on relief. How long can we tolerate this? Did I go to Guadalcanal and come back to something like this?"[46] As the audience stood and roared its approval, several men turned menacingly toward Champion.

With a tense smile, Wallace stepped to the podium.

"My message is for all," he began, "and I want all of us to be in good humor tonight." To the jeers of the audience, Champion and his two associates filed out of the room. Having averted the immediate threat of an embarrassing brawl, Wallace swung into his usual harangue, denouncing the treacherous U.S. State Department, which had abandoned the "proud and gallant Poles who fought so bravely." He paid tribute to the deep religious faith of his audience and lashed out at the godless Supreme Court, which had "outlawed Bible reading in schools and led to a move to remove references to God from the Pledge of Allegiance to the flag and the singing of the fourth stanza of 'America' in our schools." But he reserved his strongest criticism for the civil rights bill. The far-reaching measure, he warned the mostly male audience of blue-collar workers, would "destroy the union seniority system and impose racial quotas." The bill would make it "impossible for a home owner to sell his home to whomever he chose," and would plunge community schools into chaos.[47]

A Milwaukee reporter carefully tracked which lines brought the most applause: the governor's attack on the Supreme Court's school prayer decision, his opposition to open housing, and his response to the Communist *Daily World*'s attack on him the previous fall as "America's No. 1 Criminal." ("I am glad I have their opposition!") The newsman also totaled the crowd's ovations: thirty-four, in a forty-minute speech. When Wallace concluded, "a vote for this little governor will let the people in Washington know that we want them to leave our homes, schools, jobs, business and farms alone," the men in Serb Hall leaped to their feet and cheered and clapped for a full five minutes. It took the governor more than an hour to escape the throngs of autograph seekers and admirers.

For two hours he had reveled in the pleasure of absolute rapport with his audience. Not surprisingly, in the years to come he would return to that April evening again and again in his speeches and reminiscences. The utilitarian meeting room was transformed into a grand assembly hall for Milwaukee's blue-collar workers; the crowd of seven hundred mushroomed to fifteen hundred, then grew bigger yet. A decade later, Wallace reconstructed his golden moment: "Thousands of Polish-Americans had come to hear me and with them was a very fine band that kept playing, 'Way Down upon the Swanee River.' . . . Then when we were least expecting anything new, the band struck up 'Dixie' and three thousand or more voices sang 'Dixie' in Polish."[48] No wonder the memory of that evening spilled over the bounds of reality. For the man from Barbour County, Alabama, it was an epiphany. He had been right all along: these chunky Serbs and Hungarians and Poles, these hardworking Catholics, these *Yankees,* had embraced him with the same adoration that marked his passage among the masses of white Alabamians.

On election night, April 7, Wallace donned a feathered bonnet presented by Wisconsin's Winnebago Indians and began an impromptu war dance around the crowded room of his Milwaukee hotel headquarters. "We won without winning!" he shouted as jubilant followers totted up the results. In a race in which expectation was everything, the southerner captured 266,000 votes, more than a third of the 780,000 ballots cast in the Democratic primary. The governor of Wisconsin had said that 100,000 votes would be a catastrophe, recalled a jeering Wallace. "Well, I got 264,000, so there must have been three catastrophes in Wisconsin." He had promised to "shake the eyeteeth of the liberals in Washington," he said. "Consider them shook!"[49]

Political scientists and pollsters struggled to describe the exact contours of the Wallace vote. Was it the product of right-wing Republicans crossing over to endorse his "conservative" views (and to embarrass a sitting Democratic governor and President)? Was it a blue-collar "white backlash" vote, in the "ethnic" working-class districts of the state's urban communities? Or was it a combination of racial and economic conservatism centered in the growing middle-class and upper-middle-class suburbs of the state's cities? Using increasingly sophisticated computer-based methodologies, most political scientists concluded that, despite the Alabamian's dramatically visible support in working-class "ethnic" precincts, the typical Wallace voter was just as likely to be a suburban member of the Rotary Club as a regular at the union hall.[50] In the end, in a state with a small minority population and little visible urban racial conflict, more than one-fourth of almost every major identifiable bloc within the state's Democratic Party had listened to and voted for what a shocked *New York Times* called an "anachronistic Southern demagogue."[51]

Newspaper editorialists, political commentators, and liberal-to-moderate politicians outside the South struggled to explain and to minimize the Alabama governor's Wisconsin showing. It was "not too surprising in a state that let a Joe McCarthy take Bob La Follette's seat" (*New York Post*). "The Wallace vote exceeded all but the highest predictions. For that he can apparently credit the biggest Republican crossover vote on record" (*Milwaukee Journal*). With a "clearcut choice before them, two-thirds of the Democratic voters . . . in Wisconsin's elections . . . rejected an appeal to fear, prejudice and hatred" (*Chicago Daily News*). "The Wisconsin . . . election results show a considerable measure of Northern opposition to the civil rights cause, but . . . certainly they do not show that a majority opposes civil rights" (*St. Louis Post-Dispatch*).[52]

They sounded like a shaky chorus of uneasy youngsters whistling nervously as they walked past a gloomy graveyard.

How much "demagogy" could a free and normally peaceable society endure? asked Richard Rovere, one of the nation's most thoughtful journalist-historians of the 1950s and early 1960s. Senator Joseph McCarthy, at the height of his reckless and irresponsible career, had the good opinion of fifty percent of American voters. But Wallace, far more than McCarthy in his day, was a figure outside the mainstream. Despite the "current efforts of liberals to discount the Wallace showing, the fact is that there are few, if any, of them who have not been astonished and dismayed."[53]

Other journalists argued the precise level of Wallace's strength, the makeup of his emerging constituency, and the long-run implications of his unexpected showing. Unasked were even more perplexing questions. Did a third of Wisconsin's Democratic voters agree with the record he had compiled as governor of Alabama, a record marked by explicit racism and a willingness to exploit the darkest impulses of his white constituents? Or were a sizable number of voters simply willing to allow him to cut himself loose from his past and reinvent himself? There had been several "new" Nixons during the former vice president's long career. Could there be a new Wallace?

WITHIN seventy-two hours after Wallace's strong showing in Wisconsin, dozens of print and television reporters descended on Indiana in preparation for that state's May 5 primary. Walter Cronkite and CBS moved the network's evening news broadcast to a storefront in downtown Indianapolis for a series of broadcasts. By mid-April, Democratic governor Matthew Welsh's press secretary was trying to keep track of more than two dozen major journalists including NBC's Frank McGee and ABC's William Lawrence, David Broder of the *Washington Star,* Joe Cumming from *Newsweek,* Charles Bartlett of the *Chicago Sun-Times,* Robert Baker of the *Washington Post,* and Austin Wehrwein of the *New York Times.* George Wallace might or might not have "shaken the eyeteeth" of the nation's liberals, but he had certainly ignited the pack instincts of modern American journalism.

Wallace, constantly manipulating television's infatuation with visual action, dramatic confrontation, and punchy sound bites, effortlessly set his own agenda. The usual two or three minutes of air coverage allowed only a colorful charge by the challenger in a highly visual setting and a complex, defensive reaction by Governor Welsh. "Without any conscious bias," fumed the editor of the *Nation,* "the television cameras automatically focus on him and he projects very well."[54]

The men who surrounded George Wallace had little firsthand knowledge of politics north of Chattanooga, but they did know that Indiana had strong ties to white southern cultural and racial attitudes. During the 1920s, there were more Klansmen in Indiana than in any other state, and, reportedly, Wallace mistakenly believed that Indiana (rather than Georgia) was the birthplace of the modern Ku Klux Klan.[55] In the mid-1950s Asa Carter had tried to organize vigilante groups in a half-dozen midwestern cities, including industrial Gary, Indiana, and Cleveland, Ohio. Without constant attention, his cadres soon withered, but he had been encouraged by the enthusiastic response of "ethnic" blue-collar workers who resented the encroachment of blacks into their neighborhoods.[56]

In 1964, Indiana had less than a six percent minority population, much of it centered along the southern shore of Lake Michigan, just east of Chicago. (The steelmaking city of Gary hovered between forty-five and fifty percent black.) Though residents had experienced little overt conflict, they were saturated with media coverage of Chicago's growing racial unrest.[57] As the Indiana campaign got under way, Carter and fellow Klan leader Robert Shelton scouted out the state from the service-station pay phone of a sympathetic fellow Klansman.

Governor Welsh had prepared for the campaign by sending a reconnaissance team to Wisconsin. Well before the final vote, he warned that the southerner would be a formidable candidate. Unlike Wisconsin's Reynolds, who had run with little help from his state's Democratic Party, Welsh worked tirelessly to pull together factions throughout the Hoosier state. Local party functionaries, union officials, and church leaders had spoken out in Wisconsin, but in Indiana a smooth-running press operation working out of the governor's office coordinated the attack.[58] Even Lyndon Johnson, who had remained aloof from the primaries, suddenly found cause to fly to the state to be photographed arm-in-arm with the governor.[59]

Welsh was convinced that only a full-scale assault on the integrity of the Alabama governor could shake him into abandoning the mild-mannered persona that he had affected in his first primary. In a series of statewide speeches, he challenged the voters of Indiana to look behind the mask of the smiling interloper:

> *This is the man who tolerated the presence of billboards in his state before the assassination [of President Kennedy] which demanded, 'K.O. the Kennedys.'*
>
> *This is the man whose beliefs were responsible for the deaths of innocent children in the bombing of a Sunday school class in a Montgomery [sic] Church.*
>
> *This is the man who stood by while dogs were set upon human beings and fire hoses were turned on groups of peaceful demonstrators.*[60]

To each bitter assault Wallace had a stock answer: "I have the highest regard for Governor Welsh. He is a fine man."[61]

Students at Earlham, a Quaker college in Richmond, Indiana, tried the silent treatment (it badly unnerved the candidate), but at Notre Dame, hundreds of booing hecklers almost drowned out his speech in the university field house.[62] Still Wallace stuck to his campaign message: "How many of you folks are in favor of the civil rights bill?" he would ask. Hands would go up from most of the audience. "I see. And how many of you have *read* the bill?" There was always a pause while everyone turned from left to right for a quick house count. "About four or five," Wallace would announce with a grin. "You think I'm a racist because I oppose this bill. What am I to think of you, who support it without knowing what's in it?"[63]

On a late night ride from Vincennes University back to Indianapolis with Associated Press national correspondent Jules Loh, an exhausted Wallace let the mask of control and self-confidence slip. "You know what I'd like to do someday?" he said, drawing long on one of his cigars. "I'd like to go into one of these places and tell them what they expect to hear—just to see how they'd react."

"What do you think they expect to hear?" asked Loh.

"They expect me to amble out on the stage and say, 'Hi, yall. Sho good to see yall. I'm jes an ign'rant ol' hookwormy redneck from Alabama come up to visit yall. Ain't had no education and didn't wear no shoes 'til I was thirty, but I come to ask yall for yall's vote.' " He paused, then laughed sardonically.[64]

When the final returns came in on May 6 and Wallace had taken only thirty percent of the vote, Matthew Welsh claimed a great moral victory. But the state's largest newspaper, the *Indianapolis Star*, dismissed any comforting rationalizations. "If any responsible official had suggested six months ago that a segregationist from the deep South could poll such a vote in Indiana, he would have been hooted into silence and shuffled quietly into obscurity." The election results, said a disappointed editor, "speak for themselves."[65]

Back in Washington, Lyndon Johnson scoffed at the Wallace candidacy. "He got 24 percent of the vote in Wisconsin and a little less than 20 percent of the vote in Indiana." (Johnson's dubious summaries were made possible by combining the total Democratic and Republican primary votes.) "I wouldn't think that would be any overwhelming endorsement of a man's record."[66] Privately, the President was disturbed by the way in which the challenger's midwestern foray had flustered the troops on Capitol Hill. Georgia's Senator Richard Russell had pledged that southerners would "go down fighting with our boots on at the last ditch," but by the spring of 1964, he was a demoralized commander-in-chief. Wallace's strong showing in the Wisconsin primary, observed Johnson, gave white southern senators the "will to keep on fighting the civil rights measure until the liberal ranks began to crumble."[67]

By endorsing a strong civil rights bill, Johnson knew he had destroyed much of what was left of his party's old base among white voters in the South. What if the Wallace vote indicated an insurrection among northern Democrats as well? Just southeast of Chicago lay Indiana's Lake and Porter counties, dominated by the steel mills of Hammond and Gary, a Democratic stronghold in a Republican-leaning state. Even though George Wallace had not made a single stop in the two counties, he had swept past Welsh with fifty-three percent of the vote. White suburban voters there and in inner-city "ethnic" and blue-collar communities as well had flocked to the polls to protest the civil rights policies of the Johnson administration. "I've been a Democrat all my life," said one Gary union official. But he had voted for Wallace, and he would vote for Goldwater if he were nominated by the Republicans. "We've got Negroes in my union and they're O.K., but eighty-five per cent of the Negroes in this town are too pushy."[68]

By all accounts, Maryland's party leaders had scattered when the filing deadline for the state's primary approached and the President still lacked a stand-in, but the crafty Texan coaxed the slow-footed Senator Daniel Brewster into the White House for a one-on-one session. He administered the full Lyndon Baines Johnson arm-twisting-knee-squeezing treatment—"Danny, I want you to be *me* in the primary"—and then cast the glazed Brewster into the pit to do battle with a former bantamweight champion who had already bloodied two far shrewder politicians.[69]

A twice-wounded ex-Marine and a comfortably wealthy member of the gentry, Maryland's junior senator had captured almost effortlessly the state Democratic Party's Byzantine fiefdoms of big-city ethnic bosses, suburban reformers, and rural courthouse gangs of the Eastern Shore. The President's men now made certain that he had what he needed in the way of funds for advertising and a series of political photo opportunities. A joint Johnson-Brewster appearance at Pimlico's Preakness, a social affair at the White House cohosted by Mrs. Brewster and Lady Bird, "spontaneous" Brewster-Johnson film footage at the White House to be used in television advertisements—all were designed to appeal to Maryland's middle-class suburbanites, even to well-to-do moderate Republicans who knew their friend to be honorable and, in Murray Kempton's vivid phrase, "a gentleman and uncorrupted by uncomfortably immoderate brilliance."[70]

Dutifully Brewster went forth to battle on the *Today* show, first (wisely) refusing to be drawn into predictions about his opponent's strength and then (foolishly) predicting to correspondent Robert MacNeil that the Alabama governor was "on the downhill side now, he's gotten less in Indiana than he did in Wisconsin. . . . He will get a number of votes. It will not be a significant showing." No one could take George Wallace seriously as a presidential candidate, insisted Brewster. "How screwy do you get?"[71]

An exhausted Wallace staggered through a hectic ten-day series of speeches from suburban Washington to the Eastern Shore. He was clearly more on home ground in Maryland; his attacks were biting and graphic in their depiction of the horrors that awaited a nation under the heel of the President's proposed civil rights legislation. As he elaborated on its certain consequences for unions, schools, and peaceful neighborhoods, he struggled to evoke the fear of blacks without ever using the "n" word. It was as if T. E. Lawrence had sat down at his desk to write *The Seven Pillars of Wisdom* without mentioning Arabs.

If the Johnson civil rights bill was enacted, Wallace explained to a Baltimore neighborhood rally of predominantly blue-collar workers, federal officials would soon "tell an employer who he's got to employ. If a man's got 100 Japanese-Lutherans working for him and there's 100 Chinese-Baptists unemployed, he's got to let some of the Japanese-Lutherans go so he can make room for some of the Chinese-Baptists. And of course, what does that do for your seniority rights? It destroys them!"[72]

After journalists began to refer to the Wallace tour as an "oriental junket," Wallace raised the specter of an open-housing law which would force homeowners to sell to anyone, "even if it's a man with green eyes and blue teeth."[73]

As support for Wallace edged up toward forty percent among Maryland's Democratic voters, Bill Jones urged him to abandon his cautious no-risk strategy. The Dorchester County Business and Citizens Association had invited him to give a speech in the Eastern Shore town of Cambridge. In the early nineteenth century, this section of Maryland had been the heart of a slave culture as entrenched as the Deep South's; during the Civil War, thousands of whites from the region had fought for the Confederacy. One hundred years later, the state's anthem ("Maryland, My Maryland") still rang with protests over Abraham Lincoln's forcible overthrow of the pro-Confederate state legislature: "The despot's heel is on thy shore / Maryland. His torch is at thy temple door / Maryland."[74]

Resentful over its domination by the population-heavy city of Baltimore and the Maryland suburbs of Washington, the Eastern Shore remained as segregated as any Deep South community. Each year as legislators from the region gathered in the taverns of Annapolis for the sessions of the General Assembly, they sang with gusto: "We don't give a damn for the whole State of Maryland, we're from the Eastern Shore!" For the federal government, said one observer, "that goes double."[75]

Street protests begun in Cambridge in 1962 had led to the passage of a city ordinance requiring equal access to public accommodations. After white voters successfully staged a referendum to repeal the measure, angry black residents took to the streets again under the leadership of flamboyant homegrown activist Gloria Richardson. By the spring of 1964, Cambridge—rocked by round-the-clock street demonstrations, arson, and sporadic sniper fire—had come under martial law. Several hundred state Guardsmen struggled to maintain a fragile peace. A visit by Wallace, Bill Jones pointed out, would dramatize the links between his defense of segregation in Alabama and white backlash in the state of Maryland. Whites in the state who opposed integration would "know that Wallace was with them." After delaying his decision until the afternoon of May 11, the governor reluctantly concluded that a last-minute withdrawal would suggest that he was afraid to confront his opponents. Morosely, he gave aides the go-ahead.[76]

On May 11, the Wallace caravan, heavily guarded by state and local police, drove into the tense city just before nightfall. While Guardsmen patrolled the downtown, heavily armed sentries manned highway checkpoints and searched every car for weapons. To the spooked Alabama contingent, it looked like a war zone. The governor drew an overflow crowd of two thousand whites to the Cambridge firehouse, but reporters found him un-usually subdued, even distracted. He stumbled over some of his best lines, and as soon as the speech had ended, aides whisked him away from waiting fans. They lingered only long enough (said one acerbic observer) to "fairly snatch the paper box containing the collection."[77]

Within minutes of his departure, Gloria Richardson marched into the streets and was arrested with twelve of her followers. Television cameras recorded protesters lying down in the town's main street, vague distant shots of rock-throwing teenagers, and National Guardsmen lobbing a handful of tear gas canisters. Measured by the standards of demonstrations over the past two years, it was distinctly minor league. But thirty-six hours later, a two-month-old baby living near the disturbances died, and Mrs. Richardson's committee issued a statement indicating that it "appeared" that the baby had died because of the inhalation of tear gas.[78]

The last thing George Wallace wanted was a reminder of the deaths of the four young girls in Birmingham. "I told you we should not have gone to Cambridge!" he shouted at his bodyguards and aides. For the next few hours, he spoke to no one in his entourage.[79]

Within twenty-four hours, Maryland's chief medical examiner completed an autopsy: the baby had died of a congenital heart defect. And the violent confrontation outside the city auditorium between Richardson's followers and National Guard troops seemed, on balance, to have helped rather than hurt Wallace's campaign. The voters of Maryland watched the films of the angry demonstrators, one Cambridge merchant told a reporter, and then they "see Governor Wallace on TV and they can't believe the mild little man they see is the bad man they keep reading and hearing about. What he says makes a lot of sense down here."[80]

By mid-May, Daniel Brewster had written off the Eastern Shore as a lost cause, and the signs from the "ethnic" neighborhoods of inner-city Baltimore were hardly more encouraging. A much-advertised visit to eastern Baltimore's Quo Vadis Club, home of the city's Polish-American Democrats, had been an advance man's nightmare. When the candidate arrived with newsmen, they found only a half-dozen sullen club officers surrounded by several unopened kegs of beer.[81] Desperately, the senator clung to Lyndon Johnson's popularity and concentrated on the vote-rich precincts of Baltimore and the Washington bedroom communities of suburban Montgomery and Prince Georges counties. Wallace and his "pack of mindless thugs have been stewed in the vile corruption of the same ruthless power that one finds at either end of the political spectrum, right or left," railed the once-genial Danny Brewer.[82] Alabama's governor was described as a "professional liar . . . an aspiring dictator and a certain enemy of the Constitution of the United States."[83] On May 18, the night before the final vote, Maryland Democrats went all-out with a television blitz throughout the state, and Brewster managed to corral the popular Edward Kennedy for an evening of street-corner rallies throughout blue-collar Baltimore.

The next morning, nearly a quarter-million voters pulled the Wallace lever. By one estimate he carried over ninety percent of the white voters in the eight counties of the Eastern Shore.[84] They "went to the polls with big grins on their faces," said one small-town newspaper editor. "I never saw anything like it. They were going to show Uncle Sam that they had had it."[85] Wallace's strength reached across the state. He won sixteen of twenty-three counties, as well as the state capital of Annapolis. In Baltimore, "ethnic" neighborhoods that had given John Kennedy solid two-to-one majorities in 1960 went down the line for Wallace. "If it hadn't been for the nigger bloc vote," he complained, "we'd have won it all."[86]

His observation, however tastelessly expressed, was accurate. Black voters turned out in twice the numbers usual for a primary election. That turnout, combined with the solid support of white suburbanites in populous Montgomery and Prince Georges counties, and some creative vote returns from Baltimore, allowed the President's stand-in to claim a victory with fifty-three percent of the vote. Brewster's bare majority was greeted with relief and hailed as a great victory for the President. At last the mischief-maker from Alabama had done his worst: he had run out of primaries.

DANIEL Brewster had described his opponent as "sort of like a skyrocket. He's going up with a burst of speed and a lot of noise and light, and he's going to fall back down and be forgotten."[87] Even as George Wallace celebrated his near-victory on May 20, Senate Republican Minority Leader Everett Dirksen summoned the press to his office to announce that he would urge fellow

Republicans to accept the Kennedy-Johnson civil rights bill. Not only did he support the bill, but he and other moderately conservative Republicans would cooperate with liberal Democrats to invoke cloture, so ending the stonewalling of southern senators. "Wallace won't affect the final vote on this bill," Dirksen assured reporters. "On that you can stake the next two tea crops in China."[88]

On July 2, one year and twenty-three days after George Wallace's stand in the schoolhouse door, more than 150 legislators, senior members of the Justice Department, and a contingent of civil rights spokesmen led by Martin Luther King and Roy Wilkins gathered in the East Room of the White House. At 6:45 P.M., the television lights came on; Lyndon Johnson entered to polite applause and sat behind a large desk. His message to the nation was brief, less than a thousand words. "We believe that all men are created equal. Yet many are denied equal treatment . . . it cannot continue. Our Constitution, the foundation of our Republic, forbids it. Morality forbids it." He paused. "And the law I will sign tonight forbids it." With the first of seventy-one pens, Lyndon Johnson began signing the nation's most far-reaching civil rights measure since Reconstruction.[89]

FORTY-eight hours later, George Wallace joined former Mississippi governor Ross Barnett at Lakewood Park in the middle of Atlanta's largest white working-class neighborhood. The July Fourth "Patriots' Rally Against Tyranny" was sponsored by Georgia's Lester "Ax Handle" Maddox, a fanatical defender of segregation who had earned his nickname after wielding his unorthodox weapon against civil rights demonstrators in the parking lot of his chicken restaurant. Maddox had invited Ku Klux Klan Grand Dragon Calvin Craig to share the spotlight with the Alabama governor; Craig later described the Wallace effort as "the finest speech I've ever heard presented."[90] (It is not surprising that Craig responded so warmly; fellow Klansman Asa Carter had written the speech.) It lived up to its advance billing as a "no-holds-barred disection [sic] of the Communistic blueprint for the Sovietization of American society."[91]

Just before the Alabama governor stepped onstage, three black protesters—more brave than wise—began booing. Two white factory workers in the crowd of eleven thousand looked at one another and, without a word, picked up their folding chairs and began beating the men about the head and shoulders. Within seconds, they were joined by a half-dozen other white spectators who continued to kick and pummel the protesters even after they fell to the ground. The surrounding crowd shouted "Kill 'em!" "Hit 'em!" and "We want Wallace!"[92]

As police hustled the bloodied men to safety, George Wallace plunged into his speech. Gone was the smiling southerner who had jollied the Rotarians in Appleton and teased the students of Notre Dame. His shirt drenched in sweat in the ninety-five-degree temperature, his lips curled into an angry snarl, his was once again the voice that Alabamians had come to know so well: the voice of defiance and resistance.

It seemed a "cruel irony," as the nation prepared to celebrate 188 years of the principles of freedom laid out in the Declaration of Independence, "that the President of the United States has just signed into law the most monstrous piece of legislation ever enacted . . . a fraud, a sham and a hoax, this bill will live in infamy." He had tried to break through the curtain of leftist lies in his presidential campaign, he told the rapt audience, but the nation's newspapers—"run and operated by left-wing liberals, Communist sympathizers and members of the Americans for Democratic Action and other Communist front organizations"—had deceived the American people.[93] They would not tell the truth and the truth was simple: the Civil Rights Act of 1964 came straight out of the *Communist Manifesto.*

"I do not call the members of the United States Supreme Court Communists," he told his audience. "But I do say, and I submit for your judgment the fact that every single decision of the Court in the past ten years . . . has been decided against freedom and in favor of tyranny." The "chief, if not the only beneficiary of the present court's rulings, have [*sic*] been duly and lawfully convicted criminals, Communists, atheists, and clients of vociferous left-wing minority groups."

The "liberal left-wingers have passed it [the Civil Rights Act]. Now let them employ some 'pinknik' social engineers in Washington to figure out what to do with it," Wallace told the cheering crowd.[94] "We must destroy the power to dictate, to forbid, to require, to demand, to distribute, to edict. . . . We must revitalize a government founded in this nation on faith in God!"

Wayne Greenhaw of the *Alabama Journal* watched the performance with a mixture of awe and horror. Long after the Alabama governor had ended his talk, thousands of hardworking men and women stood in the blazing sun and chanted, "George! George! George!" as their hero, holding aloft both arms in the V-for-victory symbol, strutted back and forth across the stage. Wallace had delivered one of the most powerfully racist speeches he had ever heard, said Greenhaw. The governor had "never uttered the word 'nigger.'" But the code phrases were there: "the boot of tyranny," "the power to dictate," "the framework of our priceless freedoms." Whose priceless freedoms? asked Greenhaw. Those of the white people of a collapsing social order. And George Wallace "cried out for their cause."[95]

Perhaps the adulation of the crowds tilted Wallace's usually acute political antennae; perhaps he had become so addicted to being treated as a weighty presence on the nation's political scene that he refused to face reality. He had performed far better in the primaries than anyone had anticipated, but his success had been possible precisely because a vote for him had no consequences. For the disgruntled, it was the perfect temper tantrum. But as the more serious business of electing a President of the United States got under way, he was out of the national political loop.

NEITHER friends nor foes of the civil rights bill had been surprised when Barry Goldwater sided with southern senators in opposing the closing of debate. But in mid-June, as the vote neared, the Arizona senator confided to Nebraska Republican Carl Curtis and to Everett Dirksen his intention to become one of only a handful of northern conservatives voting against the legislation. Curtis, his floor manager in the upcoming Republican convention, had hoped that Goldwater would express objections to the measure and then reluctantly vote for it, thus retaining the favor of southern supporters but not alienating moderates. Dirksen had never been an arm-twister, but he warned his colleague of the negative effects upon his almost certain presidential candidacy in the fall.[96]

He "didn't convince me," said Goldwater. As early as 1961 he had bluntly told a group of Republican activists in Atlanta that the GOP was "not going to get the Negro vote . . . so we ought to go hunting where the ducks are." For disenchanted white southern voters—the ducks—to abandon traditional Democratic ties, the Republican Party would have to leave the integration issue to the states—and to the national Democratic Party. "I would not like to see my party assume it is the role of the federal government to enforce integration in the schools," he concluded.[97]

On June 18, Goldwater ended any doubts concerning his proposed vote on the civil rights bill in a brief speech which—in substance if not in tone—could have been written by George Wallace. While he personally opposed racial discrimination, national legislation would create a "federal police force of mammoth proportions." It would result in the development of an " 'informer' psychology" in which neighbors spied upon neighbors, workers upon workers, and businessmen upon businessmen. "These, the Federal police force and an 'informer' psychology, are the hallmarks of the police state and landmarks in the destruction of a free society."[98]

By every poll, Goldwater was an ideal opponent for the popular Johnson outside the South. Despite the Arizona senator's pleasant and easygoing manner, his positions placed him well outside the mainstream of public opinion in the early 1960s. At one time or another, he had come out in favor of making Social Security "voluntary," abolishing the popular Tennessee Valley Authority, and returning to the gold standard. In addition, his careless references to nuclear weapons ("I want to lob one [a nuclear missile] into the men's room of the Kremlin and make sure I hit it") left the impression that he was a genial Dr. Strangelove.[99]

But Goldwater, already the dream candidate for American conservatives who had railed against mealy-mouthed GOP moderates from Alf Landon through Dwight Eisenhower and Richard Nixon, became the hero of white segregationists across the South. Of the region's 375 Republican delegates who would go to the party's convention in San Francisco, 366 would cast their votes for the senator from Arizona. This new generation of ideologically committed southern Republicans was white, mostly male, far wealthier than the usual delegate to either party, and economically as well as racially on the far right of the political spectrum. In a post-convention survey response, eighty percent of the southern delegates rejected *any* federal action on civil rights, even when blacks were denied the right to vote, and ninety percent opposed federal funding for unemployment insurance, medical care, housing, or education. Ninety-seven percent disagreed with the statement that the "role of the political party is to reconcile different interests"; it should instead "take clear stands on issues." These were the people who responded to Goldwater's call for "a choice not an echo."[100] But Goldwatermania was not restricted to well-heeled party activists. Throughout the South, and particularly in the Deep South where the core of Wallace support lay, bumper stickers for the Republican nominee materialized on rusting old pickups as well as on the well-polished Cadillacs in country-club parking lots.

The solid backing of southerners and the careful organizing of conservative Goldwater supporters across the country paid off. By the eve of the Republican convention he was the odds-on favorite for the Republican nomination.

A GALLUP poll released on July 13 showed that support for Wallace had declined across the board except in Alabama, where he had simply banished national Democrats from the ballot. (Voters could choose either a slate pledged to Wallace under the "Democratic" label, or the Republican electors.) In a hypothetical three-way race with Goldwater and Johnson, the governor ran third among southern voters; his support outside the region collapsed to less than three percent. While the governor continued threats to mount a third-party campaign in the South, he had done little staff work and had put together no campaign organization. Only in neighboring Mississippi had state political leaders been willing to endorse his plan for placing a slate of independent electors on the ballot.

George Wallace, suddenly left high and dry, summoned legal aides Cecil Jackson and Seymore Trammell for a last-ditch gamble.

Jim Martin, a staunch Goldwater partisan, was mowing the lawn of his suburban house in Gadsden, Alabama, the day before his departure for the Republican convention in San Francisco. His wife called him inside to take a call from the governor.

Wallace told Martin that he had dispatched a state plane to the Gadsden airport. He wanted him to fly to Montgomery to meet him secretly in the governor's suite at the Jefferson Davis Hotel.

"I'm going to run down to Montgomery . . . ," Martin explained as he grabbed his car keys. "Wallace has got something he wants to see me about."

"Well, you got on your old clothes," protested Margaret Martin.

He told her not to worry, he would be right back.

Sharp-eyed security men made certain that no one saw Martin on his visit. The young Republican later described the three-hour meeting only in the most discreet generalities. Wallace, he said, had suggested himself as an ideal choice for Goldwater's vice-presidential running mate. When Martin (dumbstruck) failed to respond appropriately, the governor continued, "Now you've got to pretend that this is your original idea. . . . It didn't come from me, but you think you can persuade me."[101]

Seymore Trammell had a more colorful recollection of the encounter.

With "all my big victories of the past two years," Trammell quoted Wallace, "it must be apparent to a one-eyed nigguh who can't see good outa his other eye, that me and Goldwater would be a winning ticket. We'd have the South locked up, then him and me could concentrate on the industrial states of the North and win."[102]

Although Goldwater was the strong favorite to capture the Republican nomination, his control of the convention rested upon a narrow margin. Trammell urged Martin quietly to round up southern delegates and tell them to withhold their votes unless the Arizonan took Wallace on the ticket.[103]

A Goldwater-Wallace combination would be very strong in the South, Martin diplomatically agreed, but would be an "unknown factor" in the rest of the country. Desperate to avoid antagonizing the governor (who was technically still committed to a third-party run), Martin assured him that, when he got out to San Francisco, "I'll tell Mr. Goldwater."

"No," said Wallace emphatically. "I want you to go tonight."

Martin looked down at his yard clothes and dirty shoes. "Well obviously, I'm not prepared to go, you know. . . . I don't have any money with me; I made my plans to leave in a couple of days."

"That's no problem," said Wallace.[104]

Seymore Trammell counted out a thousand dollars in cash. Wallace loudly ordered him to stay in touch with Martin so that he could "get more money as he needs it."

Martin stuffed the money into his pocket and promised that he would "look into the matter."[105] There seemed to him to be at least a "gentleman's understanding" that, in return for his conveying the vice-presidential proposal, Wallace would abandon any notions of a third-party candidacy in the fall.[106]

After Martin's departure, Trammell said ruefully: "I think we just pissed away a thousand dollars."

"Well, goddammit, it ain't the first thousand we've pissed away, and it won't be the last," said Wallace.[107]

Martin did not rush off to San Francisco in his work pants, but he kept his promise. On Sunday afternoon, July 12, with the official opening of the convention only twenty-four hours away, Goldwater staff member Vern Stephens escorted Wallace's emissary to a secret meeting with the Arizona senator on the roof of the Mark Hopkins Hotel.

While they stood overlooking the bay, Goldwater and Stephens listened intently as Martin outlined his mission. "Mr. Wallace has suggested that he would like to be a candidate with you as your vice presidential nominee on the Republican ticket." Across the street on an adjacent roof, an enterprising freelance photographer for *Life* magazine focused his telephoto lens and began snapping away. Stephens, hands in his pockets, pensively stared down at the roof; a shirtsleeved Goldwater, tie askew, looked as though someone had just reported a death in the family.[108]

It just wasn't possible, Goldwater explained. Over the days leading up to the convention, he had used every form of flattery to persuade Wallace ("a very able man," he kept saying) to quit the race. Only that afternoon, he had emphasized to the Florida caucus just how important a Wallace withdrawal would be to his candidacy. The Alabama governor, he said, would be "a greater determinant about what the South does than either President Johnson or I."[109] But inviting him onto the ticket was another matter. Quite apart from the leverage this possibility might give to his liberal opponents, he already had the support of the South. Moreover, he added, George Wallace was still a Democrat and "this *was* a Republican convention."[110]

His assignment completed, Martin called Montgomery to relay the disappointing news.[111]

When Barry Goldwater accepted his party's nomination on July 16, he probably guaranteed his defeat with a fiery speech ("Extremism in the defense of liberty is no vice!") which offered no quarter to liberals and moderates within his own party. He also further cemented his position as the idol of conservative southerners. Strom Thurmond of South Carolina had already officially jumped ship from the Democratic party, and other conservative Democrats in the region were running for cover. Pressure increased for Wallace to abandon plans for a third-party candidacy. South Carolina textile magnate Roger Milliken, Thurmond's financial godfather and a powerful force in conservative causes, expressed his firm belief that it would be in the governor's long-term best interest to withdraw and leave the field open for Goldwater.[112]

Three days after the convention ended, George Wallace appeared before a national audience on *Face the Nation*. He did not decide to quit the race—or at least he did not disclose his decision to his aides—until the Saturday afternoon plane ride up to Washington on the eve of his television appearance. Early on Sunday morning, July 19, Bill Jones sat in the governor's room in the Washington Hotel and typed out an official statement of withdrawal with three smudged carbons on hotel stationery. When the lights came on in the Washington CBS studio, he distributed the three copies to newsmen waiting in a nearby anteroom. Wallace responded to the first question by reciting from memory almost the exact phrasing of his official statement. His goal in the campaign, he began, was not personal aggrandizement but to "get a message to the leadership of both national parties . . . to think more of states' rights and local government; to bring a halt to this destruction of individual liberty and freedom.

"Today," he continued, "we hear more states' rights talk than we have heard in the last quarter-century." Modestly, he attributed this change to the upsurge of support he had drawn in Wisconsin, Indiana, and Maryland. "I was the instrument through which this message was sent to the high councils of both major political parties."

"My mission has been accomplished. I am therefore withdrawing as a candidate for President of the United States."

As the first race riots of the decade—"Goldwater rallies," in the gloomy description of Democratic strategists—broke out in late July and early August in half a dozen northeastern cities, Lyndon Johnson's aides feared the issue might jeopardize his reelection campaign.

But the tides of racial violence flowed in both directions in the summer of 1964. Michael (Mickey) Schwerner and Andrew Goodman joined more than two hundred northern college students in Mississippi as part of Freedom Summer, an ambitious effort to register black voters in the heart of the Black Belt. Neshoba County deputy sheriff Cecil Price arrested the two on June 21 along with Mississippian James Chaney, a black co-worker. Schwerner, "the Jew boy with the beard," was the real target of the operation. Price released the men from the county jail in Philadelphia, Mississippi, just after ten P.M., then led a caravan of armed Klansmen on a high-speed chase until they forced Schwerner's station wagon to the side of a deserted two-lane road ten miles southwest of the town. The deputy sheriff shoved the men into the backseat of his police cruiser. Followed by a caravan of armed whites, he drove down a dark side road into the dense piney woods of Lowndes County and stopped.

While the three civil rights workers waited tensely, Price conferred with the vigilantes. After a few minutes, Wayne Roberts, a twenty-six-year-old former high school football star from Meridian and an ex-Marine, walked over to the car, pistol in hand. Opening the back door, he dragged Schwerner from the car so that they faced each other next to a narrow roadside ditch.

"Are you that nigger-lover?" he softly asked.

The two dozen heavily armed men who surrounded the car wore no disguises. For veteran Mississippi activist Schwerner, it must have been a terrifying tip-off to their plans. Somehow the young New Yorker—still wearing his bright blue Mets baseball cap—kept his composure and began: "Sir, I know just how you feel. . . ."

Roberts shoved the gun up against Schwerner's heart and fired. Methodically, he returned to the car, hauled a numbed Andrew Goodman to his feet, and killed him with one shot to the chest. A second Klansman, James Jordan, pulled Chaney out of the car and—in quick succession—he and Roberts shot the young civil rights worker. As Chaney lay dying on the ground, Jordan, a thirty-eight-year-old mobile home salesman, delivered a final shot into the head of his victim.

"Well," Jordan told his accomplice, "you didn't leave me nothing but a nigger, but at least I killed me a nigger."[113]

For more than six weeks, Mississippi politicians, including Senator James Eastland, repeated rumors that the three civil rights workers were alive and well and perpetrating a hoax on the state's innocent citizens.[114] (The men were most often reported to be in Cuba.) As the FBI began its search, Wallace traveled to Mississippi to join Governor Paul Johnson in addressing a huge anti–civil rights rally in Jackson. In the press conference that followed, Wallace pointedly referred to the "report by Col. Al Lingo . . . that three persons resembling the group [of missing civil rights workers] had been seen in Alabama Tuesday." [115] When newsmen pressed for further details, Johnson gave them a conspiratorial wink. "Governor Wallace and I are the only two people who know where they are," he quipped, "and we're not telling."[116]

Local whites never doubted that the men were dead. (When FBI agents dragged the Pearl River, a Neshoba County farmer suggested: "Hey, why don't you hold a welfare check over the water. That'll get that nigger to the surface."[117]) As the FBI broadened the search, additional agents monitored the harassment of Freedom Summer volunteers. By the Bureau's conservative accounting, Mississippi lawmen arrested nearly a thousand civil rights workers, often on bogus charges such as vagrancy and incitement to riot. Night riders killed six workers, wounded twenty-nine, and firebombed or dynamited a dozen black homes and churches. Finally, one week before the Republican convention in San Francisco, FBI agents—acting on the tip of an informer they paid $30,000—located the bodies of Schwerner, Goodman, and Chaney under an earthen dam on a farm only a few miles from where they had been killed.

Having cast his political fate into the hands of diehard defenders of south-ern rights and local self-government, Goldwater discovered they were a heavy load to carry in the rest of the nation. While the great white backlash that Alabama's governor had supposedly ignited was alive and well in the Deep South, outside the region it had vanished like the snows marking the Wisconsin primary.

Early in the summer, Goldwater and his southern allies had tried every form of flattery and cajolery to get Wallace to abandon his third-party effort. When he actually withdrew, however, and the senator was asked to com-ment, he said, "I never gave this Wallace thing much thought."[118] To rub salt in the wound (and a bored shrug was, to George Wallace, a mortal wound), Goldwater made it clear that he wanted nothing to do with the governor of Alabama. After Republicans announced plans for a campaign rally in Mont-gomery in late August, Bill Jones noticed that Wallace would be away on a speaking tour. In a discreet call to Goldwater headquarters, he volunteered to change the schedule so that his boss could publicly welcome the Repub-lican nominee. "I was told, quite firmly, that Goldwater would prefer for Wallace to keep his speaking engagements and be out of the state when he came in," said a bitter Jones.[119]

Although Lyndon Johnson's Democrats allowed the Alabama governor to deliver a choleric attack on the Civil Rights Act to the platform committee meeting in Miami, party leaders were almost as insulting as the Republicans. They didn't even deign to respond.[120]

By mid-October, Barry Goldwater's reckless, shoot-from-the-hip political comments had convinced most Americans that he was temperamentally unsuited for the presidency. As Lyndon Johnson put the question: Regardless of how you feel about civil rights or any other domestic issue, do you want *this* man to have his finger a few inches away from the nuclear button? Only in the Deep South did the answer seem to be a resounding yes.

In Alabama, polls indicated that Goldwater would lose the national elec-tion, but would sweep the state. Republicans cursed their lack of foresight in not putting up more candidates for office while terrified Democrats pleaded with Wallace to take the stump on behalf of endangered members of his own party. "For heaven's sake, George," one incumbent congressman reportedly told him, "you keep saying you're an *Alabama* Democrat and it's us *Ala-bama* Democrats who are getting ready to go down the chutes."[121] But for the most part the governor sat out the election, sulking, his critics agreed, because he was not allowed to play a decisive role.

Lyndon Johnson rolled to victory in one of the great landslides of the twentieth century. Barry Goldwater carried only six states—Arizona and Dixie's heartland: Mississippi, Alabama, Louisiana, Georgia, and South Caro-lina. In Mississippi, he took more than ninety percent of the white vote in silk-stocking, blue-collar, and rural white precincts. In the long run, Goldwater's win in the Deep South held great potential for the Republican party; indeed, the number of Republican congressmen from those states jumped from zero to seven.

Five of those seven came from Alabama; whites pulled the straight Republican ticket in record numbers. Gleeful opponents noted that Wallace's strategy had turned out to be too clever by half. By making it impossible for Alabamians to vote for Lyndon Johnson (the only choices at the top of the ticket were Goldwater supporters and those committed to Wallace's abandoned candidacy), he had guaranteed a spectacular Republican sweep within the state. In Alabama, the "Jacobins had begun to behead the Girondists," concluded a reporter for the *Atlanta Constitution*.[122]

Robert Sherrill of the *Nation,* one of the first journalists outside Alabama to take its governor seriously, was wary of predicting Wallace's immediate political demise. Sherrill recognized his continuing strength on his home turf. Nevertheless, he took heart from the disastrous outcome of the southerner's sortie into national politics. The smashing victory of Lyndon Johnson, who had pushed the 1964 Civil Rights Act through Congress against great odds, seemed to end Wallace's dream of a massive national white backlash. The critical moment for his career was at hand, Sherrill suggested. "Beneath the great, garish, flapping circus tent of his success are many incidental defeats that show him to be ... far from politically omnipotent." Within the South—as in the rest of the nation—deep and unresolved conflicts remained. But as black men and women, without fanfare, checked into motels, ate at restaurants, and rode the front seats of buses across the urban and border South, the outer boundaries of the region's color line collapsed without the "seas of blood" that white supremacists had confidently predicted for half a generation. By tying himself to one issue—segregation—the fiery Alabama governor ran the risk of becoming a pathetic anachronism "to be placed beside that old broken musketeer, Ross Barnett, in Dixie's wax museum."[123]

Chapter 8

"On What Meat Doth This Little Caesar Feed?"[1]

After a decade of investigations, Broward Segrest, assistant federal prosecutor for the Southern District of Alabama, concluded that the absolute power—and the level of corruption—of the Wallace administration dwarfed those of any of his predecessors.[2] That power was not made possible by a skillful manipulation of the state bureaucracy, nor by particularly ingenious methods of loosing the purse strings of the state's contractors. More effect than cause, it sprang from the governor's passionate support, a support rooted in the elemental hatreds and longtime grievances of white voters.

"Just as the people in London were soothed by the sound of anti-aircraft guns firing at nothing in the early stages of the Blitz . . ." mused Montgomery newspaper editor Ray Jenkins, "so does Wallace continue to set off impressively noisy blanks." Behind the "Wallace Maginot Line is the sea and Dunkirk," said Jenkins. Nevertheless, the people of the state continue to applaud his "fire-and-fall-back tactics."[3]

At the end of Wallace's first year in office, Jenkins concluded that "our Governor holds the Southeastern Conference title for the most desegregation in the shortest time." Almost daily an administration-backed legislator rose to introduce a piece of patently unconstitutional legislation or to praise the chief executive for filing another lawsuit in state or federal court. The script never changed. The Alabama courts upheld the legislation and the federal courts struck it down. But Jenkins understood the psychological dynamic of the Wallace modus operandi.

The willingness of whites in Alabama—and throughout the Deep South—to thrill to the smoke and thunder of the governor's rhetoric reflected a growing sense of unease and defeatism. One by one the walls of massive resistance were crumbling. But if whites could not hold back the tide, they could delay and hope for a shift in national public opinion. For George Wallace and his supporters, this meant the mobilization of white public opinion and the closing of ranks against all foes. There was no room for dissent or division.

Six days before George Wallace's 1963 inauguration, Al Lingo walked unannounced into the office of Floyd Mann, the lame-duck state public safety director. Incoming governor Wallace, Lingo told Mann, had learned that Robert Zellner was back in Montgomery and had demanded his arrest.

Mann was stunned. The elaborate surveillance system of the state and local police funneled regular reports on civil rights activists across his desk. He knew Zellner, a young white student who had been barred from Montgomery's Huntingdon College in January 1962 because, in the words of the official exclusion order, "his views on racial matters differ from that of the student body." The son of fundamentalist parents, Zellner had come to the quiet Methodist college in 1958 with little knowledge of, or interest in, the emerging civil rights movement. But step by step, with an imperceptible shift of direction that even he could not explain, he broke with his southern past. He first attended biracial meetings with black students in Montgomery and then assumed an increasingly activist role. In the fall of his senior year, he left Huntingdon and, with a small salary from the Student Nonviolent Coordinating Committee (SNCC), began visiting white college campuses in the South to "present the viewpoint of the movement to Southern white students." Arrested, beaten, and jailed in some of the toughest towns in Mississippi, Louisiana, and Georgia, by the end of 1962 he was a battle-scarred veteran.[4]

But Bob Zellner remained a distinctly secondary figure in the civil rights movement. Yet here was Al Lingo—who would be the top lawman in the state of Alabama—acting on behalf of the governor-elect to railroad a twenty-two-year-old ex-college student. "You can't just arrest somebody because you don't like 'em," Mann reminded his successor. The Montgomery County prosecutor (a close supporter of Wallace), retorted Lingo, would take care of the charges after the arrest.[5]

Lingo ordered Willie Painter, one of Mann's two plainclothes investigators with a special background in "subversion and civil rights agitation," to make the arrest. Technically, Lingo had no authority to issue orders until after Wallace was sworn into office, but Painter was well aware that within days, he would be answering to Lingo. Without telling Mann, he agreed to cooperate.

Just after seven P.M., on January 8, the detective, accompanied by Lingo, followed Zellner to Huntingdon College. As the former student stepped onto the campus, Lingo grabbed him, handcuffed him, and shoved him into Painter's unmarked state police car. Halfway to the Montgomery city jail Painter's radio suddenly squawked. "Willie B.," Mann ordered, "don't you mess with Lingo and go arresting Bob Zellner."

Painter stammered and finally blurted out: "Well, we've already got him and we're on our way downtown."

There was a long pause. "Well, goddamn," Mann said, and clicked off his transmitter.[6]

The county solicitor transferred Zellner to the Montgomery city jail and booked him for vagrancy, but the prisoner soon realized that Lingo was far more interested in discovering his "Communist connections" and driving him from the state.[7]

After a city detective learned that the civil rights activist had purchased a used 35mm camera from a Montgomery pawnshop with an eighty-five-dollar check drawn on Atlanta's Trust Company Bank, he telephoned the bank and learned that, at the moment Zellner wrote the check, he had less than fifty dollars in his account. (With its usual contempt for petty bureaucratic details, the SNCC office in Atlanta had failed to deposit Zellner's small monthly stipend.) In the days before electronic transfers, it would have taken days for a check written in Montgomery to clear an Atlanta bank, but Montgomery officials had their opening: technically, Zellner had written a check with insufficient funds. Local officials rummaged through the Alabama criminal code and came up with a charge far more serious than vagrancy: obtaining money by false pretenses. This offense carried a ten-year sentence, in the eyes of law enforcement officials a suitable punishment for civil rights agitators. When pawnbroker Harold Ehrlich refused to press charges ("If I did this to all my customers, half of them would be in jail," he told city officials), a police detective signed the complaint.[8]

In the trial a month later, Birmingham attorney Charles Morgan managed a hung jury; Zellner was convicted of trespassing on the Huntingdon College campus. His arrest and prosecution earned only a few paragraphs in the Montgomery newspaper, but his flirtation with a ten-year jail term represented the tip of an iceberg of malevolence that had turned the state's legal and political system into an all-pervasive instrument of repression. At the core of this corruption was a belief that, in the words of one of Alabama's prominent Baptist ministers, Americans had to choose between "Christian values" or the Communist doctrines of "homosexuality, degeneracy, and promiscuity" and the inevitable "amalgamation of the races." There was no place for the "broad-minded liberal" intent on protecting the constitutional rights of the "unbathed beatnik, immoral kook, [and] sign-carrying degenerate."[9]

Unwavering white unity had been the price of a slave society in Alabama and throughout the South. That tradition took on new institutional dimensions in the twentieth century as local police departments embraced the task of combating "radicalism" and "communism." During the 1930s and 1940s, the center of such police activism was Birmingham; its main targets, the labor movement in general and the activities of the state's small Communist Party. A network of informers—some paid by the city, some by U.S. Steel's subsidiaries—fed information to a special "Red Squad" of a half-dozen plainclothes detectives who used the city's vagrancy and criminal-anarchy statutes (liberally reinforced by backroom beatings) to strike at radical labor organizers.[10]

In the 1950s, the target shifted to civil rights activists. Police departments in the dozen largest Alabama cities, particularly Birmingham and Montgomery, devoted hundreds of hours to monitoring "subversives." In 1963 alone, the Birmingham antisubversive squad infiltrated and—sometimes openly, sometimes secretly—tape-recorded more than fifty "civil rights" meetings as well as a smaller number of Ku Klux Klan and National States' Rights Party gatherings. At the same time, carefully cultivated informants supplied state and local police with detailed inside accounts of meetings and decisions.

Civil rights activists were convinced their phones were tapped by the local and state authorities (most were initially not cynical enough to suspect the FBI). And they had reason to be suspicious. Police chief Laurie Pritchett later bragged that he had body-wired informants at every civil rights meeting that took place in Albany, Georgia. He had installed, as well, telephone taps on key figures under surveillance.[11]

"I had worked for years in Russia and behind the Iron Curtain and I was well aware of precautions with telephones," recalled Harrison Salisbury, who in 1960 wrote a series of articles on racial tensions in Alabama for the *New York Times*. Even when the Tutwiler Hotel staff moved him to another room, the journalist did not suspect that Bull Connor's men were taping all his calls from their command post at an old firehouse. "This was Birmingham. This was the United States," said Salisbury. "I would be careful, but I would not be paranoid." Because of what Salisbury called his "stupidity," "every single person I called from that switchboard [except Bull Connor] was summoned to the . . . [Jefferson County] grand jury," and publicly harassed.[12]

No locale, not even a federal installation, escaped the long arm of the Alabama police system. After the May 1961 assaults on the Freedom Riders, U.S. Deputy Attorney General Byron White flew to Montgomery's Maxwell Air Force Base to confer with Governor John Patterson and other state officials. During his three-day visit, the telephone operator at the federal installation transmitted to the governor complete summaries of all White's telephone conversations with Robert Kennedy and with the President. Patterson learned that White, clearly shaken by the complexity of the Montgomery crisis, had bypassed his boss and had expressed direct to the President the need for a cautious approach. The inside information emboldened the governor to take a hard-line position in negotiations.[13]

The line between surveillance and harassment was often nonexistent. Bill Cooper, a Birmingham detective who was reputedly an inside informant for the Ku Klux Klan, recounted how he had gone up to a group of picketers outside Pizitz Department Store, had written down their names, and had warned them that they would be "in trouble." The blacks, complained Cooper, simply laughed and joked on, but the two local whites were "extremely nervous." One young woman was so frightened she could not respond; when he roughly turned to the other white demonstrator, Cooper noted gleefully that the terrified young college student "staggered over to the edge of the sidewalk and vomited."[14]

Local police, as well as the state Department of Public Safety, had conducted such surveillance haphazardly. George Wallace set out to institutionalize and dramatically to increase the role of the state police. In his first week in office, he turned to Al Lingo for recommendations in establishing an agency to deal with integrationists and subversives. Lingo in turn solicited the advice of Ben Allen, the state investigator who had first infiltrated the modern Klan in the late 1940s.

Like many southern law enforcement officials, Allen drew a sharp distinction between "good niggers" and troublemakers. In 1957, six of Asa Carter's Klansmen had kidnapped and castrated "Judge" Edward Aaron, a thirty-four-year-old black Birmingham veteran, as an object lesson to civil rights activists. Governor Folsom personally assigned Allen to the case.

The detective immediately summoned Carter's henchmen and warned that if "they didn't have just cause, they'd better find 'em a damn rock to git under, because I was gonna git 'em." He discovered that Aaron was neither a rapist nor a political activist; he was known as a "white folks' nigger." Concluding that the Klansmen had "no reason whatsoever to do this man this way," Allen worked day and night to gather evidence to convict four of the men.[15]

Although he always proudly recounted his role in that case, Allen had nothing but contempt for black "radicals" and their allies, a contempt and hatred reinforced by thirty years of work in the paranoiac world of the antisubversive squad of the Alabama State Police. The memorandum Allen forwarded to Governor Wallace on January 21, 1963, was part classroom lecture, part call to arms. The people of the "Sovereign State of Alabama" faced the final stage of a crisis, which had begun in 1938 when radicals had first gathered in Birmingham and plotted the destruction of segregation. (Allen was referring to the ill-fated founding of the Southern Conference for Human Welfare, an enterprise to promote economic development and racial moderation in the region.) The problem, he emphasized, was not the black population of the state, but white liberals "contaminating the minds of those whom they come in contact with . . . confusing the minds of the Negro race" as they infiltrated the state's churches, unions, and universities. Working quietly, this fifth Column—with its northern allies—"sought to change our Southern way of life and intergrate [*sic*] the races."

Allen proposed the creation of a special committee which he incongruously entitled the Alabama Legislative Commission to Preserve the Peace. The Peace Commission, supported by broad subpoena powers and with the authority to issue contempt citations to uncooperative radicals, would have at its complete disposal the investigative division of the state police. To head off demonstrations, the commission could hold public hearings and demand that civil rights leaders furnish membership lists and full financial records. If they failed to comply, they could be cited for contempt and jailed. And if "agitators" did manage to stage significant demonstrations, the state police could arrest their leaders and hold them incommunicado for up to seventy-two hours, "leaving the rank and file to mill around . . . and allowing authorities to interview these people, thereby obtaining invaluable background information." Allen suggested that Representative John Hawkins of Birmingham (who was already serving as chairman of the Alabama American Legion's Subversive Activities Committee) head the new commission.[16]

Allen and the Alabama legislators who ultimately introduced his proposal drew their inspiration from the United States House Un-American Activities Committee, which had conducted far-reaching "antisubversive" investigations from the 1930s through the 1950s. Beginning in the mid-1950s, state officials in Virginia, Louisiana, Mississippi, Georgia, and Florida created special committees under a variety of names. Their main goal was to link Communists to the civil rights movement; Florida's notorious Johns Committee (named after state senator and former Florida governor Charley Johns) seemed equally obsessed with rooting out homosexuals.[17] These state bodies tended to focus on distributing propaganda or conducting public hearings which could be orchestrated to "expose" subversive opponents of segregation.

Allen's proposal for Alabama envisioned something far more extraordinary: the creation of an official "star chamber" backed by a state police unit. Working together, they could investigate, expose, and intimidate those who dissented from the state's position on segregation. In newspaper reports and on the floor of the House and Senate, the bill's sponsors frankly acknowledged that the purpose of the new agency was to "hold a new club over race agitators"—that is, to criminalize opposition to segregation. When senators and representatives met to iron out differences between the House and Senate versions of the bill, they denied the newly created Peace Commission broad subpoena and contempt authority, but let stand the power to expose civil rights agitators and their allies. In Alabama in 1963, the power to expose was the power to destroy.[18]

The Peace Commission was part of a larger plan by Wallace to stamp out any potential challengers. In March his legislative floor leaders quietly introduced "Bill Number 9," which gave the governor authority to bypass the attorney general's office by hiring private lawyers to represent the state "in all measures deemed in the public interest." Wallace aides, particularly Seymore Trammell, justified the action by warning that Attorney General Richmond Flowers was "soft" on integration. Radical times required radical measures.

Members of the Alabama legislature were cowed, but they were not stupid. Vaughn Hill Robison, no slouch in defending segregation, exploded in committee hearings when he read the fine print and realized the audacity of Wallace's proposal. "On what meat doth this little Caesar feed?" he shouted to colleagues as he outlined the legislation's far-reaching consequences. Bill Number 9, said Robison, was not simply an anti-integration law. It would reduce the attorney general to little more than a clerk and would give the governor a vast patronage fund to reward the hundreds of attorneys in the state who had backed him in the previous campaign.[19] With the quiet behind-the-scenes lobbying of Flowers, a handful of key representatives managed to keep the bill from the House floor, where Wallace was unbeatable on any issue that could be pitched as a defense of segregation. It was one of the few times the governor overreached himself.

Members of the legislature might be able to defend their opposition to closing down the attorney general's office; they were not about to block a measure that promised the destruction of hated integrationists and civil rights agitators. The bill to set up the Peace Commission sailed through the House and Senate.

Representative John Hawkins, a thin-lipped prophet of impending doom at the hands of the Communists (and an ardent Wallace supporter), assumed command of the Peace Commission with a promise to expose the "entire scope of the subversive apparatus" which threatened the state of Alabama. The civil rights movement was the vanguard of the revolutionary thrust of international Communism, he warned. "Communist direction is in the hands of hard-core trained red agents," explained Hawkins, but they operated through individuals sympathetic to party aims. Foremost among these, of course, was Martin Luther King, Jr., a man who "is, and has been for ten years, closely advised by Communists if not actually controlled by them."[20]

In the late summer of 1963 Wallace moved to create a second institution designed to mobilize public opinion: the Alabama Sovereignty Commission. With great fanfare, the governor and the agency's new executive secretary brought to Montgomery the directors of every civic club in the state, more than thirty local chamber of commerce directors, forty of Alabama's most prominent attorneys, heads of the state's largest labor unions, dozens of businessmen, and lobbyists from forty trade and professional associations. In a day-long meeting, Wallace pressed home the necessity for absolute unity in the struggle against the "federal juggernaut" of civil rights.[21]

A series of special memoranda written by Peace Commission staff director Ed Strickland in early 1964 were distributed on a "confidential" basis to political officials and police chiefs throughout the state. The nation, and particularly the South, faced a "grim drama," a relentless worldwide threat. The government of the United States, "speaking through President Johnson, Robert F. Kennedy and the echoing Federal Court System," was diverting attention with attacks on American patriots while "lawless bands of Negro toughs roam the jungles of New York and other major cities, openly beating, robbing, raping and killing whites in a wave of terror reminiscent of the Mau Mau." Johnson, Kennedy, and the national Democratic party had "joined hands with communist-trained Walter P. Ruther [*sic*] and a rag-tag of red front groups and opportunistic Negro leaders, to send an army of beatniks into Mississippi." These groups ("led by the National Council of Churches") supported the violent invasion of the South.[22]

A "confidential" intelligence report issued to top law enforcement officials in September of 1967 ordered their local counterparts to prepare to repel an armed assault by revolutionary black commando units. Their uprising would begin in the urban ghettos of the nation between November 20 and November 28; it would then spread to rural areas, where a "special brand of revolution" would bring havoc. The ghettos could be sealed off, but black power revolutionaries would burn and pillage rural areas "where homes were widely separated and law enforcement spread thin." The document concluded: *"We do not consider it merely a threat. We must consider this a certainty, based upon the evidence we now have."*[23] In tone and substance the Hawkins memorandum seemed remarkably similar to hysterical warnings of insurrection in the slave South.

Incompetence, indeed, sheer stupidity, characterized the day-to-day operations of the Peace Commission. The men and women who ran it were so crazed by paranoia that they could transform a Georgia workshop for training voter-registration workers into a "top secret Communist Training School" where "cadres" of revolutionaries were trained in "karate and judo" in order to "demobilize police units." And they could not get the simplest facts straight.

Commission staffers circulated hyped-up, unintentionally hilarious reports. A "profile" on Martin Luther King warned state law enforcement officials that the civil rights leader was "totally under the direction of the

Communist Party. . . . Beard Ruskin [Bayard Rustin], a Communist of some 30 years, served for 30 years as King's spokesman and brain. He became what is known as an albatross around the neck of Martin Luther King."[24]

Another memo urged an investigation into the "communist training school" conducted by the "Rev. Clarence Jordan who runs the Klinonien [sic] Farm in upper New York State." Fortunately no investigators were dispatched north, since Jordan's Koinonia was an agricultural cooperative just outside Albany, Georgia.[25]

Ralph R. Roton, a tenth-grade dropout and part-time electrician, joined the Peace Commission as an undercover operative on the personal recommendation of George Wallace. Outfitted with a phony press card from the *Birmingham Independent,* a right-wing newspaper, Roton began his duties by photographing and tape recording "Communists" in the March on Washington.

But Roton had somewhat divided loyalties. As member Number 1,638 of Confederate Lodge 11 of the United Klans of America, he had been personally tapped two years earlier by Robert Shelton to work as the Klan's special investigator. He dutifully copied materials collected by the Peace Commission and handed them over to Shelton. When a congressional committee investigating the KKK in 1966 asked him if Governor Wallace was familiar with his Klan connections, Roton claimed he could not remember if he had discussed his Klan membership with the governor. After the committee allowed him to telephone Montgomery (presumably to the governor's office), he read from a statement declaring that "to my knowledge" the governor had not been "personally" familiar with his work as a Klan investigator at the time Wallace recommended him.[26]

The real muscle behind the Peace Commission was the antisubversive unit of the state Department of Public Safety. Under the command of Major W. R. Jones, a twenty-year veteran of the patrol and a former deputy sheriff from Scottsboro, Alabama, a team of state investigators compiled materials on individuals considered to be threats to the state's "southern way of life." By October 1963, police had updated the 255 active files already in existence and had added another fifty-seven dossiers on specific individuals, as well as eighty potentially subversive organizations. Al Lingo acknowledged, even boasted, to *New York Times* reporter Claude Sitton that the antisubversive unit had created dossiers on newsmen and news-gathering organizations.

During his first term, Wallace's office routinely and haphazardly used the Sovereignty Commission, the Peace Commission, and the state Department of Public Safety to cement white unity. Citizens who feared that their ministers or other public officials had fallen under the influence of subversive forces regularly wrote their governor, who turned their inquiries over for investigation. (When a Wallace supporter expressed fears that his minister had taken part in civil rights activities, Ed Strickland volunteered that his office had compiled "hundreds" of dossiers and asked for a snapshot of the suspected minister in order to check him out—and presumably begin preparing a file on him.[27])

Wallace's defenders would later claim that the worst abuses of power stemmed from overly zealous followers, but there is ample evidence that he personally policed the boundaries of white supremacy. Jolted out of his silence on racial issues by the 1962 violence at Ole Miss, a young north Alabama Methodist minister delivered an emotional sermon which he called an "appeal to Christian thinking." Too long, C. Halford Ferrell preached, the church had either joined in oppression or remained silent; he reminded his congregation that Jesus had spoken fearlessly in defense of those who were despised and scorned. Jesus' "own people hated the Samaritans because they had foreign blood in their veins; in many cases they were 'half-breeds.' " For the people of Alabama, the "time is coming when we will be faced with the decision to curse, throw bottles, shoot a gun, or to accept the Biblical truth that God is our Father, this world is His, and all men, *regardless of color*, are His children." In the end, said Ferrell, "we must face Him, not the people we live with, not the people we do business with, and not the governor of our state."

The Alabama *Methodist Christian Advocate* published the sermon. As a leading layman, George Wallace was enraged that a fellow Methodist would imply that whites bore some responsibility for the South's racial crisis. In a personal letter he warned the minister that his "ill advised and ill timed" sermon served "only to inflame individuals." Ferrell's views, said Wallace, did not "reflect the feeling of the people of the South." Notes to prominent Methodists made it clear that the governor considered the *Advocate*'s publication of such sermons a betrayal of the cause of white solidarity in the struggle against "forced integration of the races." Ferrell's church stood behind him; others were not so fortunate.[28]

Over the years dozens of Alabamians felt the sting of the governor's displeasure. A Tuskegee bank president who criticized Wallace for closing the Macon County schools found state deposits abruptly withdrawn from his bank and given to a competitor, as did a north Alabama banker who called upon whites to extend the ballot to black voters. Moreland Smith, a Montgomery architect and supporter of the civil rights movement, was forced to leave the state when Wallace personally intervened to block commissions for his firm. The Boston-born bride of a young University of Alabama professor never learned that she had been refused a state civil service job because her father-in-law used his influence with the governor to bar her employment on the grounds that she was an "out and out integrationist."[29]

*   *   *

DEFENDERS could cite numerous examples of George Wallace's racial moderation: his service as a trustee for Tuskegee Institute, his refusal to join the Dixiecrats in their walkout from the 1948 Democratic convention; his anti-Klan position in the 1958 gubernatorial election. Even critics agreed that he compiled an exemplary record for impartiality in his six years on the bench from 1953 to 1959. Every black attorney who argued a case in Wallace's Clayton courtroom was struck by his fairness and by his refusal to engage in the kind of first-name familiarity that most white southern judges used in dealing with black lawyers.

In the fall of 1958, for example, he presided over a case involving a group of poor black Barbour County cotton farmers who had been cheated by a large cottonseed-processing company in Birmingham. When J. L. Chestnut, Jr., who in the 1950s was Selma's only black attorney, filed the suit, he waived a jury trial. The high-powered company lawyers treated him and his black clients with absolute contempt, referring to the litigants as "these people," recalled Chestnut. But every time attorneys used the phrase, Wallace "got red in the face." Finally, he interrupted. "Please refer to . . . Mr. Chestnut's clients as 'the plaintiffs' or don't refer to them at all," Wallace ordered. "George Wallace was the first judge to call me 'Mr.' in a courtroom," recalled Chestnut. The young Barbour County judge found for the plaintiffs and announced an award exceeding their original request for compensation.[30]

Birmingham attorney Arthur Shores remembered an even more astonishing breach of racial etiquette. In the mid-1950s he had agreed to travel to Clayton to defend a young black man accused of manslaughter. After the first morning's arguments, it was clear that the trial would last for several days. Wallace's bailiff told Shores that the judge wanted to see him in chambers for a "conference." When he walked into the small second-floor office, the attorney found sandwiches and iced tea for two set up on the edge of Wallace's desk. The judge knew there was no eating place for blacks in the little town. After that, each day, said Shores, "Wallace would send out and get our food, and we ate in his chambers."[31]

But no one who knew Wallace well ever took seriously his earnest profession—uttered a thousand times after 1963—that he was a segregationist, not a racist. Journalist Tom Wicker, a native-born North Carolinian with a finely tuned ear for the nuances of southern racial attitudes, saw in Wallace the "traditional Southern attitude toward Negroes—a mixture of contempt, distaste, amusement, affection, and appreciation for a valuable servant."[32]

In private, the Alabamian was, like many southern white politicians of his class and generation, simply unable to avoid using racial epithets. As late as the mid-1970s, *New York Times* reporter Jim Wooten—no virgin on the subject of racism—was as much stunned as appalled when he heard

Wallace casually refer to Edward W. Brooke, the nation's first black senator since Reconstruction, as that "nigger senator from Massachusetts."[33] Wallace "never said anything but Negro in public," recalled Tony Heffernan, a United Press International reporter in the 1960s, "but in personal conversation, they were 'niggers.' "[34]

Very occasionally an interpretive piece in the national press repeated an indiscretion ("All these countries with niggers in 'em have stayed the same for a thousand years.").[35] Even local journalists managed to convey some sense of Wallace's prejudices; when Kenya's president, Jomo Kenyatta, criticized Wallace, Ramona Martin of the *Montgomery Journal* quoted the governor's retort: "I read where a Uganda [*sic*] leader said he didn't like the Birmingham racial situation. I guess he was leaning on his spear when he said it." Wallace seemed genuinely bewildered that anyone would find such a remark offensive.[36]

Such behavior did not always accurately measure white racism in the pre–civil rights era. Even after he had committed himself to the struggle for black equality, Lyndon Johnson seemed to revel in using the "n" word in private conversations with white southern politicians. Decent, reasonably open-minded southerners like Big Jim Folsom often talked about "niggers," while more fastidious politicians like Harry Byrd of Virginia masked their racist feelings and actions behind a façade of verbal politeness.

Montgomery newspaper editor Ray Jenkins struggled to understand what prompted the governor's sometimes contradictory behavior. "I think that he wants, as much as any man that I have ever known, I think he wants to be loved by everybody." And that included blacks, said Jenkins.[37] But beneath that patina of paternalism, the need to have everyone "like" him, there was a darker subtext.

To a northern-born reporter assigned to Montgomery in 1961, the new governor seemed obsessed with race. The two mainstays of conversation for most Alabama politicians were sex and sports, but that wasn't true for George Wallace. "Didn't talk about women. We didn't talk about Alabama football," said Heffernan. "I mean, it was race—race, race, race—and every time that I was closeted alone with him, that's all we talked about."[38]

While he tolerated "good" blacks—docile, dependent, subservient—Wallace, like most white southerners of his generation, genuinely believed blacks to be a separate, inferior race. The only hope for the nation was complete racial segregation, he told a Canadian social studies teacher just after he was first elected governor of Alabama. Blacks were inherently predisposed toward criminal behavior, perhaps because a "vast percentage of people who are infected with venereal diseases are people of the Negro race." They were particularly prone to commit the most "atrocious acts of [in]humanity, such as rape, assault and murder." And they were lazy and shiftless. If blacks and whites mingled in the schools, "this mixing will result in the races mixing socially, which . . . will bring about intermarriage of the races, and eventually our [white] race will be deteriated [*sic*] to that of the mongrel complexity."[39]

Such cant made blacks subhuman, unworthy of consideration. In mid-November 1963, less than five months after he enrolled at the University of Alabama, Jimmy Hood suffered an emotional breakdown; his withdrawal from school left the soft-spoken Vivian Malone as the only black student on the Tuscaloosa campus. Shortly after Hood's departure, an explosion blasted a crater in the street outside Malone's dormitory and an anonymous caller warned that the next explosion would be in her room. On November 18, university vice president Jeff Bennett drove to Montgomery to ask the governor to use his influence to stop the bombing. Wallace, said Bennett, had been less than responsive. How long, he demanded, was it going to take "to get the nigger bitch out of the dormitory?"[40]*

As late as 1960, staff members of Alabama Senator Lister Hill's office prepared a detailed response to a letter from a Mobile woman before discovering she was a "negro maid." Embarrassed, they filed her complaint without reply, then formulated a procedure to avoid future gaffes. Staff members in doubt about a correspondent's race should simply acknowledge receipt of the letter and explain that "Senator Hill is away" during the "recess," or "hunting" or "on vacation," the Senator's office manager told his staff.[41]

Governor Wallace simply ignored correspondence, particularly complaints, from black citizens. During his first term, he received numerous reports detailing the harassment of blacks by uniformed and plainclothes state troopers. A black woman from Selma was pursued and forced off the road one night by two white men driving an unmarked car with Louisiana plates. While her three-year-old daughter wept hysterically, the two men—plainclothes investigators for the state patrol—pulled her from the car, charged her with failing to yield the right of way, and seized her driver's license. Although she wrote to the governor and pleaded for an investigation, her letter received the usual notation: "File, do not reply."[42]

Whites who wrote to protest were advised that perhaps they had "misunderstood."[43] But occasionally, Wallace had to respond. Jack Hines, a south Alabama realtor and former university classmate—someone who could not possibly be characterized as an "outside agitator"—took his son for his

---

* Three decades later, the former Alabama governor assured his official biographer that he had "ordered round-the-clock surveillance of Vivian Malone's dormitory to guard against 'anybody that threw a firecracker or made an obscene remark or made any noise or racial slur or anything.'" Stephan Lesher, *George Wallace: American Populist* (Reading, Mass.: Addison-Wesley, 1994), p. 237.

driver's test in the spring of 1965. He stood in embarrassed silence as a state trooper in the office directed "nigger" applicants to yield their place in line to whites. When a black youth timidly asked a question, said Hines, state trooper M. W. Gilmore snarlingly called him a "black son-of-a-bitch" and ordered him to "keep his damn mouth shut."

"I know this boy personally," Hines wrote in a formal complaint to Wallace, "and know his family." The black teenagers who came to take their driver's examinations were at a "very impressionable age," he warned, "and in most cases this is the first contact that these young people have with law enforcement officials. The impression that is being given here in this county, and I feel in a great majority of the counties, will leave scars that will take years to heal, if, in fact, they ever do." While the problem in the local office of the highway patrol might be corrected with a letter of reprimand to Gilmore, continued Hines, the larger issue could only be addressed by an executive order from Wallace requiring that state officials treat "Negro citizens" with the "same courtesy that is extended to white citizens." He closed his letter with a pointed request for a prompt response.[44]

After a flurry of memos, Al Lingo's Department of Public Safety relayed Trooper Gilmore's assurance that he had always "made it a practice to conduct my business affairs in a business-like manner, treating all applicants the same." Gilmore asserted that in a county with a "large negro population," occasionally "smart-aleck negro applicants" would "stir up trouble." "While it is sometimes difficult for me to hold my temper, I have always done so."[45]

In the 1950s, the ruthless force of public opinion alone had silenced most dissidents. A decade later, George Wallace's exploitation of racial fears left a scorched earth of fear and distrust. Alabama, to be sure, was never a police state. Wallace lacked the disciplined habits of a true totalitarian; he was apt to go into a rage one day and then forget the next. And the Peace Commission and Sovereignty Commission had combined budgets of less than $250,000 a year; even working in conjunction with investigators in the state Department of Public Safety and local police departments, they could hardly monitor all "subversive" activities in a state with more than three million people.

The very hysteria of their pursuit reflected weakness rather than strength. For as the bulwarks of racial segregation slowly fell in the mid-1960s, Alabamians began to hear the voices of liberals and self-professed moderates—of individuals like Jack Hines. Despite all the talk among Wallace and the white conservative establishment about "outside agitators," their real fears were directed against these homegrown dissenters who, out of moral uneasiness or pragmatic calculation, had begun to question the public institutions of racial segregation. The reach, and the limitations, of the security apparatus were about to be tested as the civil rights movement focused its attention on Dallas County. In George Wallace's Alabama, any test of seg-regation was a test of his personal power, particularly if Martin Luther King was involved.

SELMA, a peaceful Black Belt town of thirty thousand, had deep roots in the Old South. Established on the bluffs of the Alabama River in 1820, it became an important slave market and center for shipping cotton to Mobile. Al-though Federal troops burned much of the city in the spring of 1865, it slowly regained its population and prosperity as a commercial center and ginning and shipping point for cotton in the late nineteenth and early twen-tieth centuries.

The overt violence of these years—there were nineteen lynchings be-tween 1882 and 1913—declined, but Selma and Dallas County were the center of the White Citizens' Council movement in Alabama in the 1950s and early 1960s. Blacks remained a powerless majority.[46] More than fifteen thou-sand black men and women were of voting age in 1963; fewer than two hundred fifty had been able to place their names on the Dallas County voting rolls.

Community and political leaders in the county rallied to the support of embattled whites in Birmingham during the spring 1963 racial conflict. At George Wallace's request, Sheriff Jim Clark dispatched two hundred of his hated "posse" on a head-busting foray through the streets of the Steel City's black downtown community on the night of May 11. But even as Clark marched his men through the streets of Birmingham, the revolution began at home. A core of community activists formed the "Dallas County Improve-ment Association" and, with the help of two organizers from the Student Nonviolent Coordinating Committee in Atlanta, began the difficult process of convincing an intimidated black population that they, too, must mobilize and demand their political and civil rights.

The Improvement Association's goals were modest: the removal of "White" and "Colored" signs in county and city buildings, an investigation of "persistent police brutality against Negroes," and access to jobs in the town's professional and commercial establishments. The black community sought an end to the physical harassment, economic coercion, and rigged registra-tion procedures that denied most of its members the right to vote. By the fall of 1963, local activists felt bold enough to call for the formation of a biracial committee to begin the process of negotiating grievances.[47]

Local city and county officials refused even to discuss the issue.

A year later, the Improvement Association invited Martin Luther King's Southern Christian Leadership Conference and the Student Nonviolent Co-ordinating Committee to help organize a series of marches. While street demonstrations continued through January and February 1965, for a time it seemed that the tactics of restraint advocated by Selma mayor Joseph Smith-erman and police chief Wilson Baker might defuse the momentum of the movement. Local white leadership had obtained what they thought was an agreement from the unpredictable Sheriff Clark to allow Chief Baker to handle any confrontations with civil rights protesters. Even King's arrest and his week-long jailing in Selma in early February 1965 did not attract the kind of national attention that had focused on Birmingham.

The turning point came in the small town of Marion, twenty-five miles northwest of Selma. Nominally the Perry County seat, the community of four thousand hardly qualified as more than a rural hamlet. There were 3,441 eligible white voters in the county; by that ingenious electoral math practiced in much of the Black Belt, more than five thousand appeared on the voter rolls. Of 5,500 potential black voters, only a handful (in general, "white men's niggers") had been allowed to register.[48]

After a stint in the Army, Albert Turner had returned to his hometown in the late 1950s and had begun working as a brick-layer. By the early 1960s, he was making nearly six thousand dollars a year, a sizable income in impoverished Perry County. He attempted several times to register to vote, but county registrars often hid on the two days a month they were supposed to be open. When he and other potential black voters managed to catch an official in the courthouse, the clerk would bring out a huge bound volume filled with more than three hundred tests. "They had tests asking how many words [were] in the Constitution, what side the moon was on, any kind of silliness. I'm serious. It was all kinds of jive," said Turner. Though a college graduate and a successful small businessman, to county officials he was "just a nigger." Despite friendly warnings from several whites, Turner and other black community leaders began organizing voter registration workshops in the fall of 1962 and early 1963.[49]

Even after blacks obtained a federal injunction with the help of John Doar and the U.S. Justice Department's Civil Rights Division, which he headed, local officials simply thumbed their noses. Inspired by the tenacity of pro-testers in nearby Selma, Turner and his friends decided to call for outside help. On February 18, 1965, SCLC staffers C. T. Vivian and Willie Bolden arrived just after dusk at the crowded Zion Methodist Church near the center of town. More than 450 members of Marion's black community sang freedom songs and listened to speeches for nearly two hours. The rally's organizers had not made specific plans for a night march; in fact, one SCLC represent-ative had assured two state troopers that they would never risk a night march in Perry County. But the Reverend Vivian warmed up the crowd and Bolden—a charismatic speaker from Savannah—soon had the congregation on its feet. Bolden said his speech was "probably one of the best . . . I've ever made." In the exhilaration of the call-and-response from the enthusiastic crowd, "out of the clear blue, at the end of my speech, I asked how many people would like to have a march."[50]

In a body, they stood, and at nine-twenty-five P.M. all but a handful of older men and women filed out of the church and began walking toward the Perry County courthouse, less than a block away.

Marion police chief T. O. Harris, anticipating the worst, had assembled a formidable, if disorganized, force of more than two hundred: state troopers under the command of Al Lingo; county deputy sheriffs, town policemen; and a group of irregulars, civilians armed with ax handles and wooden clubs.[51] Reporters also recognized Sheriff Jim Clark and several of his men. "Don't you have enough trouble of your own in Selma?" asked one journalist. "Things got a little too quiet for me over in Selma tonight," said Clark with a wink. "It made me nervous."[52]

NBC news correspondent Richard Valeriani and his film crew; John Herbers of the *New York Times;* and a half-dozen Alabama reporters arrived just as the crowd exited the church. In the late winter evening, street lamps illuminated the black church members singing and marching slowly toward the courthouse, where the lawmen and civilian irregulars waited, billy clubs in hand.

When the crowd reached the halfway point, Police Chief Harris used his megaphone and gave the order to disperse. In the tense silence, James Dobynes, a black farmer and preacher, fell to his knees and began to pray.

Television cameramen, who had been herded into a corner beside the courthouse, switched on their battery-operated lights and other newsmen began flashing pictures. A local irregular angrily demanded that they turn out their lights; they were "blinding the officers."[53]

Surrounding the cameramen and reporters, a group of civilians led by Redge Bearden, a clerk in the local hardware store, began purposefully spraying the camera lenses with black paint. At the head of the march, Willie Bolden could see the jostling and the commotion. At almost the same moment, he and other marchers heard screams from the rear and turned to see "folk trying to run out of the church."[54] A small squad of club-wielding policemen had gone in through the back door and were herding the remaining congregation into the middle of the street.

Cager Lee, an eighty-two-year-old man too frail to join in the march, had remained in the church, but the deputies—"the men with clubs," as he called them—ordered him outside. " 'Nigger go home,' " they yelled, and when Lee did not move, they dragged him out into the street. They "hit me . . . and kicked me," said Lee. "It was hard to take for an old man."[55]

Suddenly the street lights went out. In the darkness, the eerie quiet was broken by the sickening "whack" of an ax handle as a local lumber salesman clubbed Richard Valeriani. Seconds later, a Marion service station operator grabbed a UPI photographer's camera, threw it to the pavement, then knocked him to the ground. A third club-wielding vigilante hit another television cameraman in the ribs and smashed his camera.[56] That "really seemed to get them going," said Valeriani. Reporters yelled for help, but local police officers "just stood by while they beat us."[57]

Meanwhile, deputies, policemen, and state troopers charged the terrified group of four hundred marchers. You "didn't have to be marching," remembered Turner. "All you had to do was be black."[58] Willie Bolden watched a demonstrator run past, not more than ten feet away, "and they hit him in the head, and it just bust his head wide open. Blood spewed all over," said Bolden. You "had to see it . . . it was just, just . . . you could just see folks grabbing their heads."[59]

Perry County Sheriff W. U. (Bill) Loftis, in red suspenders and cowboy hat, surveyed the mayhem while a deputy armed with a double-barreled shotgun dragged Bolden across the street to him.

"Now you see what you caused," said Loftis, as he grabbed Bolden's coat and spun him around.

The hard-bitten former street hustler began to weep, "and when I turned around he stuck a .38 snubnose right in my mouth."

"What I really need to do is blow your goddamn brains out, nigger," a furious Loftis shouted, then shoved Bolden toward a deputy. "Take this nigger over to the jail."

"There was blood on the floor," recalled Bolden. "Just literally puddles of blood leading all the way up the stairs to the jail cell."

In the distance he heard a gunshot.[60]

State troopers later claimed they had entered a local black eating spot because a "number of Negroes who had gathered inside and immediately in front of Mack's Cafe began cursing and threatening the officers." Inside they confronted (according to the official report) a ferocious gang of bottle-wielding rioters. "I saw a tall black Negro in a light-colored jacket standing across the room from us throw something in our direction," said Patrolman Frank Higginbotham, who claimed he was struck in the head as he reached for his pistol.[61]

Local marchers told a different story. Jimmie Lee Jackson, the twenty-six-year-old grandson of Cager Lee, had followed his mother, Viola Jackson, and a half-dozen other members of the march into the cafe to escape the mêlée. "I didn't see Jimmie until they had him down on the floor beating him; then they started flailing me. I didn't see anymore," said his mother.[62] Jackson later acknowledged that he threw the bottle, but he insisted that it was only after he and his mother had been clubbed. He couldn't bear it, " 'cause Mother wasn't doing anything," he told a doctor. All of the demonstrators interviewed by reporters supported Jackson's charge that the troopers had beat his mother as she lay on the floor.[63]

From that point, the accounts converge: Jackson began screaming and struck one of the troopers with his fist. A second officer, drew his .38 caliber service revolver and shot the young man once in the stomach; Jackson managed to run out of the building, but collapsed on the street. Half an hour later, Sheriff Loftis loaded him into the back of a car and drove him to the Perry County infirmary.

A local townsman approached Valeriani, who was bleeding heavily from the ax-handle blow to his head. "Are you hurt?" he asked. "Do you need a doctor?"

The NBC newsman, still in a daze, was touched by what he thought was concern for his safety.

"Yeah, I think I do. I'm bleeding," he said.

Valeriani would never forget the response. The man "thrust his face right up against mine and said, 'Well, we don't have doctors for people like you.' "[64] Within minutes, Valeriani and the other shaken newsmen, escorted by two state patrol cars, drove back toward the relative safety of Selma and Montgomery.

Though the Alabama press focused little attention on the critically wounded Jackson, editors expressed their outrage over the attack on newsmen. One state daily labeled the episode a "nightmare of State Police stupidity and brutality," and the president of the Alabama Press Association and the heads of the three major networks condemned state troopers for their failure to safeguard reporters.[65] A furious Wallace scrawled a response that accused the press of failing to cover the subversive activities of these "pro-communist agitators" and argued, in essence, that they'd gotten what they deserved. If the reporters were dissatisfied with their protection by state troopers, wrote Wallace, they could sue in an Alabama court.[66]

Although Bill Jones managed to convince his boss that to publish such a response would be impolitic, Wallace bent only slightly.[67] In a press conference he expressed perfunctory regrets, but continued to insist that the assaults on newsmen had been grossly exaggerated and to defend state troopers and local lawmen for exercising great restraint. These men, he said, were heroes. They had "put their lives on the line" to protect the people of Alabama from the "pro-communist mobsters."[68] "I'd say anything they did was necessary. It's hard for the layman to say what force was necessary in a hysterical situation. I'd say clubs were not used nearly as much here as they were in New York City." (This was a reference to tactics used against civil rights demonstrators protesting discrimination in the construction contracts for the 1964–1965 World's Fair).[69]

As they would throughout the Selma crisis, state legislators backed Wallace down the line. In a resolution adopted two days later, they condemned as "baseless and irresponsible" any suggestion that law enforcement officials had failed to protect reporters. And they endorsed Al Lingo's state troopers for their "firm and decisive actions" in handling the "threat of a violent and uncontrolled outbreak of mob violence."[70]

A decade later, Albert Turner, the acknowledged leader of Marion's black community, remembered the encounter as a decisive moment in that town. The "powers that be felt that they had to do something to stop us because they saw our determination," he explained. And the only thing they knew to do was to "give us all a good whipping." They assumed "they would beat us up, and we were supposed to stop after the good whipping. That was the theory of that time. So they did."[71]

But it didn't work. Two weeks earlier, a local black lawyer, J. L. Chestnut, Jr., had watched SNCC organizer John Lewis lead a small group of twenty marchers out of Brown Chapel and down a Selma street to the courthouse. It was an "off day" for demonstrations; no reporters or photographers were on hand to serve as a check to Sheriff Jim Clark, who had personally assumed responsibility for defending the building.

"That is as far as you can go. Turn around and go back," he ordered Lewis. "You are *not* going in the courthouse today."

"The courthouse is a public place and we have a right to go inside," replied Lewis. "We will not be turned around."

"Did you hear what I said?" snarled Clark. "Turn around and get back."

The young man never changed his impassive expression. "We are *not* going back."

The Dallas County sheriff, tapping his heavy baton in one hand, leaned forward until he was only inches away from Lewis's face. Less than a week earlier, he had sent the Reverend C. T. Vivian sprawling to the pavement in front of two network television cameras. "That boy is crazy," thought Chestnut, as he waited for what seemed forever.

Clark blinked and backed away. "Goddammit, go on in."

As Chestnut stood on the courthouse steps, the lessons of a lifetime—ingrained in black men and women in the Deep South from childhood—evaporated. "All my life I believed that white power could and would draw the line whenever and wherever it wanted and there was absolutely nothing black people could do about it." But Lewis had "stood face to face with the power of Alabama and refused on moral grounds to give in—and Alabama blinked."[72]

SEVEN days after the police riot, Jimmie Lee Jackson died. Jackson, a six-dollar-a-day pulpwood cutter, the youngest deacon in his small, rural Baptist church, had never been a leader in the local civil rights movement, but for three years he had come to all of the meetings. Five times he had walked down to the courthouse on one of the two days each month it opened for voter registration. Five times he had been rejected.[73] When they buried him, four hundred mourners packed the little A.M.E. Church in Marion, and another six hundred filled the streets outside. Within hours of Jackson's death, local blacks began to talk of a march to Montgomery to confront the man who to them had become the symbol of the repression they daily encountered: George Wallace. "We was infuriated," said Turner. "Our first plan was to go to Montgomery with Jimmie Jackson, take his body and put it on the steps of the capital," Turner later recalled. "We had decided we were going to get killed or we was going to be free."[74]

When Martin Luther King arrived in Selma for Jackson's commemorative service, he and his advisers embraced the idea of a march from Marion. Within twenty-four hours SCLC staffers, too, told reporters that there would be a "massive" march on Sunday, March 7, 1965, but from Selma, rather than Marion, to Montgomery. During a long meeting on the evening of March 3, King followed the collegial system that always guided his actions. He and his top SCLC aides, Andrew Young and Ralph Abernathy, met with local civil rights activists to thrash out the pros and cons of a march to the state capitol.

Arguments for the march seemed overwhelming. It offered an opportunity, in Abernathy's words, "to focus the attention of the nation and Congress on the State of Alabama and the plight of disenfranchised blacks." Angry black residents of Dallas and Perry counties were demanding action, and there was the irresistible allure of directly confronting George Wallace. Nothing frustrated King and his supporters more than the skill with which the governor evaded public accountability for supporting and encouraging the most violent and reactionary elements in the state. "State troopers could kill a young man in Marion and still Wallace would not be blamed," recalled a bitter Abernathy.[75]

But the death of Jackson—the first person killed in an SCLC campaign—made them cautious. In addition, King's staff had received anxious calls from the Justice Department warning that Klan members planned to assassinate the civil rights leader. At the end of the meeting the issue remained unresolved. Hosea Williams, the senior SCLC staffer, would make the final decision on whether to march on Sunday morning.

The governor's advisers were as divided as King's. Peace Commission informants within the Selma movement reported that there were no real plans to make a march to Montgomery on such short notice; demonstrators assumed they would be halted by police.[76] In a long meeting on the evening of March 4, Bill Jones outlined a devious strategy designed to embarrass King and his allies. The governor, said Jones, should issue a press release prohibiting the march. State troopers should then draw up plans in secret to close Highway 80 to all automobiles except local residents'. King and his followers would begin their walk expecting to be halted. When state troopers failed to stop them, the marchers would be totally unprepared for a fifty-mile hike. "I firmly believed my plan could make them the laughing stock of the nation and win for us a propaganda battle," Jones later recalled.[77]

At first Wallace and Lingo reluctantly seemed to agree.[78] But King and his advisers knew George Wallace better than he knew himself. As the governor conferred all day Friday with legislators, particularly those from the Black Belt counties, he began to backpedal. The proposed route would take demonstrators through Lowndes County, Alabama, a bleakly impoverished rural precinct of three thousand whites and twelve thousand blacks. Absolute white supremacy, enforced by the whip hand of Sheriff Big Otto Moorer, reigned. Not one of the county's 5,122 potential black voters was registered. Not one had ever *tried* to register in the twentieth century; whites openly boasted that the first black person who entered the county registrar's office would be dead by nightfall.[79]

Bill Jones believed that fear of violence prompted the governor to change his mind. It is also clear that he simply could not stomach the thought of appearing to give in to the despised demonstrators. By the time he met with Al Lingo late Friday afternoon, George Wallace had abandoned any idea of surrender. "I'm not going to have a bunch of niggers walking along a highway in this state as long as I'm governor," he told his advisers as they gathered in his office.[80]*

On Sunday morning, March 7, Hosea Williams and SNCC's John Lewis led demonstrators out of Brown Chapel, up Sylvan Street, and eastward toward the Edmund Pettus Bridge, which spanned the Alabama River on the road to Montgomery. A few of the marchers wore walking shoes and carried knapsacks; most were dressed in their Sunday best, and a number of the women wore high heels. They took seriously Wallace's threats to stop the march; a sympathetic doctor visiting from New York had given careful instructions on how to minimize the effects of tear gas. As Williams and Lewis reached the crest of the bridge, in the distance they could see a line of state troopers spread across the four lanes of the highway. Behind the troopers, just out of sight, nearly fifty mounted members of Jim Clark's posse checked billy clubs, electric cattle prods, and gas masks. They began unloading canisters of C-4, a particularly toxic form of tear gas designed to induce nausea and seldom used except in suppressing extremely violent mobs.

---

* According to Lingo's sworn testimony in Judge Frank Johnson's court the following week, the governor had been emphatic: "There was to be no march. I interpreted this to mean that I was to restrain the marchers."

"Regardless of what it took to do it?" Judge Johnson asked him.

"No," Lingo said. "I did not mean to kill any of them, but use the means of least force as possible to restrain them from—"

"But whatever it took to do it?" interrupted Johnson.

"Yes sir," snapped Lingo. *Williams v. Wallace,* trial transcript, 99-101.

"John, can you swim?" Williams asked Lewis, a veteran of a dozen arrests and beatings.

"No," answered Lewis.

"I can't either," whispered Williams, "and I'm sure we're gonna end up in that river."

They began their descent and walked down the east side of the bridge to within a hundred yards of the line of troopers. Lewis could see them fumbling with their gas masks, and he could hear the slap of the rubber gaskets as they snapped them on their faces. Television crews from the three major networks had found a perch in front of a local Pontiac showroom. They turned on their cameras; the unedited footage would later capture the absolute quiet of the last moment before the confrontation.

"You have two minutes to disperse," shouted Major John Cloud over his megaphone.

Williams stopped the column. "May we have a word with you, Major?" he shouted.

"There is no word to be had," said Cloud firmly. Fifty-five seconds short of his two-minute deadline, he gave the order: "Troopers advance!"

WITHIN forty-five minutes, network television and radio bulletins interrupted midday Sunday programming to announce a clash between state and local police and civil rights marchers on the Pettus Bridge. First reports were confusing and fragmentary and there were no pictures; the film had to be rushed from Selma to Montgomery before it could be developed and transmitted to New York for editing. But network editors immediately realized they had one of the most gripping pieces of film footage of the civil rights era.

ABC's premiere television showing of Stanley Kubrick's powerful story of Nazi racism, *Judgment at Nuremberg,* was the featured Sunday night movie on March 7. At nine-forty Eastern Standard Time, the film had been running for almost an hour and a half. Spencer Tracy, who played the gentle but implacable American war-crimes judge, was talking with the cook and housekeeper of his rented Nuremberg house, trying to understand how good and decent Germans had allowed the Nazis to flourish, when news anchor Frank Reynolds interrupted to announce a special news bulletin. Over the next fifteen minutes, forty-eight million viewers watched a hastily edited account of the events at Pettus Bridge; they needed no voice-over to explain the real-life drama.

The raincoat-clad figures of Williams and Lewis at the head of the column of marchers moved slowly across the bridge, then stopped. As the cameras swung to the left, they captured the shouted orders of Major Cloud and the frenzy of club-wielding troopers, swinging their billy clubs and unleashing canister after canister of tear gas. Viewers who listened closely could hear

Sheriff Jim Clark's voice: "Get those god-damned niggers! And get those god-damned white niggers!"[81] His mounted posse charged, whooping rebel yells, swinging bullwhips and ropes; one wielded a length of rubber tubing wrapped with barbed wire.

With only the tersest comments from narrator Richard Valeriani, the film rolled across television screens. Jim Benston, Arkansas-born and one of the "white niggers" who was a special target of the lawmen, later remembered little except the coughing and the vomiting from the tear gas: "It was like the world had gone away." When he staggered to his feet he found himself surrounded by Clark's vigilantes, swearing as they tried in vain to get their horses to run the marchers down.[82] Much of the violence spilled over into a four-block area beyond camera range, but microphones picked up the sound of screams, wooden clubs thudding into flesh, and the bloodcurdling yells of whites gathered to cheer the troopers.[83]

Bill Jones instantly recognized a debacle. There was "too much film. . . . Just too much film," he kept repeating. Wallace was initially unconcerned. The first reports from the scene by the state police had indicated only a "mild pushing match," but as he tuned in that evening, he, too, realized the entire episode was a fiasco.[84] He first blustered to aides that he would fire Lingo and suspend Major Cloud; secondhand accounts claimed that the governor had personally reprimanded Clark, Lingo, and Cloud the next morning.

But Lingo always insisted that the order to use force came directly from George Wallace. The governor "said that we'd teach other niggers to try to march on a public highway in Alabama," Lingo later insisted. "He said that not only to me, but to many other people who were present over a period of several days in his office while plans were being made." In an off-the-record interview with a *New York Times* reporter, one legislator supported Lingo's version of events. He even claimed to have heard Wallace authorize the use of billy clubs and tear gas. Whether or not George Wallace specifically approved the tactics of the state troopers, he never issued a single word of public criticism. A quarter-century later—while expressing regret for the injuries suffered by the marchers—he insisted that troopers had "saved their lives by stopping that march."[85]

While an overwhelmingly positive flood of mail (ten to one) encouraged the governor, neither he nor his aides had any illusions about the public relations pasting they were taking. The Pettus Bridge confrontation had "triggered an editorial barrage of condemnations seldom matched in American Journalism['s] history," complained Bill Jones.[86] What was particularly worrisome was Wallace's inability to claim any kind of rhetorical high ground. He had anticipated an angry response from moderate newspaper editors like Brandt Ayers of the *Anniston Star* and Ray Jenkins of the *Alabama Journal*. But now even the *Birmingham News*—the conservative voice of the city's business and professional community—acknowledged in a front-page editorial that blacks had no alternative except to take to the streets. If "they had to go to court case by case, individual by individual to get the vote . . . it could be years before most of those qualified were registered."[87]

No past incident, not even the Birmingham church bombing, prepared Wallace and his acolytes for the scathing attacks from the national media that followed the Pettus Bridge beatings. "George Wallace . . . has written another shameful page in his own record and in the history of Alabama," began the *New York Times* editorial on Monday, March 8.[88]

New York Republican conservative congressman Carleton J. King rushed to the House floor along with dozens of other legislators to put his revulsion on record. He was opposed to civil disobedience and "defiance of law and order," but the black men and women who stood at Pettus Bridge did not resist or throw stones; they were "gassed, clubbed and beaten at random" as they sought only to protect the most sacred right in a democracy: "their constitutional right to register and vote." Other Republican conservatives, such as Michigan's Gerald Ford, announced their support for new legislation which would use the "maximum power of the federal government to prevent further violence and to protect constitutional rights in Selma, Alabama."[89] The President's bill to guarantee voting rights—not yet submitted to Congress—was well on its way to being adopted by bipartisan acclamation.

MESMERIZED by television coverage of the state troopers' assault on demonstrators, the Reverend James Reeb, a Boston Unitarian minister, joined hundreds of other whites from all over the nation and impulsively flew to Alabama to make what he called a "personal witness." On Tuesday, March 9, less than thirty-six hours after his arrival, Reeb and two other Unitarian ministers finished their meal and walked out of Walker's Cafe, a black restaurant near SCLC's makeshift headquarters in the Brown Chapel area. Unfamiliar with Selma's dark streets, Reeb, Orloff Miller, and Clark Olsen made a wrong turn and left the relative safety of the black community. Four local whites—one carrying a stout wooden club about the size of a baseball bat—saw the three and yelled: "Hey, you niggers!" Frightened, the men turned and began walking quickly back toward Brown Chapel. Miller and Olsen looked back just in time to see a man they later identified as Elmer Cook bring his club around as though he were swinging at a high fastball. It caught Reeb squarely on the side of his head. He pitched forward into the curb without a sound.[90] Twenty-four hours later, the thirty-eight-year-old minister died of a massive cerebral hemorrhage in Birmingham's University Hospital.

Although Cook was known in the community as a violent racist—he had been arrested seventeen times for assault and battery—a Selma judge released him after his friends posted a nominal bail. That December a Selma jury would deliberate less than ninety minutes before returning a "not guilty" verdict to the boisterous cheers and applause of a packed courtroom.[91]

The death of Marion's Jimmie Lee Jackson had generated scarcely a ripple of concern, even among self-professed moderates in the state. Jackson, so the story went, was a violent black man who had assaulted state troopers as they conscientiously sought to carry out their duties. The killing of James Reeb was slightly more troublesome, but southerners had been dealing with hated Yankee abolitionist preacher-meddlers for more than a century. The Reverend Ed Folsom, pastor of a large Black Belt Presbyterian church, confided to his friend, Senator Lister Hill, "I hardly thought the fellow would die, because he seemed to have gotten along alright without using his brains up until the night he had them nearly knocked out. I figured he probably wouldn't miss them."[92]

In an "open letter" which he printed and distributed, Sheriff Jim Clark claimed that "Tommy [sic] Lee Jackson . . . had recovered from his pistol wound and was able to walk around the hospital cracking jokes and then died under very mysterious circumstances." And Reeb, the "so-called minister" had been "thrown out of one beer joint and was coming out of another," said Sheriff Clark, "when he and his companions had a fight or were beaten by some men."[93]

A committee of Selma business leaders circulated pamphlets and chain letters insisting that Jackson's black doctor in Selma had deliberately withheld antibiotics in treating the gunshot wound. Reeb, they explained, had sustained only superficial injuries in Selma. He died after fellow civil rights activists took him out on a dark road and crushed his skull.[94]

If the national press generally ignored Jimmie Lee Jackson's death, Reeb's murder was front-page news. The pressure on Lyndon Johnson as well as on Wallace began to build. A dozen demonstrators slipped into the White House on a sightseeing tour and stationed themselves in the hallway in a carefully planned sit-in to embarrass the President. From his bedroom window Johnson could hear more than six hundred picketers in Lafayette Park shouting and singing loudly through the night; their candlelit vigil demanded that he take action, some action, *any* action.

On Friday morning, March 12, Vice President Hubert Humphrey convened a meeting of the Council on Equal Opportunity to solicit suggestions for stratagems to quiet criticism that the President was being too timid in protecting the rights of black citizens. One council member proposed that the President invite Wallace to Washington. While Humphrey passed on the suggestion to Johnson later that afternoon, he acknowledged that it was highly unlikely the governor would agree to such a meeting, but the gesture would "make it clear that you had exhausted all possible avenues."[95]

Simultaneously, Wallace and his staff gloomily assembled to discuss the growing crisis and the increasing likelihood that demonstrators would march on Montgomery—this time under the protection of the federal government. On impulse, the governor's executive secretary, Earl Morgan, suggested a meeting with the President. Civil rights demonstrators, with the aid of the news media, had convinced most Americans that the issue was voting rights, he reminded his listeners. A high-level summit with Lyndon Johnson would divert attention from Selma and would allow Wallace to shift the issue from voting rights to the reckless tactics of the agitators whose "defiance of lawful state and federal authority . . . pose a threat not only to the lives and safety of our people, but to the preservation of a lawful society."[96]

It seemed like a "good idea at the time," said Earl Morgan, but he began to have second thoughts as soon as they saw the enthusiasm with which the President responded.[97] Just before Bill Jones closed up the press office Friday evening, Ben Franklin, the *New York Times* correspondent assigned to cover the Selma crisis, stopped by for a chat. "Johnson," warned Franklin, "will clobber the Governor."[98]

If granting Al Lingo a free hand in Selma had been George Wallace's first mistake, assuming he could match Lyndon Johnson one on one was his second.

JUST before noon the next day, the President welcomed Wallace and Trammell into the Oval Office with the kind of small talk that marks a gathering of politicians, even those who are sworn enemies. With a grin, Johnson told the governor that he and Martin Luther King had something in common: they were the only two men who had ever wired him for an appointment and then released the wire to the press before the President himself received it. Although often nervous and uneasy in personal confrontations, to the President's aides Wallace seemed relaxed and self-confident as he joined in the banter. Settling down on a large sofa, he tried to seize the initiative by complaining that law and order were dissolving in Alabama because of the presence of "malcontents, many of them trained . . . in Moscow or New York." It was up to the President to put a stop to the demonstrations.[99]

Johnson sat directly across from the governor in his favorite rocking chair. It seemed to him, he gently chided, that demonstrators were simply demanding the most basic right: the right to cast a ballot in a democracy. He pulled his chair closer. "You can't stop a fever by putting an icepack on your head," he admonished. "You've got to use antibiotics and get to the cause of the fever."

"You cannot deal with street revolutionaries; you can never satisfy them," retorted Wallace, "first, it is a front seat on a bus; next, it's a takeover of parks; then it's public schools; then it's voting rights; then it's jobs; then it's distribution of wealth without work."[100]

The President leaned forward until his face was only inches away from Wallace's; he gripped the governor's knee. Johnson "took the initiative," remembered White House aide Jack Valenti, "started the conversation going and never let up."[101]

For the next hour, he talked of his hopes for America, for ending racism, for decentralizing and humanizing "this godawful welfare system," for breaking the terrible cycle of poverty in the urban areas by creating satellite communities in which a more human scale of existence could be possible. "You can be a part of that," he kept saying. Stop "looking back to 1865 and start planning for 2065."

Johnson, like some Texas python, had almost wrapped himself around the governor. Wallace shrank back in his sofa seat; he seemed to Trammell to be looking increasingly forlorn and defensive. Trammell cleared his throat and interrupted the Johnson monologue. "The problem we've come to discuss," he said to the President, was "the racial agitators and the growing menace of the Communist demonstrators in Alabama."

Lyndon Johnson turned slowly. "He looked at me like I was some kind of dog mess," said Trammell. The President uncoiled himself, reached over to his desk, and picked up an inch-and-a-half-long pencil stub and a tablet. "Here!" he barked. "Take notes.

"George," Johnson asked, "why are you doing this? You ought not," he said sadly. "You came into office a liberal—you spent all your life wanting to do things for the poor. Now why are you working on this? Why are you off on this black thing? You ought to be down there calling for help for Aunt Susie in the nursing home."[102]

Trammell feebly tried again to intervene. Johnson cut him off. "Are you getting this down?" he asked accusingly. "Those goddam niggers [in Lafayette Park] have kept my daughters awake every night with their screaming and hollering." Wallace could end all the demonstrations, the President continued. "Why don't you let the niggers vote?"[103]

Under Alabama law, insisted Wallace, such decisions were "made by the county registrars, not by me."

"Well, then, George, why don't you just tell them county registrars to register those nigras?" asked Johnson.

"I don't think that would be easy, Mr. President," said Wallace miserably, "they're pretty close with their authority."[104]

Johnson's voice was suddenly stern. *"Don't you shit me, George Wallace."*[105]

In the few hours between Wallace's request for a meeting and their Saturday conference at the White House, Johnson had received a half-dozen memos from staff aides, urging a variety of tactics and arguments, but this was one session for which the President needed no coaching.[106] He understood the Alabamian because they were in many ways alike: desperately ambitious, egotistical, insecure provincials. The Kennedys had tried to intimidate and humiliate George Wallace; Lyndon Johnson knew that respectful empathy and a gentle scolding would prove far more powerful weapons.[107]

When they left the Oval Office after more than three hours, Trammell turned to his companion and held out the pencil stub. "Here, George," he said with a mischievous grin. "Don't you want this as a souvenir?"

Wallace walked on, staring at the floor.[108]

Outside in the Rose Garden, more than a hundred reporters and television correspondents waited. The President explained that Governor Wallace had come to Washington to try to stop the demonstrations in his home state. "I said that those Negro citizens of Alabama who have been systematically denied the right to register . . . should be provided the opportunity of directing national attention to their plight." The demonstrations, insisted Johnson, were a symptom rather than a cause of the crisis that Selma had come to symbolize.

"What happened in Selma was an American tragedy. The blows that were received, the blood that was shed, the life of the good man that was lost: they must strengthen the determination of each of us to bring full and equal and exact justice to all of our people." It was not a question of a conflict between the federal government and the people of Alabama: it went to the "heart and the purpose and the meaning of America itself. . . . It is wrong to do violence to peaceful citizens in the streets of our towns. It is wrong to deny Americans the right to vote."[109] George Wallace stood subdued and silent while Johnson controlled the press conference as completely as he had their meeting.

On the flight back to Montgomery, gloomy and well aware that he had taken a pasting from the President, Wallace defensively told his aides, "You know, in that Oval Office, when the President works on you, there's not a lot you can do."[110] (Although aides praised Johnson for his skillful handling of Wallace, he had second thoughts about his public domination of the Governor from Alabama. "It's like the man who wrestles his wife to the ground," Johnson said. As he "lifts his 250 pounds up off her, he says I can lick any little hundred-pound woman in the world."[111])

The Washington summit did not prove a road-to-Damascus experience. Within twenty-four hours, Wallace, back on CBS's *Face the Nation,* once again attacked the media for its use of "unmitigated falsehood" to slander the people of Alabama while ignoring the "infiltration of this so-called civil rights movement by members of the Communist conspiracy."[112] However, these were defiant shots fired in a rearguard action. The days and weeks that followed were marked by one long trail of apparent defeats for Alabama's governor.

On March 15, the President went before a joint session of Congress. In the most memorable civil rights address of his presidency, he used the events in Selma as a rallying cry for a last legislative assault on Jim Crow. "There is no constitutional issue here. The command of the Constitution is plain. . . . It is wrong—deadly wrong—to deny any of your fellow Americans the right to vote in this country." Those who heard him would remember the emotional touches: the reminiscences of his experiences with Hispanic children in a Cotulla, Texas, schoolroom; his unequivocal embrace of the civil rights movement ("And . . . we . . . shall . . . overcome"). But the groundwork had been laid by the powerful images of Pettus Bridge that had flowed across the nation's television screens. Johnson demanded that the Congress act quickly and decisively to end the decades-long practices of voter discrimination in the Deep South.[113]

Three days after the President's speech, federal district judge Frank Johnson gave judicial sanction for civil rights leaders to stage a protest march from Selma to Montgomery. Law enforcement officials, particularly Sheriff Clark and his posse, had engaged in "harassment, intimidation, coercion, threatening conduct and sometimes brutal mistreatment" of black demonstrators, mistreatment that culminated in the assault on March 7, 1965. Even though protesters were nonviolent, Sheriff Clark and Al Lingo had used tactics "similar to those recommended for use by the United States to quell armed rioters in occupied countries." Johnson seemed to go out of his way to point out that the battle plan "had been discussed with and was known to Governor Wallace."

Using a novel constitutional doctrine which he called a "theory of proportionality," Johnson brushed aside Wallace's objections and argued that the civil rights protesters had a right to march along the highways of Alabama (in this case, Highway 80) even though it might inconvenience the general population. The right to protest, said the judge, "should be commensurate with the enormity of the wrongs that are being protested and petitioned against. In this case, the wrongs are enormous. The extent of the right to demonstrate against these wrongs should be determined accordingly."[114]

Johnson's judicial order authorizing a massive civil rights march on Montgomery swept away whatever uneasiness the Pettus Bridge beatings had aroused among white Alabamians, and George Wallace's political fortunes within the state soared. Forgotten was the sight of lawmen beating and tear-gassing unarmed demonstrators; instead, Wallace once again invoked white southerners' sense of victimization. On March 18, in an angry speech before a joint session of the Alabama legislature (televised live throughout the state), the governor denounced the demonstrators as nothing more than "mobs, employing the street warfare tactics of the Communists." He flatly refused to spend state funds to protect the Selma-to-Montgomery marchers.

(President Johnson responded by federalizing the Alabama National Guard.) In the text of his prepared speech there was no direct mention of Frank Johnson, but Wallace, swept up by repeated ovations from the legislators, lashed out extemporaneously. When confronted with "riotous disorder," the federal judge "prostitutes our law in favor of that mob rule while hypocritically wearing the robes and clothed in the respect built by great and honest men."[115]

"Wallace Has Finest Hour Before Solons," headlined the *Birmingham News*. The governor received the "most resounding response ever accorded him by the legislature in his appearance," wrote longtime *Advertiser* correspondent Bob Ingram. "Several women in the audience were in tears as Wallace concluded his speech."[116] When a legislator introduced a resolution condemning the march as "asinine and ridiculous," the ayes were the "loudest answer in the state's political history," said a forty-year veteran capitol correspondent. "When dissenting votes were called for, not a single whisper could be heard."[117]

THE fifty-mile march from Selma to Montgomery, ending on March 25, 1965, was the nova of the civil rights movement: a brilliant climax, which brought to a close the nonviolent struggle that had reshaped the South. The procession was less magisterial than chaotic, mirroring a movement often stronger on inspiration than planning. (When NAACP attorney Jack Greenberg demanded to know who was in charge of logistics for the march, the SCLC's Hosea Williams—veteran of the Pettus Bridge assault and a half-dozen other beatings—proudly responded, "I am the logician.")[118]

But what it lacked in organization it made up for in enthusiasm. Ten years earlier, King had been pulled from the obscurity of his Dexter Avenue pulpit to head the bus-boycott movement; in 1958, Montgomery's city policemen had unceremoniously dragged him off to jail on a trumped-up charge of "loitering." Now, followed by more than 25,000 singing, hand-clapping followers, he led the march into the capital city of the old Confederacy like some biblical Pied Piper. And as they paraded around the fountain in Court Square, up Dexter Avenue past King's old church, and onto the square in front of the state capitol, the marchers sang out jubilantly:

Keep your eyes on the prize, hold on, hold on.
I've never been to heaven, but I think I'm right,
You won't find George Wallace anywhere in sight.
Oh, keep your eyes on the prize, hold on, hold on.[119]

Wallace had sent all women state employees home for the day (presumably to protect them from the ravages of the thousands of crazed marchers), but periodically the governor wandered into the office of his executive secretary and peered out through the closed blinds at the growing crowd. An aide teasingly suggested that he get a close view: "In a few years that may be the way the inauguration crowd looks."

"Don't say that," replied Wallace, as he returned to his office to watch one of three television sets that had been set up to monitor the final rally.[120]

Martin Luther King would always be identified with his "I have a dream" speech, but he was never more eloquent than on that warm March afternoon in 1965. As he stood on a platform before the birthplace of the slave Confederacy he looked out over an audience that, though sprinkled with several thousand northern supporters and a handful of white Alabamians, overwhelmingly reflected the transformed black community of Alabama. Even more than in his 1963 March on Washington speech, King employed the powerful cadences and themes of the southern church as he spoke to the cheering crowds.

Judgment: The authors of white supremacy had "segregated Southern money from poor whites . . . they segregated Southern churches from Christianity; they segregated Southern minds from honest thinking; and they segregated the Negro from everything."

Reconciliation: "On our part we must pay our profound respects to the white Americans who cherish their democratic traditions over the ugly customs and privileges of generations and have come forth boldly to join hands with us. From Montgomery to Birmingham, from Birmingham to Selma, from Selma back to Montgomery, a trail wound in a bloody circle has become a highway up from the darkness."

Hope and redemption: "I know you are asking today, 'How long will it take?' I come to say to you this afternoon, however difficult the moment, however frustrating the hour, it will not be long, because truth pressed to earth will rise again. How long? Not long, because no lie can live forever! How long? Not long, because you still reap what you sow! How long? Not long. Because the arm of the moral universe is long, but it bends toward justice!"[121]

As if to mock the soaring rhetoric of King's capitol steps speech, only a few hours after darkness had fallen that evening, thirty-nine-year-old Detroit housewife Viola Liuzzo lay dead. Like hundreds of other Americans, she had driven to Alabama after the Pettus Bridge incident and had offered her services and her Oldsmobile sedan to the movement. On the evening of her death she had delivered one load of marchers to Selma and was on her way back to Montgomery when four Klansmen waylaid her. Before the summer was out, Tom Coleman, a white highway department worker in Lowndes County, would be charged with the murder of Jonathan Daniels, an Episcopal seminarian from New Hampshire. (When the white jurors swiftly returned their "not guilty" verdict in the Daniels case, one of the twelve men jovially greeted Coleman: "We gonna be able to make that dove shoot now, ain't we?")[122] King had been prophet as well as preacher when he told Montgomery marchers they were "in for a season of suffering in the Black Belt counties of Alabama."[123]

Throughout the march Wallace had managed to strike a sober, even states-manlike, pose for the media. He appealed to Alabamians to stay away from the demonstrations and to avoid violence and confrontation. When terrorists planted a half-dozen bombs in Birmingham to coincide with the beginning of the march, Wallace flew to the city and personally expressed his sympathy to black residents in three of the neighborhoods hit by blasts.[124]

In an interview on the *Today* show, newsman Richard Valeriani offered the governor an opportunity to express some regret for Mrs. Liuzzo's murder. "You can't blame any one individual for the things that happen in Alabama any more than you can blame Governor Rockefeller for the murder of Mal-colm X in New York," Wallace said defensively. Besides, "It's still safer on Highway 80 in Alabama than riding the subway in New York."[125]

When NBC followed up his appearance with an interview with Mrs. Liuz-zo's grief-stricken husband, Wallace realized that he had overstepped even Alabama's elastic bounds of public decency. After all, a wife and a mother of five—however misguided—had been chased down like a wild animal and murdered on a lonely highway. Later in the day, Jones saw to it that the governor's office issued a statement promising an "around-the-clock inves-tigation of the death of Mrs. Liuzzo . . . in order to solve this outrageous crime." By nightfall Wallace was assuring reporters, "I am as angry as I can be."[126]

Despite his assurance that law enforcement officials would apprehend the murderer, the scenario that followed ranks as one of the most shameful episodes in the history of Wallace's public career. Within hours of the shootings the men who killed Liuzzo were known to federal officials; FBI informant Gary Rowe had been riding in the hit car and had pretended to take part in the killing. But state and local law enforcement officials, in concert with Ralph R. Roton, Klansman and former Peace Commission staffer, focused most of their energies not on building a case against the four Klansmen, but on uncovering evidence that could be used to discredit the victim.

Sheriff Jim Clark phoned an acquaintance in Michigan, Warren police commissioner Marvin Lane. When Clark told his fellow lawman that he had been threatened by an unnamed teamster official (Viola Liuzzo's husband was business agent for a Detroit teamster local), Lane persuaded a Detroit detective to undertake a full background investigation of Viola Liuzzo and her family.

Lane obligingly telegraphed several pages of official records on Viola Liuzzo as well as the most intimate and irrelevant details of her private life: the amount of her charge accounts, interviews with her professors at Detroit's Wayne State (where she was an excellent part-time student), and precinct registration records which indicated she had not voted in the election of 1964. The dead woman was, by all accounts, generous-hearted, if sometimes mercurial. But gossip (one neighbor said her father's senile dementia stemmed from syphilis) was piled on rumor (she was having problems with her husband). There was a "police record," to which Alabama officials repeatedly referred; it consisted of a misdemeanor, which stemmed from her decision to keep two of her children out of school in order to test the inadequacies of Michigan's compulsory school attendance law. (The Detroit school board had asked that the case be dismissed; she insisted that she be allowed to plead guilty to dramatize her objections.) State officials passed on their files to Klan leader Robert Shelton.[127] The distinction between the state and local police investigation and that of the Klan disappeared as the two swapped information in their frantic efforts to malign the victim.[128]

Working closely with the governor's office, Sheriff Clark and Al Lingo commissioned Robert Mikell, a graduate of Auburn who had majored in English and was a frustrated novelist, to write a lurid exposé of the "civil rights debauchery in Alabama which has resulted in SELMA."[129] Klan Wizard Robert Shelton offered a stomach-churning version of the character of Viola Liuzzo. "From testimony and statements from various law enforcement agencies, every time she was seen, she was in the company of the Negroes. . . . From the testimony by the examiner of her body, she did not have on any panties . . . there were high traces of barbiturate in her blood."[130]

Pamphlets, press releases, and speeches by conservative Alabamians, including George Wallace, reveal an obsession with "orgies" and "fornication" and "debauchery." More than simply a tactical effort to erase an embarrassing page from the story of Selma, the posthumous slandering of Viola Liuzzo foreshadowed the beginnings of the sexual culture wars that would resonate through American society in the 1960s and 1970s. White southerners had always been quick to talk of the "loose morals" of black men and women, but the offenders they attacked in Selma were white. As hundreds of college students gathered to demonstrate in 1965, Alabamians encountered the culture of open sexuality, which had begun in California and was sweeping in toward the heartland from each coast. Every group photograph of the college students at the Selma march was dominated by rows of neat coeds in carefully pressed jumpers and young men straight out of the late 1950s in button-down shirts, polished loafers, and close-trimmed haircuts. But there were others: young women in tight pants wearing men's shirts and sporting "long stringy hair"; young men and women of indeterminate gender who wore boots, blue jeans, and vestlike jackets and sweaters, their hair hanging down over their shirt collars.

The first shocked accounts of "depravity," described so primly that it was difficult to be sure what conduct was being condemned, appeared in the Selma newspaper. By the end of the march, however, the major newspapers of the state were filled with accounts of "petting and lovemaking between white and Negro demonstrators" and lurid descriptions of the "large number of beatniks" who were engaged in "kissing and loving and drinking."[131]

Alabama congressman Bill Dickinson claimed the floor of the House and delivered what an admirer called a "bestirring verbal intercourse." Alabama had been assaulted by "human flotsam: adventurers, beatniks, prostitutes and similar rabble." Drunkenness and "sex orgies were the order of the day in Selma, on the road to Montgomery. There were many—not just a few— instances of sexual intercourse in public between Negro and white." Thankfully, concluded the congressman, this "godless riffraff" had dispersed, leaving Alabama littered with "whiskey bottles, beer cans and used contraceptives."[132]

Working with the governor's office, Dickinson sent out more than fifteen thousand copies of his speech across the state. In mid-April, Wallace's Sovereignty Commission—with the assistance of Lingo's state police—offered a Dallas film company more than $35,000 to produce a "documentary" on the Selma March, and the Selma and Dallas County chamber of commerce distributed 100,000 copies of a pamphlet called "The Story of Selma," which contained equally lurid descriptions of the march, as well as salacious accounts of the sexual misdeeds of Martin Luther King and Ralph Abernathy. King, charged the Chamber of Commerce, "took a beautiful young lass to San Juan recently for a brief vacation," while Ralph Abernathy had once "seduced a 15-year-old girl, who was a member of his church."[133]

But the accounts of wild interracial sexual orgies were ninety-nine percent fantasy. Selma was no Woodstock. An Indiana University student wagered that there was more beer consumed in one weekend fraternity party at her campus than on the entire march. And despite Dickinson's accusations, the sworn affidavits of state troopers, Selma policemen, and Dallas County deputies described only two acts of sexual intercourse (one biracial), the shocking sight of "young Negro men and young white women walking down the street holding hands or with their arms around each others' waists," and the breathless report of a clerk in the Montgomery police department that several of the women arrested "had no underpants on."[134]

Wallace's state-funded Sovereignty Commission finished editing *The Selma to Montgomery March,* set up an elaborate distribution network, and doggedly mailed the movie around the country. But, after watching the badly produced half-hour film, which mixed hysterical narration ("We've viewed the red hand of Communism at work in this movement") and dull footage of demonstrators milling about aimlessly, disappointed viewers complained "that the picture did not show the shady side of the march." Congressman Dickinson and various Baptist and Methodist defenders of the public morality had promised debauchery and orgies—a "sex movie," said Bill Jones. Unfortunately, "we had not made a sex movie."[135]

The angry response of most Alabama whites temporarily silenced moderates in the Black Belt. Although Selma auto dealer Arthur Lewis had urged local officials to negotiate in good faith with civil rights leaders, he and his wife were Jewish and especially vulnerable to the anger of outraged bigots. He remained publicly silent; he was "yellow," he bitterly told one friend in a spasm of self-reproach. As he and his wife, Muriel, watched the footage of the club-wielding troopers and deputies, however, they resolved to speak out, regardless of the consequences.

In a letter to a group of close friends, Arthur and Muriel Lewis recounted their efforts to work behind the scenes. "We could be called moderates, but not liberals," they said, "balancing on a very thin tight-rope while trying to do what we believe is right and just." There were "decent people everywhere and this town is no exception," but the time for quiet diplomacy was over. "We must act differently, and think differently."[136]

Although the White Citizens' Council obtained a copy of the letter, which they edited to make the couple seem more radical and then circulated throughout the city, a determined Lewis invited a dozen of the wealthiest and most important white moderates to his home and urged them to sign and publish a "Declaration of Good Faith" in the *Selma Times-Journal.* Little more than an affirmation that all citizens had the right to be protected from abuse and a pledge to support interracial communication "on a basis of mutual respect," the cautious proposal set off weeks of bitter and acrimonious quarreling. The couple had steeled themselves for the hate letters, the threatening telephone calls, and the boycott of their business. The timid response of community leaders they found far more depressing. Only after Arthur and Muriel Lewis distanced themselves from active involvement in the race question did Selma's business elite—concerned over the economic implications of the continuing image of white resistance—publish a watered-down version of the resolution in the local newspaper.[137]

In late January 1965, Elinor Borawski, national field director of the Oliver Quayle Company, a firm which specialized in political consulting, had flown to Alabama at the request of incumbent Senator John Sparkman to begin an intensive survey of the political climate of the state. Sparkman feared that George Wallace might challenge him in 1966, and longtime loyalists in the state Democratic Party wondered at the future viability of their ties to the national party. Borawski's team of interviewers questioned in detail nearly eight hundred registered voters from a carefully selected statistical sample.

Responses to queries about Wallace, Borawski discovered, were unlike any she had encountered in her years of polling. The "job of being a state governor, like that of the Sergeant's in Gilbert and Sullivan's 'Pirates of Penzance,' is 'not a happy one,'" Borawski told her client. Incumbent governors usually had more unfavorable than favorable ratings. But that clearly did not apply to George Wallace. As she tried to summarize the governor's ranking with the white voters of his state, the language of the social scientist dropped away. She used words like "spectacular" and "incredible." Less than five percent of the whites in the state gave him a "poor" rating; more than half ranked his performance as "excellent." The "folks back home are ecstatic in their praise of him."[138] A mid-May poll by Lou Harris after the Selma crisis showed that Wallace's popularity stretched across much of the South; over eighty percent of white voters in the region expressed support. Once again he had shown the lasting appeal of the politics of martyrdom. George Wallace had become the unchallenged leader of an embattled people.[139]

But fanning the embers of white southerners' fears endangered his political ambitions. Throughout the 1964 presidential primaries Alabama's governor had doggedly insisted that his campaign was about "constitutional government" and property rights. Selma made a mockery of such claims. When George Wallace's club-wielding state troopers terrorized peaceful demonstrators on the Pettus Bridge, when Ku Klux Klan thugs murdered a Detroit housewife on a public highway at dusk, they challenged the most basic right in American democracy: the right to vote. Civil rights activists had mockingly anointed Birmingham's Bull Connor as the father of the Civil Rights Act of 1964; George Wallace and his policy of stubborn resistance paved the way for the passage of the Voting Rights Act of 1965.

And he proved unable to silence the outspoken resistance of a handful of white Alabamians. For each Arthur and Muriel Lewis compelled to retreat, a dozen dissidents stepped forward to take their place. "Moderation" might be a dirty word to the governor and other advocates of white resistance, but, more and more, powerful members of the South's white middle class and local community elites had begun to counsel dignified accommodation to the forces of change.[140] Elinor Borawski had not even thought it necessary to poll the black voters of Alabama in producing her 1965 survey; the passage of the Voting Rights Act of 1965 meant that white advocates of racial moderation would have more than 150,000 potential new supporters. Few were likely to support George Wallace.

His opponents had additional reason for optimism. At the turn of the century, Alabama conservatives had pushed through a new constitution aimed at permanently disfranchising blacks and substantially reducing the number of white voters. Almost as an afterthought, the framers of the document had inserted a provision prohibiting the governor from election to a consecutive term; the restriction minimized the likelihood that the state would suffer at the hands of an unruly (and perhaps adventurously activist) executive.

In less than a year George Wallace would be out of a job.

Chapter 9

"Stand Up for Alabama"

The Queen and Her Consort in a Captive State

THROUGH THE SUMMER and early fall of 1965, George Wallace sharply curtailed the frantic schedule of national speeches that had marked his first two years in office and stuck close to Montgomery, agonizing over how he could maintain control of the governor's mansion. Shortly after taking office in 1963, he had made a halfhearted attempt to push through a constitutional amendment overturning the antisuccession provision, but a handful of senators allied with his rivals skillfully buried the proposal in committee with an ease that unnerved him.[1]

For a while Wallace considered the unthinkable: giving up his control of the state government. Alabama senator John Sparkman, up for reelection in 1966, had remained unbeatable since voters sent him to Washington in 1936; his seniority on the Senate Small Business and Banking committees enabled him to channel a steady flow of federal dollars to the folks back home. But by the mid-1960s his close ties with the national Democratic Party had become a dangerous liability and, though he had dutifully supported segregation, Sparkman's dignified assaults on the federal courts struck most Alabama whites as ineffectual. To call integration a "damned imposition" no longer sufficed, said one sardonic observer of Alabama politics in the 1960s. "To keep up with him [Wallace] now it is necessary to recognize integration as a red plot."[2] Sparkman's own poll of the state's voters showed that Wallace would swamp him more than two to one in a head-to-head race.[3]

If the governor flirted with the idea of a Senate run, he always balked at the last moment. His wife did not want to take their kids out of Montgomery schools and drag them off to Washington, he insisted to newsmen. Reporters who had covered Wallace found it hard to listen to this explanation with a straight face; in twenty years of public life he had never paid the least attention to Lurleen when her concerns interfered with his political ambitions.[4] Candidly he admitted to adviser John Kohn that he had no wish to be a "small fish in a big pond" and scoffed at Kohn's insistence that the Senate could furnish a platform for his future national ambitions.[5] Few lobbyists and Alabama businessmen would line up, checkbooks in hand, to bankroll the national political campaign of a first-term senator. Some way would have to be found to hold on to the governor's mansion and the powerful economic benefits the office could channel to his planned presidential campaign.

By 1965, Wallace seemed confident that he could bully the legislature into passing a succession amendment. In his first two years as governor, he had proved a master at supplementing the political passions of racial reaction with the largesse of the pork barrel. His floor leaders had pushed through a pay raise for teachers, a substantial hike in benefits for state workers, and a massive increase in road construction. Through the late spring and summer of 1965, the legislature alternated between rubber-stamping inflammatory resolutions denouncing the U.S. Justice Department, the federal courts, and the Department of Health, Education and Welfare and enacting the governor's down-home version of the Great Society. The session funded free textbooks, another ten percent hike for teacher's salaries, and $116 million in capital projects for the state's colleges and universities. A few cynical newspaper editorialists noted that regressive taxes and state bonds, to be paid by the next generation, financed the bonanza, but most voters applauded the Wallace program. Only a handful of economic conservatives seemed uneasy that the state's bonded indebtedness had doubled since 1963. After watching another administration-sponsored measure sail through the House on a voice vote with only the most cursory hearings, one of these die-hards glumly told a Montgomery reporter, "Whatever Wallace wants, Wallace gets."[6]

Emboldened by his near-perfect record, the cocky governor brushed aside the warnings of his more cautious advisers and called submissive lawmakers together to issue his newest marching orders. "Now everybody get this straight," he told them. "No goddamn bill is gonna pass this Legislature . . . no goddamn money for any goddamn school is gonna be appropriated . . . until I get my succession bill!"[7]

In a late-September press conference, he announced an "emergency session" of the legislature to remove the antisuccession provision of the state constitution. Well aware that Wallace's last chance of intimidating legislative foes lay in going over their heads in a direct appeal to the voters, Bill Jones contacted Alabama's largest commercial television stations and suggested it would be in their best interests to broadcast the governor's speech before a joint session of the House and Senate. Almost every affiliate in the state awarded him a half-hour of air time.

At seven-thirty P.M. on September 30, viewers saw a smiling governor standing in the speaker's well beneath a marble plaque ("In this Hall the ordinance of Secession which withdrew Alabama from the Union of Sovereign States was passed Jan. 11, 1861") and waving to a clapping, chanting legislative chamber and to the galleries, carefully packed with five hundred noisy supporters. "Let the People decide," Wallace declared. The legislature must repeal the antisuccession measure and submit it to a referendum of the voters.

Two dozen hardcore opponents, half of them from the Senate, sat glumly as Wallace brought the legislature and the gallery to their feet six times. Why, he asked, did "liberal newspaper editors"—and he looked sternly at reporters off to his right—"so viciously attack the idea that your Governor might succeed himself . . . ?" The answer was simple: "The liberals . . . want the states destroyed and they want all strength, all power, all benefits to come from a centralized government. They want us to quit doing and start begging!"

The governor made no effort to be coy about his plans for a presidential run in 1968. "The liberals say that George Wallace wants to be President," he said with mock horror. "And what is wrong with that? An Alabamian is as good as most and better than some." Perhaps, he said with a grin, even as good as someone from Texas. But "men have come from Washington, D.C., and are in your Capitol tonight"—determined, he warned viewers—to make sure that the governor of Alabama was embarrassed and discredited in his home state.

While foes in the House and Senate, backed by these outsiders, sat in their comfortable armchairs, the people of Alabama "sent me north and east and west to tell the story of Americanism and the South," he continued. It would have been easy to remain in Montgomery in comfort and peace, but because he believed in the cause of freedom, "I have gone among wild-eyed fanatics. . . . I have walked through stomping crowds of screaming leftists and I have been cursed by them and I have been beat upon and their spittle has run down my face," he shouted, his fist pounding the podium for emphasis. Even though liberal newspaper reporters had "tried to trick and insinuate and revile you and me and our Southland," he concluded, "if you send me . . . *I will go again!*" The staid House chambers reverberated with rebel yells.[8]

A tall, rangy north Alabama cattleman and farmer, James Edwin Horton, Jr., sat slumped in his seat throughout the twenty-minute speech. Elected to the state Senate in 1962, he had been in office less than a year before he decided not to run again. "When I was in Montgomery, I worried about missing PTA meetings in Greenbriar," said Horton. "When I was home trying to catch up with the farm and family, I felt like I was neglecting my work in the Senate." The absence of political ambition freed him to take on the popular governor.[9]

Even though he liked Wallace personally, the governor's political antics and his hard-line defense of segregation repelled Horton. His father, James Edwin Horton, Sr., had been the presiding judge in the most famous of the Scottsboro trials. This celebrated civil rights case had begun in 1931, when two white women claimed that they had been raped aboard a freight train by nine black teenagers as they all hoboed across northern Alabama. When an all-white jury, inflamed by the Alabama prosecutor's appeal to racism, returned a guilty verdict with no recommendation for mercy, Judge Horton ordered a new trial for the Scottsboro defendants. As he had anticipated, voters turned him out in the following election. But he had never hesitated. A generation later, idealistic young Alabama lawyers still remembered Horton as a heroic figure in an Alabama judicial system tainted by racism, a true conservative who honestly believed that social order was based on the fair and impartial administration of the law.

Like his father, Edwin Horton would not be intimidated by the clamor of the mob. No-one was surprised when he joined fellow senator Bob Gilchrist to become co-leader of the Wallace opposition forces, a motley crew of little more than a dozen insurrectionists. A constitutional amendment required the approval of twenty-one of the state's thirty-five senators. While the insurrectionists struggled to win the fifteen votes needed to block the succession amendment, they filibustered, hoping Wallace would make a mistake.

Not all of the opponents of the succession bill acted out of disinterested motives. Ryan deGraffenried, defeated by Wallace in 1962, formed a tactical alliance with former Governor John Patterson. Both men were aiming for the governorship in 1966 (as was Gilchrist). From an informal command headquarters at the Albert Pick Motel in Montgomery, they secretly coordinated much of the opposition to the succession bill. "I worked undercover," said Patterson, though the coalition was hardly a secret to capital insiders. Former governor Jim Folsom warned them they were making a mistake, and urged them to let the people vote on the constitutional amendment in the fall of 1965. "If the people vote overwhelmingly for that thing, it will be a good indication for you to stay out." But deGraffenried and Patterson believed their only hopes for the governorship lay in keeping Wallace off the ticket.[10]

For seven weeks, George Wallace flailed away, a political giant surrounded by determined Lilliputian opponents. Throughout October he dragged recalcitrant senators into his office where he always began with cheerful flattery ("pattin' you, strokin' your arm, blowin' smoke up you," said one senator), then offered the usual legal political "incentives": promises of increased highway appropriations or state facilities, assurances of an open ear on patronage questions.[11] Lobbyists for state contractors were hauled in and told to use their influence with stubborn senators.

Wallace had at his disposal a critical weapon of persuasion: the state's self-insurance system. Beginning in the 1930s, Alabama provided its own insurance on rural schoolhouses in high-premium zones. To satisfy complaints by private insurers that the state's "socialistic" insurance scheme bypassed them, the legislature agreed to appropriate an amount equal to the commission fees that agents would have earned had they written equivalent policies. By 1966, annual commission fees on these phantom policies reached $600,000. In theory, the state's insurance commissioner disbursed these commissions to state insurance agents in an even-handed fashion in order to compensate them for lost income. In practice, the system provided a giant political slush fund controlled by the governor.[12]

As the campaign for the succession amendment grew more intense, Wallace authorized payouts to friendly insurance companies. In turn, they passed on "retainers" to designated senators; if the senator happened to be an attorney, such payoffs, under Alabama law, were perfectly legal. More enterprising legislators quietly paid a licensing fee, officially registered as insurance agents, and received the largesse directly.[13] In some cases the governor's men offered out-and-out bribes, a practice which they justified by claiming that Patterson and deGraffenried were also handing out cash payments. "Hell, the real problem was that half the crooks wouldn't stay bought," said one of Wallace's aides.

If positive inducements proved unsuccessful, intimidation quickly followed. "He gets to hollering and rantin' about how he's gonna take away everything in your county," said one senator who endured an hour-long Wallace harangue. These were not empty threats. In the first legislative session of his governorship, Wallace had shown that he could play hardball politics by canceling more than seven million dollars in road construction projects in the home districts of four of his opponents.[14]

After Julian Lowe, a first-term senator from south Alabama, balked at supporting the governor, a secretary called him off the Senate floor to take a telephone call from the extremely agitated head of Southern Union State Junior College in Wadley. President Walter Graham explained to Lowe that he had just received a call from the governor's office. Seymore Trammell had called his attention to the legislature's June appropriation of nearly half a million dollars for new construction at the college. With his usual bluntness, Trammell told Graham that unless Senator Lowe came out in favor of the succession amendment "the governor had found other uses for the college's capital-outlay money." Hardly a major academic institution, Southern Union was the only post-secondary school in Lowe's largely rural constituency.

Lowe returned to the Senate after taking the call, requested the floor for a "point of personal privilege," and recounted President Graham's conversation word for word while the governor and his aides listened with dismay over a desk speaker. "My vote is not for sale," announced Lowe.[15]

The prospect of defeat prompted Wallace to more and more counterproductive attempts at intimidation. When the state's largest papers ran editorials opposing the succession amendment, the governor summoned *Montgomery Advertiser* political writer Bob Ingram to his office and "raised hell for thirty minutes." Ingram, a veteran reporter with an easygoing manner and a knack for getting along with politicians, tried to disarm Wallace with a few jokes. Instead of calming down, however, the governor picked up the telephone and called Henry Gray, administrator of the Alabama Alcoholic Board of Control, the agency charged with managing the state-owned liquor stores. Tell the liquor distributors, Wallace angrily ordered Gray, that anyone who advertised in the *Advertiser,* the *Alabama Journal,* or the *Birmingham News* could forget about selling his whiskey in the state's liquor stores. Over the next three days, the advertising cancellations came pouring in. When the *Advertiser* reported the story of the ad cancellations (but not the off-the-record encounter between Ingram and Wallace), the governor professed shock that anyone should make such wild accusations and insisted that he had no knowledge of the liquor companies' decisions. "It cost us roughly a hundred thousand dollars," said *Advertiser* editor Harold Martin, who had assumed the position formerly held by Wallace's old ally, Grover Hall, Jr. The *News* began to soft-pedal its opposition and Wallace bragged to friends that the advertising cancellations had successfully "enlightened" the Birmingham newspaper. But the negative editorials continued in the *Advertiser* and *Journal.*[16]

Late on the afternoon of October 13, 1965, a telegram from the governor's office arrived at Ed Horton's north Alabama home. Although the senator was in Montgomery, just down the hall from the governor's office, the telegram brusquely announced that Wallace would fly to Florence, Alabama, the following morning to ask constituents why their senator had refused to allow them to vote on the succession amendment. Horton was welcome to join the governor on the platform if he wished to explain his position.[17]

When his wife called with news of the Wallace challenge, Horton climbed into his car for the long five-hour drive back to Greenbriar. Next morning at the Florence Holiday Inn he found a meeting room packed with more than two hundred cheering Wallace supporters, who interrupted the governor with foot-stomping ovations again and again as he accused Horton of joining hands with the national liberals.

"Huntley and Chinkley," sneered Wallace, "and Walter Contrite and all the rest are eager to report that Wallace and his fight for constitutional govern-ment have been repudiated." Horton and his fellow senators were engaged in an underhanded political effort to block the will of the people. A handful of protesters had arrived from Florence State College; armed with tips from his undercover antisubversive unit, Wallace announced to the crowd that one "pro-Horton" student leader had recently signed an advertisement in the *New York Times* urging the United States to end its involvement in Vietnam. ("That wasn't a great help to me as I got ready to speak," said a laconic Horton.) A second student, challenged by the governor, admitted that he had participated in the civil rights march from Selma to Montgomery.

Horton listened grimly, arms folded. When the governor finished his re-marks, he climbed up onto the small podium and began reading from a handful of note cards he had dictated to his wife the evening before. He denied the charge that he was associated with the candidacy of any of Wallace's political opponents. He was simply concerned over the power which the governor would be able to command if he remained in office. If the constitutional amendment were put to a vote, Wallace would mobilize every arm of the state to ensure its victory and then to guarantee his reelec-tion. As catcalls from angry listeners threatened to drown Horton out, he turned to the governor with a half-smile. "You know Governor, I now know how you felt up North." Wallace laughed appreciatively; most members of the audience did not. Horton doggedly pressed on. "In the final analysis, I must satisfy, not the governor, not the Legislature, but my own conscience. This I have done."[18] He stepped down and listened in silence for twenty minutes as constituents surrounded him and poured out their anger. An awkwardly smiling Wallace came up to Mrs. Horton and apologized. "Now you know, I like your husband; he's a fine fella; this is just politics."[19]

In nearby Huntsville, Wallace whipped the crowd of four hundred sup-porters into wild cheers with his hostile criticism of the "liberal newspapers" and their "henchmen." Senator Roscoe Roberts, another opponent of the succession amendment, received a forceful reminder of just how strongly many of his constituents felt about their governor. "He got 'em all worked up," said the senator, "and then he turned and pointed straight at me down in the crowd and said, 'There. There he is.' " A dozen hard-eyed men con-verged on Roberts, yelling " 'You sonuvabitch,' and that sort of thing," he recalled.[20] Just before Huntsville police stepped in to rescue the shaken senator, Wallace—aware that he was courting disaster—hastily called off the crowd. Other senators declined to join Wallace on the platform. "I'm glad to debate him," claimed Bob Gilchrist, "but I'm not going to do it in front of a bunch of thugs."[21]

Over the next six days, the governor broadcast a paid thirty-minute tele-cast across the state and spoke at least once in the home district of each of his Senate opponents.[22] Buoyed by the enthusiastic crowds he encountered at every stop on his whirlwind tour, he held tenaciously to the belief that he would muster the twenty-one votes he needed for victory. On October 22, he sat in his office and listened to the final debate over an intercom wired directly into the Senate chambers. All through the morning, the bad news trickled in, as one by one the undecided senators jumped ship. Neil Metcalf, a small-town attorney from Hartford and a reserve major in the National Guard, had desperately sought to avoid antagonizing Wallace while satisfying his own misgivings. He wangled an invitation for a special training session at Fort Leavenworth, Kansas, and assured the governor that although he supported him, duty called. Twenty-four hours before the final vote, Wallace dispatched an Alabama Air National Guard plane to Kansas City, but the major failed to show up for the flight back to Montgomery. Another wavering senator also disappeared on the eve of the showdown; that man was last seen, said a colleague, "loading a case of scotch in the trunk of his car and heading south." He had not stopped driving or drinking until he reached a New Orleans "sanitarium," where doctors reported he was in no condition to be moved.[23]

Any hope of pulling out an upset victory ended shortly after eleven A.M. when Kenneth Hammond took the floor. With a crewcut and hands the size of hams, the northeast Alabama senator looked like a cross between a Mafia enforcer and a lineman for Alabama's Crimson Tide. Through October he had withheld his views on the succession bill; Wallace and his advisers had used both the stick and carrot in meetings the previous week. With Hammond, as with Julian Lowe, the pressure had backfired. For thirty-five minutes, the beefy, blunt-spoken Hammond attacked the governor in one of the most vitriolic speeches ever made on the floor of the Alabama State Senate. Wallace was "no better than Adolf Hitler," he declared. The governor's opponents had only one fate: to be branded by Wallace as "nigger lovers, pinkos or communists."

Lieutenant Governor James Allen stalked out of the chamber to protest what he called "abusive and inappropriate" language. Hammond raged on. "In order to pick up support, he is going to pit the white race against the minorities of this country—the same way Adolf Hitler pitted the Jews against the master race. . . . The hatemongers may kill me before I leave the Capitol," he melodramatically warned as he reached down and placed a wrinkled cloth bag on his desk, but "This is my insurance policy." Listeners heard a heavy, ominous, clunking metal noise and the chambers fell silent. ("They just knew there was a pistol in that bag," said one senator.) His "insurance policy," Hammond confided, was the "best damn tape recorder money can buy. I've got every rotten promise George Wallace ever made me." The audience shuffled with released tension.[24]

His defection sealed the fate of the succession bill. When Lieutenant Governor Allen announced the vote shortly after three P.M., the number of opponents had increased from twelve to fourteen. Eighteen state senators—three short of the necessary sixty percent—stood with Wallace on the measure. As the exhausted members of the Senate filed out of the chamber, broadcasters interrupted regularly scheduled programming for a special news bulletin: an all-white Lowndes County jury had ignored the overwhelming preponderance of direct and circumstantial evidence and returned a not guilty verdict against Collie LeRoy Wilkins, one of the Ku Klux Klansmen who was charged with murdering Viola Liuzzo.

As usual, said Albert Brewer, Wallace's House floor leader, "nobody thought to call Lurleen after the thing failed." Brewer's wife, Martha, and the first lady were close friends. "They were very much alike in their background," said Brewer. "They were really homemakers: their families, their children were of primary importance to them." When Lurleen Wallace answered the phone late that afternoon, Brewer greeted her: "Get your running shoes on. The succession bill has failed."

"Uh-uh, not me. *You.*" She laughed. "Martha and I'll give teas all over Alabama."[25]

Brewer knew better. Several weeks before his decision to call for a special session to repeal the antisuccession ordinance, in an off-the-record session with a Montgomery reporter, Wallace had suggested that he might run his wife.[26] But even after the bill's defeat, political insiders scoffed at the idea of a Lurleen Wallace candidacy. "The idea of Wallace running his wife is so bizarre," wrote Bob Ingram, "and so very difficult to take seriously that it is not easy even to comment on it."[27]

A stand-in candidacy by a southern governor's wife was not totally unprecedented. In 1917, the Texas legislature impeached James Ferguson for misappropriating state funds and barred him from office for life. In 1924, only four years after the ratification of the nineteenth amendment, the still-popular Texas politician audaciously put up his wife as a candidate for governor. While courthouse politicians (all men) initially scoffed at the notion, they were no longer laughing by election day. Miriam, or "Ma" Ferguson as she called herself, began each rally with a brief statement promising that her husband would be her "right-hand man," and then stepped aside while he lambasted the other "look-alike, sound-alike candidates" whose vague platforms were "like the hoop skirt which covers everything and touches nothing."[28] Voters put aside their misgivings and elected James Ferguson's wife to two terms in office.

During a White House briefing for the nation's governors in 1965, Lyndon Johnson had told Wallace about the Texans' success and passed along a variation of one of Jim Ferguson's best campaign quips: challenged about his duties in his wife's administration, Ferguson told delighted listeners, "I'm gonna draw the water, tote in the wood, wind the clock and put out the cat."[29] Reporters also trotted out the tale of Pa and Ma Ferguson after the succession bill's defeat, and Texas oil billionaire H. L. Hunt had mailed the governor a lengthy memorandum describing the campaign tactics the couple had used to overcome the apprehensions of a skittish electorate.[30]

But Wallace also knew there were no other precedents, north or south, for electing a woman governor. The Wyoming Democratic State Convention had appointed Nellie Tayloe Ross to succeed her late husband in 1925, but when she tried to run on her own, voters decisively rejected her bid for office.[31] Moreover, while "Ma" Ferguson had concentrated on ceremonial duties, she had always been keenly interested in politics and, in the view of many Texans, was the equal of her husband as a tactician. Lurleen Wallace was no Miriam Ferguson. *Time* magazine and other representatives of the national media had repeatedly identified the governor's wife as a "former dime-store clerk" and a "high school graduate"; Martha Nachman, a Montgomery community activist who had known the family since her childhood, described Lurleen as a "pitiful little something." Nachman had no reservations about Lurleen's social background, but the first lady's willingness to accept her husband's casual cruelties—to accept being treated like a "whipped dog"— repelled her. She was "that way until the day she died," Nachman said. "Kind of pitiful and undernourished in every way—physically, socially, culturally, economically, intellectually undernourished."[32]

It was true that Lurleen Wallace, like many young women of her generation from working-class backgrounds, had not been able to go to college and had usually played the role of dutiful wife. She was as intelligent as and probably more capable than many of the men who ran Alabama's government; her real handicaps were her shyness in public and her total uninterest in the grubby business of politics. Tom Johnson, the Montgomery editor of the *Independent* and a friend of the Wallaces, was dumbfounded when he heard her name suggested. She was the most "unlikely candidate imaginable," he said. "It is as difficult to picture her in politics as to envision Helen Hayes butchering a hog."[33]

The soft-spoken governor's wife was equally incredulous when the issue was first broached. "Why, it never even crossed my mind that I'd ever enter politics myself," she admitted. "That was George's job . . . and my job was to stay home and raise the kids and look after the house."[34]

Slim and attractive, with just a touch of gray in her soft brown hair, the unpretentious Lurleen Wallace was, as one political columnist observed, just pretty enough to be attractive to men, but not so beautiful as to cause jealousy among women. She bought her shoes from a budget shop on State Street in Montgomery, and her clothes off the rack at a department store; for special occasions, she asked her best friend, Mary Jo Ventress, to whip up a dress from a high-style Vogue pattern. Each week a student at a local beauty college did her hair.[35]

When she was thirty-five and her husband became governor, she moved to a sixteen-room residence with a housekeeping staff and a chauffeur-driven car, but to the black prison trusties who served her, to the burly highway patrolmen who drove her on errands and watched over her, to the people who wandered through the governor's mansion on daily tours, she was one of them. Lurleen Wallace never turned her back on the working-class people of Alabama.

As one candidate after another edged toward entering the governor's race, Wallace measured the field and calculated the odds. Former governor John Patterson had trounced him in 1958 and itched for a comeback after four years of private law practice, but Patterson's popularity had declined; he was unlikely to be a serious contender, even against a surrogate candidacy by Mrs. Wallace. National Democrats pinned their hopes on Carl Elliott, the liberal ex-congressman from north Alabama, who announced his intention to run even before the succession bill failed. Vain, occasionally arrogant, the strikingly handsome Elliott was nevertheless an authentic man of the people, whose life seemed a model of exemplary public service. Like Senator Spark-man, he had worked his way up from grinding poverty. His father was a struggling tenant farmer; Elliott remembered one year when the family cleared $3.30 for ten months of backbreaking labor. In the early days of the Depression he went off to the University of Alabama with $2.80, a willingness to work ninety hours a week, and a burning ambition to make something of himself and to help the poor whites of his native hill country. As president of the student body in 1934 he had met "the man who was and who remains a political God to me—Franklin D. Roosevelt." From the time of his election to Congress in 1948, Elliott never wavered in his support for a national government that reached down to help the poor people of Alabama. An unabashed liberal and a close friend of national Democrats from Harry Truman to John Kennedy to Lyndon Johnson, he voted for public housing and increased-minimum-wage legislation, against the antilabor Taft-Hartley and Landrum-Griffin acts. And he was the key representative behind the passage of the National Defense Education Act of 1958—a measure, drafted in response to the Cold War technology race, that substantially increased federal educational funding. Over the years he had built a solid reputation as a man of unshakable rectitude, a "moderate" on racial matters, and a colorblind, pro-labor liberal on economic issues.[36]

The bad blood between Elliott and George Wallace went back to September 1962. The two shared the platform at a north Alabama meeting of Young

Democrats, three months after the governor's runoff victory over Ryan de-Graffenried. Afterward, at the urging of Bill Jones, Wallace showed up at the congressman's Jasper home. Elliott, who prided himself on his lifelong principles, had nothing but contempt for the new governor's capricious political turns. He didn't "stand for anything . . . he'd become anybody's dog that would hunt with him." But Jones, who had worked for the congressman, hoped to persuade his old boss to join hands with the state's new political powerhouse.

As Wallace started "scattering all this poppycock about how I had to join him," Elliott first tried to respond evasively. But as his guest's monologue of veiled threats and offers of support stretched into the early morning hours, his patience wore thin. "George," he said, "you don't want me because I don't want *you*." He would not be part of the effort to "tear down the judiciary and go through all this business of reinstituting a civil war." When Wallace pressed on, said Elliott, "I stopped him and ended the evening with just about the last statement of any substance that would come between us. 'George,' I said, 'don't piss on my leg [and tell me it's raining].' "[37]

Two years later, Wallace supported the White Citizens' Council, the John Birch Society, and the Ku Klux Klan in their successful campaign to block Elliott's reelection on the grounds that he was "soft on the nigger question."[38] So Elliott's gubernatorial bid was based, in part at least, on a desire for revenge. But it was also fueled by an authentic outrage over what he saw as Wallace's cynical abandonment of old-style liberalism and his embrace of the politics of racism.

On paper, the governor's most formidable challenger appeared to be his silver-haired, handsome attorney general, Richmond Flowers. Little in Flowers's background suggested that he would become the champion of racial liberalism and the point man for the Wallace opposition. The well-to-do south Alabama businessman and attorney cut his teeth on politics in the mid-1950s as a cautious Folsom supporter and was renowned for his prowess as an after-dinner speaker who regaled audiences with convoluted "darkie" stories told in dialect. He won election as attorney general in 1962 essentially by promising to be more clever than his opponents in using the court system to thwart desegregation.[39]

But Flowers had staked out a more moderate position on race on the day of Wallace's inauguration, when he chided the new governor for failing to distinguish between "a fighting chance and a chance to fight."[40] During the crisis over the stand in the schoolhouse door, he had tried to play the honest broker between Wallace and Katzenbach and had talked secretly to Attorney General Robert Kennedy.[41] While cynics attributed the attorney general's change of heart to the growing black vote in Alabama, his break with Wallace came well before substantial increases in black registration. The deaths of the four little girls at the Sixteenth Street Baptist Church touched off some deep sense of revulsion; thereafter Flowers spoke out with a new anger and passion. A month after the bombing he bluntly told a group of Birmingham businessmen that the time for the governor's antics was over. While he would continue to challenge those federal desegregation orders he felt were unreasonable, he would not do so by appealing to the contrived doctrines of interposition and state sovereignty. "The Supreme Court's decisions are the supreme law of the land and I'm *going to obey them.*"[42]

Wallace's legislative allies soon became inured to the governor's periodic rages over the indignity of being criticized by his own attorney general. In October 1965, after Flowers released a report publicizing Wallace's links with Klansman Asa Carter and accusing the governor of protecting his Klan supporters, a furious Wallace called a meeting of key senators and urged them to "impeach the son-of-a-bitch." But if Wallace despised the attorney general, he never feared him politically. White voters, he told Seymore Trammell, would never vote for a "renegade scalawag" who supported civil rights.[43]

The one opponent George Wallace feared was Ryan deGraffenried. The governor, said an aide, was "scared to death of Ryan." A journalist had dubbed the handsome Tuscaloosa attorney a "kind of Alabama John F. Kennedy," perhaps not exactly a compliment savored by many of the state's politicians, even after the President's posthumous canonization. But deGraffenried did exude an indefinable star quality. A former football great, champion debater, and decorated World War II veteran, he scarcely paused after his 1962 loss to George Wallace before he began planning for 1966. Except for a slightly greater pro-business tilt, his position on economic issues differed little from that of the incumbent, but in tone and style deGraffenried conveyed an image of calm, no-nonsense steadiness and reliability. When he talked about race relations, he usually gave the governor credit for good intentions, but argued that Wallace's cavalier defiance had accomplished nothing except the escalation of bitterness and racial hostility within the state. DeGraffenried called for a "cooling-off period" in racial tensions and promised to be a "full-time, hands-on governor"—something no one would ever say about George Wallace. He cultivated Alabama's business, educational, and labor leadership with the promise that he would "put an end to violence . . . concentrating on building the human and natural resources of our state."[44]

Though he had exhibited little overt evidence of a greater willingness to compromise on racial issues than the governor, black voters tended to support him as an acceptable moderate white candidate. Even whites committed to Wallace grudgingly viewed deGraffenried as a man of integrity who had somehow managed to avoid antagonizing his enemies—no easy task in the labyrinth of Alabama politics.[45]

All through the month of November, the governor listened to advice from his aides. One minute he would talk of running his wife, recalled Seymore Trammell. Then he would shift back to the possibility of a Senate race, and then he would embrace some "damn fool idea" like having his brother Jack run in his place.[46] Trammell and John Kohn urged him either to take Spark-man's seat or to wait it out for four years; Cecil Jackson remained undecided. Except for Wallace's old friend Ralph Adams, the only insider enthusiastic about the surrogate candidacy was Asa Carter. "What political science books have y'all read?" he demanded. "She can win. If she doesn't, she can get a million dollars' worth of publicity and it'll help the governor nationally."[47]

Even Lurleen Wallace became frustrated. After days of listening to him "kind of talk around it," she finally asked outright: "George, you want me to run?"

Patting her knee, he had replied enigmatically: "You'd make a fine candidate, sweetie."[48]

It got "right down to the lick-log," said Trammell. "He was gonna have to make a move now one way or the other."[49] Just before Thanksgiving, the equation became infinitely more complicated. Lurleen Wallace had cancer.

In the midst of the succession debates Alabama's first lady had called her Montgomery gynecologist and asked for an appointment. Her menstrual cycle had become more and more erratic and she had begun to experience abnormal bleeding, she told him. Dr. Joe Perry reassured her; she was probably having a minor reaction to the estrogen he had prescribed as she approached menopause. But he was concerned enough to begin a series of examinations and tests. The biopsy of uterine tissue confirmed his apprehensions: Mrs. Wallace definitely had cancer. Shortly after he received the lab report, Perry and the house physician came into her room at St. Margaret's Hospital and gently broke the news to her. Although Perry was upbeat and optimistic—he explained to her that uterine cancer was usually quite treatable—she had been conditioned to think of cancer as a death sentence. She tried to reach her husband, but he was unavailable, caught up in a round of frantic meetings designed to chart his political future. When Juanita Halstead, a close friend, called to ask how the tests had gone, Lurleen Wallace burst into tears. "Nita, I'm scared," she blurted out. "I've got cancer. . . . They just told me. The doctors just came and told me."

Halstead was stunned: "Are you alone?"

Still weeping, Mrs. Wallace whispered, "Yes."[50]

The diagnosis had a prior history. In April 1961, when she had delivered her youngest child, Lee, by caesarean section, an alert surgeon recognized suspicious tissue on the abdominal wall and ordered a biopsy. One pathologist concluded that it was definitely malignant or premalignant; another thought it might be a cellular malformation that sometimes occurred during pregnancy.[51] When they discussed the implications of the reports with George Wallace, he insisted that his wife not be told. His decision was not unusual for its time. A survey of oncologists made the previous year showed that ninety percent of physicians preferred not to tell patients they had cancer; instead they employed such euphemisms as "growth" or "tumor" or "hyperplastic tissue." If the patient was a woman, physicians almost invariably took their cue from her husband.[52]

A year later, Wallace enlisted Juanita Halstead in a ruse to have his wife examined by a specialist at Atlanta's Emory University Hospital. Halstead persuaded Lurleen to join her in a "routine" checkup, but the physician—because Mrs. Wallace could not be told of the earlier findings—was able to give her only a limited examination. The elaborate charade aptly captures the crushing fear of cancer which afflicted all Americans in mid-century as well as the dynamics of the roles middle-class husbands and wives played in southern society. The strong husband would make all the critical decisions; the frail wife would be shielded from her tribulations.[53]

Now, in early December 1965, physicians prescribed radiation. While Lurleen recuperated in St. Margaret's Hospital, one of her husband's friends came by to see her. Unaware that she had never been told about the 1961 biopsy (though Wallace had discussed it with his aides during the 1962 campaign), he offered his sympathy, then added offhandedly: "Well, they thought you had cancer once before."

"When Lurleen found out, it almost drove her crazy to begin with," remembered Juanita Halstead. Her anger was not eased by her husband's placating explanation: "Now honey, there was no point in you worrying about that."[54] George Wallace seems to have acted from a variety of motives. If Lurleen Wallace was to be a candidate for governor, the last thing her husband and his advisers needed were rumors that an earlier cancer had re-occurred and she was dying. The initial statements issued in November after the second biopsy were distinctly misleading. Mrs. Wallace had undergone a "minor operation," reported the governor's press secretary. She was "doing fine." Most readers who saw the brief news items assumed that it referred to some unspecified "female" surgery.[55] And when the first lady began two weeks of outpatient radiation therapy in early December, the governor's office did not report her treatment to the press.

Even though physicians were encouraged by Lurleen's response to radiation, they decided to perform a hysterectomy, major surgery requiring that she be hospitalized for over a week. Their patient had made repeated trips to St. Margaret's Hospital; more than a dozen radiologists, nurses, doctors, and hospital staff knew of her condition. So the governor's office issued a press release indicating that Mrs. Wallace would enter the hospital in mid-January of 1966 for a hysterectomy. There was no mention of cancer.

Lurleen Wallace assisted, however circumspectly, in the deception. Three days before her hospitalization, she met with Bob Ingram in the governor's mansion for a one-hour interview "to set the record straight once and for all." Off the record, she admitted that her doctors had discovered a "tumor" (she did not specify that it was malignant, and the deferential Ingram did not press her on this point). The news would be disclosed to the press after additional tests. "I've been dying of cancer for five years, if you believe all the rumors," she declared. To this day, "when I run into someone I haven't seen in a long time, they look at me and say, 'why you look real good.' "[56]

To a casual reader, the interview was bewilderingly oblique: Mrs. Wallace seemed to be denying rumors sweeping through Montgomery that she had cancer. In reality, she was seeking to conceal the fact that this might be her second brush with the disease.

On January 10, a team of three physicians, including the director of Emory University's Winship Memorial Clinic, performed the surgery, and for the first time, the governor's office acknowledged that the first lady had an "early malignant tumor." But her doctors, Wallace assured reporters, had described her long-term outlook as good. In a press release that reflected her husband's sensitivity to the issue of preexisting condition, Mrs. Wallace insisted, "All of these years people have said I had cancer, but they were wrong. I do now," she admitted, "but the doctors are certain that it was detected in time."[57]

Although the medical bulletins remained resolutely upbeat, her physician, Joe Perry, suggested that she concentrate on "enjoying the comforts of a family unit" and "let this business of a succession run its course." Her husband could wait four years and run again. In the delicate verbal dance of indirection that characterized the cancer dialogue between physician and patient in the 1960s—particularly in the South—this was as close as a doctor could come to suggesting that time might be short.

"I will think about it," was her noncommittal reply.[58]

House floor leader Brewer was well aware of the gossip about Lurleen Wallace's health; there was a "general feeling that she might not be able to serve out the term," he said. But he firmly believed that her husband would push her into the race if he thought it would keep the governor's office under his control.[59]

High winds and an opponent's impulsive decision confirmed Wallace's inclination to have his wife run as his surrogate. Ryan deGraffenried picked up the tempo of his campaign and began traveling across the state in a small twin-engine Cessna and an even smaller two-person helicopter. On February 9, after a late-afternoon appearance in Fort Payne, a town in the northeastern corner of the state, friends drove deGraffenried to the county airport, where pilot Bob Hoskins waited to make the short flight to nearby Gadsden and another speaking engagement. Twice the airport manager urged the candidate to drive the forty miles. A storm was coming in from the west, and takeoff required a steep ascent to clear the thousand-foot-tall Lookout Mountain, just south of Fort Payne. "Do you think you can make it?" deGraffenried asked. When Hoskins nodded, his passenger shrugged. "I let my pilot do the flying," he said. The two men climbed into the cockpit, and the blue-and-gray Cessna hurtled down the runway, picked up speed, and disappeared into the darkness. A black woman living in a remote cabin on the mountain's slope heard the full-throttle roar of the engines as Hoskins fought a sudden down-draft, and then a loud explosion as gale-force winds flipped the little plane on its back and slammed it into the mountain two hundred feet below the ridgeline. Pilot and passenger died instantly.[60] DeGraffenried's tragic death cleared the last obstacle for a run by Lurleen Wallace.

A week after the plane crash, *Gadsden Times* columnist Mary Hodl scathingly attacked Wallace for his callousness in foisting the race on a "woman who is essentially reserved, who has not yet recovered from major surgery and who admittedly has never wanted any part of politics." Despite the governor's tremendous popularity, predicted Hodl, the voters would rebel against this cynical ploy.[61]

Returning to the mansion uncharacteristically early on the afternoon of February 20, 1965, the day Hodl's column appeared, Wallace abruptly announced, "We're not going to run. We're going back to Clayton when my term is up."

As he must have anticipated, his wife of twenty years firmly replied, "Yes, George, we will run." Within twenty-four hours Wallace circulated the word: Lurleen would be his stand-in.[62]

Although she would always react indignantly to the suggestion that she had been forced into the race, no one who knew the Wallaces had any doubts about who made the decision. James J. Kilpatrick traveled with the couple in the mid-1960s and remembered Lurleen Wallace as "a pleasant woman—a nice smile, a nose that just misses being a pug nose, crinkly lines of middle age about her eyes." On a flight from Washington to Montgomery, George Wallace briefly left his seat; and Kilpatrick and Mrs. Wallace began talking about their shared passion for fishing. Her face "lit up," he remembered, as she began describing a recent night out on Lake Martin. Floating in the darkness, she had hooked a bass. "He wasn't real big," she exclaimed, "only about so big—" But then her husband returned, "hitching up his pants," and launched into an embittered account of how Maryland Democrats had robbed him of a victory in that state's 1964 primary.[63]

Lurleen Wallace accepted her role as candidate out of a sense of duty to her husband and with the certain knowledge that to live with George Wallace out of politics would be to replay the nightmare she had experienced after his 1958 defeat. She was honest enough to admit that she did not relish going back to the struggle that had marked her married life in the years after they left Clayton for the capital. When she remembered those months alone in an overcrowded apartment while Wallace barnstormed the state, she realized "it would be so difficult to go back to that life." "Moving into the governor's mansion was the biggest thrill of my life," she told Wayne Greenhaw. "All of a sudden, I had people to help with the children."[64]

She talked to the three still at home. Lee, at five, was too young to understand. George Junior took the news stoically. But Peggy, a high school sophomore, knew what a campaign and the governorship would entail. "Why," she asked, "do you need to do this?" Lurleen could only reply that it was a decision that she and Peggy's father had reached.[65] With Wallace's press secretary, she was more candid. "Bill," she later told him, "I did it for George."[66]

FROM the kickoff rally in Montgomery in mid-March of 1966 it was clear that Lurleen Wallace's opponents in the Democratic primary were helpless. For nearly a decade white Alabamians had turned on their televisions and had seen the national media's morality play unfold with an unchanging cast of characters: heroic black civil rights leaders and their followers beaten and abused by tobacco-chewing, pot-bellied, redneck sheriffs and thuggish-looking state policemen. Like a talented sorcerer, Wallace called forth the self-pitying paranoia that had afflicted whites since the first abolitionist had called on the people of the South to repent. They could not strike back against their tormentors, except by embracing the man who could soothe their wounded pride ("the people of Alabama are just as cultured and refined as anywhere in this nation") and promise to take the battle to the enemy ("if you support me, in 1968, I'll shake the eye-teeth of the liberals in this country").

The Wallace caravan moved through the hamlets, towns, and cities of the state in a grueling schedule of four to five rallies a day. In this Deep South state of Baptists and Methodists, the spectacle seemed almost Mediterranean, as if Lurleen Wallace were a plaster Mary being carried through the streets on a saint's day parade, preceding the faithful. The highway patrol cleared a path for the advance retinue: a bunting-draped speaker's platform flanked by Confederate and U.S. flags; two station wagons bearing Sam Smith and His Singing Alabamians, and five sound trucks—each emblazoned with "Stand Up for Alabama"—blaring out the rasping invitation, "Come to the courthouse square to hear Governor George Wallace and his lovely wife, Lurleen; come and hear Sam Smith and His Alabamians play a medley of inspirational tunes." At breakneck speed the procession moved from Opelika, to Phenix City, through Eufaula and as far south as Dothan, back up through Troy and Greenville, and on to the heart of the state. Robert Shelton roamed among the spectators and distributed Klan literature and "Never" buttons.[67]

That first campaign swing reached a triumphant climax on March 29 in

Demopolis, a beautiful small town on western Alabama's Tombigbee River. By the time the Wallaces arrived to deliver their fifth talk of the day, two thousand whites crowded the town square and spilled into the streets. They clapped and shouted as Sam Smith and the Alabamians finished up a rousing version of Hank Snow's old country-and-western hit "I'm Movin' On." As the governor glad-handed old friends, Mrs. Wallace—a fierce knot in her stomach—made her way through the crowd and accepted hugs from plainly dressed country men and women ("We're so proud of you, honey"). The band, masters at controlling a rally, first brought the crowd down a notch. "Now, folks, we want to play a little sacred number. It's Governor and Mrs. Wallace's favorite, 'Just a Closer Walk with Thee' " ("I am weak, but Thou art strong . . . ."). Then, before the scattered amens had faded away, the band whipped the crowd back to a foot-stomping crescendo with several rollicking choruses of "Dixie."

Her hands fluttering with a barely perceptible nervous tremor, Lurleen Wallace stepped up to the bank of microphones. ("One speech down and ten to go," she had grimly told one of her friends at the beginning of the campaign swing.) Carefully, she began reading from the 519-word text, delivered, as always, said one Montgomery editor, "with poise, but not with a great deal of enthusiasm—a little like a star pupil declaiming on Flag Day at the School Assembly." She ended with an explicit repudiation of her own ambition and independence: "I am grateful to be the instrument whereby you, the people of Alabama, have an opportunity to express yourself on the record compiled by the Wallace administration."

The crowd roared as George Wallace bounced across the stage, gave his wife a quick hug as she retreated to her seat, and launched into a fifty-minute laundry list of all the sufferings he and his listeners had endured. Obligatory references to the accomplishments of his administration—the free textbooks, the expansion of the trade school, the new highways—he passed over hurriedly. Wallace knew that the people of Demopolis had come to hear him exorcise the demons that tormented the God-fearing white people of Alabama: the "big city" press; the federal courts; bureaucrats; beatniks and Communists.

"I see we got the *Life* magazine and the *Saturday Evening Post* with us here," he said to a ripple of laughter. "We even got *Esquire* with us today. 'Course, they're not interested in taking our pictures; we wear too many clothes for them." His voice hardened as he spotted Ray Jenkins, his nemesis during the succession crisis. As spectators craned to see, an expressionless Jenkins—just back from a year as Nieman Fellow at Harvard—jotted down the governor's words. The editor of Montgomery's *Alabama Journal*, that "liberal, left-wing socialist newspaper that thinks Alabama people haven't got any sense," the governor declared, was "one of them Harvard-educated editors that sticks his little finger up in the air when he drinks tea and looks down his nose at the common folk of Alabama." Wallace assured his listeners, "I spoke at Harvard and I told them that the people of my state are just as cultured, refined, and educated as the people of any state."[68]

Each personal grievance was catalogued, described with sarcasm, and then transformed into an insult against the people of Alabama. "The *Wall Street Journal*"—Wallace turned to Lurleen, who handed him the clipping— "made fun of my wife on the front page because she used to be a dime-store clerk and her daddy was a shipyard worker." He looked out on the crowd, which included more than a smattering of clerks and children of laborers. "Well, I want you to remember that you're just as cultured and just as refined as those New York reporters and editors!"[69]

He did not fight just for himself. "I want to stay in public life so I can continue this campaign throughout the nation. . . . The liberal leftwing punks don't want us in public life," snarled Wallace; they want to keep all power in the hands of a "judicial dictatorship" and a "government bureaucracy run by folks a thousand miles away with beards and goatees." The "liberals and beatniks and Socialists have gotten together and said, 'We're not gonna have any more of Wallace,' and that's why the national press is here, to see if you are going to repudiate what we've done." In a lonely reference to his opponents, he promised the crowd that while other candidates for the governorship were "running about the state stressing Alabama needs better relations with Washington, . . . I'm not going to cooperate with a group of liberal pinkos!"

Arms flailing, head bobbing, he swerved back to one of the festering resentments that seemed to drive his indignation: "Why did Bobby Kennedy come to Alabama and make fun of my wife running for Governor?" demanded Wallace. "Why, he's the fellow that advocated giving blood to the Vietcong." (The charge, like most of Wallace's, was about ninety percent exaggeration. Following a speech at Tuscaloosa earlier in the month, Kennedy had deflected questions about his future ambitions with the smiling remark that his wife, Ethel, was "not going to run for President."[70] And the year before, in the wake of round-the-clock bombing of North Vietnam, Kennedy had defended the right of Americans to send blood plasma to "anyone who needs blood, including the North Vietnamese."[71] He had never advocated blood collection drives for the Vietcong, who were not civilians but soldiers.)

As Lurleen Wallace sat, hands folded, staring off into the darkness, the crowd became George Wallace's partner in a shouting, roaring defense of the Southland. "They tell you we're traitors. They tell you we're wrong to fly this flag"—he pointed to the Stars and Bars displayed at the end of the flatbed truck. "Whenever you see the Confederate flag flying, you will see people who will fight for their country with more zeal than anywhere else." Where you "find this flag, you won't find college students taking up money for the Vietcong and giving blood to the Vietcong or burning draft cards."

His last words—"God bless you, we're going to win on May third"—were lost in a roar of applause as Wallace, his wife walking slowly behind him, charged into the crowd for a last round of hand-shaking. Hundreds pushed forward, eager to press, to touch her. The self-contained Lurleen Wallace fixed one of her soft smiles on her face and steeled herself to endure the familiar embraces of hundreds of strangers. Once she reached the safety of the car, she leaned back gratefully and mused aloud, "I didn't know so many people in Alabama chewed tobacco. And they're all for me."

"Yeah," agreed her husband's longtime supporter Oscar Harper, "and they've all kissed you, too."[72]

Long after their scheduled departure, George Wallace reluctantly relinquished the handshakes and the hugs and tumbled into the backseat of the state trooper–driven Ford. In those moments of decompression, with his speech behind him and the day over, reporters who sometimes traveled with the governor could see—raw and naked—his need to win. He was half-exhilarated, half-terrified by the prospect that his gamble might fail; his words tumbled out pell-mell: "I don't believe I'll lose. I believe I'll win. I've got to win. Y'all saw 'em. Y'all saw their faces. They love me. All of 'em love me." Back at the motel, as his exhausted wife collapsed into bed, Wallace cradled the phone until one or two A.M., calling and waking supporters, occasionally issuing staccato instructions, mostly just encouraging them: "Tell 'em all hello for us. You tell all our friends hello, hear?"[73]

"It was like a damned blitzkrieg," complained 'Big Jim' Folsom, who ran a pathetically ineffectual campaign. John Patterson and Robert Gilchrist (de-Graffenried's designated successor) first attacked Wallace for fanning the flames of racial hatred and then griped that his obstinacy and inflexibility had led to more integration than was necessary. During the last week in March, only two weeks into the campaign, Patterson confided to a friend that the race was over: "There wasn't any way in the world of beating her." Men would vote for Lurleen Wallace, knowing it was simply a maneuver to allow them to support her husband. And as for women: "You had old women, eighty, ninety years old," Patterson marveled, "going and registering to vote that never voted in their life. Just so they could vote for her."[74] By the end of the month, Patterson was out of money and reduced to following the Wallaces around on their campaign tours in the hope of capitalizing on the already assembled crowds. Gilchrist, little more than a fringe figure, competed for newspaper space with a bizarre cast of kook candidates:

Charles Woods, a south Alabama multimillionaire whose face, emblazoned in living color on billboards statewide, was a mass of scar tissue from a World War II B-24 crash;

Eunice Gore, a Bible-toting retired office worker who claimed that he had "been ordered by the Lord to make this race" and who financed his campaign by passing out chances on a motorboat he hauled around the state;

A. W. (Nub) Todd, a former agriculture commissioner who got his nickname when he shot off his left arm hunting groundhogs as a boy;

Sherman Powell, a north Alabama lay preacher, lawyer, and coon hunter who—alone among the candidates—abandoned country music for a miniskirted go-go dancer in an effort to attract crowds for his speeches.

"That wasn't a slate of candidates," said William Bradford Huie as he looked back on the campaign, "it was a goddamn menagerie."[75]

Former congressman Carl Elliott threw himself into the race. Like Richmond Flowers, he realized that the number of black registered voters had risen from 110,000 to 235,000 between 1964 and 1966.[76] That figure was still less than one-fifth of the Alabama electorate, but with 200,000 votes and a third of the white electorate, Elliott thought he could topple the Wallace dynasty. He mounted his own version of the Wallace road show, with even bigger headliners: Hank Williams, Jr., and his backup band, the Cheatin' Hearts, and Hovie Lister and the Statesmen.

The campaign had scarcely begun before Elliott discovered that in the racial climate of 1966 his strategy of coalition-building was impossible. In bitterly divided Selma, he told a small rally that he had not come "to stand on the Edmund Pettus Bridge and shout *'Never!'*" Nor had he "come to stand in the Brown Chapel A.M.E church and sing 'We Shall Overcome.' " There must be a "middle ground for Alabamians." Too late, Elliott realized that Alabama had no "moderate" white constituency for any but the most cosmetic adjustments to the collapsing system of white racial domination. And audiences were hardly anxious to hear about Elliott's "liberal" economic record at a time when Wallace had made the word synonymous with treason.

To make matters worse, his plan to appeal to black voters sputtered feebly. "Before that campaign began, I assumed I *had* the black vote," said Elliott. But Richmond Flowers *did* join hands with blacks in Selma to sing "We Shall Overcome." He campaigned almost exclusively in the black community, and his message was hardly a careful attempt at mediation; his first act, Flowers told supporters, would be to "strike the colors of the Confederacy [which Wallace flew above the U.S. flag at the state capitol] and make it a museum piece." Second, "I will see to it that Negroes in this state receive their fair share of appointments to boards and commissions." He paused for effect. "And they won't be a bunch of 'Uncle Toms' either!"[77]

In early April, Elliott made a desperate pitch and asked Barney Weeks, head of the Alabama AFL-CIO and one of the few whites in the state with strong ties to the black community, to meet with Martin Luther King's aides and ask for his support. Word came back that the civil rights leader would endorse Elliott or no one at all. Within hours, however, the anxious candidate learned from a member of Lyndon Johnson's staff that King had changed his mind; the black community was set for Flowers, and King had told the President, "I've got to walk in front and let them push. There is nothing I can do about it." The following week, Elliott secretly met with the civil rights leader at the Birmingham airport, but their conference was brief; King had made up his mind, and he would not be moved. "I'm sorry about this," he told Elliott. "I understand your situation, but you must understand mine."[78]

King had concluded that who won or lost the gubernatorial race was less critical than the need to flush cautious white politicians from the shadows. He wanted no more backroom deals in which the black leadership, in return for vague promises, looked the other way when white politicians refused to appeal openly for their support. Led by King, Alabama's two largest black political groups endorsed Flowers. Those endorsements, predicted Jack Nelson for the *Los Angeles Times*, "will virtually eliminate Congressman Carl Elliott."[79]

Crowds thinned, and promises of money dried up. "I didn't stand a ghost's chance in hell after that day," Elliott admitted. And yet, with a kind of reckless, even foolhardy bravura, he disposed of his assets, mortgaged his house and car, and borrowed until he could borrow no more. In the final days of the campaign he cashed in his congressional pension and in so doing, consigned himself to a life of penury. "No power on Earth can stop us," he shouted to his dwindling audiences. "We must seize the leadership from the self-serving extremists. No one should be allowed to use the issue of race as a whipsaw for personal gain. We must have racial peace in Alabama." In the end, what drove him on was a dogged unwillingness to surrender to everything in politics he despised.[80]

Richmond Flowers posed the last threat to the Wallace victory. In racially polarized Alabama, his embrace of black issues probably doomed him in any case, but when he indiscreetly attacked the first lady in an interview with a Boston newspaper, he was finished with white voters. "You want to know if Lurleen is capable of governing," he told Jane Margold of the *Sunday Herald*, "just go to the high school she went to in Tuscaloosa and see if you find a diploma. Ain't nobody come up with it. She was sixteen when she married George and look what she's done since, worked in a dime store and been a housewife."[81] His attack was baseless: Lurleen Burns had graduated with her class in June of 1942.[82] To chivalrous Alabamians, Flowers's words were the last-gasp attacks of a desperate politician.

*   *   *

ON primary day, May 3, l966, the Wallace campaign rented the ballroom of Montgomery's Jefferson Davis Hotel and put up a huge runoff board above the speaker's platform. By ten P.M. it was all over. Nearly half a million Alabamians, almost all of them white, had cast their votes for the governor's wife. Her nine male opponents managed less than forty-five percent of the total vote. Richmond Flowers, as expected, drew the support of ninety per cent of the state's enlarged black electorate. By pollster Harris's best estimate, however, he received less than 20,000 of the state's 750,000 white votes. Carl Elliott picked up a smattering of black votes, but his 72,000 vote total, mostly from the northern tier of counties, was a stunning repudiation of his attempts to appeal to white "moderates." In his home county of Walker, which he had never failed to carry in more than two dozen primary and runoff elections, Lurleen Wallace beat him two to one.[83] The editor of the *Montgomery Advertiser* summarized the results: once the black vote was subtracted from the totals, "it is seen that, *literally,* most all white Alabamians voted for [Lurleen] Wallace."[84]

Two factors guaranteed the victory. First, while the national media headlined the enfranchisement of more than 100,000 new black voters, Wallace and his supporters quietly engineered a dramatic increase in the number of registered whites. In January 1966, the governor's office issued a red, white, and blue pamphlet to every *white* public school student in the state. The pamphlet urged parents to pay their poll tax, register to vote, and "stand up for Alabama." In the nine months preceding the primary, 110,000 new white voters were added to the polls—matching vote for vote the increase in the black electorate.[85]

And just twenty-four hours before the election, U.S. States Attorney General Nicholas Katzenbach announced on national television that he had dispatched three hundred federal observers to seven Black Belt counties to make certain that blacks were not subject to discrimination. His decision was spread across the front page of Alabama's newspapers on election day, "like we were some kind of banana republic," said one of Wallace's supporters.[86]

But pollster and political observer Samuel Lubell argued in his postmortem analysis that "it was at Selma a year ago that Wallace really won Tuesday's election." Lubell found a remarkable unanimity in the responses of whites, even those who described themselves as moderates, to the "humiliation" of the federally sanctioned Selma-to-Montgomery march: It was "like a show of force by some foreign occupying power. . . . It's rubbing salt in our wounds. . . . I've become George Wallace's man."[87]

The Republicans stood next in line for execution. In the wake of the Civil Rights Act of 1964 and Goldwater's victory in Alabama the same year, a new GOP had emerged in the state, but it was nothing like the traditional up-country Republicanism that had produced a Frank Johnson, or even the moderate pro-business Eisenhower Republicanism of the 1950s. These were the true believers: right-wing ideologues drawn by Barry Goldwater. The Arizona senator's economic conservatism and his hostility to any form of federal activism meshed comfortably with the reactionary politics of the new Republican right. In 1962, an almost unknown James Martin had nearly defeated longtime senator Lister Hill by whipping Alabama's white voters into a frenzy over the Kennedy administration's enforcement of federal court desegregation orders at Ole Miss. Two years later, the Goldwater landslide in Alabama swept five of the eight incumbent Democratic congressmen, including Carl Elliott, out of office. Encouraged by that victory, right-wing conservatives like Martin (elected to the Seventh Congressional District in 1964) believed they had succeeded in forging a new Republican majority on the basis of economic conservatism and racial segregation. Well before it was clear that Lurleen Wallace would declare her candidacy, Martin threw his hat into the ring for governor.

Although Martin blustered and condemned the federal government's newly issued school desegregation guidelines, Wallace dominated the headlines. In late July, while Republicans struggled for five minutes of local news coverage on the eve of their state convention in Montgomery, the governor called the Alabama legislature into a noisy session that soon became a media spectacle in its own right. His opening speech, broadcast live during prime time by the state's fifteen largest television stations as well as the educational television network, was billed as a blueprint for increasing highway appropriations and distributing $44 million to the state's schools—money he had conveniently found in this election year. Wallace's audience shuffled with boredom through the first ten minutes of the address before he shifted gears and began what was, in reality, the first speech of his 1968 presidential campaign.

To the enthusiastic cheers of legislators and political supporters, he detailed a series of increasingly inflammatory charges: power-hungry federal bureaucrats were intent on destroying the public schools; men in high places had "broken the law of the Constitution" and thus encouraged "every revolutionary—every thug who can assemble a mob" to go out and break the law; the federal courts had "abdicated their judicial functions as judges" and had become willing tools of the Johnson administration's plan to "tear down and subvert constitutional government." Even the "large liberal newspapers" of the state, controlled and manipulated by the "millions of dollars of foreign money" which had been "poured into this state in the past several months," had joined in the conspiracy.

The television cameras zoomed in on a stern-faced Mrs. Wallace, her eyes fixed on her husband, as he offered proof that the courts had become nothing more than "puppets of the executive branch of government." When the Kennedy administration's Justice Department had asked for an injunction in the Freedom Rider case in 1961, said Wallace, "it was immediately issued on the grounds that the channels of interstate commerce must remain free and unobstructed." But when a mob of "Communists" and a "bunch of advocates of Black Power" wanted to block the highway from Selma to Montgomery—and here Wallace curled his lip with contempt—"that same [federal court] says such conduct is constitutional."[88]

The accusation was a bizarre rendering of the state's recent history. Frank Johnson had indeed issued an injunction against the Ku Klux Klan mobs in the 1961 Freedom Rider case, and another in favor of the Selma-to-Montgomery march, but only in the hysterical atmosphere of white Alabama in the mid-1960s could one equate ax-handle-wielding Klan toughs with peaceful demonstrators struggling to obtain the right to vote. Seemingly, however, the appetite of white Alabamians for bombast was limitless. When letters and calls began pouring in ("Thank God, we've got a governor who'll stand up to Lyndon Johnson and his comunist [sic] courts"), Wallace scheduled a second speech three weeks later, again televised to a statewide audience, to urge the legislature to pass a bill that would reject the desegregation guidelines issued by the U.S. Department of Health, Education and Welfare and "tell the bureaucrats of power that they can take their federal money—and they know what they can do with it!"[89]

"Roaring Ovation Greets Governor," headlined the *Montgomery Advertiser;* "Governor's Speech Draws Standing Ovations," proclaimed another newspaper as reporters competed to describe the legislators' response to Wallace's invective. In his twenty-five-minute address, he seemed to outdo even his past performances in his overwrought charges against Washington. The "socialistic and alien" guidelines for ending segregation in the state's public schools, warned Wallace, had the "unqualified, one hundred percent support of the Communist Party, U.S.A., as well as all its fronts, affiliates and publications." Socialist bureaucrats and power-hungry politicians would not be satisfied until young boys and girls were made "pawns of sacrifice," their "beautiful spirituality of love" replaced by the "degeneracy of social planners."

Had the whole state "forgotten that we lost the Civil War, as we have lost every single neo-Confederate charge by Gov. Wallace during his administration?" demanded Ray Jenkins in the *Alabama Journal.* The governor's manipulation and exploitation of white voters' fear of change—Jenkins compared his tactics to Adolf Hitler's—and his absurd calls for interposition, his "hysterical outcries against the United States Government," were more than outrageous, they were "foolish to the point of dementia." By creating "something approaching a general psychosis in this state," said Jenkins, Wallace had accomplished all that he ever cared about: perpetuating his control of the governor's office and cynically strengthening his home base for his 1968 campaign for the presidency.[90]

Wallace kept up a steady stream of speeches and campaign appearances. Publicly he ignored his wife's Republican opponent; privately he ridiculed Martin with cruelly exaggerated imitations of his slightly pompous delivery. To the chuckles of an appreciative audience of friends, he would lean forward in his seat and puff out his chest. "He sounds just like a nigguh preacher or senator," he would explain solemnly. "Naaoww, brethrenn. . . ."[91]

In late October, William Bradford Huie watched the governor deliver his fifth speech of the day, "bright-eyed and bushy-tailed; like he'd just rolled out of bed. I mean, he was downright *wired,* he was so wound up." Not so Mrs. Wallace. E .C. Dothard, her state-trooper driver and bodyguard, remembered her fatigue. "I would go in the motel at night and she could barely walk up the stairs, she was so tired."[92]

Despite her obvious exhaustion, Lurleen Wallace seemed to blossom during the campaign. No one would ever mistake her for a great orator, but she learned to read her lines with conviction, and she responded gratefully to the outpouring of admiration and affection that greeted her at every stop. By fall, only her hurried escape for a soothing cigarette betrayed her continuing fear of crowds.

Jim Martin, singularly inept at campaigning, collapsed. He wasn't very optimistic about his chances in rural and small-town south Alabama, he confided to a group of well-dressed supporters. There was a "more informed class of people say in Huntsville [in north Alabama, and a center of the space program] than in parts of south Alabama. People with less than an eighth grade education are almost all against me." One of his listeners was the editor of the south Alabama *Prattville Progress.* Wallace campaign workers photocopied and distributed Martin's patronizing quotes on handbills and leaflets to ensure that the blunder alienated others outside the small Prattville readership.[93]

And Martin seemed to have learned nothing from Flowers's indiscreet comments about Mrs. Wallace. "We don't want any skirt for governor," he remarked smirkingly to an open meeting of Republican leaders. This casually sexist statement allowed George Wallace to become the defender of southern womanhood. "My opponents say they don't want no *skirt* for governor of Alabama. That's right—no *skirt.* Well, I want you to know, I resent that slur on the women of this state."[94] It proved to be one of his best applause lines.

Martin next took out statewide, full-page newspaper ads, which juxtaposed photographs of a stern-looking Martin and a glamorous Mrs. Wallace wearing a string of pearls and carried the headline: THE *REAL CHOICE:* A MAN OR

A WOMAN! The ad copy described Lurleen Wallace as a "nice wife, trying to do a man's job in Montgomery." Her Republican opponent, on the other hand, was a "he-man, a battler."[95] Martin was a "walking corpse" by September, bragged one gleeful Wallace campaign aide.

By mid-October George Wallace moved through the state like a victorious tribal chieftain, said then–*Newsweek* correspondent Marshall Frady. At each stop—at the courthouse steps or in a noisy high school cafeteria—he would sit and listen to local elders as they poured out news of small-town disturbances, burglaries, and break-ins ("We caught 'em and got it straightened out now. There was one colored boy with 'em"), or desperate pleas for the governor to use his influence to lure northern industry to their dying towns. Occasional lapses in the conversation allowed the governor to show off his astonishing memory for names and families as he greeted the upturned faces ("Yes, yes, yawl in the ginnin' business, I know yo folks. You tell Charlie hello for me"). It was as though, said Frady, he had "converted the entire state into his personal neighborhood . . . [and] that every community was as familiar and intimate to him as his own flesh."[96]

Virginia Durr, one of a handful of white racial liberals in Montgomery, watched the campaign with a mixture of horror and incredulity. Sister-in-law to Alabama-born Supreme Court justice Hugo Black, wife of former Federal Communications Commission chairman Clifford Durr, and a New Deal activist in her own right, Durr had returned to Alabama with her husband in 1951. (The couple had accompanied former local NAACP president E. D. Nixon to post bond for Rosa Parks when she was arrested by a Montgomery bus driver in 1955 for refusing to sit at the back of the bus; they had sheltered and defended Bob Zellner as well.) "The people adore them [the Wallaces], turn out in huge crowds and worship them," Virginia Durr wrote friends living in Puerto Rico. " 'Stand up for Alabama' does not mean one damn, single thing except to prevent integration," she continued, but it "sets people on fire," particularly white teenagers. "They pursue you downtown [in Montgomery] with Wallace stickers and it's almost your life if you refuse one, as they look at you with such hatred . . . and go on screaming 'Stand up for Alabama.' "[97]

Birmingham News columnist Hugh Sparrow, the dean of Alabama journalists, found nothing in his forty-three years of reporting to prepare him for the man from Clio. "I've never before seen a Governor who has the people so hypnotized that they believe everything he does is handed down from above," Sparrow confided to one out-of-town journalist.[98]

On November 3, election eve, George and Lurleen Wallace drove down to Clayton, where they were still registered to vote, for a last rousing rally. Nine thousand Barbour County whites—more than half of the county's white residents—jammed the courthouse square to hear the governor's promise to march on Washington in 1968 and "get the communists, socialists, beatniks and atheists out of government."[99] Back in Montgomery at midnight, the two were up again at six A.M. to return to Clayton. Though exhausted, the first lady seemed relaxed and happy. She voted, then hurried off to visit with old friends. But Wallace stayed to bask in the friendly banter of his former neighbors.

As the sun came out, fiercely bright and surprisingly warm for November, he put on a pair of dark glasses and wandered over to the small brick building that housed the Barbour County Republican headquarters. Lighting a cigarette, he looked around the square and slyly offered one of those carefully calibrated insults that only a southerner could fully appreciate. "This is the exact spot the Republicans were headquartered after the Civil War," he pointed out, and the Freedman's Bureau was "right here during Reconstruction—all them nigguhs and carpetbaggers and scalawags right here." Friends chuckled appreciatively; Republicans forced nervous smiles. "Should have mentioned that last night and watched the crowd sort of move over in this direction." He gestured toward the Republican headquarters. "Course I didn't say that last night," he added. You can "always be magnanimous when you're beating 'em."[100] He sauntered on back to the square, motioned to his bodyguard, and climbed into the car for the drive back to Montgomery.

At his semi-deserted campaign headquarters down the street from the Wallace victory party in the Jefferson Davis Hotel, a humiliated Jim Martin watched the totals go up on the bulletin board. Mrs. Wallace tallied 538,000 votes to a little over 250,000 votes for the Republican. Three of the five congressional incumbents elected in the Goldwater landslide of 1964 managed to hang on to their seats, but of the more than one hundred other candidates painstakingly recruited to challenge the Democrats, only one squeaked into office. Ironically, Lurleen Wallace drew a heavy black vote in the general election; the black leadership—anxious to support their own Democratic candidates in Black Belt counties—had urged constituents to vote a straight ticket. What one University of Alabama political scientist called a choice between a "rich man's segregationist" and a "poor man's segregationist" was no choice at all.[101]

EARLY in the debate on the succession bill, the senator from Eutaw, Alabama, announced that he could not support Wallace. Given another term in office, Charles Montgomery confided to a friend, George Wallace could become a "dictator, answerable to no one." As neighbors turned away and former friends angrily called to demand his resignation, Montgomery seemed to shrink physically and then to break. On the day he voted against the succession amendment, Montgomery had been "totally blind drunk," said one sympathetic colleague. "He could hardly talk."[102]

Four months later, as George and Lurleen Wallace made preparations for the official kickoff rally of their primary campaign, the balding Greene County farmer left his fishing cabin, drove erratically down a country road, struck a cow, and cut his arm on the broken car window. A black farmer passing by took him back to his cabin and then drove to Eutaw for medical help. Alone, Montgomery walked out to the back porch, overlooking the Black Warrior River, carefully propped a shotgun on the steps, placed the barrel in his mouth, and pulled the trigger. Those who knew him were quick to say that he had led a troubled life, with two broken marriages and a history of struggle against alcoholism. But they were equally quick to acknowledge that he had been totally unprepared for the savage hostility unleashed by his challenge to the governor.[103]

Six months after his wife's sweeping victory over Republican Jim Martin, Wallace sat in his office with James J. Kilpatrick, lit up a cigar, and replayed in his mind the sweet moment of his revenge. "You know those state senators?" Wallace said to Kilpatrick. "Not a one of them is back. They saw what the people would do to them and quit, or they ran and got whipped."[104]

The sweeping victory of Lurleen Wallace, stand-in candidate for governor, had made George Wallace the king of a captive state. Even his enemies acknowledged his triumph. "He keeps tellin' 'em, 'You the children of Israel, you gonna lead this country out of the wilderness!' " complained one of Wallace's most unbending Alabama critics, Judge Roy Mayhall. "Goddam, we're at the bottom of everything you can find to be at the bottom of, and yet we gonna save the country. We lead the country in illiteracy, and syphilis, and yet we gonna lead the damn country out of the wilderness."[105]

"I know you think I am crazy when I say he expects to be President," Virginia Durr wrote her old friend Clark Foreman. "But he actually does. He thinks the race issue is going to become more and more the central issue [of American politics], and he is going to arouse hatred all over the whole country, and then pose as their Saviour." Wallace had convinced whites in Alabama that everything they believed in was being swept away by an overbearing and oppressive federal government, that *they*—not blacks— were the victims of oppression, Durr told her brother-in-law Hugo Black. He would carry that same message across the nation.[106]

Chapter 10

"STAND UP FOR AMERICA"

THE POLITICS OF ALIENATION

STANDING IN THE January sun of an unseasonably warm Alabama day, Lurleen Wallace read her twenty-four-minute inaugural address—the longest speech she had ever given—in a firm, clear voice that showed how far she had come since she first mounted a speaker's platform in March of 1966. The new governor, elegantly dressed in a somber black cashmere suit with matching pillbox hat, vilified the "egg-heads" in Washington who "proclaim to the world that 'God is dead' " and she promised to defend the people of Alabama against the "tyranny" of the United States government (which she compared to the totalitarianism of the Soviet Union, China, and Cuba). Asa Carter had included several token references to Mrs. Wallace's "special concerns as a wife and mother," but these awkward insertions seemed only to highlight her husband's political ventriloquism. As she excoriated federal judges and Washington bureaucrats, the enthusiastic audience, which filled the street in front of the capitol, interrupted her again and again with cheers and deafening applause.[1]

Her celebration, like her husband's four years earlier, was virtually an all-white affair. Repeated choruses of "Dixie" played by no fewer than twenty-one of more than a hundred white bands drowned out the patriotic airs of the handful of black marching bands. For the first time in more than forty years, the new governor declined to host an official inaugural ball. A statement issued under Lurleen Wallace's name explained that it seemed inappropriate in the context of the escalating conflict in Indochina: "With

Alabama boys fighting in Vietnam, I consider money spent for an inaugural ball to be money wasted."

One of her husband's friends dismissed that explanation. Wallace had "told everybody it was a racial thing, that he didn't want any nigguhs showing up and dancing with Lurleen." In reality, "he didn't like the idea of not being right smack in the center of the spotlight, of having to act as the escort for the new governor."[2]

WHILE the inaugural couple greeted guests at a series of small evening receptions, two dozen Wallace supporters from across the nation gathered in a private dining room of Montgomery's Woodley Country Club for a strategy session called by Asa Carter and Jim Clark. Their agenda: how to coordinate support for Wallace's unannounced but inevitable run for the White House in 1968. With their predilection for public mayhem, Carter and Clark seemed unlikely organizers for a national political campaign. Carter usually kept a low profile as speechwriter, but he remained a man with an uncontrolled temper, often whetted by alcohol. Only months before Lurleen Wallace's inaugural, a drunken Carter had confronted a Montgomery city detective in a downtown restaurant and loudly threatened to "beat the shit" out of him if he did not stop investigating Klansmen suspected in the bombing of a local black church.[3]

Ross Barnett and Leander Perez, veterans of the 1963 summit meeting chaired by John Synon, welcomed what one guest called a who's who of "super-patriot leaders," including William Simmons of the White Citizens Council, Kent Courtney, and a representative sent by Willis Carto, head of the Liberty Lobby and publisher of the anti-Semitic magazine *American Mercury*. Courtney, a former John Bircher, publisher of the *Citizen*, and head of the newly created Conservative Society of America, had embraced Wallace after Goldwater's defeat with the fervor of a man who believed he had found the nation's redeemer.[4]

The Woodley conference delegates represented the fringe of a growing network of right-wing organizations that had emerged in the 1950s: Joseph Welch's John Birch Society, the Reverend Carl McIntire's Twentieth Century Reformation, Dr. Fred Schwarz's Christian Anti-Communism Crusade, the Reverend Billy James Hargis's Christian Crusade, Edgar Bundy's Church League of America, Dean Clarence Manion's Forum, and Texas oilman H. L. Hunt's Life Line Foundation. In rallies, "seminars," sponsored radio and television broadcasts, and dozens of magazines and newsletters, they promoted the theme elaborated by Joseph McCarthy in his heyday: liberalism equaled socialism; socialism equaled communism; therefore liberalism was only two precarious steps away from a treasonous embrace of the Communist menace. This syllogism formed the basis for the radical right's underlying grand conspiracy theory. Communist victories came not because of Marxism's ideological appeal or because of the Soviet Union's economic strength and military prowess, but because Moscow's agents, operating at the highest ranks of the United States government and supported by millions of fellow-travelers and leftist dupes, maneuvered the nation toward surrender.

Through the late 1950s, liberal activists ineffectually pointed with alarm to the rise of what they called the "ultra-right"; their fears gained credibility when Robert Welch charged in 1960 that President Dwight Eisenhower was a "dedicated conscious agent of the Communist conspiracy."[5] Sophisticated Americans seemed uncertain whether to be horrified or amused. William F. Buckley, Jr., the young guru of the respectable right, called for Welch's resignation from the society and warned conservatives to steer clear of the organization. A poll showed that more than two of every three Americans who held an opinion about the John Birch Society opposed the group.[6]

The radical right, however, seemed to feed on the contempt of mainstream community leaders. In 1959, the six largest right-wing groups—Twentieth Century Reformation, the Christian Crusade, the Church League of America, Human Events, Americans for Constitutional Action, and the John Birch Society—reported total revenues of $1,300,000. By 1964, the same organizations had budgets of $8.4 million and mailing lists that reached millions of Americans.[7]

In its crudest manifestations, this "New Right" represented a return to some of the more unsavory aspects of American history: nativism, anti-Semitism, and overt racism. All the participants in the Woodley planning conference were racist defenders of "Anglo-Saxon civilization"; the majority were vicious anti-Semites. Asa Carter's attacks against Jews went back to the 1940s; as early as the mid-1950s, Leander Perez was blaming the "Zionist Jews" for the racial problems of the South. At one of Edward Fields's National States' Rights Party rallies, Perez repeated the neo-Nazis' claim that "Communism and Zionism are almost synonymous. They're un-American co-conspirators in the drive for integration as a means of destroying both our white Christian civilization and our power to resist communism."[8]

If possible, Willis Carto represented an even more repugnant addition to the list of Wallace supporters. Born in the Midwest in 1926, Carto worked briefly as a collection agent in San Francisco in the 1940s before he found his calling as a propagandist for right-wing causes. By the mid-1950s, he had founded his own organization, "Liberty and Property" (later the Liberty Lobby), and he published a lively monthly bulletin appropriately titled *Right*. A decade later he would turn his efforts to disproving what he called the "myth of the Holocaust," but in the 1960s he understood "Blacky" (as he always referred to African Americans) to constitute the primary menace to Western civilization. Carto the Californian went far beyond Wallace the southerner in his insistence that integration ("racial amalgamation") was the conspiratorial creation of an unholy alliance of Communists, Jews, blacks, and their allies and dupes in Washington, the entertainment industry, and the mass media.[9]

Even before the Woodley conference, Carto, working with Asa Carter, had prepared a slick pamphlet headlined "Stand Up for America: The Story of George C. Wallace," which promoted the Alabamian as the only potential presidential candidate willing to confront "Blacky" and the liberal-Communist conspiracy which had seized control of the federal government.[10] The Liberty Lobby mailed 175,000 copies to its subscribers and then made an additional 150,000 copies available to the Wallace campaign. In 1964, Carto had distributed ten million copies of a vehemently anti-Johnson pamphlet, "LBJ, a Political Biography." He promised to match that figure for Wallace.

Boxes filled with "Stand Up for America" soon lined the shelves of the Wallace headquarters in Montgomery. Whenever supporters wrote from across the country to solicit his views on civil disorder or the Communist conspiracy, or to request membership information on the nearest Ku Klux Klan chapter, Wallace routinely enclosed in his replies a copy of the Liberty Lobby pamphlet as an "accurate expression of my thinking on these matters." When a Detroit newsman reported that the Alabamian's top aides had worked closely with the unsavory Liberty Lobby, both Wallace and Carto blandly denied the connection.[11]

But George Wallace's grab bag of anti-black views never amounted to a coherent racist philosophy. He was willing, even anxious, to exploit the racial fears that gripped white America, and he repeatedly toyed with conspiracy theories in his constant, albeit vague, references to the role of Communists in high places in American society. However, he usually restricted his Red-baiting to civil rights leaders, and there was nothing in his background to indicate even a hint of personal anti-Semitism. In his 1963 Washington testimony against John Kennedy's civil rights proposal, Wallace had evoked sarcastic laughter with his absurd statement that some of his "best friends" were black. But some of his best friends in Montgomery *were* Jewish business and community leaders. Quite apart from his personal opinions (which seldom stood in the way of his politics), Wallace knew that anti-Semitic statements would devastate his campaign. Hostility toward American Jews remained a persistent undercurrent in far-right politics, but only the most fanatical—the "nut-cases," as Wallace and his staff dubbed his ultra-racist supporters—openly promoted a systematic racist ideology. He never treated ethnic Americans of eastern and southern European ancestry with contempt; he embraced them as potential allies who shared his fear of blacks as well as his cultural conservatism. But just as he had enlisted key Ku Klux

Klan leaders in his 1962 gubernatorial campaign, he readily turned to the far right to furnish foot soldiers for the upcoming presidential campaign, gambling that most of his supporters feared right-wing fanatics far less than they did Communists or Black Power advocates. And he was right.

Although *Los Angeles Times* reporters Jack Nelson and Nicholas Chriss and Peter Kihss of the *New York Times* painstakingly documented the close connections between the Wallace movement and right-wing—in some cases, neo-fascist—extremists across the country, their analyses had little impact on his standing among voters.[12] When a Detroit columnist dismissed Wallace's Michigan followers as right-wing "kooks," Wallace simply laughed derisively. "The other side's got more kooks than we do," he said. Besides, "kooks got a right to vote too."[13]

In choosing to highlight the antics of a handful of political extremists, the media ignored the extent to which a revitalized evangelical movement had embraced the message of the ultra-right. During the 1950s, Billy Graham, the father of modern American revivalism, laced his sermons with anticommunist rhetoric. Karl Marx, he told a California crusade, was a "degenerate materialist," whose perverted philosophy had culminated in the "filthy, corrupt, ungodly, unholy doctrine of world socialism." Graham called for "internal security" investigations to expose the "pinks, the lavenders and the reds who have sought refuge beneath the wings of the American Eagle." But his anticommunism and his vague hints of internal subversion always remained within the American mainstream. Like other twentieth-century evangelicals, he saw the success of Communism as a reflection of America's fall from grace, a descent from a lost arcadia of small towns and small-town values to the "cesspool" of modern secularism. "America . . . is under the pending judgment of God," he warned millions of viewers, "and unless we have a spiritual revival now, we are done as a nation."[14]

By the end of the 1950s, Graham had become more pop-star evangelist than prophet, appearing regularly in television specials and serving as friend and confidant to national political leaders, particularly to Republicans, such as Richard Nixon. And he always drew back from a close identification with political extremists, a caution which earned him the contempt of emerging right-wing evangelicals like Carl McIntire, Fred Schwarz, and particularly Tulsa's Billy James Hargis.

A later generation of televangelists—Oral Roberts, Jim and Tammy Bakker, Jimmy Swaggart, Jerry Falwell, and Pat Robertson—overshadowed the Oklahoma evangelist. But in the mid-1960s, Hargis spoke to an audience of millions through as many as five hundred radio outlets and more than one hundred television stations. In 1970, he founded his own "American Christian College" in Tulsa and was well on his way to becoming the first of the big-time Christian broadcasters. Three years later, however, a disgruntled associate charged Hargis with engaging in sexual relations with both male and female students. When Hargis was forced to sever his connections with the college, his broadcasting empire quickly collapsed.[15]

But Hargis had been a pioneer in mobilizing the politics of fear. He had readily grasped the way weekly doses of apocalyptic warnings bolstered by computer-generated "personalized" mailings could help charismatic demagogues tap the pocketbooks of frightened radio listeners and television viewers. Like his better-known successors, he turned his wrath on the nation's "internal moral decay" and "collapse of moral values," a decline promoted by what he called the "powerfully entrenched, anti-God Liberal Establishment."[16]

Sophisticated Americans tended to dismiss religious ultra-conservatism as a part of America's cultural past. Hadn't Clarence Darrow finally put to rest that nonsense in the 1925 Scopes trial? But televangelists like Hargis foreshadowed the coming upsurge of religious fundamentalism in American politics. In a movement almost ignored by academicians and journalists, resurgent religious fundamentalists had begun to overtake mainline Protestant denominations in numbers even as they created a loose-knit network of orthodox evangelical colleges, publishing houses, and radio and television media outlets. Although most fundamentalists were still conditioned to avoid active involvement in politics, those restraints weakened through the 1960s.

As early as 1965, Wallace was an avid promoter of Hargis, and his staffers drew on the computer expertise of the Christian Anti-Communist Crusade to develop their own direct-mail fund-raising program.[17] By the time he launched his campaign for the presidency in 1967, the Alabamian had begun to blend the themes of the religious right into a message emphasizing the threat posed to American traditions and values by the national state and the "liberal elite" that dominated American society.

Long on rhetoric and critically short on money and experienced personnel, George Wallace needed all the help he could get. He had raised $300,000 for the 1962 governor's race and $360,000 for his first presidential campaign, but his staff had no experience in mounting a broad national effort. Ed Pearson, a statehouse reporter for the *Birmingham News* for most of Wallace's early career, found the very prospect of an organized effort ludicrous. The governor, he noted, was a "human machine of spontaneity, a nonplanner who habitually waits until the last minute before giving his supporting cast the cue."[18] Marshall Frady claimed to have seen Wallace draw up his original budget for the 1968 presidential campaign shortly after his wife's inauguration. "Let's see," said the candidate, scribbling on a memo pad. "We got better'n $380,000 when we went into three states back in '64, three goes into fifty about seventeen times—don't it?—yes, and seventeen times $380,000 that oughta be—that's $6,460,000. That oughta be enough."[19]

The Frady story has the ring of truth, for Wallace began the race without the foggiest notion of how much money would be needed. He just started collecting and depositing into the campaign bank account and hoping for the best.[20] The file drawers of his office were filled to overflowing with letters of support going back to 1963, but the whole operation was so disorganized through much of 1967 that campaign staff did little to tap the direct-mail potential that lay within their grasp. For the first few months they depended upon their usual source of support: tithes from the profitable state contracts of Alabama highway contractors and businessmen. Sometimes enthusiastically, more often grudgingly, these men furnished the seed money for Wallace's campaign and his newly created "American Independent Party."[21] Just to pay the first month's rent on a shabby headquarters office outside Montgomery, Seymore Trammell signed a personal note. But by November 1967, Trammell and Bill Jones had managed to bring some order to a new seventeen-room suite of offices. Two months later, senior aides were already projecting a budget of at least ten million dollars, an estimate that proved surprisingly close to the final cost of the third-party effort.[22]

Wallace and his staff went through the motions of drawing up a party platform and arranging state conventions to promote his candidacy, but they never made an effort to build a full-scale party from the ground up. The American Independent Party would always be little more than a personal vehicle for the former governor's ambitions. Its core remained the same handful of men who had been with Wallace since the 1962 gubernatorial race: Seymore Trammell, Cecil Jackson, and Bill Jones. Ed Ewing, Mrs. Wallace's press secretary, joined the original inner circle and spent far more time working on the Wallace campaign than on his official duties for Governor Lurleen.[23] State employees furnished much of the manpower; on one campaign swing, *Birmingham News* reporter Al Fox counted twenty-seven state officials—judges, senators, representatives, and agency heads.[24]

At Trammell's not-so-gentle insistence, business supporters funded several political operatives to work at the Wallace headquarters. Oscar Harper, who had been rewarded for past services with a series of noncompetitive contracts with the state government, continued to pay the salary of Asa Carter, still Wallace's favorite speechwriter. Klan leader Robert Shelton pocketed his sinecure from highway contractors. And Jimmy Faulkner, a wealthy south Alabama newspaper publisher, businessman, and onetime Wallace political opponent, delegated one of his editors, Jack House, to prepare literature for the 1968 campaign. While House proved competent enough, no one could ever have accused him of being a true believer. Halfway through the campaign, he bragged to an Anti-Defamation League undercover agent posing as a businessman (and secretly taping the conversation) that he thought the Wallace effort was doomed to failure; he was staying only to collect the kind of "intimate stuff" that would allow him to engineer a "million dollar thing. . . . Movie rights and everything else" on the man he called "Alabama's Little Caesar."[25]

When Tom Turnipseed came on board in the early fall of 1967, he captured the attention of northern journalists amused by his quaintly southern name. His grandfather—a dedicated Klansman in the 1920s—had received a gubernatorial pardon for killing a black man over a "trifling" matter in the 1920s. Although he knew how to play the devilish "good ol' boy," the thirty-one-year-old Turnipseed had graduated from the University of North Carolina Law School in the early 1960s. He enjoyed debating liberal faculty members, but was already turning to Goldwater Republicanism. His political baptism came with the South Carolina Republican Party in the presidential campaign of 1964. Moving on to the front line of segregationist politics, he coordinated the organization of forty-three private "seg" academies in 1965 and 1966, most of them in low-country South Carolina. (It was a "terrible damn thing—the worst . . . of all the racist things I have ever done," a repentant Turnipseed lamented a quarter-century later.[26]) His easygoing charm concealed a first-rate mind and a talent for organization, but top Wallace aides were always suspicious of his flashy good looks and his sizable ego.

In ability and commitment, most of the full-time campaign workers lay somewhere between the capable and charming Turnipseed and the cynical Jack House. As a group they would never be confused with the well-oiled public relations and campaign machines which increasingly had come to dominate the political process.

But the shifting tide of American politics had created a far more congenial climate for the Wallace campaign than anyone could have anticipated in the wake of Lyndon Johnson's 1964 landslide election. With the nation's attention riveted on the drama of the southern civil rights movement, politicians and journalists had paid little attention to the escalating crisis in northern urban ghettos created by the black migration of the twentieth century. There were a series of minor black-white clashes in the summer of 1964, but nothing prepared Americans for the explosion that began August 11, 1965. During a minor scuffle between a white California highway patrolman and a drunken black motorist in the southeast Los Angeles ghetto of Watts, a crowd of angry bystanders forced overwhelmed police to call for help. Within the hour, more than a thousand black men, most in their teens and twenties, were on the street, pelting police with rocks and bottles and shouting "Burn, baby, burn!" The next night, the rioters began systematically to loot and burn businesses in the impoverished community. By the time thousands of National Guard troops regained control of the city, thirty-four people lay dead and nearly a thousand buildings had been damaged or destroyed.[27]

Watts proved only a rehearsal for the turmoil that swept through the nation's cities, reaching a climax with the 1967 Newark and Detroit race riots. The Newark riot, which began in mid-July, was also marked by systematic looting (although black businesses were often spared). But racial tensions escalated as black "insurrectionaries" began sniping at police. Panic-stricken, poorly trained policemen and National Guardsmen responded by firing automatic weapons indiscriminately into ghetto apartment complexes and housing projects, killing twenty-four black residents.[28] Ten days later, a raid by Detroit police on an after-hours club set off a week of violence that left five thousand homeless and forty-three dead (most of them black) and did $250 million worth of damage to homes and businesses. By the end of the summer of 1967 riots in 127 cities had led to seventy-seven deaths, more than four thousand arrests, and damages of nearly half a billion dollars.

Esquire magazine commissioned classics professor–turned–freelance writer Garry Wills to examine the preparations of America's cities for future riots. Wills surveyed police departments from Cambridge, Maryland, to Los Angeles, California, and attended police conventions in which vendors proudly displayed armored personnel carriers and deadly antiriot weapons of every description. Detroit's police department had requisitioned five General Motors–made "Commando" cars—lumbering armor-plated vehicles, bristling with weapons that protruded through portholes; tested, the promoters proudly pointed out, "in the jungles of Vietnam." Philadelphia's police department under Commissioner Frank Rizzo boasted seven thousand riot-trained policemen, spearheaded by 125 sharpshooters. Specially armored police vehicles carried enough weaponry to equip a combat squad in Vietnam—two M-70 30.06 Winchester rifles with Bal-Var scopes, two M-12 anti-riot shotguns, one Thompson .45-caliber submachine gun, one .30-caliber M-1 carbine, a tear-gas gun and grenades, a gas mask, a bulletproof vest, and over a thousand rounds of ammunition. As Wills interviewed these grim policemen and read summaries of the elaborate counterinsurgency contingency plans, and as he talked with often overwrought and bombastic black "street commandos," his original assignment for *Esquire* expanded into a book whose title, *The Second Civil War: Arming for Armageddon,* captured a sense of deep foreboding.

And the new battle cry of "Black Power" seemed to encapsulate the apprehensions of white Americans, north and south. In June of 1966, James Meredith, the student who had integrated the University of Mississippi four years earlier—and who was probably the most hated black man in the state—set out on a 220-mile walk from Memphis, Tennessee, to Jackson, Mississippi, to show blacks in his home state that they could stand up for their political rights without fear. Just after he crossed the border into Mississippi, a white farmer emptied both barrels of a shotgun loaded with buckshot into Meredith, who was seriously (though not critically) wounded. In a spontaneous gesture of support, civil rights leaders converged on Mississippi to continue Meredith's march to Jackson. Stokely Carmichael, the Trinidad-born spokesman for the Student Nonviolent Coordinating Committee, skillfully turned the well-publicized march into a forum for the new brand of black nationalist militancy that had captured the imagination of young radical blacks (and the news media). As the chants of "Black Power— Black Power—Black Power" echoed through the ranks of the marchers, the civil rights movement in America turned a corner.[29]

Black moderates like Roy Wilkins, the head of the NAACP, bitterly attacked the new slogan as the "father of hatred and the mother of violence," a "reverse Hitler, a reverse Ku Klux Klan," which inevitably led to the "ranging of race against race on the irrelevant basis of skin color."[30] Martin Luther King, whose star as a civil rights leader was fading, had no use for racially exclusionary slogans; in the cries of "Black Power" he heard proof that time was running out on his attempt to use nonviolence to bridge America's racial divide. The rising tide of black separatist rhetoric encouraged him to risk more radical action: to strike at the core of racism north as well as south.

Less than a month after the Meredith march through Mississippi, King and his Southern Christian Leadership Conference carried the movement north to Chicago with a series of demonstrations designed to dramatize de facto segregation and economic deprivation in the black ghettos of the nation. On July 10, 1966, "Freedom Sunday," King joined five thousand marchers in a procession that snaked through the streets of downtown Chicago to the closed doors of Mayor Richard Daley's castle, city hall. In a reenactment of the defiance of his namesake at Wittenberg, Germany, four centuries earlier, King taped a list of the movement's demands on the massive bronze doors while dozens of television cameras and still photographers recorded the moment. Two weeks later, King and his lieutenants led another series of marches through working-class districts of Chicago; on August 3, a thousand policemen could not hold back a rock-throwing mob of angry Chicago whites who pelted demonstrators with bottles, bricks, and rocks. Eventually, demonstrators accepted a face-saving but inconclusive list of promises from Mayor Daley.[31]

For Martin Luther King, the underlying causes of the racial riots of the mid-1960s seemed as clear as they would be to a series of presidential and local commissions: poor housing, underemployment, and continued racism in America's cities. But George Wallace would have none of that. Even before the 1967 riots, Wallace realized that the civil disturbances of the mid-1960s could be linked to a whole series of powerful issues that appealed to a constituency outside the South: violence, street crime, and the danger of race war. An ongoing dialogue with one of his most effective publicists and supporters, former Montgomery journalist Joe Azbell, confirmed his hypothesis. Azbell considered himself a racial moderate in the 1950s. At a time when most southern newspapers ignored blacks or relegated them to the crime pages, he treated middle-class members of Montgomery's African-American community with civility and, in the columns of the *Advertiser*, sought to recognize what he called "positive developments in the Negro community."

But Azbell, who had covered the small but vocal Communist Party in Alabama in the 1940s, had become obsessed with the belief that the Party had created a vast conspiracy operating through America's black community, a conspiracy which would ultimately foment revolution by creating a war of the races. Although he initially admired the Montgomery civil rights leader for his courage and shrewd understanding of human nature, King's ability to stage-manage what Azbell saw as a mob of "dirt-laden hippies and beatniks, racial agitators . . . queers, prostitutes, dope addicts, priests, nuns, college dropouts and the normally peaceful black populace" during the 1965 Selma demonstrations made him the single most dangerous individual in American society, concluded Azbell.[32]

For nearly a decade, shrewd civil rights activists had manipulated the left-wing news media to create a powerful morality play with the semiliterate, tobacco-chewing white lawmen on one side and the "praying, forgiving black" on the other, said Azbell. But those same television cameras, with their vivid images of Watts's "burning, sniping, looting black mobs" shattered this carefully constructed deception, reported Azbell with no little satisfaction, "as the remainder of the nation tasted the fear . . . that had gripped the South for a decade." And whites weren't buying the explanation that America's civil disorder was due to "slums, unemployment, oppression, second class citizenship and rats." Other ethnic groups had suffered far worse deprivation, he argued, and they had responded by buckling down, going to work, and raising themselves by their own bootstraps.[33]

George Wallace shared Azbell's convictions and, indeed, much of his rhetoric. During the 1965 civil rights disturbances in Selma, he told journalist Robert Sherrill, California's governor Pat Brown had boasted in a telegram that "they knew how to live together out there—Nigger-Americans, Spanish-Americans, Polish-Americans, Italian-Americans, French-Americans and all sorts of hyphenated Americans—and while I was reading his wire, the niggers was burning down Watts." Members of his staff wanted him to wire back, an I-told-you-so, said Wallace, "but I don't believe in making political capital out of that sort of thing."[34]

The escalating racial riots, the takeover of America's city streets by thugs and hoodlums, and the lawless trampling of the U.S. Constitution by "power-hungry" federal courts were parts of a larger picture, Wallace told his fellow Alabamians after the 1966 riots. In June 1963, he had stood in the schoolhouse door to try to wake up the American people, to help them understand that if "men in high places in Washington can break the law of our Constitution, then every revolutionary—every thug who can assemble a mob—will feel that they, too, can break the law." And what had been the response of "liberal newspaper editors"? They "ridiculed that warning and ridiculed your Governor." As "guerrilla bands burn and loot and riot in Chicago, Cleveland, Los Angeles, New York, Jacksonville and other cities across the country," he sadly wished to repeat that warning.[35]

Speaking before the national convention of the Fraternal Order of Police in late August of 1966, the Alabama governor insisted that the decline in law and order and the riots in American cities had nothing to do with poverty or racism. The roots of discord could be traced directly to a "conference of world guerrilla warfare chieftains [meeting] in Havana, Cuba," where Communist leaders had made the decision to launch a program of revolutionary guerrilla warfare in American cities. Federal officials knew the identity of American radicals who received their marching orders at the conference, Wallace claimed, and were "aware—through actual demonstrations in certain cities—that a leadership capability existed to translate these plans into action.

"Why, in the face of this knowledge, did the Johnson administration fail to take required action to nip these plans in the bud?" he demanded. More important, *"why weren't the revolutionaries arrested—prosecuted—and punished?"* The one thousand delegates to the convention came to their feet as he pounded the podium. Federal "bearded beatnik bureaucrats" had laid the ground for the riots by "contributing leadership and in some instances, public funds to help finance organized discord." The federal judiciary was *"INFESTED"* with social engineers who had handcuffed law enforcement and made it impossible to place criminals behind bars. If only the "police of this country could run it for about two years," shouted the governor, "then it would be safe to walk in the parks."[36]

Wallace had outdone himself. Even the John Birchers had never claimed that federal bureaucrats took their cues from Fidel Castro. But if his rhetoric was a little overripe, millions of Americans embraced the general drift of his argument. A quarter-century after the martyrdom of Martin Luther King and the canonization of the civil rights movement, it is easy to forget the ambivalence with which white Americans responded to the turbulent changes of the 1960s. After Watts, pollsters found whites often contradictory in their assessment of the causes of racial unrest, careening back and forth from a recognition of the role of prejudice and poverty to a denunciation of lax law enforcement and the inherent lawlessness of minorities. One finding was astonishingly consistent, however: half of all Americans believed that the Communist Party in the United States played a significant role in both the demonstrations and the riots. Another quarter of those polled believed that Communists had played "some" role in racial disturbances.[37]

Wallace did not need George Gallup or Lou Harris to prove that Americans were responsive to conspiracy theories; the enthusiasm of his audiences had already told him that. Nor did he need any survey to tell him that a growing number of white voters were angry and hostile to blacks. Across the South, the much-heralded impact of growing black political participation seemed to incite whites to vote for ultra-racist reactionaries. Georgia Democrats nominated Lester Maddox, the Atlanta motel and restaurant owner who had once brandished a pistol and ax handle to chase blacks away from his businesses, as their 1966 gubernatorial candidate. Maddox decisively defeated his moderate opponent, capturing nearly seventy percent of the white vote.[38]

And by the mid-1960s, "white backlash" was no longer restricted to the South. When selfless martyrs endured assaults, even death, while maintaining their commitment to nonviolence, it was easy to be sympathetic to the cause of the civil rights movement. Whites found it more difficult to warm to SNCC's Stokely Carmichael when he told a Montgomery rally that blacks who supported the war in Vietnam were "traitors to their people." The Vietcong were not the enemy of black people, he declared; "Lurleen Wallace is your enemy." Pointing to a cluster of Montgomery policemen in riot gear, he continued: "These white helmeted cops are your enemies." Whenever the military gives a black man a gun, shouted Carmichael, "and tells him to shoot his enemy and if he don't shoot Lurleen and George and little junior, he's a fool."[39]

White northern college students who had poured into Mississippi and the Deep South during Freedom Summer, 1964, appeared to have lost all interest in the civil rights struggle. By the fall of 1966, even the most committed veterans of the movement agreed that "civil rights is fading as an issue around which students are going to rally." Stanley Feingold, a City College of New York political scientist and adviser to student civil rights groups, ruefully admitted to a newspaper reporter that the idea that white students should advocate black rights had disappeared from the nation's college campuses, in part because African-American students who espoused Black Power had made it clear they wanted no white involvement. And Feingold pointed out that it was "much easier to take a stand on civil rights when the issue was remote [in the South] or abstract." As many of the school's middle-class students saw an influx of blacks into their own neighborhoods they adopted a "vastly more critical attitude" toward civil rights issues.[40]

Mississippi's arch-segregationist Senator James Eastland opened his campaign for re-election in the fall of 1966 by boasting that the tide had turned. "The sentiment of the entire country," he triumphantly told a Forest, Mississippi, rally, "now stands with the Southern people."[41] In 1964, skittish advisers to Lyndon Johnson had referred to that summer's race disturbances as "Goldwater rallies." The hundreds of riots that marked the summers of 1966 and 1967 might well have been dubbed "Wallace rallies." The governor of Alabama had more than regained the public relations ground lost in the Selma crisis of 1965.

THE biggest task facing the Wallace presidential campaign was simply getting on the ballot in all of the fifty states as a third party. Just researching the ballot requirements required hundreds of hours of volunteer time. Barriers to the new American Independent Party varied; Colorado required a mere three hundred petition signatures, while Ohio demanded nearly half a millon. In several states outside the South, officials flatly refused to help; attorneys borrowed from a half-dozen Alabama agencies had to comb through statutes to be sure hostile bureaucrats could not eliminate the party on the basis of minor technicalities. In states like Ohio where blatantly anti-third-party legislation created insuperable barriers to getting on the ballot, the Wallace campaign put together teams of lawyers sympathetic to their movement and then persuaded them to go to court, often on a pro bono basis.[42] Eventually the campaign would collect more than 2.7 million petition signatures, an extraordinary exercise in grassroots democracy generally dismissed by unsympathetic reporters.[43] For top aides who worked in the Wallace campaign, the struggle to get on the ballot in all fifty states would become a down-home version of Mao Zedong's Long March: an epic battle pitting struggle of great heroism and courage against staggering odds.

The effort began in California in the late summer of 1967. No one was ever quite able to explain the choice of that unfriendly western state, and no one believed the Wallaceites could come close to carrying California. But there was a sense that they would not be taken seriously unless they could at least give voters a Wallace option in the nation's second most populous state.

California law barred third parties from the ballot unless they could officially register at least one percent of the state's voters as party members. In a state where even the conservative press had treated the Alabamian as a latter-day Genghis Khan, the legal requirement that Wallace persuade nearly 66,000 voters to register as members of the American Independent Party by January 1968, ten months before the election, seemed a formidable challenge.

With almost no contacts on the West Coast except for a few John Birchers, Seymore Trammell turned to his old friend Bill Simmons, head of the Citizens' Council of Jackson, Mississippi. Simmons enthusiastically recommended Robert Shearer as the man to lead the California ballot campaign.[44]

Shearer, a Republican political consultant and San Francisco publisher, was only thirty-one years old when the California Real Estate Association chose him to direct their Proposition 14 campaign against the state's fair-housing laws. Although liberal Californians initially dismissed the proposal, San Francisco conservatives skillfully played on property owners' fears of "block-busting" and lower property values while avoiding overt appeals to race. Even as Lyndon Johnson swept to victory in California in 1964, Proposition 14 carried every county in the state; seventy percent of white voters backed the anti-black measure.[45]

Encouraged by this victory and the white backlash provoked by the Watts riot, Shearer and a number of other California ultra-conservatives risked closer ties with marginal groups like the southern-based Citizens' Councils and called for an antiliberal coalition uniting southern and national conservatives. In his own weekly, the *California Statesman,* Shearer began adopting the language George Wallace had used so skillfully in his 1964 campaign. California politics—and the nation's—had become dominated by a "liberal-leftist power bloc" held together by "racial minority voting blocs."[46]

While Shearer confidently assured Trammell that rounding up 66,000 new American Independent Party members was "child's play" compared to his successful promotion of Proposition 14, his initial request for ten thousand dollars in "expense money" escalated to thirty thousand dollars, and progress reports became increasingly vague. But Trammell was preoccupied by events closer to home.

IN June 1967, Governor Lurleen Wallace had taken a break at Alabama's Gulf Shores with one of her best friends. As she and Catherine Steineker walked along the beach, Lurleen said matter-of-factly, as though she were talking about plans for the next day's fishing expedition, that she was convinced that her cancer had returned. Her doctor had assured her that recurrent stomach cramps were a side effect of the estrogen she was taking, but "I think there's more to them than just hormone problems. . . . I just don't think I'll be here a year from now."[47]

Late that month, her office released a terse statement which she had personally written. "I have been informed by my doctors that I have a malignancy which may again require surgery," she said. On the recommendations of her doctors, she had decided to go to Houston's M. D. Anderson Clinic, a leading center for cancer surgery and radiation therapy.[48] The small group of mostly Alabama reporters who covered the story rolled out all the appropriate clichés: "smiling and in good spirits" (Associated Press); "praised for her bravery and forthrightness" (*Birmingham News*); "cheerfully said goodbye to admirers as she left Montgomery's Dannelly Field" (*Montgomery Advertiser*).[49]

In private, Lurleen Wallace alternated between guarded hope and resignation. To her longtime friend Mary Jo Ventress, she poured out her fears for her children. Unspoken was the fact everyone knew: George Wallace had never been involved with their upbringing. Bobbi Jo was married and on her own, but Peggy Sue had just begun her senior year in high school, George Junior was fifteen, and Lee was only five years old. "I know that Bobbi will help George see to it that Lee's taken care of. . . . Jo . . . you know who's to get my rings . . ." By the time the governor left for Houston in early July, Ventress had a purse full of scraps of paper on which her friend had parceled out her personal belongings to those who would survive.[50]

Her husband's fund-raising trips and rallies ground to a halt. Wallace had neglected his wife for most of their married life; in 1966 she confided to close friends, with more sadness than anger, that she and her husband had not slept together for three years. Shortly after her inauguration, Wallace's old crony Glenn Curlee teased, "George, you better start sleeping with that woman."

His friend had not seen the humor of the quip. "Wouldn't it be a helluva note if she ran me off?" he responded gloomily.[51]

But he was a model husband on the trip out to Houston in August. In a two-bedroom apartment across the street from the Anderson Clinic, Lurleen Wallace and her mother unpacked the suitcases of robes, gowns, and négligées sent by friends and sniffed the Estée Lauder sachet powder that was her favorite fragrance. Wallace wandered up and down the halls of the clinic, buttonholed doctors, and talked compulsively to everyone he encountered, alternately encouraged by the optimism of hospital staff and depressed by the waiting rooms of sick and dying patients. At his favorite Houston restaurant, Trader Vic's, he rambled on almost incoherently about his wife to three aides and then—in a revelation of his apprehensions—confided: "I have hopes about Lurleen's condition."[52]

On July 10, a team of surgeons removed an egg-sized malignancy from Mrs. Wallace's colon and issued a brief but encouraging statement. The cancer was "limited," but as a "precautionary measure" the governor would undergo follow-up cobalt treatments. "We see no cause," said her surgeon, "why she should not make a complete recovery." While Alabama newspapers continued to publish optimistic accounts of her surgery and treatment, the *New York Times* reported in a brief story datelined Birmingham that there were rumors that her condition was "more serious than had been acknowledged." The governor's office denied the statement, but no one was deceived, least of all Lurleen Wallace.[53] When one of her doctors stopped by during her radiation therapy, George Wallace complained about his wife's steady pack-a-day smoking habit. "Don't you think she should cut down some on her cigarettes?"

Her physician shrugged, "Oh, I don't know. . . . We don't want to take *all* her pleasures away from her." Then he stopped, as he saw the look on her face.

To Mary Jo Ventress she bleakly confided, "The doctors might have gotten this thing now. But it will come back. . . . It will eventually get me."[54]

REPEATED trips to Texas and his wife's slow convalescence limited George Wallace's speaking schedule and made it difficult to rally the faithful. Though all the men who surrounded him were genuinely fond of Mrs. Wallace, there was the sobering consciousness that without control of the governor's office the presidential campaign would be crippled in its ability to raise money and "volunteers" from Alabama businessmen. Bereft of a national organization, Wallace supporters struggled throughout the late summer and early fall to put together a campaign staff in the fifty states.

In mid-September, Turnipseed flew to California to make a firsthand assessment of the petition drive. Shearer proudly pointed out an organizational chart showing an elaborate bureaucratic structure, with county coordinators and, within larger counties, district coordinators (eight for Los Angeles). But most positions remained unfilled, and those men whom Turnipseed met unnerved him. Even his brief exposure to the fringes of the Wallace movement had made the former Goldwater organizer acutely aware of the fine line that separated the quirky and the "genuine kook cases." Several recruits, who recounted grim warnings of Communist conspiracies and the dangers of water fluoridation, seemed more like mental outpatients than political activists.

One of the Los Angeles district coordinators had turned a suburban insurance office into a Wallace command center. "Just call me Mike," the poised and articulate Californian told Turnipseed as he described his administrative battle plan for the next sixty days. Mike's enthusiasm and organizational skill buoyed the lanky South Carolinian. Perhaps he had underestimated the California campaign. As the two closed the office and walked toward the building's parking lot, Turnipseed outlined the work they could start tomorrow. "Sorry," replied the county coordinator, as he gestured vaguely toward the mountains east of the city. He would be tied up with "maneuvers" all weekend.

"Are you in the National Guard?" asked Turnipseed.

"Naw," answered the middle-aged insurance salesman, "we got our own group." He glanced around the empty lot, opened the tailgate of his late-model station wagon, and raised a heavy army-green tarpaulin. Small arms, boxes of ammunition, two bazookas, and a "goddamn big old machine gun" filled the cargo space.

"Are you worried about the Communist takeover?" stammered Turnipseed in what he hoped was a tone of neutral interest.

Mike's eyes narrowed with suspicion. "Hell no, the Rockefeller interests—you know, the Trilateral Commission—that's what we're worried about."

That night, Turnipseed checked in with Wallace headquarters in Montgomery. The California effort was in trouble, he told Trammell. And by the way, he added, "We need to slide one of our Los Angeles coordinators over a little bit."[55]

Distracted by other crises, the Wallace headquarters ignored Turnipseed's warnings. Bill Jones, Wallace's press secretary, finally rang the alarm bells in Montgomery. In early October he flew out to California along with Ed Ewing, Mrs. Wallace's press secretary; Earl Morgan, a Jefferson County district attorney on loan to the Wallace campaign; and Joe Fine, another state employee whose duties in the state insurance commission mysteriously seemed to take him wherever the Wallace campaign surfaced. Shearer warmly welcomed the Alabama visitors, but proved remarkably vague when asked to summarize the progress of the third-party registration drive. Jones, usually affable and nonconfrontational, pressed the Californian: *Precisely* how many people had signed the sworn and notarized affidavits of party affiliation? A defensive Shearer finally admitted that, with two months gone and less than three months to go before the January 1, 1968, deadline, he had recruited fewer than two thousand of the needed American Independent Party members.

"Shearer lied," Jones reported bluntly when he called Trammell and Jackson back in Montgomery. Workers from Alabama would have to take charge and organize the campaign from the ground up. "We can get the job done," he told them, "but it's going to take a lot of money. . . . Maybe as much as half a million dollars."

Trammell didn't hesitate. "Well, okay, go ahead."

Jones was flabbergasted. Although contributions from Alabama businessmen, direct-mail solicitations, and Wallace fund-raising forays continued to bring in enough money to keep the effort moving along, the campaign was showing a deficit even as they spoke. "Damn it, Seymore," said Jones, "listen to me, what I'm saying."

As he started to go over the figures again, Seymore Trammell shouted back over the long-distance line: "Goddammit, you're not listening to me. I said go ahead."[56] Although Trammell delivered the line with great bravado, he headed straight for the nearest bar for the rest of the afternoon.

The next day, he called the governor's brother. Gerald Wallace—"Mr. Fixit," as he was known around the capital—had grown rich, thanks to his connections.[57] "I'm not signing any notes," he said flatly when told that the campaign needed seed money for the California ballot campaign. "I'm not putting my future at stake for some fool idea George has of being President." At the Central Bank of Alabama, using his Bullock County farm as collateral,

Trammell signed over to the campaign a note for $100,000. In the following twelve months, he would personally guarantee nearly $750,000 in bank loans for the Wallace campaign. Gerald never put up a nickel.[58]

Lurleen Wallace, though deathly ill, was still the governor of Alabama. With her approval, Trammell began organizing his forces. "I tell you, Alabama was just about deserted," remembered one of Wallace's supporters, referring to the last two months of 1967. In telephone calls and a series of whirlwind meetings across the state, Trammell employed a combination of veiled threats (particularly when dealing with those businessmen, lawyers, and bankers who were "sucking at the state teat") and appeals to regional patriotism to enlist an army of Alabama organizers. Workers assigned to the California team endured a blur of night flights, ninety-hour work weeks, cheap motels, and greasy takeout food. By November 12, the Wallace campaign had created forty-one local headquarters, some headed by local Californians, more by Alabamians.[59]

Back in Montgomery Ed Ewing cautioned Cecil Jackson, Wallace's executive secretary, to "be careful what you talk about [with West Coast volunteers], these phone lines may be bugged."

"Well, if they are," retorted Jackson, "I hope they'll hear everything we're saying." Otherwise, eavesdroppers "might mistakenly think we know what we're doing."[60]

Ewing and Jones realized that George Wallace alone could rally potential supporters. But the candidate was caught in a dilemma. Throughout most of September and October, he had remained with Lurleen in Houston, restlessly roaming the hospital corridors and making long telephone calls to his staff from the apartment across the street from the hospital. In October he paid a short visit to California and made weekend fund-raising trips, most of them across the South and border states. Almost weekly, the Wallaces would play out their ritual. George would announce that he was supposed to go to Arkansas or Ohio or Pennsylvania, then would add with a tone of earnest solicitation, "Honey, I'm going to cancel it." No, she would assure him; she was "just fine"; of course he should continue with his regular schedule.[61]

In November, Mrs. Wallace, gaunt and haggard, returned to Montgomery. For the first time, Alabama newspapers began to speak guardedly of her as "painfully ill" and to refer to her illness as these "tragic days." The *New York Times,* less inhibited than local sources, bluntly reported the gloomy prognosis of her closest aides.[62]

Under the circumstances, it appeared unseemly, even callous, for her husband to be out on the campaign trail. But Lurleen Wallace, ever the loyal wife and southern lady, gave him her blessing. On November 20, with fewer than 8,000 of the necessary 66,000 party registrations in hand, Wallace flew to California for one last effort to rouse the faithful. Originally scheduled for eighteen days, his trip stretched on for the next four weeks.

No novice in addressing non-southern audiences—he had been on the lecture and talk-show circuit for nearly five years now—at times Wallace still seemed awkward and ill at ease as he tried to adapt his style and message to his West Coast audiences. Some of his jokes fell flat; he seemed to grope for the most effective punch lines. On November 23, to boost public interest in the lagging campaign (which was almost ignored in the California press), Lurleen Wallace flew to Los Angeles to join her husband.

She stood by his side on November 27 as he received the most boisterous welcome of his tour from nearly eight hundred listeners who jammed the American Legion Hall in Los Angeles' Bell Gardens district. In many ways, the community was a distillation of expatriate southern culture; newsmen called it Little Dixie. And Wallace clearly played the racial theme: "How would you Californians like it if you were told you would have to bus your children out of your neighborhood?" he asked.

But most of his forty-minute speech alternated between sarcastic attacks on Washington bureaucrats and somber warnings of the breakdown of public order. Wallace wove the specter of civil disorder, street crime, the growing assertiveness of minorities, and Communist-inspired pro-Vietcong street demonstrations into an angry tapestry. "You people work hard, you save your money, you teach your children to respect the law," Wallace told his audience of primarily blue-collar workers. Then when someone goes out and burns down half a city and murders someone, " 'pseudo-intellectuals' explain it away by saying the killer didn't get any watermelon to eat when he was 10 years old." While decent people obeyed the law and taught their children right from wrong, he said, the "Supreme Court is fixing it so you can't do anything about people who set cities on fire."[63]

No Wallace speech was complete without a reference to "pro-Communist, long-haired hippies" running amok through the *"tax-supported"* university system. By 1966 most Californians condemned the state university system in general and Berkeley in particular as a hotbed of irresponsible student radicalism, violence, and sexual license. An amiable former actor, Ronald Reagan, had found attacks on the university to be the most effective lines in the script of his successful 1966 race for the governorship. In fact, when he expressed disgust at the "sit-ins, the teach-ins, the walk-outs" at the state's universities and promised a "throw-out" of the system's administrators, some of the future president's speeches sounded remarkably similar to those of Wallace.[64]

But even when Reagan voiced the most outrageous policies, his soothing, even avuncular style undercut the harshness of his message. The cruder George Wallace thrust himself forward as the authentic defender of "common" everyday folks who struggled to make a decent living, to go to church, to raise their children and to pay their taxes. And he electrified the working people of Bell Gardens and Burbank.

Educated people—the "pseudo-intellectual elites" who dominated the television and the newspapers—didn't "*say* they were out to destroy sound family values, or common sense, or tough, hard work and painfully acquired respectability," said writer Michael Novak as he assumed the voice of working-class Americans. "Educated people talk with a kind of code . . . but you know they're trying to take your world from you. You can almost feel them screwing you; you see it in their complacent eyes."[65] One of Wallace's followers clipped Novak's magazine article and sent it to him with the quote underlined.

Although Wallace sought and often obtained local television and radio time for brief interviews, most Californians drawn into the Wallace orbit saw him in person at one of more than seventy old-fashioned rallies he held in forty towns and cities from Sacramento to San Diego. Many of the local organizers drawn into the campaign were middle-class and upper-class ultra-conservatives, John Birchers, and Liberty Lobby right-wingers with the skills to coordinate a string of service club luncheons, media interviews, and outdoor rallies. But his audience was generally working class or first-generation white collar.

Typically, crowds gathered at a strip shopping center located in a white working-class neighborhood in the suburbs of Los Angeles. Other venues included county fairgrounds, the Long Beach Elks hall, a stock-car track just outside Burbank, a "drag strip" near Redwood City, a high school football stadium near Modesto, or motel-restaurant receptions along the highways leading into San Jose, Stockton, and Sacramento. After warm-up music by a local country band, master of ceremonies Chill Wills, a Texas-born actor who was proudest of his role in the Rock Hudson–James Dean film *Giant,* but best-known as the voice of Francis, the Talking Mule, would announce a concert by the four Sunshine Sisters and the Oak Ridge Boys.

Next Knoxville gospel-singer Wally Fowler would lead a rousing rendition of the Wallace campaign's version of "The Battle Hymn of the Republic," an updated ode to Alabama governor ("He stands up for God and country, against all our satanic foes"). The campaign theme song, "Stand Up for America," was equally apocalyptic. There was "rioting and looting and the cities are being burned," sang Fowler. And even though the Constitution gave the states the "sovereign right to choose," went the lyrics, the "sovereign state with rights" were "about to be destroyed" by the "Great Society."[66]

Finally, as the crowd grew increasingly restive, the candidate's motorcade would arrive. Wallace, surrounded by his out-of-uniform Alabama trooper bodyguards, would hurry to the platform, and the gravel-voiced Wills would launch himself uncertainly from his folding chair and begin his introduction. Campaign staff muttered a nightly prayer: that their candidate would get to the microphone before the bourbon-soaked Wills fell off the platform or passed out in the presence of the handful of journalists anxious for any diversion to enliven their stale recapitulation of the standard Wallace speech. Reporters nearly got their wish in a gathering outside Burbank in early December. His arm raised to heaven, Wills lurched backward and almost into the lap of the Reverend Alvin Mayall, only to recover with the grace of a veteran drunk and complete his introduction. Thereafter, Wallace's burly bodyguard Lloyd Jemison always stationed himself behind Wills, ready to keep him upright.[67] (A second near-disaster occurred when a Wallace supporter walked up to a distinctly out-of-focus Wills and asked him for an autograph for her twelve-year-old son. Sure, said the obliging Wills as he fumbled for his pen: "What's the little bastard's name?"[68])

To California newsmen who trailed the menage up the San Joaquin Valley as far north as Sacramento, then turned south to Fresno, Visalia, and Bakersfield where the children of the "Okies" of the 1930s had settled into bungalow communities, the combination of country bands, religious music, and songs of patriotic uplift seemed as incongruous as a southern gospel tent suddenly dropped into the middle of a Los Angeles shopping mall. In fact, the Wallace campaign staff knew their demography. By the 1950s Pasadena's broadcast of the *Dinner Bell Roundup* and the *Grand Ole Opry*–style *Hometown Jamboree* had made southern California a center of "hillbilly" music second only to Nashville.[69]

The *Grand Ole Opry* continued its broadcasts from Nashville's ramshackle Ryman Auditorium, its floors stained with generations of tobacco juice, but by the 1960s country music, like black music, had moved beyond its regional roots in a way that reflected the "southernization" of American culture. From the tense and impersonal world of factory and urban anonymity many of its listeners—two or three generations removed from farm and small-town America—looked back through a romanticized filter toward a lost rural arcadia. Forgotten were the blinding poverty and narrow parochialism that had propelled their parents and grandparents off the farms and into the blue-collar neighborhoods of Los Angeles, Cleveland, or Newark. Instead the music's audiences remembered families that loved and sacrificed for each other, communities that were safe, and homesteads where the old died among their children with dignity and respect.

The lyrics, derided by sophisticates for their sentimentality, captured the intensely personal preoccupations of a traditional culture: love unfulfilled or gone wrong, faithless women, bad whiskey, and the ultimate triumph of traditional morality. To the extent that there were politics in country music, they were usually the fatalistic politics of individuals conditioned to see failure and success, sinfulness and virtue as ordained by God. California's Merle Haggard might sing with compassion of the tragic outlaw or of working-class folks down on their luck, but his heroes were inevitably men who drank hard, worked harder, loved their country, and had little use for welfare cheats or unpatriotic hippies. More and more, country music was becoming the conservative voice of young white working-class Americans across America.[70]

A country music performer's success rested upon a direct and intimate relationship with the audience; a performer who "got a big head" or tried to "high-hat" fans was soon finished. George Wallace understood that, although nothing frustrated Seymore Trammell more than his boss's reluctance to break away from long-winded sessions with his admirers. "Important people would come to the governor's office," said Trammell, but Wallace would make them wait while "just talking about trash or this, that, and the other . . . [with] hayseed, ordinary, run-of-the-mill people."[71]

As the campaign reached its climax in mid-December, several state officials expressed doubt that the ballot drive would succeed, a pessimistic assessment echoed by the *Los Angeles Times*'s chief political writer, Richard Bergholz, who condescendingly described the chaos of the Wallace operation. The campaign staff must realize that their candidate, a "southerner, a segregationist"—though admittedly a "skilled demagogue"—could never carry California. A cursory telephone survey of county registrars' offices, he told the *Times*'s readers, revealed that fewer than 20,000 of the 66,000 voters needed for the new American Independent Party had signed up. The handful of true believers had already switched parties, Bergholz surmised, and the holiday crush would strip the campaign of its momentum. "Thus, it would appear that Wallace will never make it."[72]

On January 2, 1968, however, a jubilant George Wallace called a press conference in Santa Monica, and a red-faced Bergholz tersely acknowledged that it "appears the Wallace campaign has succeeded in obtaining sufficient signatures to make the ballot." In fact, Ed Ewing and his California workers had signed up more than 100,000 voters. For nearly six weeks, the rotund Ewing, with shirt sleeves rolled up and a cigarette perpetually lit, had welcomed reporters into his cluttered East Los Angeles office. When journalists probed and questioned his figures, he shuffled and scratched and turned in a prizewinning performance as the slightly bewildered good ol' boy operating totally out of his league. Unbeknownst to the press corps, friendly Wallace registrars deputized by the county clerks had, on Ewing's instructions, held back their paperwork to lull the opposition.

Not only was the American Independent Party on the ballot, a Gallup poll showed that support for Wallace in California had increased from less than two percent to eleven percent.[73] Skeptical critics sniffed that it was hardly surprising, given the candidate's commitment of resources to the California drive. But the Wallace campaign staff knew better. The expenditure of such a prodigal amount of money (nearly half a million dollars) might be questionable in the long run, but to these defensive southerners it was worth it all to watch the liberal media wipe the egg off their faces.[74]

GEORGE Wallace had little time to savor his victory. The governor's office continued to assure inquiring reporters that Mrs. Wallace was "fine," though she would have to return to Houston for periodic checkups. But during her second visit to California, on December 9, Wallace staffers had seen that she was thin and drawn. She had learned to hide the constant pain, to insist that she was better. "There's no point in his [George's] knowing about it and worrying," she told one reporter.[75]

The governor had been scheduled to campaign in California for five days, but on the second day of her stay, she nearly fainted at a Long Beach appearance, and her two bodyguards hustled her back to the airport for a flight to Houston. At the Anderson Clinic, doctors remained concerned but noncommittal. After three days of inconclusive tests, she returned to Montgomery for her last Christmas with friends and family. Only regular injections of morphine allowed her to rest for a few hours.

Just before New Year's, Mrs. Wallace, accompanied by Catherine Steineker and security guards David Harwood and Meady Hilyer, made a secret flight back to Houston for yet another round of tests. After meeting with her doctors, she sat down at a Sears department-store restaurant with her three comrades. The cancer had come back, she told them. A pelvic tumor was pressing against the nerves that extended from her back down through her right hip; that was why she had been in such agony since mid-December. (One of her Montgomery doctors later speculated that the pain actually might have been caused from damage to the lower bowel caused by the extensive radiation.) Surgery, she explained, would not be possible. Her Anderson Clinic physician had decided to try betatron treatment, a therapy which focused large amounts of radiation on a small area.

Harwood, who worshiped Mrs. Wallace, looked as though *he* had been diagnosed with a terminal illness, said Steineker. "I thought we were going to have to bury him right there in Houston." That evening, Lurleen Wallace banged on the door of Hilyer and Harwood's motel room and ordered with a smile, "Get your glad rags on!" Catherine had never been to Trader Vic's, she said, and there was nothing to be gained by lying around the motel moping.[76]

Back in Montgomery, the Wallaces attended the Blue and Gray All-Star football game, and Alabama newspaper reporters noted the physical changes brought by the governor's illness. Her weight had dropped another ten pounds and she was deathly pale; her once-smooth face was lined and drawn. Her husband had scheduled a major speech on January 11 to mark the grand opening of Houston's "Wallace for President" headquarters. Once again, the couple enacted their well-rehearsed charade.

George Wallace: "We won't go. We'd better stay here at the motel. . . . You don't feel like going."

Lurleen Wallace: "No, George. I want to go. I'd like to see the people. It'll do me good. I'm all right."

Jammed into a small, unventilated room with hundreds of supporters—one of the reporters remembered it as "one of the stuffiest rooms I've ever been in"—Wallace swung into his all-too-familiar speech. His wife, beautifully dressed in a tailored white wool dress, fixed her usual smile, but it soon faded. ("It was so hot in there. . . . I got so hot," she explained the next day.) Fired up by the adulation of his Texas true believers, Wallace galloped on for nearly thirty minutes. As he finished the last line of his speech, she whispered something to David Harwood, who pushed people aside to escort her back to the waiting car. "I caught a glimpse of her face as she left," said *Birmingham News* reporter Anita Smith; "it was ashen gray." Lurleen Wallace never again appeared in public.[77]

Even before her final trip to Texas, she had confronted her worsening illness. In the governor's mansion, as she sat before a fire with Catherine Steineker, she had sobbed uncontrollably: "Oh, Catherine, I don't want to die." One of her physicians reported, "She was up and around after she returned from Houston, but she knew the score right then." For the next four months, Mrs. Wallace struggled through a series of complications that left her weaker and weaker: emergency surgery in late February to remove an intestinal blockage and the pelvic tumor (which had shrunk, but not disappeared); another operation for an abdominal abscess; and in late March, a procedure to dissolve a blood clot in her left lung. Montgomery newspapers knew the end was near, but when she came home from the hospital on April 14, the day before Easter, they ran front-page stories quoting Mrs. Wallace's press secretary as saying that the governor was once again on the road to recovery.[78]

By late April 1968, the cancer had spread to Lurleen Wallace's liver and lungs, and she weighed less than eighty pounds. As the pain mounted, her physicians increased the doses of the morphine derivative that she had been taking since December. "We were pretty well licked, and we certainly wanted to make sure she got enough medication for her pain," said one of her doctors. Mrs. Wallace struggled to remain involved and attentive, but she drifted off into longer and longer periods of agitated sleep. Always meticulous in her appearance, she refused to see anyone except for her closest friends and family.

As oxygen tanks and intravenous carts crowded the room beside the bed, seventeen-year-old Peggy Sue persuaded herself that her mother was not going to die. She moved through the motions of her last few months at Montgomery's largest public high school—parties, the prom, the senior play, exams—never allowing herself to think about her mother's condition. "I just tried to block her illness out of my mind," she told her brother.[79]

George Junior, a quiet and sometimes withdrawn fifteen-year-old, came to his mother's room several times a day to bring her meals and beg her to eat. "Son, I would if I could," she told him in a weak whisper. Like his sister, he engaged in an elaborate process of denial. No one in the family ever addressed the final reality of the illness except in the most indirect ways. And that was how Lurleen Wallace wanted it.[80] Early in her illness, she had assured her husband, that if "worse came to worse, people meet in heaven. . . . We can meet in heaven, [too]." But for the most part, she and everyone around her maintained the illusion that hope remained until the final day of her life.[81]

Anita Smith, who had become enormously fond of Lurleen Wallace, spoke glowingly of her husband's devotion during the last stages of her illness. And it was clear that the two had grown closer. But critics of George Wallace, particularly those closest to his wife, could not forgive him as he pressed on with his campaign. Only a week after doctors at Montgomery's St. Margaret's Hospital sent their patient home for the last time on April 13, 1968, Wallace took off for a fund-raising trip to Arkansas. When reporters gingerly asked him about her condition, he claimed that her main problems were caused by complications from the treatments for her illness; as far as her cancer was concerned, "she has won the fight." Aides in Montgomery reinforced the impression that Mrs. Wallace was continuing to improve. An unidentified spokesman told reporters that she was doing "very well, eating a normal diet and has a good appetite."[82]

On April 25, Wallace returned to Texas for a three-day sweep through Wichita Falls, Amarillo, Lubbock, Midland, San Antonio, Corpus Christi, Victoria, Houston, and Dallas. Buoyed by overflow crowds at every rally, he discarded his prepared texts and returned to the themes that he had used in his California campaign: the breakdown in law and order and the threat posed by lawless mobs in America's cities. Reporters traveling with the candidate described him as "upbeat and in good humor," insisting that Mrs. Wallace was "improving."[83]

Even after his return to Montgomery, when it was apparent that his wife's condition was worsening, Wallace arranged to fly to Michigan for a series of rallies and speeches. On May 5, the morning of his scheduled departure, however, doctors warned that her condition was extremely unstable. He canceled his trip, and for the first time tried, awkwardly, to prepare his children for the inevitable. When George Junior asked (as he did every day), "Dad, how's Mother?" Wallace quietly answered, "Well, Son, your mother may not *make* it." After his father closed the door and left the room, his son cried for the first time.[84]

The following day, George Wallace was scheduled to make a statewide television address to mark his success in wresting control of the Alabama Democratic Party from the national party loyalists, but Mrs. Wallace's physician advised him to cancel the speech: his wife probably would not live through the night. They debated taking her to the hospital, but Dr. H. H. Hutchinson assured him there was no reason to subject her to the pain of a ride to St. Margaret's. Nothing could be done. Although the conversations took place out of earshot, Lurleen Wallace, still lucid, now abandoned the self-control she had maintained throughout much of her illness. "Please stay with me tonight," she pleaded with Hutchinson, then turned to her husband. "Oh, God, please let me live," she said, "because I want to live. . . . But if I can't live, please give me the strength and the faith to face whatever I have to face."[85]

Shortly after eight P.M. a member of the security detail drove to Sidney Lanier High School to bring Peggy Sue back to the mansion. At her father's insistence she had gone to one of the last practices for her senior play. She found the whole family, including her grandmother and grandfather Burns, gathered in the hall outside her mother's room.[86] Her father was sitting beside the bed, holding his wife's hand. Just after midnight, Hutchinson, stethoscope around his neck, came out into the hall. "About fifteen minutes," he said. At 12:34, her breath shortened, then stopped.[87]

THE outpouring of grief that swept Alabama in the wake of Lurleen Wallace's death seemed incomprehensible to those outside the state. Prominent public officials issued the usual statements of "profound sorrow" and "deep regret" and announced that state offices would be closed for the funeral on Thursday, May 9. But when Mrs. Wallace's body was placed in the capitol the day before the funeral, 25,000 mourners—mostly white, but a few black—waited as long as five hours to move through the six-block-long line up to the rotunda and past the silver casket, engraved with a quotation from her inaugural address: "I am proud to be an Alabamian." Every school in the state, private and public, closed the day of the funeral. Private businesses opened briefly or not at all. At a time when politicians cultivated the notion that they were "just folks," Lurleen Wallace did not have to pretend. She was genuinely unpretentious—down to earth—and the masses of people loved her for it.

The stricken faces of the family highlighted the chasm between collective public rituals and the intense private grief of those devastated by her loss.

Clio, Alabama, at the turn of the century. By the time George Wallace was born two decades later, the town showed little change. (MARY S. PALMER, MOBILE, ALABAMA)

Wallace at age fifteen at the state capitol as a Senate page. As he stood on the bronze star where Jefferson Davis had taken the oath as the Confederacy's first president, Wallace later recalled, "I knew I would return to the spot. I knew I would be governor."
(WILLIAM STANLEY HOOLE SPECIAL COLLECTIONS LIBRARY, UNIVERSITY OF ALABAMA)

Bantamweight Wallace bloodies a Tulane University opponent in 1939 on his way to setting records as a two-time Alabama Golden Gloves champion and captain of the University of Alabama boxing team. This was one of his favorite photographs.
(WILLIAM STANLEY HOOLE SPECIAL COLLECTIONS LIBRARY, UNIVERSITY OF ALABAMA)

Beginning in 1958, the politically ambitious Wallace would clash bitterly with Federal Judge Frank Johnson, but during their days at the University of Alabama, Wallace and his best friend Glen Curlee (*far right*) spent long hours with Johnson and his wife, Ruth (*center*).
(WILLIAM STANLEY HOOLE SPECIAL COLLECTIONS LIBRARY, UNIVERSITY OF ALABAMA)

Shortly before shipping out for the Pacific, Wallace joined his fellow B-29 crew members for a picnic on the white sands of Alamogordo, New Mexico. *Standing*: George Leahy, Tom Lamb; *sitting*: Jack Ray, Art Feiner, Dick Zind, Johnny Petroff, Jason Riley, Bob Bushouse, Wallace; *reclining*: George Harbinson and Emil Kott.
(COURTESY OF ARTHUR FEINER)

During his first administration, Governor "Big Jim" Folsom recognized Wallace's political skills and worked closely with him. In this photo, the young Barbour County legislator watches proudly as Folsom signs the 1951 Wallace-Cater Industrial Development Act.

(*MONTGOMERY ADVERTISER*)

Wallace and his longtime supporter *Montgomery Adviser* editor Grover Hall review the gloomy June 9, 1958, election returns the night the young Alabama politician went down to his first political defeat. Later that evening, Wallace would promise his friends that "no other son-of-a-bitch will ever out-nigger me again."

(TOMMY GILES PHOTOS)

In his second bid for the governorship in 1962, Wallace campaigned tirelessly throughout the state. Here he speaks to a crowd outside a rural country store.

(ALABAMA DEPARTMENT OF ARCHIVES AND HISTORY)

Wallace captured national attention with his January 1963 inaugural speech when he promised "Segregation now ...segregation tomorrow ...segregation forever" and made himself the leader of the white Southern resistance to integration.

Former Klan leader and white Supremacist Asa Carter—with the advice of John Kohn and Grover Hall—prepared the new governor's inaugural address. In 1972, Carter moved to Texas, assumed a new identity as "Native American" writer Forrest Carter, and wrote the controversial "autobiography" *The Education of Little Tree*.

Civil rights leaders mockingly credited the volatile Bull Connor with a major role in passing the Civil Rights Act of 1964, but George Wallace never faltered in his support of his longtime political ally. (© 1963 CHARLES MOORE/BLACK STAR)

A cameraman with a tele-photo lens captured the moment when George Wallace welcomed John Kennedy to Alabama on the President's May 1963 swing through the South. One fed-eral official later said that Kennedy "did not wish to be photographed or anything with him [Wallace]." (JOHN F. KENNEDY LIBRARY)

On the eve of the June 1963 stand in the schoolhouse door, the Wallace entourage arrived in Tuscaloosa. *Left to right:* Seymore Trammell; an unidentified security guard; the governor's brother Gerald Wallace; bodyguard and driver, E. C. Dothard; adviser John Kohn; legal assistant Cecil Jackson; the governor; and two unidentified individuals. (COURTESY OF SEYMORE TRAMMELL)

Wallace and his staff choreographed the stand in the schoolhouse door for the benefit of the news media. Most television viewers and newspaper readers saw a stern Wallace squaring off with Assistant Attorney General Katzenbach.

The more telling angle would have been this photo. *Left to right:* U.S. Attorney Macon Weaver, Katzenbach, Federal Marshal Peyton Norville, and Wallace.

Three months later, Klansmen bombed Birmingham's Sixteenth Street Baptist Church, killing four young black girls. *Time* magazine linked Wallace to this grisly event by superimposing his stern profile over the church's blown-out stained-glass window. In a national television interview, Wallace denounced the cover as "defamation by photography."
(© 1993 TIME INC)

For his 1964 presidential campaign, Wallace substituted an American flag for one of the two rebel flags normally painted on the fuselage of his official airplane. And the logo, "Stand Up for Alabama," became "Stand Up for America." Here, Seymore Trammell; Wallace; and his executive secretary, Earl Morgan, pose on the eve of the governor's withdrawal from the race.
(EARL ROBERTS PHOTO)

Al Lingo (*center*), head of Alabama's state troopers during the first Wallace administration. Here he leads his troopers into Notasulga in September 1963 to block integration of the Macon County schools.
(WILLIAM STANLEY HOOLE SPECIAL COLLECTIONS LIBRARY, UNIVERSITY OF ALABAMA)

In the midst of the Selma crisis, President Lyndon Johnson and George Wallace met in the Oval Office for a three-hour summit. Afterwards, a subdued Wallace listened as the President eloquently supported Alabama's black citizens in the campaign for the vote. (UNITED STATES ARCHIVES)

On March 25, 1965, Martin Luther King led a triumphant procession of 25,000 civil rights demonstrators past his old church on Montgomery's Dexter Avenue and up to the steps of the state capitol. *Left to right:* King, an unidentified marcher, Coretta Scott King, and the Reverend Ralph David Abernathy. (© 1963 CHARLES MOORE/BLACK STAR)

As the marchers gathered outside the capitol, Seymore Trammell (*left*) and Wallace aides Cecil Jackson (*right*) and Ed Ewing (*center rear*) peeked out through the blinds. One of his advisers teasingly warned the governor that in a "few years that may be the way the inauguration crowd looks."
(COURTESY OF SEYMORE TRAMMELL)

Frustrated in his effort to repeal the Alabama law barring him from a second consecutive term as governor, Wallace ran his wife, Lurleen.
(ALABAMA DEPARTMENT OF ARCHIVES AND HISTORY)

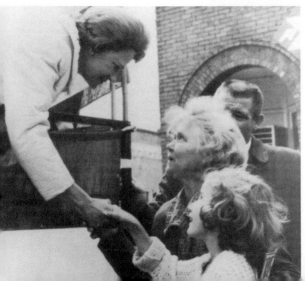

Not surprisingly, men supported Lurleen Wallace as a stand-in candidate for her husband. What stunned former Governor John Patterson was her appeal to women voters; "you had old women, eighty, ninety years old," Patterson recalled, "going and registering to vote that never voted in their life. Just so they could vote for her."
(ALABAMA DEPARTMENT OF ARCHIVES AND HISTORY)

Postelection analysis showed that the over-whelming majority of Alabama whites voting in the Democratic primary threw their support to the Wallace ticket. In this South Alabama rally, the crowd roared its support as George Wallace called upon them to "Stand Up for Alabama."
(ALABAMA DEPARTMENT OF ARCHIVES AND HISTORY)

Although no one had any illusions about who was in charge during the administration of Lurleen Wallace, she surprised her husband at a 1966 Christmas party by presenting him with an apron so that he could handle his "new chores as 'the governor's spouse.'"
(TOMMY GILES PHOTOS)

Lurleen Wallace had asked for a closed casket, but her husband decided to follow southern custom. Here he and his family gather at the open coffin in the capitol rotunda in May 1968. *Left to right*, Wallace son-in-law Jim Parsons, daughter Bobbi Jo Parsons, daughter Peggy Sue, George Wallace, Jr., and youngest daughter Lee in Wallace's arms.
(TOMMY GILES PHOTOS)

Outside the South during his 1968 presidential campaign, Wallace spoke only of defending states' rights, but as late as August of that year, he was still appearing at segregationist rallies in the region. Here he joins Louisiana's Leander Perez (*standing*) and Roy Harris at a Citizens' Councils "White Monday" rally in Montgomery.
(*JACKSON CLARION-LEDGER*)

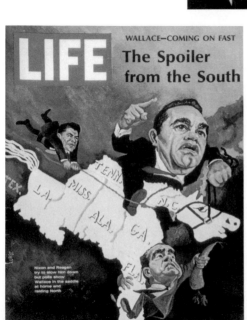

While most political observers initially dismissed Wallace's 1968 third-party campaign, by mid July it was apparent that the Alabama governor would make a strong showing. On this August cover of *Life* magazine, cartoonist Ranan Lurie dramatically depicted Wallace's role in setting the stage for the Southern Strategy which would dominate Republican politics for the next quarter century.
(RANAN LURIE, *LIFE* MAGAZINE © TIME INC.)

In his 1968 campaign, Wallace attracted angry protests as well as enthusiastic crowds. At this St. Louis rally, Wallace and Press Secretary Bill Jones watch apprehensively as police separate scuffling civil rights demonstrators and Wallace supporters.

(LYNN PELHAM, *LIFE* MAGAZINE © TIME INC.)

HERBLOCK'S CARTOON   OCT -

"So Much For Domestic A nd Foreign Problems — "

After Wallace's disastrous press conference introducing the trigger-happy Curtis LeMay as his running mate, *Washington Post* cartoonist Herblock gleefully skewered the Alabama ex-governor and the former Air Force general.

(COPYRIGHT 1968 BY HERBLOCK IN *THE WASHINGTON POST*)

Albert Brewer (*left*) served as Wallace's House majority leader from 1963 to 1967 and as lieutenant governor during Mrs. Wallace's administration. After his wife's death, Wallace insisted that he would not oppose Brewer for the governorship in 1970. Here Wallace shares the podium with Brewer, Lieutenant Governor James Allen (*second from left*), and University of Alabama President Frank Rose at a 1965 education conference in Birmingham.

(WILLIAM STANLEY HOOLE SPECIAL COLLECTIONS LIBRARY, UNIVERSITY OF ALABAMA)

WAKE UP, ALABAMA!
(JUNE 3 COULD BE TOO LATE)

IS THIS
THE
IMAGE
YOU
WANT?

This Could Be Alabama Four Years From Now! Do You Want It?

BLACKS VOW TO TAKE OVER ALABAMA

But Wallace, the perennial candidate, needed the governorship as a base for his projected 1972 presidential bid. In the 1970 Democratic primary runoff, his supporters distributed thousands of racist leaflets in a successful effort to defeat the racially moderate Brewer. (AUTHOR'S COLLECTION)

Richard Nixon secretly poured $400,000 into the 1970 Brewer campaign in an unsuccessful attempt to derail Wallace's future as a third-party candidate. By 1971, however, the two men were edging toward a rapprochement. (UNITED STATES ARCHIVES)

As Wallace began his campaign for the 1972 Democratic nomination, an unemployed busboy and janitor from Milwaukee named Arthur Bremer began stalking him. In this photo taken at a Michigan rally on May 12, a Kalamazoo photographer inadvertently captured Bremer in the cheering audience (*standing left, with glasses*).

(© *KALAMAZOO GAZETTE*/RICK CAMPBELL)

Three days later at a Maryland shopping center, George Wallace overrode the warnings of his Secret Service detail and strode into the waiting crowd. CBS news cameraman Laurens Pierce, less than five feet behind the Alabama governor, recorded Bremer as he began firing into Wallace at point-blank range.

(AP/WIDE WORLD PHOTOS)

According to Wallace, entertainer Elvis Presley, who admired and often talked with the Alabama governor, threatened to kill Bremer after the shooting. Here the two meet in Montgomery after a Presley performance in 1974.
(WILLIAM STANLEY HOOLE SPECIAL COLLECTIONS LIBRARY, UNIVERSITY OF ALABAMA)

Paralyzed below the waist and in constant pain, Wallace turned back to religion. Here, in a 1974 photograph, he sits praying with his second wife, Cornelia, and his daughter Lee at Jerry Falwell's Liberty Baptist Church in preparation for his "testimony."
(AP/WIDE WORLD PHOTOS)

Fellow southerner Jimmy Carter understood the critical role of the Alabama governor in galvanizing regional voters. Here the Democrats' 1976 nominee, developing his own Southern Strategy, meets Wallace at the Alabama capitol as the presidential campaign begins.
(COPYRIGHT © BY THE BIRMINGHAM NEWS COMPANY 1995)

The popular Ronald Reagan became the heir to the conservative Democratic voters Wallace had attracted in the 1960s and 1970s. Here, on a 1986 campaign swing to drum up support for Republican candidates, Reagan greets—and warmly praises—the Alabama governor. (UPI/BETTMANN)

On the thirtieth anniversary of the Selma march, Wallace—no longer a defender of segregation—joined hands with Southern Christian Leadership Conference Secretary Joseph Lowery as veterans of the 1965 demonstrations gathered on the steps of the capitol. (MARK MILLER/MONTGOMERY ADVERTISER 1995)

Lurleen Wallace was close to all her children, but Peggy Sue seemed most affected. For years she would work to sort through the complexity of her feelings: pain, loss, even frustrated anger at the way her mother (however unwillingly) had left her at a vulnerable moment in her life. She was proud of her father, but never close to him. Peggy Sue's mother was the center of her life, and she was gone. Twenty years later, one close friend of the family remembered little of the funeral. But he could still vividly recall the sight of Peggy Sue, standing alone, even aloof, from the rest of the family, comforted only by a boyfriend who remained by her side.

Lurleen Wallace had carefully planned her own funeral service with her minister, John Vickers, and she had been emphatic: despite the widespread southern custom of "viewing" the deceased, she wanted a closed casket. But George Wallace decided to override his wife's decision. Although she was "very thin she still looked like herself," said George Junior, who agreed with his father.[88]

Peggy Sue did not. Her worst moments came on the day of her mother's funeral. Under the glare of television lights and flashing strobe units from news photographers, she walked with her family into the capitol rotunda and up to the bier and open coffin. She saw placed over her mother's body a glass bubble, the perfect symbol for that lack of privacy, that fishbowl existence that she had always hated.

"Modesty is the citadel of beauty and virtue," said Vickers in his eulogy the next day. "Our governor was one of modesty and humility," he told the hushed crowd in St. James's Methodist Church. She was first and foremost "a wife, a mother, a servant to her state and a friend."[89]

IN the days following her inauguration, Lurleen Wallace had read in the *Montgomery Advertiser* a story outlining the horrendous overcrowding and understaffing in the state's mental hospital and its school for the retarded, both in Tuscaloosa. Determined to judge for herself, the governor announced that she would inspect conditions at the Bryce State Hospital and the Partlow State School in late February 1967. Partlow administrators scheduled a series of briefings, but Mrs. Wallace insisted on visiting the oldest and most crowded of the dormitories, where dozens of young inmates lay in beds that lined long, barracklike rooms. When school officials reluctantly opened the door to one third-floor ward, the governor walked in and was nearly overcome by the stench of excrement and stale urine. An overweight and severely retarded nine-year-old moaning "Mama! Mama!" attempted to hug her before attendants pulled her away. Mrs. Wallace, fighting for control, began silently weeping as she walked out of the building.[90] In the brief time that she served as governor, she struggled to persuade her husband to increase appropriations for Bryce and Partlow.

Her minister, public officials who praised the governor, and newspaper editorials returned again and again to the story of the weeping Lurleen Wallace, moved by the sight of suffering children. They eulogized her as the authentic southern lady, a woman who "lived by a rule as old as civilization: The family comes first."[91]

Virginia Durr, the grande dame of the handful of white civil rights activists in Montgomery, never concealed her contempt for George Wallace, but she felt only compassion for his wife. "She was sweet, you know, one of those sweet southern women that did everything that had to be done."[92] And Durr understood the loss that the people of the state felt. "She seemed to symbolize to so many people all they think a 'Southern Woman' should be: pretty, dainty, a good mother and certainly an obedient wife, brave under suffering and doomed." But Durr found something repugnant about the mourning, "something macabre in the recitation of her sufferings and the detailed description of her illness . . . and death." So "many Southerners are in love with death, especially women. Their highest ambition, it seems to me, is to be known as a 'brave sufferer.' I hate it."[93]

Within seventy-two hours of the funeral, Wallace moved out of the governor's mansion and into the modest ranch-style house in suburban Montgomery that he and Lurleen had bought the previous year. The children were dispersed to friends or family. For days he moped around the house alone, and friends saw him daily at his wife's gravesite in Greenwood Cemetery. A little more than a week after the burial, he called Bob Ingram, who had taken a post in the new Brewer administration, and asked him to bring the former lieutenant governor over to his house.

Wallace, red-eyed from weeping, seemed to Ingram depressed to the point of complete inertia. He led his visitors through the living room and comfortable den into a small, spare room with a single bed, three chairs, and a closet overflowing with thousands of plaques and framed certificates of gratitude and congratulation given him by civic clubs, chambers of commerce, and fraternal orders across America. When Governor Brewer attempted to express his condolences, Wallace blurted out that he was "already hearing talk about how I am going to run against you in 1970. Let me tell you this," he insisted, "the only Wallace candidate who will be running for governor in 1970 will be you."[94]

Ingram thought it inappropriate to be talking politics a week after Lurleen Wallace's death. Brewer, seldom at a loss for words, mumbled that he was simply trying to get through the difficult period of transition; he hadn't even thought of future elections. But Wallace wouldn't stop. "Lurleen told me many times how kind and considerate you were to her. You were really special to her," he added. "She would never forgive me if I were to run against you."[95]

George Wallace was never close to his children, but there was one piece of advice he constantly hammered home to them on the few occasions when he sat around the dinner table and waxed philosophical. "The only thing that counts," he would say, "is money and power."[96] He had never cared about money. With the death of his wife, and his promise to longtime ally Albert Brewer not to run in 1970, Wallace seemed to have cut himself loose from the critical sources of political and economic power. But he could still draw to his side millions of frustrated Americans. On May 27, 1968, two weeks after his conversation with Governor Brewer and Bob Ingram, and three weeks after the death of his wife, Wallace announced his return to the presidential campaign trail.[97]

Chapter 11

RICHARD NIXON, GEORGE WALLACE, AND THE SOUTHERNIZATION OF AMERICAN POLITICS

AFTER HIS HAIRBREADTH loss to John Kennedy in 1960, Richard Nixon had played the role of the magnanimous loser, congratulating Kennedy and discouraging supporters who wanted to challenge questionable election returns from precincts in Mayor Daley's Chicago. Two years later, faced with another heartbreaking loss to California governor Pat Brown, his mask of control slipped; exhausted, hung over, and trembling with rage, he had stalked into the press room of his campaign headquarters and lashed out at assembled newsmen in rambling remarks so incoherent that reporters—who are not noted for their empathy for wounded politicians—sat in silent embarrassment. For ten minutes (though it seemed like hours to his staff) the former vice president alternated between mawkish self-pity and bitter attacks on the press, which he blamed for his defeat. He closed with the line memorable for its unintended irony: "Well, you won't have Nixon to kick around anymore, because, gentlemen, this is my last press conference. . . ." As stunned aides Herbert Klein and H. R. Haldeman pulled him from the room, the defeated candidate was unrepentant. "I finally told those bastards off, and every Goddamned thing I said was true."[1]

By December 1967, memories of his losses had faded. With the determination that had led his Duke Law School classmates to dub him Richard the Grind, Nixon fought his way back to political center stage. As a former vice president and presidential candidate with political and business connections abroad, he traveled often to Europe and Asia in the mid-1960s. Occasionally foreign leaders like Charles de Gaulle received him with the pomp and ceremony normally awarded a head of state; more often he was shunted off to mid-level officials. Despite such rebuffs, he doggedly sought the public eye with regular press conferences and articles designed to establish his credentials as the Republican Party's steady hand on foreign policy. As a whole, Nixon's efforts were long on rhetorical warnings, short on specifics, often wrongheaded in their predictions, and only marginally indicative of the kind of bold departures in foreign policy that would mark his presidency. Such deficiencies were more than offset by the ex cathedra predictions and grand observations that demonstrated what the Romans called *gravitas*. This was a man to be taken seriously.[2]

If there was a turning point in the political recovery of Richard Nixon, it had come in 1964. Faced with the likelihood that his party would nominate conservative standard-bearer Barry Goldwater (and the certainty he would suffer a smashing defeat), the former vice president introduced the Arizona senator at the convention and then dutifully delivered more than one hundred and fifty speeches for Republican candidates in thirty-six states, always emphasizing his support for Goldwater even as he distanced himself from the nominee's more extreme positions. By the time the votes were counted in the Johnson landslide, Nixon had compiled a staggering number of chits from conservative and moderate Republicans. When he embarked on an equally aggressive speaking schedule for party candidates in the 1966 off-year elections, he became the odds-on favorite for the GOP nomination in 1968.[3] And the long-coveted prize—the presidency—appeared within reach as the Democratic Party seemed to implode.

WHEN Lyndon Johnson committed United States airpower and troops to support the tottering South Vietnamese government in 1964 and 1965, only a small minority of intellectuals and students challenged him. As the number of ground troops rose from fifty thousand in 1964 to nearly half a million in January of 1967, as casualties mounted, as the cost of the war doubled, tripled, then quadrupled, members of the antiwar movement, frustrated and impotent, escalated their tactics, from teach-ins to rallies to raucous street

demonstrations. The war in Vietnam and the explosion of the antiwar movement, coupled with summer after summer of civil disorder, left the incumbent Democratic administration discredited and the nation deeply divided.

On January 30, 1968, 85,000 Vietcong guerillas and their North Vietnamese
allies—supposedly on the verge of collapse—launched their devastating
"Tet" offensive, attacking at will throughout South Vietnam. It took American
forces twenty-six days to dislodge the Vietcong from their last stronghold in
the Imperial citadel in Hué. The American public finally said, "Enough." In
the month after Tet, pollster George Gallup found that the number of self-
described "hawks" had plummeted from sixty percent to forty percent, while
the number of "doves" rose from twenty-four percent to forty-two percent.[4]
If the majority of voters rejected a further escalation of the war, they had little
stomach for accepting humiliating defeat at the hands of a ragtag army of
pajama-clad peasants. Richard Nixon skillfully positioned himself to take
advantage of the frustrations of middle-class and working-class Americans
by holding out the chimerical promise that he could win the war by relying
upon airpower rather than increasing the number of American ground
troops.

But first he had to win the Republican nomination. And in that process, the
South played a critical role.

To most political reporters, Richard Nixon's "Southern Strategy" was simply a continuation of Barry Goldwater's efforts to woo disgruntled whites in
the old Confederacy, but Nixon adamantly rejected the notion that he had
picked up where Goldwater left off. "The idea that Goldwater started the
Southern Strategy is bullshit," he told biographer Herbert Parmet. Everyone
seemed to forget that Eisenhower had been the first modern Republican to
campaign seriously in the South, in 1952 and 1956, and he had made significant inroads in the region. Goldwater's campaign was a detour, insisted
Nixon. The federal government's desegregation policies and the rise of the
civil rights movement had spurred angry whites in the Deep South to all-out
resistance, and Goldwater had been drawn to that unstable constituency like
a moth to a flame. As a result, Nixon concluded, Goldwater "ran as a racist
candidate . . . and he won the wrong [southern] states": Mississippi, Georgia,
Alabama, Louisiana, and South Carolina.[5]

The Arizonan's huge majorities in the Deep South had made possible the
election of dozens of Republican officeholders for the first time since the
post–Civil War Reconstruction era, but his identification with hard-line segregationists weakened his party's appeal to moderates in the border states
and in the North. The GOP, argued Nixon, should reach out to the South's
emerging middle-class suburban constituency, more in tune with traditional
Republican economic conservatism than with old-style racism.

If Nixon's analysis showed a shrewd grasp of the long-term weaknesses of the 1964 GOP campaign, it was disingenuous to pretend that his own manipulation of the politics of race bore no resemblance to that of Barry Goldwater. The political demands of the hour required him to walk a precarious ideological tightrope—to distance himself from Goldwater's explicit appeal to southern white racism while reaping the benefits of such a strategy. There was little incentive to court the die-hard white racist vote in the South. The Democrats would surely renominate Lyndon Johnson and most white southerners, racists and moderates alike, would never vote for the man who had made a point of including the battle cry of the movement, "We shall overcome," in his speech introducing civil rights legislation. The votes of these white southerners would fall to a Republican—even to a moderately conservative Republican—by default.

Nixon realized he couldn't be *too* moderate. Most southern GOP leaders were considerably to the right of the national political mainstream on economic, social, and racial issues. The majority of their mid-level and lower-level cadres had entered the party on the wave of the Goldwater campaign, and—while they were chastened by the Johnson landslide of 1964—they were not about to abandon their conservative and ultra-conservative views. To gain their allegiance required a deft political hand.

In the two years after the 1964 election, Nixon traveled 127,000 miles, visited forty states, and spoke to four hundred groups, nearly half of them in the South. On his southern swings, he was conservative, but not too conservative; a defender of civil rights, but always solicitous of white southerners' "concerns." He often prefaced his remarks with a reminder that he had supported the Supreme Court's decision in 1954 as well as the Civil Rights Acts of 1964 and the Voting Rights Act of 1965. His bona fides established, he would then launch into a stern lecture on the problem of "riots, violence in the streets and mob rule," or he would take a few swings at the "unconscionable boondoggles" in Johnson's poverty program or at the federal courts' excessive concern for the rights of criminals. The real culprits in the nation's racial conflicts were the "extremists of both races," he kept saying.[6]

Sometimes he shifted away from racial issues to the traditional Republican themes of economic conservatism and limited government. More often, he stood on the lofty ground of foreign policy. The testosterone levels of southern Republicans seemed to rank just below those of NFL linemen, and Nixon early learned that a little tub-thumping patriotism and a defense of military muscle went a long way toward deflecting their worry about civil rights.[7] In a May 1966 speech in Birmingham, for example, he sounded perilously close to the "old" Richard Nixon when he told a cheering crowd of Alabama Republicans that "thousands of American boys wouldn't be dead today" if Lyndon Johnson had bombed North Vietnam from the beginning of the conflict.[8]

During one of those southern forays in the spring of 1966, Nixon traveled to Columbia, South Carolina, for a fund-raising dinner for the South Carolina GOP. Senator Strom Thurmond had easily assumed command of the state's fledgling Republican Party when he officially switched to the GOP during the Goldwater campaign. In the years after his 1948 presidential run, he modulated his rhetoric and shifted the focus of his grim maledictions to the "eternal menace of godless, atheistic Communism." He had even learned (when pressed) to pronounce the word "Negro" without eliciting grimaces from his northern fellow Republicans. But race remained his subtext; he continued to Red-bait every spokesman for civil rights from Whitney Young of the Urban League to Stokely Carmichael of the Black Panthers. For the traditional southern campaign chorus of "Nigger-nigger-nigger," he substituted the Cold War battle cry: "Commie-Commie-Commie." On the eve of Nixon's visit, Thurmond was still attacking the civil rights movement, still accusing the Supreme Court of fostering "crime in the streets" and of promoting "a free rein for communism, riots, agitation, collectivism and the breakdown of moral codes."[9]

The senator assigned Harry Dent to act as the vice president's host. Despite Nixon's reputation as wooden and aloof, he charmed Thurmond's aide by bluntly acknowledging his presidential aspirations and soliciting advice. He had no illusions about the difficulties of getting the nomination and defeating Lyndon Johnson, he told Dent. But the man he feared most was George Wallace.[10]

In his public statements, Nixon always professed to be unconcerned about the Alabama governor. As a third-party candidate, Wallace might hurt the GOP in the South, argued Nixon, but he would draw an equal number of votes from normally Democratic blue-collar voters in the North. "I don't think he'll get four million votes," said Nixon, who pointed to the dismal past experience of third-party candidates.[11] Four million votes would translate into less than six percent of the expected turnout.

He was considerably more frank in his conversation with Dent. The Alabama governor, said Nixon, undercut one of the basic assumptions of his Southern Strategy: that angry whites, when faced with a choice between any conceivable national Democrat and Richard Nixon, would reluctantly side with the GOP, thus freeing him to appeal to moderates in the border states and the North. If Wallace should "take most of the South," Nixon told Dent, as the Republican candidate he might be "unable to win enough votes in the rest of the country to gain a clear majority." Once the election went to the Democratic-controlled House of Representatives, the game was over.

Dent argued that Thurmond was the key to gaining the support of southern Republicans. Conservatives might privately deride the South Carolina senator as an egotistical fanatic, but his very estrangement from the traditional political process—his refusal to cooperate or compromise with fellow senators—made him the ideological measuring stick for southern GOP leaders baptized in the ideologically pure waters of Goldwater Republicanism.

At an afternoon press conference, Richard Nixon went out of his way to praise the former Dixiecrat. "Strom is no racist," he told reporters; "Strom is a man of courage and integrity." To Thurmond, laboring under the burden of his past as the "Dr. No" of American race relations, it was like being granted absolution from purgatory by the pope of American politics. Almost pathetically grateful, the senator seldom wavered in his support for Nixon in the years that followed.[12]

Nixon's careful cultivation of southern white sensibilities and of power brokers like Thurmond paid off at the 1968 Republican convention. Nelson Rockefeller mounted a last doomed challenge from the old eastern wing of the party, but the real threat came from the media-savvy governor of California. Ronald Reagan captured the emotional commitment of conservatives across the country, particularly in the South. Although Nixon later spoke confidently about the "coolness and confidence" with which his campaign manager, John Mitchell, controlled the convention, the Reagan challenge was his most vulnerable moment in his fight for the nomination. Southern delegations controlled 356 convention votes, more than half the number required for the nomination. Nixon went into the convention with the support of 298 of those delegates.[13] A shift of as few as thirty-five delegates would block his first-ballot nomination and open the way for a Reagan victory.

Flanked by his impassioned sidekick, Strom Thurmond, Nixon summoned the southern delegations to his suite at the Hilton Plaza for a virtuoso performance. (The meeting was captured on tape by an enterprising *Miami Herald* reporter who persuaded a Florida delegate to carry a concealed recorder into Nixon's suite.) Nixon first reaffirmed his commitment to economic conservatism and a foreign policy resting upon equal parts of anti-communism and military jingoism. Still, the issue of race preoccupied the group. Once again, Nixon showed that he was the master of the wink, the nudge, the implied commitment. Without ever explicitly renouncing his own past support for desegregation, he managed to convey to his listeners the sense that, as President, he would do the absolute minimum required to carry out the mandates of the federal courts. In a Nixon administration, there would be no rush to "satisfy some professional civil-rights group, or something like that."[14]

Although some members of his audience believed that George Wallace had the right solution ("take those bearded bureaucrats and throw them in the Potomac") or that the golden-tongued Reagan was the more authentic conservative, the bitter memories of the Goldwater debacle made them pause and listen to Thurmond. "We have no choice, if we want to win, except to vote for Nixon," he insisted. "We must quit using our hearts and start using our heads." Believe me, he said, "I love Reagan, but Nixon's the one."[15]

After the convention, Texas Republican senator John Tower described Nixon's southern brigade as the "thin gray line which never broke."[16] A more appropriate analogy might be found in Margaret Mitchell's *Gone With the Wind*. Like so many Scarlett O'Haras, Nixon's Dixie delegates reluctantly turned their backs on the dashing blockade-runner and resigned themselves to a marriage of convenience with the stodgy dry-goods merchant.

They received their first reward with Nixon's announcement that Spiro Agnew would be his running mate.

A few weeks before the convention, the candidate had accompanied his old law partner, John Mitchell, to an Annapolis restaurant to meet Maryland's governor. Afterward, Nixon told an aide: "That guy Agnew is really an impressive fellow. He's got guts. He's got a good attitude."[17] Although he concealed his decision to the last to gain maximum leverage, it was a done deal.[18]

Woodrow Wilson's 1916 running mate, Thomas Marshall, is best remembered for his insistence that "What this country needs most is a really good five-cent cigar," but his assessment of the vice presidency was no less insightful. The poor wretch imprisoned in this meaningless office endures four years in a "cataleptic state," said Marshall. "He cannot speak; he cannot move; he suffers no pain; and yet he is perfectly conscious of everything that is going on about him."[19] He might have added that the position required little mental heavy lifting beyond an ability to read a speech (written by the President's speechwriters) and to assume a posture of adoration at the mere mention of the chief executive's name.

The former Maryland governor seemed perfectly suited for the job. His ignorance of a wide range of subjects proved breathtaking to those hastily assigned to shepherd him through the 1968 campaign. In an interview many years later, Nixon defensively insisted that "Agnew was not a lightweight. Agnew was a heavyweight."[20] If so, the fact escaped most of those who surrounded him. He had been a petty bribe-taker from the time he was first elected to public office in Baltimore County.[21] (When federal prosecutors eventually disclosed the payoffs, Wallace's men chuckled at Agnew's lack of imagination: the "sonofabitch oughta look around and see what the architects are kicking back in Alabama!"[22])

It is not clear whether Mitchell or Nixon had any knowledge of, or interest in, Agnew's ethical lapses. What was important was that he was a malleable, "saleable" product who could help marginally in the border states without demonstrably hurting the ticket elsewhere. He had earned a reputation as a

moderate in the Maryland gubernatorial contest when his opponent, a vociferous segregationist, promised to turn the clock back on civil rights. With
his typical "on the one hand and on the other hand" rhetoric, Nixon insisted
that he chose Agnew because he was a "progressive" border-state Republican who took a "forward-looking stance on civil rights, but . . . had firmly
opposed those who had resorted to violence in promoting their cause."[23]

What really sold Nixon, however, was the Maryland governor's performance during the five-day Baltimore race riot that followed Martin Luther
King's assassination in April 1968. As the city returned to some degree of
normality, Agnew summoned one hundred mainstream black city leaders—
respected community organizers, middle-class preachers, lawyers, businessmen, and politicians—to a conference in Annapolis. Instead of holding a
joint discussion, the governor lashed out at his audience's failure to condemn
the "circuit-riding Hanoi-visiting . . . caterwauling, riot-inciting, burn-
America-down type of leader[s]" who, he said, had caused the rioting in the
city. Pointing his finger for emphasis, he accused the moderates of "breaking
and running" when faced with the taunts of "Uncle Tom" from black radicals
like Stokely Carmichael and H. Rap Brown. Three fourths of his audience—
many still exhausted from long days and nights on the street trying to calm
the rioters—angrily walked out of the meeting.[24] These were the "very people who were trying to end the riots," pointed out the executive director of
the city's Community Relations Commission, but Baltimore's television stations reported a flood of telephone calls supporting the governor.[25]

Twenty years later when he defended his vice-presidential choice to Herbert Parmet, the only substantive mention Nixon made of Agnew's record as
governor was a glowing account of his performance after the Baltimore
riots.[26]

IN the spring of 1968, when polls had shown that Nixon would tie either of
the most likely Democratic nominees, Robert Kennedy or Hubert Humphrey, the South (and George Wallace) seemed critical to his campaign. By
the end of August, the importance of southern electoral votes had receded in
the wake of the Democrats' self-immolating convention in Chicago, a fitting
(if ignoble) culmination to a year of misery for the party and a salutary
reminder of the ephemeral nature of political victory. In November 1964,
Lyndon Johnson had stood like a Texas colossus. Three and a half years
later, beset by civil disorder and growing economic crises at home and the
war in Vietnam, he withdrew from the presidential race after Minnesota
senator Eugene McCarthy humiliated him in an early primary. When Robert
Kennedy eclipsed McCarthy as the Democratic front-runner, only to be
gunned down in California, the stage was set for disaster. In a convention
marked by violent clashes in the street between Chicago police and antiwar

demonstrators, and only slightly less bitter conflict on the convention floor, Hubert Humphrey—who had not won a single primary—assumed the discredited leadership of a tattered political party. Even the Russians seemed to cooperate in Nixon's game plan, with their decision to invade Czechoslovakia and crush democratic reforms a week after the Republican convention. "Makes it kind of hard to be a dove," chortled the candidate's top advertising pundit.[27]

Calculation had figured in Richard Nixon's successful rehabilitation and return to national prominence, but chance had proved equally critical to his good fortune. By the time Nixon and his staff retreated to Mission Bay, California, in mid-August to make their plans for the fall campaign, he led Humphrey by fifteen points and was pulling away. Nor was financing the presidential race a problem. Mitchell and his chief fund-raiser, Maurice Stans, confidently assured the candidate they would reach their goal of a $24 million war chest.

By the end of August, George Wallace held a commanding lead in the Deep South and trailed Nixon narrowly in much of the remainder of the region. In the long run, Nixon believed, Dixie's heartland—Mississippi, Alabama, Louisiana, and Georgia—would come home to the Republican Party because the national Democrats, sensitive to their black constituency, could not appeal to the region's racially conservative white voters. In the meantime, the GOP nominee abandoned his original goal of a southern sweep and adopted a modified Southern Strategy. Thurmond would give him South Carolina; he would work to carry the border South.[28] His main weapon would be Spiro Agnew, who soon began sounding like a rather dignified clone of George Wallace.[29]

The Nixon team decided to concentrate on what they called the Big Seven: New York, Pennsylvania, California, Texas, Illinois, Ohio, and Michigan. As the GOP candidate in 1960, Nixon had won only two of these states, but in mid-August of 1968 he held a substantial lead in all seven. Together, they provided 210 of the 270 electoral votes necessary for victory. With his revised Southern Strategy, the capture of all (or most) of these large states would assure him a clear-cut majority in the electoral college.

More than a year before, H. R. Haldeman had prepared a memorandum detailing television's critical role in the Nixon comeback. Political rallies and repeated exposure to opponents' supporters ("and paid troublemakers") were counterproductive. Political campaigning must "move out of the dark ages and into the brave new world of the omnipresent eye," explained Haldeman.[30] Television, according to the conventional wisdom of the new political handlers, allowed the maximum manipulation of the electorate. For most voters, agreed Nixon speechwriter Raymond Price, the decision to support a candidate represented a "gut reaction, unarticulated, nonanalytical, a product of the particular chemistry between the voter and the *image* of the candidate." It's "not what's *there* that counts, it's what's projected," and that projection "depends more on the medium and its use than it does on the candidate himself."[31]

There was little that could be described as revolutionary in either the tactics or the techniques used by Nixon's media advisers. What they brought to their undertaking was a new level of professional sophistication and vast resources. John Mitchell took charge of the campaign, with advertising director Harry Treleaven as field commander. They deployed a team of ninety advance men and public relations specialists with one goal: to project a hazy "aura" of warmth, competence, and invincibility in an issueless campaign, the political equivalent (in Joe McGinniss's memorable metaphor) of an indoor stadium "where the wind would never blow, the temperature never rise or fall, and the ball never bounce erratically on the artificial grass."[32]

As early as 1938, Joseph Kennedy had told an assistant that "the only thing that counts is the image you create for the public."[33] But his son John's skills as a natural television performer made it possible to conceal his self-conscious manipulation of the media. Each time Nixon appeared behind a podium or before a television camera, anxious to appear natural, likable, and in command, voters—and viewers—had an uneasy sense that stagehands and makeup artists were scurrying around just off camera. Too often Haldeman's "omnipresent eye" simply confirmed adman Roger Ailes's devastating description of Richard Nixon as the boy who got a briefcase for Christmas when other kids got footballs—and loved it.[34]

If he never became an all-out convert to television—"I'm not going to have any damn image experts coming telling me how to part my hair," he once told his staff—the candidate's own thinking soon mirrored the assumptions of his Madison Avenue handlers.[35] Nixon soon complained to Haldeman that the White House staff was spending far too much time worrying about his position on issues rather than shaping his "public appearance— presence." He could accomplish far more if aides restricted his contact with the press and made sure he was presented in a statesmanlike setting to a "naive type audience" ("no Jewish groups," he admonished). The important thing to remember, he would tell Haldeman, was that "speech is obsolete as a means of communication."[36]

He did his best to prove his point in a series of addresses and stump speeches which, even by the standards of modern campaign rhetoric, were stultifyingly vacuous. Nixon's chartered jet, *Tricia*, moved serenely from city to city, followed at a distance by two equally smoothly operating press planes on which aides distributed the candidate's speeches, handouts, and position papers with terrifying efficiency. Communication facilities were state-of-the-art; the canapés on the plane and at hotel hospitality suites inevitably fresh and appetizing; the bar always open on the ground or in the air. The enormous Republican war chest allowed John Mitchell to purchase the best campaign that money could buy.

"Reporters and columnists who had covered Presidential campaigns for many years began to be assaulted by a sense of unreality," wrote Godfrey Hodgson, chief American correspondent of the *Observer* of London; the press corps "fell into a state of what one can only call astounded torpor."[37] The attempt by Nixon (and Kennedy before him) to shape a campaign— indeed, to govern—on the basis of controlled photo ops reinforced the skepticism of reporters, who responded by becoming increasingly adversarial, even cynical, in their accounts and analyses of politicians and their messages. In such a context, Wallace's blunt, often crude language had even greater potential appeal. Repeatedly, voters told journalists that they might not always agree with George Wallace, but that, as one Youngstown steelworker said, "You don't have to worry about figuring out where he stands. He tells it like it really is."[38]

ON June 12, five weeks after his wife's death and less than a week after Sirhan Sirhan assassinated Robert Kennedy in Los Angeles, George Wallace had returned to the hustings for fund-raising tours through Tennessee, Virginia, the Carolinas, Florida, Georgia, Louisiana, Mississippi, and Texas. He squirmed a bit when reporters asked him about his abbreviated period of mourning and acknowledged that he wished he "could have waited a little longer" before returning to the race, but there was work to be done. The liberal "sob sisters" and "bleeding-heart sociologists" were still on the loose and there was nothing to indicate that the Democrats or Republicans ("there isn't ten cents' worth of difference [between them]") had heard the call of the hardworking people of America.[39]

A Chattanooga Baptist preacher heralded Wallace's reemergence on the campaign trail with an apocalyptic invocation: "Outside the visible return of Jesus Christ," shouted the Reverend John S. Lanham, "the only salvation of the country is the election of George Wallace." In the city's ramshackle municipal auditorium six thousand Tennessee farmers, factory employees and white-collar workers, small businessmen and retirees gave the Alabamian eleven standing ovations as he laid out his lambasted back-alley muggers, urban rioters, HEW bureaucrats, federal judges, and—most of all—the "out-of-touch politicians" who led the Democratic and Republican parties. "You could put them all in an Alabama cotton picker's sack, shake them up and dump them out; take the first one to slide out and put him right back into power and there would be no change." Although Wallace scorned Republicans and Democrats alike, he seemed to save his choicest barbs for Nixon. The former vice president and members of his party had been fighting to capture the "colored vote" since 1953, when Eisenhower had appointed Earl Warren to write the *Brown v. Board of Education* school decision. "Nixon is just like the national Democrats. He's for all this Federal invasion of the state's right to run their [*sic*] own affairs."[40]

Alabama reporters covering the former governor saw an immediate trans-formation in his personality. Gone was the Wallace who had moped around Montgomery after the death of his wife. "Once he got a dose of the crowds, he was the same old George," said one of his followers, "full of vinegar and ready to take on those brief-case totin' bureaucrats in Washington."[41] His handlers had only to point Wallace in the direction of a set of microphones or a speaker's platform and stand out of the way.

It was clear that his brief absence from national politics had not weakened his appeal to voters. In that first June speaking tour, five months before the general election, Wallace drew large and enthusiastic crowds throughout the South. Ten thousand stood two hours in the blistering Memphis sun to hear him promise to return control of the nation's schools to local government instead of "some bearded Washington bureaucrat who can't even park a bicycle straight." Four thousand gathered in Columbia, six thousand in Pensacola, eight thousand in Jacksonville, ten thousand in Baton Rouge, and twelve thousand in Jackson. Outside Dallas, fifteen thousand Wallace sup-porters jammed a small high school stadium and waited through a Texas-sized downpour to cheer the man the warm-up speaker called "America's divinely appointed savior."

Even more heartening was the financial response to his appeal for funds. During one three-day swing concluding with a June 21 rally in Jackson, Mississippi, Wallace volunteers collected $450,000 in cash and checks. Cam-paign finance director Dick Smith commandeered an ex–Mississippi State football player to "stomp down" on the checks and cash so that they could squeeze the booty into twelve oversized mail bags.[42] By the end of June, Wallace had erased a campaign debt of half a million dollars, raised an additional million, and was well on his way toward his goal of ten million dollars, a figure that fell far short of Nixon's high-rolling effort, but came close to that of Hubert Humphrey's.[43]

The Citizens' Council raised a quarter-million dollars and managed to conceal the source of the money by having more than three hundred indi-viduals write checks for contributions of a thousand dollars or less. Several wealthy right-wingers made contributions ranging from five thousand dollars to as much as thirty thousand dollars; an administrative aide told one news-man that John Wayne had sent them three checks for ten thousand dollars each, the last inscribed "Sock it to 'em, George."[44]

Enterprising reporters repeatedly printed rumors that H. L. Hunt had se-cretly bankrolled the Wallace campaign. Hunt, an eccentric Texas oilman widely described as the richest man in the world (and a bigamist, as well, managing to juggle three wives and families and a bevy of young mistresses), had avoided the spotlight until the 1950s. As the decade wore on, however, he seemed to relish his notoriety and made no secret of his support for ultra-conservative causes. He put up nearly $150,000 in 1952 in an unsuccessful attempt to promote a Republican draft of General Douglas MacArthur and spent as much as $1 million a year to fund the two virulently anticommunist radio series, *Facts Forum* in the early 1950s and *Life Line* in the late 1950s and early 1960s.[45]

George Wallace had captured Hunt's attention early in the 1960s, and he began writing the Alabama governor to offer advice on a variety of issues. Wallace answered the old man's letters graciously, and the two men met informally (and openly) a half-dozen times in Dallas and in Montgomery during the Texan's business trips to Alabama.

But reporters were looking in the wrong direction. As Bill Jones sardonically (and truthfully) said, the "only thing we ever got from H. L. Hunt was $500, two cases of liquor and a whole stack of pamphlets"—not even anticommunist pamphlets, at that. By 1968, Hunt, slipping into his dotage, was passing around health-food leaflets extolling the brain-building virtues of peanut butter and apricots.[46]

The real source of support was his son, Bunker.

While Bunker Hunt maintained a much lower profile, he was, if possible, even more politically reactionary. Though he shunned publicity, he was well on his way to becoming enormously wealthy from his own oil ventures by the mid-1960s. Friends described the rotund oilman (five feet eleven inches, three hundred pounds) as an appealing teddy bear of a man who just happened to be hopelessly paranoid. In addition to various religious enthusiasms—he funded an unsuccessful search for Noah's ark and gave millions to support the conservative evangelical Campus Crusade for Christ—he became one of the largest contributors to the John Birch Society and followed in his father's footsteps by bankrolling the ultra-right-wing radio series, *Manion Forum*. A casual anti-Semite ("Never look a Gift-Jew in the mouth," he cryptically warned his associates), he openly financed right-wing political campaigns and distributed funds to various ultra-conservative candidates like Strom Thurmond.[47]

Wallace, sensing that Bunker might be ready to give more substantive support to the campaign, dispatched Seymore Trammell to Texas with instructions to ask for three million dollars. This was a little too much even for Hunt, but in early summer he sent his lawyer to Montgomery to meet with Trammell and Cecil Jackson at the Jefferson Davis Hotel. Hunt's representative brought with him a large briefcase filled with hundred-dollar bills; in later years, the total was put at $250,000 to $300,000. Wallace told his top advisers that this was their "rainy day" fund to be used in an emergency.[48]

More than eighty percent of the nine million dollars raised by the campaign came from small contributions of less than fifty dollars, solicited by the increasingly slick direct-mail fund-raising techniques of televangelists and, more important, by fund-raisers where Wallace was present to press the flesh. Instead of the discreet private "occasions" favored by leading Democratic and Republican candidates, at which donors were asked to contribute from five thousand dollars on up, the Wallace staff emphasized smaller contributions. A typical campaign day began with a civic club breakfast, followed by a morning press conference. In cities with substantial donors (primarily in the oil and natural-gas states of Louisiana and Texas), some twelve to fifteen "guests" sat around and chatted with the former governor over lunch for a thousand dollars a plate. After a quick flight to the next city, Wallace squeezed in an afternoon press conference or small rally, followed by a large-scale fund-raising dinner from six to seven-thirty P.M. at which the faithful—for only twenty-five dollars a ticket—gathered in church halls, motel meeting rooms, and Elks Lodges to hear his message. (Even at twenty-five dollars, the dinner was hardly a bargain, complained one Wallace loyalist when he saw the paper plate of cold, overcooked chicken, mushy lima beans, day-old white bread, and iceberg lettuce drowned in French dressing.)

The governor then hurried to the final rally of the evening where campaign hawkers sold bumper stickers, buttons, and campaign souvenirs, and volunteers manned rickety card tables and appealed to Wallace partisans to give five, ten, or twenty-five dollars and perhaps to become "petition workers" for the candidate. (Supporters who accepted money-raising petition forms were told to solicit friends and workers who would give small amounts—$5 and $10—for the Alabama candidate. More than half of the six thousand petitions were returned, with an average enclosure of $257 each.) If the crowd bypassed the phalanx of fund-raisers outside, pretty young "Wallace girls" inside passed buckets up and down the aisles for petty cash contributions.[49]

Reporters dismissed the passing of the campaign bucket as a down-home public relations ploy to make poor voters believe they were seriously contributing and therefore had a stake in Wallace's election drive. But Alabama's ex-governor John Patterson joined his former opponent at a June rally in central Texas—it was one of more than twenty held through the South that month—and was astounded at the willingness of poor working-class people to open up their wallets. He watched aides tally $35,000 in change and small bills on the three-hour flight back to Montgomery.[50]

Wallace was not the first American political candidate to attract small donors through direct mailings and television appeals, but he broke new ground in the effectiveness of his campaign. In the early spring of 1968, an Alabama-based advertising agency, Luckey and Forney, threw together a half-hour television film, *The Wallace Story*. Little more than a crudely edited summary of the candidate's best applause lines delivered at rallies across America, the narrative was interrupted repeatedly with pleas for viewers to send in their dollars so that George Wallace could "stand up for America." When the agency marketed the film on small television stations in the South and in relatively inexpensive media markets in the Midwest and the Rocky Mountain states, even the Wallace people were stunned at the response. "The money is just coming in by the sackfuls," said an awed Jack House in April 1968. Most of it, he confided, was in small contributions from a dollar to a hundred dollars. "It's a gold mine."[51]

In August Trammell authorized the prime-time broadcast of *The Wallace Story* on NBC and CBS at a cost of nearly half a million dollars. When the program aired in mid-September with a request for contributions, viewers mailed nearly $600,000 to the Montgomery campaign offices. The return names and addresses, added to those on the hundreds of thousands of letters that had come into the governor's office during the 1960s, created a potentially lucrative list for direct-mail solicitations. More than two hundred automatic typewriters churned out thousands of "personalized" letters to Wallace supporters across the nation.[52] By November, the country boys from Alabama had raised more than nine million dollars in an authentic grassroots campaign.

To leave the impression that George Wallace had set off on his quest for the presidency without any preparation or strategic planning would be unfair. The foundation of his campaign was inevitably a version of *his* Southern Strategy. Wallace felt comfortably sure that he could top Nixon and Humphrey in the states Goldwater had carried in 1964, as well as Arkansas, and his own instincts coupled with nationally published polls showed him within striking distance of a plurality in the very border states that Nixon hoped to take. In a very close three-way campaign, a candidate could throw the election into the House of Representatives with as few as 180 electoral votes. *If* Wallace carried the entire old South (128 electoral votes) and *if* he carried the entire border South (49 electoral votes) it would take only one or two narrow wins in a few midwestern states like Ohio and Indiana to put him over the top. And the Congress, he insisted, would not have the temerity to award the presidency to a second-place finisher.[53]

The Alabama governor sought to maintain the illusion that he was a serious threat, and his campaign headquarters released varying scenarios of just how he could be elected President of the United States. All were fantasies, and in his unguarded moments Wallace was considerably more candid.

Whether he won or lost, he said, the third-party campaign could "influence the outcome of the presidential race and win concessions for the South."[54]

On June 30, 1968, Wallace again appeared on *Meet the Press*. He spelled out to host Lawrence E. Spivak just what concessions would be necessary in order for him to abandon the race. First, he told the national television audience, any candidates who sought his support would "have to turn back local institutions to the state." Second, they must "cut out foreign aid to the enemies of our country." Third, they would have to promise to "stop this academic freedom talk that allows people to call for Communist victory in this nation, because I am sick and tired of American servicemen being killed by the Communists on the one hand" while pro-Communist college professors were allowed to "raise money, blood and clothes in this country and call for their victory . . . which boosts the morale of the Communists." Finally, he told the panel, any candidate he supported would have to agree to name conservative judges to the Supreme Court, judges who would respect the rights of the states in contrast to the sitting members of the court who had done so much to "destroy constitutional government in the country."[55]

The national news media groped with the problem of just what to make of Wallace as a presidential candidate. Was he an entertaining con man? A political spoiler? America's own would-be Mussolini? A serious contender for the White House? A reporter for London's *Observer* concluded that many large American newspapers had initially played down their coverage of Wallace, "like parents who refuse to look when their child is doing something naughty for fear it might encourage him to show off."[56] But, as the crowds grew in intensity and number and the polls showed a steady rise in his support, an ever-increasing entourage of network correspondents and journalists joined the American Independent Party candidate as he hop-scotched across America in an obsolete, prop-driven DC-6 whose Number 3 engine was alarmingly inclined to stall on landings and takeoffs. One reporter was seen to kneel and kiss the tarmac after the pilot had feathered an engine and made a particularly terrifying three-bounce landing. The charter company "ought to give it to him [Wallace] rather than charge him for it," said Jack House, who refused to risk his life by flying with the candidate.[57] Even when finances improved, the most the campaign could afford was a refurbished Electra turbo-prop.

The logistics of a presidential campaign simply overwhelmed the advance teams hastily recruited from across Alabama. In comparison with the Wallace operation, Hubert Humphrey's chaotic road show was a model of organization, said one weary newsman who took to carrying a change of underwear in his typewriter case after the Wallace staff mislaid his luggage two nights running. Richard Cohen, a Brown University student writing an independent-study project, traveled with the governor on a week-long midwestern swing. Within twenty-four hours he was giving orders and making suggestions. "I firmly believe that if I had been with the campaign another week or two," recalled the twenty-year-old Cohen, "I could have been appointed as press secretary."[58]

Correspondents could endure the abysmal communications system, the lack of an advance text for Wallace's speeches (not really a problem since he usually gave the same one), the constantly revised scheduling, the third-rate hotels and motels along the way, even the dried-out cheese or peanut butter sandwiches handed out by smiling Wallace volunteers. What they found impossible to believe was that, once they had settled into the worn seats of the prop jet, the only drinkable liquids on board were paper cartons of orange juice or chilled bottles of Dr. Pepper and Coca-Cola.

Some of the press had covered him for years. They may have despised his demagoguery, but it was hard for many of them to dislike a politician who once opened a telephone conversation with a newspaper editor by merrily explaining, "I just called up to kiss your ass some more."[59] Southern-born reporters like Jack Nelson and Tom Wicker enjoyed jousting with Wallace, and David Braaten of the *Washington Star* called him "my favorite bigot." Halfway back to Montgomery from one hurried raid into enemy territory, newsmen who had managed to sneak several bottles of whiskey aboard began reprising the spirited version of "We Shall Overcome" that had greeted Wallace at his last rally. After dispatching state police bodyguard E. C. Dothard with a flyswatter to silence the heretics, the candidate ambled back to the rear of the plane. "Good Lord, here I am trying to save the world and everybody's drunk," he mockingly reprimanded them. And it is hard to imagine Richard Nixon (or even Hubert Humphrey) instructing photographers (as Wallace did in St. Louis), "Y'all be sure to get a shot of me shakin' my fist. Or picking my nose." Laughing with little-boy glee, he had struck a pose: one fist in the air, the other delicately picking his nose.[60]

Walter Pincus of the *Washington Post* found a certain charm in the "All-American, innocent—almost totally non-political—atmosphere" of the third-party entourage. The well-groomed young men and women from the University of Alabama who passed out Tom's Toasted Peanuts and Dr. Peppers on the plane, even the state policemen and Secret Service agents who guarded the candidate, seemed relaxed and more at ease than the tight-lipped men guarding Nixon and Humphrey.[61]

Other reporters were less generous. Their coverage constantly included references to Wallace's crudeness: his tendency to spit in a handkerchief when distracted, his less-than-refined table manners, his outdated "greasy hair." Theodore H. White—alumnus of Boston Latin School, summa cum laude graduate of Harvard—described the Alabamian with the thinly veiled disgust of the well-bred when forced into contact with the lower orders. "A big gold ring glistened on his finger, and in repose his somber face glowered. Occasionally he would run a comb through his sleek, glossy hair . . . and his close-set eyes were shrunken into deep, dark hollows under the great eyebrows. He was a very little man . . . his hands twitch[ed] when he spoke."[62] Repelled by the general tawdriness of the candidate, White told his friend Joseph Alsop, "I've had enough of this" and abandoned the campaign halfway through his scheduled tour.[63]

Even Garry Wills, who understood the Wallace phenomenon far better than most observers, relished describing the sour working-class, struggling middle-class aura of the Alabama governor and his followers: "They vomit laughter. Trying to eject the vacuum inside them." The columnist's description of Wallace—"the old crotch-scratcher"—at a Chicago Civic Center rally in the early stages of the campaign was an evocative piece of writing, but it told almost as much about Wills as it did the victim. The governor of Alabama, he wrote, had the

> *dingy attractive air of a B-movie idol, the kind who plays a handsome garage attendant. . . . He comes out rubbing his hands on an invisible garage rag (most of the pit grease out of his nails), smiling and winking, Anything-I-can-do-for-you-pretty-girl? His hair is still wet from careful work with comb and water in the gas station's cracked mirror (main panel in the men's room tryptych, rubber machine on one side, comb-and-Kleenex dispenser on the other).*[64]

Sometimes there was something more: pure contempt for the good ol' boys who were trying to crash a party reserved for establishment candidates. Richard Cohen, the twenty-year-old student, disdainfully assessed the Wallace caravan: the candidate himself, with his "slicked-back hair" and "unctuous smile," looked like a small-town policeman who had never been able to rise above the "lower-middle class background in which he was raised"; Wallace's genial advance man, George Mangum, had an "illiterate face" and should return to his old trade of "spinning hillbilly music" rather than trying to play a role in national politics. Cohen simply dismissed the "honey-faced, somewhat stupid 'Wallace Girls'" with their teased and carefully sprayed bouffant hairstyles. After a local advance man failed to reserve enough rooms for newsmen, a young woman in the Wallace entourage gamely, but ineffectually, struggled to complete the task of booking accommodations. "Undoubtedly," the Ivy Leaguer smirked, "she was a student at the University of Alabama."[65]

As the funds poured in, Wallace's national campaign headquarters in Montgomery exploded from a small downtown suite to a thirty-thousand-square-foot building on the outskirts of the city. As late as May 1967, the campaign had been staffed by a handful of paid employees and a dozen high-ranking state officials who doggedly maintained the fiction that they were working on their vacation time. By mid-summer of 1968, as Trammell and Jackson struggled to coordinate an unwieldy organization of hundreds of paid staff and thousands of Alabama volunteers and nationwide Wallace supporters, they often found themselves overwhelmed by factional infighting among local ultra-conservatives and exploited by sharp-eyed opportunists drawn to the Wallace show as an ideal setting for a quick con. California, where they had begun so promisingly, was a snake pit by mid-summer. Trammell and Jackson soon suspected that the head of the original Wallace-for-President organization was raking off funds for his own local right-wing movement. They replaced him with the Reverend Alvin Mayall, a Bakersfield John Bircher, only to discover that Mayall, head of California's notoriously anti-Semitic "Christian Nationalist Crusade," had far more interest in Jew-baiting than in electing George Wallace.[66]

Mayall, or "Benedict Arnold" as Montgomery staffers began referring to him, proved to be one of dozens of what the Wallace people privately called the "nut cases." Jesse Todd, president of Alabama's Mammy's Pancake Houses and Mrs. Todd's Cafeterias and a dedicated Wallace volunteer, struggled to recruit "high type" folks into the campaign, but he proudly reported that he also made use of the hard-edged men who offered their services. He had been able to "work with them at night," so they "wouldn't be seen during the day by the folks that we were proud of."[67]

Staffer Tom Turnipseed dealt with many of these loose cannons. Robert Shelton caused a flap early in the campaign when an ABC television camera crew recorded him warmly shaking hands with his old friend George Wallace. Newsmen had repeatedly described the close connection between the Alabama governor and the Klan leader, but George Wallace knew that this film was worth more than a thousand words. One of his Alabama troopers wrested the camera away from the newsman, opened the film spool, and exposed it to the light.[68] Shelton, seeming oblivious to the problems his presence created for a campaign staff anxious to distance their candidate from his gamier associates, continued to call almost weekly to offer his political advice. Finally Turnipseed hit upon a tactful way to handle the problem: "I said, 'Well, you know, Robert, you probably shouldn't be calling in here, 'cause they [the FBI] tap your phone, don't you reckon?' " The Klansman simply snorted and ignored the hint.[69]

Turnipseed also found himself at cross-purposes with the head of Montana's Wallace campaign. "I hadn't been in town two days," he recalled, "before he was telling people that I was a Moscow-trained agent." Too late, Turnipseed learned that their man in Montana was a mental case who had been expelled from the local John Birch Society for "extremism."[70] C. L. (Bill) West of Catoosa, Oklahoma, confided to staffers in Montgomery that he had no idea how many "paranoiac-schizophrenics" were running around loose in the country until he published an advertisement inviting volunteers to work in the Wallace campaign.[71]

Beginning in 1965, Robert Welch had used Selma's sheriff, Jim Clark, as a go-between to pass along the names of key Birchers across the nation anxious to help George Wallace "save our country from being taken over by the Communists."[72] White Citizens' Council members had been critical to the Wallace effort in the early stages of the 1964 California ballot drive; the Bakersfield Birchers, as well, superbly trained at organization and propaganda, had put together one of the most efficient local operations and had signed up 3,900 new party members in a matter of days.[73] In state after state outside the South, dedicated Birchers stepped into the organizational void in the 1968 campaign; they dominated the Wallace movement in nearly a dozen states from Maine to California.

Wallace recognized the delicate balance between the critical role right-wingers played in running the local drives and the damage they could do if he were seen as the creature of these extremists. The strategy was always to accept the support of such groups, but to insist—as he did to one of his more fastidious supporters—that it was "hard to control who supports you in this country" and to promise "I will determine the policies and not some [of my followers] who sound . . . like half-wits."[74]

The amateurism, the divisions, the chaos would have swamped a lesser candidate, yet there Wallace was, drawing crowds at least as big as Nixon's and Humphrey's and "twice as enthusiastic." The media suddenly woke up to the fact that his third-party effort was not collapsing in the stretch, and the Alabamian pulled a politician's hat trick in late September when *Life* magazine joined the nation's two largest newsweeklies, *Time* and *Newsweek,* to feature him in cover stories. The publicity was hardly positive. George Wallace had not "one constructive proposal to offer a troubled nation," lectured *Time* editors, who struggled to come up with new words and phrases to condemn the candidate ("simplistic," "atavistic," "bantam-cock posture," "billingsgate," "portentous appeals to patriotism," "pugnacious," "political profit in fear and hate. . .").[75]

"Not since Theodore Roosevelt's Bull Moose Party emerged in 1912 has a third party so seriously challenged the two party system," *Newsweek* editors proclaimed. Polls consistently showed the support of more than a fifth of the electorate. If they were understating the southerner's appeal, as one North Carolina analyst cautioned, the Wallace campaign might be like a "floating iceberg—there's a lot more to it than shows on the surface and what's beneath is the dangerous part." And if Humphrey should bounce back in the polls, warned *Time*'s editors, there was a very real possibility that the election would be decided by the House of Representatives for the first time since 1825.[76]

*   *   *

AT historical moments of social and economic crisis, a minority of Americans had always been willing to embrace demagogues like Huey Long or Joseph McCarthy. With Wallace's increasing popularity, the question observers had to ask was a troubling one: Just how large was this minority?

The candidate's appeal, said NBC's Douglas Kiker, a native southerner, was transparently simple. George Wallace had seemingly looked out upon those white Americans north of Alabama and suddenly been awakened by a blinding vision: "They all hate black people, all of them. They're all afraid, all of them. Great God! That's it! They're all Southern! The whole United States is Southern!"[77]

Of course George Wallace repeatedly insisted, with great indignation, that he was no racist. After a week on the campaign trail, cynical reporters accompanying him took to soundlessly mouthing the phrase he undoubtedly recited in his sleep, since he parroted it in almost every speech he ever delivered: "I have never in my public life in Alabama made a speech that would reflect upon anybody because of race, color, creed, religion, or national origin."

Wallace, like most politicians, had a remarkable capacity for self-deception, but it is difficult to imagine how even he was able to repeat this statement daily, each time with his voice quivering in outrage. He had built his career in Alabama on the bedrock of white supremacy, and every survey of his followers showed that one of the major sources of his national appeal lay in the perception that he was antiblack. And yet, more than simply a spokesman for the white backlash, Wallace transcended the usual categories of "liberal" or "conservative."

He was often described as a "populist," though by the mid-1960s the term had become so elastic it had little meaning. Most mainline reporters and liberal academics shared a romantic notion of a tradition reaching back to the late nineteenth century in which virtuous but impoverished farmers rejected the false issues of racism and struggled against the economic oppression of corporations and malefactors of great wealth.[78] By such reckonings, the early Tom Watson of Georgia was an archetypical southern populist: an authentic reformer derailed by the powerful forces of racism and reaction.

But in 1957 Columbia University historian Richard Hofstadter saw populism through a darker lens. His influential essay "The Paranoid Style in American Politics" identified a dangerous tendency toward extremism which had its origins in the nativist and anti-Catholic Know-Nothing movement of the 1840s, then stretched forward to the Ku Klux Klan of the 1920s and the McCarthy Red-baiters of the 1950s. A significant minority (frequently Anglo-Saxon Protestants) had responded to social upheaval by embracing fantastical notions of shadowy conspirators—Wall Street bankers, Catholics, Jews, Communists—bent on corrupting the values of Christian Americans. In more recent years, this minority had ominously turned to charismatic but author-itarian leaders: Huey Long and Father Charles Coughlin in the 1930s, Joe McCarthy and General Douglas MacArthur in the 1950s.[79]

At least a dozen articles that appeared during the 1968 campaign com-pared Wallace to Louisiana's "Kingfish," Huey Long. Both were authoritar-ian, but the Kingfish rejected the politics of race. In speech after speech Wallace knit together the strands of racism with those of a deeply rooted xenophobic "plain folk" cultural outlook which equated social change with moral corruption. The creators of public policy—the elite—were out of touch with hardworking taxpayers who footed the bill for their visionary social engineering at home and weak-minded defense of American interests abroad. The apocalyptic rhetoric of anticommunism allowed Wallace to bridge the gap between theocratic and "moral" concerns and the secular issues of government economic policy, civil rights, and foreign policy.

Despite the opportunity it offered for a crusade against godless, atheistic Communism, the Vietnam War was never very popular with Wallace sup-porters. Their quarrel was with the antiwar protest movement, led by "silver-spooned brats" who rejected a whole constellation of American cultural and religious values, of which "patriotism" was the core. Wallace offered a sim-ple solution: he would turn the problem over to the Joint Chiefs of Staff, ask them what needed to be done, and then "get on with doing it." Humphrey couldn't criticize his boss, the President; Nixon had to be reasonably respon-sible in order to appeal to a broad range of American voters. Wallace had no such inhibitions.[80]

And on the flickering television screen and in dozens of personal appear-ances he offered to those frightened and insecure millions a chance to strike back—if only rhetorically—at the enemy. As almost every observer sensed, a Wallace rally was an act of communion between the speaker and his audience, for he was one of the last grandmasters of the kind of foot-stomping public speaking that characterized American politics, particularly southern politics, in the age before television. A Wallace speech excited the kind of nonanalytical emotional response that media advisers had always sought to evoke. But in his influential 1964 book, *Understanding Media,* social critic Marshall McLuhan had laid down what quickly became the gospel for all political consultants: television performers—and politicians were simply television performers, hawking themselves rather than laundry detergent—were only effective if they understood the intimate nature of the new technology. Television was a "cool" medium, which required under-statement and self-control. Any appeal that was grossly exaggerated, caustic, "hot," was likely to turn off most voters, who were drawn to the cooler and controlled images of the new television age.

If George Wallace was limited by his raw, angry edge, thousands of stump speeches from county fairs to Kiwanis Clubs had given him an unerring sense of what would play. He was, in the vocabulary of students of rhetoric, the perfect mimetic orator, probing his audiences' deepest fears and passions and articulating those emotions in a language and style they could understand. On paper his speeches were stunningly disconnected, at times incoherent, and always repetitious. But Wallace's followers reveled in the *performance;* they never tired of hearing the same lines again and again.

With faintly concealed disdain, the Miami *Herald*'s John McDermott compared Wallace's public appearances with an old-time southern camp meeting: the opening hymns, the fervent prayers ("We come to Thee tonight, our Lord and Savior Jesus Christ, thanking Thee and praising Thee for this great turnout"), the summons to a struggle between the people of the Word and the godless atheistic enemies who had breached the gates of Christian America ("Get on your sword of righteousness and like Gideon, lead us against the enemy. The battle of Armageddon is approaching and we are ready to stand by your side against the hosts of Satan").[81]

If a Wallace rally featured the sacred—God, Mother, and Country—it also included the profane: the speech itself, in which the energy flowed back and forth between Wallace and his audience in a performance molding rage, laughter, and sheer sexual energy into an emotional catharsis. His appeal was closer to that of the outlaw country singer Waylon Jennings than to that of the suave John Kennedy, whom Wallace had envied for his effortless grace. Many of his listeners—whether men or women, northern or southern—responded with the wary thrill of middle-class southern girls drawn to, and yet terrified by, the ducktailed, T-shirt-wearing macho rednecks who ambled down the hallways of their high school.

Gonzo journalist Hunter Thompson saw Wallace's power for the first time when he covered a rally at Milwaukee's Serb Hall, the venue of the Alabamian's initial successful foray into "ethnic" America during his 1964 presidential campaign. Thompson arrived a half hour before the scheduled five P.M. start; nearly a thousand locals had already squeezed into a room that could comfortably seat less than half that number. Several hundred more milled around outside.

The air was electric. By the time Wallace was halfway through his speech the audience of Polish and Serbian Americans was stepping on his best lines, laughing, shouting, exhilarated by the furious energy of his snarling attacks against hippies, civil rights "agitators," welfare recipients, atheists, beatniks, antiwar protesters, Communists, street toughs who had "turned to rape and murder 'cause they didn't get enough broccoli when they were little boys." To a jaded Thompson, it was awe-inspiring, a political "Janis Joplin concert" in which "the bastard had somehow levitated himself and was hovering over us."[82] The nakedly primitive power of those rallies unnerved the reporters who covered Wallace. As long as he remained safely contained in the back-waters of southern politics, there was little reason to be concerned. But as his support grew from ten percent to fifteen percent to twenty percent of the population, it became impossible to dismiss him simply as a fringe figure, regional or otherwise.

THE trick, for candidates who hoped to benefit from the "Wallace factor," was to exploit the grievances he had unleashed while disentangling themselves from the more tawdry trappings of his message. The Republican number-crunchers knew the figures by heart: eighty percent of southern Wallace voters preferred Nixon to Humphrey; by a much narrower margin, northern Wallace voters preferred Humphrey to Nixon. How could they drive the southern Wallace voters into the GOP without disturbing those in the North? That balancing act was proving more difficult than Nixon had imagined, particularly since he wanted to run a nondivisive campaign.[83]

The counterattack against the Wallace threat to the Southern Strategy was executed by Strom Thurmond's assistant Harry Dent. In an indication of Nixon's continued caution, Dent was never officially brought on board the Nixon team. He was placed in charge of an ostensibly southern operation for the general election with the unlikely title "Thurmond Speaks for Nixon-Agnew," though he coordinated strategy with the Nixon campaign and cleared every major decision through John Mitchell.

Dent repeatedly insisted that neither the Southern Strategy nor Nixon's generally conservative emphasis in 1968 was racist. And, in fact, he (like other members of the Nixon team) scrupulously avoided explicit references to race. The problem with the liberalism of the Democrats, Dent charged, was not that it was too problack, but that it had created an America in which the streets were "filled with radical dissenters, cities were literally burning down, crime seemed uncontrollable," and the vast social programs of the Democrats were creating an army of the permanently dependent even as they bankrupted the middle class. The rising tide of economic and social conservatism clearly complemented opposition to federal activism, north and south.

But the political driving force of Nixon's policies toward the South was *not* an abstract notion about the "preservation of individual freedom"; almost every aspect of the 1968 campaign was tightly interwoven with issues of race.[84] The economy seemed to favor Humphrey. The inevitable conse-quences of Johnson's refusal to choose between guns and butter were still on the horizon. Fueled by the military buildup in Vietnam, industrial pro-duction was at an all-time high; unemployment was less than three percent and income was up. But voters remained uneasy over the long-term direc-tion of the American economy. Between 1947 and 1965 the purchasing power of middle- and lower-middle-income voters rose forty percent, at an average of more than two percent per year. That steady progression faltered in the mid-1960s. Between 1965 and 1968, a combination of accelerating price increases and sharp hikes in the payroll and income taxes led to stagnation (some economists said an actual decline) in real wages for the average worker. Family income rose, but primarily because of the increasing movement of women into the work force. Families were working harder in order to stay in place. American middle-class and working-class families had reached the crest of the boom years of the postwar era.

Higher taxes and inflation also hurt black and Hispanic Americans; nevertheless nonwhites made remarkable economic as well as political gains. It would become an accepted truism that the civil rights legislation of the 1960s primarily benefited upwardly mobile and middle-class blacks. In reality, there were significant increases for working-class blacks as well. For the years between 1961 and 1968, aggregate income for whites increased fifty-six percent, while the total for nonwhites went up 110 per cent. Most of that increase came as black Americans—particularly in the South—entered higher-wage occupations at a dramatic pace. During that same period, the federal government transferred approximately $121 billion to individuals living below the poverty line, with over thirty percent of those funds going to black Americans. Had poor and middle-income white Americans retained that amount, it would have added less than three-eighths of one percent to their disposable income; but that was not the public perception in the 1960s. The poor, particularly the black poor, became scapegoats.[85]

In much the same way, racial fears were linked to concerns over social disorder in American streets. The threat of crime was real; every index of criminality showed an increase in the number of crimes against property and in crimes of violence. Americans were still more likely to be maimed or killed by their friends and relatives than by strangers, but the growth of random, brutal urban violence—an escalation of black-on-white violence attracted the most attention—made law and order an inevitable issue in the 1960s.

And Wallace simply erased the line between antiwar and civil rights protests, between heckling protesters and street muggers. By the fall, Nixon and even Humphrey were attempting to play catch-up with the crime issue, although both went to great lengths to insist that the issue was nonracial. (As the former vice president pointed out on several occasions, blacks were far more likely to be the victims of crime than whites were.) Occasionally, the façade slipped. Early in the campaign Nixon had taped a television commercial attacking the decline of "law and order" in American cities. As he reviewed it with his staff, he became expansive. That "hits it right on the nose," he said enthusiastically. "It's all about law and order and the damn Negro–Puerto Rican groups out there." Nixon did not have to make the racial connection any more than would Ronald Reagan when he began one of his famous discourses on welfare queens using food stamps to buy porterhouse steaks. His audience was already primed to make that connection.[86]

For nearly a hundred years after the Civil War, politicians had manipulated the racial phobias of whites below the Mason-Dixon line to maintain a solidly Democratic South. To Nixon it seemed only poetic justice that the tables should be turned. The challenge lay in appealing to the fears of angry whites without appearing to become an extremist and driving away moderates.

Economist Eliot Janeway had applied the term "backlash" as early as the summer of 1963, when he warned of the potential for social conflict between black and white blue-collar workers. As automation reduced the number of entry-level positions in the workplace, Janeway predicted a scrambling for the kind of jobs that low-income blacks and whites traditionally had shared.[87] By the mid-1960s, everyone agreed that white backlash existed. The race riots and the increasing federal pressure to integrate northern schools and housing made it apparent that there was capital·to be made in the North as well as in the South among discontented white Democrats. But the question remained: How pervasive and deeply rooted was the reaction to black political and economic advancement?

National attitudes on race are notoriously difficult to measure; even the dramatic increase in polling in the 1950s and 1960s often failed to distinguish between momentary responses to headline-grabbing racial incidents and long-term attitudinal changes. The currents of racial tolerance and racial hatred seemed to ebb and flow. But as the decade progressed, Lou Harris, George Gallup, the Roper Research Associates, and the University of Michigan Survey Research Center documented what dozens of contemporary reporters and political leaders sensed: whites outside the South might support federal action to destroy legal segregation and guarantee the right to vote, but they resisted change in their own neighborhoods.[88]

Political observer Samuel Lubell was one of the first to point out that Wallace support among northern voters was strongest in white neighborhoods that abutted heavily black districts. Ironically, prosperity, not poverty, had intensified this racial polarization. As income for African Americans rose in the 1940s and 1950s, black families pressed outward from their circumscribed neighborhoods toward accessible and affordable housing, often in marginal white communities. Visiting these urban areas, said Lubell, was like "inspecting a stretched-out war front," with each Wallace precinct "another outpost marking the borders to which Negro residential movement had pushed."[89]

And as the federal courts began to shift their focus from striking down legal discrimination in the South to ending de facto segregation in the North, voters in the suburbs as well as in in-town white neighborhoods rebelled. Polling throughout the early 1960s showed that white northerners were more comfortable with limited desegregation than were southern whites, but once the figures approached a fifty percent black student population, the gap between the two regions disappeared. Always in the past, said Lubell, the assumption had been that the South would come to resemble the North. "Wallace raised the prospect that the North, as it changes, may become southernized."[90]

Nixon would need to move just to the right of a Democratic Party which had to be mindful of its black constituency. Nowhere was his caution more evident than in his handling of the critical question of school desegregation. Floating a trial balloon in mid-September, Nixon agreed to an interview with two Charlotte television newsmen. There were no members of the national media present. Although he reiterated his long-standing position that he "supported the Supreme Court decision outlawing segregation," Nixon bluntly attacked federally mandated school desegregation plans. It was counterproductive to bus "slum" (by which he meant black) children into schools in wealthier areas: "All you do is destroy their ability to compete." The best solution, he suggested, was to be found in "freedom of choice" plans such as those which southern communities had developed over the past two years.[91] (Under so-called freedom of choice, minority students had to take the initiative in desegregation by requesting transfers to predominantly white schools. Theoretically, such plans were color-blind, but everyone knew that whites would never ask to have their children transferred to all-black schools. The federal courts had repeatedly ruled that such schemes were subterfuges designed to maintain de facto segregation.)[92]

It was a nuanced but measurable shift in Richard Nixon's position. His support for the *Brown* decision outlawing school segregation had always been perfunctory and relatively unenthusiastic, but now, for the first time, he publicly gave voice to the argument raised by many whites that desegregation hurt blacks (because of their supposed deficiencies) as well as whites. Even more significantly, he openly embraced the "freedom of choice" plans.

But his shift was a little too subtle. Local television reporters did not seem to recognize that the Republican candidate's statements marked a departure in his public position on the issue, and the *Charlotte Observer* buried his explicit endorsement of "freedom of choice" plans in their coverage of the story.[93] Dent anxiously waited for a reaction which never came. Nixon denied his southern strategist permission to use excerpts from the Charlotte interview in regional television and radio advertisements and continued to hesitate over making school desegregation an issue.

As the campaign headed into the final stretch, Wallace remained a threat, but one easily contained so long as Humphrey's support barely topped thirty percent. Twice burned, Nixon kept warning his staff against overconfidence. There was always the danger of an October surprise: a breakthrough in the U.S.–North Vietnamese negotiations by Lyndon Johnson would convince the American people that peace was at hand. And old Democratic Party loyalties, he reminded Haldeman and Ehrlichman, ran deep. Still, even to a pessimist like Nixon, the possibility that Humphrey might resuscitate his campaign seemed a fantasy. On September 27, hundreds of antiwar protestors in Portland, Oregon, had drowned out the Democratic candidate's speech with shouts of "Murderer!" "Racist!" "Stop the war!" When Humphrey took refuge in his hotel, aides disclosed that only twenty-seven percent of the voters continued to back him; Nixon's lead in the polls had widened to fifteen points. Support for George Wallace had topped twenty percent. If the numbers continued to grow until the election, warned the editors of *Newsweek*, the former Alabama governor could well surpass Humphrey.

No one could ever pinpoint the precise moment when the campaign turned; Humphrey believed it was the last day of September. Party chairman Larry O'Brien had scraped together $100,000 for a half-hour of prime television time on NBC during which the Democratic candidate was to make a major policy statement on Vietnam and foreign relations. In some curious way, the complex issue of Humphrey's relationship to the albatross of Lyndon Johnson and the Vietnam War had come down to a simple question: Should the massive bombing of North Vietnam—which Johnson had resumed after an earlier pause —be stopped as a peace gesture? Or would a bombing halt be regarded as a sign of weakness and a failure of will, as Johnson and die-hard supporters of the conflict like Nixon argued?

Response to the final version of the speech hinged on one critical paragraph in which Humphrey told his television audience: "As President, I would be willing to stop the bombing of the North as an acceptable risk for peace." He left himself an out by insisting that he would expect, in return, some evidence of North Vietnam's willingness to respect the demilitarized zone between South and North Vietnam.[94] This flabby compromise satisfied few of his advisers, but in the context of Humphrey's slavish support for Johnson's hard-line policies it marked a new willingness on his part to become his own man. The speech infuriated Lyndon Johnson. "Nixon is following my policies more closely than Humphrey," he complained to one of his aides. But the vice president's timid assertion of independence offered an opening for the peace wing of the Democratic Party to come home. The heckling subsided, and almost overnight Humphrey seemed revitalized.

And the labor movement—traditional mainspring of the Democratic Party—came to life. The AFL-CIO leadership had received a jolt on September 10, when Flint, Michigan's Local 326 of the United Auto Workers—one of the union's largest—overwhelmingly endorsed the Wallace candidacy. A secret AFL-CIO survey in mid-September showed that one of every three union members supported the Alabama governor, and a *Chicago Sun-Times* poll taken the same week showed that forty-four percent of all white steelworkers in that city backed Wallace; Humphrey was a distant second, with less than thirty percent. Al Barkan, the director of labor's Committee for Political Action (COPE) called it the "Wallace Infection."[95]

Traditional appeals to economic self-interest had weakened in the heightened social tensions of the 1960s, but there was still a case to be made against the upstart Alabama governor. In his four years in office (six, counting Lurleen's half-term) Wallace had done for economic theory what the Pentecostals did to systematic theology. On the stump and in his American Independent Party platform he called for limited government and lower taxes—at least at the federal level. Back home he had funded dramatic increases in social spending for his middle-class and lower-middle-class supporters, but at the cost of borrowing hundreds of millions of dollars and acquiescing in dramatic increases in the state's regressive sales and gasoline taxes even as corporate and business interests escaped unscathed. By October, a steady stream of mailings from COPE headquarters warned thirteen million union members that Wallace was luring northern jobs to Alabama, a low-wage, right-to-work state, whose programs relied heavily on regressive taxes which would hit the workingman harder than the well-to-do. (Understandably, COPE did not emphasize that Wallace had publicly opposed anti-union "right-to-work" laws.)[96]

Northern blue-collar union members began to turn away from Wallace, and Humphrey's crowds grew visibly larger and more enthusiastic in those industrial states central to the GOP's electoral strategy.

Nixon's aides sensed danger. When the Republican most needed his border state reserves, Wallace—who had assembled an insurmountable lead in Alabama, Louisiana, and Mississippi—edged ahead in Arkansas, Georgia, and North Carolina, and threatened Nixon's lead in Florida, Tennessee, and South Carolina.

But at the critical moment when Wallace's chances for throwing the election into the House of Representatives seemed dramatically to improve, his campaign faltered.

When Bill Jones and Seymore Trammell dropped in on the Wallace campaign in mid-September for a conference with their boss, they immediately noticed a stunning blonde given to skintight silver and gold lamé cowboy outfits. Of "indeterminate age," but with a strikingly beautiful face "purchased in stores and a body saved from age by tender care" (she gave her age as "nearly forty" but was forty-eight), Ja-Neen Welch had worked in a Hammond, Indiana, advertising agency charged with arranging publicity for a Wallace campaign rally. When the entourage passed through Hammond in mid-August, Welch joined the campaign, traveling on the candidate's plane and appearing as a regular at all the rallies. When Wallace discovered she had missed the bus to the airport after a stop in New Orleans, he had personally ordered the pilot to return to the terminal and wait for her.[97]

She would kick off the bucket-fund-raising part of a rally by seductively stroking the microphone and shouting to the audience: "I want *you* for the Wallace rebellion!" (Her routine was a rather heavy-handed takeoff on a popular commercial of the late 1960s in which a voluptuous blond cowgirl called on television viewers to "join the Dodge Rebellion" by purchasing a Dodge Charger.) During her first few appearances, Ja-Neen Welch promised big givers a bonus: "If you'll raise your hand, and you got a hundred-dollar bill to contribute, I'll come give you a hug and a kiss."

"I'm telling you hands would go up all over the place," remembered Wallace's aides. "Hell, she was sexy looking. . . . She had those damn boobs out there."[98]

Bill Jones decided this was a little too crude for a presidential campaign and toned down Welch's routine, but he admitted that she raised a lot of money. "She made those guys put the bills in that hat, she sure did. Each one of them thinking they were going to get with her that night, I guess."[99]

Trammell, who sometimes edged toward paranoia on matters of security, immediately decided that she was a spy for the Nixon camp, and invited her to join him and Earl Morgan for a drink of scotch in their hotel suite. Suspicions that she might be an undercover Nixon operative were quickly allayed. As Trammell somewhat ungallantly phrased the matter, she "had more looks than brains." Without the slightest sense of embarrassment, she explained her contribution to the campaign. "I go in there"—nodding toward Wallace's suite—"every night . . . for a few hours . . . and make love." She was concerned, she told Trammell and Morgan, about the candidate's mental state. "He's very nervous, and sometimes he won't even take his coat off when we're making love, he's in such a hurry." But she added, "If I was just married to him, if I was his wife, I could calm him down and . . . make him the best lover you ever saw."[100]

Trammell and Morgan conferred with Bill Jones. "We were all concerned," said Jones, about the potential problem Welch posed for the campaign, but "knowing the Governor as we did," recalled Trammell, we knew "he was going to have to have somebody so it might as well be her as anybody else. At least she was helping the campaign, making an awful lot of money."

Before peephole journalism became the order of the day, there was little danger that newsmen would report on the former governor's after-hours diversions. The real problem was that Ja-Neen Welch had become fixated on becoming the second Mrs. Wallace. In early October, a Cleveland newswoman reported her breathless prediction that she and Wallace were in love and were "going to get married."[101]

"I stayed out of Wallace's sex life," said Bill Jones. But he was delegated the sorry task of getting rid of Welch. When she protested, Jones was gentle, but firm: "You go home, Ja-Neen, that's it."[102]

In one of his famous "not for attribution" interviews with reporters, Wallace explained that Ms. Welch had been separated from her "limited role" in the campaign because her "erratic behavior caused our security to have serious skepticism about her. . . ." (Wallace often prefaced the most innocuous observations with the phrase, "Now, you can't quote me on this boys, but. . . ." Reporters soon learned, as in this case, to ignore his admonition.) "Ms. Welch has never been within twenty feet of George Wallace," a press spokesman added gratuitously. Anxious for a reconciliation, Welch was nonetheless miffed; she retaliated by releasing a series of photographs which showed her in smiling poses considerably closer to the governor than twenty feet. In one shot she passionately kissed a rather awkward-looking Wallace. But reporters let her—and the story—drift into obscurity.[103]

L'affaire Ja-Neen, as one reporter dubbed it, was an overnight embarrassment; the Alabamian's appointment of a running mate proved to be a full-bore disaster.

George Wallace trusted no one, he confided in no one, and nothing better illustrated this trait than the process by which he chose a vice president. Former Georgia governor Marvin Griffin, a genial political has-been and lifelong segregationist, had accepted temporary anointment as the American Independent Party's candidate to allow Wallace to comply with laws in several states which required a running mate, but no one had any illusions about his permanent status. While all of Wallace's advisers agreed that it was important to broaden his Deep South base, they wanted to reach out for a national figure who might give the ticket credibility outside the region. The names most commonly mentioned were Ezra Taft Benson, secretary of agriculture in the Eisenhower administration; retired general Curtis LeMay, chief of staff of the Air Force in the Eisenhower and Kennedy administrations; the FBI's J. Edgar Hoover; and—in all seriousness—Colonel Sanders of Kentucky Fried Chicken fame. Benson and LeMay expressed interest from the outset. Hoover did not even deign to respond to Wallace's discreet inquiries; he had always kept his distance because of what he privately termed Wallace's "psychoneurotic tendencies."[104]

In June, Trammell and Earl Morgan traveled to Washington and sounded out several congressmen and senators. Not one was even politely interested in signing on as George Wallace's sidekick. On the way home, said Trammell, as the two men began running down a list of ex-governors and retired politicians, they came to the name of former Kentucky governor A. B. (Happy) Chandler. Both had the same immediate reaction: "That's it, that is *it*. He's the one."[105]

The seventy-year-old Chandler was the kind of border-South political figure who could strengthen Wallace's position in the states where he was within striking distance of a plurality. Kentucky voters had elected him at age thirty-five as their youngest governor in history. He later served a term in the U.S. Senate, resigned to become baseball commissioner, and then returned to Kentucky to serve a second term as governor in the mid-1950s. Even though Chandler had been out of office for more than a decade, he remained a beloved figure in Kentucky and was almost equally popular in nearby Tennessee.

Wallace reacted cautiously. "Well, you know, that fellow's liberal now, Seymore. And . . . he's the one, the commissioner that integrated baseball."[106]

The facts may have been a little more complicated, but Wallace's political memory was on target. In 1946, Branch Rickey, owner of the Brooklyn Dodgers, had announced his decision to bring Jackie Robinson into baseball as the first black major league player; the remaining fifteen baseball owners had voted unanimously to oppose Rickey. Chandler had just settled into his position as baseball commissioner, and most sports observers predicted that the Southern politician would bring Rickey to heel. In later years, Chandler claimed that he had looked Rickey in the eye and told him that, if Jackie Robinson came to the big leagues, he would be treated like any white player. "Plenty of Negro boys had offered to fight and die for this country" in the Second World War; "if they couldn't engage in baseball after the war that just wasn't right."[107] While he may have exaggerated his own role in the Robinson affair, there is no doubt that Chandler, unlike his predecessor, Kenesaw Mountain Landis, offered Rickey at least passive support.[108]

A second test had come in his final term as governor in 1955 when federal courts had ordered the integration of the public schools in Sturgis and Clay, two small western Kentucky towns. Four days before the scheduled opening of schools, Clay's mayor, Herman Clark, who virtually owned the town of sixteen hundred—had called Chandler at the governor's mansion. "Albert," he warned his old friend, "I just want to tell you . . . no nigger [is] going to school here." The next morning, Clay's citizens awakened to the sound of a Kentucky State National Guard tank and three thousand Guardsmen marching down the town's two-block-long main street and on out to the high school. In a crowded press conference, Chandler explained his decision: "It's not my job to put blacks in the school, but if they show up, it's my job to see they are protected." He made the first high-level black political appointment in Kentucky in the twentieth century, integrated state parks with a stroke of the pen, repeatedly counseled Kentuckians to respect the decisions of the federal courts even when they disagreed with them, and bluntly told constituents that the court's decision outlawing segregation was "morally correct."[109]

Chandler was proud of his role in bringing Jackie Robinson to baseball and scornful of the kind of die-hard segregationist antics that had marked Wallace's career. But he also missed the excitement of politics. "Dammit, how much golf can you play anyway?" he complained after a decade of quiet retirement.[110]

Over a period of weeks, Trammell, Morgan, and Cecil Jackson gradually wore down Wallace, though he kept returning to Chandler's apostasy on race. It would enrage many of his supporters, he warned.

It was precisely because he was a moderate that Chandler would be so valuable to the ticket, countered the three. "We have all the nuts in the country," argued Trammell. "We have all the Ku Klux Klan, we have the Birch Society. We have the White Citizens' Council." With Chandler, "we could get some decent people—you working one side of the street and he working the other side."[111]

In early August, an uneasy Wallace finally gave the go-ahead and a promise that the campaign would not be based on racial issues. Chandler agreed to join the ticket. By early September, word of his selection leaked to reporters who described it as a "done deal."[112]

And then the phones started ringing in Montgomery. The chairman of Wallace's campaign in Kentucky denounced Chandler as an "out-and-out integrationist" and resigned. Seven other Wallace electors followed him, and hard-right activists in the John Birch Society voiced furious opposition. Wallace panicked, particularly when large contributors began calling in. Of the telephone calls he received, none was more critical than Bunker Hunt's.

Hunt's first choice for Wallace's running mate had been Ezra Taft Benson, a leading spokesman for right-wing causes in the 1960s. But Benson was a senior member of the Quorum of the Twelve Apostles, the ruling body of the Church of Jesus Christ of Latter-day Saints. While a number of Mormon leaders quietly sympathized with many of Wallace's positions, they realized that Benson's selection would inevitably cause public relations problems for the Mormon Church and barred him from accepting a position on the third-party ticket.[113]

Hunt could not stomach a traditional mainstream Democratic politician like Happy Chandler. Trammell and Tom Turnipseed insisted at the time and in later years that Hunt's veto alone determined the decision to drop Chandler; more likely it was simply the last straw. On September 9, less than thirty-six hours before the Washington news conference Wallace had scheduled to announce the appointment, Morgan, Jackson, and Trammell flew to Kentucky to tell the former governor that Wallace would have to renege on his promise to name him as running mate.[114]

Embarrassed by the newspaper headlines, which raised questions about his political judgment, Wallace next dispatched Trammell to Los Angeles, where General Curtis LeMay divided his time between playing golf, socializing with fellow retired military officers, and fulfilling his ceremonial obligations as chairman of the board of Networks Electronics Corporation.

It was no accident that filmmaker Stanley Kubrick had used LeMay as a model for the simple-minded Air Force general Buck Turgidson (played by George C. Scott) in *Dr. Strangelove or: How I Learned to Stop Worrying and Love the Bomb*. The bluff, square-jawed, and absolutely humorless Curtis LeMay, chewing away on a cigar, was a figure who seemed destined for parody. He was the "bomber man," a fanatical booster of airpower, who had been a key figure in the development of nonevasive bombing techniques in the European theatre in 1943, and had eventually, as chief of staff of the Strategic Air Forces in the Pacific, presided over the massive destruction of Japanese cities in the last year of the war.

LeMay's success as commander of operations for the famous Berlin airlift in 1948 led to his appointment as the first head of the U.S. Strategic Air Command. This elite all-jet bomber force, loaded with hydrogen bombs, was soon flying round-the-clock missions around the world, ready at a moment's notice to launch a nuclear strike against the Soviet Union. No one doubted the general's technical abilities or his skills in molding a corps of elite airmen capable of maintaining the nation's nuclear arsenal at a high state of readiness.

And no one doubted that he seemed to have a screw loose on the subject of nuclear weapons—"Several," insisted one Defense Department official acidly. John Kennedy had reluctantly promoted LeMay to chief of staff of the Air Force in 1961; he regretted the decision to the end of his life. Every time the President had to see him, "he ended up in a sort of fit," said Kennedy's deputy secretary of defense, Roswell Gilpatric. "I mean he [Kennedy] would just be frantic at the end of a session with LeMay," who would spin off at a moment's notice into a poetic description of the advantage of nuclear strikes or some other "outrageous proposals."[115] After his retirement in 1965, LeMay had insisted that his reputation as a mad bomber was unfair. As an air commander he had tried to steer his planes "away from hospitals, prison camps, orphan asylums, nunneries and dog kennels. I have sought to slaughter as few civilians as possible."[116]

When Trammell tried to persuade him to join the Wallace ticket, the general was interested, but cautious. Three years of retirement had left him frustrated and far from the center of power. Despite his uneasiness about the Alabama governor and his own lack of political experience, LeMay concluded that this was a chance to—as he put it—stand up for the only candidate who was committed to "turning the Vietnam war effort over to the military" and at the same time to stand against the "anti-war demonstrators, the anarchists and left-wingers in this country who have been giving aid and comfort to the Communist enemy."[117]

When LeMay's boss threatened to fire him from his $50,000-a-year job if he joined the Wallace campaign, Trammell flew to Dallas and persuaded Bunker Hunt to put up a secret $1 million trust fund to compensate the general for the expected loss of his salaried position. On September 27, LeMay rendezvoused in Chicago with Wallace—the first time the ex-sergeant had talked with his old Pacific commander. It took the skillful politician only a few minutes to learn the right buttons to push.[118] He denied that he was a racist and promised to give LeMay a free hand in commenting on defense issues during the campaign. He admitted that there was little chance a Wallace-LeMay ticket could win the election, but it was an opportunity to educate Americans on the dangers they faced from Communist subversion abroad and at home. The most important assurance Wallace saved for last: he was "damn sure going to try to keep [Hubert] Humphrey from being elected." If the race went into a deadlock in the electoral college, said Wallace, they would have "enough strength there to defeat Humphrey."[119]

He would be proud to serve, LeMay told Wallace. After a hasty telephone conference with Jackson and Trammell in Montgomery, Bill Jones scheduled the official announcement for ten A.M. October 3 in Pittsburgh, where Wallace was already scheduled to deliver a major speech.

Eighteen hours before the news conference, the governor's top aides huddled with LeMay in his suite in the Pittsburgh Hilton to prepare him for the grilling he would receive the following day. As Ed Ewing, Cecil Jackson, and Earl Morgan gently suggested a series of evasive responses he might use to deflect reporters' troublesome questions, they learned that the general was far more interested in offering his blunt views on the "phobia" Americans had about nuclear weapons than in listening to advice from a lifelong civilian and two former second lieutenants.[120] As the evening wore on, Jackson summoned Bill Jones and Seymore Trammell as reinforcements. At four-thirty A.M., the Wallace staff was still trying to explain why it was absolutely essential that LeMay stay away from the "atomic warfare" issue to avoid any snares laid by devious newspaper reporters. Rightly or wrongly, Ewing told the general, Americans *did* have a phobia about hydrogen bombs.[121]

The press conference was broadcast live on all three networks from the Grand Ballroom of the Pittsburgh Hilton. Morgan, LeMay, and Jones positioned themselves behind the bank of microphones, while at the podium Wallace paid tribute to his new running mate as a man of courage and conviction who still found time to appreciate the "tender and the trivial." The general responded with an innocuous statement written by the Wallace staff.

At 10:18, Bill Jones announced to the more than one hundred reporters gathered in the ballroom that "General LeMay will take a few questions."

Jack Nelson of the *Los Angeles Times* was on his feet. "General," he asked, "do you think it is necessary to use nuclear weapons to win the war in Vietnam?"

Earl Morgan tensed as he watched LeMay lean toward the microphone. "We can win this war without nuclear weapons," he began and Morgan exhaled with relief.

However, the general plunged resolutely onward: "But I have to say that we have a phobia about nuclear weapons."

"Oh, damn," mumbled Morgan, as he watched the reporters jerk forward in their seats.

"I think there may be times when it would be most efficient to use nuclear weapons. However, the public opinion in this country and through the world throw up their hands in horror when you mention nuclear weapons just because of the propaganda that's been fed to them."

One of the reporters overturned a chair as he barreled up the aisle in the race for a telephone to call in the story. The politically tone-deaf LeMay continued his seminar. ("All he needed was a pointer and a couple of flip charts and he would have been happy as a clam," said Morgan.)

"I've seen a film of Bikini Atoll [in the Pacific] after twenty nuclear tests," lectured the general, "and the fish are all back in the lagoons, the coconut trees are growing coconuts, the guava bushes have fruit on them, the birds are back."

For once in his life, George Wallace was speechless; he edged up to LeMay, a look of pain on his face, his mouth opening and shutting.

In all fairness, LeMay continued, he should acknowledge that some experts thought there might be a problem with the island's crustaceans. "They get minerals from the soil, I guess, through their shells, and the land crabs are a little bit hot." But, he added as if to offset this gloomy observation, "the rats are bigger, fatter, and healthier than they ever were before."

Wallace edged him gently away from the microphones. "Now, let me say gentlemen, now let me say, General LeMay hasn't *advocated* the use of nuclear weapons, not at all. He is just *discussing* nuclear weapons with you."

But Jack Nelson was relentless. ("Damn his sorry hide," said Bill Jones, remembering.) "If you found it necessary to end the war, you would use them, wouldn't you?"

"If I found it necessary, I would use anything we could dream up—*anything that we could dream up,*" the general repeated for emphasis.

Frantically, Jones whispered to Wallace, "Let me just stop the news conference; tell them we've got to catch a plane." But Wallace was intent on clarifying his running mate's disastrous gaffe.

"All General LeMay has said, and I know you fellows better than he does because I have to deal with you, he said that if the security of the country depended on the use of any weapon in the future he would use it. But . . . we can win and defend in Vietnam without the use of nuclear weapons."

LeMay pulled away from Wallace and leaned forward into the microphones, trying to be heard above the noise of the ballroom. "Let me make one more statement. Wait a minute now. I know I'm going to come out with a lot of misquotes from the campaign. . . . I'll be lucky if I don't appear as a drooling idiot whose only solution to any problem is to drop atomic bombs all over the world. I assure you I'm not."

A distraught Wallace blurted, "General, we got to go," as he finally managed to end the press conference.

Jones had seen his boss angry, but never like this. "Wallace, oh Wallace was mad, God, he was so infuriated, he was just livid." Two hours later when they reconvened in the Wallace suite to coordinate their efforts at damage control, the sight of Ewing, Jones, Trammell, and Morgan seemed to set him off again. "I should never have listened to you people," he yelled, conveniently forgetting that he had been LeMay's biggest booster. Only Earl Morgan seemed unperturbed; he had headed straight for the hotel bar after the news conference and was falling-down drunk.[122]

Even when Hubert Humphrey began referring gleefully to the Wallace-LeMay ticket as "the Bombsey Twins," the campaign staff kept up a brave front. They insisted that the Pittsburgh press conference was a minor flap, that LeMay's views had been, in Wallace's words, "blown all out of proportion" by the unfair news media. And there was an upsurge of supporting letters and contributions. Even though the "pinko, near-red, and all-red press" might "make you appear to be a drooling idiot," wrote two of the general's followers, their unfairness just made true Americans "love you [and Governor Wallace] more and they get millions more votes for both of you."[123]

Jones and Trammell assigned no fewer than three of their steadiest staff members to serve as watchdogs, and LeMay suddenly found himself speaking in some of the most remote venues in the continental United States, delivering hard-hitting speeches with such titles as "Preserving Our Natural Resources for the 21st Century."

But no spot was sufficiently remote for the general. Two weeks after his political baptism, his handlers decided to risk a speech on the environmental policies of a future Wallace administration before a small crowd at the Yale University School of Forestry. General LeMay worked hard on the speech; next to bombing Communists, preserving the environment lay closest to his heart. The audience, clearly surprised by the thoughtfulness of his presentation, responded warmly, and one faculty member asked a general question on the subject of population control.

"I've seen plenty of big fools in my life, but not many ever topped Curtis LeMay," said one of his chaperones. "He didn't know one hoot in hell about politics."[124] The general presented a thoughtful analysis of the relationship between overpopulation and the excessive exploitation of natural resources, then added, "There are many cases where abortion is proper and that choice should be left up to the judgment of the people concerned and the physicians."[125] The week before, Wallace had learned the price tag for the Boeing 727 jet his imperious running mate had demanded to fulfill his campaign duties: $127,000 a week, twelve times the cost of Wallace's own turboprop. "God damn," he had exploded, "he's either spending all our money or dropping atomic bombs."[126] But this was more than money; blue-collar northern Catholics were crucial to the third-party campaign. Wallace shuttled LeMay off to Vietnam for a "confidential" fact-finding tour of the troops, with vague instructions to "listen to our boys and pick up some ideas about how to end this thing."[127]

The LeMay fiasco (as the original press conference was thereafter called by the governor and his aides) should never have happened. George Wallace was not a regular reader of *Esquire* magazine, but that spring, one of his many admirers had mailed him a copy of an article which had appeared the previous fall. Clarence Mohr, a *New York Times* reporter who had covered the Goldwater debacle in 1964, summed up his impressions of the Arizonan's inept campaign with his sarcastic title, "Requiem for a Lightweight." The piece contained the usual Monday morning quarterbacking: acidic descriptions of inept aides, poor scheduling, and tactical campaign blunders. But Mohr had put his finger on the root cause of Goldwater's repeated campaign disasters.

Even after he was nominated for the presidency, the Arizona Republican continued to speak off-the-cuff as though he were talking to golfing buddies in the locker room of the Flagstaff Country Club. He would casually talk about making Social Security voluntary on Monday and would then withdraw the idea on Tuesday, said Mohr, or would insist that he was not trigger-happy on defense issues even as he suggested that fear of nuclear war was somehow "silly and sissified." When reporters pointed out these contradictions, he would rail that the press was "twisting" his words. Goldwater self-destructed, argued Mohr, because he was essentially a superficial and frivolous man who never understood that both journalists and voters took the statements of a presidential candidate seriously. The voters would not forgive him for either his "threat to their interests or his inconsistency." Wallace underlined Mohr's conclusion and scrawled in the margin: "Clip & Make copies for ST/CJ/JH"—Seymore Trammell, Cecil Jackson, and Jack House.[128]

That was the lesson Wallace understood, but seemed to forget in his choice of LeMay: his embattled constituency wanted him to strike out against enemies in language as bitter and angry as possible—thus LeMay could echo Wallace's claims that American soldiers were "bleeding and dying in Vietnam . . . because our leaders have tied their hands behind their backs."[129] But Americans *did* have a phobia about nuclear weapons, and most regarded LeMay's cavalier willingness to consider hydrogen bombs as the ultimate potential betrayal of their "interests."

The LeMay press conference helped to crystallize the misgivings of voters who had been cautiously leaning toward George Wallace. Ultimately, an enormous gender gap emerged: women, particularly non-southern women—proved far less willing than men to vote for the Alabama politician. In the eleven states of the old Confederacy, half of the men and forty percent of the women were ready to vote for Wallace in late September, at the high-water mark of his campaign. In the North, one-fifth of white males claimed he had their vote, but less than half that number of women supported him.[130]

Cultural and regional differences undoubtedly played a role, but the reason women most often volunteered for opposing Wallace was that he was "dangerous." In his public performances—the speeches and rallies—Wallace often teetered along a razor's edge of violence. Where Nixon and Humphrey hated the hecklers and demonstrators, particularly the antiwar demonstrators, who appeared on the campaign trail, Wallace welcomed them, and had become a master at manipulating them. His retorts grew hackneyed ("Son, if you'll just shut up and take off your sandals, I'll autograph one of them as a souvenir"), but they never failed to delight his followers.

In the impassioned atmosphere of the 1968 campaign, however, it proved far more difficult to predict the outcome of the intricate minuet of insult and response. While most followers were satisfied just to listen to Wallace's talk of "skinning heads" and "popping skulls," others wanted the real thing. Tom Turnipseed got a taste of that dark side when he stopped in a small working-class district outside Webster, Massachusetts, in mid-September to arrange a Wallace rally at a local Polish-American club. Their members, club officers told him after a few drinks at a local bar, were one hundred percent behind the Alabama governor. "Now let's get serious a minute," said the club president. "When George Wallace is elected president, he's going to round up all the niggers and shoot them, isn't he?"

"Naw," replied Turnipseed, laughing, "nothing like that. We're just worried about some agitators. We're not going to shoot anybody." He looked around at the grim, determined faces. "This guy got pissed," remembered Turnipseed, "and he said, 'Well, I don't know whether I'm for him or not.' "[131]

These were the "night people." And in one rally after another, Wallace's angry rhetoric ignited fist-swinging, chair-throwing confrontations between these hardcore followers and antiwar and civil rights demonstrators, who on occasion pelted the candidate with various objects. Wallace was hit by rocks, eggs, tomatoes, pennies, a peace medallion, Tootsie Rolls, a sandal, and a miniature whiskey bottle. By October, television crews always set up two cameras: one to focus on the stage, the other to capture the mêlées and bloodied demonstrators in the audience.

Wallace's troubles gave Nixon the opening he needed.

On October 7, in a highly publicized interview with UPI editors in Washington, Nixon responded to a question on the issue of school integration by endorsing "freedom-of-choice" plans and repeating his opposition to "forced busing," which he had first expressed in his mid-September Charlotte television interview. Two days later Humphrey, speaking to the same group of journalists, attacked "freedom-of-choice" plans as a "subterfuge for segregation." For the first time, the line between Humphrey on one side, and Wallace and Nixon on the other, was clearly drawn. On October 14, regional ads comparing Nixon and Humphrey's positions began appearing on southern radio and television stations.[132]

At the same time, Harry Dent's careful polling revealed Wallace's Achilles' heel: angry white southerners feared that a vote for the Alabama governor would allow Hubert Humphrey to win the election. Fred LaRue, a Mississippi Republican who had cut his political teeth on southern Goldwater-GOP politics, put together a commercial with Dent in which country music star Stuart Hamblen sang a sad song of southerners who chased a rabbit— George Wallace—while the real enemy of the South, Hubert Humphrey, waltzed into the White House. Patiently, LaRue tried to tutor Harry Treleaven, the Nixon campaign's director of advertising, on the content and positioning of special "southern" radio and TV spots. "You got to get . . . [them] on or adjacent to country and western programs. Either that or wrestling," he directed.[133]

Aghast at the notion of buying advertising time from Buck Owens, Ernest Tubb, the Wilburn Brothers, or the Wally Fowler Gospel Hour, Treleaven stalled. The frustrated Dent appealed directly to South Carolina textile industrialist Roger Milliken, whose long career as a union buster had given him a finely honed sense of his workers' cultural tastes. Within twenty-four hours, he and four fellow textile manufacturers had raised the money for Dent's down-home campaign, and country music legends Roy Acuff, Tex Ritter, and Stuart Hamblen began practicing the Nixon jingle, "Bring Our Country Back."[134]

During the last two weeks of the campaign, Nixon took to the air himself in advertisements specifically tailored to white southern voters: "There's been a lot of double-talk about the role of the South"—by which he meant the white people of the South—"in the campaign of nineteen sixty-eight, and I think it's time for some straight talk," he told his listeners. Without mentioning Wallace by name, Nixon warned that a "divided vote" would play into the hands of the Humphrey Democrats. "And so I say, don't play their game. Don't divide your vote. Vote for . . . the only team that can provide the new leadership that America needs, the Nixon-Agnew team. And I pledge to you we will restore law and order in this country. . . ."[135]

The Nixon counterattack devastated Wallace. In the immediate aftermath of the LeMay fiasco, polls had shown a slight erosion of Wallace support outside the South. But the late-October Harris and Gallup polls reflected a precipitous decline. In the eight-day period from October 13 to October 20, the percentage of voters committed to Wallace dropped from twenty percent to fifteen percent; most of that loss came in the North and border states. Approximately half the Wallace defectors in the North shifted to Humphrey, who—nationwide—showed his first significant improvement since the Democratic convention; he climbed from thirty-one percent to thirty-six percent in the polls. But the good news for the Nixon people was that he was getting half of the Wallace voters in the North while border South supporters of the Alabama governor were abandoning their candidate and choosing the Republican nominee three to one over Vice President Humphrey.[136]

Stung by the daily headlines proclaiming his drop in the polls, Wallace accused the media of trying to "stampede" his supporters into believing that he had no chance to be elected.[137] After all, the crowds had remained enormous and enthusiastic through September and October: fifty thousand waited two hours on the Boston Common to hear the Alabama governor, and ten thousand to fifteen thousand supporters packed each Wallace rally in the unlikely cities of Detroit, Pittsburgh, Portland, San Diego, Phoenix, and Minneapolis. Reporters attributed the gloomy mood of the Wallace staff to the polling results, but Trammell, Jackson, and Jones had never expected to win. They were far more preoccupied by internal chaos and division within the top ranks of the campaign.

Gerald Wallace had initially regarded his brother's second try for the presidency with derision, but his attitude changed dramatically as the money begin to roll into Wallace headquarters. On a sunny August morning, he drove out to Trammell's farm south of Montgomery, where Trammell and Jackson had met to review the progress of the campaign. Gerald, never noted for his finesse, charged: "I know y'all are stealing. You either take me in," he threatened, "or I'll take over the money. George says I can."

The following day, Wallace scheduled a conference with Jackson, Trammell, and Earl Morgan. He was not questioning their integrity, he insisted, but "just figured Gerald could relieve y'all of the burden of handling all that money." He had transferred check-signing authority to his younger brother, Jack, and his old University of Alabama crony Ralph Adams. Neither Jackson nor Trammell questioned Jack's honesty, but both were openly contemptuous of Adams and were convinced that the Machiavellian Gerald would easily manipulate the two men for his own ends. "Gerald only wants to steal," Trammell complained to Wallace. "He wants to stop spending and start shoveling the money into bank vaults."[138]

Even Jack Wallace acknowledged that his brother was a problem. Halfway through the campaign, Tom Turnipseed had asked him point-blank: "Jack, why in the hell does Gerald keep wanting to come in here and be involved with [issuing] the checks?"

Jack had paused for a moment. "He's my brother and I love him." But Gerald had "always been too greedy. . . . That's been his problem in life, he's too greedy." When Gerald died, said Jack, "they're going to have to screw him in the ground . . . , he's so crooked."[139]

But George Wallace would not be moved. Jack Wallace and Ralph Adams—with Gerald hovering in the background—were given complete control over the campaign's disbursements. Within two weeks of the shift in financial control, George Wallace sent Trammell a memorandum ordering him to cut back on advertising—a sharp departure from the past practice of spending up to the last penny. "I do not want any commitments made [for television] that we don't have the money for. . . . I want enough money held back in the bank for the purpose of finalizing the campaign after it is all over, win or lose."[140]

Trammell found himself unable to authorize expensive advertising in key states at the very moment when the campaign faltered. To him as well as to Jones and Jackson, a realistic strategy meant a concentrated effort on Florida, the Carolinas, Georgia, and Tennessee, all of which were leaning in their direction; there Wallace had the greatest chance of capturing electoral votes.[141] But Wallace vetoed the schedule his top aides proposed; he was running a "national campaign." He began a backbreaking final series of rallies in thirty-three northern cities from Boston to San Diego, but made only one brief stop in Tennessee (a critical swing state), another in North Carolina, and a third in Atlanta.

OCTOBER 24, 1968, was overcast and drizzly, but unseasonably warm for New York City. More than a thousand police—a hundred of them on horseback— lined up on Seventh Avenue between West Thirty-first and West Thirty-third streets as the crowds began to pour into Madison Square Garden. Twenty thousand of the faithful packed the arena by eight P.M. for the largest political rally held in New York City since Franklin Roosevelt had denounced the forces of "organized money" from the same stage in 1936. At eight-twenty,

George Wallace stepped out into the lights and the audience erupted. Although the campaign had another week to run, for Wallace, the evening was the emotional climax of his race for the presidency.

Across the street an astonishing collection of fringe groups gathered: a caravan of Ku Klux Klansmen from Louisiana who had driven all the way to New York; a delegation of followers of the "Minutemen of America," paramilitary ultra-rightists with neatly printed signs and armloads of brochures; a dozen jackbooted members of the American Nazi Party sporting swastika armbands and "I like Eich" buttons worn in memory of Adolf Eichmann, who had been sentenced to death by an Israeli court for his role in supervising the murder of millions of Jews during the Holocaust. New York police maintained an uneasy peace between the far-right contingent and the more than two hundred members of the Trotskyite Workers' World Party and several hundred members of the radical Students for a Democratic Society, bearing the black flag of Anarchy. Altogether, two thousand protesters—most in their early twenties—waved their picket signs and screamed their battle cries. Radical demonstrators mocked: *"Sieg heil! Sieg heil!"* The right wing countered: "Commie faggots! Commie faggots!"

Inside the Garden, while a brass band played a medley of patriotic songs, Wallace strode back and forth across the stage, saluting the crowd, which roared his name again and again in a chant that could be heard by the demonstrators half a block away. Soon he was joined by Curtis LeMay and his wife, Helen.

After more than fifteen minutes, Wallace finally brought his followers to order by having a country singer perform "God Bless America." Apparently overwhelmed by the fervor of the crowd, he began his speech awkwardly. In the southwest balcony of the Garden, a squarely built black man stood and held up a poster proclaiming "Law and Order—Wallace Style." Underneath the slogan was the outline of a Ku Klux Klansman holding a noose. Another demonstrator at his side suddenly turned on a portable bullhorn and began shouting: "Wallace talks about law and order! Ask him what state has the highest murder rate! The most rapes! The most armed robberies." The overwhelmingly pro-Wallace crowd exploded in rage, and police hurried to rescue three suddenly silent black demonstrators who were surrounded by a dozen Wallace followers shouting "Kill 'em, kill 'em, kill 'em."

The heckling seemed to ignite the Alabama governor: "Why do the leaders of the two national parties kowtow to these anarchists?" he demanded, gesturing toward the protesters in the balcony. "One of 'em laid down in front of President Johnson's limousine last year," said Wallace with a snarl. "I tell you when November comes, the first time they lie down in front of my limousine it'll be the last one they'll ever lay down in front of; their day is *over!*"

The crowd was on its feet for the first of more than a dozen standing ovations.

"We don't have a sick society, we have a sick Supreme Court," he continued, as he scornfully described "perverted" decisions that disallowed prayer in the classrooms even as they defended the right to distribute "obscene pornography."

Fifteen minutes into his talk, he shed his jacket as he weaved and bobbed across the stage, his right fist clenched, his left jabbing out and down as if he were in the midst of one of his youthful bantamweight Golden Gloves bouts. "We don't have riots in Alabama," shouted Wallace. "They start a riot down there, first one of 'em to pick up a brick gets a bullet in the brain, that's all. And then you walk over to the next one and say, 'All right, pick up a brick. We just want to see you pick up one of them bricks, now!' "[142]

Richard Strout, the influential columnist for the *New Republic,* sat in an upper balcony. For more than forty years, he had reported on the American political scene under the by-line "T.R.B. from Washington," but nothing had prepared him for the spectacle he encountered in the Garden that night. "There is menace in the blood shout of the crowd," he wrote to his readers. "You feel you have known this all somewhere; never again will you read about Berlin in the 30's without remembering this wild confrontation here of two irrational forces." The American "sickness" had been localized in the person of George Wallace, the "ablest demagogue of our time, with a bugle voice of venom and a gut knowledge of the prejudices of the low-income class." He would not win, said Strout, and his strength was declining, "but sympathy for him is another matter."[143]

ON election night, November 4, Wallace settled down in the pine-paneled den of the brick rambler Lurleen Wallace had insisted they buy for the day when they would no longer be in the governor's mansion. While members of the family, speaking in hushed voices as though they were just back from a funeral service, slipped in and out, Wallace switched back and forth between the three networks, trying to be polite to guests who dropped in, but mesmerized by the unfolding totals. Long before the polls had closed on the West Coast, with only seventeen percent of the vote counted, Walter Cronkite announced authoritatively that the former Alabama governor had "gone down to ignominious defeat." Angrily, Wallace ground one of his everpresent cigars in an ashtray. "A deep Southerner getting that many votes is not ignominious," he growled to the silent knot of friends and family, then switched the channel.

The news from NBC and ABC was equally definitive. Halfway across town in the cavernous municipal auditorium rented in the flush of September's enthusiasm, Dick Smith, co-chair of fund-raising, watched and tersely spat out the mantra of every wounded and profane politician: "Son of a bitch . . . son of a bitch . . . son of a bitch . . ."[144] Polls as late as October 3 had showed Wallace winning more than one of every five voters. But in the end, only the Deep South remained steadfast. His support had weakened in the border states and had plummeted from thirteen percent to less than eight percent in the North in the last month of the campaign. The final Harris and Gallup polls had accurately predicted his election day total: fourteen percent. He captured only fifty-eight electoral votes, from the same southern states (plus Arkansas, minus South Carolina and Arizona) that Goldwater had carried in 1964.

Cecil Jackson called from the downtown auditorium. The faithful were waiting restlessly. Throughout the evening, Wallace had maintained a relentless optimism, putting the best face on his defeat: "We're doing real good, real good, don't you think? We'll get ten million votes . . . a mighty good vote. A third-party movement from the Deep South . . ." But he was suddenly slack and tired. "I just don't want to go," he protested quietly, almost like a child forced to take his medicine. "I want to stay here."

Shortly before eleven P.M., after a second call from Jackson, Wallace took a deep breath and stood up. He asked Bobbi Jo to bring him two aspirin, woke his youngest daughter, Lee, and began the fifteen-minute drive to greet the two thousand followers who crowded down in the front seats of the auditorium, sullenly watching the banks of television screens. Once on stage, he was smiling and upbeat as he generously thanked his followers and supporters. (LeMay, in contrast, looked as though he had been thrown from one of his beloved bombers without a parachute. "It was a miserable mess," he later said in one of his few comments on the campaign.)[145] The two hundred reporters who surrounded Wallace concentrated almost entirely on trying to unravel the positive spin Wallace put on the numbers as he talked about how the other candidates (particularly Nixon) had begun stealing his speeches.[146]

Almost unmentioned by the press was the recurrent theme of Wallace's remarks to his fellow Alabamians: that he had shown the people of Detroit, San Francisco, Philadelphia, and New York that the people of Alabama were "just as refined and good and intelligent and courageous and cultured as the people of any state in the union."[147] The newsmen were focused on concrete results; what Wallace understood was that, for the people of Alabama and the South, the election was about respect and regional pride.

Not until early the next morning were the seesaw election results final and Nixon declared the victor. The margin was close: 43.4 percent of the popular vote for Nixon to 42.7 percent for Humphrey. The returns from the three-way race would furnish raw material for political scientists and pollsters for years to come. Who had voted for Wallace? Who had supported him and then defected at the last minute? What was the impact of his candidacy on the race?

Like most third-party movements, Wallace's American Independent Party had faltered, and his base of support had dwindled to his Deep South bastion. Political commentators breathed a sigh of relief. A southern demagogue they could understand, but Wallace as a national figure was genuinely unnerving. In their obituary for the Alabama governor and his political uprising, *Newsweek* editors declared that the Wallace movement, as a national threat, was "fatally" wounded; Nixon had successfully coopted the domestic issues—law and order, school desegregation, an increasingly conservative position on court appointments—that had given the southerner's candidacy such initial appeal.[148]

Richard Nixon harbored no such illusions.

Wallace did have his strongest support within the South, but he had succeeded in attracting a surprising eight percent of voters outside the region. Far less than one percent of northern voters had supported Strom Thurmond's Dixiecrats in 1948.[149]

And the Alabamian had come close to achieving his real goal. Despite the late-September optimism of Trammell, Jackson, and Jones, Florida was beyond the reach of their candidate. (Nixon carried the state handily with forty-four percent of the vote; Wallace ran third). But North Carolina and Tennessee slipped away to Nixon by statistically insignificant margins. Had Wallace carried either of these states, a shift of less than one per cent of the vote in New Jersey *or* Ohio from Nixon to Humphrey would have thrown the election into the House of Representatives.[150]

Even more ominously, George Wallace threatened the southern foundation of the future Republican majority Nixon hoped to build. The most salient numbers to emerge in the wake of the 1968 election came from pollsters Richard Scammon and Ben Wattenberg: four of every five Wallace voters in the South would have voted for Nixon with Wallace out of the contest. (In the North, Wallace voters divided almost evenly in choosing between Nixon and Humphrey, but even these non-southern Wallace supporters gave a slight edge to Nixon as their second choice.)[151]

A WEEK after the election, Trammell came into Wallace's campaign office carrying Bunker Hunt's briefcase—which still bulged with a quarter of a million dollars in cash. The Texas oilman must have been aware that the campaign had slowed its spending in the last few weeks, Trammell suggested, and he would be more likely to help in future campaigns if they returned part of the money. Wallace agreed but told his aide to distribute bonuses of three thousand to thirteen thousand dollars to the staff members who had worked most unselfishly on the campaign. For a few days, the Hunt briefcase was like a rather ample cookie jar. Bill Jones reached in and "got ten thousand dollars out of it," he said, and he had no apology. He had been working sixteen-hour days, seven days a week for less than twenty thousand dollars a year. Altogether Trammell paid out $82,000 to top workers.[152]

When he flew to Dallas with Wallace and returned the famous briefcase, they expected some sign of gratitude. Instead Hunt simply grunted, "How much is left?" When Trammell told him, Hunt reached down into the brief-case, pulled out eighteen thousand dollars, and handed it to Wallace, who stuffed it into his coat pocket.[153]

Some bitter campaign workers claimed that the Hunt funds were only a part of the treasury which floated away after the election.[154] (On November 4, the American Independent Party had over a million dollars—Wallace himself later put the figure at nearly two million dollars—in its coffers.[155] And federal prosecutor Broward Segrest expressed skepticism that any of the cookie jar was returned to Hunt.[156]) One mid-level staff member who worked in the "money room" where solicitations were opened, cash placed in a vault, and checks arranged for deposit, claimed to have seen Gerald Wallace arrive late one evening with two of his employees and wait until all the workers had left. The next morning, the vault, which contained the cash from the campaign, was empty.

Dick Smith, co-chairman of the campaign contribution committee and one of the true believers of the 1968 drive, had worked day and night without financial reimbursement. Nearly four years later, he bitterly added a footnote to the campaign's sordid financial denouement. "I'm not accusing anybody of stealing," he said sarcastically, "they just didn't turn it all in."[157]

Two days after his defeat, Wallace sat in his office with his closest advisers, Ed Ewing, Cecil Jackson, Seymore Trammell, and Bill Jones, and listened as they told a few last stories and talked of their plans. Within six weeks, all four would begin lives without George Wallace. Jones and Ewing formed an advertising agency, Jackson returned to his law firm in Selma, and Trammell started his own law firm and began to consider an independent political career.

Wallace mockingly outlined his future. "Maybe I'll sit under the Confed-erate statue [in Clayton] and play checkers. . . . I s'pose that I'll practice a little law, something. . . ."[158]

His aides did not even bother to snigger. They knew Wallace would run for governor, not because he wanted to be governor, but because he could not exist outside the campaign trail. And they knew he had already begun dreaming of the governor's race in 1970 and another run for the presidency in 1972. Critics might now dismiss George Wallace as a Dixie demagogue, but he knew better. He had kindled the deep discontents of an embittered national political minority.

Chapter 12

THE WARS OF RICHARD NIXON

THE SURVIVAL OF GEORGE WALLACE, 1969–1970

LIKE GEORGE WALLACE, Richard Nixon cared little for the troublesome details of domestic governance. "Domestic controversy involved the unsolvable, passion-laden issues ... and the damnable special interest groups who always demand and demand more but never show gratitude," recalled Nixon domestic adviser John Ehrlichman.[1] But the thirty-seventh President understood that some domestic issues—particularly those that touched on the emotional hot-button issues—were critical for his political survival. None triggered stronger emotions than questions of race and power. During his first eighteen months in office, however, Nixon failed to develop any consistent legislative or administrative (or political) strategy as he sent out a steady stream of conflicting signals.

In an August 1970 meeting with southern congressmen and senators he explained that he was in favor of desegregation, but against integration, a semantic distinction which apparently meant that he was against segregation in theory, but would block any policies that might bring about racial integration in schools or neighborhoods.[2] Even as he rhetorically reassured the opponents of desegregation, Nixon appointed his relatively liberal friend Robert Finch as secretary of the U.S. Department of Health, Education and Welfare; Finch in turn supported the aggressive team of civil rights enforcers he had inherited from the Johnson administration. John Ehrlichman believed that during his five and a half years in the White House Richard Nixon changed dramatically on many issues, but little in his basic assumptions about race. He "always couched his views in such a way that a citizen could avoid admitting to himself that he was attracted by a racist appeal," said Ehrlichman. Privately, the President told his domestic adviser that "America's blacks could only marginally benefit from Federal programs because blacks were *genetically inferior* to whites."[3]

There were times, particularly in the first year or two of his administration, when Nixon seemed to differentiate, however hazily, between the politics of getting elected and the politics of governing. That meant a need to "do something" about the increasing racial polarization of American society. In that process he was critically influenced by an ambitious young New York politician, a neo-liberal Democrat who proved to be a master at finding common ground with the President: Daniel Patrick Moynihan.

The ebullient Irish Catholic Moynihan, who had been a reformer within the New York Democratic Party in the 1950s, was a rare blend of political operative and scholar-intellectual: the professorial politician. When his party regained the White House in 1960, he had joined the Kennedy team and served as one of Lyndon Johnson's most important advisers on the problems of urban America. Although it is tempting to see his alliance with Nixon as a matter of pure self-interest, well before the 1968 election Moynihan had begun to question some of the assumptions of Lyndon Johnson's Great Society as it sought to deal with the problem of black poverty in America.

He had been badly burned in 1965 when he authored what later came to be called the "Moynihan Report on the Black Family." The growing crisis in the black community, he argued, lay in the collapse of the traditional two-parent family. The disappearance of the black father figure and a sharp rise in the number of out-of-wedlock births (twenty-five percent for blacks in 1965, but three percent for whites) were more than moral questions for Moynihan; they were the fundamental factors in the creation of a permanent black underclass. "Men must have jobs," Moynihan had argued, even if the nation had to "displace" black females. While the sexism of this analysis went almost unnoticed in the mid-1960s, civil rights leaders condemned the report as an example of "blaming the victim." The document, designed to lay the groundwork for one of Lyndon Johnson's much beloved White House conferences, became a public relations fiasco, and Moynihan resigned his position in the Johnson administration.[4]

As the nation seemed to come apart in the violence of the race riots of the summers of 1965–1967 and the growing dissent over the Vietnam War, Moynihan's concern over a general breakdown in American civic life reinforced his apprehensions over the disintegration of the black family and the growth of a black underclass. Although quick to acknowledge the powerful and painful legacy of slavery and racial discrimination, he sternly insisted that the nation could "simply not afford the luxury of having a large lower class that is at once deviant and dependent."[5]

In the fall of 1967, the Americans for Democratic Action, a liberal activist organization closely linked to the Democratic Party, invited him to speak to their annual convention. His address, entitled "The Politics of Stability," laid out three criteria for what Moynihan called a "new" liberalism. First, Democratic liberals had to "see more clearly that their essential interest is in the stability of the social order." They must reject the fringe elements within their party and move toward an alliance with responsible conservatives who shared a concern over social disorder and division. While liberals sometimes served as the conscience of the nation, the difficult problems of race and poverty "may well be more amenable to conservative solutions than to liberal ones—or to solutions carried out by conservatives."[6]

Second, liberals should abandon their blind faith in the notion that welfare programs administered by the federal government would ameliorate social problems. Conservatives, he conceded, had a point in arguing that the national government was too distant and too out of touch with local problems to bring about effective change. Moynihan proposed the decentralization of social welfare programs, whenever possible by giving state and local government increased resources through revenue sharing.

Finally, liberals had to stop "defending and explaining away" the problems in the black community as nothing more than the product of racism. Moynihan edged up to the traditional conservative argument that improvements in black life could only come from within, then veered away, perhaps remembering the uproar that had greeted his 1965 report.[7]

The speech (printed later as an article) caught Richard Nixon's attention and led to a first meeting in Key Biscayne, Florida, shortly after the 1968 election. The two immediately hit it off, and—despite his many sardonic comments on old friends as well as enemies—Nixon always retained his fondness for Moynihan.[8] Although the Democrat's views shifted to the right, he never abandoned his belief that catastrophic conditions required federal intervention if the nation was to prevent what he saw as the continuing disintegration of the black family and the rise of welfare dependency. To resolve the crisis in race relations, politicians must lower the rhetoric and place the problem of black Americans in the larger context of supporting lower-income families across the board.

Moynihan wasted no time. Even before the President took the oath of office, the policymaker laid out an agenda that skillfully played to Nixon's contempt for the welfare bureaucracy. In his speech to the ADA, Moynihan had attacked what he called the "service" approach to solving the problems of poverty, an approach which a cynical person "might describe . . . as one of feeding the sparrows by feeding the horses."[9] The solution was not to abandon the poor, but to bypass this parasitic and wasteful welfare bureaucracy. As John Ehrlichman sarcastically (and rather imperfectly) paraphrased Moynihan's strategy: "Cut out the social workers (. . . mostly Yale graduates with pangs of conscience) who pandered to black malingerers. Just send the entitled poor a check each month, Pat argued, and blue-collar workers would begin to feel better."[10]

In a major televised address in August 1969, Richard Nixon proposed the boldest domestic innovation of his presidency: a federally funded "Family Assistance Plan" designed to break the cycle of welfare dependency in America. In return for a work commitment, impoverished families—even those in which the father was present in the household—would receive a direct payment guaranteeing a minimum standard of living. By establishing automated procedures similar to Social Security the plan would drastically reduce red-tape costs and phase out many of the social workers and personnel who (he argued) profited most from the existing welfare system.[11]

During his first year in office, Nixon also created the Office of Minority Enterprises to promote black capitalism; he backed the beginning of so-called "set-aside" programs, which required that a fixed percentage of government contracts be guaranteed to minority businesses; and, through the Department of Labor, his administration instituted the "Philadelphia Plan," which required companies doing business with the federal government to establish goals and timetables for hiring and promotion of minorities, even if such mechanisms interfered with longtime seniority practices.

But the centerpiece of the Nixon program remained the Family Assistance Plan—a bold measure by any standard. By the administration's own calculations, it would add from ten million to thirteen million Americans to the nation's welfare rolls; no one was exactly certain of the numbers. Even under the most optimistic projections, welfare costs would increase by four billion dollars during the first year, with unknown costs in future years. According to one study (never made public), the plan would have had a particularly powerful impact on southern blacks, increasing benefits forty percent within the fourteen states of the region.

In the end, the program stalled in Congress. Nixon blamed liberal Democrats, who supposedly knuckled under to the lobbying efforts of professional welfare workers and such radical groups as the National Welfare Rights Organization. In fact, neither Republican conservatives nor Nixon's own cabinet demonstrated much enthusiasm for the FAP; the powerful U.S. Chamber of Commerce, as well, came out in bitter opposition. But the real problem lay in the political equation. The plan did nothing to strengthen the coalition Nixon saw as essential for his own reelection in 1972.[12]

*   *   *

IF the civil rights movement had characterized the early 1960s, the discovery of the "forgotten American" marked the end of the decade. Novelist and would-be political analyst Norman Mailer foreshadowed the future in a self-indulgent reflection on the Republican convention of 1968 (written, as always, in the third person). Waiting in a press room for a long-overdue appearance by Martin Luther King's SCLC successor, Ralph Abernathy, the writer was seized by a disquieting awareness. He was "heartily sick of listening to the tyranny of soul music, so bored with Negroes triumphantly late for appointments, so depressed with Black inhumanity to Blacks in Biafra, so weary of being sounded in the subway by Black eyes. . . ." So jaded was he, in fact that he secretly found himself cheering "Yeah man, yeah, go!" when "flatulent old Republicans got up in Convention Hall to deliver platitudes on the need to return to individual effort." For Mailer, the evidence was unmistakable: "He was getting tired of Negroes and their rights." And if he felt this way, what about the buttoned-down voters of suburban America? Even if they were "not waiting for Georgie Wallace," mused Mailer, was it possible they were ready for "Super-Wallace"—a dressed-up, more sophisticated and refined salesman for the venom and bitterness that too many whites felt toward blacks?[13]

After George Wallace's strong showing in the 1968 election, scholars—sociologists, political scientists, historians—began to pore over the polling data and election returns in an attempt to define a nation in the middle of political upheaval. By the end of Nixon's first year in office the media had jumped on the bandwagon; *Newsweek* devoted almost an entire issue in the early fall to "The Troubled American: A Special Report on the White Majority." The weekly's polling results showed that half of all white Americans blamed high rates of unemployment in the black community on black laziness; two-thirds described crime as one of the most serious problems they faced and overwhelmingly identified blacks with street crimes; three-fourths opposed any further integration in schools; ninety percent were against the integration of their neighborhoods; and ninety-eight percent expressed their hostility to busing.[14]

Negative racial attitudes among whites reached across class lines from inner-city ethnic neighborhoods to those in suburbs. But magazines of liberal and conservative opinion like the *New Republic* and the *National Review,* as well as the tonier *Harper's, Atlantic,* and *The New Yorker,* and even special features sections of the leading newspapers of the nation appeared most fascinated with the smoldering discontents of the working class.

Some writers managed to hear the anguish of dislocation and upheaval—the sense of powerlessness and fear—among white working-class Americans without ignoring the casual and frightening racism which too often accompanied it. Robert Wood, an MIT urban planner who was undersecretary of housing and urban development in the Johnson administration, created a statistical profile of this alienated group of twenty-three million American families, once the backbone of the nation, the heroes of the nation's civics books. "The working American lives in the gray area fringes of a central city or in a close-in or very far-out cheaper suburban subdivision of a large metropolitan area." He earned between $6,000 and $7,500 (above the poverty line in the mid-1960s). With the help of installment credit, he was likely to own his own home and even more likely to own his own car. Only six percent of those in his social and economic class had any education beyond high school; nearly half had never gone to school beyond the eighth grade.[15]

Americans—poor, working-class, middle-class, and rich—looked back to a year like 1910, said Pete Hamill, himself a son of the post–World War II working class. His parents and his parents' friends longed for a time "when there were harvests in the fall and feasts in the spring, when kids went swimming in the old swimming hole and played baseball and respected God, Flag and Country. Most of all they want to return to a time in America when you lived in the same house all of your life and knew everybody you would ever care to know on the street where you were born."[16]

Such nostalgia rested upon an illusion. Through most of the nation's history, the American working class had lived on the edge of survival, one accident away from dependence on the mercy of family and friends, one layoff away from destitution and hunger. But if there had not been a golden age, families had enjoyed at least two and a half decades of constantly rising incomes and expectations in post–World War II America. Suddenly, the ground had shifted, and all the signposts of a generation seemed to have been swept away in a revolution made all the more menacing by the electronic visions of turmoil and upheaval flashed across their living rooms each evening. Most whites living in working-class communities, said Hamill, saw blacks only as "militants with Afros and shades, or crushed people on welfare." The video message tended to picture most blacks "threatening to burn down America or asking for help or receiving welfare or committing crime."[17]

Television had played a powerful role in the acceleration of the civil rights movement in the first half of the 1960s; it furnished an equal impetus to the counterrevolution of the late 1960s and early 1970s. Marshall Frady saw it when he interviewed voters in the white working-class precincts of Gary, Indiana, after the 1968 election. For much of the decade, they had watched the stories of rising crime and racial tensions, the burning of great American cities, and the emergence of a black leadership demanding—not asking for—a place at the table of American democracy. Their community, their neighborhood, might be relatively calm, but, through the "immediacy of television, [they] feel menaced by confrontations and figures remote from their existences, which in another time would have remained quite abstract to them."[18]

The chaos and disorder seen on their flickering television screens reminded working-class Americans that the vaunted American virtues of mobility and choice—*control*—belonged to another world, said essayist Peter Schrag. While young executives and well-educated Americans on the way up might welcome risk and opportunity, the average working-class and lower-income white-collar worker found it difficult to imagine major change for the better. He (or she) had no problem envisioning change for the worse. And yet, "for a decade he is the one who has been asked to carry the burden of social reform, to integrate his schools and his neighborhood, [he is the one who] has been asked by comfortable people to pay the social debts due to the poor and the black."[19]

Other liberals wrote out of a frustration born of contempt. In the pages of the *New York Review of Books*, the *Little Red Book* of America's eastern intellectuals, novelist and essayist Elizabeth Hardwick described the joyless, soulless American lumpen-proletariat drawn to tacky politicians like Wallace. The typical white working-class American "comes home to his payments on the car, the mortgage on his house in the bland development, to his pizzas and cottony bread and hard-cover pork chops, to his stupefying television, his over-heated teenage daughter, his D-in-English, car-wrecking son: all this after working himself to exhaustion." Dulled by the "misery of the working class, its joyless patriotism, its stunting deprivations," he could only lash out blindly at educated whites above him and blacks just below. When a poor black welfare mother thought about education for her children, said Hardwick, "she hopes for something more alive, original and creative"; working-class whites only wanted to " 'stomp on'—the kind of term they like—the free and inspired teacher, bottle up the flow of ideas, further degrade the already bad textbooks."[20]

Even columnist Pete Hamill, the self-described "son of the white working class," could not conceal his uneasiness over the dark side of those "cabdrivers, beauticians, steelworkers, ironworkers and construction-men so beautifully romanticized by generations of dreamy socialists" (and by George Wallace). In reality, said Hamill, they could be an "ugly bunch of people."[21]

If liberals fretted over the reactionary tilt of their former New Deal allies, politicians and pragmatists had to deal with the world as it was. In the two years between the presidential campaign of 1968 and the off-year election of 1970, political analysts Richard Scammon, Ben Wattenberg, and Kevin Phillips outlined the strategies for political survival.

In *The Real Majority*, published in early 1970, Scammon and Wattenberg— old-style Democrats—argued that George Wallace had it right: the Democratic Party had lost touch with the mainstream of the American electorate, which was white, middle-aged, and working/middle class. While they did not coin the term, Scammon and Wattenberg popularized a catch-phrase that would soon become a staple in the political lexicon: the "Social Issue" (with capital letters). Although it had many dimensions, most critical was the belief that American society faced a crisis in terms of the rise of street crime and social unrest: the breakdown of "law and order" *and* the erosion of the cultural values that underlay the social system.[22] Somewhere between a "fifth and a third of the electorate . . . [was] up for grabs largely on the basis of the Social Issue," said Scammon and Wattenberg. That swing vote was centered in the Wallace movement, they argued, but Wallace supporters— like the Nixon voters—increasingly viewed "law and order" as more important than economic issues. And they responded with more enthusiasm to attacks on black radicals and antiwar demonstrators than to pleas for new spending (and taxes) to ameliorate social problems. Unfortunately for the Democratic Party, they argued, its "pro-black stance" and its refusal to take a hard-line attitude toward street crime and antiwar protesters had chained the party to the losing side of the emerging Social Issues. In chastened form it might be possible to continue the social welfare traditions of the old Democratic Party, but the party had to stop scolding Americans about the Bill of Rights and take a tough line opposing crime in the streets, campus disruptions, drugs, and pornography. Above all else, they insisted, the party had to disentangle these issues from that of race.[23]

There was a certain deceptive appeal to such a prescription. There were too many political exhibitionists in the Democratic leadership who equated egocentric proclamations with thoughtful action. And a concern over crime in the streets was not necessarily a reflection of inherent fascism; it was, after all, often blacks who suffered from violence. The notion of running a campaign on the platform of "law and order *with justice*" had a nice theoretical ring.

It might be possible, as Scammon and Wattenberg argued, to separate race from the Social Issue. Theoretically. But in reality, fears of blackness and fears of disorder—interwoven by the subconscious connection many white Americans made between blackness and criminality, blackness and poverty, blackness and cultural degradation—were the warp and woof of the new social agenda.

Kevin Phillips made no bones about the importance of race. A twenty-seven-year-old graduate of Colgate and of Harvard Law School, Phillips was Bronx Irish, a self-proclaimed streetwise city kid who had begun drawing maps of voting patterns when he was in high school, one of the first of that generation of young conservatives who would reshape American politics in the 1980s. Joe McGinniss, who savagely chronicled the 1968 Nixon television ad campaign, mocked Phillips, "pale and dour" from hours huddled over his computers and charts, hurrying through the halls of Nixon headquarters, trailing reams of computer printouts and breathing a kind of clarified cynicism.[24]

But no one denied his brilliance. Throughout 1968 and into early 1969 he labored away at a book which would have a profound impact on his party's future political strategy: *The Emerging Republican Majority*. Phillips was one of the first political demographers to grasp the political significance of the growth of the conservative Sun Belt and to recognize the political dynamite embedded in the social and cultural conflicts that dominated the 1960s. Like Scammon and Wattenberg, he emphasized the essential conservatism of first-generation and second-generation European immigrants, and he was perfectly willing to take advantage of the anti-intellectualism that Wallace had brilliantly illuminated in his 1968 campaign. But Phillips bluntly recognized the critical role fear in general, and white fear of blacks in particular, would play in guaranteeing the emerging Republican majority.

Understanding what makes politics tick wasn't so difficult, Phillips had confided to author Garry Wills in the middle of the 1968 election. Who hates whom—"That is the secret."[25] In the traditional Democratic heartland—the urban Midwest—the assertiveness of black Democrats was driving whites into the Republican Party despite their lingering attachments to loyalties forged during the New Deal. And in the South, the enfranchisement of blacks and their movement into the Democratic Party had already triggered the flight of white conservatives away from the party of their fathers and toward the once-hated Republicans. "Populist" Republicans could "hardly ask for a better target than a national Democratic Party aligned with Harvard, Boston, Manhattan's East Side, Harlem, the New York *Times* and the liberal Supreme Court."[26] Phillips urged his party to work vigorously to maintain and expand black voting rights in the South, not as a moral issue, but because it would hasten the transfer of whites—north *and* south—to the Republican Party.[27]

Millions of Americans, particularly traditional working-class Democrats, were politically "in motion" in the 1960s, concluded Phillips; the GOP should use the emotional issues of culture and race to achieve what Phillips's mentor and boss, John Mitchell, called a "positive polarization" of American politics. (By "positive" Mitchell meant that the Republicans would end up with more than fifty percent of the voters once the electorate was divided into warring camps.) In the long run, Wallace would be a big help. "People will ease their way into the Republican Party by way of the American Independents. . . . We'll get two-thirds to three-fourths of the Wallace vote in nineteen seventy-two."[28]

Phillips's book came off the press in early September. Harry Dent, who headed what Nixon called his "Wallace-watch," urged the President to develop a racial policy conservative enough to entice white southerners, but not so radical as to repel the "nominally Democrat white middle class vote in the swing states of California, Ohio, Illinois, Pennsylvania, and New Jersey." The "only fly in the ointment is George Wallace," he warned, but a sufficiently conservative policy would be enough to make southerners realize that Wallace was "not a viable alternative and turn to Republicanism in droves." In short, said Dent, the Republican Party should "follow Phillips' plan," though—he hastened to add—they should "disavow it publicly."[29]

Over the 1969 Christmas holidays, Nixon read the book; he shared Dent's enthusiasm. In his daily meeting with H. R. Haldeman on January 8, 1970, the President issued his marching orders: "Use [Kevin] Phillips as an analyst—study his strategy—don't think in terms of old-time ethnics, go for Poles, Italians, Irish, must learn to understand Silent Majority . . . don't go for Jews & Blacks."[30]

A month later, Alexander Bickel, a distinguished Yale law professor, published a bluntly critical assessment of school desegregation in the New Republic, American liberalism's flagship magazine. Significant racial integration in the schools was impossible, Bickel argued. When African Americans formed a significant minority, the "whites move, within a city or out of it into suburbs . . . or else they flee the public school system altogether, into private and parochial schools." Given that inescapable reality, it was "not very fruitful to ask whether the whites behave as they do because they are racists, or because everybody seeks in the schools some sense of social, economic, cultural group identity." When federal authorities demanded integration, the only whites left in these biracial schools were the very poor in urban areas or rural and small-town southerners. "The government is thus seen as applying its law unequally and unjustly, and is therefore fueling the politics of George Wallace."

Bickel's essay captured the new spirit of "realism," which pervaded much writing by neo-conservatives on the issue of race relations. The goal of an integrated public-school system was an illusion; the nation should accept significant segregation as an inevitable creation of intransigent cultural mores. The "vanguard of black opinion, among intellectuals and political activists alike," Bickel suggested, was increasingly "oriented more toward the achievement of group identity and some group autonomy than toward the use of public schools as assimilationist agencies."[31]

As a disciple of Supreme Court Justice Felix Frankfurter, the great advocate of judicial restraint, Bickel had always emphasized the importance of limited federal power and what he called "local diversity."[32] For the Nixon White House, which saw the Ivy League as a hotbed of radicalism and left-wing extremism, Bickel's influential voice gave political cover to the administration's retreat on the issue of school integration. Nixon had the article copied and made required reading for all White House staff; he quoted (and misquoted) Bickel's arguments in his conversations with aides.[33] And when *Washington Star* columnist Richard Wilson wrote an equally bleak assessment of the fate of school desegregation in the District of Columbia ("integration has led only to disillusion and dispair"), Nixon passed the Wilson piece along as well with the comment: "a very astute analysis." It would be impossible to come out in overt opposition to further court-ordered integration, he told H. R. Haldeman, but "the government can interpret the Court [orders] in a very narrow way, and we must."[34]

By the spring of 1970, Nixon had formulated his reelection strategy: he would concentrate upon recruiting Catholic ethnics, blue-collar workers, and, particularly, southern whites. (As one reflection of the winds of political change, Nixon ordered Haldeman to begin recruiting country music stars like Johnny Cash to perform for White House galas.)[35]

But as President, Nixon could go only so far. Wallace would always be on his right flank, ready to criticize any changes in policy as halfhearted and ineffective. Far preferable would be the destruction of the third-party challenger.

WHEN Montgomery newsman Ray Jenkins had probed a Wallace insider for details of the governor's "leadership-style" in the spring of 1963, the state senator had shrugged off the question. There was not much to tell, he said: "We eat Baby Ruths and cuss niggers."

"No, no, be serious," said Jenkins.

"All right," replied the legislator. A few days earlier, "we had a $110 million bond issue that we were trying to get through the legislature and we had everybody . . . holding a strategy session. . . . [The 1963 highway bond issue was actually $100 million.] We were talking about spending $110 million of the taxpayers' money and I looked around and the Governor of this state was gone . . . he was standing over by the window eating a Baby Ruth."

Wallace was "about ten notches above most Governors that I have ever known in intelligence," said Jenkins. Just by "half doing it, he could make things run pretty well."[36]

But he was often unwilling to give even half his time to the process. He "loved being governor and he loved running," said Albert Brewer, who not only succeeded Lurleen as governor but had been Wallace's first-term legislative floor leader, "but . . . he was just an administrative disaster because he wouldn't take time with it."[37]

Wallace had come into office on the crest of an economic upturn that lasted through the 1960s; without tax increases, state revenues rose nearly fifteen percent each year from 1963 to 1968. "My oh my, it was fun to spend that money," recalled Albert Brewer as he wistfully reflected on those palmy days of ever-rising state budgets. When these funds proved inadequate for

Wallace's ambitious programs, he proposed a modest increase in corporate and income taxes. The "folks from the Black Belt counties and the Big Mules" found a sales tax far preferable, said Brewer, since "their approach was 'This is the only taxes that niggers would pay.' "[38] Wallace publicly insisted that he was opposed to regressive sales taxes, but Birmingham's corporate lobbyists reported with some satisfaction that the governor's lieutenants had made no effort to kill a proposed sales tax, nor had Wallace made any effort to push through a corporate tax increase in the Senate even though the House had passed a modest increase.[39] When the legislature hiked the sales tax so that it became one of the highest in the region, Wallace quietly signed the revenue measure. And the legislature followed the governor's lead by funding most of his program with a quarter-billion dollars in long-term bonds (doubling the state's indebtedness).[40]

The actual business of running state government was, in the words of a Mobile state senator, "a hell of a bother,"[41] but Wallace paid close attention to those details that translated into votes. He was extraordinarily responsive to constituent mail, as Al Lingo learned from a stream of personal memos ordering the restoration of drivers' licenses of individuals convicted of driving under the influence. A reinstated driver, drunk or sober, was a Wallace voter. And what other governor personally monitored regional highway patrol dispatch centers to make sure they used the wrecker services of his supporters?[42]

Teachers as well as state employees (who doubled in number in the 1960s) looked with renewed affection on their governor each year as salary and fringe benefits climbed steadily. Highway and bridge construction became one of the major growth industries in the state, and the governor received the public relations boost that came from hundreds of road signs, emblazoned with Confederate and Alabama state flags, trumpeting "THE WALLACE HIGHWAY PROGRAM. Largest in Progressive Alabama's History." Absent was the American flag or any reference to the fact that ninety percent of the funds came from the federal government.[43]

There were a few malcontents. Thoughtful educators groused over the neglect of the state's two flagship schools, Auburn and the University of Alabama, and the diversion of limited resources into the dozens of two-year schools. "Hell, they got junior colleges some places . . ." said John Patterson, "you can almost hit three of them with a rock."[44] And the governor ignored the desperate and overburdened prison system and mental health programs; there were fewer votes to be found in funding these enterprises.

For George Wallace the governorship was simply the platform from which he ran for office. As the ex-governor began planning his 1972 run for the presidency, he discovered to his chagrin just how critical that platform was. Alabama contractors and business supporters—deprived of any quo for their quid—were suddenly uninterested in bankrolling his ambitions.

When his wife died in the spring of 1968, George Wallace had given his pledge to Albert Brewer that he would not be a candidate for governor in 1970, an assurance he not only repeated privately but also, indiscreetly, in the presence of several television cameras and microphones.[45] He had meant every word of his promise. But as he contemplated the end of his national as well as state political prospects, he no longer meant it.

In mid-July 1969, he used his old friend Grover Hall to launch a trial balloon. "The signs abound that George C. Wallace has decided to repossess the Alabama governor's chair from his protégé, Gov. Albert Brewer," wrote Hall. This was not, Hall said, because Wallace had any great interest in the governorship per se. It was simply a "move to firm his footing for the 1972 presidential race."[46]

Wallace made his first gambit to regain the governor's mansion with characteristic flair. During the first week of September 1969, while the hapless Brewer was meeting with other southern governors in Williamsburg, Virginia, Wallace summoned legislative leaders to his home in Montgomery. He presented them with an inflammatory resolution which called upon parents to ignore court-ordered desegregation orders by appearing at the school of their choice, a move that amounted to a wholesale revolt against federal guidelines. Wallace admitted that his plan would probably "come to naught," but "then we can say we've tried. And that's a whole lot more than some of these sissy folks have done." As one of Brewer's people said: "Guess who's the main 'sissy' he has in mind."[47]

Despite the uncomfortable opposition of Brewer's floor leaders, the proposal swept through the legislature with great whoops and applause. The grandiloquent call for massive defiance was soon forgotten, but in Alabama Wallace had drawn the battle lines for the next year's campaign.[48]

Even before his emergence as a challenger to Brewer, the White House anticipated the worst. "Old George is layin' low like Br'er Rabbit in his briar patch," Dent had told syndicated columnist Stewart Alsop in mid-summer. "But we know he's in there."[49] And with his decision to retake the governorship as a prelude to another presidential run, concluded Alsop, Wallace had become the "ghost of Banquo to Nixon's Macbeth ('Hence, horrible shadow! Unreal mockery, hence!')." The President understood that George Wallace was a candidate who could "smell votes as a pig smells truffles." His haunting presence was "what the much-touted 'Southern strategy' is really all about."[50]

As Nixon looked ahead to his reelection campaign, the Democrat he most feared was Teddy Kennedy, but he had been given a reprieve from another Nixon-Kennedy clash on July 18, 1969, when the Massachusetts senator drove off the end of a bridge on Chappaquiddick Island and swam to safety, leaving staffer Mary Jo Kopechne dead or dying in the submerged car. Although Kennedy had managed to avoid prosecution and to cover up some of the more embarrassing details of the accident, Nixon knew that Chappaquiddick could be turned into "one of his greatest liabilities if he decided to run for President in 1972."[51]

Maine senator Edmund Muskie, Humphrey's vice-presidential running mate, had emerged as the unexpected star of the 1968 campaign. At a time when political cynicism was on the rise, he radiated a Lincolnesque image of rectitude and old-fashioned values. Theodore White, the semi-official chronicler of American elections in the 1960s and 1970s, gave his benediction to the senator in *The Making of the President—1968*. "Muskie had proven himself an almost immeasurable asset to the [Democratic] campaign.... Muskie, a low-key, extraordinarily effective speaker in the New England style, had made trust—trust of people for government, trust of black for white and white for black, trust of Americans in Americans—his keynote."[52] Nixon, who had spent much of his career trying to live down the nickname "Tricky Dick," did not want the 1972 presidential election to rest upon the issue of who the voters trusted most.

But Ed Muskie was not his greatest problem. Nor was George McGovern ("the easiest Democrat to beat"); "my concern was about Wallace," Nixon later wrote.[53]

That concern was reflected in the steady stream of memos that moved back and forth between Nixon and Harry Dent.[54] Nixon immediately saw in the Wallace-sponsored legislative resolution the first salvo in the hard-fought battle for the votes of the white South as well as those of blue-collar northerners. He glimpsed in Albert Brewer the faint possibility of undercutting his Deep South challenger. He had made a point of seeking out the Alabamian for a brief chat during a presidential visit to the 1969 Governors' Conference in Williamsburg. Nixon prided himself on his ability to quickly size up individuals, and having taken the measure of George Wallace during the 1968 campaign, he was not impressed by Brewer's mild demeanor and uncharismatic personality. If Harry Dent shared the President's doubts about Brewer's chances, he reminded Nixon of the stakes. Wallace was well on his way toward "exploiting the race question to a fare-thee-well on the way to the Governor's chair" and, once in power, he would have a bully platform to "begin transferring the blame from the courts to us."[55] Nixon told Dent that he was "interested in helping [Brewer] in any way possible."[56]

But when his impresario of southern affairs proposed a private meeting between Brewer and the President, the cautious Nixon balked. Instead, he decided to keep his political options open. He remained doubtful that anyone could defeat the former governor on his home turf, a skepticism shared by journalists and businessmen who followed state politics.[57] If Brewer continued to show strength, the White House might quietly channel support his way. (There was also the faint possibility that Wallace might join Strom Thurmond and move over to the Republican Party, or at least accept some rapprochement with the Nixon administration).[58]

Ironically, almost everyone who followed Alabama politics agreed that Brewer was one of the most capable chief executives his state had known in the twentieth century. Unlike his opponent, he cared deeply about the details of government and worked hard to recruit first-rate, honest administrators. Even the small minority of white Alabama liberals and the larger number of blacks who faulted Brewer for his early association with Wallace recognized him as a man of uncommon decency, integrity, and administrative ability. But few believed he could win a race with Wallace.

Brandt Ayers, editor of the *Anniston Star,* privately and publicly supported Albert Brewer; he briefly dared to hope that the soft-spoken north Alabama politician might finally rid Alabama of its obsession with Wallace's lost causes. But he always worried that Brewer looked too much like that grade-school classmate everyone remembered—someone whose mother sent him off each day immaculately dressed, who "never has a wrinkle, never has a spot; he never stubs his toe or gets his britches dirty or scrapes his elbow." And when he got to school, he was the "kid who's in the front row and his hand is in the air."[59] In a campaign against a "macho" candidate like Wallace, Ayers feared that Brewer would be done in by what he called the "wimp issue." It was no accident that Wallace constantly sneered at "sissies" too cowardly to stand up for Alabama.

Postmaster General Winton Blount, Nixon's point man in Alabama, was convinced that Brewer could win.[60] A wealthy businessman with a nose for ferreting out lucrative government contracts, Blount had made his millions as a construction contractor in the postwar South. During the 1963 civil rights crisis in Alabama, he had worked quietly with the Kennedys to defuse the potential for violence during the stand in the schoolhouse door crisis. He had officially switched to the GOP after the 1964 election, but unlike many Goldwater Republicans who combined economic conservatism with hard-line white-only politics, Blount proved to be a racial moderate. While other Alabama businessmen ran for cover, Blount had shown considerable courage in challenging Wallace and urging peaceful compliance with unpopular judicial decisions through the 1960s.[61]

His smooth unbroken movement up through the business world and into the Nixon cabinet left him serenely self-confident and blind to the raw and elemental passions that still drove the politics of his home state. Robert Vance, the head of Alabama's Democratic Party through the late 1960s and early 1970s, was a bitter partisan but a shrewd judge of Blount's limitations. Some men of wealth and power had enough self-control to be a "prick and maybe act like something else," said Vance. But Blount "doesn't know how to get on the common man's level." Vance added caustically: "He doesn't want to. He's an arrogant prig."[62]

IN March 1970, Wallace officially launched his campaign with a thirty-one-point program that promised both increased expenditures for state services *and* lower taxes; a woman in the state cabinet; and a campaign to "rid the state of filthy literature and narcotics."[63] At the same time, he began groping for the issues that would mobilize the faithful. After military prosecutors charged twenty-six-year-old Army Lt. William Calley with commanding a unit responsible for the execution of more than one hundred Vietnamese civilians, candidate Wallace hustled over to the stockade in Fort Benning, Georgia, to express his solidarity with Calley and to complain that "every time a soldier seeks out the enemy, he will be tried for murder." There probably hadn't been a massacre, said Wallace, but if there had, "anyone killed is a direct result of the North invading South Vietnam."[64]

Few constituents seemed to see the Calley case as a burning issue in Alabama's gubernatorial campaign. Throughout February and into March, Wallace experimented with new lines of attack. He tossed barbs at his opponent for lining up with the "outside militants from Detroit and Atlanta and Chicago." In one speech he suggested that Brewer and Judge Frank Johnson were in cahoots; in another he linked his old legislative floor leader with Richard Nixon. Although the crowds were large and occasionally as enthusiastic as in the old days, reporters—particularly those who secretly longed for a Wallace comeuppance—began to note an uncharacteristic coolness.

When he paid a brief visit to the University of Alabama campus, a noisy group of students calling themselves "Weirdos for Wallace" greeted him with whistles and cheers. As he began recounting steps taken by his administration to improve education in Alabama, a male cheerleader in a suit and horn-rimmed glasses led a rousing chant: "We're No. 50. . . . We're No. 50. . . . We're No. 50,"—a not-so-subtle reminder that Alabama ranked toward the bottom of the nation in support of higher education. Wallace abruptly ended his speech and stalked off the stage.[65]

Brewer underwent an astonishing metamorphosis. No one could ever accuse him of being a spellbinder, but—buoyed by support from newspapers, business and labor leaders, and college students from across the state—he began bringing his audiences to their feet with the slogan "Full time for Alabama," and the decidedly unsexy rhetoric of aggressive competence, honest government, and an "open door for all Alabama's citizens" (an oblique reference to his willingness to listen to the complaints of the state's black voters). A Huntsville civic center crowd of four thousand—with several hundred black supporters scattered through it—interrupted him again and again with outbursts of applause and chants of "Brewer . . .

Brewer . . ."[66] At the University of Alabama, several thousand students welcomed their governor with a series of roaring ovations that left the self-contained Brewer almost overcome with emotion. It was a "tremendous experience . . . a happening," he recalled. "I won't *ever* forget it."[67]

On March 10, Postmaster General Blount was driven to the White House for a long meeting with the President and John Ehrlichman. The upcoming legislation revamping the postal service occupied the first few minutes of their discussion, but most of the ninety-minute session focused on one issue: the Alabama gubernatorial race and the possibility of financial support for the Brewer campaign.

Blount outlined the encouraging news from home. A poll taken by Oliver Quayle in January in Alabama's Second Congressional District—strong Wallace country—showed incumbent Governor Brewer with an eight-point lead. The postmaster general had also learned that a secret Wallace survey based on interviews with six hundred likely Democratic primary voters gave Brewer an astonishing fifty-three-to-thirty-four-percent lead, a figure made even bleaker for Wallace by the fact that two-thirds of his supporters were low-income whites, who traditionally turned out in smaller numbers.[68] But with the first primary face-off two months away, Brewer was running out of money.

Nixon outlined a public relations campaign to get out the word to Alabamians that his administration would be responsive to the incumbent's efforts to sidestep further integration. As the meeting drew to a close, he instructed chief of staff H. R. Haldeman to talk with Blount "re money needed."[69] The Nixon reelection campaign kitty bulged with cash collected and squirreled away before the Campaign Reform Act of 1970; through his personal attorney, Herbert Kalmbach, the President had access to millions of dollars in slush funds including $1.9 million in cash (mostly hundred-dollar bills) in one safe-deposit box alone.[70] The only real danger was public disclosure of his administration's involvement in the race.

Two days later, when a Brewer poll confirmed that the governor's three-to-two lead over Wallace was holding, Blount called the White House.[71]

Even with the good news from Alabama, Nixon hesitated. Gut instinct told him that Wallace could not be cornered on his home turf, but two national voter surveys in mid-March tipped the balance. While the Alabama ex-governor's nationwide strength was down to twelve percent, he still held the allegiance of one out of three southern voters, said the Gallup poll. Of those, more than eighty percent named Nixon as their second choice over any Democrat.[72] On March 19 the syndicated political column by Rowland Evans and Robert Novak was headlined: "Wallace Appears to Be in Trouble in Race for Alabama Governor"; the results of their unscientific polling of a number of working-class communities in Alabama indicated surprising support for

Brewer in former Wallace strongholds. Two hours after the *Washington Post* arrived at the White House, Nixon sat in the Oval Office for his regular morning meeting with his chief of staff. In the yellow tablet on which he carefully recorded presidential commands, Haldeman tersely summarized Nixon's decision: "Forward with Brewer."[73] That night, Haldeman wrote in his diary that the President, encouraged by the polls, was willing to put in $100,000.[74]

Within twenty-four hours, Blount phoned Albert Brewer and explained that he could "raise some money for the campaign."[75] Brewer was not naïve; he assumed that the funds were coming from wealthy Republican contributors anxious to help the President by using a proxy to defeat his southern rival. He asked his press secretary, Bob Ingram, to fly to Washington to confer with Blount about details of the transfer of funds. The governor emphasized that he did not know "how much it was nor how it had been raised."[76] And he made it clear that the less he knew the better.

By this time, rumors were rife around Montgomery that Republicans intended quietly to support Brewer; Ingram had heard that funds might be coming from a group of Canadian contractors who were bidding on a new highway tunnel to be built in Mobile.[77] As he flew to Washington on March 23, he read still another Evans and Novak column reporting the administration's critical interest in the outcome of the Alabama race, and a second story reporting the Wallace campaign's charges that Nixon planned to spend $700,000 to defeat him.[78] Comfortably settled in Blount's Watergate complex apartment that Sunday evening, Ingram, tongue in cheek, expressed his gratitude for the promise of $700,000.

"You'll be lucky if you get ten percent of that," snorted his stone-faced host.[79]

Two days after the Blount-Ingram meeting, Nixon gave the final approval to Haldeman: "Blount—100 G for Brewer. Move on this."[80]

Ingram, a longtime writer and columnist for the *Montgomery Advertiser,* had signed on with Brewer after the death of Lurleen Wallace. He had been around; he had no illusions about the connections between business and politics. But when Brewer outlined the plan for the pickup of funds the first of April in New York City, alarm bells began to go off. Ingram was to go to the Sherry Netherland Hotel at 11:45 A.M. A man holding a briefcase in his lap would be seated in the lobby. "I was to approach him and ask: 'Are you Mr. Jensen of Baltimore?' "

His contact would reply, "No, I'm Mr. Jensen of Detroit."

Ingram checked into his hotel and began his walk down to the Sherry Netherland, imagining himself wandering through a huge hotel lobby—it would be filled with dozens of men gripping their obligatory briefcases—mumbling, "Are you Mr. Jensen . . . ?" Fortunately, the Sherry Netherland, a residential hotel, had only a small lobby occupied by a tall man with a "dour expression on his face," clutching a very expensive leather briefcase.

" 'Are you Mr. Jensen from Baltimore?' I asked, trying to keep a straight face," Ingram later recalled.

"No, I am Mr. Jensen of Detroit," snapped Herbert Kalmbach. If the White House contact man found the use of a code amusing, said Ingram, he managed to conceal his hilarity.

"Where's your briefcase?" demanded Kalmbach.

"I didn't bring one," admitted a suddenly panicky Ingram. "I figured you would give me that one."

Kalmbach fixed a contemptuous glare on the stocky Ingram.

"I'm not about to give you my briefcase," he snapped. The lawyer flipped the leather case open enough to give a glimpse of the stacks of hundred-dollar bills removed that morning from the Nixon-controlled safe-deposit box at New York's Chase Manhattan Bank, then pulled a frayed manila envelope from the briefcase pocket and began jamming the money inside.

Ingram looked around. Standing no more than twenty feet away, a half-dozen waiters from the hotel restaurant ("everyone looking like the Mafia"), watched intently. "I sensed that every one of them . . . [was] already contemplating how they would take that envelope from me and dispose of my body."[81]

Kalmbach shoved the envelope into Ingram's hand and stalked out of the hotel. As Brewer's press secretary rushed out of the hotel and crossed the street, a taxi nearly ran him down. For a moment, said Ingram, the future flashed before him—he saw himself lying on the pavement, the manila envelope ripped open, and hundreds of hundred-dollar bills floating down the street toward Central Park.

On the same day that Nixon authorized the cash transfer for Brewer he moved on a second front against his Alabama nemesis. H. R. Haldeman asked Clark Mollenhoff, former investigative reporter and now special counsel to the President, for a report on the status of an ongoing Internal Revenue Service investigation into charges of corruption in the Wallace administration; the charges focused specifically on the activities of the former governor's brother Gerald.

Richard Nixon always complained that, despite his reputation, he did not invent the practice of using the nation's tax system to harass political enemies. During the Roosevelt and Kennedy administrations in particular, representatives of the executive branch had abused the tax system by triggering politically motivated audits. But if Nixon and his staff did not invent intimidation by audit, they raised it to an art form. Shortly after he assumed office, recalled Nixon, he learned that the IRS had performed routine audits of John

Wayne and Billy Graham, and he had "hit the ceiling." "Get the word out down to the IRS," he instructed his White House assistants, "I want them to conduct field audits of those who are our opponents, if they're going to do in our friends."[82]

In July 1969, White House assistant Tom Huston pressured the IRS into forming the so-called Special Services Staff, designed to target and investigate leftist political individuals and organizations. By 1970 the SSS had compiled an "enemies list" of more than a thousand institutions and four thousand individuals, prime targets for harassment by audit.[83] Many of the individuals targeted by Nixon-initiated tax probes were innocent victims of hardball politics. George Wallace, his brother, and many of his supporters were guilty victims of hardball politics.

By early spring of 1970, IRS investigators were convinced that they were on the trail of serious illegalities in a half-dozen areas, from illegal campaign financing to kickbacks that state contractors gave to Wallace cronies. And the biggest crony of all was Gerald Wallace, who, investigators suspected, had repeatedly taken bribes and failed to report them as income. Assistant IRS Commissioner Roger Bacon sent Clark Mollenhoff a brief summary investigation; he emphasized that his staff had not yet assembled enough hard evidence to convene a grand jury.

On March 20, hours after Mollenhoff told H. R. Haldeman that he had received a preliminary IRS report, the President's counsel answered a telephone call from one of Nixon's hatchet men, Murray Chotiner, demanding a copy of the report. Chotiner, said Mollenhoff, was a "likeable scoundrel," but a scoundrel nevertheless. He knew from conversations with Haldeman that Chotiner had a "special arrangement" to make inside White House information available to selected columnists like Jack Anderson. Mollenhoff refused to hand over the confidential report.

Within minutes, Haldeman called and demanded his compliance. Increasingly apprehensive, Mollenhoff balked. He asked that the President personally authorize Chotiner's access to the records; Haldeman haughtily replied that when he called "it was always for the President." Mollenhoff forwarded the report to Haldeman.[84]

Three weeks later, in his April 13 "Washington Merry-Go-Round" column (syndicated in more than three hundred newspapers), Jack Anderson published a synopsis of the IRS allegations against Gerald Wallace and his friends. Reprints of the Anderson piece soon filled Alabama newspapers.[85] As Mollenhoff had suspected, Haldeman had passed on the report to Chotiner, who in turn handed it over to the muckraking columnist. And, as everyone at the White House knew, H. R. Haldeman did not sneeze without making sure he had the President's approval.[86] An angry Gerald Wallace admitted he was under investigation and blamed it all on Richard Nixon.

"Why did they wait until three weeks before the election to publish them [the preliminary audit reports]?" he asked. "The reason is obvious—politics of the dirtiest sort."[87] But the leak of the IRS files was so heavy-handed, so obviously a White House–engineered operation, it backfired in Alabama. In the meantime, George Wallace had finally found the spark to ignite his flagging gubernatorial campaign.

LATE March and early April 1970 had been the low point for the candidate and his badly shaken advisers. The Anderson column had come fresh on the heels of a series of articles in the *Montgomery Advertiser* describing with specific detail the widespread abuse of government agencies by the Wallace administration in 1963 and 1964.[88] Aides found their boss depressed and withdrawn; for several days, said one friend, "George was so down in the dumps . . . he wouldn't leave his house to campaign for the runoff."[89] Instead of the dependable trio—Cecil Jackson, Seymore Trammell, and Bill Jones—who had guided him through the 1960s, he had been forced to rely on his brothers, and on Taylor Hardin, a former Army officer and businessman who had served as adjutant general in his first administration. Wallace had always "run scared," but the most recent polls only confirmed the bleak reports he had been getting from around the state. One capitol secretary who knew the former governor only casually was stunned when she received an after-midnight telephone call. "He was obviously depressed, scared, calling himself defeated, grasping for someone to talk to. . . . It was pathetic."[90]

But the secret survey of Alabama voters Wallace had commissioned in January had showed that though Brewer was more popular, a substantial number of working-class and rural voters were fearful that his administration would be "soft on integration."[91] During the final month of the campaign a blitz of television and radio commercials and hard-hitting speeches focused almost entirely on the issue of race. Wallace denounced Brewer as a "sissy britches" politician who "used to stand on this platform behind me and my wife . . . who rode her skirttails to power [and now has] joined together with black militants to defeat me." He pleaded with white voters to "save Alabama as you know Alabama." Should Brewer win, warned Wallace, the state would be ruled by a "spotted alliance" of blacks and "sissy britches from Harvard who spend most of their time in a country club drinking tea with their finger stuck up."[92]

As the first primary results came in on May 5, his desperate attacks appeared to have failed. Brewer had not captured a majority of the votes, but he was the front-runner, leading Wallace 422,000 to 414,000, with 180,000 votes divided among the other five candidates. (Asa Carter, Wallace's old Klan speechwriter, drew 15,000 votes.) For Brewer, the prize was in sight; no twentieth-century gubernatorial candidate in Alabama had ever come back to win after placing second in the primary. A frantic Blount called Nixon aide Lawrence Higby and passed on rumors that H. L. Hunt had thrown a half-million dollars into the Wallace campaign. He pleaded with the White House for an additional $300,000 for Brewer's runoff campaign.[93] After consulting with Nixon, Haldeman passed on a typically terse set of instructions to Higby. "OK," he said. "Call Kalmbach and set it up."[94]

Ingram flatly refused to serve as bagman a second time, so Brewer enlisted James R. (Jim Bob) Solomon, a mid-level state official and loyal supporter trusted for his honesty and integrity. Solomon flew to New York, where H. R. Haldeman's brother-in-law, France Raine, handed over $200,000—again in the lobby of the Sherry Netherland. Back in Alabama, Solomon dumped the money into the hands of State Representative Drexel Cook of Elba, Alabama, another Brewer supporter. When Mrs. Cook opened her refrigerator and found two thousand hundred-dollar bills neatly stacked in the vegetable hydrator, she panicked and demanded that her husband get the money out of the house. For more than a week, Brewer's aides juggled the stash, uncertain as to just how they were going to launder nearly a quarter of a million dollars. Finally the governor's staff deposited the cash directly into one of the accounts they used to pay for radio and television ads.[95]

By the time Solomon rendezvoused with Kalmbach in mid-May at the Los Angeles Bank of California to pick up the last $100,000, procedures were down pat. But the state bureaucrat lacked the sangfroid of a 007. Obsessed with the fear that his plane might crash and his wife be disgraced, he pinned a note to his underwear explaining that the $100,000 in untaxed cash in his briefcase was for the Brewer campaign.[96]

Ultimately the $400,000 furnished nearly a third of Brewer's campaign budget, but not even these infusions of presidential cash could save him. Wallace pulled out the stops with a reckless disregard for the image—non-racist defender of states' rights—that he had cultivated in the 1968 presidential contest. On the night of his brother's loss in the first primary, Gerald Wallace had stood in campaign headquarters and watched intently as Brewer's lead steadily increased. "What are you going to do now?" UPI correspondent Tony Heffernan had asked. Gerald Wallace smiled self-confidently. "We'll just throw the niggers around his neck."[97]

He was as good as his word. By all accounts, the run-off two weeks later hit a low point even for Deep South race-baiting. Tom Turnipseed, who had once been given a firsthand lesson from South Carolina's Strom Thurmond in how to print and distribute "unofficial" campaign tabloids ("or 'hate sheets,' as we jokingly called it") remembered the grim meeting that kicked off the final phase of the campaign. Wallace issued no detailed battle plan, said Turnipseed. He just looked around the table and said: "You've gotta do what needs to be done."[98] Off the record, another aide spelled out the strategy to a reporter: "Promise them the moon and holler 'Nigger.' "[99]

The underground campaign became a raw sewer as thousands of "unau-thorized" leaflets poured into rural and small-town Alabama and into the working-class districts of Mobile, Montgomery, and Birmingham. One dis-tributed statewide showed a photograph of Brewer supposedly meeting with Cassius Clay (soon to be Muhammad Ali) and Black Muslim leader Elijah Muhammad. (The governor's press secretary quickly recognized a Brewer photo op with singer Johnny Cash and his agent. Skilled Wallace operatives had superimposed pictures of Clay and Muhammad.) Another broadside, released by a Selma-based Wallace committee, headlined: "WAKE UP, ALABAMA! BLACKS VOW TO TAKE OVER ALABAMA," and showed a beautiful, blond five- or six-year-old girl wearing only her bathing trunks and seated on a beach, surrounded by seven smiling black boys. The caption read: "This Could Be Alabama Four Years From Now! Do You Want It?"[100]

Faced with a choice between his former boss and the man he labeled the state's "number one white nigger," Carter reenlisted with Wallace. His Klan splinter group distributed, among other scurrilous materials, a fake photo-graph of Brewer's two daughters which purported to show them pregnant by black men.[101]

At the same time, the incumbent's campaign found itself the target of relentless sabotage. Martha Brewer, an attractive and effective spokesperson, traveled throughout the state from March through May, targeting women's groups and representing her husband when he faced scheduling conflicts. On at least a half-dozen occasions, a distraught "aide" would arrive just minutes after she had left, asking worriedly, "Was she okay? . . . I mean, she wasn't slurring or anything, was she?"[102]

Late in the campaign, members of a hastily formed group called Women for Wallace telephoned nursing homes around the state, claimed to repre-sent Brewer's office, and arranged visits from Mrs. Brewer. "You know how it is at a place like this," said the director of one home in Birmingham. "The women got themselves all gussied up and we even planned to sing, 'For she's a jolly good fellow.' " Of course Mrs. Brewer never showed.[103]

Gone was the coyness of Wallace's earlier references to the fact that black voters supported Albert Brewer. The governor was now the "tool of black militants" who would turn the state over to black revolutionaries. After black leader John Cashin demanded that Brewer endorse the hiring of at least fifty black highway patrolmen, there appeared this Wallace radio ad: ominous music, the sound of a police siren, and then the pitch: "Suppose your wife is driving home at 11 o'clock at night. She is stopped by a highway patrolman. He turns out to be black. Think about it. . . . Elect George C. Wallace."[104]

As he cranked up the race issue, the challenger subtly linked the age-old cry of "Nigger, nigger" with a devastating attack on Brewer's runoff alliance of blacks and upper-middle-class white voters. Tom Turnipseed remembered a night in Opelika, Alabama, late in the campaign when Wallace seemed to "take flight." Standing on the back of a flatbed Ford truck, he warned of the dangers of black rule and again lashed out at the "spotted alliance": the newspaper reporters in their ivory towers; the well-to-do whites who had joined hands with blacks to support his opponent.

"They look down their noses and call us peapickers, and peckerwoods and lint heads and rednecks." Well, Wallace snarled, "let them call us rednecks if they mean our necks might be red from a good honest day's toil in the summer sun!" The decent working-class people of Alabama—those whose "fierce contact with life" had taught them the realities of struggle and work and survival—would not be deceived.

"You all ever heard of Mountain Brook?" Wallace asked listeners, his voice dripping with sarcasm. "Mountain Brook's a lily-white town . . . where the rich folks live in the suburbs up across the mountain from Birmingham." The men who worked there drove downtown in their "chauffeur-driven limousines and they go on back to Mountain Brook to the big old houses . . . and they go on up there to the . . . Mountain Brook Country Club, and they'll sit up there and sip on those martinis with their little fingers up in the air . . ."

Wallace paused and held up his little finger in a mincing imitation.

". . . and they say"—his voice became simpering—" 'Oh, we must have progress, we must have school integration.' " His voice suddenly harsh and angry: "And guess where their children go to school? They go to a lily-white private school. They've bought above it all!"[105]

Although Brewer complained of the "gutter politics" of his opponent, he made a fatal decision to "hug the ground and pray," to wait for a backlash among voters against Wallace's crude racial appeals, said one of his aides. Any effort to respond to the race-baiting would only keep the issue front and center, insisted the governor.[106]

On election morning, June 2, a tense Wallace made one last dash through his home county to rally the faithful. "Now don't let them niggers beat us, you hear?" he greeted a supporter out rounding up last-minute votes. And he warned Barbour County tax assessor Stanley Baker, "If I don't win, the niggers are going to control this state."[107]

He need not have worried. In the end, the election became a referendum on Alabama voters' admiration for macho politicians *and* their fear of blacks. Harold Martin, publisher of the *Montgomery Advertiser* and a strong Brewer partisan, commissioned a poll shortly after the election to probe the source of Wallace's support. "Even his enemies put he's a racist or he's a dictator and then over on the back part where it says what do you admire about him, they would put in there: 'We admire the way he fights for what he thinks is right.' " That was ultimately the decisive factor in tipping the balance against Brewer, said Martin: "He wouldn't fight."[108]

A jubilant Wallace hailed his followers as they gathered in a downtown hotel and watched his majority steadily climb from twenty thousand to twenty-five and eventually to thirty thousand votes. As expected, Brewer overwhelmingly carried black voting precincts around the state and did well in upper-middle-class and upper-income districts. But the real story of the election was the turnout in rural and small-town Alabama and in the white working-class districts of the state. Even in the relatively "progressive" northern half of the state around Florence, Huntsville, and Decatur, the race magic had worked. Wallace tweaked the national reporters who had been cautiously predicting a Brewer win. With a sly dig at Richard Nixon he explained that had he lost, "I was gonna say in my concession speech, 'Well, I won't have y'all [newsmen] to kick around any more.' "[109] He insisted that he had no hard feelings toward his opponent. "I consider Gov. Brewer and his family my personal friends and I wish him success in whatever future endeavor he is involved in. I say that sincerely."[110]

At his campaign headquarters Brewer greeted dispirited followers and offered the usual gracious thanks to campaign aides and his loyal family. He knew the rules of Alabama politics: no matter how despicable the tactics and methods of an opponent, voters did not like "sore losers." But when he sat down with a sympathetic CBS interviewer and was asked about the personal attacks on his wife and daughters, he could no longer contain his bitterness. "It was nigger, nigger, nigger, all over again," he said, his face a mask of anger. "I hoped race wouldn't become an issue in this campaign, but it boiled down to a hate and smear issue. And if that's what it takes to win, the cost is too high."[111]

Six months later, longtime Wallace adviser John Kohn expressed regrets for his role in urging Wallace to use "racist" tactics against Brewer, whom he described as an "honest . . . self-made man and a gentleman." Added Kohn: "I am not proud of my participation in a racist-type campaign. . . . I make a public apology."[112]

George Wallace never did.

THE first significant returns did not reach Washington until nearly eleven P.M. Richard Nixon called his chief southern strategist for details. When Dent explained that returns were fragmentary, Nixon asked for the vote from several Jefferson County precincts. When Dent gave him the figures, the President called the results. The gamble had failed. "Get some sleep, and have a full report on my desk by 7 A.M.," he ordered.[113]

Nixon tried to take heart from the Alabama governor's bruising victory. "Wallace poses problems to our Dem. friends"; he would "force them further left," Nixon told Haldeman in his post-election analysis. And he would be weaker nationally because his campaign was "*pure* racist—[he] avoided that in '68."[114] But—as was often the case when Nixon was dealing with Wallace—this upbeat assessment reflected wishful thinking. Even though the national media focused almost all their coverage of the gubernatorial contest on Wallace's shameless race-baiting, a post-election Gallup poll showed that the Alabamian's "highly favorable" rating among national voters had *increased* to fourteen percent from ten per cent the previous year.[115]

The New Yorker's Washington correspondent, Richard Rovere, exaggerated only slightly when he argued that the Nixon administration would "gladly have traded off a defeat for Wallace in Alabama for just about any political or legislative victory they have lately sought." The new governor was a disaster for the Democrats in Alabama, and, in the long run, a corrosive force within the national party. So long as Wallace remained a third-party candidate, however, he was a dagger pointed at the heart of a Nixon reelection bid. "In 1972, the Democrats will not have to explain away Lyndon Johnson or make any defense of the war; they will be free to blame the Republicans for everything that has gone wrong," argued Rovere. If Democrats recaptured the big industrial states and Wallace took the Deep South, Nixon would find it difficult to put together his electoral majority. Wallace had established an "awesome and disquieting presence in national politics." The once and future governor of Alabama "may turn out to be a larger figure in American history than he has ever dreamed of being."[116]

In his first post-election memo, Harry Dent warned that Wallace would soon begin gearing up for the 1972 race, and he would be able to "show statistically that the Nixon Administration has done far more to bring about desegregation in the South than the Democrats." At the same time, Dent predicted, Wallace, remembering the lessons of his 1968 campaign, would move beyond the race question to fan the winds of discontent on a broad range of issues: inflation, high taxes, and the rising crime rate.[117]

Patrick Buchanan, Nixon's right-wing conscience, agreed. Wallace, said Buchanan, had discovered the "social issues"—"drugs, demonstrations, pornography, disruptions, 'kidlash,' permissiveness, violence, riots, crime." Unless the President preempted the Alabama governor's agenda, Wallace would "take seven million votes from Nixon and three million from the Democrat," in a repeat of the 1968 campaign.[118] Buchanan urged the President to go all-out for the Wallace vote and to take a hard-line conservative position, even to the extent of admitting that his administration had made mistakes in carrying out school-desegregation plans.

The Wallace victory reinforced Nixon's drift to the right. The "mixing of the races" in the nation's schools was "about as wise as compulsory mixing of Greeks and Turks on the island of Cypress," the President told his aides. Integration should not be "forced upon them [Americans] or their children."[119] The White House staff had been "affected too much by the unreal atmosphere of the D.C. press, social and intellectual set." Wallace was on the right track: "emphasize anti-crime, anti-demonstrations, anti-drugs, anti-obscenity. We must get with the mood of the country which is fed up with the liberals."[120] While his administration would try to ease the tensions of court-ordered school desegregation in the South by offering federal aid and mediation, Nixon told Haldeman, everyone had to understand that "everything we do, all decisions and statements, must consider first their effect on [the election in] November."[121]

But Richard Nixon could never bring himself to admit that the strutting little ex-boxer from Alabama was playing him like a marionette; the President's southern strategist understood that part of his boss's personality better than Buchanan. And so, even as Dent outlined a variety of suggestions for coping with the Wallace threat, from playing down desegregation measures in the region to arranging a series of appearances in the region by Nixon, Agnew, and John Mitchell, he emphasized that it was essential that Wallace "be ignored on his statements and challenges. To do otherwise would be submitting to political blackmail."[122]

"I agree," scrawled Nixon on the memo, and then promptly began to follow a strategy which seemed suspiciously responsive to Wallace's statements, challenges, and "political blackmail." Now came the ill-fated Supreme Court nominations of southern conservatives Clement Haynsworth and G. Harrold Carswell, and the purging of key HEW liberals like Nixon's old friend HEW secretary Bob Finch, and of Leon Panetta, director of the Office for Civil Rights. Finch was allowed the dignity of a face-saving retreat to a powerless position on the White House staff, but Nixon subjected Panetta to a publicly humiliating ouster.[123]

In April 1970, when Democratic senators (with the help of a handful of moderate Republicans) managed to block the nominations of Haynsworth and Carswell, the chief executive turned the issue to his advantage. To place a southerner on the court who was a strict constructionist would be impossible, he angrily told reporters at the White House. "When you strip away all the hypocrisy," said Nixon, the "real reason for their rejection was their legal philosophy . . . [and] the accident of their birth." He could well understand the "bitter feeling of millions of Americans who live in the South about the act of regional discrimination that took place in the Senate"; never again would he "nominate another Southerner and let him be subjected to the kind of malicious character assassination accorded both Judges Haynsworth and Carswell."[124]

His statement was fifty percent nonsense. While Haynsworth was qualified for the court, Nixon's own aide Bryce Harlow had pointed out that Republicans as well as Democrats opposed Harrold Carswell for his demonstrated record of incompetence and racism. "They think he's a boob, a dummy," said Harlow. "And what counter is there to that? He is."[125] But the President's appeal to white southerners' sense of victimization was a superb variation on the theme that Wallace had exploited so well; Nixon's popularity in the region jumped sharply.

By the fall of 1970, only the most dim-witted political observers could fail to see the shift in the President's policies. He soon hit the road campaigning for Republican candidates in the off-year elections and, in a series of arm-waving, shouting speeches, linked the Democrats with lawless, foul-mouthed antiwar demonstrators, crime in the streets, the rise of pornography in America, and the mindless bureaucrats who would "bus children clear across town to achieve an arbitrary racial balance."[126] Although conservative Republicans following the Nixon line won in two well-publicized senatorial races, and the President claimed an ideological victory when conservative Democrats replaced more liberal opponents in other races, voters across the nation responded coolly to many of his charges. The mindless bureaucrats condemned by Nixon were, after all, *his* mindless bureaucrats.

Adviser Ray Price shrewdly put his finger on the fatal flaw in the President's efforts to outdo Wallace at his own rhetorical game. Voters instinctively recoiled from the image of the strident Nixon, the same man who had promised to "bring us together" in 1968. The one strong card held by Democrat Edmund Muskie—Nixon's likely opponent—was the Maine senator's appeal to a national yearning for stability and calm. The "trick for us [Nixon's team] is to play it first, and better: to persuade the people that we can calm the passions."[127]

If the implementation of the strategy was flawed—and two years later Nixon did not repeat his error in trying to "out-Wallace" the Alabama governor on the stump—the President never doubted the political advantages of his conservative tilt. As Nixon looked ahead to 1972, he ordered his aides to review domestic issues, "scrape away all the crap and just pick three issues that will give us a sharp image." They "shouldn't be concerned if it is something we will actually accomplish," he announced ("JFK was doing all of his progress building on phony issues"). "Rather, we should look in terms of how we create issues. We need an enemy."[128]

The Family Assistance Plan had been Richard Nixon's centerpiece program for solving the crisis of a racially divided America. As the off-year congressional elections approached, Moynihan pleaded with the President to throw his support behind the FAP, which had passed the House but was bottled up in the Senate by a coalition of liberal Democrats and conservative Republicans. It was now or never, argued Moynihan. What Moynihan did not know was that Nixon had already decided his bold gambit was a mistake. Privately, he told Haldeman to make a "big play for the plan," but to "be sure it's killed by [the] Democrats." Whatever happened, said Nixon, they could not let it pass.[129] The Family Assistance Plan died a quiet death in the Congress, though its corpse stayed around for another year and a half. In April 1972, when a cabinet member asked what should be done about the proposal, "Flush it," Nixon replied with a shrug. "Blame it on the Budget," he said as he went on to other issues.[130]

His withdrawal of support for the Family Assistance Plan was one of those little-noticed turning points in Nixon's heretofore moderate approach toward issues of race, welfare, and economics. In the final analysis the President's bold departure in federal policy was less a victim of the budget than of the growing racial tensions in American society and the need to maintain the Republican base within the South and among those conservatives outside the region who would eventually be described as Reagan Democrats. Nixon continued to preface his remarks on social and racial issues with a formulaic rejection of the "extremists of the left" and the "extremists of the right," but in his rhetoric and in his policies, the drift was to the right. The President who had promised to "bring us together" would develop a political campaign which emphasized his commitment to containing welfare costs, his opposition to busing, quotas, and affirmative action (including the repudiation of many of the programs begun by his own administration), and the theme that the Democratic Party was out of touch with mainstream values in American society.

Speechwriters should prepare "uplifting" lines which "direct attention to the hopes and dreams that unite us rather than the hates and fears that divide us," he instructed H. R. Haldeman. But then, recalled his aide, he "shifted into his regular spiel on the thing that people don't love each other and we're not all the same and we can't approach things on that basis." The whole "secret and philosophy" of their political strategy had to be based on a recognition of the deep and corrosive differences among Americans.[131] Kevin Phillips had it right the first time. Who hates whom: "That is the secret."

As Dent had predicted, Alabama's governor-elect once again hit the southern speakers' circuit with Richard Nixon as his primary target. Voters, said Wallace, had supported the Republican because of his promise to embrace a true "freedom-of-choice" program which would end the "uncertainty, doubt, confusion and frustration" created by the Johnson administration. After two years it was obvious that the President had retreated to a "chorus of confusing platitudes" while he presided over an "all-out onslaught to force integration regardless of the consequences." Although Nixon extended the olive branch in his public statements on integration, his "HEW bureaucrats use every tactic existing to ram their guidelines down our throats."[132] Wallace, said one Alabama editor, had outdone the South's most famous dem-

agogue, Huey Long. Long had promised to make "Every Man a King. . . .
George would not only make every man a king, but would also make all his
supporters members of a regicidal lynching bee."[133]

In mid-July Nixon sat down with his ever-present yellow legal pad and
outlined the next stage of his political strategy. At the top of the page he
wrote and underlined: "Need to Handle Wallace."[134] Jack Anderson's attack
on their governor and his problems with the IRS had not fazed Alabama
voters; an indictment and trial of George or Gerald Wallace was something
else. The President began pressing his staff to accelerate the investigation.
While IRS commissioner Randolph Thrower was a stickler for maintaining
his agency's independence from the White House, he now agreed that the
initial investigation justified an increase in resources. By August 1970 more
than seventy-five men and women were examining returns in what John
Mitchell's Justice Department dubbed the Alabama Project. Agents pored
over the past tax returns of Wallace, his brothers, and virtually every financial
supporter who had done business with the state. They examined the records
of state agencies as well, in an attempt to link the awarding of state contracts
to political contributions.[135]

From Franklin Roosevelt through Lyndon Johnson, IRS investigations
which involved high-level political figures (particularly opponents) had always drawn special attention from the White House, but rarely had the
stakes been higher. Even if the Alabama Project turned up nothing on George
Wallace, a successful prosecution of his brother for political corruption could
embarrass and potentially destroy the governor. Attorney General Mitchell,
Nixon's closest friend and one of the few advisers in whom he placed
absolute trust, appointed Will Wilson, head of the Criminal Justice Divison,
to oversee the inquiry and to protect White House interests. The Wallace
investigation was one of a number of politically sensitive cases managed for
Nixon by the sixty-four-year-old Wilson, who had a long and colorful career
in Texas politics—spent mostly as a conservative Democrat—as a state Supreme Court justice, state attorney general, and senior partner in an influential Dallas law firm. Despite his successful organization of the Kennedy-
Johnson campaign in Texas in 1960, he ran afoul of Lyndon Johnson in a
typical Texas-style clash of egos and ambitions; after he backed Goldwater
in 1964, he was finished with the Democratic Party and cut off from any
future political options in his home state.

When Richard Nixon named Wilson to head the criminal-justice division of
the Justice Department, he dangled a prize the Texan had coveted since
serving on his own state's high court: a seat on the U.S. Supreme Court.
Wilson proved a loyal Nixon soldier. In the early spring of 1970 when the
President tried to force aging justice William O. Douglas off the court, Wilson
was the man who furnished Gerald Ford with the necessary derogatory

information. (Wilson later complained that "Ford took the material we gave him and screwed it up. Ford blew it.")[136]

Unlike Mitchell, who had jousted only with fellow bond-market lawyers before joining the Nixon cabinet, Wilson was a battle-hardened veteran of three decades of Texas political wars. His broad background in civil and criminal law and his unwavering loyalty to Nixon made him an ideal choice to shepherd the Wallace project to a successful conclusion. As the investigation continued into the fall of 1970, Wilson and his assistant William Sessions (later head of the Federal Bureau of Investigation) conferred almost weekly with federal prosecutors and IRS investigators in Montgomery. In turn, Wilson passed along his findings and recommendations to assistant attorney general Richard Kleindienst and his boss, John Mitchell.[137]

If the Alabama Project offered great promise, it carried equally dangerous risks. Ira DeMent, U.S. attorney for the Middle District of Alabama, recused himself from the day-to-day operation of the case because he had earlier represented Seymore Trammell, a prime target in the investigation. But he kept in constant touch through his assistant, Broward Segrest, the prosecutor in charge of assembling the evidence. Initial reports from IRS investigators convinced Segrest and DeMent that they had the potential for a crippling case against the Wallace administration. But as DeMent frankly acknowledged, "In 'political' cases, I was always willing to accept direction—unless it was a heinous crime or there was clear-cut evidence of abuse of justice." And tax cases were by their very nature "political."[138] Segrest, too, knew that there was no way to avoid weighing political considerations in the conduct of the investigation. If both were practical politicians as well as prosecutors, however, each had established a reputation for integrity. The line between "direction" and control was a fine one, but it existed in their minds. They had no intention of throwing overboard a solid case against Wallace, for Richard Nixon or for anyone else.[139]

Alabama's state government had a long tradition of financial kickbacks and outright corruption between contractors and political leaders. During his eight years in office, Big Jim Folsom cheerfully acknowledged his affection for what he called the "emoluments of office," and his administration was remembered for petty (and sometimes not-so-petty) graft.[141] Neither Folsom nor Wallace seems to have personally benefited in a significant way from the flow of funds (though one of Wallace's aides from the 1960s acknowledged that a little money might have slipped into the governor's pocket occasionally—"nothing big.")

But when critics accused Folsom of various forms of malfeasance during the 1954 campaign, he answered by mounting a speaker's platform in Mobile and dramatically defending himself with one of the most unusual arguments ever used by a cornered politician. "I plead guilty to stealing. That crowd I got it from, you had to steal. . . . Shore I stole. I stole to build hospitals. I stole to build schools. I stole to build roads." And, pointing at his followers: "I stole for you—and you—and you."[141]

Wallace, in contrast, had promised to appoint an "honest, God-fearing finance director" who would end the "stinking political payoff system" with a strict competitive bidding system for all state contracts.[142] "Every dollar wasted on political payoffs in Alabama takes a dollar away from the old people, the school children, the blind and mentally ill . . ." he told supporters on the eve of his 1962 campaign. "I shall not use the office of governor to make me and my family or political cronies rich. Incorruptible state government will be our source of strength in the future."[143]

Despite his promises, the governor-elect granted his old friend Montgomery businessman Oscar Harper exclusive rights to the "Official Inauguration Program." Assembled by Asa Carter, the glossy three-hundred-page paperback combined profiles and photographs of Wallace and his family with dire warnings that it was thirty minutes to midnight, with white civilization standing on the edge of "disappearance into the vast sea of the world's colored majority."[144] The two-dollar purchase price paid the cost of printing and distribution. Contractors, office suppliers, automobile and truck dealers, insurance agents, engineers, and asphalt dealers who hoped to do business with the state ponied up more than $85,000 for 170 pages of glossy ads—all clear profit for the enterprising Harper, who was known to have the new governor's ear.[145]

Within a few months, Wallace had embraced the Folsom tradition of graft and kickbacks, doubled, tripled, and quadrupled the take, and compounded it all with breathtakingly cynical press releases boasting of reductions in the mansion's liquor fund. Overnight, his old cronies developed expertise in the asphalt business.[146] David Silverman, a jeweler whose Montgomery apartment had been a regular hideaway for the governor's assignations during the 1950s, received checks totaling ten thousand, one hundred dollars from the Tuscaloosa Pre-Mix Company. A decade later, Silverman could not recollect his association with the company until an enterprising reporter refreshed his memory with photostatic copies of two checks documenting his payoff (or "referral fee," as the jeweler preferred to describe it). Even then Silverman "could not recall what services he had performed in return for the fee."[147]

Instead of acting as an agent or buying into a firm, Oscar Harper started up his own company and managed to sell $2.4 million of asphalt to the state highway department. He proved a man of many entrepreneurial talents, spinning off companies at the drop of a state contract. Early in the first Wallace administration, Harper and his brother printed up letterheads for Alastar Office Outfitters. The company sold the state twenty-nine expensive copy machines to be placed in (as yet unbuilt) junior colleges and trade schools and then promptly went out of business. The head of the state education department huffily defended the purchase as an example of good planning and denied the "unfounded accusation" that the copying machines would be outdated by the time the schools were built.[148]

Every state program was subject to a slice for the Wallace political machine and its supporters, from "referral" legal fees tacked onto the quarter of a billion dollars in new bonds, to under-the-table kickbacks from window-sash manufacturers who hoped to bid on the new trade schools and junior colleges, all intertwined with an elaborate system requiring state architects, engineers, and contractors to hire designated "agents" who performed no services and whose only requirement was loyalty to the governor.[149] And when election time for Lurleen Wallace rolled around, businessmen and professionals who did business with the state received serially numbered campaign pledge cards accompanied by a letter of solicitation from the state's purchasing agent. (He was technically "on leave" at the time he signed the letters.) With the numbered cards, the traditional "I gave at the office" alibi disappeared.[150]

After especially embarrassing newspaper exposés, Wallace might dash off a note to agency heads insisting that contractors doing business with the state should not "pay any fee to anyone connected with this Administration—for instance Gerald Wallace."[151] But press secretary Bill Jones bluntly defended the practice of rewarding friends: "Somebody has got to finance the political campaigns, somebody's got to do it."[152] By the mid-1960s, the perpetual Wallace campaign was receiving hundreds of thousands of dollars a year in political paybacks.

In his gaudy heyday in Louisiana politics, Huey Long had sought to maintain the distinction between payoffs for the system and personal graft. Under the Kingfish, the "deduct box" became an integral fixture of Louisiana politics as aides constructed ever more elaborate systems to siphon off money from state contractors to support the Long political machine. Long even countenanced a minimal amount of corruption, "relatively little stuff," said one of his retainers, "enough to make a good living." If the corruption became too widespread, however, the voters would lose confidence in the system, and the political machine would collapse. Large-scale graft was thus "politically immoral."

But there was a thin and often nonexistent line between naked personal greed and raking off a commission for the political machine or even rewarding political contributors who would be expected to return the favor in the next campaign. On the eve of his death in 1935 Long predicted to his secretary that his minions would be "stealing the emblems off the capitol pretty soon."[153] He could have had George Wallace's brother Gerald in mind when he made his prediction.

Gerald Wallace was not a man without virtues. While his brothers Jack and George escaped to Tuscaloosa and followed their careers in law and politics, the dutiful middle son stayed on with his mother and baby sister. For three long years, he walked the dusty roads of Alabama as a lowly "rod man" for the state highway department and shared his meager earnings with Mozelle and Marianne Wallace. His mother was not a demonstrative woman, but when anyone mentioned Gerald, her voice took on an unexpected tenderness. "He was a marvelously loyal son," she told one reporter. He "always made sure Marianne and I were doing okay."[154]

After a stint in the Navy during World War II, Gerald finally had his chance at the University of Alabama, only to collapse from exhaustion. Doctors in Tuscaloosa diagnosed a severe case of tuberculosis. After two lung operations and more than six years of hospitalization in an overcrowded state sanatorium, he returned to the university in the mid-1950s, and in 1958 passed the bar examination. His grades as a law student were excellent, but over the next thirty years no one would ever accuse him of any interest in the grubbier details of a legal practice. Gerald was a fixer.

His blunt embrace of the fast chance and his surly attacks on newsmen soon soured reporters. Their acrid thumbnail portraits ("a weasel-like underweight man with sunken cheeks and a cadaverous complexion") were usually accompanied by thinly veiled accusations of dishonesty. His name seldom appeared without an uncomplimentary qualifying phrase: "influence peddler"; "ghostly presence"; "power behind the throne in the Wallace administration."[155] He would not, he acknowledged to one reporter, describe himself as a "good sweet man." The burden of caring for his family and the long years of hospitalization had left him bitter, cynical, and greedy. George was "interested in political things," said Gerald. "I have always been interested in material things, not only for security reasons . . . it's my nature to be interested in material things."[156]

With his brother in office, new vistas opened. Since Alabama's legislature had never passed ethics legislation, and the state's professional associations (including the bar association) had no restrictions on "referral" fees, a license to practice law, to sell real estate, or to work as an insurance broker offered a perfectly legal way to launder money obtained through influence peddling. By mid-1963, Gerald Wallace was licensed to practice law, to serve as a real estate broker, and to sell life, casualty, and medical insurance. In the first four years of his brother's administration, he officially reported a four hundred percent increase in his income, from less than $30,000 a year to more than $125,000. Such an increase was essential to support a lavish lifestyle which included regular trips to the gambling tables of Las Vegas. (On one December evening, he dropped more than $25,000 playing blackjack at the Tropicana Club.)[157]

The governor's brother periodically defended himself against charges of outright corruption, but Gerald Wallace recognized that slander in small doses was his best advertisement. Who, after all, would want to pay his inflated "legal" fees if he were incapable of peddling influence?

"I couldn't keep Gerald out of the government," complained Seymore Trammell. In 1963, Wallace had appointed his former campaign adviser to the post of state finance director, the most powerful nonelective office in Alabama, which—given his boss's disinterest in detail—made him the de facto administrator of the state government. Dealing with Gerald's shakedown operations, said Trammell, was like trying to douse the efforts of a particularly ingenious pyromaniac. "I would stop whatever he had started, whether an insurance scandal or something . . . and I'd be damned if it wouldn't be a week before [George] Wallace would say: 'Well, I don't believe Gerald's too involved in this, Seymore. And it *does* sound like a good idea.' " That would only mean Gerald had maneuvered his brother into endorsing another one of his get-rich schemes, said Trammell. "Gerald could manipulate everything in the world." Most of all, "he could manipulate George Wallace."[158]

With an investment of three thousand dollars Gerald purchased a quarter-ownership in a Selma asphalt-producing company and promptly began making a sham of the state's bidding process. During his brother's first term as governor, Gerald's company sold $2.9 million worth of asphalt to the state in four Black Belt counties even though it charged a $2.50-per-ton premium over the going price.[159]

When the state paid more than a quarter of a million dollars to Birmingham's most prestigious law firm for handling the paperwork on Alabama's $200 million highway and education bond issues in 1963, the firm's senior partner, Alfred Rose, promptly kicked back sixty thousand dollars to Wallace's speaker of the House, Rankin Fite. Fite had performed no legal services, but Rose was no fool. Neither was Fite. He passed on a third of his share of the boodle to the governor's brother.[160] And when the state decided to offer employees a chance to purchase supplementary life insurance through a payroll checkoff plan, no one in Montgomery was surprised to learn that Gerald was a broker for the selected company.[161]

By the end of the summer of 1970, Broward Segrest and his staff and the district attorney's office had hundreds of examples of what they were convinced were corrupt activities. Shortly after the June runoff, John Mitchell had confided to Charles Colson that Wallace was in a "peck of trouble." He seemed confident that the IRS investigation would immobilize Wallace. "I remember thinking to myself, 'Boy, that's good news,' " Colson later recalled, " 'because that'll get him out of the way for 1972.' "[162]

But Wallace and the men who surrounded him seemed unperturbed. Even with the Justice Department breathing down their collective necks, Wallace's brother Gerald and other friends of the incoming administration were launching new schemes for collecting money from business groups. Wallace placed John Pemberton, clerk of the House of Representatives, in charge of the 1971 inauguration. Pemberton promptly began soliciting cash contributions from lobbyists and businessmen likely to have future business connections with the incoming Wallace administration.[163]

When longtime Wallace adviser John Kohn heard of the Pemberton activities and learned of new schemes by Gerald Wallace, it was the last straw. The Alabama aristocrat, who had been called the "Svengali" of the first Wallace administration, bitterly terminated his longtime connections to the politican he had advised for so long. By refusing to rein in the corruption and greed of Gerald and other corrupt cronies, said Kohn, "I am convinced that you have already failed the people of Alabama. . . . I want to formally disassociate myself from you. . . ."[164]

Those Alabama insiders who had been following the progress of the Justice Department investigation were convinced that it would soon bring down the Wallace administration. But Broward Segrest and the other members of the investigating team had begun to run into unexpected roadblocks. "I concede, we were a little green" in approaching the investigation, acknowledged Segrest twenty years later. His main tool was his staff's ability to dig out evidence of unreported (and presumably illegal) income. They depended heavily on the state tax office's criminal division to identify lower-level offenders and then "go back up the ladder" in a series of plea bargains.[165]

And Gerald Wallace was ready for that one. "Just remember," he repeatedly reminded his friends, "Al Capone got caught because he didn't pay his taxes."[166] Ira DeMent recalled the same line: "Gerald told me over and over again: 'I always pay my taxes.'" Even, DeMent added sarcastically, "on the stuff he stole."[167] According to one IRS agent who worked on the investigation, many of Gerald Wallace's apparent payoffs had come in the form of "legal fees" for which he performed no services, but—whenever he received payment in the form of a check he religiously reported it on his income-tax returns.

"We were also convinced that he had obtained significant amounts of cash money from businessmen doing business with the state," said the investigator, but whatever cash he received, it was "never invested openly and we could never establish anything more than a pattern." Agents later speculated that at least some of the cash—which they assumed had been put back into his business enterprises—had disappeared on the gaming tables of Las Vegas. Gerald and his partners may have been crooks, concluded one examiner, "but they weren't stupid."

IRS personnel were convinced that public officials had used rigged bidding procedures to channel state contracts to selected companies that gave money to the various Wallace political campaigns. Technically, these violations could be prosecuted under the Corrupt Campaign Practices Act of 1925, but that law was so ridden with loopholes and exceptions that it offered a shaky foundation for the hard-hitting prosecution the Justice Department wanted to undertake. (The Racketeer Influenced and Corrupt Organizations—RICO—Act had just passed the Congress, but it was still seen as a weapon to be used against organized crime; nearly a decade was to pass before federal prosecutors routinely used the act to prosecute political extortionists.) Given the weakness of the 1925 law, the massive loopholes in Alabama's competitive bidding rules, and the absence of any conclusive testimony documenting the connection between campaign contributions and state contracts, only the accumulation of circumstantial evidence could guarantee success. And Wallace's continuing popularity, feared Segrest, would make it difficult to find a jury that would go along with such a case.

The prosecution needed an insider who would turn state's evidence. In midsummer of 1970, a Mobile, Alabama, advertising executive who had handled Lurleen Wallace's campaign agreed to testify that Seymore Trammell had instructed him to present a series of phony vouchers to campaign contributors, who could then write off their contributions as tax-deductible business expenses. The IRS had also discovered that a building contractor with lucrative state contracts had built Trammell an expensive swimming pool. George Wallace's former finance commissioner had neither paid for the construction nor reported it as in-kind income on his tax returns. While these violations were relatively minor in the grand scheme of statewide corruption, they gave investigators a needed wedge.

Trammell seemed ripe for turning state's evidence. After the 1968 presidential run he and Wallace had parted in a clash of egos, and when Trammell announced his candidacy for state treasurer in 1970, his former boss had called a press conference and announced he would "not even vote for Trammell, much less lend him his support."[168] Trammell failed to make the runoff. Publicly he insisted that Wallace and Brewer were "fine men"; privately he passed on inside information about corruption in the Wallace administration to *Montgomery Advertiser* editor and publisher Harold Martin, who made Trammell's tips the basis for his articles in the middle of the final gubernatorial runoff. Although voters turned out to be more concerned about racial issues than phony tire invoices, Trammell's well-known involvement in the leaks confirmed his break with Wallace.[169]

Shortly after the finale of that campaign, Trammell called Blount to discuss a business deal, but Nixon's postmaster general had politics on his mind. He made it clear to Trammell that he thought they had overlapping interests.

George Wallace planned to run again in 1972 as a third-party candidate, and the Nixon administration was intent on stopping him. Even if the IRS investigation reached a dead end, Blount confided, it might frighten away some of Wallace's major campaign contributors and make it difficult for him to get his race off the ground. Would Trammell be willing to fly to Washington to talk with Will Wilson about the developing tax case? The postmaster general made an indirect but pointed reference to Trammell's potential legal problems by reassuring him that the Nixon people were interested only in derailing Wallace. As Trammell recalled the conversation, "I was in no danger of being indicted because Nixon knew that Wallace and I were no longer together."[170] He agreed to meet with the head of the Criminal Justice Division.

Will Wilson could be tough, even ruthless, but he also had an uncanny ability to inspire confidence and trust. When Trammell met with him in late June 1970 he was instantly attracted to the gregarious and blunt-talking Texan. Wilson and his assistant, Bill Sessions, talked to Wallace's former top assistant for hours with only the faintest hint of a threat; after outlining twenty-two areas of investigation from asphalt contracting to campaign financing, they asked for his cooperation. Trammell was hooked. Without consulting an attorney (after all, he was a lawyer), he agreed to meet with Broward Segrest.[171]

That decision was a fatal blunder. Trammell was usually a shrewd political operator, but by the summer and fall of 1970, his life seemed to be falling apart. His investments (and his marriage) had gone sour; he had failed at a political career. Always a two-fisted drinker, he had never before let alcohol get the best of him, but as he began his conversations with Broward Segrest, his judgment was impaired by alcohol, depression, and an uncontrollable desire to destroy Gerald Wallace, whom he blamed for many of his problems.[172]

In later years, Segrest expressed a grudging admiration for Trammell. "He hated Gerald Wallace, but it was as though he could not bring himself to implicate his old colleagues. He gave us nothing we didn't already have." Meanwhile, said Segrest, "he just undressed himself."[173] By the time Trammell belatedly brought in his old friend Robert Alton as attorney, he was in deep difficulty.

In April 1971, federal prosecuting attorneys began presenting the results of their two-year probe. Despite the supposed confidentiality of the proceedings, knowledgeable local reporters learned that, while George Wallace would not be named, the Montgomery grand jury planned to indict Gerald and at least a dozen major Wallace business supporters who had made millions off their contracts with the state government.[174]

Tom Turnipseed ran into Gerald Wallace at the Diplomat, a favorite drinking spot for capital city politicians. "Sag [Gerald's nickname] looked like hell; he was drinking and depressed," he remembered. "What in the hell is wrong with you?" asked Turnipseed.

"It's those damn IRS boys, Tom. I think they've got me this time."[175]

In fact, the case was at a crossroads. On April 30, Segrest announced a recess in the presentation of witnesses to the grand jury, a recess which would last through the summer. Although the investigation was still in progress, Segrest laid out the case to his Washington superiors. They had not been able to gather substantial evidence directly incriminating George Wallace. Wallace would be able to claim that he was simply the piano player at the whorehouse; "he doesn't know what goes on upstairs." Segrest thought they had a strong case against Gerald, but he readily acknowledged that there was no smoking gun and no guarantee they would obtain a conviction in view of the governor-elect's popularity in the state. "Most of the witnesses," as Segrest wrote in his memorandum to the Justice Department, "whose testimony is essential to expose such practices as bribery and kickbacks to state officials are businessmen who are still benefitting from the system and will not, therefore, blow the whistle."[176]

THE late spring of 1970, at the time of the Brewer-Wallace runoff, had marked a low point in the polls for Nixon; he trailed Democratic front-runner Edmund Muskie by six points: forty-four to fifty percent, with six percent undecided. With Wallace in the race and drawing eleven percent of the vote, said pollster Lou Harris, the figures were worse. Muskie's lead increased eight percent and Nixon dropped below the forty percent mark.[177] A year later, as the White House considered whether to go forward on the Alabama tax investigation, George Gallup charted a rebound for the President. In a head-to-head race with any of the three most likely Democratic nominees—Muskie, Ted Kennedy, or Hubert Humphrey—Nixon held a four- to six-point lead. But his margin dropped to one percent when Wallace was factored into the race as a third-party candidate. And most of the President's advisers feared that the Alabama governor's strength would rebound once he hit the campaign trail.[178]

On May 25, three weeks after the Segrest briefing, Nixon traveled to Alabama with what reporters described as "all the flavor and trappings of a Presidential campaign." In remarks in Mobile and Birmingham, he praised southerners for their progress in desegregating schools and scolded the "double, hypocritical standards of those Northerners who look at the South and say: 'Why don't those Southerners do something about their race problem?'" At the same time, he warmly encouraged efforts of community groups to "resolve their differences in a peaceful and constructive way."[179]

Blount was anxious to have the President meet with the governor, but Nixon had always been sensitive to charges that Wallace had dictated the Republican Southern Strategy. He solved the problem by inviting a klatch of southern governors along for a brief luncheon on Air Force One during the flight from Mobile to Birmingham. The light and informal conversation seemed to ease some of the tension resulting from the tax investigation. (Wallace still did not know about Nixon's $400,000 contribution to the Brewer campaign.) Nixon thought the meeting had gone well.

Four days later, Washington columnists Evans and Novak reported breathlessly that a "tenuous line of communication has now been opened between agents of President Nixon and Gov. George Wallace." Even before the flight, they said, Wallace had sent word through Postmaster General Blount that "he and the Nixon administration have a common interest—to keep a liberal Democrat out of the White House." Novak had traveled to Alabama as part of the large presidential press corps, but had remained in Montgomery for a series of quiet background conversations. While Evans and Novak were known for their access to White House tidbits, this one bore all the earmarks of a leak from the office of the postmaster general, "tough, able" Winton Blount. The two columnists made no mention of the tax investigation under way, but emphasized that the "new line of communication between Montgomery and Washington runs from some of Wallace's most confidential political aides into the Justice Department offices of Att. Gen. John Mitchell . . . and his deputy, Richard Kleindienst"—precisely the two men who would make recommendations to the President on whether or not to prosecute Gerald Wallace's friends.[180]

Shortly after the column appeared, Tom Turnipseed once again encountered Gerald Wallace at the Diplomat. Wallace was sitting with New York fixer-attorney Roy Cohn, who represented a New York insurance company and was making his pitch for a joint shakedown of Alabama state employees. In contrast to his downcast mood in early April, the governor's brother was cheerful and in great spirits. His tax problems, he implied, were over.[181]

The following week, Turnipseed returned to Montgomery from a Texas third-party fund-raiser and drove to the governor's office to report on the take from the evening of speech-making and entertainment. The Hunts had bought several tables of tickets, he told Wallace, and the groundwork was laid for the 1972 election. But the governor seemed preoccupied and uninterested. "I'm tired of these kooks in this third-party business," he announced without preamble. "It's crazy. I'm thinking about going back into the Democratic Party." Turnipseed was momentarily shaken; all the planning had been aimed toward a repeat of the 1968 third-party run. But he was a loyal soldier and used to Wallace's secretive decision-making. "That's fine with me," he said. "But if we're going to do it, I need to get moving so we can work with some of our friends in the southern legislatures so that we can set up some early southern primaries."

With this casual conversation, George Wallace renounced the third-party effort Richard Nixon so feared and set out on a journey through the Democratic primaries which would rip the party apart.[182]

ON August 10, 1970, Broward Segrest met in Washington with Will Wilson and learned that the administration had tentatively abandoned the case against Gerald Wallace. Within twenty-four hours, James K. Polk, the Washington journalist who had followed the case most closely, quoted an unnamed Justice Department official, either Wilson or ne of his aides: "You don't jump into a bear pit with a bear unless you make damn sure that you've got him by the tail." If they went forward with the indictment and trial of Gerald Wallace and lost, his brother would be able to claim that he was being "politically persecuted," and his grievances against the administration would be even greater.[183]

In late August, Attorney General Mitchell dramatically shuffled his staff. Without notice or explanation, he transferred Bill Sessions to a Justice Department operation in Texas. Will Wilson, embroiled in a bitter feud with Texas congressman Henry Gonzales, became another one of the many Nixon appointees left "twisting slowly in the wind," watching his dreams of a Supreme Court appointment disappear and his reputation suffer.[184] Assistant Attorney General Richard Kleindienst, who had always regarded Wilson as the chief threat to his position as Mitchell's heir-apparent, moved adroitly to undermine his rival's influence with the attorney general and to convince him that the Texas Democrat-turned-Republican was an unnecessary political liability. (In light of the many charges made against his integrity as assistant and later attorney general, Kleindienst's rationale for throwing Wilson overboard was rich with irony: "Regardless of the truth or falsity of the charges . . ." he said, "the public's confidence in the nonpolitical administration of the federal criminal laws has to be maintained.")[185] In October, Wilson would resign from office, but in the meantime, the final decisions on the Wallace prosecution were made by John Mitchell, operating on direct instructions from Richard Nixon.

Although DeMent was ostensibly not a part of the day-to-day operation of the case, he and Segrest made one last attempt to help Trammell, whom they had increasingly come to see as a kind of scapegoat for the broad corruption of the Wallace administration. On at least two occasions, the Assistant District Attorney Segrest presented a deal on Trammell's behalf to Kleindienst. But after checking with Mitchell and the White House, the acting attorney general insisted that the prosecution go forward.[186] Indicted and then convicted the following year, Wallace's former assistant was sentenced to a four-year term in a minimum-security federal prison camp on the grounds of Maxwell Air Force Base in Montgomery. Although a handful of other Wallace supporters were indicted, most cases were dismissed; only Trammell served any time in prison.

In later years, Richard Nixon—like everyone else in his administration who was involved in the case—professed total amnesia when questioned about the IRS investigation against the Wallaces.[187] After Trammell was released, former attorney general John Mitchell began serving his eighteen-month term for Watergate crimes in the same Maxwell facility. Trammell left word for Mitchell that "I could bring him a newspaper . . . on Sundays just as my yard man, Bubba, had done for me."

A few days later, Mitchell returned the call and thanked Trammell. "Seymore," he volunteered, "I want you to know that I had nothing to do with your being sent to prison. . . . Your case was handled directly out of the White House."[188]

On January 12, 1972, the Justice Department issued a terse announcement that it was dropping its investigation of Gerald Wallace and dismissing the grand jury that had spent nearly eighteen months probing corrupt financial practices in Alabama. Officials declined any comment except to say that "[the] statement speaks for itself."[189] Twenty-four hours later, George Wallace held a press conference in Tallahassee, Florida. *Washington Post* staff writer George Lardner, Jr., began his front-page lead: "Alabama Gov. George C. Wallace put his third-party movement on the shelf today and announced his candidacy for the Democratic presidential nomination."[190] With that announcement, Wallace enormously improved Richard Nixon's chances of reelection, a prospect the Alabamian himself recognized. A week earlier, he had jokingly told an old Republican friend: "Tell the President I'm going down to Florida and kick hell out of those Democrats."[191]

Even before the Justice Department had officially announced its decision to abandon the tax investigation, Wallace began telling reporters in Montgomery that he was going to run as a Democrat in Florida. When CBS newsman Dan Rather joined a group of journalists for a televised New Year's "conversation" with the President, he bluntly asked about the suspicious circumstances surrounding the Wallace about-face. Nixon tried to turn the question aside by telling Rather to "ask the Democrats," but Rather came right back.

"Mr. President," he said sharply, "I'm not asking the Democrats. I'm asking you."

Rather's persistence clearly provoked Nixon. Within hours of the televised exchange, White House staffers Charles Colson and Jeb Magruder went to work generating "spontaneous" telegrams, letters, and telephone calls from across the country to Dan Rather, "complaining about his treatment of the

President last evening."[192] Nixon was further angered when the New York fashion magazine *Women's Wear Daily,* which had begun including controversial hard-news pieces, published an article by Kandy Stroud elaborating on Rather's theory that the Nixon people had worked with Wallace because he was a "man who can be bought."[193] The President had earlier tried to lift Stroud's press credentials (he referred to her as that "kike girl" in his early-morning briefing with Haldeman), and Charles Colson awarded her an honored position on the White House opponents list.[194] But in the absence of hard-and-fast evidence of an arrangement, reporters moved on to other subjects.

It may very well be that the Justice Department decision not to go forward with an indictment of Gerald Wallace was made on the basis of simple political calculation (as the carefully engineered Justice Department leaks insisted). Will Wilson pointed out that although Richard Nixon might secretly scheme and maneuver to destroy his opponents, he took a consistently cautious approach toward actually indicting and trying political foes. On more than one occasion, said Wilson, Kleindienst had been emphatic: "We don't indict enemies of the President unless there is overwhelming evidence."[195]

When Seymore Trammell heard the back-to-back news of the Justice Department's announcement and Wallace's decision to abandon his third-party run, however, it confirmed—for him at least—his darkest suspicions that he was the sacrificial goat. "Nixon and Wallace made a deal after the two-year investigation of the Wallaces," said a bitter Trammell. And "that deal was for Wallace and his brother Gerald to be indicted or face prison or for Wallace to kill the third party. The third party *was* George Wallace."[196]

Trammell was not alone in his suspicions. A week after the Alabama governor's declaration of his Democratic candidacy, Evans and Novak returned from a trip to Montgomery and reported that there was "pervasive opinion here that a deal has been made between Wallace and the White House."[197] Veteran journalist Michael Dorman flatly insisted that several sources in the White House told him that "Nixon agreed to kill the investigation of the Wallace brothers themselves, but not of their associates." In return, said Dorman, "Wallace pledged to refrain from a third-party race in 1972." The journalist even went so far as to claim that "the deal was sealed" aboard Air Force One, during the short flight on which Wallace accompanied Nixon on his May 1971 visit to Mobile.[198]

For those with a taste for political theater, there is something immensely appealing in the image of Wallace and Nixon dramatically sealing their secret bargain as Air Force One winged its way from Mobile to Birmingham. But there has always been something wrong with this particular part of the scenario: the two men were never alone together. When Garry Wills asked

Wallace about the widespread rumors that there was an airborne deal, the Alabama governor seemed more annoyed than defensive.

"Deal! Shee-it!" said a contemptuous Wallace. "The only time I was with the President was at the lunch on that plane, and [Kentucky governor] Louie Nunn was there, and [Florida governor] Reubin Askew, [Mississippi governor] John Bell Williams, Harry Dent, Red Blount, Tricia Nixon, and Julie, and David Eisenhower—some deal I'm going to make with all them sittin' around." Wallace added, "If they had anything on me or my family, they'd use *that* to get rid of me, not make no *deal*."[199]

For the most part, signed and sealed agreements between political opponents are the currency of Hollywood scriptwriters, not the coin of politicians' dealings. But if it is unlikely that any arrangement was consummated aboard Air Force One (or elsewhere), there was motive and opportunity for a wary cease-fire in which each side drew back step by step from a direct confrontation.

Certainly Nixon himself longed for a deal. As early as February 1971, H. R. Haldeman's daily diary tantalizingly hinted at such a possibility. Reporting on a two-hour meeting between John Mitchell and the President, Haldeman cryptically summarized their discussion of Wallace: It "appears that Wallace is interested in making a deal of some kind that will make it unnecessary for him to run for President." Mitchell was still uncertain over the Alabamian's long-term impact on the race, but the President "felt very strongly that, under any circumstances, it would be better for us to have him out and that we should try to work this out."[200]

It was the last entry in the Haldeman diary on the subject. Even after Nixon's death, his lawyers continued to block the release of documents and records that might throw light on the issue. The key figures who apparently acted on Nixon's behalf—Winton Blount, Charles Colson, Will Wilson, and Richard Kleindienst—have consistently refused to discuss the case or have professed complete amnesia.

Whether or not an explicit agreement was made, Wallace had established quiet links with the Nixon White House, which would be strengthened over the next two and a half years. And his decision to abandon his third-party candidacy was an act of extraordinary importance for the Nixon reelection campaign strategy. Now Wallace was the Democrats' problem.

Chapter 13

"SEND THEM A MESSAGE"

VARIATIONS ON A THEME

WEARILY MAKING THE ROUNDS on his fourth chronicle of a presidential campaign, journalist Theodore White was as hostile to George Wallace as ever. In his survey of American presidential politics in 1982, White would dismiss the Alabama Democrat with one savagely descriptive line: "a Southern populist of the meanest streak." This was only a slight improvement over his 1964 assessment of Wallace as a "narrow-minded grotesquely provincial man."[1] But in 1972 even White took note of a physical transformation. "The hair that used to curl out in a ducktail slicked back with brilliantine, like the cartoons of Senator Claghorn, was now neatly cut, if somewhat sprayed." And the governor had "shed the old undertaker's uniform—dark suit, narrow black necktie—of Southern courthouse politicians, and was garbed now in bright shirts, fashionable double-knit suits, broad colorful ties."[2]

Most reporters credited the spruced-up Wallace to his stunning new wife. Cornelia Snively was no stranger to politics: her uncle was Big Jim Folsom. When Folsom, a widower, moved into the Governor's Mansion in 1947, he had asked Cornelia's mother, the flamboyant "Big Ruby" Folsom Austin, to serve as the state's first lady. Eight-year-old Cornelia had peered down through the balusters to watch George and Lurleen Wallace as they left early from one of her uncle's famous late-night parties. Over the next twenty-two years, she entered the Miss Alabama beauty contest (and placed second while still in high school); attended Rollins College in Winter Park, Florida; and tried her hand at songwriting, country-and-western singing (a disaster), and summer-stock acting (forgettable) before she found brief stardom as the lead attraction of the Sunshine State's Cypress Gardens water-skiing extravaganza.

Marriage to a wealthy Florida citrus grower, John Snively III, had seemed to offer a storybook ending for a beautiful young southern woman of the 1950s. But two children, an elegant home with servants, and afternoons of bridge at the Winter Park Country Club held no allure for Cornelia Snively. She was addicted to the excitement of center stage, and by the late 1960s her marriage had ended. She moved back to Montgomery, financially strapped and determined to land "the most eligible man in town," George Wallace.[3] "Poor George," she later recalled with a laugh. "He never had a chance."[4]

In her autobiography, she claimed to have persuaded her brother to introduce her to Wallace in 1969, after her divorce from Snively was final. In fact, Cornelia had traveled as part of the Wallace entourage during the 1968 presidential campaign and had found herself in the midst of a spirited competition among a half-dozen suitors for the candidate's favors. On one flight to California, Wallace insiders feared "woman trouble" on board when they noticed Cornelia squaring off with Maida Persons, Wallace's former secretary, and Lisa Taylor, a striking young country-music singer, half of the team of "Mona and Lisa—the Singing Sisters."

Lisa Taylor quickly abandoned the competition, but every time he glanced toward the back of the plane, Wallace crony Oscar Harper remembered, Cornelia Snively and Maida Persons had inched forward a few more seats. Finally Wallace motioned to his security aide:

"You go tell Ruby Folsom Austin's daughter [Cornelia] and Maida Persons they better get their asses to the back of this plane or I'm gonna send them back to Montgomery when we land."[5]

By 1970, however, Wallace and Cornelia had become inseparable. In Montgomery, the two kept company until the early hours of the morning. Fearful of public gossip, she never campaigned in the Wallace-Brewer race, but as soon as George Wallace returned to his motel room, he'd "head for that telephone like a dog that treed a squirrel," recounted an adviser. "He was crazy about that woman."[6]

After recapturing the governorship, Wallace confided to a number of his friends and to Gerald that he was going to marry Cornelia Snively. While they professed to be concerned about the impact of marriage to a divorcee (after all, the well-publicized divorce and remarriage of Nelson Rockefeller had been a key factor in his loss to Barry Goldwater as late as 1964), their real hostility stemmed from the well-founded apprehension that Cornelia would brook no competition in the race to sit at the political right hand of her husband. She fancied herself—not without justification—a shrewd political operator in her own right, and she recognized the dangers posed by the governor's old supporters.

The first test of wills came in late November when Gerald Wallace and Oscar Harper tried to persuade the governor-elect to postpone his wedding until after his January 1971 inauguration. Cornelia had her wedding, as scheduled. Montgomery newsmen gleefully observed that the arrival of the beautiful and vivacious new wife had caused an upheaval among the Wallace staff. When Tom Turnipseed resigned as head of the 1972 campaign, one account fixed the blame on his indiscreet promise to make Cornelia "the Jackie Kennedy of the rednecks," a remark that annoyed the hypersensitive Wallace but amused his wife. (Actually, Turnipseed's departure as head of the campaign was triggered by other more weighty disagreements with Gerald).[7] And the governor's bodyguards, who had worshiped the gentle Lurleen, despised the independent-minded (and sometimes imperious) Cornelia.[8]

WALLACE had a new wife and, increasingly, a new image. Less than a month before his inauguration in early 1971, he told the National Press Club that he had "always been a moderate" and no longer believed segregation was desirable. The nation, he told his audience, "ought to have non-discrimination in public schools" as well as "public accommodations open to all."[9] Bending to the changing political winds, he began greeting and signing photographs for integrated school groups as they toured the state capitol.

Privately, Wallace remained as racially insensitive as ever. A flabbergasted *New York Times* correspondent traveling with the Alabama governor in the spring of 1972 reported Wallace's casual references to the "big nigger vote" and his laughing apology to aides after one speech that he "didn't give them much nigger talk today. . . . Shoot, folks are going to start saying that I've gone soft."[10] But almost every observer agreed that Wallace had abandoned the hard-line segregationist views he had espoused before his near defeat in 1970.

Even his speech-making seemed less strident and angry. Absent were provocative references to "popping skulls" and "skinning heads" and his oft-stated promise to use the presidential limousine to run over unruly hippies. Wallace ruefully recalled the shouting confrontations that had marked his 1968 run for the presidency. "Those big crowds . . . here's a little girl listening to me, and some extremist is shouting foul language over her head, and her daddy can't stand it any longer, and he picks up a chair, and so that's what the news media tell about, and not what I said."[11]

The crowds too had changed. The "gas-station men in blue coveralls were still there, the workers with muscular biceps," noted White, but now they sat side by side with "men in neckties and white shirts, with the sour breath of office workers; women in housedresses with their babies; . . . old ladies with their gray hair sprayed into a blueish set."[12]

The media—particularly the television networks—seemed unable to agree on just how to describe Wallace. "The sideburns are longer, the neckties wider, the suit a stylish double-knit with button-down pockets," but "underneath the cosmetics, George Corley Wallace has changed very little," argued George Lardner, Jr., of the *Washington Post.* The Alabamian might bask in a wider spotlight, but even though he had become the prophet of the "Social Issue," it was still the same tangle of racial and physical fears summoned up by the words 'law and order,' and 'busing.' " [13]

Not so, insisted *Newsweek* correspondent Stephan Lesher in January 1972 on the eve of the Florida primary. Voting for the Alabama governor was just a harmless way of letting off a little steam. He had become a "force for good" by becoming the "hard-hat's cathartic, playing Santa Claus instead of Satan by passing out beribboned nostrums for the shadowy cholers afflicting middle America."[14]

Wallace was quick to tell reporters that he had not changed. "It's just that I don't have to yell as loud now as when I was first elected. . . . Like the old story about the farmer who had to knock the mule down to get his attention." Now, "you all listen to what I say, so I can talk a little softer."[15] And as the campaign began, they listened because of one critical issue: busing.

By early 1972, a series of federal court decisions seemed to mandate that extraordinary measures had to be taken to end de facto segregation, even if integration meant busing children away from their neighborhood schools into adjacent counties or inner-city schools. For whites who had fled to the suburbs, there seemed no escape.[16] On one level, George Wallace's embrace of the busing issue reinforced the traditional perception of voters that he was fixated on the subject of race. As he geared up for yet another presidential run in the late summer of 1971, an adviser identified the main problem Wallace faced as a national candidate: voters in "Colorado or Iowa . . . think George is against niggers."[17] But Wallace's all-out opposition to busing also helped him stake out a position as the most forceful spokesman for a national backlash. Busing proved to be one of those rare political issues that amount to a nonnegotiable demand for the majority of voters, and Wallace had an open field within the Democratic Party. Initially, few mainstream candidates could stomach the thought of trying to "out-Wallace" him. If black voters—a constituency critical to Democats—were sometimes ambivalent on the issue of busing, they knew from bitter experience that segregation, whether mandated by law or residential patterns, led to inferior black schools. And it required no great insight for them to see that hostility to busing often masked overt racism. Anxious to avoid antagonizing black voters, the leading Democratic contenders—Muskie, Humphrey, and McGovern—stood paralyzed like so many deer frozen by the bright lights of an oncoming car.

*   *   *

As Wallace campaigned across balmy Florida in early March, seventy men and women, drawn by a small newspaper ad appealing for volunteers to help the Alabama governor in the upcoming Wisconsin Democratic presidential primary, ignored snow emergency warnings and crowded into a small meeting room at Milwaukee's Red Carpet Airport Inn. Longtime aide John DeCarlo stood at the door and greeted gray-haired retirees, two dozen blue-collar workers, a few curious teenagers, a local construction engineer, a Milwaukee lawyer, the Sheboygan owner of a chain of service stations, and a shy twenty-one-year-old part-time janitor and busboy who identified himself as Arthur Bremer. As DeCarlo outlined the upcoming Wallace campaign in Wisconsin, Bremer sat quietly in one corner of the room, but at the end of the evening he picked up a bundle of posters and bumper stickers and a Wallace lapel button.

The next morning, in a dreary mixture of sleet and snow, the young volunteer drove to the lakefront section of the city and began pasting posters on the lampposts. Returning to his sparsely furnished two-room apartment, he taped a National Rifle Association cardboard target on his kitchen door, centered the Wallace button on the bull's eye, and began writing in a lined notebook: *"Now* I start my diary of my personal plot to kill by pistol either Richard Nixon or George Wallace. I intend to shoot one or the other while he attends a champange [*sic*] rally for the Wisconsin Presidential Preference Primary."[18]

Arthur Bremer's father was a hard-drinking Milwaukee truck driver. Gossipy neighbors recalled seeing his mother, depressed and withdrawn, wandering around in her housecoat and slippers well after noon. She routinely locked her husband out of the shabby apartment and loudly announced to anyone who would listen that she was not going to cook any more meals.[19] Bremer dreaded the late afternoons, when he returned from school to hear his father screaming at his mother. "Dad would swear and my younger brother would cry," he recounted. As his parents raged through the tiny living room and kitchen, he retreated to an imaginary world in which he pretended "I was living with a television family and there was no yelling at home and no one hit me."[20] Between 1952 and 1968 his parents appeared at least three times in Milwaukee Children's Court to show cause why one or more of their four sons should not be taken from their custody for abuse and neglect."[21]

At Milwaukee's South Division High school, I.Q. tests suggested that Bremer was above average in intelligence; his grades in English and history were adequate despite the fact that he spelled atrociously. But all his teachers remembered him as a pathetic loner with a disconcerting habit of laughing inappropriately. Fellow students who recalled him did so only because of his awkward laughter and his inability to engage in small talk. "He'd walk down the corridor, talking to himself, shaking his head and smiling to himself," said one classmate. "Weird" was the word most used to describe him.[22]

In a burst of self-pity, he described his isolation. "No English or History-test was ever as hard, no math final exam ever as dificult as waiting in a school lunch line alone, waiting to eat alone & afterward reading alone in the auditorium while hundreds huddled and gossiped and roared and laughted and staered at me, and planned for the week and laughed and laughed."[23]

In the two years after graduation from high school, Bremer lived with his parents while he worked as bagger at a local grocery, as a part-time janitor, and as a part-time busboy at the Milwaukee Athletic Club. Although he enrolled in several courses at a local community college, he usually failed to show up after the first few classes. He did finish one darkroom course and briefly talked about becoming a professional photographer, but he began quarreling with his younger brother Roger, who complained to his family that Arthur was "strange." Finally, in October 1971, Bremer slapped his father and stormed out of his parents' house. He moved into a two-room apartment near Milwaukee's big Miller Brewing Company complex and cut all ties with his family.

Most of the tenants in the small apartment building came to know him by sight. He seemed pleasant enough, said the apartment manager's wife, but he was "very much a loner"; in the six months he lived there she never saw him bring anyone up to his flat. With money saved while living at home, he bought a battered 1967 two-door Rambler sedan for seven hundred dollars, and through the fall and winter often drove slowly through the darkened streets of the city, then parked in McKinley Park on Lake Michigan and spent hours staring out over the water. His mother attempted to visit him several times, often disturbing other tenants with her banging and shouting. He always refused to answer his door.[24]

In mid-November of 1971, just after he had moved out on his own, he filed a complaint with the city's Community Relations Commission complaining of "discrimination and harrassment" by the Milwaukee Athletic Club. (His supervisor had transferred him to kitchen duty after patrons complained that Bremer hummed and loudly talked to himself as he cleared tables.) Bremer "appears to bottle up anger but will sometime let it go," wrote the commission's investigator in his report. "I assess him as bordering on paranoia." Although he dismissed the young man's complaint, he offered to arrange professional help. When he called Bremer's apartment in an effort to set up an appointment, no one answered.[25]

A week later, Bremer rented a firing lane in the basement shooting gallery of Milwaukee's Flintrop Arms Center. With a recently purchased five-shot .38

caliber snub-nose revolver, a weapon often used by plainclothes policemen, he blasted away at the two-foot target seventy-five feet away; other patrons watched with amusement. Several shots lodged in the ceiling, sending a shower of dust and plaster to the floor. After more than a hundred rounds, an embarrassed Bremer finally put one bullet in the outer ring of the target. "Still can't believe it," he later wrote. "How does anybody hit with one of those things?"[26]

Exhausted by the strain of aiming and firing the heavy handgun, he cruised aimlessly around the city until nine-thirty P.M., when he parked in front of a synagogue in the northern Milwaukee suburb of Fox Point. Just before ten P.M., police spotted him asleep behind the wheel of his car in a no-parking zone. One officer shined his light into the car and saw .38 cartridges scattered across the seat. Bremer, incoherent and irrational, finally admitted that he was carrying a pistol in his coat pocket.[27] After a cursory examination by an overworked general practitioner who handled psychiatric evaluations for the police, he pled guilty to the minor misdemeanor of disorderly conduct and paid a thirty-eight-dollar fine.[28]

Shortly after the Fox Point arrest, Arthur Bremer's life took a hopeful turn; he met and became infatuated with an attractive fifteen-year-old. It was the first time he had ever shown any interest in a girl. Joan Pemrich was not sure what to make of the blond-haired, blue-eyed "Art," as he called himself. He was a bit short (five feet, six inches), but "kinda cute," and she was flattered by the attention of a twenty-one-year-old. But three dates spent listening to his nonstop monologues convinced her that her new boyfriend was "weird." He "talked crazy," she told her mother, and constantly boasted of his vast knowledge of human psychology and his plans for the future as a professional photographer. She did not confide Bremer's other interests. He "tried to take me to dirty movies," she later admitted. "He always liked dirty movies." Although she balked at going out with him again, her suitor continued to come by her house almost every day and sent her flowers, candy, and Christmas presents.[29]

Early in January, his apartment manager's wife did a double-take when she saw a bald Bremer in the halls. He had "shaved his whole head—the whole thing, clean off."[30] In his diary, he confided his plan to go to a high school dance, catch his ex-girlfriend off guard, "and show her that inside I felt as empty as my shaved head, stop her in her tracks, just to talk."[31] But Joan Pemrich failed to show up. Instead, she sent her girlfriends, who took one look at the forlorn Bremer and burst out laughing. Humiliated, he left the gymnasium.[32]

At first Pemrich's mother had felt sorry for the young man who followed her daughter around "like a little lost puppy." But shortly after he shaved his head, she intercepted one of his compulsive late-night telephone calls.

"Look, Art," she told him bluntly. "Joanie doesn't want to see you. She doesn't want to have anything to do with you."[33]

On January 13, 1972—the day George Wallace officially announced his candidacy for the presidency—Bremer drove from his downtown Milwaukee apartment to a gun shop less than a block from his parents' house and purchased a .38 caliber Charter Arms revolver to replace the pistol confiscated by the Fox Point police; two weeks later, he bought a Browning nine-millimeter semi-automatic pistol. On both occasions he meticulously filled out the Treasury form, truthfully stating that he had never been convicted of a felony.[34]

Over the next few days he began to plan a dramatic gesture to impress his former girlfriend. "I would blow my brains out on her front lawn," he wrote.[35] Then he constructed elaborate fantasies of a public massacre, which would culminate in a melodramatic suicide, something which was "BOLD AND DRAMATIC, FORCEFULL & DYANIMIC. A STATEMENT OF MY MANHOOD FOR THE WORLD TO SEE."[36] In early February, he donned a heavy overcoat, pocketed his two guns and two hundred rounds of ammunition, and walked to the busiest bridge intersection crossing the Milwaukee River in the middle of the city. After sitting for more than an hour, he lost his nerve and returned to his apartment.[37]

He intensified his practice sessions at two local firing ranges during the rest of the month; his baldness made it easy for several gun owners to remember seeing him methodically firing at silhouette targets.[38] Co-workers had always described him as an "odd duck," but his supervisor at the athletic club became unnerved when Bremer began to "simulate firing of a gun with his hand . . . as well as engaging in other erratic behavior."[39] The club reduced his working hours and in late February Bremer simply failed to show up. He had already quit his part-time janitorial position; he had about fifteen hundred dollars in savings.

He became a regular around the Wallace for President campaign headquarters in Milwaukee's midtown Holiday Inn. He "hung around a lot," recalled Grey Hodges, a full-time Wallace worker from Montgomery. Hodges found the young man oddly withdrawn, but a "damn good worker." One evening, a handful of volunteers and paid staff gathered in one of the motel's rooms to watch television. Bremer sat quietly on the floor with a large paperback in his lap. "He'd look up, read that book, look up at the television and then read some more," said Hodges, who finally leaned forward to see the title. Bremer was reading the Warren Commission's report on the assassination of President John Kennedy.[40]

THROUGH the winter and spring, Richard Nixon occupied himself with the heady maneuvers of geopolitics. The landmarks of his administration, in Nixon's view, included the opening of relations with China in 1971, his conclusion of the Strategic Arms Limitation Treaty with the Soviet Union in 1972, and his success in staving off the inevitable collapse of South Vietnamese forces until after the election of 1972. "Peace and foreign policy generally still have to be at the top of the list," he argued to aides as he determined his reelection strategy; the "substance of domestic policy is not as critically important as the substance of foreign policy." There was no future, he decreed, in trying to peddle such "tepid issues" as revenue sharing and government reorganization.[41]

Though voters might respond to pollsters by ranking the war in Vietnam as the nation's major problem, the President recognized they were likely to *vote* on the basis of their immediate, personal problems: the growing gap between paycheck and groceries, a break-in and the mugging of a neighbor, the threat of seeing their children bused out of neighborhood schools.

As the 1972 campaign approached, Nixon issued a steady stream of memos to Ehrlichman and Haldeman, emphasizing the importance of publicizing his administration's opposition to "forcibly integrated housing or forcibly integrated education."[42] He was "fixated on the issue," said Ehrlichman.[43] When the Boston patrician Elliot Richardson became Secretary of Health, Education and Welfare in 1971 and seemed to show an undue readiness to support federal courts' busing decrees, Nixon ordered Ehrlichman, "I want you personally to jump Richardson and Justice and tell them to *Knock off this Crap.* I hold them personally accountable to keep their left wingers in step with my express policy—Do what the law requires and not *one bit more.*"[44]

Throughout the fall and winter of 1971, Nixon constantly pressed his staff to come up with a plan for antibusing legislation or a constitutional amendment banning busing. Ehrlichman argued that it was ludicrous to place language into the Constitution of the United States dealing with schoolbuses. And it seemed unseemly for the President of the United States to urge outright defiance of the federal courts. "I know it's not a good idea," admitted Nixon, "but it'll make those bastards [in the Democratic Party] take a stand and it's a political plus for us."[45]

Still, he hesitated, paralyzed by the taunts of the Alabama governor. "If I win in Florida, you just watch," Wallace had told a group of reporters gathered around his desk in Montgomery in mid-January. The White House would—within a week—come down "both feet" against "cartin' children to Kingdom come."[46] Hell, Wallace prophesied, we'll "have Mr. Nixon himself taking the batteries out of the buses."[47]

Pollsters expected George Wallace to run well in the northern and more rural regions of Florida; almost every observer agreed the Alabama governor would capture a plurality of votes in the field of a dozen candidates. But only his most optimistic supporters anticipated the ease with which he overwhelmed his eleven Democratic opponents on March 15. Piling up forty-two percent of the vote, running ahead in Cuban-American and posh suburban districts as well as in rural Florida, only in black precincts and a handful of heavily Jewish areas of Miami did he fail to lead the ticket. By one estimate, nearly sixty percent of the nonblack voters of the state pulled the Wallace lever. Floridians also cast their ballots on a nonbinding referendum calling for the enactment of a constitutional amendment prohibiting busing and guaranteeing the sanctity of the neighborhood school. Three out of every four voters (and nearly ninety percent of all white voters, according to the *Miami Herald*), supported the measure.[48]

"A Jarring Message from George" and " 'They Have to Listen Now' " head-lined the cover stories in *Time* and *Newsweek*.[49] For an electorate increasingly reliant upon television, the shift in tone by the nation's three networks was even more critical. In their initial coverage of the Florida primary, the networks had generally treated busing as an artificial issue whipped up by a demagogue.[50] Wallace's sweeping victory legitimized it.

If journalists had begun to take Wallace seriously as a presidential candidate, most remained bemused by his campaign's religious trappings. Attending a rally for the Alabamian meant "traveling backwards in a time machine . . . back to a time when Americans thought of themselves as innocents," reported the Associated Press national correspondent at the end of a brief tour through Florida. After a "foot-stomping rendition of 'Give Me That Old Time Religion' " and a long-winded invocation, a Wallace rally seemed "more like a revival than a political appearance."[51] *The Washington Post*'s George Lardner, Jr., barely suppressed a smirk as he recounted how *Grand Ole Opry* country singer Billy Grammer warmed up crowds by "plumping for prayer in the public schools and telling how 'the Lord Jesus Christ saved my soul in New Orleans, La.' several years ago."

Wallace's own secret polls showed that well over half of the nation's voters saw him as an unacceptable candidate. But the easy assumption of journalists that Wallace represented the past rather than the future seemed questionable. The same Florida electorate that gave him a forty-two percent plurality and voted three to one for an antibusing amendment supported a constitutional amendment reinstituting school prayer *ten to one*. The governor from Alabama understood and voiced the longing of millions of white middle-class and working-class voters for a stable world in which work was rewarded, laziness punished, blacks knew their place, men headed the household, women were men's loyal helpmates, and children were safe from vulgar language.

In the week before the Florida primary, editors of the *Washington Post* had questioned the leading Democratic contenders. When they pressed Wallace to name the top academic and business leaders who might help him shape governmental economic policy, he had fumbled defensively: "I got a breakdown [on economic policy] from a group of college professors at Troy State University the other day. . . . I got a blue book, a blue paper on it, and I read it."

Who would advise him on military and foreign affairs?

"Well, at the University of Alabama I've discussed foreign affairs. . . ." The candidate turned to his press secretary. "What about Dr. Harper? He's my nuclear adviser, isn't he?"

And then Wallace suddenly righted himself. What was so awe-inspiring about these experts, anyway? he demanded. "We've had four wars in the last 50 years, and we're in debt and we're involved all over the world. . . . I don't know whether the advice [from policy experts] has been so good or not," he said sarcastically. "Maybe a fellow just ought to advise himself from the seat of his pants, just what his common sense tells him, instead of sitting down with someone who told us to get in this [Vietnam] war."[52]

It was vintage Wallace—straight from a long tradition traceable at least as far back as Andrew Jackson, a tradition in which Americans rebelled against the notion that government was the province of experts and bureaucrats. The issues might shift from state to state and region to region, but—whether he was talking about busing, taxes, or prayer in the schools—George Wallace reached back to the language of his nineteenth-century populist fore-bears as he celebrated the "producers" of American society: the "beauticians, the truck drivers, the office workers, the policeman and the small business-men," who had formed the heart of the Democratic Party, "the bulk of its strength and vitality."

Instead of the New York bankers and moneyed interests feared by his nineteenth-century counterparts, Wallace warned of the danger to the American soul posed by the "so-called intelligentsia," the "intellectual snobs who don't know the difference between smut and great literature," the "hypo-crites who send your kids half-way across town while they have their chauf-feur drop their children off at private schools," and (in his favorite line) the "briefcase-carrying bureaucrats" who "can't even park their bicycles straight."[53] But the contrast between the common people and the elites—whether moneyed or cultural—was the same. And Wallace's 1972 campaign slogan—"Send them a message"—shrewdly played upon voters' ambiva-lence. They could send a message, and not have to live with the unaccept-able consequences of George Wallace as President.

Before the Florida vote, Nixon's press secretary, Ron Ziegler, had assured reporters that the President would never make an antibusing speech on television because the issue was "too complex and emotional."[54] On March 17, less than forty-eight hours after the Florida primary votes were in, Nixon made a televised national address, calling upon Congress to impose a "mor-atorium" on the federal courts to bar them from ordering any new busing to achieve racial balance. Back in Montgomery, Wallace gleefully reminded newsmen of his January prediction.[55]

Nixon's speech set the tone for the rest of the spring. His reflections on the 1968 presidential race and the 1970 congressional campaign had helped him define in his own mind the segments of the old Democratic constituency ripe for recruitment: white southerners (that had been clear even before the 1968 election), traditional blue-collar workers (particularly Catholics and "ethnic" voters), and that first generation of insecure suburbanites who had just escaped from the inner city. The President had been particularly intrigued by the election of New York's James Buckley, who had won a seat in the U.S. Senate in 1970 as a third-party "Conservative" candidate. Buckley had defeated his Democratic and Republican opponents by ignoring the traditional conservative emphasis upon economic policies and focusing on "hot" issues: "law and order," "pornography," and "old-fashioned patriotism."[56]

Wallace's Florida victory confirmed Nixon's views. The "gut" issues of the coming election would be crime, busing, drugs, welfare, inflation, he told his staff. All of these, said Nixon with some satisfaction, were "issues the Democrats [Wallace excepted] hate."[57] The busing issue was the Alabama governor's most potent weapon—the "only issue," claimed White House counsel Charles Colson, and the one to which Richard Nixon returned again and again in his memos on campaign strategy and tactics, always fretting that the public might not understand his views. The liberal media had been successful in "so confusing the issue that many people are not aware . . . that we are really against busing," he complained to Haldeman.[58] He urged his chief of staff to coordinate the Republican attack so that "our major effort should be to put our Democratic friends strongly on record in favor of busing and us on record against it."[59]

Wallace was now legitimate. The impossible task for the last serious Democratic contenders, Hubert Humphrey and George McGovern, was to hang on to the traditional Democratic coalition and somehow draw Wallace voters back into the fold. But the voters were angry with the Democratic Party; no sleight-of-hand rhetoric could change that fact.

"WE started out running [in] the primaries in 1972," recalled Wallace's campaign manager, Charles Snider, "and we didn't even know what the Democratic National Committee was." When Snider and press secretary Billy Joe Camp first met with party chairman Larry O'Brien and other party leaders, "they thought we were from outer space."[60] Snider, a thirty-nine-year-old ex–building contractor and developer, had begun working with Wallace during the 1968 campaign and, with the departure of Trammell, Jackson, and Jones, moved quickly to the top of the Wallace organization.

Overwhelmed by the pressures of mounting a national campaign, Snider and his assistants failed to master the Democratic Party's arcane delegate-selection rules, which seemed cunningly contrived for manipulation by those slick lawyers and bureaucrats so despised by Wallace's followers. (By mid-May, the McGovern operatives, led by whiz kid Gary Hart, would turn 2.2 million votes into 410 delegates. Wallace, by contrast, would rack up 3.35 million votes but could claim only 325 delegates.[61])

In early February, Snider and Camp argued that it was critical to move North. A run in the Wisconsin, Indiana, Michigan, and Maryland races, coupled with campaigns in half a dozen southern primaries, could establish their boss as a legitimate Democratic contender. But Wallace remained curiously reluctant to take the gamble. The stakes might be higher than he had anticipated; a misstep might be fatal. And Taylor Hardin, his state finance director and chief fund-raiser, urged a cautious approach. Busing was not an issue in Wisconsin, and polls showed Wallace with the support of less than eight percent of the state's Democratic voters, far behind Humphrey, McGovern, and Muskie.[62] Despite the Alabama governor's strong showing in the 1964 Democratic primary, the Wallace-LeMay ticket had drawn less than ten percent of the vote in the Badger State in the 1968 election.

In the end, Snider and Camp had an invaluable ally in the ambitious Cornelia. With an almost religious faith in the ability of her husband to build support, she cajoled, flattered, and ultimately succeeded in convincing the apprehensive Wallace that he would run well in both Wisconsin and Michigan.[63] On February 24, he gave the go-ahead for entering the presidential primaries in half a dozen northern states, beginning with the April 4 Wisconsin race. But he remained in Montgomery, fearful that if he made an all-out run in Wisconsin and was trounced, his romp through the political campaign would end. Less than two weeks before the primary, he finally opened a frantic ten-day campaign with a March 23 rally in Milwaukee's civic auditorium.

"I applauded loudly & laughed & stood up to applaud," recounted Arthur Bremer. Toward the end of Wallace's speech, Bremer managed to work his way to the front of the crowd and stood less than thirty feet from the candidate. "After he gave the liberals hell, he stood in the open & waved & smiled. . . . I moved in & for the first time saw his face." If he had brought his gun, Bremer wrote in his diary the next day, *"That would of been IT."*[64]

Wallace ran his usual chaotic campaign and often charged onto a stage with little of the background briefing considered essential in barnstorming. In Milwaukee's Serb Hall, site of raucous and enthusiastic rallies in 1964 and 1968, he once again brought members of the audience to their feet. Gone were all but the most fleeting references to busing or race. A tax revolt was brewing across the nation, and Wallace skillfully emphasized the disparity between Wisconsin and his own state. "In Alabama, here's what we pay in [property taxes]. . . . For a $30,000 home, $130 a year." His listeners gasped. And the real crowd-pleasers were many of the secondary themes he had honed in his Florida campaign: short, snappy punch lines attacking federal bureaucrats, know-it-all newsmen, "welfare loafers," and wasted foreign aid. "I'm sick and tired of giving up 50 percent of my income to the United States to waste half of it on nations that spit on us and half of it on welfare, I'm sick of permissiveness in this society!"[65]

Michael Novak, the social critic and chronicler of ethnic Americans, followed the candidate through the Wisconsin primary and left each rally "exhausted and excited as if it had been a championship basketball game." The country was safe from George Wallace, he argued. "He lacks the seriousness, the class, Americans like to see in their President." But—however "grossly and mendaciously"—Wallace understood the hidden anger of a working and marginal middle class besieged by change.[66]

Muskie's chief adviser, John English, became increasingly unnerved in the week before the election as his volunteers began calling eight thousand voters a day to drum up support for the senator from Maine. Less than ten percent of the voters contacted said they supported Wallace, but phone canvassers found that more than a quarter of the respondents claimed to be undecided or refused to name their preference. (In a relatively liberal state like Wisconsin, voters were often reluctant to admit they were supporting George Wallace, even a spruced-up and suddenly respectable George Wallace.) "I don't know what Wallace has here," concluded a wary Muskie campaign adviser, "but there's something for him out there. It could be the tip of an iceberg we're seeing."[67]

These apprehensions proved to be well-founded. Wallace did not win in Wisconsin; George McGovern took first place, and leaped to the front of the pack of Democratic contenders. But the Alabama governor came in second, ahead of Humphrey and a collapsing Muskie. With one week of campaigning, his support had tripled, going from less than eight percent to more than twenty-two percent of the voters; even his most bitter enemies within the national Democratic Party acknowledged he would be a powerful force by convention time in Miami.

On the night of his second-place finish, volunteer workers and well-wishers gathered in the Milwaukee Holiday Inn to cheer a grinning Wallace, who acted as though he had won the election. "I'm a 'viable' candidate," he told his followers as he mockingly thanked the reporters present for their earlier dismissal of his entry into the Wisconsin race. "I didn't even know what that word 'viable' meant until I got to you writers."[68]

Arthur Bremer, like most of the Wallace volunteers, had asked campaign director Grey Hodges about meeting the governor. But the taciturn young man failed to show up for the reception.[69] By primary day he was far more interested in a front-page article that appeared in both Milwaukee newspapers as a sidebar to the campaign political coverage. President Nixon would be in Ottawa for a series of meetings with Canadian officials and an address on United States–Canadian relations before that nation's parliament. "I don't think I['ll] waste myself on Wallace, although he'll be a more active campaigner," Bremer had written in his diary. "Why lower myself to this? I want the big bastard."[70]

RICHARD Nixon kept in constant touch with his domestic operatives on the shape of the upcoming fall political campaign, but in early April he was immersed in the far more congenial chess game of foreign policy. While his February visit to China to meet with Chinese premier Chou En-lai and party chairman Mao Zedong had been an unqualified success, his attempts to prop up the South Vietnamese government until after the 1972 election were suddenly in jeopardy. On March 30, intelligence officials told the President that the North Vietnamese army had launched an assault (the worst since the 1968 Tet Offensive, which had politically crippled the Johnson administration) across the demilitarized zone separating North and South Vietnam. Secretly, Nixon began preparing for a massive sea bombardment and—for the first time—the use of B-52's against North Vietnam.[71] Just as Kennedy had made no changes in his public appearances as the Cuban missile crisis unfolded, Nixon kept to his schedule. He would fly to Canada on the evening of April 13, returning on the fifteenth. The stepped-up bombing raids would be announced in the middle of his Canadian visit.

Bremer first considered flying to Syracuse, New York, renting a car, and driving into Canada. (He had learned from research at the library that he would not be able to fly into Canada with his pistols.) As he packed his bags he abruptly changed his plans and decided to "detour to N.Y. city & SCREW some of the ladies. They take out big ads in the porno papers. I got a right to some before—"[72]

And so Bremer boarded a flight to New York City and wandered across Manhattan in a series of joyless attempts at a last fling before his rendezvous with history. He took a helicopter ride from Jamaica Plains (where he stayed the first night) to Wall Street, rented a "Lincoln Continnetal [Nixon was in one today]" for a tour of the city, and checked into the Waldorf-Astoria. For his last night in New York he decided to go to the Victoria, a massage parlor three blocks from his hotel. He paced back and forth past the entrance: "I felt like I was going to get raped . . . I twisted my guts for hours . . . with fear and anticipation." At last he walked up to the reception desk and paid thirty dollars for a half-hour session. After he awkwardly undressed and lay on the table, a bored bikini-clad masseuse named "Alga" chatted aimlessly while she masturbated him. Desperate, he pleaded with her to "do it another way."

Primly she explained that the rules of the house prevented sexual intercourse. After half an hour, a resigned Bremer told her she could "push & pull on that thing for a week & I couldn't come." It was his longest conversation with another person since Joan Pemrich's mother had intercepted his telephone call in early January.[73]

He was no more successful in the rest of his plans. He was a twenty-one-year-old without a credit card; no one would rent him a car for the drive to Canada. "I could of, should of been in Ottawa by then," he scrawled in his diary. He caught a flight back to Milwaukee, packed suitcase and guns into the trunk of his Rambler, and began the fourteen-hundred-mile drive to the Canadian capital. By the time he arrived in Port Huron, Michigan, twenty-four hours later, he was exhausted.[74] Collapsing in his Howard Johnson room, he began distractedly playing with his Browning semi-automatic. Suddenly it went off with a deafening roar.

"My entire head rang from the powerful blast. . . . I felt sure the woman who rented me the room would come running & pound on my door," he wrote. The bullet had just missed his right foot and had gone through the blanket, the sheets, the mattress, and the shag carpet, into the plywood subfloor. Shaken, he had the presence of mind to turn on his television loudly; no one came to investigate.

The next morning Bremer prepared to cross the border by hiding his Browning semi-automatic in an opening he had scouted out in front of the right rear wheel well of his Rambler. "A mistake," he laconically recorded that night. The gun slipped through the opening and into the fire wall, a cavity that could be reached only by tearing the fender off the Rambler.[75] Bremer's quest for a place in history seemed doomed by awesome incompetence. In one twenty-four-hour period, he had tried (and failed) to lose his virginity, seen his elaborate plan for crossing the border into Canada from New York collapse, nearly shot his foot off, and lost the most deadly of his two handguns.

In Ottawa his luck did not improve.

Threats of anti–Vietnam War demonstrations against Nixon, coupled with the physical assault on visiting Soviet premier Aleksei Kosygin in 1971 by a fanatical Hungarian-Canadian émigré, had made the Canadians paranoically fearful.[76] As Bremer drove down the streets of Ottawa on April 14, he saw uniformed snipers, part of a huge contingent of Canadian civilian and military security forces drawn into the capital city, scattered across rooftops. Along the parade route, police units meticulously examined each storm-drain manhole, then waited while welders sealed the steel covers; firemen even turned their hoses on snowbanks to melt potential hiding places for bombs.[77]

Bremer parked on the route from the airport, carefully pinned on one

"Vote Republican" button and a second with a picture of the President, and walked up behind one of the Royal Canadian Mounted Police who lined the route. "Fantasied killing Nixon while shooting right over the shoulder of that cop," he later wrote. But suddenly, without warning, the President's car sped past in the early-evening cold.

"He went by before I knew it," said Bremer, "Like a snap of the fingers. A dark shillowet, waving, rushing by in the large dark car. 'All over,' someone said."

During the next thirty-six hours, he saw the President a half-dozen times; twice he was less than sixty feet away when Nixon's motorcade passed, but the would-be assassin knew that the presidential Lincoln was armor-plated.

An hour after Air Force One lifted off from the military airport south of Ottawa, Bremer packed up his belongings and drove southward to Washington in a halfhearted stalking attempt. A drive past the heavily defended White House sent him into despair, and he stayed in Washington less than twenty-four hours before giving up and starting the long trip back to Wisconsin. "ALL MY EFFORTS & NOTHING CHANGED. Just another god Damn failure." In his diary he raged: "Shit! I am thruorly pissed off. About a million things. . . . My fuse is about burnt. There's gonna be an explosion soon."[78]

For the next two weeks, he remained in his apartment, venturing out only to pick up groceries and for long walks along the lakefront.

IF George McGovern's Wisconsin victory established the South Dakota senator as the front-runner for the Democratic nomination, Wallace's strong second-place showing in the state sent the party into a nervous semi-convulsion. In mid-April party leaders in Michigan staged a gala Jefferson-Jackson Day fund-raising dinner. They invited George McGovern, Hubert Humphrey, and Edmund Muskie to speak and pointedly ignored the governor of Alabama.

Wallace had made a career out of responding to personal slights from national political leaders. With Charley Snider's approval, local supporters rented a drafty auditorium at the state fairgrounds outside Detroit and invited voters to come for his counter-rally. As Wallace drove in from the Detroit airport he fidgeted and fumed that he was "gonna be humiliated when nobody showed up." But two miles from the fairgrounds, the traffic slowed to a crawl; it took almost half an hour to cover the last thousand yards. By the time the southerner stepped onto the stage, five thousand men and women jammed the small arena. Wallace bounded up the steps two at a time, reported the *Detroit News,* and within minutes had turned the packed auditorium into a roaring pep rally. "There were people in the aisles, lining the walls, pushing up against the platform in front and some were trying to squeeze in the doors in the back," said an awed Cornelia Wallace.[79]

Outside, police estimated another six thousand to eight thousand surrounded the arena. Although the Alabama governor had already given three speeches earlier in the day, the adulation of the crowd rejuvenated him. Bitter complaints of welfare fraud and abuse ("I read in a Milwaukee paper about one woman collecting six welfare checks—that's paid for with your tax dollars") prefaced a backhanded slap at his main Democratic opponents for their criticism of the war ("They've got the brass of an army mule to come and tell you that they're against the war. They're the ones . . . passed the resolution that got us in."). The closer was a show-stopping account of a supposed conversation between President Nixon and Chairman Mao on the subject of busing. Wallace told the rapt crowd that he understood that Mao told the President he couldn't advise Americans on busing, because "when we take a notion to bus, we don't ask anybody about it."

"And do you know what the President could have told him?" Wallace wound up. " 'We do the same thing!' "[80]

By the end of the forty-minute speech, his voice rasped with fatigue and occasionally broke. But Wallace removed his coat and loosened his tie while the hall emptied and filled to overflowing again for a second celebration of the power of the people over the judges with their "asinine busing decisions" and "briefcase-carrying bureaucrats who are trying to run your lives."[81]

Across town, a gloomy unease settled over Democratic Party leaders as they gathered in the cavernous Cobo Hall, the tables carefully spaced to minimize the fact that fewer than three thousand of the faithful had gathered. Humphrey, McGovern, and Muskie, the party's "three chosen gladiators[,] merged into a composite portrait of a panic," wrote one Detroit newspaper columnist.[82] Although no one mentioned Wallace by name, his shadow lay over the proceedings. George McGovern made a spirited appeal to Wallace voters by echoing the Alabama governor's attacks on the "establishment center" which had "drifted so far from our founding ideals that it bears little resemblance to the dependable values of the Declaration of Independence and the Constitution."[83] But if disgruntled traditional Democrats were unhappy with the "establishment center," there was little evidence that they identified with McGovern's call for withdrawal from Vietnam and a massive reallocation of federal resources to social-welfare programs.

Labor leaders at the Jefferson-Jackson dinner privately conceded to newsmen that Wallace might carry as much as forty-five percent of the state's unionized voting public. "The rank and file just won't listen to us on this Wallace thing," said a top United Auto Workers official off the record. "We just hope that they come back into the regular Democratic fold in November."[84]

Inside the White House, Nixon and his aides could scarcely believe how well their plans for the campaign were falling into place. If the Wallace and Nixon camps were not working hand in glove, both found it in their mutual interest to cooperate as each stage of the campaign evolved. Harry Dent, Nixon's chief southern operative, met regularly with Tom Turnipseed. Although Turnipseed had resigned as head of the campaign effort, he remained a Wallace consultant. In memos to his boss, H. R. Haldeman, White House aide Gordon Strachan bragged that access to Turnipseed allowed them to monitor the Wallace effort from the inside. The clear impression conveyed to the President and the attorney general was that Turnipseed was a White House spy, an implication that later came back to haunt the South Carolina lawyer during the Watergate disclosures.[85]

In fact, Wallace personally approved the relationship between Turnipseed and White House aides. Dent and his aide, Wallace Henley, fed Turnipseed White House polls to help Wallace gauge his moves in choosing the primaries he would enter and offered advice on just how to exploit the vulnerability of other Democratic candidates. After the Alabama governor's success in the Wisconsin primary, Patrick Buchanan urged party operatives to repeat the tactics in Michigan. Since crossover voting was allowed, "Again, our people should go for Wallace and McGovern."[86]

In return for the secret White House support and political intelligence, Turnipseed passed on vague and contradictory hints about the one thing that most concerned Nixon: whether Wallace would remain as a Democrat through the election or (the President's greatest nightmare) finish up the primaries and then cut back into the campaign as a third-party candidate.[87]

On the afternoon of May 3, Arthur Bremer bought copies of the *Milwaukee Sentinel* and the *Journal* and read about Wallace's landslide in Alabama and his surprisingly strong second-place showing in Indiana, where he trailed Humphrey by fewer than forty thousand votes in a primary drawing 700,000 voters.[88] Then he wandered through the zoo, walked along the lakefront, and drove to the Mayfair Shopping Center Cinema to see *A Clockwork Orange.* He "thought about getting Wallace all thru the picture—fantasing my self as the Alek on the screen come to real life." (Alex was the homicidal protagonist of the Stanley Kubrick film.) Wallace, Bremer had decided, would have the "honor" of becoming his victim.

Ironically, it was Nixon Bremer despised; Wallace was simply a more convenient target. "I don't expect anybody to get a big thobbing erection from the news," he complained. "Who the hell ever got buried in 'Bama for being great. . . ? SHIT! I won't even rate a T.V. enteroption in Russia or Europe when the news breaks—they never heard of Wallace."[89]

Using the Milwaukee newspapers, he plotted out Wallace's campaign schedule for Michigan's May 16 primary. And he checked out of the local

library Robert Blair Kaiser's *"R.F.K. Must Die,"* a biography of Robert
Kennedy's assassin, Sirhan Sirhan. "Really like it," he wrote in his diary. "A
good man with a pen."[90]

The morning after Bremer made his diary entry, George Wallace settled
into his Flint, Michigan, hotel room for an interview with Detroit *News* correspondent Michael Wendland. When Wendland asked about the rigors of
campaigning, the Alabama governor leaned forward and spoke intently. It
wasn't simply that the daily grind of the speeches and interviews took its toll,
he said, there was also the lingering fear of who might be waiting in the
audience. "Somebody's going to get me one of these days . . ." he said. "I can
just see a little guy out there that nobody's paying any attention to. He
reaches into his pocket and out comes the little gun, like that Sirhan guy that
got [Robert] Kennedy."

Then as if he realized how apprehensive he had sounded, he chewed for
a moment on the end of his cigar and gave a big grin. "See what I mean?" he
told Wendland with a wink. "All that worrying can really get to you."[91]

When Wallace arrived in Dearborn, Michigan, on the night of May 9, six
thousand supporters had overflowed the community youth center and surrounded the building. The white working-class suburb of Detroit was a
center of antibusing resistance in the state, and Wallace handlers had anticipated a good turnout. An hour and a half before the governor's scheduled
appearance, the hall was filled and Wallace organizers frantically searched
for loudspeakers to set up outside the auditorium.

By the time the jubilant Wallace and his wife walked onto the stage at
eight-thirty P.M., even the jaded Detroit reporters assigned to the campaign
were impressed by the boisterous enthusiasm. From the moment local auto
workers presented Wallace with an official union jacket, until the candidate
wound up with his patented punch line—"Busing is the most asinine cruel
thing I've ever heard of"—supporters cheered, yelled, stamped their feet,
and waved hats and signs.[92] For twenty minutes after his speech Wallace
seemed unable to break away from the delirious crowd; he wandered back
and forth across the stage of the auditorium, waving, snapping his quick
jerky salutes.

Outside the back of the auditorium, Arthur Bremer managed to inch his
way through the crowd to a position at a window overlooking the area
behind the stage. A half-dozen onlookers later recalled his distinctive dress:
his shirt, socks, and tie were all vivid red, white, and blue stripes set off
against a dark blue suit. "He looked like a flag," remembered one man who
stood next to him.[93] Just before the rally began, Bremer had watched Wallace walk within five feet of the window and wave to excited followers
pressed against the glass. During the half-hour speech, Bremer waited until
one of the spectators moved and then carefully positioned himself directly in

front of the window. "The thin glass was weakly reinforced with wire mesh. But no trouble for a bullet at all." He opened his jacket and felt for his gun.

Suddenly the speech was over, and Wallace was striding down the back steps, directly by the window, moving toward his waiting car. "He took less time to wave good-bye than he did to wave hellow," wrote a startled Bremer. As he started to draw his gun, two teenaged girls leapt to their feet and blocked the window. Bitterly he wrote in his diary, "I let Wallace go only to spare these 2 stupid innocent delighted kids." Though Bremer had failed, he had seen for himself that—unlike the tight net around Nixon—Wallace's security was light, even lackadaisical. "There'd be other times."[94]

Over the next twenty-four hours Bremer came close to his target as he trailed the candidate back and forth across the state. At a surprisingly flat rally in the north Michigan town of Cadillac, cameramen filming the crowd picked up Bremer at least twice as, standing and shouting, he tried to rouse the crowd to the enthusiasm he had seen in Dearborn. He attempted to ease his way down to the front of the auditorium, but rally organizers had roped off the first four rows for local dignitaries. "I am, at the very most, 35 feet from my target," Bremer later wrote, reliving the frustrating moment. But he recalled those frustrating hours on the firing range. "Too far to risk. Need a sure shot."[95]

His last chance to catch Wallace in Michigan had slipped away. Newspapers published the Alabama governor's final primary itinerary: a whirlwind tour through the Eastern Shore of Maryland, a quick flight back to Montgomery for two days of badly needed rest, and then a last round of appearances on election eve in suburban Maryland. But Maryland was seven hundred miles away and Bremer now had less than a hundred dollars of his painfully saved nest egg. A week earlier, leaving Milwaukee, he had packed all his clothes, a pillow, a blanket, and sheets into the back of his Rambler. He would have to sleep in the car on the way to Maryland. But he seems to have given no thought to turning back.

ON the morning of May 15, George Wallace woke up in the Montgomery governor's mansion in a foul mood. Always tense just before a primary election, he was particularly put out at his heavy schedule in suburban Maryland. He quarreled with his daughter Peggy Sue, and at one point threatened to leave Cornelia behind when she lingered over her makeup. All polls showed he was the front-runner in both Maryland and Michigan. Why risk a public rally in which a gaffe (or an unfriendly audience) could dominate the headlines on election morning? he groused to press secretary Billy Joe Camp.

His first speech, in Wheaton, just north of Washington, D.C., seemed to confirm his premonitions. Two dozen college students threw pennies, a bar of soap, and a couple of tomatoes toward the speaker's platform. Wallace made light of the incident. "I see some members of the audience are still undecided," he told his followers with a mocking grin.

When one attractive young woman began shouting obscenities ("about as foul as any I had ever heard in any army latrine," Wallace recalled), he snapped back with a grin: "Is that what they teach you at the college you attend?"[96] For the most part, the heckling and the crowd's laughing responses to the well-rehearsed put-downs seemed good-natured and hardly menacing. As CBS cameraman Laurens Pierce filmed the rally, he focused on one devotee clad in a distinctive red-white-and-blue shirt and tie, leading the audience in cheers. Toward the end of the speech, the young man pleaded unsuccessfully with a policeman holding back the crowd. "Could you get George to come down and shake hands with me? I'm a great fan of his."[97] But a renewed shower of pennies sent Wallace, surrounded by a dozen bodyguards, scurrying to his limousine. Pierce stepped in front of the short, blond-haired young man. "Haven't I filmed you before at another Wallace rally?" he asked.

Arthur Bremer emphatically shook his head, then briskly walked away.[98]

While Wallace wolfed down a hamburger steak at a nearby Howard Johnson's, his Maryland campaign chairman hurried to confirm arrangements near Laurel, one of the many middle-class communities that melt together in the suburbs which stretch almost unbroken between Washington and Baltimore. When he reached the small shopping strip just before two P.M. he found Wallace's bulletproof podium in place, the sound system already checked out by a local country-music band, and more than a thousand supporters gathering behind the roped-off spectators' area. There were no hecklers or anti-Wallace signs in sight.

An hour later, the candidate plunged gamely into his standard speech, rambling over the familiar terrain of busing, tax benefits for the working class, and foreign aid and welfare handouts, but his voice was failing—he had to stop repeatedly for water—and although all the punch lines were in place, there was no rhythm, no buildup. He even stumbled over his best law-and-order line ("If somebody gets knocked in the head when they walk away from this shopping center today, the person who gets knocked in the head, uh, knocks you in the head, is out of jail by some federal judge's edict before you get to the hospital.") At three-fifty P.M., sensing that he was disappointing his audience, Wallace abruptly ended his talk. "I want to apologize to you for being here a little late and apologize to you for my voice," he said, "but it's been a long strenuous campaign." If the audience wanted to "shake up" the left-wingers in the Democratic party, he concluded, "and you want to give them the Saint Vitus Dance, the best way to do it is to vote for George Wallace tomorrow. Thank you very much."[99]

As he moved away from the platform toward the waiting convoy of cars, the fans began calling to their hero.[100]

"I suppose I had better shake hands," he told James Taylor, the Secret Service man in charge of the security detail.[101]

Taylor winced as he looked out over the milling crowd. "Don't go, Governor," he argued.

"That's all right," said Wallace. "I'll take the responsibility."[102]

Secret Service agent Nick Zarvos stayed a step ahead as the candidate reached across the rope barricade to touch the hands of smiling followers; Alabama state police captain E. C. Dothard walked a step behind. When they reached the end of the rope barricade and began moving back toward the cars, Arthur Bremer—partially shielded by a middle-aged couple in the front row—shouted: "Hey, George, let me shake hands with you!" Wallace turned in the direction of the voice and extended his hand.

Less than three feet away, Bremer began firing. One bullet ripped through Wallace's forearm and shoulder; another entered his right abdomen and stomach, while a third bullet pierced his right rib cage and lodged in his spine.

The next twenty seconds, recorded by an alert television cameraman, were a chaotic replay of a scene familiar to Americans in the 1960s: the assassin wrestled to the ground, the shouts of the bystanders, the screams, first of fear and then of outrage.

Ross Speigle, a forty-six-year-old crane operator who was first to tackle the gunman, began pounding Bremer's head into the pavement ("I really wanted to hurt him and hurt him bad," said Speigle). Finally three county policemen wrestled a bloody Bremer away and dragged him to a waiting squad car while the crowd shouted in frustration, "Get him! Get that bastard!"[103]

Lying on the ground, George Wallace felt no immediate pain but knew instantly that he was badly wounded. "I tried to move my legs, but nothing happened. It was as though they didn't belong to me at all."

Cornelia reached him first. Screaming, she threw herself prone across her husband.

"I'm shot," he said to her in a flat breathless voice. "I've been shot."

Thirty minutes later in the emergency room of Silver Springs's Holy Cross Hospital, a team of surgeons examined Wallace, who was still lucid, though in agonizing pain.

"Governor, move your legs," the chief surgeon kept asking him. Finally, Cornelia Wallace, who had been allowed into the area, broke in. "He can't hear you," she said. "He has a bad hearing problem."

She spoke loudly. "George, move your legs."

"I can't," Wallace said in a whispery voice. "I've been shot in the spine."[104]

Jammed between two policemen, Arthur Bremer sat quietly as he was driven to the Prince Georges County jail in Hyattsville. Only once did he speak. "Do you think they'll want to buy my book?" he asked. When the police inventoried his pockets, they found his car keys, a pocket comb, and $1.73—all that remained of his savings.[105]

MAY 15 had been a busy day for the President. In addition to the usual ceremonial "in and outs"—the brief presentation of diplomatic credentials by four new ambassadors—John Connally, his secretary of the treasury, had decided to resign. The two men met during the day to discuss a joint press conference on the sixteenth. Nixon still had hopes of placing the former Texas Democrat on the ticket in place of Agnew, and he planned to use the occasion to emphasize his great regard for Connally. But just before five P.M., Haldeman called the President into the office adjacent to the Oval Office.

"We just got word over the Secret Service wire that George Wallace was shot at a rally in Maryland," said Haldeman. Details were sketchy. They knew only that Wallace was still alive and the assailant white. (The White House staff had always feared that the assassination of Wallace by a black gunman would trigger a race conflict.)

Nixon immediately ordered an elaborate security watch in the jail to prevent a repetition of Oswald's murder after the Kennedy assassination. At Connally's suggestion, the President also increased the number of Secret Service agents guarding Democratic candidates and extended protection to Ted Kennedy. Although Kennedy was not officially a Democratic candidate, he was a likely choice for a deadlocked convention, and in any case the brother of John and Robert Kennedy was considered a lightning rod for potential kooks.

Such precautions were understandable. But it soon became clear that the President of the United States was interested in far more than calming the public and safeguarding the integrity of an investigation. First and last, he intended to use the incident to protect and advance his political fortunes.

The shooting of Wallace came at a critical moment of upheaval within the FBI. J. Edgar Hoover, its longtime chief, had been dead for less than two weeks, and while Nixon had appointed faithful political operative L. Patrick Gray as acting director, Gray was out of the loop during the first critical hours after the Wallace shooting. Instead, W. Mark Felt, assistant FBI director and the ranking career officer in the Bureau, took charge of the case. Technically, Felt was not a political appointee, but twenty years at Hoover's elbow had taught him the importance of remaining in the good graces of the White House. The very week of the Wallace shooting, he had persuaded Acting Director Gray to authorize a series of illegal burglaries in an attempt to locate radical members of the Weather Underground—the so-called Weathermen—accused of planting bombs in their campaign against the war in Vietnam. (A federal jury convicted Felt of approving the burglary in 1980; Ronald Reagan pardoned him the following year.[106])

And Felt had a trusted contact: White House counsel Charles (Chuck) Colson. The forty-one-year-old lawyer and ex-Marine had come on board in the fall of 1969 to head the Office of Public Liaison. He soon proved particularly skilled at mobilizing "spontaneous" public opinion in support of the President's policies and even more adept at coordinating a repertoire of increasingly illegal dirty tricks against Democratic opponents. Colson was "tougher than hell, smarter than hell, meaner than hell," recalled one White House aide who worked closely with him during these years.[107]

These characteristics wedded to his unfailing talent for sycophancy soon earned him Richard Nixon's attention and admiration. Early in his tenure at the White House, Colson successfully planted in a tabloid newspaper a photograph of Teddy Kennedy leaving a nightclub arm-in-arm with a voluptuous young woman clearly not his wife. Thereafter, remembered Haldeman, one of Colson's prime assignments was to "catch him [Kennedy] in the sack with one of his babes." And from that moment on, said Haldeman, "as far as the President was concerned, *Colson was Mr. Can-Do.*"[108]

While he technically answered to Haldeman, Colson was soon spending hours with Nixon endorsing and elaborating on the President's self-destructive efforts to "destroy" his political enemies. Haldeman and Ehrlichman often modified or even ignored orders issued in the heat of their chief's periodic temper tantrums; Colson never questioned his boss. He was the man aptly described by a Senate staffer as someone who would "walk over his own grandmother if he had to" in order to reelect Richard Nixon. Although Colson, in his born-again-Christian post-Watergate reincarnation, complained (correctly) that the quote had been inaccurately attributed to him, it stuck precisely because it had such a chilling ring of truth.[109]

Ninety minutes after the shooting the investigation exploded into a jurisdictional nightmare as Colson and Nixon conspired to use the incident to embarrass the man they were increasingly coming to see as their most likely opponent: George McGovern.

Between five P.M. and eleven P.M., Colson conferred with Felt at least a half-dozen times; twice the President spoke on the phone to the FBI assistant director. From the very first conversation with Felt, Colson and the President knew the identity of the accused assassin. (Bremer was carrying his wallet with a Wisconsin driver's license.) Under Title 18, Section 245, of the U.S. Code, the attack on Wallace as a political candidate was a violation of his civil rights as a candidate for federal office, so Pat Gray assumed from the outset of the case that the Bureau would control the investigation, and he bluntly shoved state and local police officials aside. After a brief examination less than an hour after the shooting, a Prince Georges County psychiatrist had urged officials to place the suspect under a suicide watch. In his judgment Bremer was a "mental case." But the young man's refusal to talk with arresting officials was troubling. Was Bremer—as it appeared—simply another in the long line of sociopaths who had acted alone? Or was he part of a larger, politically motivated conspiracy organized to kill the fiery Alabama presidential candidate?

Just after five P.M., Thomas Farrow, head of the Baltimore FBI office, called his counterpart in Milwaukee (where it was an hour earlier) and told him to check out the address listed on Bremer's driver's license: 2433 West Michigan Street in Milwaukee. Within minutes, two agents from the office arrived at the twenty-two-unit building. The Bureau's field agents were famous for investigation by the book; lacking a search warrant, the two men began systematically interviewing other residents in the apartment building.

But James Rowley, head of the Secret Service, had different priorities. As the agency charged with protecting the President and presidential candidates, the Secret Service was primarily concerned over the potential danger to Nixon and to other candidates. Without consulting the President or clearing his actions with the FBI, Rowley ordered one of his Milwaukee agents to investigate Bremer's apartment. The agent had no difficulty obtaining entry with the cooperation of the building caretaker, and had no compunctions about entering the premises without a warrant. In the two small and poorly furnished rooms, jumbled with dirty clothes, piles of paper, and overdue bills, he found a handwritten note containing a reference to suicide, another listing the presidential primaries, and others that appeared "incoherent in nature." The debris scattered through the apartment—a Confederate flag, a gun magazine, a pamphlet published by the Black Panther Party, a handout from the American Civil Liberties Union—suggested something less than a hard-bitten professional assassin. Of perhaps more relevance were materials that reflected—in the words of a later memo—an "interest directed toward abnormal sexual behavior." (Later investigators seemed particularly fascinated by a comic book which showed a "pig in a pigpen named Arthur Herman, who apparently had sexual designs on the other pigs in the pigpen.") The Secret Service agent placed two handwritten notes in an envelope to take back to Washington—"do a bang-up job of getting people to notice you," one began—for further examination.[110]

As he leafed through the material, he heard a firm knock at the door. His FBI counterparts had heard footsteps and rustling papers in Bremer's apartment. At this point, according to the official Secret Service report, "investigative jurisdiction was discussed between representatives of both enforcement agencies on the scene."[111] John Ehrlichman described the conflict somewhat more vividly. "The Secret Service and the FBI were at each other's throats," he recalled. "I thought they were going to shoot each other!"[112]

In the Oval Office, the President laid it out from the beginning, recalled

Colson. "Whose side is he on—right or left-winger?"[113] If Bremer had "ties to the Republican Party or the Nixon campaign," a worried Nixon hypothesized to Colson and Haldeman, it could easily cost him the election.[114] Nixon had made it clear to Felt that he wanted to know about Bremer's background. Was he involved in "any demonstrations or similar activity?" he asked. The President seemed particularly disturbed that some of the materials in Bremer's apartment had slipped into the hands of the Secret Service; he issued a firm order that any materials removed from the apartment be returned immediately to the FBI.[115]

The eventual criminal prosecution of Wallace's assassin was irrelevant, Nixon told Haldeman and Colson. "What matters for the next 24–48 hours is the story regarding the guy and so on." They should not worry about conducting White House operations "by the book," the President instructed; "it's all PR at this point, not a matter of who wins the case."[116] "We were constantly saying, 'Can we do this or that?' " Colson admitted two decades later. "Like catching Teddy Kennedy in bed. It was both of us. We were spontaneous combustion."[117]

As in every case where the political interests of his administration seemed at risk, Richard Nixon's first instinct was to step outside the bureaucracy. Bureaucrats always had their own interests and agendas, and they had a frustratingly shortsighted view of the importance of following rules, regulations, and laws. During the first of many conversations with the White House, Felt had mentioned to Colson that Bureau agents would not search the apartment until they had obtained a warrant the next morning. That important piece of information laid the foundation for a scheme which—even by the rather elastic standards of Nixon's White House—was as audacious as it was illegal.

While Colson and Nixon sat in the Oval Office waiting for another call from the FBI, Nixon leaned back, cocktail in hand, and mused out loud: "Wouldn't it be great if . . . oh, wouldn't it be great if they [*sic*] had left-wing propaganda in that apartment?" Too bad, he said, "we can't plant McGovern literature."[118] With one master stroke, they could sow bitter division within the ranks of the Democrats by linking Wallace's would-be assassin with the party's likely nominee.

Colson had just the man he needed for this operation. Fourteen months earlier, he had recruited E. Howard Hunt for special White House assignments. Hunt, a Washington public-relations operative and former Central Intelligence Agency officer, had never engaged in actual espionage or counterintelligence operations; his specialty lay in spreading "disinformation" against supposed foreign-policy foes. But he had also written a number of novels—including several thrillers—under his own name and a variety of pen names, and he was at heart a frustrated if extraordinarily incompetent espionage agent.[119]

Colson had used Hunt to perform a variety of covert (and illegal) operations for the Nixon White House. Over the previous Labor Day weekend, Hunt and his team of Cuban-Americans had burglarized the offices of a Los Angeles psychoanalyst in an attempt to obtain the files of Daniel Ellsberg, the former State Department official who had leaked the Pentagon Papers and had, in the process, become one of Nixon's obsessions.

Hunt and Colson had worked even more closely together in an operation designed to embarrass Ted Kennedy by slandering his late brother. On Colson's instructions, Hunt had forged a series of State Department telegrams that purported to show that President Kennedy had engineered the 1963 assassination of South Vietnamese president Ngo Dinh Diem and his brother, Ngo Dinh Nhu. Colson showed the forged cables to a *Life* magazine reporter, but the savvy newsman refused to write a story unless he was allowed to subject the telegrams to analysis by an intelligence expert, an analysis Colson knew would reveal them as spurious.[120] All this was simply a warm-up to Hunt's fateful—and astonishingly botched—break-in at the Watergate complex later that spring.[121]

If his record as a successful operative was a bit shaky, by his own assessment he had one great advantage: he was willing to do anything to curry favor with Colson and with the President. Colson ordered Hunt to go home and prepare to fly to Milwaukee and break into the Bremer apartment on a top-secret White House assignment.

Hunt later insisted that he had expressed misgivings about the mission from the outset. The apartment might be guarded by police or locked. And how was he supposed to get in? An irritated Colson told him to "bribe the janitor or pick the lock."[122] Hunt returned to his suburban Virginia home, assembled his CIA-issued disguise kit and false identification papers, and began calling airlines with service to Milwaukee. His wife, Dorothy, berated him for involving himself in another one of Colson's schemes. "He's got to be *insane,*" she warned.[123]

While Hunt packed his bags, Colson was on the phone laying the groundwork for the Bremer disinformation operation. He explained to Felt that the President had heard rumors that Bremer "had ties with Kennedy or McGovern political operatives, that obviously there could be a conspiracy."[124] He then talked to the Associated Press White House correspondent, a reporter from the *Washington Post,* and Gerald terHorst, chief Washington correspondent for the *Detroit News.* (Colson had cultivated a regular relationship as an "inside source" with terHorst). The White House aide told the newsmen there was evidence that Bremer had "allied himself with 'left-wing causes.' "[125] He also suggested that Bremer was connected to the campaign of Senator George McGovern.[126]

While the *Post* account of the Wallace shooting failed to include any of

Colson's tidbits, terHorst did report that "sources close to the investigation" had told him that Bremer was a "dues-paying member of the Young Democrats of Milwaukee, one of the most liberal in the party," an accusation echoed in the Associated Press story. This was, of course, completely untrue.[127]

Even as Colson laid the groundwork for linking George Wallace's would-be assassin with George McGovern, his plans fell apart.

Felt relayed to Colson the embarrassing news that, in the one hour and twenty minutes when Secret Service and FBI agents had abandoned the apartment during their jurisdictional squabble, newsmen had persuaded the building superintendent to allow access to Bremer's quarters. While they had not disturbed the evidence, they had photographed and inventoried the cluttered materials in the three rooms. But Felt proudly assured Colson that he would seal the room and maintain a round-the-clock guard until they obtained a search warrant.[128]

Nixon, furious over the missed opportunity to link McGovern with Bremer, berated his counsel for failing to control the FBI investigation, while Colson's secretary called Hunt to give him the welcome news. "You don't have to travel, Howard," Joan Hall said. "Chuck says thanks, anyway."[129]

If the enigmatic Bremer could not be turned into a political bonanza, he remained a worrisome threat to the White House. When agents searched the blue Rambler, they discovered a 137-page handwritten diary, which the suspect had kept from April 4 through May 13. Within hours, a team of nearly two dozen transcribers had been assembled to decipher the scrawled, often incoherent document. FBI agents learned that the would-be assassin had stalked Nixon through the spring of 1972, had given up in frustration because of the tight security around the President, and had then turned to Wallace as his target. (He had even briefly considered shooting McGovern.) But the President and his men were far more concerned about the diary's first entry, which contained an enigmatic reference to an earlier manuscript buried somewhere in Milwaukee. Just a week before his attack on Wallace, Bremer had referred again to a hidden portion of the diary:

Hey world! Come here! I wanna talk to ya!

If I don't kill—if I don't kill myself I want you to pay through the nose, ears & belly button for the beginning of this manuscript. The 1st pages are hidden & will preserve [for] a long time. If you don't pay me for them, I got no reason to turn 'em over—understand punk!?[130]

While the semiliterate, misspelled musings seemed to suggest that Bremer was simply an unbalanced individual desperately seeking recognition and fame, during those first hours after Wallace had been shot near panic existed among White House staff. What if the missing diary linked Bremer—even indirectly—to the Republican campaign? worried Nixon.

The first order of business was to make certain that no information about the document leaked to the press. So tightly did the White House seek to control the diary that twenty-four hours after its transcription, James Rowley, head of the Secret Service, had not yet gained access to make certain that it did not contain critical information concerning future threats to Nixon and other presidential candidates. Patrick Gray finally agreed to allow Rowley's men to read the document, but only under conditions of absolute security.[131]

On orders from Nixon, Ehrlichman ordered the FBI to avoid any mention of the document in their internal memoranda. Bureau officials, however, had already sent out five memos referring to the diary. Within twenty-four hours after receiving Ehrlichman's order, FBI officials reported back that "letters and enclosures to the President, Acting Attorney General, Deputy Attorney General, AAG, Civil Rights Division and AAG, Criminal Division, [mentioning the diary] have been destroyed and supplemental letters prepared for transmittal to each [in which] all references to diary [are] deleted." As Nixon could have anticipated, however, R. I. Shroder, the high-ranking FBI official ordered to alter intragovernmental communications, dutifully prepared a memo for the files ("for record purposes") describing the potential obstruction of justice and explaining that he had altered the records only upon explicit orders from the White House. He distributed copies of the document through the Bureau.[132]

But there was no political bombshell in the portion of the diary they recovered from Bremer's car. And as the Bureau began to check and recheck the gunman's background and to correlate their investigation with his diary, it became more and more likely that Bremer was exactly what he appeared to be, a pathetic misfit and loner who followed the classic pattern of the political assassins of the 1960s: Lee Harvey Oswald, Sirhan Sirhan, and James Earl Ray. By the time he came to trial in June 1972, the White House had shifted its energies to exacerbating the self-destruction of the McGovern campaign. When the Maryland jury, which deliberated for less than thirty minutes after Bremer's three-day trial, found the would-be assassin guilty, and the presiding judge sentenced him to sixty-three years in prison, Arthur Bremer was quickly forgotten by the public.

Almost a month to the day after Bremer's attempted assassination of George Wallace, Washington, D.C., police apprehended five men as they sought to install listening devices in the Watergate offices of the Democratic National Committee. In the years that followed, historians, politicians, and journalists have argued over the President's precise involvement. As Tennessee senator Howard Baker repeatedly asked at the Watergate hearings, "What did the President know and when did he know it?"[133] But Richard

Nixon's response to the Wallace shooting showed beyond any doubt that the Watergate break-in faithfully reflected a President's contempt for the constraints of the law. As he prepared for his reelection campaign, nothing mattered except winning: "It's all PR at this point. . . ."

THE euphoria at the results of the May 15 Michigan and Maryland Democratic primaries swept away the White House preoccupation with Bremer. Pollsters had projected Wallace as the winner in both states, but no one anticipated his stunning margin of victory, particularly in Michigan, where he swept suburban as well as white working-class precincts and racked up a fifty-one percent majority, handily outdistancing George McGovern, who drew only a quarter of the state's Democratic voters. The key to the seriously wounded southerner's victory in both states was crossover voting by suburban Republicans, who needed no encouragement from the White House to choose Wallace as their vehicle for sending a message: No more busing. They might be irritated with court-ordered busing, but they could hardly turn to the Democrats for relief in November.

The "Mich[igan] Wallace thing is fantastic," Nixon told Haldeman as he went over the returns. Now perhaps, everyone on his staff would "believe [the] busing issue."[134] As longtime Nixon backer Robert Finch had argued in March, the "entire strategy . . . depends on whether George Wallace makes a run on his own."[135] With Wallace fighting for his life in Maryland's Holy Cross Hospital, the threat seemed over.

But Richard Nixon had not made it to the edge of a triumphant reelection without covering every contingency. Two days after the primary, Nixon had already put together what Haldeman called the "tentative plan on Wallace." It began with a carefully choreographed presidential hospital visit. (Cornelia Wallace recalled with just a touch of sarcasm that the commander in chief arrived wearing television makeup.)[136] Nixon confided in his diary his less-than-positive feelings about Wallace ("a demagogue"), but he instinctively understood that the Alabama governor, above all else, wanted to be treated with respect. In their twenty-minute meeting, he promised to send Alexander Haig over to the hospital to brief the governor on the upcoming presidential trip to Moscow. Wallace praised Nixon for his efforts to speed the withdrawal of American troops from Vietnam. The President pointed to a floral flag arrangement that had been placed by Wallace's bed and told him to "keep the flag flying high." (Like most southerners, Nixon generalized, Wallace was "somewhat sentimental in terms of his strong patriotism.") The emotional Wallace gave a weak salute. "I saluted back and left the room," Nixon wrote in his diary that night.[137]

As the President walked down the hall, he leaned over to Cornelia Wallace and said with a smile: "From what I hear, you've been good for the Governor. He has the determination to overcome this thing."

446 THE POLITICS OF RAGE

"Yes, sir, I know he will," she returned with an impish smile. "We expect to be out there running against you in November."[138]

Which was precisely what Cornelia Wallace had in mind. Even as surgeons struggled to treat her husband's multiple wounds, she had begun plotting his political survival with Billy Joe Camp. "Tomorrow is Election Day," she had told Camp, "and people just won't vote for a dying man."[139] Shortly after nine P.M., she appeared before a television camera and, flanked by the governor's children, assured reporters that "my husband is in very good condition. . . . I feel very optimistic about him." Smiling, she continued, "You know his nature. He didn't get the title of the Fighting Little Judge for nothing." She had made no mention of his probable paralysis.[140] The next morning she staged a carefully posed photograph of a smiling Wallace brandishing the front page of the *Baltimore Sun* with its banner headline: "Wallace Wins in Maryland, Michigan; Hospital Takes Him off the Critical List."

Over the next three weeks, she worked quietly behind the scenes to fan the impression that, if the Democrats failed to nominate Wallace, he would revive his third-party campaign. Simultaneously, close supporters of the Alabama governor entered into negotiations with a Hubert Humphrey desperate to block the impending nomination of McGovern. Wallace, briefed at his hospital bed, apparently believed that Humphrey was willing to put him on the ticket as his running mate and assigned one of his closest friends to try and negotiate a deal. (The former vice president later admitted that the bait had been dangled by an intermediary, but said he never had any intention of joining forces with Wallace.)[141]

The Republicans' elaborate network kept Nixon informed of every move in the Democrats' preconvention maneuvering. (Within twenty-four hours after Humphrey sent an intermediary to see a Wallace aide, Nixon knew the details of their meeting.[142]) Through the Secret Service, the FBI, and inquiries by White House physician William Lukash, Nixon had obtained detailed information on the governor's medical condition. There was little or no chance that he would ever walk again; that much was known to the public within forty-eight hours after the shooting. But Nixon and his aides also knew that the Alabama governor was in much worse condition than his press secretary's optimistic bulletins would suggest. George Wallace had no control of his urinary or excretory functions; he had lost twenty percent of his body weight; he was in continuous and excruciating pain from the spinal injury. Moreover, the bullets that struck him in the stomach and nicked his lower bowel had triggered the first of what would be a series of debilitating abscesses, each requiring additional surgery.

Even the calendar was on the President's side. The Alabama governor had already missed the deadline for filing as an independent candidate in seventeen states. Although Colson predicted that Wallace would run in a number of other states, Nixon and John Mitchell were skeptical.[143]

By mid-June, the White House plans for the 1972 campaign were almost complete. Nixon's expansion of the air war against North Vietnam had bought enough time to postpone the collapse of the South Vietnamese until safely after the election. More importantly, the Democrats seemed committed to nominating George McGovern, the one opponent the President felt certain he could easily beat. Still Nixon continued to fret. A Wallace third-party run—even if it were halfhearted—remained a possibility, and White House polls continued to show that a three-way race would reduce the President's victory margin by at least four percentage points.

Nixon decided to make certain that Wallace got to Miami Beach for the Democratic National Convention to keep the Democrats off-balance and on the ropes. When he learned that the governor might have difficulty making the trip, the President proposed that the Air Force furnish—on "humanitarian" grounds—a C-147 hospital plane. Mitchell and Dent opposed the move on the grounds that the public would recognize the gesture as a cynically transparent White House political ploy, but Nixon overrode their objections.[144] And for a time, the maneuver seemed well worth the risk. After an emotional detour to Montgomery, Wallace arrived at the convention center in a cloud of belligerent press releases threatening the Democratic Party with dire consequences if it failed to heed his warnings. But, exhausted and debilitated, he quickly retreated to his hotel suite, where round-the-clock nurses anxiously monitored his weakening condition. Four Alabama doctors accompanying him assumed that the hectic pace of activities had worn out their patient; in fact, he was suffering from the early stages of a severe abdominal abscess, which would require surgery as soon as the convention had ended. Without firm instructions or direction from Wallace, most of his delegates milled about aimlessly.[145]

Democratic Party leaders, anxious to avoid a rancorous and open split, had agreed to give the Alabama governor twenty minutes of prime television time on the second night of the convention to present his minority planks on defense, taxes, busing, and welfare reform. Waiting in a stuffy backstage area, Wallace became queasy and nearly had to cancel his talk. While his family and his doctors watched apprehensively, the candidate, gray and sweating heavily, clung to the arms of his wheelchair as his bodyguards pushed him up a narrow ramp that brought him to the proper height at the speaker's stand.

The national Democratic Party platform was on the road to disaster, he warned the delegates. The only hope for the party was to turn its back on wasteful domestic welfare programs and reject plans for relegating the United States to the status of a "second-rate power." If anything was clear from the political primaries of the spring and early summer, he reminded his audience, it was the opposition of voters to the "senseless, asinine busing of . . . school children to achieve racial balance throughout the United States." (The

McGovernites had made the defense of busing a litmus test for racial commitment; the final Democratic platform insisted that the "transportation of students" was "another tool" which had to be used to eliminate segregated public schools.) If the Democratic Party remained hostage to the "intellectual pseudo-snobbery that has controlled it for some years," said Wallace, it would inevitably be rejected by the "average citizen who works each day for a living and pays his taxes and holds the country together."[146]

On paper, the speech breathed fire and defiance, but even though the governor managed to bring some vigor to his voice when he raised the busing issue, it was clear to delegates, and even clearer to the millions of television viewers, that the gaunt figure in the wheelchair was not the same Wallace who had roused his followers to rebellion. The McGovernites, anxious to avoid needless conflict, listened respectfully, applauded politely at the conclusion of the speech, and then overwhelmingly voted down Wallace's substitute planks for the party platform. Wallace was fast asleep in his hotel suite when exuberantly undisciplined Democrats finally nominated McGovern halfway between midnight and dawn on the morning of July 13.

THROUGHOUT June and early July, Nixon's aides struggled to maintain their lines of communication with the fractured Wallace campaign.[147] Colson worked through with one faction led by Snider and Bill France. (France, head of the National Association for Stock Car Auto Racing [NASCAR], had been Wallace's main money raiser in the 1972 campaign). Colson reported that Snider and other key Wallace people were ready to use their influence with the Alabama governor to discourage any third-party run and to work quietly for Nixon's reelection, but in return they wanted "$750,000 to keep their staff on through the election."[148]

Meanwhile Harry Dent was in touch with Tom Turnipseed and Cornelia Wallace, who seemed intent on pushing through a third-party campaign unless the Nixon people made significant concessions. For the White House, the problem was to know who really spoke for Wallace. We've "got to figure out whose deal is for real and how to handle it," reported Haldeman after one frustrating meeting between Nixon and Colson.[149] Ultimately, Nixon authorized payment of an undisclosed sum to the Wallace people for the "financial support of their staff needs."[150]

But in the political chess game of 1972, the members of the Wallace entourage were limited by the inescapable fact that they were planning a gambit without a knight. Several followers in Montgomery privately admitted to reporters that the hints of a third-party run were made only to keep the flow of contributions pouring into campaign headquarters in Alabama. George Wallace was exhausted, depressed, and totally uninterested in throwing himself into the race.[151]

Even had he wished to make the run, he was hemmed in by the passionate commitment of his own followers to defeating George McGovern. The Wallace delegates at the Democratic convention, wrote Ray Jenkins, seemed honestly to believe that President McGovern would "put marijuana in vending machines, make our daughters have abortions whether they need them or not, turn Fort Knox over to the National Welfare Rights Organization, and rent the Pentagon to the Red Chinese for an Embassy."[152]

"I think he's a tool of the Communist party," Wallace himself remarked in an off-the-record comment to a *New York Times* reporter on the eve of the convention. If the voters had really understood his position, "he wouldn't have gotten one delegate."[153] Three times, McGovern met with the Alabama governor and asked for his endorsement. Wallace was cordial, but he candidly outlined his many disagreements with his party's nominee, and he reminded his opponent of the political realities: "You know, the problem, George, is that our people, even if I was to endorse you, I couldn't get them to support you."[154] McGovern's staff wrote off the South as hopeless.

Nixon had watched the unruly Democratic convention with ill-concealed glee. In his diary, he concluded that he had a "chance not just to win the election, but to create the New Majority we had only dreamed of in 1970. Only organized labor and George Wallace remained in doubt."[155] Less than a week after the convention ended, the AFL-CIO—for the first time in its history—decided not to make a political endorsement in the campaign of 1972.

Nixon seemed to think it unseemly for him to attempt to close the sale on Wallace's tacit endorsement of the Republican ticket. All through June and into July, he considered which of his followers was best positioned to make the pitch. Billy Graham "has a line to Wallace through Mrs. Wallace who has become a Christian," reported Haldeman.[156] Nixon had already used him in 1968 in an unsuccessful attempt to persuade Wallace to withdraw his third-party candidacy. And Graham had passed along to Wallace White House polls which showed that three of every four Wallace voters would turn to Nixon if the only choice was McGovern. According to Graham, Wallace swore that he would never do anything to help McGovern.[157]

But the more Nixon thought about it, the more he concluded that the perfect man for the job was his former secretary of the treasury. John Connally had met Wallace at several governors' conferences, and the Texas politician's wife, Nellie, had become friends with Cornelia. (The first call Cornelia Wallace took after her husband's shooting came from Nellie Connally.)[158] "Go down there and see him, and let me know what he wants," Nixon instructed.[159]

On July 25, Secret Service agents hustled the President's emissary through a back entrance into Spain Rehabilitation Clinic in Birmingham. Connally found Wallace sitting up in his hospital bed, still recovering from the latest in a series of operations necessary to drain infections caused by the gunshot wounds to his abdomen. Although alert and decisive in his comments, recalled the Texan, he was also unmistakably depressed and concerned about his recovery and rehabilitation. Wallace would not categorically abandon his third-party run, "but he did say he would not do anything to help McGovern."[160] Both men agreed that defeating McGovern was a common priority. Despite his oft-stated argument that his third-party candidacy hurt both parties equally, Wallace understood that he would draw the majority of his votes from Republicans. He extracted no specific promises from Connally. He told him that he would make his official announcement within the week and, while he would not openly endorse the President, he would make it clear to his followers that he was not supporting George McGovern. Back in Texas, Connally called to pass on the good news to the White House.

That same afternoon, George McGovern's press secretary released a brief statement announcing that the Democratic Party's vice-presidential nominee, Thomas Eagleton, had been hospitalized three times for severe depression, had twice received shock treatments, and was still taking medication for his condition. Although McGovern insisted that he was "1,000 percent" behind his running mate, in a matter of days Eagleton withdrew from the ticket, setting the stage for the total collapse of the Democratic presidential campaign of 1972.[161] July 25, John Connally later decided, marked the beginning of the end for George McGovern. The Eagleton debacle, the AFL-CIO's refusal to support the Democratic ticket, and George Wallace's weary acknowledgment that his role as a player in the political drama of 1972 was over gave the President the equivalent of a political hat trick. "We might well say that this was the day the election was won."[162]

Richard Nixon agreed. Even before the votes were counted, he was savoring his triumph. The sweep of the South was the most important development in the election of 1972, he told three of his close advisers, "and getting Wallace out was the most important single event." Removing Wallace from the political playing field made it possible for him to build a "New American Majority" on the solid foundation of the conservative South. Elitists might "look down their noses" on southerners, but in fact they were "Americans to the core," a people who had never been "poisoned by the elite universities and the media" so that they retained their "patriotism," "strong moral and spiritual values," and "anti-permissiveness."[163]

George Wallace could not have said it better.

"ATTENTION MUST BE PAID"

THE LEGACY OF GEORGE WALLACE

FEAR THAT HER HUSBAND'S political career might be over haunted Cornelia Wallace as she sat in the Holy Cross Hospital emergency room. She could not bear to "take him home crippled and to take him out of politics—I might as well have left him to die on the ground at that shopping center."[1] After twenty-six years of nonstop office-seeking, he had no life beyond the campaign trail.

As his doctor would later attest, only the governor's superb physical condition made it possible for him to survive the devastating gunshot wounds he had received at close range. A paramedic still remembered with awe the high-speed ambulance sprint from the Laurel Shopping Center to Holy Cross Hospital. George Wallace had repeatedly pushed away the oxygen mask on his face and complained that it was "too hot in here," she recalled. Absorbed with her efforts to stanch his bleeding, she ignored him. Finally, her fifty-three-year-old patient rose up, unlatched the window, and shoved it open.[2]

But physical toughness could not allay the depression that soon gripped him. "Why has this happened to me? If I were a mean man, maybe I could understand it," he told his wife, "but I've never done anything to hurt anybody. I didn't deserve this."

This was "part of God's plan for you," Cornelia suggested. No one will be able to "hate you now. Everyone will be sympathetic." Maybe, she said, "maybe God is giving you the greatest challenge of your life."[3]

With friends and important visitors, he remained upbeat. After the Nixon visit, a parade of celebrities and politicians trooped out to Holy Cross hospital to visit with the stricken governor: Ethel Kennedy, wife of the late Robert Kennedy, came; so did black congresswoman Shirley Chisholm and presidential aspirants Hubert Humphrey and George McGovern. Elvis Presley, a longtime admirer of Wallace, called and offered to retaliate against Bremer. (Wallace later said he told Presley to forget about such ideas; it would "ruin your career," he told the entertainer.)

To all these visitors, he seemed upbeat and hopeful; with family and close friends, he was far less cheerful. Two weeks before his flight to the Democratic convention, Wallace—racked by round-the-clock pain—began a series of what his wife tactfully called "crying spells." His surgeon briefly prescribed a mood elevator and pain medication, but Dr. Joseph Schanno was an old-fashioned physician concerned with the dangers of dependency and addiction. Spinal victims had to learn to live with a level of "ongoing discomfort," he bluntly told his patient.

Increasingly, Cornelia Wallace became the main target of her husband's angry and despairing outbursts. In the long hours between daily therapy sessions, he brooded over the shooting, playing and replaying the nightmarish episode in his mind. Initially, his wife held back any information on Arthur Bremer, but Wallace soon demanded everything he could find about his assailant. He was particularly disturbed by rumors in the press that, in the weeks before the shooting, Bremer had been spotted meeting a tall, handsome man with a short mustache.[4]

As the Watergate conspiracy and cover-up began to unravel in the spring of 1973, E. Howard Hunt became one of the first of the conspirators to tell all to congressional investigators. In a series of private interviews he described a half-dozen "dirty trick" operations mounted from the White House; almost offhandedly he referred to the Wallace shooting and Colson's orders to break into Arthur Bremer's apartment. Within days, a team of *Washington Post* reporters, Robert Woodward and Carl Bernstein, leaked a summary of Hunt's closed-door testimony—as well as Charles Colson's vehement denials. When Hunt and Colson testified before Congress that summer, the Watergate Committee had a golden opportunity to get to the bottom of the story, but senators and staffers bumbled the interrogation. Colson, in particular, was never challenged about the inconsistencies in his sworn statements.

At first, said Cornelia Wallace, she had blamed the assassination attempt on a "very Communist liberal element" among McGovern's supporters. But as she watched the Eagleton debacle and the collapse of the Democratic campaign, "I think McGovern in a sense was done in, too. And the man that ended up President was Richard Nixon. So I don't know."[5]

The publication of the last half of Bremer's diary shortly after the testimony of Hunt seemed to confirm Wallace's belief that he had been the victim of a White House–directed conspiracy. He soon gained additional ammunition for his theory. In late 1973, Gore Vidal published a long piece in the *New York Review of Books* mocking the FBI's claim that Bremer was a lone assassin. After reviewing Hunt's involvement in past cloak-and-dagger work, the novelist engaged in an elaborate exegesis of the mixture of sophistication and banality in the Bremer diary and darkly suggested that the document had been the work of Nixon-inspired CIA forgers, intent on covering the tracks of the real gunman.[6]

It was difficult to tell if he was writing tongue-in-cheek or seriously, but Wallace found his argument convincing. Paraphrasing Vidal, the governor suggested to reporters that the diary had a "contrived tone to it as though it were deliberately written to throw off inquiry into a possible conspiracy."[7] When Martha Mitchell, the estranged wife of Nixon's attorney general John Mitchell, visited George and Cornelia Wallace in Montgomery in May 1974, she insisted that her husband, deeply disturbed by a Colson-Bremer connection, had asked repeatedly: "What was Charles Colson doing, talking with Arthur Bremer four days before he shot George Wallace?"[8]

No evidence has ever been introduced to support a possible conspiracy. Martha Mitchell, who was drinking heavily by 1972 and sometimes behaved erratically, may simply have misunderstood her husband's response to the news that Colson had ordered a break-in of Bremer's apartment. But her story persuaded the governor to go public with his misgivings. Bremer seldom made more than thirty dollars a week, Wallace confided to one reporter. "How can he buy an automobile, buy two guns? Stay at the Waldorf Astoria, go to massage parlors, rent limousines, go to Canada, . . . follow me all around?" Where, he asked pointedly, did his assailant get the money? And why did this community-college dropout just happen to write a diary which "proved" that he was acting alone?[9] In a backhanded assurance of his faith in Nixon's personal innocence, the Alabamian told a nationwide television audience: "I never would imply that the President of the country knew anything about it." But he continued to reject the notion that Bremer had acted alone.[10]

If Wallace drew back from drawing a direct line from the President to the assassination plot, he remained intrigued by the possibility that faithful Nixon underlings had acted on their own. He kept remembering what Tom Turnipseed had recounted about his conversation with Nixon aide Harry Dent just two weeks before the attempted assassination. Supporting the Wallace candidacy had been a key part of the GOP strategy, Dent had told Turnipseed, "but those guys [Haldeman and Colson] think we may have created a monster. They're worried."[11] No one ever accused England's Henry II of ordering the murder of the Archbishop of Canterbury, Turnipseed pointed out, but when the king cried out, "Will no one rid me of this turbulent priest?" members of his court needed no specific instructions.[12]

Floundering in the morass of Watergate, the President and his top aides were far more concerned about the political fallout from those high crimes and misdemeanors that Colson and other Nixon aides *had* successfully carried out. The sloppiness of Watergate's congressional investigators and the tenacious refusal of the FBI to resolve the conflicting Hunt-Colson testimony allowed a successful cover-up of the Nixon-Colson-Hunt caper.

But the mystery of just what the White House had attempted on the night Wallace was shot soon came back to haunt Nixon. In the spring of 1974, *Los Angeles Times* correspondent Jack Nelson visited Montgomery and listened as the Alabama governor laid out his suspicions. Nelson had heard other rumors: that the man with the mustache whom Bremer had met on a Lake Michigan Ferry while he stalked Wallace looked suspiciously like G. Gordon Liddy, the White House specialist in dirty tricks who had been part of the Watergate break-in team.[13] And films taken of the Laurel shooting showed a figure in the background who also bore a resemblance to Liddy. In May, Nelson presented to the FBI a list of questions which outlined various conspiracy theories but focused on the discrepancy between Colson and Hunt's testimony. Wallace's public hints of his dissatisfaction with the initial investigation made it difficult for FBI director Clarence Kelley to dismiss the journalist's request for reviewing the investigation.[14]

Through June and July, the Bureau tenaciously fought off any efforts to resolve the conflicts between the Hunt allegations and the Colson denials. In internal memos, FBI officials suggested that Wallace might be pushing the conspiracy theory in an effort to gain press coverage.[15] There is no evidence that Kelley was taking direction from the White House or even consulting Nixon; his primary concern seems to have been protecting the Bureau from embarrassment. As he told his fellow administrators, "Our review may turn out later to be wrong. We cannot be put in such a position."[16]

In early July, while the FBI continued to stonewall Nelson's persistent requests for information, the Watergate investigation of Richard Nixon moved toward a showdown. White House congressional liaison Bill Timmons continued to encourage Nixon's hopes for holding on to the presidency. He based much of his optimism upon the support of the three southern Democrats on the Judiciary Committee: Walter Flowers of Alabama, James Mann of South Carolina, and Ray Thornton of Arkansas. On the morning of July 23, 1974, however, Timmons learned that all three southern Democrats (as well as Republican Lawrence Hogan of Maryland) had decided to vote for impeachment.

"This was stunning news," recalled Alexander Haig, who had replaced Haldeman as Nixon's chief of staff. "All three were close to Governor George Wallace of Alabama who was regarded as a staunch Nixon supporter in the impeachment issue."

Earlier in the spring, the governor's top assistant, Taylor Hardin, had assured Haig that the President "had only to call on Wallace if there was anything he could do to help." The time had come to take him up on his offer. Perhaps, Nixon suggested, "the Alabama governor would be willing to call his fellow Alabamian Walter Flowers and remind him that party loyalty need not include supporting the radical surgery of removing a President from office."

Haig placed the call. When one of Wallace's top staffers answered, Haig was told: "I don't think the governor will take your call, Al. You'll have to have the President call him personally."

Haig walked across to the Oval Office. When the governor took the phone, Nixon came straight to the point and asked him to talk with Flowers.

"George, I'm just calling to ask if you're still with me."

Wallace said, "No, Mr. President, I'm afraid I'm not."

"George, isn't there some way we can work this out?" asked Nixon.

"I don't think so, Mr. President," replied the governor.[17]

In his diary, Nixon reported that while Wallace expressed sorrow that "this had to be brought upon me," he did not waver.

"I'm praying for you . . ." he told Nixon. "But I don't feel that I can really talk to Flowers."[18]

The President hung up the phone and turned to his chief of staff.

"Well, Al, there goes the presidency."[19]

Nixon and his chief of staff always believed that Wallace's decision was triggered by the machinations of liberal Democrats. The wire services had reported a "scurrilous item" out of Montgomery which indicated that Wallace had been "told by unnamed sources that the CIA, acting in concert with Nixon, had been involved in an attempt on his life during the 1972 campaign that left him a paraplegic." There were "reports that Senator Edward Kennedy had been in touch privately with Wallace."[20] In reality, what provoked the governor was the ongoing refusal of the Nixon White House to divulge the details of the actions of Nixon and Colson on the night of his shooting. The cumulative weight of public revulsion—not the failure of Alabama's governor to call a handful of southern Congressmen—triggered Richard Nixon's downfall. But, for Wallace, that telephone conversation must have brought some measure of satisfaction.[21]

DESPITE his continuing struggle with the physical effects of his injuries, Wallace drifted toward another run for the presidency. For Charley Snider and his staff, running a national political campaign in 1972 had been a bruising introduction to the big time. In the spring of 1973, Snider made a critical move and hired one of the nation's most effective direct-mail fund-raisers. Richard Viguerie of Falls Church, Virginia, had begun his career raising money for right-wing political groups in the 1960s. As conservative evangelicals began to move into the political arena, his direct-mail computer banks became the genesis of a dynamic period of ideological cross-fertilization. As Viguerie quickly discovered, the fields were ripe for a harvest of fear.

"You see," he told a reporter in a rare interview, "in an ideological cause like this, people give money not to win friends, but to defeat enemies." People, he argued, "are more strongly motivated by negative issues than positive ones."[22]

Not surprisingly, Viguerie proved a master at welding the peculiarly moral intensity of born-again evangelicals to the social agenda of the new political right. He focused heavily on the threat of secularism to traditional "family values." Crime and law and order had been hot issues since the mid-1960s, but Viguerie and other right-wing publicists were able to up the take on their fund-raising campaigns with lurid accounts of evil at work in America: abortionists ("Abortion means killing a living baby . . . with burning deadly chemicals or a powerful machine that sucks and tears the little infant from its mother's womb") and homosexuals ("When the homosexuals burn the Holy Bible in public . . . how can I stand by silently," began a letter mailed out in support of singer Anita Bryant's Save Our Children, Inc. "Do you realize what they want? They want to recruit our school children under the protection of the laws of our land!").[23]

"Since about 50 percent of the mail the Governor receives has some sort of religious reference in it," explained Snider in mid-1973, Viguerie's operation seemed a logical choice for raising money for the Wallace effort.[24] Within eighteen months, the fund drive had brought in more than $3.5 million. More importantly, Viguerie culled from the vast Wallace files and other sources a list of a quarter-million true believers—followers of the Alabama governor who could be expected to contribute again and again.[25] To Snider, Viguerie confidently predicted that he would double that list to guarantee another ten million dollars before the 1976 election. Whatever problems Wallace might encounter, money would not be one of them.

At the same time, his vulnerability on the charge of racism had lessened. Many black political leaders still opposed him, but in May 1974, in the first Democratic gubernatorial primary campaign after his near-assassination, Wallace received thirty percent of the black vote, this despite the fact that he was opposed by a liberal opponent. (Alabama's antisuccession law had been overturned by voters in 1968.) Increasingly, black Alabamians seemed ready to put aside their misgivings and to vote for him. Perhaps Cornelia had been right; the shooting had cleansed much of the anger and hatred toward him.

Wallace himself seemed to sense that his moment as a national figure had passed. During one session in his office in Montgomery in the fall of 1975, his brother Gerald finally exploded. "God dammit, George, you gotta do it!"

An equally exasperated Wallace shot back angrily: "Gerald, why don't you get your ass shot at, get bricks thrown at you, with your wife at one end of the country and you at the other. You give me your list of girls you see at all the bars in town, and I'll stay there."[26]

In the end, he ran. He would always run if there was even a remote chance of a respectable showing. As he geared up for another presidential campaign, there was the same flurry of frightened editorials by liberals. With Gerald Ford in the White House, the chances for a Democratic victory seemed promising. The last thing the party needed was a replay of the disruptive Wallace campaign of 1972. But, despite the money and the organization, the campaign went awry from the start as questions about his health multiplied. And Wallace, it became clear, was not the same candidate who had electrified national audiences for a decade.

After he broke his leg during physical therapy in late June of 1975, the governor had to curtail his activities for weeks. His failure to realize that he had broken a bone until he developed an embolism served as a reminder of his precarious health.[27] When he announced his candidacy in November 1975, he read without much animation a dull prepared statement, and his strategy to push just to the right of center of the Democratic Party failed to stir listless and apathetic crowds, though he could still rally the faithful with an angry call to save the great American middle class from the evils of liberals and big government. But at times he seemed ill at ease in exploiting the social agenda he had done so much to foster. He harped on the evils of abortion in one speech and attacked the Equal Rights Amendment in another, then dropped the issues, perhaps recalling that he had publicly endorsed the ERA when it was first introduced and that he was on record as a defender of *Roe v. Wade*.[28]

When he did lash out, he often seemed to have lost his touch. After Judge Frank Johnson issued a court order in November 1975 requiring Alabama to improve the hellish conditions in its state prisons, Wallace exploded at a press conference with a torrent of abusive language, suggesting that his old nemesis needed a "good barbed wire enema." However colorful the comment, it hardly suited his new image and simply reinforced the impression that he was thrashing his way through the campaign.[29]

By mid-February 1976, Wallace's support was slipping not only throughout the nation but also—critically for his chances—in the South, where a soft-spoken peanut farmer and former Georgia governor named Jimmy Carter was pulling ahead.[30] Despite spending huge sums of money in the Florida primary, Wallace lost the Sunshine State to Carter. Dispirited and demoralized, he pushed on to North Carolina, a state that had traditionally given him strong support, but a week before the Democratic primary, the *Montgomery Advertiser*'s editor and publisher Harold Martin reported the obvious to his readers: "The Wallace campaign organization is falling apart." And Alabama's governor could do nothing to stop its demise or the new southern contender.[31]

After his North Carolina loss to Carter, he was first bitter, then philosophical. When it became clear that the choice was between the Georgian and more liberal Democratic challengers, Wallace surprised most observers by endorsing Jimmy Carter and furnishing the decisive votes to put him over the top. If he could not become President, he could at least take credit for helping to elect a fellow southerner. On the night of Carter's nomination, Wallace was in an unusually introspective frame of mind; as he talked with ABC newsman John Snell, he frankly admitted that his quest for the White House had always been a chimera. "I had to do things—say things to get elected in Alabama, that made it impossible for me to ever be President."[32]

THROUGHOUT the campaign, news reports had hinted at growing estrangement between Wallace and his wife. A little over a year after his shooting, one Alabama newspaper editor who knew him well had predicted that for a man like Wallace, paralysis, sexual impotence, and marriage to a beautiful woman like Cornelia would be a devastating combination. "I suspect the day is going to come when he is going to think that his wife is running around with other men," said Ray Jenkins. "He may already think that."[33] Just two months before the 1976 presidential election, Montgomery newspapers breathlessly announced the couple's separation; Wallace discovered that his wife had installed an elaborate recording system, which had taped hundreds of his telephone calls over an eighteen-month period. Off the record, security aides told reporters they had taken hundreds of neatly boxed reels, put them in a weighted bag, and dumped them in the Alabama River.

Cornelia Wallace claimed that she had bugged George to confirm her suspicions that Gerald Wallace had "spread rumors that I have slept with every State Trooper around."[34] To her surprise, she claimed, she had discovered that her husband had spent long hours on the telephone engaging, as one of her lawyers primly told reporters, in the "kind of conversations a married man ought not to be having with other women."[35]

Alabama's media scrambled to satisfy the public's fascination with the latest details of the First Family's disintegrating marriage. Had Wallace ordered security personnel to shadow Cornelia, as she claimed? What was the nature of the allegedly salacious telephone calls between Wallace and his late-night girlfriends? Had his wife foiled the governor's mansion guards by secretly making backup copies of her tapes, as she implied? Cornelia Wallace kept up a steady stream of off-the-record interviews with local reporters, while Wallace—though he refrained from making any statements—made no effort to muzzle aides and security men who dropped hints of infidelities by his wife. "Alabama's First Lady claims the governor has threatened and abused her," announced a local television reporter in one breathless promo filmed outside the gates of the mansion. "Details at ten."

But Cornelia Wallace learned that, in the clutch, a sitting governor is not without resources. Divorce proceedings were normally filed with the clerk of Family Court in the relevant county and then assigned at random to one of the sitting circuit judges. Wallace's attorney ignored these procedures and filed his petition with Montgomery County judge John W. Davis III, who was not only a Wallace appointee, but also the son of a lifelong friend and physician to Wallace. Moreover, Judge Davis's father-in-law, a wealthy real estate developer, had extensive dealings with the state highway department and was a longtime political supporter and personal friend of the governor. But Davis indignantly denied that such matters would affect his judgment and he refused to recuse himself.[36] After fighting all the way to the Alabama Court of Civil Appeals, attorneys for the governor's wife managed to dislodge Davis, but hours before her day in court, Cornelia was told by Wallace's lawyers that they had proof that she had *not* kept copies of her tapes of the governor's late-night telephone calls. She collapsed and was rushed to a Montgomery hospital; her lawyers agreed to a modest out-of-court settlement.[37]

In the summer of 1974, Wallace had made a much-heralded visit to the Lynchburg, Virginia, Liberty Road Baptist Church, home of the burgeoning "Moral Majority" movement led by the Reverend Jerry Falwell. Before a national television audience on *The Old-Time Gospel Hour*, the governor listened somberly as Falwell hawked deluxe large-type Bibles, proceeds to support the newly created Liberty Baptist College ("We teach patriotism, discipline and love of mom and dad . . . and every professor is a Bible-carrying Christian"), before he introduced the guest speaker.

Wallace began by describing his childhood memories: traveling to camp meetings in Georgia and the Florida Panhandle, beginning each day with a devotion at breakfast and listening again as his parents read Scripture before bedtime.[38] His home was in the Bible Belt, he told the rapt crowd of five thousand, and "I know some people refer to it sneeringly." But it had been the rock which allowed him to survive the troubled times of his life.

"I have been through the valley of the shadow of death. I know that when I was there, I asked God to spare me if it be his will; if not then I cast my lot with him." For reporters who had covered Wallace for years, his quiet intensity was an eerie counterpoint to the harsh language he had made his own in twenty-five years of campaigning. As he came to the end of his brief testimony, his eyes filled. He had learned the age-old truth of his faith, he declared. Whether rich or poor, healthy or infirm, "if you have Jesus in your heart and soul, then you are by worldly standards a multimillionaire. . . . If he has you in the hollow of his hand, you are whole . . . and I *am* whole . . . through the grace of our Lord and Savior, Jesus Christ." After an emotion-filled moment of silence, the Liberty Baptist Church exploded in a chorus of amens and an ovation that continued as an aide rolled Wallace's wheelchair up the red carpet and out into the sunlight, where an overflow crowd waited to greet him.

A writer for *Rolling Stone* saw in that response a foretaste of the growing evangelism that would prove such a force in the late 1970s and 1980s. Falwell's church was a "safe haven of 100% Americanism for people who didn't understand things like dope and abortion and riots. It was the religious equivalent of George Wallace." As Joe Klein watched the crowded buses roll out of the huge parking lot, the people inside staring straight ahead, he glimpsed the new and untested army of Christian warriors leaving for the front to take their place in the struggle against the forces of secularism.[39]

Wallace had never exhibited any compunction about using Christian morality as a political drawing card; he was the first politician to testify in favor of a constitutional amendment allowing prayer in the schools. But in the years that followed, he seemed reluctant to talk about his personal religious faith in the way that was to become commonplace among other politicians from Jimmy Carter to Ronald Reagan. Friends nevertheless reported that he was spending more time reading the Bible and praying and reflecting on those he had wronged, particularly on those black people he had wronged, in his climb to power. Barred from reelection in 1978, because Alabama still limited consecutive terms to two, Wallace accepted a position as consultant to the rehabilitation center of the University of Alabama Medical School in Birmingham. And he began to seek forgiveness.

John Lewis, a courageous black veteran of hundreds of civil rights marches and a half-dozen beatings in Alabama, later remembered the call he had received in 1979. The former governor requested a meeting when Lewis (then a city councilman in Atlanta) returned to visit his mother in Troy, Alabama. Lewis initially hesitated. He knew that when the heroine of the Montgomery bus boycott, Rosa Parks, stopped in to meet Wallace in the mid-1970s, a photographer was waiting. Although she was too polite to leave, Parks had always resented Wallace's use of the photograph to curry favor with black voters.[40]

But no photographer waited in Troy when the two men met in Mrs. Lewis's small living room. They sipped coffee and then George Wallace poured forth a halting defense ("it was all a question of states' rights") and a rueful listing of all the things he regretted he had done. "I've come to ask your forgiveness," he told Lewis. "I want to ask your forgiveness for anything I've done to wrong you."

It was "like a confession," said Lewis. As though he were a priest, he was being asked to grant absolution. They grasped hands and prayed together.[41]

Wallace picked up the telephone and made his calls, one by one. The politicians came first: black mayors and elected officials accustomed to making deals with the devil. But E. D. Nixon, founder of the Montgomery bus boycott committee, also forgave him. The Reverend Ralph Abernathy, Martin Luther King's successor, shared a platform with him in 1974 as both received honorary degrees from all-black Alabama State University. Even Coretta Scott King managed to find a good word for George Wallace.

Most Alabamians—most Americans—willed his redemption. In 1974, Dr. Robert M. Dickerson, the pastor of Martin Luther King's Dexter Avenue Baptist Church, invited him to speak to the predominantly black Alabama Progressive Baptist State Convention. In later years, that historic occasion still echoed in the memories of those present and those who had only heard of the event secondhand. The *Charlotte Observer* described what it called the former governor's "impromptu" appearance at Martin Luther King's old church in Montgomery and described how Wallace had related his own suffering to the suffering of black people and asked for their forgiveness.

"When he came in, in his wheelchair, it was an event that I shall never forget," remembered Dr. Dickerson twenty years after the event. "He [Wallace] said some things there that some thought he would not ever say. . . . People stood—blacks and whites—and cried. It was a time when people could vent their tears with shouts with the raising of hands, with a standing ovation. . . . I thought it was a time of healing."[42]

Such is the power of memory.

Contemporary newspaper accounts tell a somewhat different story. Far from being unannounced, the Wallace visit was a carefully choreographed media event with print and television reporters present. John Cochran covered the occasion for NBC. News accounts give no hint that Wallace explicitly asked for forgiveness. He simply stated what was, at that time, his standard line: His remarks about segregation had all been misunderstood. He had stood in the schoolhouse door because of his commitment to states' rights, not because of any racist feelings.[43]

But the memories were real. Black Alabamians wanted Wallace to be forgiven.

Ruth and Frank Johnson could neither forgive nor forget the pain he had caused them. Wallace had first called Ruth to make his case. "I just want to tell you I'm sorry," he said when Mrs. Johnson picked up the phone, "sorry for all the heartache I've caused you and all the trouble I've given you for things I said. I was wrong."[44]

As he talked, she remembered their student days at the University of Alabama. "People think the Depression was just hard times," she recalled, "but we didn't mind the work and the lack of money. We were young and idealistic. And we loved George for his enthusiasms." Wallace had turned his back on the idealism of their youth as he callously whipped up the "violence, hatred and hysteria of the 60's and 70's in Alabama."

But that, at least, Ruth Johnson could understand. What she could never forgive were the personal attacks on her family. When her husband's rulings on school desegregation had angered many Alabamians, they had enrolled their only son, Johnny, in a private school to try to protect him from intimidation and isolation. Shortly afterward, Wallace pilloried the Johnsons for their decision. Frank Johnson was anxious to make sure that the white people of Alabama sent their children to school with blacks, said Wallace, but he had "different ideas about his own son." With a $22,500-a-year job as a federal judge, "he can afford to send his son to a private school, but there are a lot of white people who aren't so fortunate as to have such a good job."[45]

Johnny Johnson's tragic suicide some years later seems to have been related to mental illness unconnected to the harassment of his father. Still, the governor's bitter attacks on her husband frightened Ruth Johnson, particularly after a Ku Klux Klansman planted a bomb at the home of her mother-in-law. "I was never frightened for myself," she recalled, "but I was so afraid for my son." No matter how she had tried to shield him, "on every hand he heard the sneering, yelling voice of George Wallace maligning his father—'integratin', carpetbaggin', scalawaging liar'—and worse. That is hard for a mother to forgive."[46]

She heard Wallace out. But when he sent word by Glen Curlee that he wanted to talk with her husband, the response was brief. "I sent him a message that if he wanted to get forgiveness, he'd have to get it from the Lord," said Judge Johnson. "And I never heard from him again."[47]

By embracing black voters and by holding onto the core of his old hardshell constituency, Wallace eked out another gubernatorial victory in 1982—his fifth, counting Lurleen's race, since 1962. But he was a shell of a man during his last four years in office. He seldom appeared in public, delegated administrative duties to his appointees, and spent much of his time in bed. Newspaper reporters had long hinted that the governor was a heavy user of a variety of painkillers and antidepressants, but in 1983, the *New York Times* reported that he had been taking methadone for almost two years. Three years later, the *Montgomery Advertiser* used the word "dependence" to describe his reliance upon the powerful drug which was occasionally used as a painkiller, but more commonly as a substitute for heroin.[48]

After his divorce from Cornelia Wallace in 1978, he began a romantic relationship with a thirty-two-year-old Dolly Parton look-alike. As a teenager, Lisa Taylor had performed with her sister for the Wallace campaign in 1968 as half of the Singing Sisters, "Mona and Lisa," and had achieved modest success as a country-and-western singer. She had been born into poverty; her father was (she later said) hard-drinking and abusive. But with the discovery that their farm sat on some of the most valuable coal lands in Alabama, the Taylor family had suddenly become wealthy. From rags to riches, through a marriage, one child, and a divorce, Lisa had remained smitten with George Wallace. Mere weeks after his divorce was final, the governor later claimed, she began telephoning and proposing marriage. He insisted that he had tried to put her off, but "I finally gave in."[49]

Within months after their marriage in 1981, processors served the state's first lady with a lawsuit filed by her father, James Taylor. The Walker County coal magnate claimed that, as he lay in a coma in a Birmingham hospital near death, his son and three daughters (including Lisa) had signed between two and three million dollars' worth of his property over to themselves. When he unexpectedly recovered, Lisa refused to return her portion. Eventually the two settled their embarrassingly public squabble without going to trial, but not until the news media had once more had a field day. During Wallace's last two years in office, his wife made little effort to maintain even the illusion of a functioning marriage and spent most of her time at her Jasper, Alabama, home or at the official governor's cottage on the Gulf. The couple divorced without fanfare in early 1987.[50]

As election year, 1986, rolled around, all signs pointed toward another gubernatorial campaign. Gerald Wallace bluntly told his brother that he was not physically up to the effort, but confessed to reporters that George "does not share that opinion with me."[51] With pressure growing on all sides for him to step down, Wallace appeared in the House chambers of the old state capitol in April 1986 to announce his plans. In his pocket he had two speeches: one announcing his decision to run for reelection, a second confirming rumors that he would end his forty-year political career.

The crowd of three hundred of the still-faithful cheered as his attendant pushed him to the speaker's dais, but they grew somber as he began speaking. His words muffled by deafness and his voice barely audible, he acknowledged that he had wanted to run again, but friends and family had convinced him that because of his health problems he had to step down. Halfway through his seven-minute announcement, his hands began to shake and his voice quavered as tears welled up. After much "prayerful consideration," he had decided it was over for him. "I have climbed my last political mountain."[52] As he drove back to the governor's mansion with his son, George Junior, he broke the silence of the short journey only once.

"I hope the rich and powerful don't take over now," he said.[53]

*   *   *

IN the years after his retirement, Wallace occasionally gave interviews, but reporters found the process laborious and not very rewarding. Questions had to be written out because of his deafness, and he usually responded with little more than a halting rerun of the same phrases and words he had used for thirty years. In 1988 and 1992, Democratic presidential candidates trooped out to his modest Montgomery ranch house for a brief photo opportunity, moments in the limelight which he relished even when he was sickest.

During his last term in office, Wallace had often talked of devoting his time and energy to writing an autobiography once he retired. He and former *Newsweek* correspondent Stephan Lesher struck a financial deal in early 1987 to work together on a book for a highly respected trade publishing company, W. W. Norton. Once he had received his share of the advance, Wallace dutifully taped his interviews with Lesher. But the former governor had always lacked the kind of reflective temperament essential to writing a revealing self-portrait. Except for a few tidbits about his relationship with Lurleen, his recollections offered little that was not already on the public record. In 1994, Lesher released a conventional biography under his own name with Addison-Wesley. Although Wallace appeared for an autographing session in Montgomery, Lesher's book made no acknowledgment of his financial arrangements with the former Alabama governor.

In the years after his shooting, George Wallace grew closer to his four children. They faithfully visited, occasionally joined by a few old friends who dropped by to reminisce. But Wallace spent most of his time alone, watching television and brooding over the past. Three years after she had left Wallace, one visitor remained haunted by the memory of the last time she saw him. He sat in his den chair, headphones blaring away through his deafness a Hank Williams tune he and Lurleen had loved when they were young. "He was all hunched over in the dark, the tears just streaming down his face. Lord, do I remember it."

Virginia Durr, a lifelong campaigner for civil and human rights, watched the rise and the fall of George Wallace with a horrified fascination. In the winter of 1994, she sat in her living room in Montgomery and tried to sort through the meaning of his life and his place in American history. "I feel sorry for him now," she said. "I know he's old and sick and he really seems to be sorry." But that didn't erase the past, she said: the blind hatred and fear of black people that he had aroused, not just in Alabama, but across the country. At ninety-one, Virginia Durr had lived through most of the twentieth century, long enough to see "civilized people like the Germans go mad over Jews" and to watch on her television the senseless slaughter in the Balkans. Wallace's appeal must have something to do with the basic insecurity of

Americans in the 1960s and 1970s, she believed: they had to "blame some-body else."

"Men's hearts are concealed," the English biographer John Boswell wrote to Samuel Johnson. "But their actions are open to scrutiny." Virginia Durr understood the consequences of his actions firsthand, but she could not let go of her effort to understand what drove her fellow Alabamian on his remarkable journey. "He was a tragic figure, don't you think?" With his intelligence and energy, he could have been a great figure in Alabama and in the nation. But he compromised himself when he faced political annihi-lation in the late 1950s. That moral failure she could understand, she mused, but long after he was politically secure, he just kept on going. "I just don't know, I wish I could understand why Wallace or anybody feels so good about humiliating other people," she said as she sat in her favorite rocking chair.[54]

ARTHUR Miller, in his memorable play *Death of a Salesman,* says of a washed-up Willy Loman: "Attention must be paid." What he was talking about, said the Democrats' 1972 presidential candidate, George McGovern, "was the frustration of the little guy, the little salesman that couldn't make the sale." George Wallace tapped into that anger and that desperation. Long before journalists and pundits had coined the term "silent majority," said McGovern, Wallace understood that there might not be a majority, but there were "millions of Americans who felt that nobody was paying any attention to them, that nobody cared about their frustrations."[55]

Richard Nixon always saw the Alabama governor as the key to under-standing the reshaping of American politics. Nearly twenty years after the former President left office in disgrace, historian Herbert Parmet interviewed him for a biography, *Richard Nixon and His America.*[56] At the end of his fourth and last question-and-answer session, Parmet methodically outlined the conservative shifts Nixon had made after 1970 to placate the Wallace constituency.

"Your point is that we had to move to the right in order to cut Wallace off at the pass?" asked Nixon.

"Absolutely," replied Parmet.

"Foreign policy was my major concern. You start with that," said Nixon. "To the extent that we thought of it [the Wallace movement] at all—maybe subconsciously—anything that might weaken my base because of domestic policy reasons had to give way to the foreign policy priorities." There was "no question that all these things must have been there. . . . I think," he added, "it's a pretty clear-headed analysis." It was as close as the proud Nixon would ever come to admitting that, when George Wallace had played his fiddle, the President of the United States had danced Jim Crow.[57]

In the decorous landscape of upscale malls, suburban neighborhoods, and prosperous megachurches that has become the heartland of the new conservatism, Ronald Reagan, not George Wallace, is the spiritual godfather of the nineties. During such moments of racial crisis as the spectre of cross-district busing, surburbanites occasionally turned to George Wallace in the 1960s and early 1970s to voice their protest, but he was always too unsettling, too vulgar, too overtly southern. With the exception of a few hard-line right-wingers like Patrick Buchanan, the former Alabama governor has been a prophet without honor, remembered (if at all) for his late-life renunciation of racism.

Even the religious right, which has shared many of his attitudes and rhetoric about the "moral decline" of America, has resisted identification with the legacy of George Wallace. In his defense of religious conservatism, the executive director of the Christian Coalition candidly acknowledged the historical links between the early Wallace and evangelicals of the 1960s. "George Wallace may have stood in the door," admitted Ralph Reed, "but evangelical clergy provided the moral framework for his actions." Reed compares today's resurgent religious conservatism to the civil rights movement "whose allegiance was to God and whose strategy and intelligence were the eloquently simple dictates of conscience." Martin Luther King, not George Wallace, is the preferred historical model.[58]

But two decades after his disappearance from national politics, the Alabama governor seems vindicated by history. If he did not create the conservative groundswell that transformed American politics in the 1980s, he anticipated most of its themes. It was Wallace who sensed and gave voice to a growing national white backlash in the mid-1960s; it was Wallace who warned of the danger to the American soul posed by the "intellectual snobs who don't know the difference between smut and great literature"; it was Wallace who railed against federal bureaucrats who not only wasted the tax dollars of hardworking Americans, but lacked the common sense to "park their bicycles straight." Not surprisingly, his rise to national prominence coincided with a growing loss of faith in the federal government. In 1964, nearly 80 percent of the American people told George Gallup's pollsters that they could trust Washington to "do what is right all or most of the time." Thirty years later, that number had declined to less than 20 percent.[59]

If George Wallace did not create this mood of national skepticism, he anticipated and exploited the political transformation it precipitated. His attacks on the federal government have become the gospel of modern conservatism; his angry rhetoric, the foundation for the new ground rules of political warfare. In 1984, a young Republican Congressman from Georgia explained the facts of life to a group of young conservative activists. "The number one fact about the news media," said Newt Gingrich, "is they love fights. You have to give them confrontations."[60] And they had to be confrontations in a bipolar political system of good and evil, right and wrong. The greatest hope for political victory was to replace the traditional give-and-take of American politics with a "battleground" between godly Republicans and the "secular anti-religious view of the left" embodied in the Democratic Party.[61]

The notion of politics as a struggle between good and evil is as old as the Republic; that moral critique of American society lay at the very core of populism in the late nineteenth century. But angry reformers of an earlier generation had usually railed against the rich and powerful; Wallace turned the process on its head. He may have singled out "elitist" bureaucrats as symbols of some malevolent abstraction called "Washington," but everyone knew that his real enemies were the constituencies those federal officials represented: the marginal beneficiaries of the welfare state. The "populism" embraced by conservatives in the 1990s was little more than a public relations maneuver, an effort to use an appealing rhetorical slogan to cloak the Republican Party's unappealing image as the advocate of the privileged.

Much has changed in southern and American politics in the years since 1958 when George Wallace promised his friends that he would "never be out-niggered again." Middle- and upper-income suburbanites have fled the unruly public spaces of decaying central cities and created (or tried to create) a secure and controlled environment. Isolated from the expensive and frustrating demands of the growing urban underclass, suburbanites could control their own local government; they could buy good schools and safe streets—or at least better schools and safer streets than the inner city. "Big" government—the federal government—they complained, spent *their* hard-earned taxes for programs that were wasteful and inefficient and did nothing to help them.[62]

Halfway around the world, Polish writer Ryszard Kapuściński traveled through the Soviet Empire during its last days from 1989 through 1991, and watched the unsettling costs of social upheaval. As the Communist Party, the state security apparatus, and the crude but reassuring cradle-to-grave welfare system disintegrated, the peoples of Moscow's unraveling *imperium* desperately looked for shelter from the storms of change. "In the face of encircling affiliations and threats of reality," wrote Kapuściński, they remembered a "past which seems a lost paradise."[63]

But this retreat came at great cost, for the three horsemen of nationalism, racism, and religious fundamentalism were the driving forces of this flight into nostalgia. Those most afflicted with these "plagues" were beyond reason. In their eyes burned a "sacred pyre that awaits only its sacrificial victims," wrote Kapuściński at the end of his journey. Such men and women had no sense of the complexity of the world, no appreciation for "the fact that human destiny is uncertain and fragile." Above all, they were free of the anxiety that comes from asking the question: "Am I right?" Their world was a simple and reassuring one: "on one side we, the good people, on the other they, our enemies."[64]

George Wallace had recognized the political capital to be made in a society shaken by social upheaval and economic uncertainty. As the conservative revolution reached high tide, it was no accident that the groups singled out for relentless abuse and condemnation were welfare mothers and aliens, groups that are both powerless and, by virtue of color and nationality, outsiders. The politics of rage that George Wallace made his own had moved from the fringes of our society to center stage.

He was the most influential loser in twentieth-century American politics.

NOTES

PREFACE

1. *New York Times,* January 15, 1963; *Montgomery Advertiser,* January 15, 1963; *Birmingham News,* January 14, 15, 1963.
2. Taylor, *Me 'n' George,* 28–29.
3. Ibid.
4. *Birmingham Post-Herald,* January 15, 1963; *Montgomery Advertiser,* January 15, 1963. A photostatic copy of Wallace's inaugural address is in the Alabama Department of Archives and History.
5. The words may have been Asa Carter's, but they reflected Wallace's views. Six months after his inaugural, he endorsed the showing of the viciously racist film *Birth of a Nation,* and he angrily denounced what he called the nation's double standard toward the South: "What about all the times in Africa when the white people get hacked to death? No civil liberties boys made noise about that." Montgomery, *Alabama Journal,* June 18, 1963.
6. Novak, *Choosing Our King,* 231.
7. Haygood, "George Wallace Faces His Demons," 69.
8. John Cashin, author's interview.
9. William Cowper (1731–1800), "There Is a Fountain."
10. Goldfield, *Black, White and Southern,* 233.
11. *New York Times,* April 4, 1986.
12. *Time,* October 11, 1982.
13. Lesher, *George Wallace,* xvii, ix–xi, 504–506.
14. Haygood, "George Wallace Faces His Demons," 72.
15. Author's conversation with John Kohn, January 12, 1988.

CHAPTER 1: THE MUSE OF HISTORY

1. Robert D. Dortch (Birmingham-Southern vice president for admissions) to author, July 24, 1992.
2. Jackson, *Clio,* 2; White, *The Making of the President, 1968,* 343.
3. This profile of Mozelle Wallace is based on Cooper, "The Rise of George Wallace," 17–18; Church Home Record Book, 1915–[1919], Wilmer Hall Records, USA Archives; 1910 census, Mobile; 1900, 1910, 1920 census; Birmingham; 1910 census, Montgomery; Montgomery City Directories, 1911–1916; Mobile City Directories, 1900–1915; Birmingham City Directories, 1906–1915.

4. Alabama Department of Archives and Records, Civil War Pension Records, Company A, 57th Alabama Infantry.
5. *Clio Free Press,* February 4, 1908.
6. *Montgomery Advertiser,* June 18, 1962.
7. *Clio Free Press,* March 1, 1918.
8. Frady, *Wallace,* 58.
9. *Montgomery Advertiser,* June 18, 1962.
10. Frady, *Wallace,* 58.
11. *Historical Statistics of the United States,* Part 1, 516–17.
12. *Birmingham Post-Herald,* March 20, 1992. Frady, *Wallace,* 61; Wallace, *Stand Up for America,* 11.
13. Wallace, *The Wallaces of Alabama,* 19–20.
14. Jackson, *Clio,* 163–64.
15. *Montgomery Advertiser,* June 18, 1962.
16. Frady, *Wallace,* 61.
17. Ibid.
18. Dorman, *The George Wallace Myth,* 173; Frady, *Wallace,* 56–57.
19. Frady, *Wallace,* 59.
20. Ibid., 54.
21. Tindall, *Emergence of the New South,* 354–55.
22. Flynt, *Poor but Proud,* 294.
23. Johnson, *Statistical Atlas of Southern Counties,* 43.
24. Flynt, *Poor but Proud,* 50.
25. Vance, *All These People,* 120.
26. Wallace, *Stand Up for America,* 15. In his later recollections, he put the figure at five thousand dollars. Lesher, *George Wallace,* 27.
27. Wallace, *Stand Up for America,* 16.
28. Frady, *Wallace,* 69.
29. *Columbus* (Ga.) *Ledger,* March 4, 1968.
30. Wallace, *Stand Up for America,* 12.
31. *Montgomery Advertiser,* June 19, 1962; Wallace, *The Wallaces of Alabama,* 56.
32. Gorn, " 'Gouge and Bite, Pull Hair and Scratch,' " 22.
33. *Birmingham News,* September 21, 1980.
34. *Columbus* (Ga.) *Ledger,* March 4, 1968. Frady, *Wallace,* 71.
35. Wallace, *Stand Up for America,* 20–21; *Montgomery Advertiser,* May 3, 1964; *Birmingham News,* January 15, 1975.
36. *Montgomery Advertiser,* June 19, 1962; Frady, *Wallace,* 72.
37. Greenhaw, *Watch Out for George Wallace,* 92–93.
38. Frady, *Wallace,* 59.
39. Wallace, *Stand Up for America,* 15.
40. *Montgomery Advertiser,* June 18, 1962.
41. *Alabama Official and Statistical Register, 1935,* 235.
42. *Montgomery Advertiser,* June 19, 1962.
43. McDowell Lee, author's interview.
44. Lesher, *George Wallace,* 34.
45. *Journal of the Alabama Senate, 1935,* vol. 1, 10–11.
46. Wallace, *Stand Up for America,* 25; Frady, *Wallace,* 74; *Stand Up for Alabama,* 213; *Montgomery Advertiser,* June 19, 1962.

47. Mabel Amos, APT interview.
48. Greenhaw, *Watch Out for George Wallace,* 94.
49. Ibid., 23; Frady, *Wallace,* 80.
50. Wallace, *Stand Up for America,* 24–25.
51. Smartt, *History of Eufaula, Alabama,* 290.
52. Owen, *History of Alabama,* vol. 4, 1715; Jennie Kendall Dean, "A Sketch of Anne Kendrick Walker," Eufaula, Alabama, Carnegie Library.
53. Elizabeth D. Rhodes Diary, December 19, 1860, Eufaula, Alabama, Carnegie Library.
54. Walker, *Backtracking in Barbour County,* passim.
55. Walker, *Backtracking in Barbour County,* 261. Despite her sympathy for local whites, Walker presented evidence on both sides in her book. The best collection of information on the riots may be found in the majority and minority reports of February 23, 1875, submitted to the Select House Committee on Elections.
56. Rogers, "Reuben F. Kolb: Agricultural Leader of the New South," 109–19.
57. Woodward, *Origins of the New South,* 188.
58. *Columbiana* (Ala.) *People's Advocate,* July 21, 1892.
59. Rogers, *The One-Gallused Rebellion,* 219.
60. Cammack, "Reuben Francis Kolb," 21–27.
61. *Union Springs* (Ala.) *Herald,* quoted in *Birmingham Daily News,* July 12, 1892.
62. *Eufaula Daily Times,* August 2, 1892.
63. Rogers, *One-Gallused Rebellion,* 212–26; Summerell, "A Life of Reuben F. Kolb," 77.
64. Sparkman, "The Kolb-Oates Campaign of 1894," 15–16; Rodabaugh, "Fusion, Confession, Defeat and Disfranchisement," 131–53; Going, "Critical Months in Alabama Politics, 1895–1896," 272–81.
65. McMillan, *Constitutional Development in Alabama, 1798-1901,* 361–63; Kousser, *The Shaping of Southern Politics,* 130–38, 165–71.
66. Grafton and Permaloff, *Big Mules and Branchheads,* 53.
67. *Columbus* (Ga.) *Ledger,* March 4, 1968.
68. Frady, *Wallace,* 63; Wallace, *Stand Up for America,* 25.
69. Wallace, *The Wallace Family,* 28–29.
70. Frady, *Wallace,* 81.
71. Ibid.
72. Walker, *Backtracking in Barbour County,* 342.
73. McGill, "George Wallace," 5.
74. *Alabama: A Guide to the Deep South,* 343.
75. Lesher, *George Wallace,* 12.
76. Jackson, *Clio,* 43.
77. Frady, *Wallace,* 149.

CHAPTER 2: STUDENT AND SOLDIER: "I'VE DONE MY PART"

1. Wolfe, *The University of Alabama,* 158–71. Doyle, "Cause Won, Not Lost," 231–55.
2. Norrell, *A Promising Field,* 98–99.
3. *Crimson-White,* February 3, 1939.
4. Glen Curlee, APT interview.
5. Bill Jones, APT interview.

6. Photographs courtesy of Jim Reed, Tuscaloosa, Alabama.
7. "Fact-Sheet on George Wallace prepared for newsmen by Bill Jones, January 6, 1963," copy in possession of the author.
8. Frady, *Wallace,* 81.
9. Sachs, *George Wallace,* 9.
10. Glen Curlee, APT interview; Ralph Adams, APT interview.
11. Glen Curlee, APT interview.
12. Bass, *Taming the Storm,* 50.
13. Dodd and Dodd, *Winston: An Antebellum and Civil War History,* 94–95, 268.
14. Sikora, *The Judge,* 72–74; Yarbrough, *Judge Frank Johnson,* 1–5.
15. Bass, *Taming the Storm,* 49–50.
16. Yarbrough, *Judge Frank Johnson,* 9.
17. Letter from Frank M. Johnson, Jr., to author, February 10, 1994; "We didn't go": Yarbrough, *Judge Frank Johnson,* 47.
18. Letter from Ruth Johnson to author, February 2, 1994.
19. *Crimson-White,* February 9, 1940; March 1, 1940.
20. Ibid., April 5, 1940.
21. Ibid, April 11, 1941.
22. Bill Jones, APT interview.
23. Elliott, *The Cost of Courage,* 78.
24. Wolfe, *The University of Alabama,* 172.
25. Barnard, *Dixiecrats and Democrats,* 17–22.
26. Wallace, *Stand Up for America,* 50.
27. *Stand Up for Alabama,* 11.
28. *Birmingham News,* September 21, 1980.
29. Letter from Ruth Johnson to author, February 2, 1994.
30. Letter from Ruth Johnson to author, February 10, 1994.
31. Frady, *Wallace,* 84; Sachs, *George Wallace,* 14.
32. Lesher, *George Wallace,* 45.
33. House, *Lady of Courage,* 5–7.
34. Ibid., 7.
35. *Birmingham Post-Herald,* November 2, 1966.
36. Frady, *Wallace,* 84.
37. *Tuscaloosa News,* June 5, 1942.
38. Wallace, *Stand Up for America,* 36–37.
39. Marriage license, Tuscaloosa County, from Alabama Department of Vital Records.
40. Lesher, *George Wallace,* 49.
41. *Montgomery Advertiser,* June 22, 1962.
42. Frady, *Wallace,* 85.
43. Wallace, *Stand Up for America,* 37.
44. *Hot Springs* (Ark.) *Sentinel Record,* January 23, 1967; House, *Lady of Courage,* 10–11.
45. Wallace, *Stand Up for America,* 40.
46. Richard Zind, author's interview.
47. Robert Bushouse, author's interview.
48. House, *Lady of Courage,* 11.
49. Letter from Arthur Feiner to author, June 21, 1993.

50. Greenhaw, *Watch Out for George Wallace,* 194.

51. Herbert, *Maximum Effort,* 22–24; George Leahy to author, June 19, 1993.

52. Letter from George Leahy to author, June 19, 1993.

53. Letter from Jack Ray to author, August 6, 1993.

54. Wallace, *Stand Up for America,* 41.

55. Letter from Jack Ray to author, June 1, 1994.

56. Robert Bushouse, author's interview.

57. Letter from George Leahy to author, June 19, 1993.

58. Letter from George Leahy to "Mom," April 28, 1945, copy in possession of author.

59. "Consolidated Statistical Summary of Combat Operations," 58th Wing, WG-58-SU-OP-S, 486th Group, 58th Wing, 20th Air Force, January 1–August 14, 1945, MAFRI.

60. Herbert, *Maximum Effort,* 34.

61. Lesher, *George Wallace,* 54.

62. Wallace, *Stand Up for America,* 41.

63. Letter from Arthur Feiner to author, May 28, 1994.

64. LeMay, *America Is in Danger,* 263; Hawk Johnson, author's interview.

65. LeMay, *Superfortress,* 123.

66. Herbert, *Maximum Effort,* 48.

67. Letter from Arthur Feiner to author, June 21, 1993.

68. Robert Bushouse, author's interview.

69. Herbert, *Maximum Effort,* 62.

70. Robert Bushouse, author's interview.

71. Frady, *Wallace,* 230.

72. Robert Bushouse, author's interview.

73. Letter from George Leahy to author, February 18, 1993.

74. Richard Zind, author's interview; letter from Arthur Feiner to author, May 28, 1994.

75. Hawk Johnson, author's interview.

76. Wallace, *Stand Up for America,* 45.

77. George Bushouse, author's interview.

78. Ibid.

79. Letter from Jack Ray to author, August 6, 1993.

80. Frady, *Wallace,* 87.

81. "Consolidated Statistical Summary of Combat Operations," 58th wing, from WG-58-SU-OP-S, "History of the 58th Bombardment Wing, 1-August, 1945 through 31-August, 1945," pp. 14–16, MAFHI.

82. Wyden, *Day One,* 242–45.

83. Letter from George Leahy to author, June 19, 1993.

84. Wallace, *Stand Up for America,* 47.

85. Ibid., p. 48.

86. Ibid.

87. Robert Bushouse, author's interview; George Leahy to author, June 19, 1993.

88. *Congressional Record,* 88th Congress, 1st session, vol. 109, September 5, 1963.

89. Letter from George Leahy to "Betty," September 17, 1945, copy in possession of author.

90. Letter from George Wallace to Arthur and Alice Feiner, June 3, 1991, copy in possession of the author.
91. Letter from Arthur Feiner to author, July 21, 1993.

CHAPTER 3: THE MORAL COMPASS OF AMBITION

1. Michie and Rhylick, *Dixie Demagogues,* 143.
2. Grafton and Permaloff, *Big Mules and Branchheads,* 72.
3. Taft, *Organizing Dixie,* 51, 162.
4. Barnard, *Dixiecrats and Democrats,* 7.
5. Ibid., 31–37.
6. Sims, *The Little Man's Big Friend,* 31–32.
7. Grafton and Permaloff, *Big Mules and Branchheads,* 73.
8. *Speeches of Governor James E. Folsom,* 94.
9. Taylor, *Faulkner: Jimmy, That Is,* 83.
10. *Speeches of Governor James E. Folsom,* 94.
11. Barnard, *Dixiecrats and Democrat,* 39–41.
12. *Speeches of Governor James E. Folsom,* 183.
13. Grafton and Permaloff, *Big Mules and Branchheads,* 73.
14. Ibid., 68.
15. Barnard, *Dixiecrats and Democrats,* 41.
16. John Patterson, Bass-Devries interview, 33.
17. Wallace, *Stand Up for America,* 52.
18. Frady, *Wallace,* 89.
19. *Clayton Record,* May 17, 1946.
20. McDowell Lee, author's interview.
21. Frady, *Wallace,* 97.
22. *Alabama Journal,* May 6, 1949.
23. *Montgomery Advertiser,* May 1, 1947; Montgomery *Alabama Journal,* May 6, 1949.
24. Seymore Trammell, author's interview, November 28, 1988.
25. Wallace, *The Wallaces of Alabama,* 31–32.
26. *Birmingham News,* May 23, 1951.
27. McDowell Lee, author's interview.
28. Cobb, *The Selling of the South,* 35–63.
29. Kennedy, "New England and the South," 36.
30. Elliott, *The Cost of Courage,* 213.
31. *Birmingham News,* February 26, 1956.
32. *Clayton* (Ala.) *Record,* January 5, 1951.
33. Frady, *Wallace,* 118.
34. Wallace, *Stand Up for America,* 52–53.
35. Ibid., 58.
36. Wallace, *The Wallace Family,* 40–41.
37. *Birmingham Post-Herald,* November 3, 1966; House, *Lady of Courage,* 10–14.
38. Letter from George Wallace to James B. Folsom, June 13, 1953, Folsom Papers, ADAH.
39. Sims, *The Little Man's Big Friend,* 131.
40. Letter from George C. Wallace to O. H. Finney, April 13, 1954, Folsom Papers, ADAH.

41. Sims, *The Little Man's Big Friend,* 41.
42. " 'Y'all Come,' Original Scrip [*sic*] by Judge George Wallace," video copy of 1954 Folsom television commercial; copy in possession of the author.
43. Greenhaw, *Alabama on My Mind,* 27.
44. Bartley, *The Rise of Massive Resistance,* 107; McMillen, *The Citizens' Councils,* 5–137.
45. Elliott, *The Cost of Courage,* 177.
46. Grafton and Permaloff, *Big Mules and Branchheads,* 188–89.
47. *New York Post,* February 8, 1956.
48. *Birmingham News,* February 6, 1956.
49. Ibid., February 9, 1956.
50. Montgomery *Alabama Journal,* February 9, 1956.
51. *Montgomery Advertiser,* November 5, 1955.
52. Sims, *The Little Man's Big Friend,* 176.
53. Frady, *Wallace,* 109.
54. Sims, *The Little Man's Big Friend,* 208.
55. *Montgomery Advertiser,* March 1, 1956.
56. *Clayton Record,* May 16, 1956.
57. *Birmingham News,* March 10, 1956.
58. Frady, *Wallace,* 110.
59. *Birmingham News,* September 1, 1957.
60. Harry Ashmore, author's interview.
61. Bass, *Unlikely Heroes,* 73, 65.
62. Bartley, *The Rise of Massive Resistance,* 126 ff.
63. *Montgomery Advertiser,* January 26, 1956.
64. Ibid., March 1, 1956.
65. Sims, *The Little Man's Big Friend,* 185–86.
66. Hamilton, *Lister Hill,* 217.
67. Grafton and Permaloff, *Big Mules and Branchheads,* 201.
68. *Montgomery Advertiser,* August 5, 1956.
69. *Clayton* (Ala.) *Record,* April 30, 1948.
70. *Montgomery Advertiser,* July 15, 1948.
71. Letter from George C. Wallace to Gladys King Burns, September 18, 1964, Burns Papers, UAL; Burns, "The Alabama Dixiecrat Revolt of 1948," 152–63.
72. *Stand Up for Alabama,* 17; Taylor, *Me 'n' George,* 10.
73. Taylor, *Faulkner: Jimmy, That Is,* 86.
74. Brown, *Democracy at Work,* 280; *Birmingham News,* July 15, 1948.
75. *Montgomery Advertiser,* August 13, 1956; *Birmingham News,* August 13, 1956.
76. Thomson and Shattuck, *The 1956 Presidential Campaign;* Parmet, *The Democrats,* 138–41; Bendiner, "The Compromise on Civil Rights—I," 11–12.
77. *Montgomery Advertiser,* July 18, 1956.
78. Brown, *Democracy at Work,* 399–400; *Columbia State,* August 17, 1956.
79. *Montgomery Advertiser,* August 17, 1956, September 13, 1956, October 14, 1956.
80. *Hearings Before Subcommittee No. 5 of the Committee on the Judiciary, House of Representatives,* 85th Congress, 1st Session, 799.
81. Greenhaw, *Watch Out for George Wallace,* 111; McDowell Lee, author's interview.
82. Taylor, *Me 'n' George,* 13.

83. Frady, *Wallace,* 124.
84. Taylor, *Me 'n' George,* 16.
85. McLean, "From the Ashes: Phenix City, Alabama," 140–48; John Patterson campaign television advertisement, ADAH.
86. Powledge, *Free at Last,* 145.
87. John Patterson, Bass-DeVries interview.
88. Murphy, "The South Counterattacks," 376.
89. Raines, *My Soul Is Rested,* 135.
90. *State of Alabama ex rel. John Patterson, Attorney General, v. NAACP,* June 1, 1956; Lucille Black to Roy Wilkins, October 29, 1964, "Memorandum re: Birmingham Meeting," NAACP Papers, Group III, Series C, Branch Files, Box l, LC.
91. Powledge, *Free at Last,* 173.
92. Murphy, "The South Counterattacks," 371–90.
93. Author's transcript, John Patterson 1958 television advertisements, ADAH.
94. *Montgomery Advertiser,* October 20, 1965.
95. Informant Report, January 23, 1961, Box 3, Alabama ADL Papers, BPL.
96. Long, "The Imperial Wizard Explains the Klan," 8, 25–26; Wade, *The Fiery Cross,* 312–16.
97. Long, "The Imperial Wizard," 8, 25–26.
98. Raines, *My Soul Is Rested,* 304; *Atlanta Journal,* May 16, 1958; *Birmingham Post-Herald,* September 1, 1960.
99. Frady, *Wallace,* 125.
100. *Montgomery Advertiser,* May 7, 1958.
101. Ibid., May 15, 1958.
102. Greenhaw, *Watch Out for George Wallace,* 115.
103. Montgomery *Alabama Journal,* May 16, 17, 1958.
104. *Florence* (Ala.) *Times,* April 28, 1958.
105. John Patterson, Bass-DeVries interview.
106. Yarbrough, *Judge Frank Johnson,* 64.
107. *Montgomery Advertiser,* June 10, 1958.
108. Taylor, *Me 'n' George,* 16.
109. Dallek, *Lone Star Rising,* 518.
110. Ibid., 526.
111. Seymore Trammell, author's interview, November 28, 1988.
112. Ibid.
113. Seymore Trammell, author's interview, August 15, 1989.
114. Ibid.
115. Seymore Trammell, author's interview, August 28, 1988.
116. Seymore Trammell, author's interview, November 28, 1988.
117. Yarbrough, *Judge Frank Johnson,* 65.
118. Bass, *Taming the Storm,* 81.
119. *Browder v. Gayle,* 142 F. Supp. 707, 715–17.
120. *Montgomery Advertiser,* December 22, 1956.
121. Bass, *Taming the Storm,* 93.
122. *Birmingham News,* January 8, 1957.
123. Bass, *Taming the Storm,* 189.
124. Sikora, *The Judge,* 88–89.

125. Bass, *Taming the Storm,* 189. "I hate to say he lied," Wallace told a biographer in the late 1980s, but "what he said is not correct or true at all." Lesher, *George Wallace,* 136. As far as I have been able to determine, other than George Wallace no one—friend or foe of Frank Johnson—has ever suggested that he is capable of falsehood.

126. Sikora, *The Judge,* 89.

127. Seymore Trammell, author's interview, November 28, 1988.

128. Ibid.

129. Huie, "Humanity's Case Against George Wallace," 3.

130. Seymore Trammell, author's interview, November 28, 1988.

131. *Montgomery Advertiser,* January 28, 1976.

132. *United States of America v. George C. Wallace,* Transcript of Testimony before Judge Frank M. Johnson, January 26, 1959, 11.

133. Ibid., 31–33.

134. *Birmingham News,* January 27, 1959.

135. Sikora, *Judge Frank Johnson,* 90.

136. Greenhaw, *Watch Out for George Wallace,* 105.

137. John Synon, *Profile of a Presidential Candidate,* 42 ff.

138. Greenhaw, *Watch Out for George Wallace,* 198–99.

139. Lesher, *George Wallace,* 32.

140. Greenhaw, *Watch Out for George Wallace,* 198–99. Journalist Steven Brill remembered that the first time he ever saw Wallace, it was the fall of 1958 and the defeated Wallace was extremely drunk. Brill, "George Wallace Is Even Worse Than You Think He Is," 23.

141. Ray Jenkins, Bass-DeVries interview, SHC, 60.

142. Wallace, *The Wallaces of Alabama,* 57–58.

143. Greenhaw, *Watch Out for George Wallace,* 198.

144. Lesher, *George Wallace,* 117. *Birmingham News* reporter Anita Smith later confronted Lurleen Wallace with off-the-record statements from close family friends that she had threatened to divorce Wallace if he did not pay less attention to politics and more to his family. She did not deny the story. Smith, *The Intimate Story of Lurleen Wallace,* 78.

145. Frady, *Wallace,* 189.

146. Greenhaw, *Watch Out for George Wallace,* 198.

147. *Montgomery Advertiser,* March 11, 1962; *Birmingham Post-Herald,* March 11, 1962.

148. *Montgomery Advertiser,* March 8, 1962.

149. *Lee County Bulletin* (Ala.), March 16, 1962.

150. Fadeley, "George Wallace," 59; *Montgomery Advertiser,* March 11, April 23, 12, 1962.

151. Frady, *Wallace,* 131.

152. *Montgomery Advertiser,* April 7, 1962.

153. Frady, *Wallace,* 131.

154. Harper, *Me 'n' George,* 58.

155. *New York Times,* March 11, 1956; *Montgomery Advertiser,* March 11, 1956; Huie, *Three Lives for Mississippi,* 18–34; Cook, *The Segregationists,* 140–44; *Birmingham Post-Herald,* October 30, 31, November 1, 8, 1957; *Birmingham News,*

March 11, 1956; *Birmingham Post-Herald,* January 24, 25, 29, 1957; New York *Herald Tribune,* April 24, 1957.

156. *Birmingham News,* January 23–29, March 26, 1957.
157. Greenhaw, *Watch Out for George Wallace,* 162.
158. *Montgomery Advertiser,* January 8, March 14, 1962.
159. Benjamin Muse, confidential memorandum, July 13, 1961, SRC Papers, AU; *Montgomery Advertiser,* April 7, 1962.
160. Ibid., April 11, 12, 1962; March 14, 1962.
161. Grafton, *Big Mules and Branchheads,* 234; *Montgomery Advertiser,* May 3, 1962; Sherrill, *Gothic Politics in the Deep South,* 272.
162. Grafton, *Big Mules and Branchheads,* 236.
163. Wooten, "George Wallace: The Island of his Exile," 13. As he told Howell Raines in 1979 in commenting on his inaugural address: "I made a mistake in the sense that I should have clarified my position more. I was never saying anything that reflected upon black people, and I'm very sorry that it was taken that way." *New York Times,* January 21, 1979.
164. Report from Benjamin Muse, February 6, 1964, Benjamin Muse Reports, SRC Papers, Trevor Arnett Library, AU.

CHAPTER 4: "THE THREADS RAN THROUGH": THE KENNEDYS FACE THE GOVERNOR

1. Burke Marshall memo, November 30, 1962, Box 17, Burke Marshall Papers, JFK Library.
2. Lord, *The Past That Would Not Die,* 140; *Jackson Clarion-Ledger,* September 26, 1963.
3. Branch, *Parting the Waters,* 668.
4. Robert F. Kennedy, JFK interview, 23.
5. Erskine, "The Polls: Race Relations," 145; Erskine, "The Polls: Kennedy as President," 336.
6. Nicholas Katzenbach, JFK interview, 20–21.
7. *Birmingham News,* June 5, 1988.
8. Burke Marshall memo, November 30, 1962, Box 17, Burke Marshall Papers, JFK Library.
9. Kirby, *Fumble,* 142. J. Jefferson Bennett to Burke Marshall, March 4, 1963; Burke Marshall, "Memorandum re: University of Alabama," March 19, 1963; and memorandum, D. Robert Owen to Burke Marshall, June 6, 1963; Box 17, "Alabama" file, Burke Marshall Papers, JFK Library. Robert F. Kennedy and Burke Marshall, JFK interview.
10. Frank Rose, author's interview.
11. Seymore Trammell, author's interview, November 28, 1988.
12. *Chattanooga Times,* April 16, 1963; Clark, *The Schoolhouse Door,* 179–80.
13. Burke Marshall, "Memorandum re: University of Alabama," March 19, 1963, in Marshall Papers, Box 17, JFK Library.
14. Clark, *The Schoolhouse Door,* 180.
15. *Southern School News,* August, 1962, 2.
16. *Birmingham News,* February 9, 1963.
17. *Birmingham Post-Herald,* May 22, 1963.

18. "There were several people he talked to about various things. To say that he completely confided in one person? I don't believe he ever did." Bill Jones, author's interview.
19. Seymore Trammell, author's interview, November 28, 1988.
20. Seymore Trammell, author's interview, January 11, 1988.
21. Burke Marshall, "Memorandum to the File, re: University of Alabama," March 19, 1963, Burke Marshall Papers, JFK Library.
22. Robert Kennedy and Burke Marshall, JFK interview, 107.
23. Letter from Harrison Salisbury to author, July 20, 1991; *New York Times,* April 12, 1960.
24. Nunnelley, *Bull Connor,* 9–68.
25. Eskew, "But for Birmingham," 101–102.
26. Ibid., 118.
27. Morgan, *A Time to Speak,* 59.
28. Eskew, "But for Birmingham," 202.
29. Garrow, *Birmingham, Alabama, 1956–1963,* 140. Even for Connor, his response to the bombing of three black Birmingham churches in January of 1963 was an audacious exercise. At one of the three churches, a member of the congregation smelled the burning dynamite fuse and sounded the alarm. Connor immediately issued a statement announcing that "We know that Negroes did it." The proof, he said, was the fact that witnesses "saw Negroes running from the churches." *Birmingham Post-Herald,* February 1, 1963; *New York Times,* February 1, 1963.
30. Lesher, *George Wallace,* 195.
31. *Birmingham Post-Herald,* April 4, 1963.
32. Sherrill, *Gothic Politics in the Deep South,* 212.
33. Robert Kennedy and Burke Marshall, JFK interview, 528; Brauer, *John F. Kennedy and the Second Reconstruction,* 253.
34. *Montgomery Journal,* August 14, 1962; *Birmingham News,* July 26, 1959; *Montgomery Advertiser,* May 17, 1963.
35. *South: The Magazine of Dixie,* April 29, 1963.
36. *Montgomery Advertiser,* April 21, 1963.
37. *Birmingham Post-Herald,* April 17, 1963.
38. Robert F. Kennedy, JFK interview, 518.
39. Sikora, *The Judge,* 164–65.
40. Robert F. Kennedy, JFK interview, 518.
41. *Birmingham News,* April 25, 26, 1963; *Montgomery Advertiser,* April 21, 26, 1963; *New York Times,* April 26, 1963.
42. Guthman, *We Band of Brothers,* 268; Robert F. Kennedy, JFK interview, 518.
43. Audiotape of conversation among Robert F. Kennedy, George Wallace, Seymore Trammell, Burke Marshall, and Ed E. Reid, April 25, 1963, JFK Library. All quotes that follow are from the tape, not the printed transcript, which has numerous errors.
44. Robert F. Kennedy and Burke Marshall, JFK interview, 519.
45. Frady, *Wallace,* 169. Guthman gives the quote as "Well, I suppose I can understand Wallace's position politically. But that Trammell is something. He really wants trouble." Guthman, *We Band of Brothers,* 211.
46. Sikora, *The Judge,* 165.

47. Eskew, "But for Birmingham," 375.
48. *Montgomery Advertiser,* May 8, 1963.
49. Nunnelley, *Bull Connor,* 147.
50. *Birmingham Post-Herald,* May 8, 1963.
51. Raines, *My Soul Is Rested,* 165.
52. *New York Times,* May 11, 1963.
53. Raines, *My Soul Is Rested,* 176.
54. Ibid., 177.
55. "nigger son of a bitch": Branch, *Parting the Waters,* 793; "I ain't going to protect . . .": Fred Powledge, *Free at Last,* 512.
56. Bishop, *The Days of Martin Luther King, Jr.,* 304.
57. *New York Times,* May 13, 24.
58. *Birmingham News,* May 13, 1963; *New York Times,* May 13, 1963; *Newsweek,* May 20, 1963, 25.
59. *New York Times,* May 13, 1963.
60. Garrow, *Birmingham, Alabama,* 190; "I hope that": Powledge, *Free at Last,* 511.
61. *Montgomery Advertiser,* May 13, 1963.
62. Presidential Recordings, Civil Rights, 1963, Audiotape 86.2, May 12, 1963, JFK Library.
63. Jones, *The Wallace Story,* 83–84; Pierre Salinger, "Memo of Conversation between President [John F.] Kennedy and Governor GW of Alabama," President's Office Files, "Civil Rights—Alabama. 5/17/63," Box 96, JFK Library.
64. A quarter-century later, in his authorized biography, George Wallace denied that he had made such statements, and his biographer insisted that it "stretches credulity to believe that he would have gratuitously laid himself open to a foe by using the word *nigger* and referring to the stereotyped sexual appetites of black men, ministers or no." Lesher, *George Wallace,* 199. But Pierre Salinger, who wrote the memo within hours of the conversation, was emphatic. These were the words and the sentiments expressed by Wallace, and he still remembered them well. Letter from Pierre Salinger to author, January 21, 1991.
65. Paul Dixon, JFK interview, 49; *Montgomery Journal,* May 19, 1963.
66. *Montgomery Advertiser,* May 19, 1963.
67. According to Eddie Reid, in a telephone call passed on to Burke Marshall. Robert F. Kennedy and Burke Marshall, JFK interview, 532.
68. [J. Russel Anders] "Outline of Program," April ?, 1963; Burke Marshall, "Memorandum to the Members of the Cabinet," May 21, 1963, in BM Papers, Alabama File, Box 17, JFK Library; letter from William H. Orrick, Jr., to Attorney General Robert Kennedy, May 29, 1963, Alabama Civil Rights Files, 299.l.5.l.8, BPL.
69. *New York Times,* October 30, 1963.
70. Winton (Red) Blount, author's interview.
71. George LeMaistre, author's interview.
72. *Florence* (Ala.) *Times,* May 22, 1963.
73. George LeMaistre, author's interview.
74. Clark, *The Schoolhouse Door,* 124–25.
75. Greenhaw, *Watch Out for George Wallace,* 130.
76. Clark, *The Schoolhouse Door,* 176.
77. Raines, *My Soul Is Rested,* 328–29.

78. Greenhaw, *Watch Out for George Wallace,* 130–31; Raines, *My Soul Is Rested,* 329.

Chapter 5: "We Dare Defend Our Rights": The Stand in the Schoolhouse Door

1. Sidey, *John F. Kennedy,* 406; Salinger, *With Kennedy,* 101.
2. In their taped recollections, Burke Marshall and Robert Kennedy placed the White House meeting on the weekend of the schoolhouse-door stand, but White House records show that it was June 1, a week earlier. President John F. Kennedy's Appointment Books, June 1–17, 1963, JFK Library.
3. Schlesinger, *Robert Kennedy,* 639.
4. "Ninety percent": Presidential Recordings, Audiotape 88.6, May 21, 1963; Negroes . . . "are getting mad": Presidential Recordings, Audiotape 88.6, May 20, 1963, JFK Library.
5. Burke Marshall, JFK interview, JFK Library, 83.
6. Presidential Recordings, Audiotape 88.6, May 20, 1963, 6, JFK Library.
7. Robert Kennedy and Burke Marshall, JFK interview, 539.
8. Presidential Recordings, Audiotape 90.3, June 1, 1963, JFK Library.
9. Greenhaw, *Alabama on My Mind,* 55–57.
10. Letter from Grover C. Hall, Jr., to Horace Hall, May 19, 1958, Grover C. Hall, Jr., Papers, ADAH.
11. Ibid.; *Montgomery Independent,* October 24, 1968.
12. *Montgomery Independent,* October 24, 1968; *New York Times,* June 3, 1963.
13. *Mobile Press-Register,* May 3, 1964.
14. James J. Kilpatrick, "What Makes Wallace Run?" 406.
15. Transcript, *Meet the Press,* June 2, 1963, Lawrence E. Spivak Papers, LC.
16. Greenhaw, *Alabama on My Mind,* 57–58.
17. *Alabama Journal,* June 5, 1963.
18. Mrs. Lister Hill, author's interview; letter from Brooks Hayes to John F. Kennedy, November 30, 1962, RFK Papers, JFK Library.
19. A week before the stand-down, Shelton's assistant, Al Sisk, called President Rose and assured him that the Klan—while scheduled to hold a rally outside Tuscaloosa June 10—would not be on campus. Letter from D. Robert Owen to Burke Marshall, June 6, 1963, Burke Marshall Papers, "Alabama" file, Box 17, JFK Library; *Birmingham News,* June 7, 8, 9, 1963.
20. E. R. Fields to author, July 26, 1993.
21. Stanton, *Klanwatch,* 175ff.
22. "Desegregation Memo," 5-28-63, Burke Marshall Papers, Alabama Folder, Box 18, JFK Library.
23. *Tuscaloosa News,* June 9, 1994.
24. Ibid.
25. Rowe, *My Undercover Years with the Ku Klux Klan,* 81–91. Portions of the material in Rowe's book are contradicted by official and other sources.
26. Mikell, *Selma,* 177.
27. Ibid., *Birmingham News,* June 9, 1963; "Testimony of Herbert Eugene Reeves," U.S. Congress, Hearings on KKK Organizations, 89th Cong., 1st Sess., House Committee on Un-American Activities, 1965, 3086–88.

28. "Memorandum for the Attorney General by William H. Orrick, Jr.," June 6, 1963, Box 18, Burke Marshall Papers, JFK Library.
29. Letter from Nicholas deB. Katzenbach to the Attorney General, May 31, 1963, in RFK-Alabama Civil Rights Files, 299.1.5.1.8, Birmingham Public Library. *Birmingham News,* June 5, 1983.
30. Kohn, *The Cradle,* 59.
31. Transcript of telephone conversation between Attorney General Robert Kennedy, Cecil Jackson, and John Peter Kohn, June 8, 1963, 4:40 P.M., copy in possession of the author.
32. *Washington Post,* June 11, 1963.
33. Dorman, *The George Wallace Myth,* 122–25.
34. Ibid, 127.; Robert F. Kennedy, JFK interview, 20.
35. Watson, *The Expanding Vista,* 128–52; Watson, "Kennedy Live," 53–66.
36. Earl Morgan, author's interview.
37. Raines, *My Soul Is Rested,* 330–31.
38. From *Crisis: Behind a Presidential Commitment,* an ABC documentary aired October 21, 1963.
39. Letter from "Mother Mae" Wallace to Lurleen Wallace, June ?, 1963, "Miscellaneous" letters, Wallace Family Papers.
40. Kohn's published version, in *The Cradle,* was more diplomatic. "Governor, suppose they did jail you in an integrated jail," he wrote. "Then you would be in a ridiculous situation." *Cradle,* 63–64.
41. Winton (Red) Blount, author's interview; draft of Trustees Resolution, prepared by Governor Wallace's Office, in Alabama Governor's Papers, "Standing in the Doorway" File, Drawer 443, GW Papers, ADAH; *Birmingham News,* June 11, 1963.
42. Winton (Red) Blount, author's interview.
43. Nicholas Katzenbach, LBJ interview, 13–14; *Montgomery Advertiser,* April 3, 1986.
44. From *Crisis: Behind a Presidential Commitment,* a documentary aired October 21, 1963; *Montgomery Advertiser,* June 12, 1963; *Atlanta Constitution,* June 12, 1963.
45. Peggy Sue (Wallace) Kennedy, author's interview.
46. Confidential interview.
47. Raines, *My Soul Is Rested,* 331.
48. Ibid., 341.
49. Robert F. Kennedy and Burke Marshall, JFK interview, 528.
50. *Montgomery Advertiser,* April 3, 1986.
51. *New York Times,* June 12, 1991; *Birmingham News,* June 12, 1991; *Montgomery Advertiser,* June 12, 1991; Robert F. Kennedy and Burke Marshall, JFK interview, 523; Nicholas Katzenbach, LBJ interview, 13.
52. Watson, *The Expanding Vista,* 148.
53. Raines, *My Soul Is Rested,* 341.
54. *Birmingham News,* June 5, 1983; Raines, *My Soul Is Rested,* 341.
55. *Montgomery Advertiser,* June 12, 1963; Drew, *Crisis: Behind a Presidential Commitment,* author's transcript.
56. Guthman, *We Band of Brothers,* 217–18.
57. Whalen, *The Longest Debate,* 153. *Washington Post,* June 12, 1963 and Sidey, *John F. Kennedy,* 401.
58. Sidey, *John F. Kennedy,* 401.

59. *New York Times,* June 12, 1994.
60. Robert Kennedy and Burke Marshall, JFK interview.
61. Ibid.; "not bothered": Burke Marshall, LBJ interview, 544.
62. *New York Times,* June 12, 1963.
63. McIlhany, *Klandestine,* 38. In his 1994 retrial for the Evers murder, six people who knew Beckwith swore under oath that he had repeatedly bragged about killing the Mississippi civil rights leader. *New York Times,* February 2, 1994.
64. George Wallace to John F. Kennedy, June 12, 1963, June 13, 1963; John F. Kennedy to George Wallace, June 14, 1963, George Wallace to John Kennedy, June 17, 1963, "University of Alabama—Segregation" file, Drawer 443, George Wallace Papers, ADAH.
65. *Birmingham News,* June 16, 1963; *Citizen,* July–August 1963.
66. Erskine, "The Polls: Kennedy as President," 339; Erskine, "The Polls: Speed of Racial Integration," 513–14; Brauer, *John F. Kennedy,* 263.
67. Memorandum from Don Jones to Burke Marshall, June 19, 1963, "Alabama" file, Box 17, Burke Marshall Papers, JFK Library.
68. Sorensen, *Kennedy,* 246.
69. Basler, ed. *Collected Works of Abraham Lincoln,* VII, 282.

CHAPTER 6: "ALL OF US ARE VICTIMS"

1. *Birmingham News,* September 16, 1962.
2. "Playboy Interview, Martin Luther King"; Rather, *The Camera Never Blinks,* 100.
3. Jack Nelson, APT interview.
4. *Harrisburg Patriot,* July 3, 1963.
5. Hearings before the Committee on Commerce, U.S. Senate, 88th Congress, First Session, July 15, 16, 1963. Since the constitutional justification for the proposed civil rights legislation rested upon the Constitution's interstate commerce clause, initial hearings were held before the commerce committee.
6. Parks, *Rosa Parks: My Story,* 106.
7. John Salmond, *A Southern Rebel,* 179–97.
8. Salmond, " 'The Great Southern Commie Hunt,' " 438–52.
9. *Birmingham News,* July 15, 1963.
10. *Hearings Before the Committee on Commerce,* July 15, 1963.
11. "Statement by George C. Wallace Before the Senate Committee on Commerce, July 15, 1963," ADAH Speech Collection. The colloquy on the photograph is from the official record of the Committee hearings and from the Montgomery *Alabama Journal* and *Birmingham News,* July 15, 1963. Favorable estimates of Wallace are from the *Birmingham News,* July 16, 1963 and the *Washington Post,* July 16, 1963.
12. "Speech by George C. Wallace . . . before the South Carolina Broadcasters Association, July 15, 1963," ADAH Speech Collection; *Charleston News and Courier,* July 16, 1963; *Columbia* (SC) *State,* July 16, 1963.
13. "Speech of George C. Wallace before the Citizens' Council of Louisiana, Inc., August 10, 1963," ADAH Speech Collection.
14. Norrell, *Reaping the Whirlwind,* 128–43.
15. *Montgomery Advertiser,* August 29, 1963; "communists and sex perverts": *Alabama Journal,* September 14, 1963.

16. Freyer, *The Little Rock Crisis,* 115–17.

17. Bartley, *The Rise of Massive Resistance,* 265.

18. *Montgomery Advertiser,* August 25, 1963.

19. Ibid., August 28–30, 1963; *Birmingham News,* August 28–30, 1963.

20. Alabama *Code,* 1962, Title 14, Section 407.

21. *Tuscaloosa Graphic,* quoted in *Montgomery Advertiser,* September 15, 1963.

22. Wilson and Harris, "Hucksters of Hate—Nazi Style," 11.

23. Cook, *The Segregationists,* 136, 172–86; Wilson and Harris, "Hucksters of Hate—Nazi Style," 11–17.

24. Bull Connor File, 105-65138-14, FBI.

25. McMillan, "The Birmingham Church Bomber." Throughout his article, author George McMillan refers to Stoner as "Mr. X." "He has a distinguishing physical characteristic," a detective told McMillan, "and he always tells his buddies it's too dangerous for him to be seen, that *he* would be noticed, marked and remembered." Stoner was a childhood victim of polio and walked with a limp. Longtime Atlanta police chief Herbert Jenkins confirmed to me in 1987 that he was the source for much of McMillan's article, including the quote about Stoner's proximity to various bombings.

26. Raines, *My Soul Is Rested,* 167–71. FBI officials suspected him of direct involvement in dozens of racial bombings, but his only conviction came at the hands of Alabama Attorney General William Baxley in 1980 when an all-white jury convicted him of the Bethel bombing and sentenced him to a long prison term.

27. McMillen, "The Birmingham Church Bomber," 18.

28. *Montgomery Advertiser,* September 23, 1964.

29. *Thunderbolt,* November 1962, 4; March, 1963, 7.

30. "Notes," January 28, 1964, Folder 38, Box 3; Jones, "Summary of the Activities of the National States Rights Party during the year of 1963 and spring of 1964 in Birmingham Alabama," May 1964, William C. Hamilton Papers, 3.35, BPL.

31. Letter from Edward R. Fields to author, July 26, 1993.

32. Letter from Edward R. Fields to George Wallace, August 24, 1963; letter from George Wallace to Edward Fields, August 27, 1963, from "Segregation" file, Drawer 339, George Wallace Papers, ADAH.

33. *Montgomery Advertiser,* September 1, 4, 1963.

34. *Alabama v. Robert E. Chambliss,* trial transcript, 474, BPL.

35. Letter from Lieutenant Thomas H. Cook to Chief Jamie Moore, July 18, 1963, Boutwell Papers, 20.38, BPL.

36. FBI Interview with Robert Chambliss, October 1, 1963, BAPBOMB File, BPL.

37. *Mongomery Advertiser,* March 21, 1959; *Birmingham Post-Herald,* March 21, 1959. For a detailed outline of his various brushes with the law, see *Alabama v. Chambliss* transcript, 581 ff, BPL.

38. "Press Release, September 1, 1963, 1 A.M.," Boutwell Papers, BPL.

39. Birmingham Police Department Inter-office Communication, September 5, 1963, BPL. The informant's report was used to bring a conspiracy indictment against Fields and J. B. Stoner on September 23, 1963. *New York Times,* September 24, 1963.

40. Sikora, *Until Justice Rolls Down,* 55–57; FBI Sixteenth Street Baptist Church Bombing Investigation Files, 1963–1965, BPL, FBI Report, October 4, 1963, 1308.1.1, BPL.

41. Law-and-order quote from "Birmingham Police Department Inter-office Communication, September 5, 1963, in Hamilton Papers, BPL; other quotes from *Montgomery Advertiser,* September 3, 1963.

42. Norrell, *Reaping the Whirlwind,* 144–45; *Birmingham News,* September 3, 1963.

43. Crass, *The Wallace Factor,* 61.

44. *Birmingham News,* September 13, 1963.

45. "Telephone Conversation, September 3, 1963—Approximately 10 A.M.—Governor Wallace calling Mayor Albert Boutwell," Boutwell Papers, 20.40, BPL.

46. Birmingham Police Department Inter-office Communication, September 9, September 10, 1963, Boutwell Papers, 20.38, BPL; *Birmingham News,* September 4, 1963; *Montgomery Advertiser,* September 5, 1963.

47. *Alabama v. Chambliss,* trial transcript, 247, BPL; *Birmingham News,* October 9, 1963.

48. Telegram from "Imperial Wizard" Robert M. Shelton to Mayor Albert Boutwell, September 4, 1963, in Boutwell Papers, 20.38, BPL.

49. Marcus A. Jones, Birmingham Police Department Inter-office Communication, September 9, 1963 [Account of meeting at Redmont Hotel, September 4, 1963], Boutwell Papers, 20.38, BPL.

50. *New York Times,* September 6, 1963.

51. Raines, *My Soul Is Rested,* 348; "If I had stepped": Powledge, *Free at Last,* 484; *New York Times,* September 5, 1963.

52. "Statement from Chief Moore . . . meeting with the Birmingham School Board . . . September 5, 1963," Boutwell Papers, 20.38, BPL.

53. *Birmingham News,* September 5, 1963.

54. Ibid., September 10, 12, 13, 15.

55. *Montgomery Advertiser,* September 20, 1963.

56. Ibid., September 8, 1963.

57. *New York Times,* September 24, 1963.

58. Letter from Edward R. Fields to author, July 26, 1963. By October, all the charges against the States' Rights Party leaders had been dismissed.

59. For example, on his statewide telecast to the people of Alabama on September 8, 1963, he insisted that he wanted no violence. "If we resort to bombing, if we resort to harming the hair on a single person's head in this State, we cannot win this fight." *Montgomery Advertiser,* September 9, 1963.

60. Bill Jones, author's interview.

61. *New York Times,* September 6, 1963.

62. *Alabama v. Chambliss* trial transcript, 261–62, 272, 275, BPL.

63. Ibid., 516.

64. Ibid, 312 ff.

65. In the course of one of his interrogations, Chambliss volunteered an elaborate description of how to make a "drip method bomb." FBI agents were convinced from the limited evidence recovered that this was the method used. *Alabama v. Chambliss* trial transcript, 250, BPL.

66. Raines, "The Birmingham Bombing," 25.

67. Sikora, *Until Justice Rolls Down,* 105.

68. Ibid.

69. Cobbs/Smith, *Long Time Coming,* 90–91.

70. *Alabama v. Chambliss* trial transcript, 94–95, BPL.

71. Ibid., 524.
72. Ibid, 64–65.
73. *Newsweek,* September 30, 1963, 21.
74. *Alabama v. Chambliss* trial transcript, 67, BPL.
75. Ibid., 68.
76. *New York Times,* September 16, 1963.
77. *Birmingham News,* September 18, 1963.
78. Ibid.
79. Ibid., September 16, 1993.
80. Ibid.
81. Garrow, *Bearing the Cross,* 292.
82. *New York Times,* September 16, 1963.
83. Fairclough, *To Redeem the Soul of America,* 159.
84. *New York Times,* September 19, 1963; *Atlanta Constitution,* September 19, 1963.
85. *Nashville Tennessean,* June 22, 1972.
86. Ibid., September 17, 1963; author's conversation with Phillip Sullivan of the *Tennessean.*
87. Robert F. Kennedy and Burke Marshall, JFK interview, 595.
88. *New York Times,* September 17, 1963.
89. *Birmingham News,* September 16, 1963.
90. Raines, *My Soul Is Rested,* 181–83.
91. *New York Times,* September 17, 1963. See Morgan, *A Time to Speak,* 10–14.
92. Charles Morgan, author's interview, July 11, 1994; Morgan, *A Time to Speak,* 14.
93. *Birmingham Post-Herald,* October 3, 1963; *Montgomery Advertiser,* October 3, 1963.
94. Letter from George Wallace to Robert C. Floyd, Jr., October 15, 1963, "Segregation" file, Drawer 399, GW Papers, ADAH.
95. *Montgomery Advertiser,* September 16, 1963. Nor were such musings restricted to Alabamians. U.S. Senators Willis Robertson of Virginia and Richard Russell of Georgia frankly speculated that the bomb had been planted by civil rights activists. *Montgomery Advertiser,* September 26, 1963; O'Reilly, *"Racial Matters,"* 111.
96. *Montgomery Advertiser,* September 19, 1963. See also "Racial Files," Lister Hill Papers, Gorgas Library, UA; and "Letters to the Editor" sections of the *Montgomery Advertiser, Birmingham News,* and *Birmingham Post-Herald,* September 18–25, 1963.
97. *Montgomery Advertiser,* September 22, 1963.
98. Spencer, "Judgment Without Trial," September 29, 1963, Folder 7, Box 5, Boutwell Papers, BPL.
99. Thornton, "Challenge and Response in the Montgomery Bus Boycott of 1955–56," 218.
100. *Alabama v. Chambliss* trial transcript, 277, BPL.
101. Audiotape No. 111.7, September 19, 1963, JFK Library.
102. Audiotape No. 112.5, September 23, 1963, JFK Library.
103. Burke Marshall interview, JFK interview, 100.
104. *Birmingham News,* September 27, 1993.
105. *Montgomery Advertiser,* September 28, 1963.

106. Garrow, *Birmingham,* 141.
107. "Memo to Chief Jamie Moore, April 2, 1967," William Hamilton Papers, Folder 38, Box 3, BPL.
108. *Alabama v. Chambliss* trial transcript, 525, BPL.
109. McMillen, "The Birmingham Church Bomber," 17.
110. Raines, "The Birmingham Bombing," 24.
111. Sikora, *Until Justice Rolls Down,* 115.
112. Detective M. A. Jones report, September 24, 1963, Hamilton Papers, BPL.
113. McMillen, "The Birmingham Church Bomber," 17.
114. *Montgomery Advertiser,* September 30, 1963.
115. *New York Times,* October 1, 1963.
116. Raines, "The Birmingham Bombing," 25. In his public statements, Shelton always claimed that he was opposed to violence. But, in a 1987 civil lawsuit, lawyers for the mother of a young black man lynched in Mobile, Alabama, convinced an all-white jury that Shelton and other Klan leaders covertly incited internal Klan cells to commit acts of violence (including the murder of her son) even as they professed nonviolence. Stanton, *Klanwatch: Bringing the Klan to Justice,* pp. 213–16.
117. J. Edgar Hoover to Attorney General Robert Kennedy, September 30, 1963, BAPBOMB File, FBI, No. 333. O'Reilly, *"Racial Matters,"* 110–13.
118. *New York Times,* February 18, 1990; *Atlanta Constitution,* October 30, 1985.
119. Cobbs/Smith, *Long Time Coming,* 101.
120. Ibid., 202-03. The author photocopied the document (as well as a reporter's later account of the meeting) and attached it as an appendix to *Long Time Coming.*
121. *Montgomery Advertiser,* October 8, 1963.
122. *New York Times,* October 3, 1963.
123. *Los Angeles Times,* October 1, 1963; *Birmingham Post-Herald,* October 1, 1963. In his story, William O. Bryant of the *Washington Post* quoted Birmingham police chief Jamie Moore as saying that he knew "absolutely nothing" about the arrests. Otherwise, there was no hint that the arrests might be a charade. *Washington Post,* October 1, 1963.
124. Langner quote from *Birmingham Post-Herald,* October 9, 1963; "common in Birmingham": *Time,* October 18, 1963.
125. Robert Kennedy and Burke Marshall, JFK interview, 595.
126. *New York Times,* October 9, 1963. In their November 8 issues, the *Washington Post* and the *Chicago Daily News* had given extensive coverage to the bombing and the arrest of Chambliss by Wallace's state police. The *Post* described Chambliss's misdemeanor conviction in a two-paragraph story; the *Daily News* did not even mention the outcome of the case. A survey of eight national newspapers from Boston to Los Angeles showed a similar pattern.
127. Claude Sitton, author's interview.
128. *New York Times,* February 18, 1980.
129. O'Reilly, *"Racial Matters,"* 114.
130. *Birmingham News,* September 29, 1963; *Birmingham Post-Herald,* September 29, 1963.
131. Letter from George Wallace to Retired Admiral Lawton Ford, January 6, 1964, in "B'ham Bombing File," Drawer 399, George Wallace Papers, ADAH.

132. Sikora, *The Judge,* 90.
133. *Atlanta Constitution,* October 8, 1968.
134. William Baxley, author's interview.
135. Raines, "The Birmingham Bombing," 12ff.; *Atlanta Constitution,* October 30, 1985.

CHAPTER 7: A TREMOR, NOT AN EARTHQUAKE: GEORGE WALLACE AND THE PRESIDENTIAL CAMPAIGN OF 1964

1. Huie, "The U.S. *Must* Say No to George Wallace," 17.
2. Fitzhugh, *Cannibals All!,* xiii; Simkins, *"Pitchfork" Ben Tillman,* 393–407.
3. Sherrill, *Gothic Politics,* 184.
4. Joe Azbell, author's interview.
5. *Montgomery Advertiser,* November 5, 1963.
6. The text of the speech, including its hard-line racist portions, was distributed early in the evening of November 4 and appeared in several Alabama newspapers. It became one of the most oft-cited examples of Wallace's racism. See Frady, *Wallace,* 173; Jones, *The Wallace Story,* 112–13; Lesher, *George Wallace,* 263. Ironically, it was never delivered in this form. The actual speech as Wallace delivered it can be found in the NAACP Papers. "A Major Fraud: Governor Wallace's Speech at Harvard U.," NAACP Papers, Group III, Container 329, GW Folder, LC.
7. *Boston Globe,* November 5, 1963.
8. Grossman, "Harvard Looks Back on Gov. Wallace's Visit," 3.
9. *Harvard Crimson,* November 5, 1963.
10. *Alabama Journal,* November 5, 1963.
11. *Harvard Crimson,* November 5, 1963.
12. Irwin Hyatt, author's interview; letter from Frederick J. Elsas to author, January 22, 1988.
13. George Wallace Speech, June 1966, GW Film, APT Footage, Reel 403.
14. *Harvard Crimson,* November 9, 1963.
15. Seymore Trammell, author's interview, November 28, 1989.
16. *Birmingham News,* November 5, 1963.
17. *Huntsville* (Ala.) *Times,* November 8, 1963.
18. Huie, "The U.S. *Must* Say No to George Wallace," 17.
19. *Birmingham News,* November 23, 1963.
20. Earl Morgan, author's interview.
21. "Red" Holland to Edwin Guthman, November 30, 1963, Burke Marshall Papers, Box 17, JFK.
22. *Birmingham News,* January 16, 1964.
23. *Montgomery Advertiser,* February 2, 1964.
24. *Tacoma* (Wash.) *Tribune,* January 15, 1964.
25. *Montgomery Advertiser-Journal,* November 24, 1963.
26. McMillen, *The Citizens' Councils,* 289; Cook, *The Segregationists,* 195.
27. "John J. Synon—Biog," Alabama ADL papers, BPL.
28. Epstein and Forster, *The Radical Right,* 34.
29. Jones, *The Wallace Story,* 330.
30. *The Daily Cardinal,* February 21, 1963.

31. Taylor, *Me 'n' George,* 24.

32. Frady, *Wallace,* 172.

33. *New York Times,* March 29, 1964.

34. Haney, "Wallace in Wisconsin," 261–62; Forster and Epstein, *Danger on the Right,* 164–71; *Montgomery Advertiser,* August 24, 1963.

35. Schuyler A. Baker, Elena Vorbovia interview.

36. *Birmingham News,* March 31, 1964.

37. *Milwaukee Sentinel,* March 17, 1964.

38. *Milwaukee Journal,* March 17, 1964.

39. Haney, "Wallace in Wisconsin," 262–63.

40. *Madison* (Wisc.) *State Journal,* March 12, 1963.

41. Jones, *The Wallace Story,* 193.

42. *Madison* (Wisc.) *State Journal,* March 11, 1964.

43. *Birmingham News,* March 26, 1963.

44. George Wallace, Wisconsin speech, March 1964, ADAH Speech Collection.

45. Watson, *The Expanding Vista,* 131.

46. *Birmingham News,* April 2, 1964.

47. George Wallace Wisconsin speech, ADAH Speech Collection; *Milwaukee Journal,* April 2, 1964.

48. Wallace, *Stand Up for America,* 89.

49. *New York Times,* April 8, 1964; Englehart, "Wallace in Indiana," 451.

50. Rogin, "Wallace and the Middle Class," 107–108; Carlson, *George C. Wallace and the Politics of Powerlessness,* 27–44; Hixson, *Search for the American Right Wing,* 113–74.

51. *New York Times,* April 9, 1963.

52. *Montgomery Advertiser,* April 14, 1964. (The *Advertiser* reprinted editorials from almost every major newspaper in the country that commented on the election.)

53. Rovere, "Letter from Washington, May 16, 1964," 195, 197, 193.

54. *Nation,* May 4, 1964, 449.

55. *Mobile Press-Register,* May 3, 1964.

56. *Southerner,* I (April–May, 1956), 1a.

57. Rogin, "Politics, Emotion and the Wallace Vote," 27–49.

58. Welsh, "Civil Rights and the Primary Election of 1964," 14.

59. *Washington Star,* May 1, 1964.

60. *Indianapolis Star,* April 15, 1964.

61. *Time,* April 24, 1964, 22.

62. *Montgomery Advertiser,* April 21, 1964; *Birmingham News,* April 30, 1964; *New York Times,* April 30, 1964.

63. *Indianapolis Star,* May 3, 1964.

64. *Mobile Press-Register,* May 3, 1964.

65. *Indianapolis Star,* May 6, 1964.

66. *Washington Post,* May 7, 1964.

67. Johnson, *The Vantage Point,* 159.

68. Hoffman and Strietelmeier, "Gary's Rank-and-File Reaction," 29.

69. Kempton, "The State of Maryland," 6.

70. Mike Manatos to Walter Jenkins, May 2, 1964, WHEF Name Files, GW, Box 45, LBJ Library; *Washington Post,* April 27, 1964; Kempton, "The State of Maryland," 7.

71. "NBC-TV *Today Show* transcript, May 6, 1964, ADAH Speech Collection.

72. Makay, "The Speaking of Governor George C. Wallace," 128.

73. Makay, "The Rhetorical Strategies of Governor George Wallace," 174.

74. Johnson, "Maryland," 16–99.

75. *Washington Star,* May 13, 1964.

76. Jones, *The Wallace Story,* 279–81.

77. Kempton, "The State of Maryland," 8.

78. *Baltimore Sun,* May 12, 13, 14, 1964.

79. Jones, *The Wallace Story,* 285.

80. *Washington Star,* May 13, 1964.

81. Kempton, "The State of Maryland," 6.

82. *Birmingham News,* May 10, 1964.

83. *New York Times,* May 8, 1964.

84. *Cambridge* (Md.) *Daily Banner,* May ? [date illegible], GW clipping files, ADAH.

85. *U.S. News & World Report,* June 1, 1964, 31.

86. *New York Times,* May 21, 1964.

87. NBC-TV *Today Show* transcript, May 6, 1964, ADAH Speech Collection.

88. *New York Herald-Tribune,* May 13, 1964.

89. *Public Papers of the Presidents, LBJ,* II, 843–44; *New York Times,* July 3, 1964; *Washington Post,* July 3, 1964.

90. Greenhaw, *Watch Out for George Wallace,* 150.

91. Handbill advertising "Patriot Day," July 4, 1964, copy in possession of the author.

92. *Atlanta Journal-Constitution,* July 5, 1964.

93. George C. Wallace Speech, Atlanta, Georgia, July 4, 1964, ADAH Speech Collection.

94. *Birmingham News,* July 4, 1964.

95. Greenhaw, *Watch Out for George Wallace,* 155–56.

96. Whalen, *The Longest Debate,* 213.

97. Bass and DeVries, *The Transformation of Southern Politics,* 27.

98. *Congressional Record—Senate,* June 18, 1964, 14318.

99. Mohr, "Requiem for a Lightweight," 120.

100. Cosman, *Republican Politics,* 242–43.

101. James Martin, APT interview; *Gadsden Times,* January 16, 1968.

102. Huie, "Humanity's Case Against George Wallace," 3.

103. *Huntsville Times,* July 30, 1992.

104. James Martin, APT interview.

105. Huie, "Humanity's Case Against George Wallace," 4.

106. *Huntsville Times,* July 30, 1992.

107. Huie, "Humanity's Case Against George Wallace," 3. Bill Jones gives a slightly different version of the meeting. Jones, *The Wallace Story,* 324–25.

108. *Huntsville Times,* July 30, 1992; July 24, 1964, 20.

109. *Birmingham News,* July 13, 1964.

110. James Martin, APT interview.

111. *Birmingham News,* January 21, 1968.

112. *New York Times,* July 20, 1964.

113. Because the autopsy showed that the three men—particularly Chaney—had

numerous broken bones, most civil rights activists believed they had been savagely beaten. But the crushed bones were more likely caused by the earth mover used to bury them under an earthen dam. Cagin and Dray, *We Are Not Afraid,* 294–95.

114. *Washington Post,* July 23, 1964.
115. *Birmingham News,* June 26, 1964.
116. Cagin and Dray, *We Are Not Afraid,* 356–57.
117. O'Reilly, *"Racial Matters,"* 232.
118. *New York Times,* July 20, 1964.
119. Jones, *The Wallace Story,* 343.
120. *New York Times,* August 22, 1964.
121. *Birmingham Post-Herald,* October 22, 1964.
122. Cleghorn, "Aftermath in Alabama," 34.
123. Sherrill, "Wallace and the Future of Dixie," 272.

CHAPTER 8: "ON WHAT MEAT DOTH THIS LITTLE CAESAR FEED?"

1. "Upon what meat doth this our Caesar feed, / That he is grown so great?" *Julius Caesar,* I, ii.
2. Broward Segrest, author's interview, January 11, 1989.
3. Montgomery *Alabama Journal,* March 16, 1964.
4. Love, "Claiming a Right to Choose," 34–36.
5. *Zellner v. Lingo* file, Drawer 519; letter from John P. Kohn to George Wallace, n.d., "Kohn: Attorney's Fees" file, Drawer 510, GW Papers, ADAH.
6. Robert Zellner, author's interview.
7. Morgan, *A Time to Speak,* 135–46.
8. *Montgomery Advertiser,* January 9, 10, 11, 1963; Love, "Claiming a Right to Choose," 36; Morgan, *A Time to Speak,* 139–41. Quote from *Zellner v. Lingo* file, Drawer 510, GW Papers, ADAH.
9. Reverend Bob Marsh Radio Address, March 28, 1965; distributed by the Alabama Sovereignty Commission, Box 5, Alabama Sovereignty Commission Papers, ADAH.
10. Kelley, *Hammer and Hoe,* 72–73.
11. Powledge, *Free at Last,* 415.
12. Letter from Harrison Salisbury to author, July 20, 1991. "This was Birmingham": Salisbury, *A Time of Change,* 50. In a calculated attempt to drive unfriendly media out of the region, Birmingham's officials sued Salisbury for slander for more than three million dollars and demanded nearly seven million dollars from the *New York Times.* Encouraged by the prospect of sympathetic all-white juries, local governments in adjoining states adopted the strategy against others covering the civil rights movement. It would take three years of trials and appeals and a landmark Supreme Court decision (*New York Times v. Sullivan*) to halt this new form of harrassment.
13. Raines, *My Soul Is Rested,* 310; John Patterson, JFK interview, 33–37.
14. Notes: April 17, 1967, Folder 38, Box 3, William Hamilton Papers, BPL.
15. Raines, *My Soul Is Rested,* 170–71.
16. Letter from Ben L. Allen to Albert J. Lingo, January 21, 1963, "Commission to Preserve the Peace" file, Drawer 406, GW Papers, ADAH.

17. *Miami Herald,* July 4, 1993; *New York Times,* July 4, 1993.

18. *Birmingham News,* March 11, 1956, May 14, 1959, April 19, 1959, May 25, 1963; Ben L. Allen to Albert J. Lingo, January 21, 1963, "Commission to Preserve the Peace" file, Drawer 406, GW Papers, ADAH; "hold a new club": *Birmingham News,* April 19, 1963; "Biennial Report of the Alabama Legislative Commission to Preserve the Peace," spring 1965, Drawer 406, GW Papers ADAH.

19. "Goggins Report," *South,* July 8, 1963, 6; "On what meat": Sherrill, "Wallace and the Future of Dixie," 270.

20. "Report of the Alabama Legislative Committee to Preserve the Peace," "Committee to Preserve the Peace" file, Drawer 406, GW Papers, ADAH; *New York Times,* February 17, 1964.

21. Minutes of the State Sovereignty Commission, March 2, 1964, "State Sovereignty Commission" file, Drawer 406, GW Papers, ADAH.

22. "Staff Study, Alabama Legislative Committee to Preserve the Peace, July 1964, "Selma March, Affidavits" file, Drawer 406, GW Papers, ADAH.

23. Alabama Legislative Committee to Preserve the Peace: S.A.I. Report, *Confidential,* September 15, 1967," Drawer 406, GW Papers, ADAH.

24. Letter from Edward Strickland to Mayor Albert Boutwell, April 30, 1964, File 3.28, Hamilton Papers, BPL.

25. John Hawkins and Ed Strickland, "Communist Goals . . ." May 19, 1964; "Notes," May 17, 1965, File 3.28, Hamilton Papers, BPL.

26. Letter from John H. Hawkins, Jr., to John Buchanan, February 9, 1966, and "Summaries of Witnesses," February 8, 1966, Buchanan Papers, BPL. Roton's statement is quoted from "Activities of the Ku Klux Klan Organizations in the United States," Part 3; Hearings Before the Committee on Un-American Activities, House of Representatives, 89th Cong, 2nd Session, 3109–231.

27. "Committee to Preserve the Peace" file, Drawer 406, GW Papers, ADAH.

28. The Reverend C. Halford Ferrell, "An Appeal for Christian Thinking: Sermon of the Week," *Methodist Christian Advocate,* November 13, 1962; letter from George Wallace to C. Halford Ferrell, April 9, 1963, "Segregation" files, Drawer 399, GW Papers, ADAH. For other examples of Wallace's harassment of white Alabamians who counseled moderation, see the following files in the Alabama Governors' Papers: "Segregation" files, Drawer 399; "1963–64 Civil Rights" files, Drawer 406; "Public Safety" files, Drawer 412; "Civil Rights" file, Drawer 415; "SCEF" files, Drawer 506, GW Papers, ADAH.

29. Alan Parker, Bass-Devries interview, 9; letter from Clyde Butler to George Wallace, April 8, 1965, "1964–65 Civil Rights" file, Drawer 406, GW Papers, ADAH; *Atlanta Constitution,* June 27, 1989; letter from J. S. Palmer to George Wallace, May 30, 1966, "Civil Rights" file, Drawer 415, GW Papers, ADAH; The Rev. Walter Telfer, author's interview.

30. Chestnut, *Black in Selma,* 117.

31. Jack Bass, *Taming the Storm,* 185. "Wallace would send out": Arthur Shores, William A. Elwood interview, transcript in possession of the author.

32. Wicker, "George Wallace: A Gross and Simple Heart," 47.

33. *New York Times,* May 7, 1972.

34. Raines, *My Soul Is Rested,* 375; Anthony Heffernan, author's interview.

35. *Newsweek,* June 1, 1964, 18.

36. *Montgomery Journal,* June 18, 1963.

37. Ray Jenkins, Bass-Devries interview, 56.

38. Raines, *My Soul Is Rested,* 375.

39. Letter from Art Wallace to George Wallace, August 13, 1963; letter from George Wallace to Art Wallace, September 13, 1963, "Segregation" file, Drawer 399, GW Papers, ADAH. Wallace's official biographer, Stephan Lesher, seeks to explain away the harsh racist language of some of Wallace's correspondence as the product of overzealous staffers who had written and prepared responses. But, as Lesher acknowledges, whether or not Wallace personally dictated the letter to Art Wallace, this and other racist letters were sent "with his permission and, presumably, with his broad support of the sentiments expressed." Lesher, *George Wallace,* 204.

40. Clark, *Segregation's Last Stand,* 246. "To: Tuscaloosa File, November 16, 1963," Box 17, Burke Marshall Papers, JFK.

41. "Memo from Mr. Cronin to Office Staff," February 15, 1960, "Racial" file, Senator Lister Hill Papers, UAL.

42. Letter from Mrs. Cora Thomas to George Wallace, July 24, 1965, "1965 Public Safety Department" file, Drawer 412, GW Papers, ADAH.

43. Letter from Major Harry B. Ansted to George Wallace, March 5, 1964; letter from George Wallace to Harry Ansted, March 12, 1964, "Segregation" file, Drawer 399 GW Papers, ADAH.

44. Letter from Jack W. Hines to George W. Wallace, March 19, 1965, "Public Safety" file, Drawer 404, GW Papers, ADAH.

45. Letter from Trooper M. W. Gilmore to Colonel Albert J. Lingo, March 23, 1965, copy in "Public Safety Department" file, Drawer 412, GW Papers, ADAH.

46. Eagles, *Outside Agitator,* 30–33.

47. *Montgomery Advertiser-Journal,* September 22, 1963. Voting figures from Garrow, *Protest at Selma,* 31.

48. Voter Education Project, *Voter Registration in the South,* 3.

49. Raines, *My Soul Is Rested,* 188; *New York Times,* March 26, 1968.

50. Raines, *My Soul Is Rested,* 191.

51. File No. 51-23: Report of Major W. R. Jones, February 18–19, 1965, "RE. Marion, Alabama, Registrations" file, Drawer 412, GW Papers, ADAH.

52. Fager, *Selma,* 74.

53. Ibid.

54. Raines, *My Soul Is Rested,* 191.

55. *New York Times,* February 22, 1965.

56. *Birmingham News,* March 20, 1965. Only two whites were charged in the mêlée. One was fined $75 and $3.75 court costs for assaulting Valeriani with an ax handle; the second was assessed a $50 fine since he had used his fist instead of a club. *Montgomery Advertiser,* March 6, 1965.

57. Valeriani was quoted in the *Birmingham News,* February 20, 1965. File No. 51-23: Report of Major W. R. Jones, February 18–19, 1965, "RE. Marion, Alabama, Registrations" file, Drawer 412, GW Papers, ADAH.

58. Raines, *My Soul Is Rested,* 189.

59. *New York Times,* February 22, 1965.

60. Raines, *My Soul Is Rested,* 192.

61. File No. 51-23: Report of Major W. R. Jones, February 18–19, 1965, "RE. Marion, Alabama, Registrations," file, Drawer 412, GW Papers, ADAH.

62. Adams, "Young Man Tried to Register," 18.

63. *New York Times,* February 20, 21, 22, 1965; Mendelsohn, *The Martyrs,* 133–52. "Mother Wasn't": Mendelsohn, *The Martyrs,* 147.

64. Williams, *Eyes on the Prize,* 271.

65. Montgomery *Alabama Journal,* February 20, 1965.

66. Undated draft of telegram to ABC News by George Wallace, in "RE. Marion, Alabama, Registrations" file, Drawer 412, GW Papers, ADAH.

67. Memo from Hugh Maddox to Bill Jones, March 3, 1965, "Re. Marion, Alabama, Registrations" file, Drawer 412, GW Papers, ADAH.

68. *Anniston Star,* February 21, 1965.

69. *Birmingham News,* February 20, 1965.

70. *Montgomery Advertiser,* February 26, 1965.

71. Raines, *My Soul Is Rested,* 188.

72. Chestnut, *Black in Selma,* 201.

73. Adams, "Young Man Tried to Register to Vote," 18.

74. "We was infuriated" and "We had decided we were going": Williams, *Eyes on the Prize,* 267; "Our first plan": Raines, *My Soul Is Rested,* 194.

75. Abernathy, *And the Walls Came Tumbling Down,* 325–26.

76. "Confidential Memorandum," Ed Strickland to George Wallace, March 8, 1965, "Committee to Preserve the Peace" files, Drawer 406, GW Papers, ADAH.

77. Jones, *The Wallace Story,* 356.

78. "Confidential Memorandum," Ed Strickland to George Wallace, March 8, 1965, "Committee to Preserve the Peace" files, Drawer 406, GW Papers, ADAH. *Montgomery Advertiser,* March 6, 1965; Jones, *The Wallace Story,* 358–59; Seymore Trammell, author's interview, January 11, 1988.

79. Eagles, *Outside Agitator,* 89–117; Jones, *The Wallace Story,* 357.

80. Greenhaw, *Watch Out for George Wallace,* 169.

81. Fager, *Selma, 1965,* 95.

82. Hinckle and Welsh, "Five Battles of Selma," 28.

83. Based on a viewing of the ABC and CBS footage.

84. "Too much film": Nelson Benton interview in Raines, *My Soul Is Rested,* 386. *Montgomery Advertiser,* March 14, 1965.

85. *Birmingham News,* April 13, 1966; Greenhaw, *Watch Out for George Wallace,* 174; *New York Times,* March 9, 1965; Lesher, *George Wallace,* 326.

86. Jones, *The Wallace Story,* 363.

87. *Birmingham News,* March 13, 1965.

88. *New York Times,* March 8, 1965.

89. Garrow, *Selma,* 89.

90. Williams, *Eyes on the Prize,* 276–77.

91. Mendelsohn, *The Martyrs,* 172–73.

92. Letter from the Reverend Ed Folsom to Lister Hill, March 12, 1965, "Racial" file, Lister Hill Papers, UAL.

93. "An open letter from Sheriff James G. Clark, Jr., April 24, 1965," Box 5, Alabama Sovereignty Commission Papers, ADAH. The letter is reprinted in Mikell, *Selma,* 245–50.

94. Sol Tepper's "Ten Big Questions Regarding the Death of Reverend Reeb in Selma, Alabama," January 3, 1966, and the publications of the Selma Committee for Better Understanding, "Civil Rights File: Selma," Drawer 412, GW Papers, ADAH.

95. Memo from Hubert Humphrey to Lyndon Johnson, March 12, 1965, "Legislative Background: Voting Rights Act of 1965," Box 2, LBJ Library.

96. Jones, *The Wallace Story*, 375–76; letter from George Wallace to Lyndon B. Johnson, March 12, 1965, White House Central Files, Ex HU 2/ST1, LBJ Library.

97. Earl Morgan, author's interview.

98. Jones, *The Wallace Story*, 381.

99. Miller, *Lyndon*, 430. No record of the three-hour meeting was made. My reconstruction is based on an account leaked to White House correspondent Marianne Means; my interview with Seymore Trammell; the interviews of Jack Valenti, Burke Marshall, and Nicholas Katzenbach conducted by the LBJ Library; Johnson's account in his autobiography, *The Vantage Point;* Richard Goodwin's recollections in his book *Remembering America;* and Wallace's interview for the LBJ Library and his account as given in his authorized biography by Stephan Lesher.

100. Jones, *The Wallace Story*, 377, 380.

101. Jack Valenti, LBJ interview, IV, 9.

102. Seymore Trammell, author's interview, February 14, 1989; "Aunt Susie": related by Horace Busby in Middleton, *LBJ*, 86.

103. Lesher, *George Wallace*, 332.

104. Goodwin, *Remembering America*, 322.

105. Katzenbach's recollection was that the discussion was over school desegregation rather than voting rights, but everyone present remembered Johnson's barnyard remonstrance. Raines, *My Soul Is Rested*, 339.

106. Letter from Douglas Cater to Lyndon Johnson, March 13, 1965; letter from Nicholas Katzenbach to Lyndon Johnson, March 13, 1965; letter from Lee White to Lyndon Johnson, March 12, 1967; letter from Harry McPherson to Lyndon Johnson, March 12, 1987. All in "Legislative Background: Voting Rights Act of 1965," Box 2, LBJ Library.

107. Juanita Roberts, who helped Johnson write his autobiography, *The Vantage Point,* remembered that the President seemed genuinely fond of Wallace, far more regretful about his apostasy than angry. Juanita Roberts LBJ interview, IV, 10.

108. Seymore Trammell, author's interview, February 14, 1989.

109. *New York Times,* March 14, 1965, 62.

110. Bill Jones, author's interview.

111. Harwood, *Lyndon*, 107.

112. Transcript, *Face the Nation,* March 14, 1965, copy in possession of the author.

113. Johnson, *The Vantage Point,* 165.

114. *Williams v. Wallace,* trial transcript, 194.

115. *Birmingham News,* March 19, 1965; *New York Times,* March 19, 1965.

116. *Montgomery Advertiser,* March 19, 1965.

117. *Birmingham News,* March 19, 1965.

118. Bass, *Taming the Storm,* 249.

119. Wofford, *Of Kennedys and Kings,* 193.

120. Jones, *The Wallace Story,* 432.

121. *New York Times,* March 26, 1965.

122. Eagles, *Outside Agitator,* 244.

123. *New York Times,* March 26, 1965.

124. *Birmingham Post-Herald,* April 23, 1965.

125. Jones, *The Wallace Story,* 436–37.

126. Montgomery *Alabama Journal,* March 26, 27, 1965; Jones, *The Wallace Story,* 437.

127. "Activities of the Ku Klux Klan Organizations in the United States," part 3, Hearings Before the Committee on Un-American Activities, House of Representatives, 89th Cong., 2nd Session, 3109–231.

128. Copies of the Michigan police investigation results were mailed to *hundreds* of prominent Alabamians. The results are reprinted in Mikell's *Selma,* 136–42.

129. The governor's office arranged complete access for Mikell to Lingo and his investigation; all the photographs that appeared in the book came from the files of the state police and the Peace Committee. When the book was published, Wallace and his staff personally worked to arrange national distribution for it. "Re Selma March Film" file, Drawer 413, GW Papers, ADAH.

130. Mikell, *Selma,* 181.

131. For a compilation of these articles distributed by the Selma and Dallas County chamber of commerce see "The Story of Selma: or 'The Other Side of the Coin.'"

132. *Congressional Record,* March 30, 1965, vol. III, 57ff.

133. "The Story of Selma," 19.

134. Persons, *Sex and Civil Rights,* 4ff.

135. Saturnalia quote: The Reverend Bob Marsh, radio address, March 28, 1965; "red hand of Communism": *Selma to Montgomery March* filmscript; Complaints: letter from J. K. Callaway to Eli H. Howell, November 26, 1965. All in Box 5, Alabama Sovereignty Commission Papers, ADAH; Jones, *The Wallace Story,* 451.

136. Fager, *Selma, 1965,* 181.

137. Ibid, 183–87.

138. Oliver Quayle and Company, "A Survey of the Political Climate in Alabama—Confidential," Study #219, February 1965, Roy Mayhall Papers, BPL.

139. *Birmingham News,* May 24, 1965.

140. Chappell, *Inside Agitators,* 189–211.

Chapter 9: "Stand Up For Alabama": The Queen and Her Consort in a Captive State

1. "Speech Delivered by Governor George C. Wallace . . . August 6, 1964," ADAH Speech Collection; *Montgomery Advertiser,* August 7, 1964.

2. Sherrill, "Portrait of a 'Southern Liberal' in Trouble," 53.

3. Oliver Quayle Company, "A Survey of the Political Climate in Alabama—Confidential," Study #219, February 1965, Roy Mayhall Papers, BPL.

4. *Birmingham News,* May 30, May 31, 1965.

5. Letter from John Kohn to George Wallace, December 3, 1969, Kohn Family Papers. Copy in possession of the author.

6. *Montgomery Advertiser,* August 7, 1965; *Birmingham News,* August 22, 1965; *New York Times,* May 23, 1965; *Montgomery Advertiser-Journal,* August 29, 1965; Cooper, "The Rise of George C. Wallace," 196–99.

7. Huie, "Humanity's Case Against George Wallace," 3.

8. "Speech Delivered by Governor George C. Wallace . . . September 30, 1965," ADAH Speech Collection; *Montgomery Advertiser,* October 1, 1965.

9. James Edwin Horton, Jr., author's interview.

10. John Patterson, Bass-DeVries interview.

11. Frady, *Wallace,* 182.

12. William Baxley, author's interview; Wicker, "George Wallace: A Gross and Simple Heart," 47.

13. Wicker, "George Wallace: A Gross and Simple Heart," 47.

14. *Birmingham News,* April 13, May 7, 1963; Seymore Trammell, author's interview, January 18, 1988.

15. *Montgomery Advertiser,* October 11, 1965.

16. Ibid., October 15, 1965. Harold Martin, Bass-DeVries interview; Ray Jenkins, author's interview, July 10, 1992.

17. Letter from Hugh Maddox to Edwin Horton, October 13, 1965, copy in "1965–66 Democratic Party" file, Drawer 416, GW Papers, ADAH.

18. *Florence* (Ala.) *Times,* October 14, 1965; quote from *Huntsville Times,* October 14, 1965.

19. *Montgomery Advertiser,* October 15, 1965; *Huntsville Times,* October 15, 1965; James Edwin Horton, Jr., author's interview.

20. Frady, *Wallace,* 184.

21. *Florence* (Ala.) *Times,* October 14, 1965.

22. *Birmingham News,* October 19, 1965; *Mobile Register,* October 19, 1965.

23. *Birmingham News,* October 22, 23, 1965.

24. Quotes from the Hammond speech are from the *Montgomery Advertiser,* October 23, 1965; *Birmingham News,* October 22, 1965; and the *Montgomery Journal,* October 22, 1965; "They just knew": Frady, *Wallace,* 186–87.

25. Albert Brewer, author's interview.

26. *Montgomery Advertiser,* August 27, 1965.

27. *Montgomery Advertiser-Journal,* October 24, 1965.

28. *Dallas News,* July 18, 1924; McKay, *Texas Politics,* 54–77, 129–59, 186–246, 324–36.

29. Lesher, *George Wallace,* 359.

30. *Birmingham News,* April 23, 1967. In his official biography, Wallace claimed to have learned of the Ferguson campaigns for the first time from Lyndon Johnson at a White House briefing.

31. Wayne Greenhaw, *Watch Out for George Wallace,* 190. When Franklin Roosevelt appointed Alabama senator Hugo Black to the United States Supreme Court in 1937, Governor Bibb Graves named his wife, Dixie, to fill out the unexpired term as a tactical move to avoid a bitter fight within the state's Democratic Party, but Mrs. Graves served only briefly in the role of caretaker.

32. Quoted in Bass, *Taming the Storm,* 202–203.

33. *Birmingham News,* February 21, 1966.

34. Smith, *The Intimate Story of Lurleen Wallace,* 77.

35. Frady, *Wallace,* 188.
36. Silveri, "Pushing the Fence Back Too Far," 3–5.
37. Elliott, *The Cost of Courage,* 232. The quote "tear down the judiciary" is from Greenhaw, *Watch Out for George Wallace,* 261.
38. Elliott, *The Cost of Courage,* 232.
39. Frady, *Wallace,* 206–207.
40. *Birmingham News,* January 19, 1963.
41. Frady, *Wallace,* 141.
42. *Montgomery Advertiser,* October 3, 1963.
43. *New York Times,* October 17, 1965; "impeach the son-of-a-bitch": *Alabama Journal,* January 7, 1966; "scalawag": Seymore Trammell, author's interview, January 18, 1988.
44. *Montgomery Advertiser,* February 10, 1966; Montgomery *Alabama Journal,* February 10, 1966.
45. *Montgomery Advertiser,* February 11, 1966.
46. Smith, *The Intimate Story of Lurleen Wallace,* 9.
47. Seymore Trammell, author's interview, November 28, 1988; Taylor, *Me 'n' George,* 78–79.
48. Greenhaw, *Watch Out for George Wallace,* 200.
49. Frady, *Wallace,* 190.
50. Smith, *The Intimate Story of Lurleen Wallace,* 9.
51. Summary of medical information obtained from Anita Smith, Jack House, and interview with Peggy Sue (Wallace) Kennedy. Dr. Joseph Perry agreed to review the material (telephone conversation, July 10, 1992) and to make corrections. He offered no corrections to the material I sent him.
52. Oken, "What to Tell Cancer Patients," 1120–28. Twenty years later, fewer than twenty percent of physicians *ever* concealed a cancer diagnosis—even a diagnosis of terminal illness—from their patients. Lear, "Should Doctors Tell the Truth?" 17.
53. House, *Lady of Courage,* 44.
54. Ibid.
55. *Montgomery Advertiser,* November 24, 1965.
56. Ibid., January 9, 1966.
57. *Alabama Journal,* January 10, 1966; *Montgomery Advertiser,* January 10, 11, 1966.
58. House, *Lady of Courage,* 26; *Alabama Journal,* January 10, 1966; *Montgomery Advertiser,* January 11, 1966.
59. Albert Brewer, author's interview.
60. *Birmingham Post-Herald,* February 11, 1966; *Birmingham News,* February 10, 1966; *Montgomery Journal,* February 10, 1966; *Montgomery Advertiser,* February 11, 1966.
61. *Gadsden Times,* February 20, 1966.
62. House, *Lady of Courage,* 31; Robert Ingram, author's interview.
63. Kilpatrick, "What Makes Wallace Run?" 407.
64. Greenhaw, *Watch Out for George Wallace,* 199.
65. Ibid., 201; House, *Lady of Courage,* 31; Peggy Sue (Wallace) Kennedy, author's interview.

66. Lesher, *George Wallace*, 357.
67. Coverage in *Birmingham News* and *Post-Herald, Montgomery Advertiser, Alabama Journal*, and *Tuscaloosa Graphic* for March 24–30, 1966.
68. Ray Jenkins, APT interview.
69. Jenkins, "Mr. and Mrs. Wallace Run for Governor of Alabama."
70. *Birmingham News*, March 19, 1966.
71. *Los Angeles Times*, November 6, 1965.
72. Taylor, *Me 'n' George*, 79.
73. Greenhaw, *Watch Out for George Wallace*, 192; Wicker, "George Wallace: A Gross and Simple Heart," 43.
74. John Patterson, Bass-DeVries interview.
75. *Birmingham News*, November 7, 1966; William Bradford Huie, author's interview.
76. *New South*, 21 (winter 1966), 88–89.
77. *Birmingham News*, April 13, 1966; *Montgomery Advertiser*, April 16, 1966.
78. Elliott, *The Cost of Courage*, 283–84; Douglas Cater, author's interview.
79. *Birmingham News*, April 8, 12, 1966; *Los Angeles Times*, April 13, 1966.
80. *Anniston Star*, March 15, 1989.
81. *Boston Herald*, March 29, 1966. House, *Lady of Courage*, 45.
82. *Tuscaloosa News*, June 5, 1942.
83. *Birmingham News*, May 4, 1966; *Montgomery Advertiser*, May 4, 5, 1966; Brink and Harris, *Black and White*, 103; *Birmingham Post-Herald*, May 10, 1966.
84. *Montgomery Advertiser*, May 5, 1966.
85. Alabama Governors' Papers, "Registration of Voters" file, Drawer 412, GW Papers, ADAH.
86. *Huntsville Times*, May 5, 1992.
87. *Birmingham Post-Herald*, May 6, 1966.
88. "Speech . . . by George C. Wallace . . . July 26, 1966," ADAH Speech Collection; *Montgomery Advertiser*, July 27, 1966.
89. "Speech . . . by George C. Wallace . . . August 9, 1966," ADAH Speech Collection.
90. *Alabama Journal*, August 20, November 7, 1966.
91. Frady, *Wallace*, 32–33; Seymore Trammell, author's interview, January 18, 1988.
92. "Jim Martin" file, Drawer 412; GW Papers, ADAH; 1965–66 "Democratic Party" file, Drawer 416, GW Papers, ADAH; William Bradford Huie, author's interview; George Wallace, Jr., *The Wallaces of Alabama*, 97.
93. *Prattville Progress*, October 6, 1966; "Jim Martin" file, Drawer 411, GW Papers, ADAH.
94. John Grenier, Bass-Devries interview; Frady, *Wallace*, 193.
95. Undated Martin advertisement, *Birmingham Post-Herald*, copy in "Jim Martin" file, Drawer 411, GW Papers, ADAH.
96. Frady, *Wallace*, 26–30.
97. Letter from Virginia Durr to Clark and Mairi Foreman, October 25, 1966, Durr Papers, Radcliffe University Library.
98. *Washington Post*, October 2, 1966.
99. *Clayton* (Ala.) *Record*, November 10, 1968.
100. Frady, *Wallace*, 197–99; *Montgomery Advertiser*, November 4, 1966.

101. Donald S. Strong, "Alabama," 453–58.
102. Frady, *Wallace,* 184–85.
103. Ray Jenkins, APT interview; Frady, *Wallace,* 204; *Birmingham News,* March 19, 1966.
104. Kilpatrick, "What Makes Wallace Run?," 407.
105. Frady, *Wallace,* 19. Frady identifies the speaker simply as an "Alabama judge," but it is clearly Mayhall who publicly used the same remark (minus the profanity) in a speech the following year (*Birmingham News,* November 28, 1967).
106. Letter from Durr to Clark Foreman, May 13, 1966, Durr Papers Radcliffe University Library. Letter from Durr to Hugo Black, September 23, 1965, Black Papers, Library of Congress.

CHAPTER 10: "STAND UP FOR AMERICA": THE POLITICS OF ALIENATION

1. *Montgomery Advertiser,* January 17, 1967; *New York Times,* January 17, 1967; *Atlanta Constitution,* January 17, 1967.
2. Frady, *Wallace,* 202.
3. Jack Show, author's interview.
4. Witcover, "George Wallace Isn't Kidding," 23; *Los Angeles Times,* September 17, 1968.
5. Forster and Epstein, *Danger on the Right,* 40–41.
6. Lipset, "Three Decades of the Radical Right," 421–39.
7. Jorstad, *The Politics of Doomsday,* 83.
8. Cook, *The Segregationists,* pp. 202–203.
9. Mintz, *The Liberty Lobby,* 70ff.
10. *Liberty Lobby Presents,* 2–44.
11. "KKK" file, Drawer 443; "Committee to Preserve the Peace" file, Drawer 406; "Anti-Communism" file, Drawer 419. All in GW Papers, ADAH. *Detroit Free Press,* October 21, 1965; *Birmingham News,* October 24, 1965.
12. *Los Angeles Times,* September 17, 1968; *New York Times,* September 13, 1968. The Anti-Defamation League of B'nai B'rith issued detailed biographies of the unsavory backgrounds of dozens of prominent Wallace supporters across the country. The report attracted little attention except among liberals already hostile to Wallace. ADL Press Release, September 13, 1968, Alabama ADL Papers, BPL.
13. *Atlanta Journal and Constitution,* November 12, 1967.
14. Frady, *Billy Graham,* 235–37.
15. Redekop, *The American Far Right;* 15–26; Hill, ed., *Encyclopedia of Religion in the South,* 319.
16. Lipset, *The Politics of Unreason,* 274.
17. Letter from George C. Wallace to Ed Strickland, June 17, 1965, "Committee to Preserve the Peace" file, Drawer 406, GW Papers, ADAH. See also the Hargis correspondence in the "H" file, Taylor Hardin Papers, BPL.
18. *Birmingham News,* December 11, 1966.
19. Frady, *Wallace,* 13.
20. Seymore Trammell, author's interview, January 18, 1988.
21. *New York Times,* April 28, June 18, 1967.
22. *Birmingham News,* November 5, 17, 1967.

23. Frady, *Wallace*, 215.
24. *Birmingham News,* December 11, 1967.
25. "Ronald Cohn Memo of Tape Recording of Jack House," April 29, 1968, Folder X-1, Alabama ADL Papers, BPL.
26. Tom Turnipseed, author's interview, July 21, 1988.
27. Matusow, *The Unraveling of America,* 360–61; Conot, *Rivers of Blood,* 6–22, 415–30.
28. O'Neill, *Coming Apart,* 175.
29. Carson, *In Struggle,* ; Good, "The Meredith March," 11–13; Good, "A White Look at Black Power," 116; Kopkind, "The Birth of Black Power," 6ff; Garrow, *Bearing the Cross,* 498ff; Adam Fairclough, *To Redeem the Soul of America,* 309–330.
30. Wilkins, "Steady as She Goes," 295.
31. Garrow, *Bearing the Cross,* 475–524.
32. Azbell, *The Riotmakers,* 30, 50.
33. Ibid., 68.
34. Sherrill, *Gothic Politics in the Deep South,* 263.
35. George C. Wallace Speech, July 26, 1966, Dan Dowe Documents, BPL.
36. "Address . . . Miami, Florida, August 29, 1966," transcript, Fadely, "George Wallace: Agitator Rhetorician," 245–51; *Montgomery Advertiser,* August 30, 1966.
37. Erskine, "The Polls: Demonstrations and Race Riots," 664–69.
38. *New York Times,* September 29, 30, 1966.
39. *Birmingham News,* June 14, 1967.
40. *New York Times,* October 24, 1966.
41. *Jackson* (Mississippi) *Daily News,* September 30, 1966.
42. Letter from Hugh Maddox (Wallace legal adviser) to Bill Jones, September 27, 1967, Wallace Presidential Campaign Materials, Box 67-B. At the time I examined these Presidential Campaign Materials, they were housed in the Mervin Sternes Library of the University of Alabama–Birmingham. They are now under the control of the George Wallace Foundation and available to scholars only with special permission from the foundation.
43. Chester, Hodgson, and Page, *An American Melodrama,* 284–85.
44. Seymore Trammell, author's interview, January 11, 1988.
45. Gallup, *The Gallup Poll,* vol. 3, 2079; *New Republic,* January 16, 1965, 18; Shearer, "California Voters Win Big Victory," 9–10.
46. McMillen, *The Citizens' Council,* 145.
47. Smith, *The Intimate Story of Lurleen Wallace,* 5.
48. *Birmingham News,* June 27, 1967.
49. *New York Times,* September 12, 1967; *Birmingham News,* July 12, 1967; *Montgomery Advertiser,* July 5, 1967.
50. Smith, *The Intimate story of Lurleen Wallace,* 12.
51. Frady, *Wallace,* 202.
52. Smith, *The Intimate Story of Lurleen Wallace,* 17.
53. *New York Times,* September 18, 1967.
54. Smith, *The Intimate Story of Lurleen Wallace,* 47, 23.
55. Tom Turnipseed, author's interview, July 21, 1988.
56. Bill Jones, author's interview; Ed Ewing, Elena Vorbovia interview.
57. *Montgomery Advertiser,* April 16, 1970.

58. *Montgomery Advertiser-Journal,* May 24, 1970. Central Bank and Trust Company–Seymore Trammell Promissory Notes. Copies in possession of the author.

59. Chester, *An American Melodrama,* 286; Seymore Trammell, author's interview, January 11, 1988; *Los Angeles Times,* November 18, 1967.

60. Ed Ewing and Schuyler Baker, Elena Vorbovia interview.

61. Smith, *The Intimate Story of Lurleen Wallace,* 80–81.

62. *New York Times,* November 21, 1967.

63. *Los Angeles Times,* November 24, 27, 1967; *Montgomery Advertiser,* November 25, 1967.

64. Cannon, *Ronnie and Jessie,* 131.

65. Novak, "Beyond the Fringe," 79.

66. *Los Angeles Times,* November 12, 1967; Chester, *An American Melodrama,* 651.

67. The description is based on news coverage in the *Los Angeles Times* for November and December, 1967; Tom Turnipseed, author's interview, July 21, 1988; and Wayne Greenhaw, *Watch Out for George Wallace,* 28–29.

68. Taylor, *Me 'n' George,* 44.

69. Carney, "From Down Home to Uptown," 104–110; Malone, *Country Music U.S.A.,* 200–204.

70. Freedman, "The Sociology of Country Music"; Cobb, "From Muskogee to Luckenbach"; DiMaggio, "Country Music: Ballad of the Silent Majority"; Lund, "Fundamentalism . . . in Country Music"; DiMaggio and Petersen "From Region to Class."

71. Seymore Trammell, author's interview, January 11, 1988.

72. *Montgomery Advertiser,* December 21, 1967; *Los Angeles Times,* December 12, 1967.

73. Gallup, *The Gallup Poll,* vol. 3, 2093.

74. *Los Angeles Times,* December 28, 1967.

75. Smith, *The Intimate Story of Lurleen Wallace,* 81.

76. Ibid., 34, 96.

77. *Houston Chronicle,* January 12, 1967; *Birmingham News,* January 12, 1967; Smith, *The Intimate Story of Lurleen Wallace,* 80–81.

78. Ingram, *That's the Way I Saw It,* 9; *Montgomery Advertiser-Journal,* April 15, 1968; *Birmingham News and Post-Herald,* April 15, 1968.

79. Peggy Sue (Wallace) Kennedy, author's interview.

80. Wallace, *The Wallaces of Alabama,* 116.

81. Smith, *The Intimate Story of Lurleen Wallace,* 108.

82. *Montgomery Advertiser,* April 21, 24, 1968.

83. Ibid., April 21, 1968; "upbeat": *Birmingham News,* April 26, 1966, and Ingram, *That's the Way I Saw It,* 9; *Montgomery Advertiser,* April 26, 1966.

84. Wallace, *The Wallaces of Alabama,* 117.

85. Smith, *The Intimate Story of Lurleen Wallace,* 112.

86. Peggy Sue (Wallace) Kennedy, author's interview.

87. Wallace, *The Wallaces of Alabama,* 118.

88. Ibid., 120.

89. *Montgomery Advertiser,* May 10, 1968.

90. Mobile *Register,* February 25, 1967; Greenhaw, *Alabama on My Mind,* 37.

91. *Montgomery Advertiser,* April 9, 1968. Similar editorials appeared in the *Birmingham News* and *Post-Herald.*

92. Virginia Durr, Paul Stekler interview.
93. Letter from Virginia Durr to Jim Dombrowski, May 14, 1968, Virginia Durr Papers, Radcliffe College.
94. Ingram, *That's the Way I Saw It*, 10–11.
95. Albert Brewer, author's interview.
96. Peggy Sue (Wallace) Kennedy, author's interview.
97. *Montgomery Advertiser*, May 28, 1968.

CHAPTER 11: RICHARD NIXON, GEORGE WALLACE, AND THE SOUTHERNIZATION OF AMERICAN POLITICS

1. *Los Angeles Times*, November 4, 1962; Haldeman, *The Ends of Power*, 113.
2. Nixon, "Khrushchev's Hidden Weakness"; Nixon, "Needed in Vietnam: The Will to Win."
3. Nixon, *Memoirs*, 259–65; Ambrose, *Nixon*, 50–57.
4. Scammon and Wattenberg, *The Real Majority*, 91.
5. Richard Nixon, Herbert Parmet interview.
6. *New York Times*, September 30, 1966; Witcover, *Resurrection of Richard Nixon*, 130–40.
7. Thurmond had not demanded concessions on civil rights before his June endorsement; he was more intent on obtaining Nixon's support for funding an anti-ballistic missile system and an overall American military buildup. Nixon, *Memoirs*, 304–305.
8. Witcover, *The Resurrection of Richard Nixon*, 147.
9. "Strom Thurmond Reports to the People," vol. 11, no. 21 (May 31, 1965); Thurmond, *The Faith We Have Not Kept*, 31–36, 107–34; Sherrill, *Gothic Politics in the Deep South*, 235–55.
10. Dent, *The Prodigal South Returns to Power*, 77; Harry Dent, author's interview.
11. *Washington Post*, April 21, 1968.
12. Dent, *The Prodigal South Returns to Power*, 76–77.
13. Chester, *An American Melodrama*, 435.
14. *Miami Herald*, August 7, 1968.
15. Chester, *An American Melodrama*, 447.
16. Nixon, *Memoirs*, 309
17. Witcover, *The Resurrection of Richard Nixon*, 321.
18. Nixon, *Memoirs*, 311–12.
19. Chester, *American Melodrama*, 483.
20. Richard Nixon, Herbert Parmet interview.
21. Cohen and Witcover, *A Heartbeat Away*, 92–96.
22. Huie, "Humanity's Case Against George Wallace," 3.
23. Ibid., 313.
24. *Baltimore Sun*, April 12, 13, 1968; *Washington Post*, April 13, 1968.
25. *Baltimore Sun*, April 12, 18, 1968; *Washington Post*, April 12, 13, 1968.
26. Richard Nixon, Herbert Parmet interview.
27. McGinniss, *The Selling of the President*, 49.
28. Nixon, *Memoirs*, 316.
29. Lippman, *Spiro Agnew's America*, 149–50.
30. Haldeman seems to have been blissfully ignorant of the chilling implications of his literary allusions. In *Brave New World* (1934), Aldous Huxley portrayed a

totalitarian future in which society disregarded individual dignity and worshiped science and the machine while George Orwell's bleak dystopian novel,
1984 (1949), described how "Big Brother" used the "omnipresent eye" to
enslave a passive and deluded population.

31. Ibid., 38–39.
32. McGinniss, *The Selling of the President*, 39.
33. From *The Kennedys,* a WGBH/Boston documentary aired September 20–21,
1992.
34. McGinniss, *Selling of the President*, 103.
35. Chester, *An American Melodrama*, 618.
36. McGinniss, *The Selling of the President,* 39, 103; H. R. Haldeman notes of
meetings with Richard Nixon, March 15, 1970, Box 41, H. R. Haldeman Papers,
Nixon Presidential Materials.
37. Chester, *An American Melodrama*, 689.
38. *New York Times,* March 10, 1968.
39. Ibid., June 12, 1968; *Montgomery Advertiser,* June 12, 1968.
40. *Birmingham Post-Herald,* June 25, 1968; *Chattanooga Times,* June 13, 1968.
41. *Montgomery Independent,* June 28, 1968.
42. *Montgomery Advertiser,* July 26, 1993.
43. *Birmingham Post-Herald,* June 25, 1968.
44. Seymore Trammell, author's interview, January 11, 1989; Smith, "How 'Amateurs' Raised Nearly $10 million," 27; "Sock it to 'em": Chester, *An American
Melodrama,* 666.
45. Forster and Epstein, *Danger on the Right,* 134–38.
46. Chester, *An American Melodrama,* 666; Seymore Trammell, author's interview,
January 11, 1989.
47. Hurt, *Texas Rich,* 371.
48. Seymore Trammell, author's interview, January 11, 1989; Bill Jones, author's
interview. Former Governor Wallace's official biographer denied that the Alabama governor had received money from H. L. Hunt; he concluded that H. L.'s
son, Bunker, had contributed only to Wallace's later campaigns. Lesher, *George
Wallace,* 409. As federal prosecutor Broward Segrest notes, however, the existence of the Bunker Hunt 1968 cash contribution became a matter of public
record in the 1971 tax evasion trial of Seymore Trammell, and details of the fund
eventually became common knowledge among Wallace workers by 1972. Broward Segrest, author's interview, February 16, 1994; Tom Turnipseed, author's
interview, March 3, 1994.
49. Smith, "How 'Amateurs' Raised Nearly $10 Million," 27.
50. John Patterson, APT interview.
51. Secret tape recording of Jack House conversation, April ?, 1968, Folder X-1
Alabama ADL Papers, ADAH.
52. "Lucky and Forney" folder, Taylor Hardin Papers, ADAH.
53. The Wallace Campaign, "George Wallace *Can* Be Elected President," August 28,
1968, Box 67-B, Wallace Private Papers. In 1969, Governor Wallace received a
$30,000 federal tax deduction for donating his papers to the state of Alabama.
I was able to examine them when they were housed at the main library at the
University of Alabama, Birmingham, but they are currently unavailable to schol-

ars. In 1984, the Wallace family reclaimed the materials and announced the formation of the Wallace Foundation and plans to build a $10–$14 million George and Lurleen Wallace Center for the Study of Southern Politics in Montgomery. The family has promised to make these materials available to scholars at some time in the future.

54. *Birmingham Post-Herald,* June 22, 1968.

55. Transcript, *Meet the Press,* June 30, 1968, Container 114, Lawrence Spivak Papers, LC.

56. Chester, *An American Melodrama,* 293.

57. Secret tape recording of Jack House conversation, April ?, 1968, Folder X-1, Alabama ADL Papers, BPL.

58. Cohen, "A Week with the Wallace Campaign," 25.

59. *Montgomery Independent,* October 24, 1968. The words in the article were "I just called to kiss your gluteus maximi some more," but Grover Hall explained that he had made the substitution because "you have to be a Yale demonstrator to get away with those three-lettered words."

60. Gardner and Loh, "The Wonderful World of George Wallace," 110.

61. *Washington Post,* August 11, 1968.

62. White, *The Making of the President, 1968,* 348.

63. Cohen, "A Week with the Wallace Campaign," 47.

64. "crotch-scratcher": Wills, "Can Wallace Be Made Respectable?" 32; Wills, *Nixon Agonistes,* 49.

65. Cohen, "A Week with the Wallace Campaign," 7, 25.

66. Letter from William K. Shearer to Cecil Jackson, February 6, 1968, Box 67B, Wallace Private Papers; ADL Report, "Wallace and the Radical Right," September 13, 1968, Alabama ADL Papers, BPL; "Benedict Arnold": letter from Jesse T. Todd to James T. Hardin, February 14, 1969, "T" file, Taylor Hardin Papers, ADAH.

67. Letter from Jesse T. Todd to James T. Hardin, February 14, 1969, "T" file, Taylor Hardin Papers, ADAH.

68. *New York Times,* June 28, 1968.

69. Tom Turnipseed, author's interview, March 3, 1994.

70. Tom Turnipseed, author's interview, July 21, 1988.

71. Letter from C. L. West to James T. Hardin, March 13, 1969, Taylor Hardin Papers, ADAH.

72. Letter from Robert Welch to George C. Wallace, December 6, 1966, Box 45, Wallace Private Papers.

73. *Decatur* (Ala.) *Daily,* September 29, 1968.

74. Letter from George Wallace to Mr. and Mrs. Ken Krippene, September 29, 1967, Box 67B, Wallace Private Papers.

75. *Time,* July 19, 1968, 17.

76. *Newsweek,* September 23, 1968, 28–29; *Time,* September 27, 1968, 14–15.

77. Kiker, "Red Neck New York," 25.

78. While such impressions were based upon C. Vann Woodward's influential biography of Tom Watson, Woodward's portrait was much more subtle and nuanced.

79. Hofstadter, *The Paranoid Style,* 3–40.

80. Wallace and his followers had decidedly ambiguous views on the war. He often urged more aggressive prosecution of the war but, as a group, Wallace voters in 1968 were much more likely than Humphrey or Nixon to agree with the proposition that the United States should never have become involved in the Vietnam conflict. Lipset and Raab, *The Politics of Unreason,* 384–99.

81. *Miami Herald,* July 28, 1968; Gideon quote from *Denver Post,* October 5, 1966.

82. Thompson, *Fear and Loathing on the Campaign Trail,* 156.

83. Gallup, *The Gallup Poll,* vol. 3, 2099, 2130, 2134, 2139–41, 2143–54, 2163, 2167–69; *Washington Post,* September 17, 1968.

84. Dent, *The Prodigal South,* 75–76.

85. Budd, *Inequality and Poverty,* 50–90; Levy, *Dollars and Dreams,* 101–110, 192–217; Danzier and Portney, *The Distributional Impacts of Public Policies,* passim; Brimmer, "Inflation and Income Distribution in the United States," 37–48; Miller, "Sharing the Burden of Change," 279–93. In contrast, Edgar Browning, a University of Virginia economist, has argued that government and academic economics have exaggerated the plight of the poor by underestimating the "in-kind" transfer of income to the poor. Brown, *Redistribution and the Welfare System,* 7–30.

86. McGinnis, *Selling of the President, 1968,* 23; Ehrlichman, *Witness to Power,* 223.

87. White, *Making of the President, 1964,* 233.

88. Erskine, "The Polls: Negro Housing," 482–98; "The Polls: Demonstrations and Race Riots," 655–67; "The Polls: Negro Employment," 132–53; and "The Polls: Speed of Racial Integration," 513–24.

89. Lubell, *The Hidden Crisis,* 105.

90. Ibid., 86.

91. *Charlotte Observer,* September 13, 1968.

92. *Atlanta Constitution,* June 1, 2, 1968; Dent, *The Prodigal South,* 82.

93. *Charlotte Observer,* September 13, 1968.

94. *New York Times,* October 1, 1968.

95. Campaign Policy Committee minutes, September 16, 1968, Box 1146, Humphrey Papers, MDH.

96. *New York Times,* September 24, 1968, 53; "COPE, AFL-CIO, 1968 Elections, Preliminary Report," n.d. (1968), copy in possession of the author.

97. Bill Jones, author's interview.

98. "I want you": *Ramparts,* October 26, 1968; "sexy-looking": Tom Turnipseed, author's interview, July 21, 1988; background on Ja-Neen Welch: *Los Angeles Times,* September 13, 1968, Montgomery *Alabama Journal,* May 4, 1969.

99. Bill Jones, author's interview.

100. Seymore Trammell, author's interview, January 11, 1989.

101. *Newsweek,* October 7, 1968, 22.

102. Bill Jones, author's interview.

103. *Newsweek,* October 7, 1968, 23.

104. O'Reilly, *"Racial Matters,"* 172.

105. Seymore Trammell, author's interview, January 11, 1989.

106. Ibid.

107. Allen, *Jackie Robinson,* 91–92.

108. Tygiel, *Baseball's Great Experiment,* 82–83.

109. Bowles and Tyson, *They Love a Man in the Country,* 181; "Morally correct": *Birmingham News,* September 10, 1968; *New York Times,* September 10, 1968.
110. *Louisville Courier-Journal,* September 10, 1968.
111. Seymore Trammell, author's interview, January 12, 1989.
112. Ed Ewing, Elena Vorbovia interview.
113. Secret tape recording of Jack House conversation, April ?, 1968, Folder X-1, Alabama ADL, BPL. Seymore Trammell, author's interview January 11, 1988, Ed Ewing, Elena Vorbovia interview; Epstein and Forster, *The Radical Right,* 54–55, 142, 187, 200–201, 209.
114. *Louisville Courier-Journal,* September 10, 1968.
115. Schlesinger, *Robert Kennedy and His Times,* 449–50.
116. LeMay, *Mission with LeMay: My Story,* iii.
117. Statement of General Curtis E. LeMay, October 3, 1968, D-3, LeMay Papers, LC.
118. *Los Angeles Times,* October 6, 1968; "Response, filed February 3, 1971, in Los Angeles Superior Court by Networks Electronics Corp. in re: *Curtis E. LeMay v. Networks Electronics Corp.,*" copy in possession of author; Tom Turnipseed, author's interviews, July 21, 1988, August 20, 1992.
119. Coffey, *Iron Eagle,* 445.
120. Ed Ewing, Elena Vorbovia interview.
121. Ibid.; Bill Jones, author's interview.
122. "We got to go": *Newsweek,* October 14, 1968, p. 31; "Damn": Earl Morgan, author's interview. LeMay's other quotes from *An American Melodrama* and Alabama Public Television interview with Jack Nelson; author's interviews with Seymore Trammell, January 11, 1989, and Bill Jones.
123. Letter from Homer I. Henderson to Curtis LeMay, October 9, 1968; letter from Mrs. Cecil W. Mason to Curtis LeMay, October 4, 1968, Box D-1, LeMay Papers. The date of the Mason letter is obviously in error since she refers to events that occurred on October 6, 1968.
124. Greenhaw, *Watch Out for George Wallace,* 211.
125. *New York Post,* November 2, 1968.
126. Witcover, *Marathon,* 266.
127. *New York Post,* November 2, 1968.
128. Mohr, "Requiem for a Lightweight," 120.
129. LeMay Speech, Washington Press Club, October 14, 1968, Box D3, LeMay Papers.
130. *Birmingham Post-Herald,* November 1, 1968. Seymour Martin Lipset and Earl Raab had access to the raw polling data compiled by George Gallup before and after the 1968 election and were able to clearly identify those groups that supported Wallace at each stage of the campaign. Lipset and Raab, "The Wallace Whitelash," *Transaction,* December, 1969, 6.
131. Tom Turnipseed, author's interview, July 21, 1988.
132. *Charlotte Observer,* September 13, 1968; Dent, *The Prodigal South,* 111–14.
133. McGinnis, *Selling of the President,* 122.
134. Dent, *The Prodigal South Returns to Power,* 110–11; McGinniss, *The Selling of the President,* 122–23; Harry Dent, author's interview.
135. McGinniss, *The Selling of the President,* 21.
136. Gallup, *The Gallup Poll,* vol. 3, 2162–2169; *Birmingham News,* October 26, 1968; Scammon and Wattenberg, *The Real Majority,* 183.

137. Wallace claimed larger figures in almost every case in his campaign pamphlet, "The George C. Wallace Presidential Campaign Souvenir Photo Album" (Selma: Dallas Publishing Co, 1970). I have used the more conservative numbers furnished by police officials to the media.
138. Huie, "Humanity's Case Against George Wallace," 2.
139. Tom Turnipseed, author's interviews, July 21, 1988, March 3, 1994.
140. "Confidential Memorandum," George Wallace to Seymore Trammell, September 16, 1968, copy in possession of the author; Huie, "Humanity's Case Against George Wallace," 3.
141. Seymore Trammell, author's interview, January 11, 1989; Bill Jones, author's interview.
142. *New York Post,* October 25, 1968; *New York Times,* October 25, 1968.
143. "T.R.B. from Washington," *New Republic,* November 9, 1968, 4.
144. Lardner and Lott, "The Wonderful World of George Wallace," 106.
145. Coffey, *Iron Eagle,* 447.
146. *New York Times,* November 5, 1968; *Montgomery Advertiser,* November 5, 1968; *Birmingham News,* November 5, 1968.
147. Transcript of Wallace remarks to campaign workers and volunteers, November 5, 1992, copy in possession of the author.
148. *Newsweek,* November 18, 1968, 51.
149. Cohodas, *Strom Thurmond,* 190.
150. Nor was that the only permutation that would have led to an election debacle. In Ohio and New Jersey, where Nixon squeaked by Humphrey, Wallace faded badly in the week preceding the election. Much of that last-minute voter switch was from Wallace to Humphrey. An additional two percent shift of Wallace voters to Humphrey would have had the same disastrous results for Nixon by throwing Ohio and New Jersey into the Democratic column and blocking a Nixon majority in the electoral college.
151. Scammon and Wattenberg, *The Real Majority,* 182–83.
152. Bill Jones, author's interview; Huie, "Humanity's Case Against George Wallace," 2.
153. Huie, "Humanity's Case Against George Wallace," 2.
154. Greenhaw, *Watch out for George Wallace,* 225; Lesher, *George Wallace,* 427.
155. Lesher, *George Wallace,* 427.
156. Broward Segrest, author's interview, February 16, 1994.
157. Montgomery *Alabama Journal,* March 23, 1972.
158. Loh, "Lonesome George," 106.

CHAPTER 12: THE WARS OF RICHARD NIXON: THE SURVIVAL OF GEORGE WALLACE, 1969–1970

1. Ehrlichman, *Witness to Power,* 181.
2. Harry Dent Memo, August 6, 1970, Dent Files, Nixon Presidential Materials.
3. Ehrlichman, *Witness to Power,* 196–197. At the time Ehrlichman published his autobiography, a number of critics questioned his assignment of overtly racist feelings to Nixon, but the publication of H. R. Haldeman's diary more than confirmed Ehrlichman's assertions. See, for example, Haldeman, *The Haldeman Diaries* (CD-ROM), April 28, 1969.

4. Moynihan, *Maximum Feasible Misunderstanding;* Rainwater and Yancey, *The Moynihan Report.*

5. Moynihan, "The President and the Negro," 33, 45.

6. Ibid., 44.

7. Moynihan, *Coping,* 185–94.

8. Nixon, *Memoirs,* 341–42.

9. Moynihan, "The President and the Negro," 40.

10. Ehrlichman, *Witness to Power,* 220.

11. Wicker, *One of Us,* 531–38.

12. Parmet, *Richard Nixon,* 549–61; Ambrose, *Nixon: The Triumph of a Politician,* 293–94, 345, 366–67, 402–406, 657–58.

13. Mailer, *Miami and the Siege of Chicago,* 51–53.

14. *Newsweek,* October 6, 1969, 28–73.

15. Schrag, "The Forgotten American," 27–28.

16. Hamill, "Wallace," 47.

17. Hamill, "Revolt of the White Lower Middle Class," 28.

18. Frady, "Gary, Indiana," 37.

19. Schrag, "The Forgotten American," 30.

20. Hardwick, "Mr. America," 3–4.

21. Hamill, "Wallace," 48.

22. Scammon and Wattenberg, *The Real Majority,* 62; 96–100, 166–68, 284–86.

23. Ibid., 286–88.

24. McGinniss, *The Selling of the President,* 123–24.

25. Wills, *Nixon Agonistes,* 265.

26. Phillips, *The Emerging Republican Majority,* 239.

27. Ibid, 287.

28. Wills, *Nixon Agonistes,* 267.

29. Letter from Harry Dent to Richard Nixon, October 13, 1969, Box 2, Dent Files, Nixon Presidential Materials.

30. H. R. Haldeman Notes, January 8, 1970, Box 41, H. R. Haldeman Papers, Nixon Presidential Materials.

31. Bickel, "Where Do We Go From Here?," 20–22.

32. Bickel, *The Supreme Court and the Idea of Progress,* 112–13.

33. Ehrlichman, *Witness to Power,* 203.

34. *Washington Star,* February 11, 1970; Memorandum from Richard Nixon to John Ehrlichman, February 18, 1970, "Presidential Memos to Ehrlichman, 1970," Box 83, White House Special Files, Nixon Presidential Materials; Haldeman, *The Haldeman Diaries* (CD-ROM), February 19, 1970.

35. Memorandum from Richard Nixon to Bob Haldeman, February 9, 1970, H. R. Haldeman Files, Box 229, Nixon Presidential Materials.

36. Ray Jenkins, Bass-Devries interview, 54.

37. Albert Brewer, author's interview.

38. Ibid.

39. *South: The Magazine of Dixie,* April 29, 1963, 6.

40. Cooper, "The Rise of George Wallace," 198.

41. Pierre Pelham, Bass-Devries interview, 16.

42. "Public Safety Department Files, 1964–65," Drawer 412, GW Papers, ADAH.

43. Sherrill, "Wallace and the Future of Dixie," 267.
44. John Patterson, Bass-Devries interview, 40.
45. "I have no intention to run for any office in my state ever again." *Charlotte* (N.C.) *Observer,* June 5, 1968.
46. *Montgomery Advertiser,* July 14, 1969.
47. *Birmingham Post-Herald,* September 4, 1969.
48. *Montgomery Advertiser,* September 5, 1969.
49. *Alabama Journal,* July 9, 1969.
50. *Newsweek,* November 10, 1969, 128.
51. Nixon, *Memoirs,* 543.
52. White, *The Making of the President, 1968,* 359.
53. Nixon, *Memoirs,* 542; Richard Nixon, Herbert Parmet interview.
54. Dent, *The Prodigal South,* 161.
55. Memorandum from Harry Dent to Richard Nixon, January 19, 1970, February 13, 1970, Box 4, Dent Files, Nixon Presidential Materials; memorandum from Richard Nixon to John Ehrlichman, February 18, 1970, White House Special Files, Box 83, "Presidential Memos to Ehrlichman, 1970," Nixon Presidential Materials.
56. Nixon, *Memoirs,* 440–41; "interested in helping": memorandum from Harry S. Dent to Dwight Chapin, September 11, 1969, White House Central Files, Executive HU2-1/ST1, Nixon Presidential Materials.
57. *Birmingham News,* January 1, 1970.
58. Haldeman, *The Haldeman Diaries* (CD-ROM), February 19, 1971.
59. Brandt Ayers, APT interview.
60. Syndicated columnists Frank Mankiewicz and Tom Braden reported in the fall of 1969 that Blount was openly raising money for Brewer from among his fellow Republicans, a clumsy move that infuriated Robert Vance. *Los Angeles Times,* November 21, 1969.
61. *Atlanta Constitution,* October 19, 1988; Winton Blount, author's interview.
62. Robert Vance, Bass-Devries interview.
63. *The Life of George C. Wallace,* 24.
64. *Montgomery Advertiser,* February 21, 1970.
65. *Alabama Journal,* March 17, 1990.
66. *Birmingham Post-Herald,* April 14, 1970.
67. Albert Brewer, author's interview.
68. "Attitudes and Preferences of Voters in 1970 Race for Governor of Alabama." Confidential report prepared for Jimmy Faulkner, January 1970, by Louis, Bowles and Grace, Inc., p. 46. Wallace Family Papers.
69. John Ehrlichman Notes: Meeting between Richard Nixon and Postmaster General Blount, March 10, 1970, Ehrlichman Files, Nixon Presidential Materials.
70. *Alabama Journal,* May 29, 1973.
71. "President Richard Nixon's Daily Diary," March 12, 1970, Box FC-20, WHCF FN Papers. When I interviewed Blount, he could not recall his role in the Nixon-Wallace standoff.
72. *Washington Post,* March 19, 1970.
73. H. R. Haldeman Notes, March 19, 1963, Box 41, Haldeman Files, Nixon Presidential Materials.
74. Haldeman, *The Haldeman Diaries* (CD-ROM), March 19, 1970.

75. Lawrence N. Higby Deposition, 43–48, Democratic National Committee Papers, USA. Confidential interview.
76. Ingram, *That's the Way I Saw It,* 20–21.
77. Bob Ingram, author's interview.
78. *Washington Post,* March 23, 1970.
79. Bob Ingram, author's interview.
80. H. R. Haldeman Notes, Box 41, Haldeman Files, Nixon Presidential Materials.
81. "Mafia": *Montgomery Advertiser,* June 22, 1992; "I sensed that": Ingram, *That's the Way I Saw It,* 20–21.
82. *Newsweek,* April 16, 1984, 37. Nixon periodically repeated his instructions to get the IRS to review the returns "of all Democratic candidates and start harassment of them, as they have done of us." Haldeman, *The Haldeman Diaries* (CD-ROM), September 27, 1970.
83. Kutler, *The Wars of Watergate,* 105–107.
84. Mollenhoff, *Game Plan for Disaster,* 108–109.
85. *Washington Post,* April 13, 1970.
86. Mollenhoff, *Game Plan for Disaster,* 112–13. For a reprint of the relevant documents in the case, see "Statement of Information and Supporting Evidence: Internal Revenue Service," in Watergate Hearings: Committee on the Judiciary, 35–42. After Chotiner's death, Jack Anderson confirmed that it was Chotiner who had given him a copy of the IRS records. *Birmingham News,* July 17, 1974.
87. *New York Times,* April 16, 1970.
88. *Montgomery Advertiser,* April 1–8, 1970.
89. Taylor, *Me 'n' George,* 97.
90. *Montgomery Advertiser,* September 19, 1976.
91. "Attitudes and Preferences of Voters in 1970 Race for Governor of Alabama." Confidential report prepared for Jimmy Faulkner, January 1970, by Louis, Bowles and Grace, Inc., p. 46, Wallace Family Papers.
92. *Birmingham Post-Herald,* April 30, 1970; *Montgomery Advertiser,* April 30, 1970.
93. H. R. Haldeman Notes, May 7, 1970, Box 41, Nixon Presidential Materials. Kalmbach gave a sketchy description of the hand-over of the second and third installments in his testimony before the Senate Watergate Committee, vol 1, 2142–44.
94. Lawrence N. Higby Deposition, 43, in case files of *Democratic National Committee v. James McCord,* Democratic National Committee Papers, USA.
95. Montgomery *Alabama Journal,* June 13, 1973; *Birmingham News,* June 14, 1973; Bob Ingram, author's interview.
96. Lukas, *Nightmare,* 147; *Washington Post,* June 28, 1973.
97. Anthony Heffernan, author's interview.
98. Tom Turnipseed speech, Milwaukee, Wisconsin, October 16, 1986. Copy in possession of the author; Tom Turnipseed, author's interview, July 7, 1988.
99. *Newsweek,* June 15, 1970, 27.
100. Copy in possession of the author.
101. *New York Times,* May 4, 1970; *Time,* June 15, 1970.
102. Tom Turnipseed, author's interview, July 21, 1988.
103. *Newsweek,* June 15, 1970, 29.
104. Ibid., 27.

105. Tom Turnipseed, author's interview, July 7, 1988.

106. Bob Ingram, author's interview.

107. *New York Times,* June 3, 1970.

108. Harold Martin, Bass-Devries interview.

109. *Newsweek,* June 15, 1970, 29.

110. *Huntsville Times,* June 3, 1970.

111. *Birmingham News,* June 3, 1970.

112. "Kohn Tells It," 6; *Montgomery Advertiser,* December 7, 1971.

113. Dent, *The Prodigal South,* 164.

114. Haldeman Notes, June 3, 1970, Box 41, Haldeman File, Nixon Presidential Materials.

115. *Washington Post,* July 23, 1970.

116. Rovere, "Letter from Washington," June 13, 1970, 113–14.

117. Memorandum from Harry S. Dent to Richard M. Nixon, June 16, 1970, Dent Memoranda, WHSF: POF Handwriting, Box 6, June 1–16, 1970, Nixon Presidential Materials.

118. Patrick Buchanan to Richard Nixon, August 24, 1970; President's Personal File, Box 6, Nixon Presidential Materials.

119. John R. Brown III, transmitting report from Richard Nixon to John Ehrlichman, Leonard Garment, John Price, March 17, 1970, White House Special Files, Box 83, "Presidential Memos to Ehrlichman, 1970," Nixon Presidential Materials. As H. R. Haldeman wrote in his diary, Nixon "wants me to tell all staff P[resident] is a conservative, does not believe in integration." *The Haldeman Papers* (CD-ROM), July 23, 1970.

120. Memorandum from Richard M. Nixon to·John Ehrlichman, September 8, 1970, White House Special Files, Box 83, "Presidential Memos to Ehrlichman, 1970," Nixon Presidential Materials.

121. Haldeman, *The Haldeman Diaries* (CD-ROM), July 11, 1970.

122. Memorandum from Harry S. Dent to Richard M. Nixon, June 16, 1970, Dent Memoranda, WHSF: POF Handwriting, Box 6, June 1–16, 1970, Nixon Presidential Materials.

123. Panetta and Gall, *Bring Us Together,* 1–3, 350–367.

124. *Public Papers of the President, 1969–1972,* 345–46.

125. Ehrlichman, *Witness to Power,* 126.

126. *New York Times,* October 25, 1970.

127. Stephen Ambrose, *Nixon: The Triumph of a Politician,* 397.

128. Haldeman, *The Haldeman Diaries* (CD-ROM), June 9, 1971.

129. Ibid., July 13, 1970.

130. Parmet, *Richard Nixon,* 559.

131. Haldeman, *The Haldeman Diaries* (CD-ROM), October 14, 1972.

132. *Wallace Newsletter,* July 1970.

133. *Montgomery Advertiser,* May 3, 1970.

134. Nixon Notes, July 19, 1970, PPF, Nixon Presidential Materials.

135. *Washington Post,* April 13, 1970; Polk, "Looking Backward: Wallace Money," 17–19.

136. Kutler, *Wars of Watergate,* 150.

137. Will Wilson, author's interview; letter from Will Wilson to author, May 26, 1993.

138. Ira DeMent, author's interview.
139. Broward Segrest, author's interview, January 11, 1989.
140. Sims, *The Little Man's Big Friend,* 190.
141. Grafton, *Big Mules and Branchheads,* 170.
142. *Montgomery Advertiser,* March 8, 1962.
143. Dorman, *The George Wallace Myth,* 28.
144. *Stand Up for Alabama,* 231.
145. *Montgomery Advertiser,* September 22, 1963.
146. *Waugh Asphalt Co., Inc. v. Seymore Trammel* [sic] *et al.,* Alabama Governors' Papers, File Drawer 519, GW Papers, ADAH.
147. *Tuscaloosa News,* April 14, 1970.
148. Ibid.; *Birmingham News,* November 21, 1965.
149. *United States of America* v. *Seymore Trammel,* 1972, Transcript, II, 313–14, 321–22, 398–401. One of the most lucrative forms of payola was employed by the highway department: engineering firms and paving companies were required to hire Wallace agents designated by Seymore Trammell. Letter from Rex M. Whitton (federal highway administrator) to George C. Wallace, September 9, 1964, Alabama Highway Department Investigation, File Drawer 505, GW Papers, ADAH.
150. *Birmingham News,* October 4, 1968. Morton Biehl, a "loyalist" national Democrat and bitter opponent of Wallace, furnished detailed information on the not-so-subtle Wallace solicitation to muckraker Drew Pearson, who in turn made it the basis for one of his many anti-Wallace columns. Memorandum from Morton O. (Moe) Biehl to Drew Pearson, October 7, 1968, Drew Pearson Papers, Wallace File G302, LBJ Library.
151. Letter from George Wallace to Walter Houseal (Superintendent of Insurance), Dec. 27, 1967, File Drawer 104, Wallace Family Papers.
152. Bill Jones, author's interview.
153. Williams, *Huey Long,* 820.
154. Greenhaw, *Watch Out for George Wallace,* 218.
155. Ibid., *Birmingham News,* January 22, 1984. When Gerald Wallace did not respond to my written request for an interview, I asked Sam Webb, an Alabama attorney and history professor, to intervene on my behalf. Gerald heard him out, thought for a moment, and then said: "Why should I talk to him? What's in it for me?"
156. *Montgomery Independent,* January 10, 1974.
157. *Montgomery Advertiser,* April 16, 1970.
158. Seymore Trammell, author's interview, June 11, 1988.
159. *Montgomery Advertiser,* March 29, April 19, 1970.
160. Initial news leaks claimed that Fite had split his sixty-thousand-dollar fee, fifty–fifty; Gerald Wallace indignantly claimed the fee was only ten thousand dollars. The final figure is from the report of the Alabama Bar Association's complaint against Wallace and Fite for unethical conduct. *Birmingham News,* February 28, April 10, June 8, 1973; *Montgomery Independent,* January 10, 1974; *Montgomery Advertiser,* March 1, 1973.
161. *Montgomery Advertiser,* March 29, April 19, 1970.
162. Charles W. Colson interview, June 15, 1988, Nixon Presidential Materials.

163. Representative Bert Nettles to John Pemberton, December 31, 1970; Nettles to John Kohn, January 3, 1971; copies in possession of the author.

164. John P. Kohn to George C. Wallace, January 20, 1971, copy in possession of the author.

165. Broward Segrest, author's interview, February 16, 1994. Ira DeMent and Broward Segrest were reluctant to comment about some aspects of the case, but both men pointed to an article written in April 1971 by James R. Polk, an Associated Press reporter operating out of Washington. Polk, said Segrest, had a direct line to Strother, head of the tax division's criminal division, and to John Clark, a Justice Department attorney who concentrated upon campaign finance violations under the Corrupt Practices Act. The article, which appeared in the *Washington Star* on April 27, 1971, and the *Birmingham News* the following day, was "absolutely accurate in its details," said DeMent, with emphasis, in our interview, and I have relied upon it in outlining my summary of the IRS investigation.

166. Tom Turnipseed, author's interview, July 21, 1988.

167. Ira DeMent, author's interview.

168. *Birmingham Post-Herald,* September 27, 1971.

169. Seymore Trammell to author, December 12, 1993.

170. Seymore Trammell, author's interview, August 15, 1989.

171. Ibid. In my interview with Will Wilson, he did not dispute Trammell's account, but he insisted that he had no recollection of the specifics of the meeting. Will Wilson, author's interview.

172. Seymore Trammell, author's interview, January 11, 1989.

173. Broward Segrest, author's interview, January 11, 1988.

174. *Birmingham News,* April 10, 11, 18, 30, 1971.

175. Tom Turnipseed, author's interview, July 7, 1988.

176. Polk, "Looking Backward," 18.

177. *Washington Post,* May 1, 1971.

178. Gallup, *The Gallup Poll,* vol. 3, 2309; Montgomery *Alabama Journal,* November 7, 1971.

179. *New York Times* and *Montgomery Advertiser,* May 26, 1971.

180. *Washington Post,* May 31, 1971.

181. Tom Turnipseed, author's interview, July 7, 1988.

182. Ibid., July 21, 1988.

183. *Birmingham News,* August 11, 1971.

184. Will Wilson, author's interview.

185. Kleindienst, *Justice,* 140.

186. Seymore Trammell, author's interview, August 15, 1989; Robert Alton, author's interview; Broward Segrest, author's interview, January 11, 1989; Ira DeMent, author's interview.

187. When Herbert Parmet outlined the public facts surrounding the IRS investigation in his 1988 interview with Nixon, the former President interrupted sharply: "I didn't know about that." Beginning with the leaking of IRS materials from the Oval Office in the spring of 1970, the evidence seems conclusive that the entire anti-Wallace operation—the "Wallace watch," as Nixon called it—was run out of the President's office. None of the former White House aides I have inter-

viewed believe that Haldeman or anyone else in his office would have under-taken an operation this politically delicate without Nixon's knowledge. Richard Nixon, Herbert Parmet interview, November 16, 1988.

188. Seymore Trammell, author's interview, August 15, 1989.
189. *New York Times,* January 13, 1972.
190. *Washington Post,* January 14, 1972.
191. Charles Bartlett, "Wallace Reaches for Respectability in Primaries with an Eye on '76," *Washington Post,* February 26, 1972.
192. Memorandum from Jeb S. Magruder to Charles W. Colson, January 3, 1972, Colson Files, Box 17, Nixon Presidential Materials.
193. Stroud, "Rather Outspoken," 4–5.
194. Haldeman Notes, March 19, 1970, Box 42; Alexander P. Butterfield to H. R. Haldeman, July 8, 1971, Haldeman Memos, Nixon Presidential Materials.
195. Will Wilson, author's interview.
196. Seymore Trammell, author's interview, August 15, 1989.
197. *Washington Post,* January 19, 1972.
198. Dorman, *The George Wallace Myth,* 47.
199. Wills, "Can Wallace Be Made Respectable?" 35. "Well, Tricia [the President's daughter] and Governor [Reubin] Askew [of Florida] were on there, too, he told R. W. Apple of the *New York Times.* I tell you this much. I wouldn't make any deal in front of them." *New York Times,* February 20, 1972.
200. Haldeman, *The Haldeman Diaries* (CD-ROM), February 4, 1971.

CHAPTER 13: "SEND THEM A MESSAGE": VARIATIONS ON A THEME

1. White, *America in Search of Itself,* 288; White, *The Making of the President, 1964,* 233.
2. White, *The Making of the President, 1972,* 92.
3. Information on financial problems from Wallace Family Papers; Wallace, *C'Ne-lia,* 133–225.
4. Cornelia Wallace, author's interview.
5. Taylor, *Me 'n' George,* 95.
6. Ibid., 96.
7. Tom Turnipseed, author's interview, July 7, 1988; Cornelia Wallace, author's interview.
8. Taylor, *Me 'n' George,* 102.
9. *Birmingham News,* December 7, 1971.
10. *New York Times,* May 7, 1972.
11. *Birmingham News,* July 30, 1969.
12. White, *The Making of the President, 1972,* 92.
13. *Washington Post,* February 6, 1972.
14. Lesher, "Who Knows What Evil Lurks in the Hearts of 'X' Million Ameri-cans?" 9.
15. Perry, *Us and Them,* 108–109.
16. *Bradley v. Richmond School Board,* 456 F.2d 6 (4th Cir. 1972). *Swann v. Charlotte-Mecklenburg Board of Education,* 402 U.S. 1, 91 S.Ct. 1267 (1971).
17. *Washington Post,* August 30, 1971.
18. Arthur Bremer diary, March 2, 1972, UAB Reynolds Library.

19. *New York Times,* August 6, 1972.
20. *Milwaukee Journal,* May 16, 1972.
21. Ibid., May 21, 1972.
22. Ibid., May 16, 1972.
23. Arthur Bremer Diary, March 14, 1972, UAB Reynolds Library.
24. *Milwaukee Journal,* May 16, 17, 1972; Wittner, "A Boy Who Shut Everyone Out," 32–33.
25. Ibid., May 16, 1972.
26. Arthur Bremer Diary, March 14, 1972, March 5, 1972, UAB Reynolds Library.
27. Memorandum from Acting FBI Director Patrick Gray to Acting Attorney General Richard Kleindienst and President Richard Nixon, May 17, 1972; "Summary Memo," May 22, 1972, WALSHOT File, FBI.
28. *Milwaukee Journal,* May 16, 1972.
29. Ibid., May 16, 17, 1972; "dirty movies": *Washington Post,* May 16, 1972.
30. *Milwaukee Journal,* May 16, 1972.
31. Arthur Bremer Diary, March 14, 1972, UAB Reynolds Library.
32. *Milwaukee Journal,* May 16, 17, 1972; Wittner, "A Boy Who Shut Everyone Out," 32–33.
33. Ibid., May 16, 1972.
34. Memorandum from Acting Director, FBI [Patrick Gray] to Acting Attorney General [Richard Kleindienst], May 18, 1972, WALSHOT File, FBI.
35. Arthur Bremer Diary, March 14, 1972, UAB Reynolds Library.
36. Ibid., March 2, 1972.
37. *Washington Post,* August 2, 1972; Arthur Bremer Diary, March 14, 1972, UAB Reynolds Library.
38. *Milwaukee Journal,* May 16, 1972; Acting FBI Director Patrick Gray to Acting Attorney General, May 18, 1972 (copy to the President), WALSHOT File, FBI.
39. "Personal Characteristics [of Arthur Bremer]," Memo of Acting Director Patrick Gray to Acting Attorney General Richard Kleindienst, May 17, 1972, WALSHOT File, FBI.
40. *Montgomery Advertiser,* October 25, 1972.
41. Memorandum from Richard Nixon to Bob Haldeman, April 11, 1972, Box 163; memorandum from Richard Nixon to John D. Ehrlichman, April 9, 1972, Box 163, Haldeman Files, Nixon Presidential Materials.
42. Ambrose, *Nixon: The Triumph of a Politician,* 522.
43. John Ehrlichman, author's interview.
44. Richard Nixon notation, on Herb Klein memorandum to Richard Nixon, July 3, 1971, Nixon Presidential Materials.
45. John Ehrlichman, author's interview.
46. *Washington Post,* January 14, 1972.
47. *Birmingham News,* February 5, 1972.
48. For surveys of the election, see the *Washington Post, New York Times,* and *Miami Herald* for March 15, 16, 1972.
49. *Time,* March 17, 1972, 22–27; *Newsweek,* March 27, 1972, 22–28.
50. Perry, *Us and Them,* 109–115.
51. *Montgomery Advertiser,* March 12, 1972.
52. *Washington Post,* March 5, 1972.

53. Quotations are from the Wallace newsletter; his op-ed piece in the *New York Times,* March 1, 1972; and speeches in the Florida campaign, reported in *Birmingham Post-Herald* and *Montgomery Advertiser* in February and early March.

54. *New York Times,* March 7, 1972.

55. Ibid., March 17, 1972.

56. White, *The Making of the President, 1972,* 48–51. Feigert, "Conservatism, Populism and Social Change," 272–77.

57. Memorandum from Richard Nixon to John Ehrlichman, April 8, 1972, Box 163, Haldeman Files, Nixon Presidential Materials. See also memorandum from Nixon to Ehrlichman, May 17, 1972, Box 163, Haldeman Files, Nixon Presidential Materials.

58. Memorandum from Charles Colson to Richard Nixon, May 19, 1972, Colson Files, Box 15, Nixon Presidential Materials; memorandum from Richard Nixon to Bob Haldeman, March 27, 1972, Haldeman Files, Box 163, Nixon Presidential Materials.

59. Richard Nixon to Bob Haldeman, April 11, 1972, Box 163, Haldeman Files, Nixon Presidential Materials.

60. Carlson, *George C. Wallace and the Politics of Powerlessness,* 185.

61. Scammon, *America Votes,* 23.

62. *Los Angeles Times/Washington Post* News Service dispatch, April 11, 1972, Wallace Family Papers.

63. Cornelia Wallace, author's interview.

64. Arthur Bremer Diary, March 23 [sic], 26 [sic], 1972, UAB Reynolds Library. From this point on in his diary, Bremer's dates are sometimes inaccurate. It seems likely from internal evidence that this first entry was written March 24, the second March 29.

65. Quotes are from the *Milwaukee Journal* and *Milwaukee Sentinel,* March 31, 1972.

66. Novak, *Choosing Our King,* 209.

67. *Los Angeles Times* News Service dispatch, March 30, 1972, Wallace Family Papers.

68. *Washington Post,* April 6, 1972.

69. *Montgomery Advertiser,* October 25, 1972.

70. Arthur Bremer Diary, March 8, 31, 1972, UAB Reynolds Library. (See n. 64.)

71. Nixon, *Memoirs,* 586–87.

72. Arthur Bremer Diary, March 23 [sic], 1972, UAB Reynolds Library. (See n. 64.)

73. Ibid.

74. Bremer, *An Assassin's Diary,* 46.

75. Ibid., pp. 52, 57. "Summary Memo," May 22, 1972, WALSHOT File, FBI.

76. *New York Times,* October 19, 1971.

77. Ibid., April 15, 1972.

78. Bremer, *An Assassin's Diary,* 93–96.

79. *Detroit News,* April 16, 1972; Wallace, *C'Nelia,* 83.

80. *Detroit News,* April 16, 1972.

81. *Milwaukee Journal,* April 16, 1972.

82. Undated clipping from the *Detroit News,* Wallace Family Papers.

83. McGovern, *Grassroots,* 183.

84. *Birmingham News,* May 11, 1972.

85. Memoranda from Gordon Strachan to H. R. Haldeman, January 18, February 16, May 16, 1972, in Hearings Before the Committee on the Judiciary, vol. 1, 75–76, 84–86; Senate Watergate Committee Hearings, 1672–73.

86. Memorandum from Patrick Buchanan/Ken Khaghigian to John Mitchell, and H. R. Haldeman, April 12, 1972, Senate Watergate Committee Hearings, 1228.

87. Tom Turnipseed, author's interview, March 3, 1994; Harry Dent, author's interview.

88. *Milwaukee Journal,* May 3, 1972.

89. Bremer, *An Assassin's Diary,* 104–105.

90. Ibid., 121.

91. *Detroit News,* May 16, 1972.

92. Ibid., May 10, 1972.

93. *New York Times,* May 29, 1972.

94. Bremer, *An Assassin's Diary,* 126–28.

95. Ibid., 132.

96. Wallace, *Stand Up for America,* 5–6.

97. *Newsweek,* May 29, 1972, 21.

98. *Milwaukee Journal,* May 17, 1972.

99. Transcript of audiotape recording of May 15 speech, WALSHOT File, FBI.

100. Wallace, *Stand Up for America,* 7.

101. Statement of Special Agent James Taylor, May 16, 1972, WALSHOT File, FBI.

102. Wallace, *Stand Up for America,* 7.

103. *Newsweek,* May 29, 1972, 22.

104. Wallace, *C'Nelia,* 42. The recollection of the chief surgeon, Dr. Joseph Schanno, was that, when he questioned Wallace, the Alabama governor responded, "I've been shot in the spine, my legs are paralyzed." Joseph Schanno interview, May 18, 1972, WALSHOT File, FBI.

105. *Washington Post,* March 17, 1972.

106. Powers, *Secrecy and Power,* 487; O'Reilly, *"Racial Matters,"* 352–53.

107. Kelly, "David Gergen," 68.

108. Haldeman, *The Ends of Power,* 93.

109. *Wall Street Journal,* October 15, 1971; Colson, *Born Again,* 57.

110. Acting Director, FBI [Patrick Gray] to the Acting Attorney General [Richard Kleindienst], May 17, 1972, WALSHOT File, FBI.

111. Memorandum from James J. Rowley, Director, U.S. Secret Service, to Eugene T. Rossides, Assistant Secretary, Department of Treasury, May 16, 1972; Memorandum from C. L. McGowan to Mr. Gebhardt, June 4, 1974, WALSHOT File, FBI.

112. John Ehrlichman, author's interview.

113. Hersh, "Nixon's Last Cover-Up," 76.

114. *Washington Post,* June 21, 1973.

115. Memorandum from C. W. Bates to Mr. Shroder, May 15, 1972, WALSHOT File, FBI. When Felt told him that the Secret Service agent who entered Bremer's apartment had removed a number of documents, Nixon ordered that they be returned immediately and placed under the control of the FBI.

116. Haldeman, *The Haldeman Diaries* (CD-ROM), May 16, 1972. When Haldeman edited his diaries for the slightly abbreviated book version, he deleted the

President's self-incriminating statement (without informing the reader with eli-sion marks) in his book. Haldeman, *The Haldeman Diaries* (book version), 460–61.

117. This reconstruction is based on the account by Seymour Hersh, which appeared in the *New Yorker* magazine; on the FBI and Secret Service memos contained in the FBI's WALSHOT file; on the Nixon Daily Diary and telephone log for May 15; and on the recently released *The Haldeman Diaries*. The late President Nixon successfully blocked the release of the files and tapes of all conversations dealing with the Wallace shooting.

118. Colson has given three accounts of that evening conversation, varying slightly in detail, but identical in their essence. In 1988, when he was originally inter-viewed by Nixon Project staffer Frederick J. Graboske, Colson first insisted that he could not remember the President ordering the planting of material. By the time filmmaker Fred Emery interviewed Colson in 1993, however, Colson in-sisted that it was Nixon who suggested the planting of McGovern material. Charles Colson interview, June 15, 1988, Nixon Project; Hersh, "Nixon's Last Cover-Up," 76; Emery, *Watergate*, 116.

119. Vidal, "The Art and Arts of E. Howard Hunt," 9–19; Szulc, *Compulsive Spy*, 47–108.

120. Szulc, *Compulsive Spy*, 134–35.

121. Szulc, *Compulsive Spy*, 138 ff.

122. Testimony of E. Howard Hunt, Ex. Sess., Senate Watergate Committee, July 25, 1973, Senate Watergate Committee Hearings, 129. In his testimony before the Watergate Committee and in his book *Undercover*, 216–17, Hunt says that he talked with Colson the morning after the shooting, but in his interview with the FBI he more accurately places the sequence of events on the evening of the fifteenth. See memorandum from Baltimore FBI Office to Director, FBI, Sep-tember 10, 1974, "Report on Hunt Interview," WALSHOT File, FBI.

123. Hunt, *Undercover*, 217.

124. Ibid.

125. *Washington Post*, May 17, 1972.

126. Ibid., June 21, 1973.

127. *Detroit News*, May 16, 1972; *Birmingham News*, May 16, 1972; *Washington Post*, May 17, 1972.

128. "Running Log of Telephone Conversations. . . ." May 15, 1972, WALSHOT File, FBI.

129. Hunt, *Undercover*, 218.

130. Bremer, *An Assassin's Diary*, 118.

131. Memorandum from W. M. Felt to Acting Director Pat Gray, May 19, 1972, WALSHOT File, FBI.

132. Memorandum from R. I. Shroder to Mr. Bates, May 18, 1972, WALSHOT File, FBI.

133. Kutler, *The Wars of Watergate*, 361.

134. H. R. Haldeman Notes, May 17, 1972, Box 45, Haldeman Files, Nixon Presiden-tial Materials.

135. Vidal, "The Art and Arts of E. Howard Hunt," 17. White, *The Making of the President, 1972*, 235–38.

136. Memorandum for the President's File, May 19, 1972, Re: Visits to Governor

George Wallace and [Secret Service Agent] Mr. Nick Zarvos, WHSF: POF, Box 88, Nixon Presidential Materials; Wallace, *C'Nelia,* 79.

137. Nixon, *Memoirs,* 609.
138. Wallace, *C'Nelia,* 80.
139. Ibid., 57.
140. *Baltimore Sun,* March 16, 1972.
141. Taylor, *Faulkner: Jimmy, That Is,* 192–93; Ray Jenkins, author's interview, January 23, 1994.
142. H. R. Haldeman Notes, May 17, 1972, Box 45, Haldeman Files, Nixon Presidential Materials.
143. C. Colson notes of meeting w/President, June 30, 1972, Box 16, Colson Files, Nixon Presidential Materials.
144. Memorandum from Gordon Strachan to H. R. Haldeman, June 27, 1972, Haldeman Files, Box 99, Nixon Presidential Materials.
145. Annie Laurie Gunter, author's interview.
146. *Birmingham News,* July 12, 1972.
147. Charles Colson notes of meeting with President, June 30, 1972, Box 16, Colson Files, Nixon Presidential Materials.
148. Haldeman, *The Haldeman Diaries* (CD-ROM), July 18, 1972.
149. Ibid., July 18, 1972.
150. Ibid., August 2, 1972.
151. Montgomery, *Alabama Journal,* July 12, 13, 1972.
152. *Montgomery Advertiser,* July 16, 1972.
153. *New York Times,* July 4, 1972.
154. McGovern, *Grassroots,* 234.
155. Nixon, *Memoirs,* 657.
156. Haldeman, *The Haldeman Diaries* (CD-ROM), June 19, 1972.
157. Ambrose, *Nixon: The Triumph of a Politician,* 587.
158. Wallace, *C'Nelia,* 47–48.
159. Nixon, *Memoirs,* 657.
160. Haldeman, *The Haldeman Diaries* (CD-ROM), July 25, 1972. In his memoirs, Nixon remembered that Connally had told him that he was "definitely not going to run for President on a third-party ticket." Nixon, *Memoirs,* 658.
161. *New York Times,* July 26, 27, 1972.
162. Nixon, *Memoirs,* 658.
163. Haldeman, *The Haldeman Diaries* (CD-ROM), October 14, 1972.

Epilogue: "Attention Must Be Paid": The Legacy of George Wallace

1. Wallace, *C'Nelia,* 43.
2. *Washington Post,* May 16, 1972.
3. Wallace, *C'Nelia,* 73.
4. Cornelia Wallace, author's interview.
5. *Christian Science Monitor,* November 24, 1975.
6. Vidal, "The Art and Arts of E. Howard Hunt," 18–19.
7. *Montgomery Advertiser,* September 22, 1976.
8. Cornelia Wallace, author's interview. *Birmingham News,* May 16, 1974; Brendan P. O'Regan, author's interview.

9. *Chicago Sun-Times,* May 29, 1974.

10. *Birmingham News,* December 6, 1973.

11. Tom Turnipseed, author's interview, July 7, 1988.

12. Ibid., July 21, 1988. The exact remark attributed to Henry II is "Will no one revenge me of the injuries I have sustained from one turbulent Priest?" Lyttelton, *History of the Life,* vol. 4, 353.

13. Wallace's son, George Junior, told a Montgomery reporter that in the twenty years after the shooting, the Wallace family had "heard on different occasions that Bremer was seen on a ferry in the state of Michigan—where he did stalk my father at one time—with someone who worked directly for President Nixon." *Montgomery Advertiser,* December 13, 1992.

14. Jack Nelson, author's interview.

15. Such media interest would be far greater if "he was the victim of some mysterious conspiracy rather than the mere victim of an uninspiring figure such as Bremer," said an unnamed staffer. "Questions Presented to the Director, 5/28/74 by Jack Nelson ... relative to the Shooting of Governor George C. Wallace ..." WALSHOT File, FBI.

16. Heim to McDermott Memorandum, August 5, 1974, WALSHOT File, FBI.

17. Haig, *Inner Circles,* 470–71.

18. Transcript, CBS *Sixty Minutes,* April 16, 1984, copy in possession of the author.

19. Nixon, *Memoirs,* 1050.

20. Haig, *Inner Circles,* 470–71.

21. Hersh, "Nixon's Last Cover-Up," 76.

22. Thimmesch, "The Grass-Roots Dollar Chase," 58.

23. Crawford, *Thunder on the Right,* 52.

24. *Birmingham News,* August 28, 1973.

25. Thimmesch, "The Grass-Roots Dollar Chase," 60.

26. Witcover, *Marathon,* 169.

27. *Montgomery Advertiser,* July 3, 1975; *New York Times,* July 3, 1975.

28. Letter from Phyllis Schafly to Jean Robinson [Governor Wallace's secretary], April 17, 1973, "Mrs. Phyllis Schafly" file, Drawer 514, GW Papers, ADAH; letter from George C. Wallace to James F. Dowd, June 29, 1971, "Legislation: Abortion Law" file, Drawer 547, GW Papers, ADAH.

29. *New York Times,* November 13, 1975; *Time,* November 25, 1975.

30. *New York Times,* March 3, 1976.

31. Montgomery, *Alabama Journal,* March 21, 1976.

32. John Snell to author, July 24, 1991.

33. Ray Jenkins, Bass-DeVries interview.

34. *Birmingham News,* November 23, 1986.

35. *Montgomery Advertiser,* September 9, 1977.

36. Ibid., October 5, November 1, 1977.

37. *Montgomery Advertiser,* January 5, 1978; Cornelia Wallace, author's interview.

38. *Birmingham Post-Herald,* August 19, 1974.

39. Klein, "The Ministry of George C. Wallace."

40. Parks, *Rosa Parks: My Story,* 106.

41. John Lewis, author's interview; John Lewis, APT interview.

42. Dr. Robert M. Dickerson, author's interview. Dickerson was pastor of the Dexter

Avenue Baptist Church from 1973 to 1977 and president of the Progressive Baptist Association in 1974 and 1975.

43. *Montgomery Advertiser,* November 7, 1974; *Birmingham News,* November 7, 1974.

44. Bass, *Taming the Storm,* 462.

45. *Montgomery Advertiser,* February 6, 1964.

46. Ruth Johnson, author's interview; letter from Ruth Johnson to author, February 2, 1994.

47. Bass, *Taming the Storm,* 462.

48. The governor's extensive use of the drugs was reported in the *New York Times* on April 5, 1983, and in the *Birmingham News,* May 8, 1983. Two years later the press began to refer explicitly to his "dependency" upon various drugs, including methadone, to help control the pain. *New York Times,* August 29, 1985; *Montgomery Advertiser-Journal,* January 26, 1986; *Birmingham News,* April 3, 1986.

49. *Montgomery Advertiser,* March 11, 1981; *Birmingham News,* November 23, 1986. Quote from Lesher, *George Wallace,* 497.

50. *Athens* (Ala.) *News Courier,* October 25, 1981.

51. *Montgomery Advertiser-Journal,* January 26, 1986.

52. *Montgomery Advertiser,* April 3, 1986.

53. George Wallace, Jr., Elena Vorbovia interview.

54. Virginia Durr, Paul Stekler interview.

55. George McGovern, APT interview.

56. (Boston: Little, Brown and Company, 1990).

57. Richard Nixon, Herbert Parmet interview.

58. Reed, "The Faith Factor in American Life," remarks before the National Press Club, Washington, D.C., October 12, 1994, transcript in possession of the author.

59. Phillips, *Arrogant Capital,* 7.

60. Osborne, "Newt Gingrich," 15.

61. *New York Times,* November 16, 1994; Remnick, "Lost in Space," 86.

62. Schneider, "The Suburban Century Begins," 37.

63. Kapuściński, *Imperium,* 371.

64. Ibid.

BIBLIOGRAPHY

BOOKS

Abernathy, Ralph David. *And the Walls Came Tumbling Down: An Autobiography.* New York: Harper & Row, 1989.

Alabama: A Guide to the Deep South. New York: Richard M. Smith, 1941.

Alexander, Herbert C. *Financing the 1968 Election.* Lexington, Mass.: Lexington Books, 1971.

Allen, Maury. *Jackie Robinson: A Life Remembered.* New York: Franklin Watts, 1987.

Ambrose, Stephen A. *Nixon: The Triumph of a Politician, 1962-1972.* New York: Simon & Schuster, 1989.

Azbell, Joe. *Black Dynamite: The Facts About the Red Conspiracy to Turn Negroes Against America.* Montgomery: Freedom Banner Publishers, 1951.

———. *The Riotmakers.* Montgomery: Oaktree Books, 1968.

Barnard, William D. *Dixiecrats and Democrats: Alabama Politics, 1942–1950.* University, Ala.: University of Alabama Press, 1974.

Barrett, Russell H. *Integration at Ole Miss.* Chicago: Quadrangle Books, 1965.

Bartley, Numan V. *The Rise of Massive Resistance: Race and Politics in the South During the 1950's.* Baton Rouge: Louisiana State University Press, 1969.

——— and Hugh D. Graham. *Southern Politics and the Second Reconstruction.* Baltimore: The Johns Hopkins University Press, 1975.

Basler, Roy P., ed. *The Collected Works of Abraham Lincoln.* 8 volumes. New Brunswick, N.J.: Rutgers University Press, 1953.

Bass, Jack. *Taming the Storm: The Life and Times of Judge Frank M. Johnson, Jr., and the South's Fight over Civil Rights.* New York: Doubleday, 1993.

———. *Unlikely Heroes.* New York: Simon & Schuster, 1981.

——— and Walter DeVries. *The Transformation of Southern Politics: Social Change and Political Consequences Since 1945.* New York: Basic Books, 1976.

Bell, Daniel, ed. *The Radical Right: The New American Right.* Expanded and updated edition. New York: Anchor Books, 1964.

Bennett, David H. *The Party of Fear: From Nativist Movements to the New Right in American History.* Chapel Hill: University of North Carolina Press, 1988.

Bickel, Alexander. *The Supreme Court and the Idea of Progress.* New York: Harper & Row, 1970.

Bishop, Jim. *The Days of Martin Luther King, Jr.* New York: G. P. Putnam's Sons, 1971.

Black, Earl. *Southern Governors and Civil Rights: Racial Segregation as a Campaign*

Issue in the Second Reconstruction. Cambridge, Mass.: Harvard University Press, 1976.

———— and Merle Black. *Politics and Society in the South.* Cambridge, Mass.: Harvard University Press, 1987.

Black, Merle, David M. Kovenock, and William C. Reynolds. *Political Attitudes in the Nation and the States.* Chapel Hill: Institute for Research in Social Science, 1974.

Botsch, Robert Emil. *We Shall Not Overcome: Populism and Southern Blue-Collar Workers.* Chapel Hill: University of North Carolina Press, 1980.

Bowles, Billy, and Remer Tyson. *They Love a Man in the Country: Saints and Sinners in the South.* Atlanta: Peachtree Publishers, 1989.

Branch, Taylor. *Parting the Waters: America in the King Years, 1954–1963.* New York: Simon & Schuster, 1988.

Brauer, Carl. *John F. Kennedy and the Second Reconstruction.* New York: Columbia University Press, 1977.

Bremer, Arthur Herman. *An Assassin's Diary.* New York: Harper's Magazine Press, 1973.

Brewer, W. *Alabama: Her History, Resources, War Record, and Public Men. From 1540 to 1872.* Montgomery: Barrett & Brown, 1872.

Brink, William, and Louis Harris. *Black and White: A Study of Racial Attitudes Today.* New York: Simon & Schuster, 1967.

————. *The Negro Revolution in America: What Negroes Want, Why and How They are Fighting For it; Whom They Support; What Whites Think of Them and Their Demands.* New York: Simon & Schuster, 1964.

Broder, David. *The Party's Over: The End of Politics in America.* New York: Harper & Row, 1972.

Brown, C. Edgar, ed. *Democracy at Work: Being the Official Report of the Democratic National Convention . . . 1948.* Philadelphia: Local Democratic Political Committee of Pennsylvania, 1948.

Browning, Edgar K. *Redistribution and the Welfare System.* Washington, D.C.: American Enterprise Institute, 1975.

Budd, Edward C., ed. *Inequality and Poverty.* New York: W. W. Norton & Company, 1967.

Button, James W. *Black Violence: Political Impact of the 1960s Riots.* Princeton, N.J.: Princeton University Press, 1978.

Cagin, Seth, and Philip Dray. *We Are Not Afraid: The Story of Goodman, Schwerner, and Chaney and the Civil Rights Campaign in Mississippi.* New York: Macmillan, 1988.

Canfield, James Lewis. *A Case of Third Party Activism: The George Wallace Campaign Workers and the American Independent Party.* Washington, D.C.: University Press of America, 1984.

Cannon, Lou. *Ronnie and Jessie: A Political Odyssey.* New York: Doubleday, 1969.

Carson, Clayborne. *In Struggle: SNCC and the Black Awakening of the 1960s.* Cambridge, Mass.: Harvard University Press, 1981.

Carlson, Jody. *George C. Wallace and the Politics of Powerlessness: The Wallace Campaigns for the Presidency, 1964–1976.* New Brunswick, N.J.: Transaction Books, 1981.

Cason, Clarence. *90 Degrees in the Shade.* Univ., Ala.: University of Alabama Press, 1983.

Chalmers, David. *And the Crooked Places Made Straight: The Struggle for Social Change in the 1960s.* Baltimore: The Johns Hopkins University Press, 1991.

———. *Hooded Americanism: The First Century of the Ku Klux Klan, 1865–1965.* New York: Doubleday, 1965.

Chappell, David L. *Inside Agitators: White Southerners in the Civil Rights Movement.* Baltimore: The Johns Hopkins University Press, 1994.

Chester, Lewis, Godfrey Hodgson, and Bruce Page. *An American Melodrama: The Presidential Campaign of 1968.* New York: Viking, 1969.

Chestnut, J. L., Jr., and Julia Cass. *Black in Selma: The Uncommon Life of J. L. Chestnut, Jr.* New York: Farrar, Straus and Giroux, 1990.

Clark, E. Culpepper. *The Schoolhouse Door: Segregation's Last Stand at the University of Alabama.* New York: Oxford University Press, 1993.

Cleghorn, Reese. *Radicalism, Southern Style: A Commentary on Regional Extremism of the Right.* New York: American Jewish Committee, 1968.

Cobb, James C. *The Selling of the South: The Southern Crusade for Industrial Development.* Baton Rouge: Louisiana State University Press, 1982.

Cobbs, Elizabeth [Hood]/Petric J. Smith. *Long Time Coming: An Insider's Story of the Birmingham Church Bombing that Rocked the World.* Birmingham: Crane Hill Publishers, 1994.

Coffey, Thomas M. *Iron Eagle: The Turbulent Life of General Curtis LeMay.* New York: Crown, 1986.

Cohodas, Nadine. *Strom Thurmond and the Politics of Southern Change.* New York: Simon & Schuster, 1993.

Cohen, Richard, and Jules Witcover. *A Heartbeat Away: The Investigation and Resignation of Vice President Spiro T. Agnew.* New York: Viking, 1974.

Colson, Charles. *Born Again.* Old Tappan, N.J.: Chosen Books, 1976.

Conot, Robert. *Rivers of Blood, Years of Darkness.* New York: Morrow, 1968.

Cook, James Graham. *The Segregationists.* New York: Appleton-Century-Crofts, 1962.

Cosman, Bernard, and Rubert Huckshorn, eds. *Republican Politics: The 1964 Campaign and Its Aftermath for the Party.* New York: Praeger, 1968.

Crass, Philip. *The Wallace Factor.* New York: Mason/Charter, 1976.

Crawford, Alan. *Thunder on the Right: The "New Right" and the Politics of Resentment.* New York: Pantheon Books, 1980.

Dallek, Robert. *Lone Star Rising: Lyndon Johnson and His Times, 1908–1960.* New York: Oxford University Press, 1991.

Danzier, Sheldon H., and Kent E. Portney. *The Distributional Impacts of Public Policies.* New York: Macmillan, 1988.

Davis, Hugh Graham. *The Civil Rights Era: Origins and Development of National Policy.* New York: Oxford University Press, 1990.

Dean, John W., III. *Lost Honor.* Los Angeles: Stratford Press, 1982.

Dent, Harry S. *Cover Up: The Watergate in All of Us.* San Bernardino: Here's Life Publishers, Inc., 1986.

———. *The Prodigal South Returns to Power.* New York: Wiley, 1978.

Dodd, Donald B. *Historical Atlas of Alabama.* University, Ala.: University of Alabama Press, 1974.

Dodd, Donald B., and Wynelle S. Dodd. *Winston: An Antebellum and Civil War History of a Hill County of North Alabama.* Jasper, Ala.: Northwest Alabama Publishing Company, 1970.

Dorman, Michael. *The George Wallace Myth.* New York: Bantam, 1976.

Doyle, Andrew. "Causes Won, Not Lost: College Football and the Modernization of the American South," International Journal of the History of Sport, II (August, 1994).

Durr, Virginia Foster. *Outside the Magic Circle: The Autobiography of Virginia Foster Durr.* Edited by Hollinger F. Barnard. University, Ala.: University of Alabama Press, 1986.

Eagles, Charles. *Outside Agitator: Jon Daniels and the Civil Rights Movement in Alabama.* Chapel Hill: University of North Carolina Press, 1993.

Egerton, John. *Speak Now Against the Day: The Generation Before the Civil Rights Movement in the South.* New York: Knopf, 1994.

Ehrlichman, John. *Witness to Power.* New York: Simon & Schuster, 1982.

Elliott, Carl, Sr., and Michael D'Orso. *The Cost of Courage: The Journey of an American Congressman.* New York: Doubleday, 1992.

Emery, Fred. *Watergate: The Corruption of American Politics and the Fall of Richard Nixon.* New York: Times Books, 1994.

Epstein, Benjamin R., and Arnold Forster. *The Radical Right: Report on the John Birch Society and its Allies.* New York: Random House, 1967.

Evans, Rowland, Jr., and Robert D. Novak. *Nixon in the White House: The Frustration of Power.* New York: Vintage Books, 1972.

Fager, Charles E. *Selma, 1965: The March that Changed the South.* 2nd ed. Boston: Beacon Press, 1974.

Fairclough, Adam. *To Redeem the Soul of America: The Southern Christian Leadership Conference and Martin Luther King, Jr.* Athens, Ga.: University of Georgia Press, 1987.

Fite, Gilbert C. *Richard B. Russell, Jr.: Senator from Georgia.* Chapel Hill: University of North Carolina Press, 1991.

Fitzhugh, George. *Cannibals All! Or Slaves without Masters.* Edited by C. Vann Woodward. Cambridge, Mass.: Harvard University Press, 1960.

Forster, Arnold, and Benjamin R. Epstein. *Danger on the Right.* New York: Random House, 1965.

———. *Report on the Ku Klux Klan.* New York: Anti-Defamation League, 1965.

Frady, Marshall. *Billy Graham: A Parable of American Righteousness.* Boston: Little, Brown, 1979.

———. *Wallace.* 2nd ed. New York: New American Library, 1976.

Freyer, Tony. *The Little Rock Crisis: A Constitutional Interpretation.* Westport, Conn.: Greenwood Press, 1984.

Gallup, Dr. George H. *The Gallup Poll: Public Opinion, 1935-1971.* 3 vols. New York: Random House, 1971.

Garrow, David J. *Bearing the Cross: Martin Luther King., Jr., and the Southern Christian Leadership Conference.* New York: William Morrow, 1986.

———. *The FBI and Martin Luther King, Jr.: From "Solo" to Memphis.* New York: W. W. Norton, 1981.

———. *Protest at Selma: Martin Luther King, Jr., and the Voting Rights Act of 1965.* New Haven, Conn.: Yale University Press, 1978.

Garrow, David J., ed. *Birmingham, Alabama, 1956–1963: The Black Struggle for Civil Rights.* New York: Carlson Publishing, 1989.

The George C. Wallace Presidential Campaign Souvenir Photo Album. Selma, Ala.: Dallas Publishing Co., 1970.

Gitlin, Todd. *The Sixties: Years of Hope, Days of Rage.* New York: Bantam Books, 1987.

Glad, Betty. *Jimmy Carter: In Search of the Great White House.* New York: Norton, 1980.

Goldfield, David R. *Black, White and Southern: Race Relations and Southern Culture 1940 to the Present.* Baton Rouge: Louisiana State University Press, 1990.

Goodwin, Richard. *Remembering America: A Voice from the Sixties.* Boston: Little, Brown and Co., 1988.

Grafton, Carl, and Anne Permaloff. *Big Mules and Branchheads: James E. Folsom and Political Power in Alabama.* Athens, Ga.: University of Georgia Press, 1985.

Graham, Hugh Davis. *The Civil Rights Era: Origins and Development of National Policy.* New York: Oxford University Press, 1990.

Greenhaw, Wayne. *Alabama on My Mind.* Montgomery, Ala.: Sycamore Press, 1987.

———. *Elephants in the Cottonfields: Ronald Reagan and the New Republican South.* New York: Macmillan, 1982.

———. *Watch Out for George Wallace.* Englewood Cliffs, N.J.: Prentice Hall, 1976.

Gregory, James N. *American Exodus: The Dust Bowl Migration and Okie Culture in California.* New York: Oxford University Press, 1989.

Guthman, Edward. *We Band of Brothers.* New York: Harper & Row, 1971.

——— and Jeffrey Shulman, eds. *Robert Kennedy in His Own Words: The Unpublished Recollections of the Kennedy Years.* New York: Bantam Books, 1988.

Hacker, Andrew. *Two Nations: Black and White, Separate, Hostile, Unequal.* New York: Charles Scribner's Sons, 1982.

Hay, Alexander M., Jr., with Charles McCarry. *Inner Circles: How America Changed the World. A Memoir.* New York: Warner Books, 1992.

Haldeman, H. R., with Joseph DiMona. *The Ends of Power.* New York: Quadrangle Press, 1978.

———. *The Haldeman Diaries: Inside the Nixon White House.* New York: G. P. Putnam's Sons, 1994.

———. *The Haldeman Diaries: Inside the Nixon White House.* CD-Rom. Monterey, Cal.: Sony Imagesoft.

Hamilton, Virginia Van der Veer. *Hugo Black: The Alabama Years.* Baton Rouge: Louisiana State University Press, 1972.

———. *Lister Hill: Statesman from the South.* Chapel Hill: University of North Carolina Press, 1987.

Harvey, James C. *Black Civil Rights During the Johnson Administration.* Jackson, Miss.: University and College Press of Mississippi, 1973.

Harwood, Richard, and Haynes Johnson. *Lyndon.* New York: Praeger, 1973.

Havard, William, ed. *The Changing Politics of the South.* Baton Rouge: Louisiana State University Press, 1972.

Herbert, Kevin. *Maximum Effort: The B-29's Against Japan.* Manhattan, Ks: Sunflower University Press, 1983.

Hixson, Walter. *Search for the American Right Wing: An Analysis of the Social Science Record, 1955–1987.* Princeton, N.J.: Princeton University Press, 1992.

Hofstadter, Richard. *The Paranoid Style in American Politics and Other Essays.* New York: Knopf, 1965.

House, Jack. *George Wallace Tells It Like It Is.* Selma, Ala.: Dallas Publishing Co., 1969.

———. *Lady of Courage: The Story of Lurleen Burns Wallace.* Montgomery: League Press, 1969.

Huie, William Bradford. *Three Lives for Mississippi.* New York: WCCC Books.

Humphrey, Hubert. *The Education of a Public Man.* Garden City, N.Y.: Doubleday, 1976.

Hunt, E. Howard. *Undercover: Memoirs of an American Secret Agent.* New York: Berkley, 1974.

Hurt, Harry, III. *Texas Rich: The Hunt Dynasty from the Early Oil Days Through the Civil Crash.* New York: W. W. Norton, 1981.

Ingram, Bob. *That's the Way I Saw It.* Montgomery, Ala.: B & E Press, 1986.

Jackson, Alto L. *Clio, Alabama: A History.* Eufala, Ala.: np, 1979.

Jacoway, Elizabeth, and David R. Colburn, ed. *Southern Businessmen and Desegregation.* Baton Rouge: Louisiana University Press, 1982.

Jamieson, Kathleen Hall. *Packaging the Presidency: A History and Criticism of Presidential Campaign Advertising.* 2nd ed. New York: Oxford University Press, 1992.

Jeansonne, Glen. *Gerald L. K. Smith: Minister of Hate.* New Haven, Conn.: Yale University Press, 1988.

Johnson, Charles S. *Statistical Atlas of Southern Counties.* Chapel Hill: University of North Carolina Press, 1941.

Johnson, Lyndon Baines. *The Vantage Point: Perspectives of the Presidency, 1963–1969.* New York: Holt, Rinehart and Winston, 1971.

Jones, Bill. *The Wallace Story.* Northport, Ala.: American Southern Publishing Company, 1966.

Jorstad, Erling. *The Politics of Doomsday: Fundamentalists of the Far Right.* Nashville, Tenn.: Abingdon Press, 1970.

Kapuściński, Ryszard. *Imperium.* Translated by Klara Glowecewska. New York: Alfred A. Knopf, 1994.

Kelley, Robin D. G. *Hammer and Hoe: Alabama Communists During the Great Depression.* Chapel Hill: University of North Carolina Press, 1990.

Kennedy, Robert Francis, Jr. *Judge Frank M. Johnson.* New York: G. P. Putnam's Sons, 1978.

Key, V. O., Jr. *Southern Politics in State and Nation.* New York: Knopf, 1949.

Kirby, James. *Fumble: Bear Bryant, Wally Butts and the Great College Football Scandal.* New York: Harcourt Brace Jovanovich, 1986.

Kleindienst, Richard. *Justice: The Memoirs of Attorney General Richard Kleindienst.* Ottawa, Ill.: Jameson Books, 1985.

Kohn, [John] Peter. *The Cradle: Anatomy of a Town—Fact and Fiction.* New York: Vantage Press, 1969.

Kolkey, Jonathan Martin. *The New Right, 1960–1968: With an Epilogue, 1969–80.* Washington, D.C.: University Press of America, 1983.

Kousser, J. Morgan. *The Shaping of Southern Politics: Suffrage Restriction and the Establishment of the One-Party South, 1880–1910.* New Haven, Conn.: Yale University Press, 1974.

Kovenock, David M., James W. Prothro, et al. *Explaining the Vote: Presidential Choices in the Nation and the States, 1968.* Chapel Hill: Institute for Research in Social Sciences, University of North Carolina, 1973.

Kunstler, William. *Deep in My Heart.* New York: Morrow, 1966.

Kutler, Stanley I. *The Wars of Watergate: The Last Crisis of Richard Nixon.* New York: Knopf, 1990.

Ladd, Everett Carl, Jr. *American Political Parties—Social Change and Political Response.* New York: W. W. Norton, 1970.

Lawson, Steven F. *Black Ballots: Voting Rights in the South, 1944–1969.* New York: Columbia University Press, 1976.

———. *In Pursuit of Power: Southern Blacks & Electoral Politics, 1965–1982.* New York: Columbia University Press, 1985.

LeMay, Curtis E. *America Is in Danger.* New York: Funk & Wagnalls, 1968.

——— and MacKinlay Kantor. *Mission with LeMay: My Story.* New York: Doubleday, 1965.

Lesher, Stephan. *George Wallace: American Populist.* Reading, Mass.: Addison-Wesley Publishing Company, 1994.

Levy, Frank. *Dollars and Dreams: The Changing American Income Distribution.* New York: Russell Sage Foundation, 1987.

Liberty Lobby Presents: Stand Up for America. The Story of George C. Wallace. Washington, D.C.: Liberty Lobby, 1965.

Lienesch, Michael. *Redeeming America: Piety and Politics in the New American Right.* Chapel Hill: University of North Carolina Press, 1993.

The Life of George C. Wallace: "Our Kind of Man." Clayton, Ala.: Friends of George C. Wallace, 1970.

Lineback, Neal G., and Charles T. Traylor. *Atlas of Alabama.* University, Ala.: University of Alabama Press, 1973.

Lippman, Theo, Jr. *Spiro Agnew's America.* New York: W. W. Norton, 1972.

Lipset, Seymour, and Earl Raab. *The Politics of Unreason: Right Wing Extremism in America, 1790–1970.* New York: Basic Books, 1970.

Lord, Walter. *The Past That Would Not Die.* New York: Harper & Row, 1965.

Lubell, Samuel. *The Hidden Crisis in American Politics.* New York: W. W. Norton, Inc., 1970.

Lukas, J. Anthony. *Nightmare: The Underside of the Nixon Years.* New York: Viking Press, 1973.

Lyttelton, Lord George. *History of the Life of King Henry the Second and of the Age in Which He Lived.* 4 vols. Oxford, England: J. Dodsley, 1769–1773.

Magruder, Jeb Stuart. *An American Life: One Man's Road to Watergate.* New York: Athenaeum Press, 1974.

Mailer, Norman. *Miami and the Siege of Chicago.* New York: World Publishing Company, 1968.

Malone, Bill C. *Country Music U.S.A.* Revised edition. Austin: University of Texas Press, 1985.

———. *Southern Music: American Music.* Lexington, Ky.: University of Kentucky Press, 1979.

Matusow, Allen J. *The Unraveling of America: A History of Liberalism in the 1960s.* New York: Harper & Row, 1984.

May, Ernest R., and Janet Fraser, eds. *Campaign '72. The Managers Speak.* Cambridge, Mass.: Harvard University Press, 1973.

McGinniss, Joe. *The Selling of the President, 1968.* New York: Trident Press, 1969.

McGovern, George S. *Grassroots: The Autobiography of George McGovern.* New York: Random House, 1977.

McIlhany, William H., II. *Klandestine: The Untold Story of Delmar Dennis and His Role in the FBI's War Against the Ku Klux Klan.* New Rochelle, N.Y.: Arlington House, 1975.

McKay, Seth Shepard. *Texas Politics, 1906–1944.* Lubbock, Tex.: Texas Tech Press, 1952.

McKinney, John C., and Edgar T. Thompson, eds. *The South in Continuity and Change.* Durham, N.C.: Duke University Press, 1965.

McMillan, Malcolm. *Constitutional Development in Alabama, 1798–1901: A Study in Politics, the Negro, and Sectionalism.* Chapel Hill: University of North Carolina Press, 1955.

McMillen, Neil A. *The Citizens' Councils: Organized Resistance to the Second Reconstruction, 1954–1964.* Urbana, Ill.: University of Illinois Press, 1971.

Mendelsohn, Jack. *The Martyrs: Sixteen Who Gave Their Lives for Racial Justice.* New York: Harper & Row, 1966.

Michie, Alan A., and Frank Rhylick. *Dixie Demagogues.* New York: Vanguard Press, 1939.

Middleton, Harry. *LBJ: The White House Years.* New York: Abrams, 1990.

Mikell, Robert M. *Selma.* Charlotte, N.C.: Citadel Press, 1965.

Miller, Merle. *Lyndon: An Oral Biography.* New York: G. P. Putnam's Sons, 1980.

Mintz, Frank P. *The Liberty Lobby and the American Right: Race, Conspiracy and Culture.* Westport, Conn.: Greenwood Press, 1985.

Mollenhoff, Clark R. *Game Plan for Disaster: An Ombudsman's Report on the Nixon Years.* New York: W. W. Norton, 1976.

Morgan, Charles, Jr. *A Time to Speak.* New York: Harper & Row, 1964.

Moynihan, Daniel Patrick. *Coping: On the Practice of Government.* New York: Random House, 1973.

———. *Maximum Feasible Misunderstanding.* New York: Free Press, 1969.

Murphy, Reg, and Hal Gulliver. *The Southern Strategy.* New York: Charles Scribner's Sons, 1971.

Nixon, Richard. *The Memoirs of Richard Nixon.* New York: Grosset and Dunlap, 1978.

Norrell, Robert J. *A Promising Field: Engineering at Alabama, 1837–1987.* University, Ala.: University of Alabama Press, 1990.

———. *Reaping the Whirlwind: The Civil Rights Movement in Tuskegee.* New York: Knopf, 1985.

Novak, Michael. *Choosing Our King—Powerful Symbols in Presidential Politics.* New York: Macmillan, 1974.

Nunnelley, William A. *Bull Connor.* University, Ala: University of Alabama Press, 1991.

O'Neill, William L. *Coming Apart: An Informal History of American in the 1960's.* Chicago: Quadrangle Books, 1971.

O'Reilly, Kenneth. *"Racial Matters": The FBI's Secret File on Black America, 1960–1972.* New York: The Free Press, 1989.

Osborne, John. *The Nixon Watch*. New York: Liveright, 1970.

Oudes, Bruce, ed. *From the President: Richard Nixon's Secret Files*. New York: Harper & Row, 1989.

Owen, Thomas McAdory. *History of Alabama and Dictionary of Alabama Biography*. 4 vols. Chicago: S. J. Clarke, 1921.

Owsley, Frank L., Jr. *Struggle for the Gulf Borderlands: The Creek War and the Battle of New Orleans, 1812–1815*. Gainesville: University of Florida Press, 1981.

Panetta, Leon, and Peter Gall. *Bring Us Together: The Nixon Team and the Civil Rights Retreat*. Philadelphia: J. B. Lippincott, 1971.

Parks, Rosa, with Jim Haskins. *Rosa Parks: My Story*. New York: Dial Books, 1992.

Parmet, Herbert S. *Richard Nixon and His America*. Boston: Little, Brown, 1990.

———. *The Democrats: The Years After FDR*. New York: Macmillan, 1976.

Peirce, Neal R. *The Deep South States of America*. New York: W. W. Norton, 1974.

Perry, James M. *Us & Them—How the Press Covered the 1972 Election*. New York: Clarkson N. Potter, 1973.

Persons, Albert C. (Buck). *Sex and Civil Rights: The True Selma Story*. Birmingham: Esco Publishers, 1965.

Phillips, Kevin P. *The Emerging Republican Majority*. New Rochelle, N. Y.: Arlington House, 1969.

———. *Arrogant Capital: Washington, Wall Street, and the Frustration of American Politics*. Boston: Little, Brown and Co., 1994.

Pierce, Truman M., and James B. Kincheloe, R. Edgar Moore, Galen N. Drewry, and Bennie E. Carmichael. *White and Negro Schools in the South: An Analysis of Biracial Education*. Englewood Cliffs, N.J.: Prentice-Hall, 1955.

Powers, Richard Gid. *The Life of J. Edgar Hoover: Secrecy and Power*. New York: Free Press, 1987.

Powledge, Fred. *Free at Last: The Civil Rights Movement and the People Who Made It*. New York: Harper Perennial, 1991.

Price, Raymond. *With Nixon*. New York: Viking Press, 1977.

Raines, Howell, ed. *My Soul Is Rested: The Story of the Civil Rights Movement in the Deep South*. New York: G. P. Putnam's Sons, 1977.

Rainwater, Lee, and William L. Yancey. *The Moynihan Report and the Politics of Controversy*. Cambridge, Mass.: Massachusetts Institute of Technology Press, 1967.

Rather, Dan, with Mickey Herskowitz. *The Camera Never Blinks*. New York: Morrow, 1977.

Redekop, John Harold. *The American Far Right: A Study of Billy James Hargis and Christian Crusade*. Grand Rapids, Mich.: Eerdmans, 1968.

Reed, Ralph. *Politically Incorrect: The Emerging Faith Factor in American Politics*. Dallas: Word Publishing, 1994.

Ribuffo, Leo P. *The Old Christian Right: The Protestant Far Right from the Great Depression to the Cold War*. Philadelphia: Temple University Press, 1983.

Rogers, William Warren. *The One-Gallused Rebellion: Agrarianism in Alabama, 1865–1896*. Baton Rouge: Louisiana State University Press, 1970.

Rowe, Gary Thomas, Jr. *My Undercover Years with the Ku Klux Klan*. New York: Bantam Books, 1976.

Sachs, Patricia, ed. *George Wallace: A Rebel and His Cause*. New York: Universal Publishing, 1968.

Safire, William. *Before the Fall: An Inside View of the Pre-Watergate White House.* New York: Doubleday, 1975.

Salinger, Pierre. *With Kennedy.* New York: Doubleday, 1966.

Salisbury, Harrison. *A Time of Change: A Reporter's Tale of Our Time.* New York: Harper & Row, 1988.

Salmond, John A. *Conscience of a Lawyer: Clifford Durr and American Civil Liberties.* Tuscaloosa: University of Alabama Press, 1990.

————. *A Southern Rebel: The Life and Times of Aubrey Willis Williams, 1890–1965.* Chapel Hill: University of North Carolina Press, 1983.

Scammon, Richard M. *America Votes: A Handbook of Contemporary American Election Statistics (1972).* Washington, D.C.: Government Affairs Institute, 1973.

———— and Ben J. Wattenberg. *The Real Majority: An Extraordinary Examination of the American Electorate.* New York: Coward-McCann, 1970.

Schlesinger, Arthur M., Jr. *Robert Kennedy and His Times.* Boston: Houghton Mifflin, 1978.

————. *A Thousand Days: John F. Kennedy in the White House.* Boston: Houghton Mifflin, 1965.

Sherrill, Robert. *Gothic Politics in the Deep South: Stars of the New Confederacy.* New York: Grossman, 1968.

Sidey, Hugh. *John F. Kennedy.* Rev. ed. New York: Athenaeum, 1964.

Sikora, Frank. *The Judge: The Life and Opinions of Alabama's Frank M. Johnson, Jr.* Montgomery, Black Belt Press, 1992.

————. *Until Justice Rolls Down: The Birmingham Church Bombing Case.* Tuscaloosa: University of Alabama Press, 1991.

Silver, James W. *Mississippi: The Closed Society.* New York: Harcourt Brace, 1963.

Simkins, Francis. *"Pitchfork" Ben Tillman: South Carolinian.* Baton Rouge: Louisiana State University Press, 1944.

Sims, George E. *The Little Man's Big Friend: James E. Folsom in Alabama Politics, 1946–1958.* Tuscaloosa: University of Alabama Press, 1985.

Smartt, Eugenia Persons. *History of Eufaula, Alabama.* Eufaula, Ala.: no publisher, 1930.

Smith, Anita. *The Intimate Story of Lurleen Wallace: Her Crusade of Courage.* Montgomery: Communications Unlimited, 1969.

Solberg, Carl. *Hubert Humphrey: A Biography.* New York: W. W. Norton, 1984.

Sorensen, Theodore. *Kennedy.* New York: Harper & Row, 1963.

Speeches of Governor James E. Folsom. Wetumpka, Ala: Wetumpka Press, n.d.

Stand Up for Alabama: The Official Inaugural Program Honoring Governor George C. Wallace, 1963–1967. Montgomery: National Services, 1963.

Stanley, Harold W. *Senate vs. Governor: Alabama, 1971: Referents for Opposition in a One-Party Legislature.* University, Ala: University of Alabama Press, 1975.

Stanton, Bill. *Klanwatch: Bringing the Ku Klux Klan to Justice.* New York: Grove Weidenfeld, 1991.

Steed, Robert P., Laurence W. Moreland, and Todd A. Baker, eds. *Party Politics in the South.* New York: Praeger, 1980.

Steffgen, Kent H. *The Bondage of the Free.* Berkeley, Cal.: Vanguard Books, 1966.

Steinfels, Peter. *The Neo-Conservatives: The Men Who Are Changing America's Politics.* New York: Simon & Schuster, 1979.

The Story of Selma: or "The Other Side of the Coin." Selma, Ala.: The Selma and Dallas County Chamber of Commerce, 1965.

Strong, Donald S. *Registration of Voters in Alabama.* University, Ala.: University of Alabama Press, 1956.

Synon, John J., ed. *George Wallace: Profile of a Presidential Candidate.* Kilmarnock, Va.: MS, Inc., 1968.

Szulc, Ted. *Compulsive Spy: The Strange Career of E. Howard Hunt.* New York: Viking Press, 1974.

Taft, Philip. *Organizing Dixie: Alabama Workers in the Industrial Era.* Rev. and ed. by Gary Fink. Westport, Conn.: Greenwood Press, 1981.

Taylor, Sandra Baxley. *Faulkner: Jimmy, That Is.* Huntsville, Ala.: The Strode Publishers, 1984.

———. *Me 'n' George: A Story of George Corley Wallace and His Number One Crony, Oscar Harper.* Mobile: Greenberry Publishing, 1988.

Thompson, Dr. Hunter S. *Fear and Loathing on the Campaign Trail '72.* San Francisco: Straight Arrow Books, 1973.

Thompson, Mattie Thomas. *History of Barbour County, Alabama.* Eufala, Ala.: By the Author, 1939.

Thomson, C. A. H., and F. M. Shattuck. *The 1956 Presidential Campaign.* Washington, D.C.: The Brookings Institution, 1960.

Thurmond, J. Strom. *The Faith We Have Not Kept.* San Diego: Viewpoint Books, 1968.

Tindall, George B. *The Emergence of the New South, 1913–1946.* Baton Rouge: Louisiana State University Press, 1967.

Tygiel, Jules. *Baseball's Great Experiment: Jackie Robinson and His Legacy.* New York: Vintage Books, 1984.

Vance, Rupert. *All These People: The Nation's Human Resources in the South.* Chapel Hill: University of North Carolina Press, 1945.

Voter Education Project. *Voter Registration in the South, Summer, 1966.* Atlanta: Voter Education Project, Southern Regional Council, 1966.

Wade, Wyn Craig. *The Fiery Cross: The Ku Klux Klan in America.* New York: Simon & Schuster, 1987.

Walker, Anne Kendrick. *Backtracking in Barbour County: A Narrative of the Last Alabama Frontier.* Richmond: Dietz Press, 1941.

Wallace, Cornelia. *C'Nelia.* Philadelphia: Holman, 1976.

Wallace, George. *Stand Up for America.* Garden City, N.Y.: Doubleday, 1976.

Wallace, George, Jr., as told to James Gregory. *The Wallaces of Alabama: My Family.* Chicago: Follett Publishing Co., 1975.

Watson, Mary Ann. *The Expanding Vista: American Television in the Kennedy Years.* New York: Oxford University Press, 1990.

Wattenberg, Ben J. *The Real America: A Surprising Examination of the State of the Union.* Garden City, N.Y.: Doubleday, 1974.

Whalen, Charles and Barbara Whalen. *The Longest Debate: A Legislative History of the 1964 Civil Rights Act.* Cabin John, Md.: Seven Locks Press, 1985.

White, Theodore. *America in Search of Itself: The Making of the President, 1956–1980.* New York: Harper & Row, 1982.

———. *The Making of the President, 1964.* New York: Atheneum, 1965.

———. *The Making of the President, 1968.* New York: Atheneum, 1969.

————. *The Making of the President, 1972.* New York: Atheneum, 1973.

Wicker, Tom. *One of Us: Richard Nixon and the American Dream.* New York: Random House, 1991.

Williams, Juan. *Eyes on the Prize: America's Civil Rights Years, 1954–1965.* New York: Penguin, 1987.

Williams, T. Harry. *Huey Long.* New York: Knopf, 1969.

Wills, Garry. *Nixon Agonistes: The Crisis of the Self-made Man.* Boston: Houghton Mifflin, 1969.

————. *The Second Civil War: Arming for Armageddon.* New York: Signet Books, 1968.

Witcover, Jules. *Marathon: The Pursuit of the Presidency, 1972–1976.* New York: Viking Press, 1976.

Wofford, Harris. *Of Kennedy and Kings: Making Sense of the Sixties.* New York: Farrar Straus & Giroux, 1980.

Woodward, C. Vann. *Origins of the New South, 1877–1913.* Baton Rouge: Louisiana State University Press, 1951.

————. *Tom Watson: Agrarian Rebel.* New York: Macmillan, 1938.

Wolfe, Suzanne Rau. *The University of Alabama.* University, Ala.: University of Alabama Press, 1983.

Wooten, James. *Dasher: The Roots and the Rising of Jimmy Carter.* New York: Summit Books, 1978.

Wright, J. Leitch, Jr. *Creeks and Seminoles: The Destruction and Regeneration of the Muscogulge People.* Lincoln, Neb.: University of Nebraska Press, 1986.

Wyden, Peter. *Day One: Before Hiroshima and After.* New York: Simon & Schuster, 1984.

Yarbrough, Tinsley E. *Frank Johnson and Human Rights in Alabama.* University, Ala.: University of Alabama Press, 1981.

ARTICLES

Adams, Alvin. "Young Man Tried to Register to Vote 5 Times Before Death," *Jet,* March 18, 1965.

Alsop, Stewart. "Mr. Nixon's Horrible Shadow," *Newsweek,* November 10, 1969.

Bass, Jack. "A Prophet of the New Politics," *Philadelphia Inquirer Magazine,* December 25, 1988.

Bendiner, Robert. "The Compromise on Civil Rights—I," *Reporter,* September 6, 1956.

Bickel, Alexander M. "Desegregation: Where Do We Go from Here?" *New Republic,* February 7, 1970.

Brill, Steven. "George Wallace Is Even Worse Than You Think He Is," *New York,* March 17, 1975.

Brimmer, Andrew F. "Inflation and Income Distribution in the United States," *The Review of Economics and Statistics* 53, February 1971.

————. "The Wallace Watch," *New York,* June 30, 1975.

Black, Earl, and Merle Black. "The Demographic Basis of Wallace Support in Alabama," *American Politics Quarterly* I, July 1973.

Buckley, William F., Jr. "An Hour with George Wallace," *National Review,* March 12, 1968.

Bullock, Paul. "Rabbits and Radicals: Richard Nixon's 1946 Campaign Against Jerry Voorhis," *Southern California Quarterly* 55, fall 1973.

Caddell, Patrick, and Robert Shrum. "White Horse Pale Rider," *Rolling Stone,* October 24, 1974.

Carney, George O. "From Down Home to Uptown: The Diffusion of Country-Music Radio Stations in the United States," *Journal of Geography* 76, March 1977.

Chmaj, Betty E. "Paranoid Patriotism: The Radical Right and the South," *Atlantic Monthly,* November 1962.

Cleghorn, Reese. "Aftermath in Alabama," *Reporter,* December 3, 1964.

Cobb, James C. "From Muskogee to Luckenbach: Country Music and the 'Southernization' of America," *Journal of Popular Culture* 16, winter 1982.

Cole, Dollie. "Thou Shalt Not Kill George Wallace," *Saturday Evening Post,* March 1975.

Conway, M. Margaret. "The White Backlash Re-examined: Wallace and the 1964 Primaries," *Social Science Quarterly* 49, December 1968.

Cramer, M. Richard. "School Desegregation and New Industry: The Southern Community Leaders' Viewpoint," *Social Forces* 41, May 1963.

Crespi, Irving. "Structural Sources of the George Wallace Constituency," *Social Science Quarterly* 52, January 1971.

Danzig, David. "The Radical Right and the Rise of the Fundamentalist Minority," *Commentary,* April 1962.

DiMaggio, Paul, and Richard A. Peterson. "From Region to Class, the Changing Locus of Country Music." In R. Serve Denisoff and Richard A. Peterson, eds., *The Sounds of Social Change.* Chicago: Rand McNally and Company, 1972.

DiMaggio, Paul, Richard A. Peterson, and Jack Esco, Jr. "Country Music: Ballad of the Silent Majority." In R. Serve Denisoff and Richard A. Peterson, eds., *The Sounds of Social Change.* Chicago: Rand McNally and Company, 1972.

Dykeman, Wilma, and James Stokely. "The Klan Tries a Comeback," *Commentary,* January 1960.

Englehart, Gordon. "Wallace in Indiana," *Nation,* May 4, 1964.

Erskine, Hazel. "The Polls: Demonstrations and Race Riots," *Public Opinion Quarterly* 31, winter 1967–68.

———. "The Polls: Race Relations," *Public Opinion Quarterly* 26, spring 1962.

———. "The Polls: Speed of Racial Integration," *Public Opinion Quarterly* 32, fall 1968.

"Estimated Negro Voter Registration in the South," *New South* 21, winter 1966.

Feigert, Frank B. "Conservatism, Populism and Social Change," *American Behavioral Scientist* 17, no. 2, 1973.

Frady, Marshall. "Gary, Indiana," *Harper's,* August 1969.

Freedman, Alex S. "The Sociology of Country Music," *Southern Humanities Review* 3, fall 1969.

Gardner, George, Jr., and Jules Loh. "The Wonderful World of George Wallace," *Esquire,* May 1969.

Going, Allen J. "Critical Months in Alabama Politics, 1895–1896," *Alabama Review* 5, October 1952.

Good, Paul. "The Meredith March," *New South,* summer 1966.

———. "A White Look at Black Power," *Nation,* August 8, 1966.

Gorn, Elliot J. " 'Gouge and Bite, Pull Hair and Scratch': The Social Significance of Fighting in the Southern Backcountry," *American Historical Review* 90, February 1985.

Grasmick, Harold G. "Rural Culture and the Wallace Movement in the South," *Rural Sociology* 39, winter 1974.

Grossman, Edward A. "Harvard Looks Back on Gov. Wallace's Visit," *Harvard Alumni Bulletin* 66, November 23, 1963.

Hacker, Andrew. "Is There a New Republican Majority?" In Louise Kapp Howe, ed., *The White Majority: Between Poverty and Affluence.* New York: Random House, 1970.

Haggerty, Brian A. "Direct-Mail Political Fund Raising," *Public Relations Journal,* March 1979.

Hamill, Pete. "The Revolt of the White Lower Middle Class," *New York,* April 14, 1968.

———. "Wallace," *Ramparts,* October 26, 1968.

Haney, Richard C. "Wallace in Wisconsin: The Presidential Primary of 1964," *Wisconsin Magazine of History,* summer 1978.

Hardwick, Elizabeth. "Mr. America," *New York Review of Books,* November 7, 1968.

Haygood, Wil. "George Wallace Faces His Demons," *Boston Globe,* December 2, 1993.

Hersh, Seymour. "Nixon's Last Cover-up: The Tapes He Wants the Archives to Suppress," *New Yorker,* December 14, 1992.

Hinckle, Warren, and David Welsh. "Five Battles of Selma," *Ramparts,* June 1965.

Hoffman, Victor, and John Strietelmeier. "Gary's Rank-and-File Reaction," *Reporter,* October 8, 1964.

Hollis, Daniel W., III. "The Hall Family and Twentieth-Century Journalism in Alabama," *Alabama Review* 32, April 1979.

Huie, William Bradford. "Alabamians Against Wallace," *Look,* April 30, 1968.

———. "Humanities Case Against George Wallace," *Genesis,* March 1976.

———. "The Truth About the Lie That Made George Wallace Famous," *Village Voice,* January 12, 1976.

———. "The U.S. *Must* Say No to George Wallace," *True: The Men's Magazine,* July 1968.

Jenkins, Ray. "George Wallace," *New York Times Magazine,* April 7, 1968.

———. "Mr. and Mrs. Wallace Run for Governor of Alabama," *New York Times Magazine,* April 24, 1966.

———. "The Queen of Alabama and the Prince Consort," *New York Times Magazine,* May 21, 1967.

Johnson, Bradley. "Maryland." In Clement Evans, ed., *Confederate Military History,* vol. 2. Atlanta: Confederate Publishing Co., 1899.

Kazin, Michael. "The Grass-roots Right: New Histories of U.S. Conservatism in the Twentieth Century," *American Historical Review* 97, February 1992.

Kelly, Michael. "David Gergen, Master of the Game," *New York Times Magazine,* October 31, 1993.

Kempton, Murray. "The State of Maryland," *New Republic,* May 23, 1964.

Kennedy, John F. "New England and the South: The Struggle for Industry," *Atlantic Monthly,* January 1954.

Kiker, Douglas. "Red Neck New York: Is This Wallace Country?" *New York,* October 7, 1968.

Kilpatrick, James Jackson. "What Makes Wallace Run?" *National Review,* April 18, 1967.

Klein, Joe. "The Ministry of George Wallace," *Rolling Stone,* October 24, 1974.

"Kohn Tells It Like It Is," *South: The News Magazine of Alabama,* March 1971.

Kopkind, Andrew. "The Birth of Black Power," *Ramparts,* October 1966.

Lear, Martha Weiman. "Should Doctors Tell the Truth? The Case Against Terminal Candor," *New York Times Magazine,* January 24, 1993.

Lesher, Stephan. "John Schmitz Is No George Wallace," *New York Times Magazine,* November 5, 1972.

———. "Who Knows What Evil Lurks in the Hearts of 'X' Million Americans? George Wallace Knows—and He's Off and Running," *New York Times Magazine,* January 2, 1972.

Lipset, Seymour. "Three Decades of the Radical Right: Coughlinites, McCarthyites and Birchers." In Daniel Bell, ed., *The Radical Right: The New American Right; Expanded and Updated.* New York: Anchor Books, 1964.

——— and Earl Raab. "The Wallace Whitelash," *Trans-Action* 7, December 1969.

Loh, Jules. "Lonesome George," *Esquire,* October 1972.

Long, Margaret. "The Imperial Wizard Explains the Klan," *New York Times Magazine,* July 5, 1963.

Love, Edgar A. "Claiming a Right to Choose: A Profile [of Robert Zellner]," *Motive,* November 1982.

Lund, Jens. "Fundamentalism, Racism and Political Reaction in Country Music." In R. Serve Denisoff and Richard A. Peterson, eds., *The Sounds of Social Change.* Chicago: Rand McNally and Company, 1972.

Makay, J. J. "The Rhetorical Strategies of Governor George Wallace in the 1964 Maryland Primary," *Southern Speech Journal* 36, 1970.

McDonnell, Richard A. "The Direction of the Wallace Vote in 1972 and 1976," *Presidential Studies Quarterly* 11, fall 1981.

McGill, Ralph. "George Wallace: Tradition of Demagoguery," *West (Los Angeles Times* magazine), December 17, 1967.

McMillan, George. "The Birmingham Church Bomber," *Saturday Evening Post,* June 6, 1964.

Miller, S. M. "Sharing the Burden of Change." In Louise Kapp Howe, ed., *The White Majority: Between Poverty and Affluence.* New York: Random House, 1970.

Mohr, Clarence. "Requiem for a Lightweight," *Esquire,* August 1965.

Moynihan, Daniel P. "The Politics of Stability," *New Leader,* October 9, 1967.

———. "The President and the Negro: The Moment Lost," *Commentary,* February 1967.

Mueller, Samuel A. "Busing, School Prayer, and Wallace: Some Notes on Right Wing Populism," *Christian Century,* April 19, 1972.

Murphy, Warren. "The South Counterattacks: The Anti-NAACP Laws," *Western Political Quarterly* 12, June 1959.

Nixon, Richard M. "Khrushchev's Hidden Weakness," *Saturday Evening Post,* October 12, 1963.

———. "Needed in Vietnam: The Will to Win," *Reader's Digest,* October 1967.

Norrell, Robert J. "Labor at the Ballot Box: Alabama Politics from the New Deal to the Dixiecrat Movement," *Journal of Southern History* 57, May 1991.

Northrop, John, Jr. "Teaching Educational TV a Lesson," *Southern Exposure* 2, winter 1975.

Novak, Michael. "Beyond the Fringe: Why Wallace," *Commonweal,* October 18, 1968.

Oken, Donal, M.D. "What to Tell Cancer Patients: A Study of Medical Attitudes," *Journal of the American Medical Association* 175, April 1, 1961.

Osborne, David. "Newt Gingrich: Shining Knight of the Post-Reagan Right," *Mother Jones,* November 1984.

Orum, Anthony M. "Religion and the Rise of the Radical White: The Case of Southern Wallace Support in 1968," *Social Science Quarterly* 51, fall 1970.

Pettigrew, Thomas F., Robert T. Riley, and Reeve D. Vanneman. "George Wallace's Constituents," *Psychology Today* 5, February 1972.

Playboy Interview: "Martin Luther King," *Playboy,* January 1965.

Playboy Interview: "Governor George Wallace," *Playboy,* November 1964.

Polk, James R. "Looking Backward: Wallace Money," *New Republic,* June 10, 1972.

Raines, Howell. "Alabama Bound," *New York Times Magazine,* June 3, 1990.

———. "The Birmingham Bombing," *New York Times Magazine,* July 24, 1983.

Ransford, H. Edward. "Blue Collar Anger: Reactions to Student and Black Protest," *American Sociological Review* 37, June 1972.

Remnick, David. "Lost in Space," *New Yorker,* December 5, 1994.

Robinson, Michael J., and Clifford Zukin. "Television and the Wallace Vote," *Journal of Communication* 26, spring 1976.

Rodabaugh, Karl Louis. "Fusion, Confession, Defeat and Disfranchisement: The 'Fade-out of Populism' in Alabama," *Alabama Historical Quarterly* 34, summer 1972.

Rogers, William Warren. "Reuben F. Kolb: Agricultural Leader of the New South," *Agricultural History* 32, 1958.

Rogin, Michael. "Politics, Emotion and the Wallace Vote," *British Journal of Sociology* 20, March 1969.

———. "Wallace and the Middle Class: The White Backlash in Wisconsin," *Public Opinion Quarterly* 30, spring 1966.

Rovere, Richard. "Letter from Washington," *New Yorker,* May 16, 1964.

———. "Letter from Washington," *New Yorker,* June 13, 1970.

Salmond, John. " 'The Great Southern Commie Hunt': Aubrey Williams, the Southern Conference Educational Fund and the Internal Security Subcommittee," *South Atlantic Quarterly* 86, August 1978.

Scammon, Richard M. "How Wallace Will Run His Third-Party Campaign," *Reporter,* October 19, 1967.

Schneider, William. "The Suburban Century Begins," *Atlantic Monthly,* July 1992.

Schoenberger, Robert A., David R. Segal, and Ira M. Wasserman. "The Ecology of Dissent: The Southern Wallace Vote in 1968," *Midwest Journal of Political Science* 15, no. 3, 1971.

Schrag, Peter. "The Forgotten American," *Harper's,* August 1969.

Shearer, William K. "California Voters Win Big Victory in Battle Against Mixed Housing!" *Citizen* 9, November 1964.

Sherrill, Robert G. "Portrait of a 'Southern Liberal' in Trouble," *New York Times Magazine,* November 7, 1965.

———. "Wallace and the Future of Dixie," *Nation,* October 26, 1964.

Silveri, Louis. "Pushing the Fence Back Too Far: The Defeat of Congressman Carl Elliott in 1964," *Alabama Review* 45, January 1992.

Smith, Dick. "How 'Amateurs' Raised Nearly $10 Million in Nine Months," *Montgomery Independent,* November 28, 1968.

Strong, Donald S. "Alabama: Transition and Alienation." In William C. Havard, ed.,

The Changing Politics of the South. Baton Rouge: Louisiana State University Press, 1972.

Stroud, Kandy. "Rather Outspoken," *Women's Wear Daily,* March 14, 1972.

Thimmesch, Nick. "The Grass-Roots Dollar Chase—Ready on the Right," *New York,* June 9, 1975.

Thornton, J. Mills, III. "Challenge and Response in the Montgomery Bus Boycott of 1955–56," *Alabama Review* 33, July 1980.

Vidal, Gore. "The Art and Arts of E. Howard Hunt," *New York Review of Books,* December 13, 1973.

"The Wallace Vote: Maryland Editors Say This—," *U.S. News & World Report,* June 1, 1964.

"Wallace: 'Welcome Home You Living Doll,' " *Newsweek,* June 1, 1964.

Watson, Mary Ann. "Kennedy Live," *Washington Journalism Review,* October 1990.

Welsh, Matthew E. "Civil Rights and the Primary Election of 1964 in Indiana: The Wallace Challenge," *Indiana Magazine of History* 75, 1979.

White, Theodore H. "Texas: Land of Wealth and Fear," *Reporter,* May 25, June 8, 1954.

Wicker, Tom. "George Wallace: A Gross and Simple Heart," *Harper's,* April 1967.

Wittner, Dale. "A Boy Who Shut Everyone Out," *Life,* May 26, 1972.

Wills, Garry. "Can Wallace Be Made Respectable?" *New York,* March 6, 1972.

Wilson, Joseph, and Edward Harris. "Hucksters of Hate—Nazi Style," *Progressive,* June 1964.

Witcover, Jules. "George Wallace Isn't Kidding," *Reporter,* February 23, 1967.

Wooten, James. "George Wallace: The Island of His Exile," *Washington Post Magazine,* April 1, 1984.

———. "Wallace's Last Hurrah?" *New York Times Magazine,* January 11, 1976.

Wright, Gerald C., Jr. "Contextual Models of Electoral Behavior: The Southern Wallace Vote," *American Political Science Review* 71, June 1977.

DISSERTATIONS AND THESES

Burns, Gladys King. "The Alabama Dixiecrat Revolt of 1948." M.A. thesis, Auburn University, 1965.

Cammack, Ruth S. "Reuben Francis Kolb: His Influence on Agriculture in Alabama." M.A. thesis, Alabama Polytechnic Institute (Auburn University), 1941.

Clark, Wayne Addison. "An Analysis of the Relationship Between Anti-Communism and Segregationist Thought in the Deep South, 1948–1964." Ph.D. diss., University of North Carolina at Chapel Hill, 1976.

Cohen, Richard. "A Week with the Wallace Campaign." Undergraduate thesis, Brown University, January 26, 1969. (Copy in "1968 Election File," Drawer 416, GW Papers, ADAH.)

Cooper, James Pershing. "The Rise of George C. Wallace: Alabama Politics and Policy, 1958–1966." Ph.D. dissertation, Vanderbilt University, 1987.

Corley, Robert Gaines. "The Quest for Racial Harmony: Race Relations in Birmingham, Alabama, 1947–1963." Ph.D diss., University of Virginia, 1979.

Eskew, Glenn Thomas. "But for Birmingham: The Local and National Movements in the Civil Rights Struggle." Ph.D. diss., University of Georgia, 1993.

Fadely, Lawrence Dean. "George Wallace: Agitator Rhetorician. A Rhetorical Criticism of George Corley Wallace's 1968 Presidential Campaign." Ph.D. diss., University of Pittsburgh, 1974.

Makay, John Joseph. "The Speaking of Governor George C. Wallace in the 1964 Presidential Primary." Ph.D. diss., Purdue University, 1969.

McLean, William Campbell, IV. "From the Ashes: Phenix City, Alabama, and Its Struggle with Memory." M.A. thesis, Emory University, 1995.

Newberry, Anthony Lake. "Without Urgency or Ardor: The South's Middle-of-the Road Liberals and Civil Rights, 1945–1960." Ph.D. diss., Ohio State University, 1982.

Sparkman, John. "The Kolb-Oates Campaign of 1894." M.A. thesis, University of Alabama, 1924.

Summerell, Charles Grayson. "A Life of Reuben F. Kolb." M.A. thesis, University of Alabama, 1930.

Thompson, Jan Gregory. "A History of the Alabama Council on Human Relations: From Roots to Redirection, 1920–1968." Ph.D. diss., Auburn University, 1983.

Wagnon, Judy Means. "Grover C. Hall, Jr.: Profile of a Writing Editor." M.A. thesis, University of Alabama, 1975.

OFFICIAL AND SEMI-OFFICIAL PUBLICATIONS

Alabama Official and Statistical Register, 1935 (Wetumpka, Ala.: Wetumpka Printing Company, 1935).

Biennial Reports of the Alabama Legislative Commission to Preserve the Peace, 1964–1968.

Birmingham City Directories, 1900–1920.

Democratic National Committee v. James McCord, in Democratic National Committee Papers, United States Archives.

Final Report, Select Committee on [Watergate] Presidential Campaign Activities, U.S. Senate, 93 Cong., 2 Sess.

Hearings Before the Committee on Commerce, U.S. Senate, 88th Congress, 1st session, 1963 (civil rights bill hearings).

Hearings before the Select Committee to Study Government Operations with Respect to Intelligence Activities, 109th Congress, 1st session, 1975 (Ku Klux Klan investigation hearings).

Historical Statistics of the United States. Washington, D.C.: Bureau of the Census, 1975.

Journal of the Senate of the State of Alabama, Regular Session of 1935.

Mobile City Directories, 1900–1915

Presidential Campaign Activities of 1972 [Watergate] Hearings, Select Committee on Presidential Campaign activities, U.S. Senate, 93 Cong., 1 Sess.

Public Papers of the Presidents; Lyndon B. Johnson, 1963–64, vol. 2 (Washington, D.C.: U.S. Government Printing Office, 1965).

Republican National Committee, *The 1968 Elections: A Summary Report with Supporting Tables.* Washington, D.C.: RNC Research Division, 1969.

Statement of Information [Watergate] Hearings, Committee on the Judiciary, H.R., 93 Cong., 2 Sess.

Testimony of Witnesses [Watergate] Hearings, Committee on the Judiciary House of Representatives, 93 Cong., 2 Sess.

United States of America v. George C. Wallace, U.S. District Court, Middle District of Alabama, Northern Division (1959). Trial transcript in possession of the author.

United States of America v. Seymore Trammell, U.S. District Court, Middle District of Alabama, Northern Division (1972). Transcript copy in possession of the author.

United States Census (Alabama) 1900, 1910, 1920, 1930.
Hosea Williams v. George Wallace, 1965, U.S. District Court, Montgomery, Alabama, Civil Action 2181-N (1965), File # B0150841, Box 125, Federal Records Center, East Point, Georgia.
Robert Zellner v. Albert Lingo, U.S. District Court, Middle District of Alabama, Northern Division, Civil Action 1896-N (1963), Drawer 510, GW Papers, ADAH.

NEWSPAPERS

Atlanta Constitution
Atlanta Journal
Baltimore Sun
Birmingham Age-Herald
Birmingham News
Birmingham Post-Herald
Boston Globe
Cambridge (Md.) *Daily Banner*
Charleston (S.C.)
  News and Courier
Charlotte (N.C.) *Observer*
Chattanooga Times
Chicago Daily News
Chicago Sun
Clayton (Ala.) *Record*
Cleveland Plain Dealer
Columbia (S.C.) *State*
Clio (Ala.) *Free Press*
Columbiana (Ala.)
  People's Advocate
Columbus (Ohio) *Ledger*
Dallas Morning News
Detroit Free Press
Detroit News
Eufaula (Ala.) *Daily Times*
Florence (Ala.) *Times*
Harrisburg (Pa.) *Patriot*
Hot Springs (Ark.)
  Sentinel-Record
Huntsville (Ala.) *Times*
Indianapolis Star

Lee County (Ala.) *Bulletin*
Louisville Courier-Journal
Memphis Commercial Appeal
Miami Herald
Milwaukee Journal
Milwaukee Sentinel
Mobile Press-Register
Montgomery *Alabama Journal*
Montgomery *Advertiser*
Montgomery *Independent*
Nashville Tennessean
New York Herald-Tribune
New York Post
New York Times
Philadelphia Inquirer
Pittsburgh Courier
Richmond (Va.) *Times Dispatch*
Saint Louis Post-Dispatch
Tacoma Tribune
University of
  Alabama Crimson-White
Tuscaloosa Graphic
Tuscaloosa News
Union Springs (Ala.) *Herald*
Wall Street Journal
Wall Street Journal
Washington (D.C.) *Post*
Washington (D.C.) *Evening Star*
Wisconsin *State-Journal*
Worcester (Mass.) *Sunday*
  Telegram

MANUSCRIPT COLLECTIONS

Alabama Department of Archives and History, Montgomery, Alabama (ADAH)

Alabama Sovereignty Commission Papers
James K. Folsom Papers (private)

Governor James K. Folsom Papers (official)
Grover Hall Papers
Taylor Hardin Papers
Governor John Patterson Papers
Speech Collection
Governor George Wallace Papers
Governor Lurleen Burns Wallace Papers

Birmingham Public Library, Archives and Manuscripts, Birmingham, Alabama (BPL)

Alabama Anti-Defamation League Papers
Alabama v. Robert E. Chambliss trial transcript
Birmingham 1963 Bombing, FBI File (BAPBOMB)
Albert Boutwell Papers
John Buchanan Papers
Bull Connor Papers
Dan Dowe Documents
William C. Hamilton Papers
Arthur J. Hanes Papers
Ray Hurlburt Papers
Robert F. Kennedy Alabama Civil Rights Files
Roy Mayhall Papers
J. T. Waggoner Papers

Emory University, Woodruff Library Special Collections, Atlanta, Georgia

Ralph McGill Papers
  Newsweek, Atlanta Bureau Collection

Eufaula, Alabama, Carnegie Library, Eufaula, Alabama

"A Sketch of Anne Kendrick Walker," unpublished manuscript
  Elizabeth D. Rhodes Diary, unpublished manuscript

Federal Bureau of Investigation Files and Records, Washington, D.C. (FBI)

Alabama Freedom Rider Files
Bull Connor File
Viola Liuzzo File
George Wallace Shooting File (WALSHOT)
Mississippi Burning File (MIBURN)

Jimmy Carter Library, Atlanta, Georgia (JC)

Jimmy Carter Papers

John F. Kennedy Library, Boston, Massachusetts (JFK)

John F. Kennedy Papers
Robert F. Kennedy Papers
Burke Marshall Papers
Lee White Papers
JFK Audiovisual Materials
1963 Civil Rights White House Tapes, May 12, 20, 21; June 1; July 9; August 8;
    September 19, 23.
Tape of RFK–GW Meeting, April 25, 1993

Library of Congress, Washington, D.C. (LC)

Hugo Black Papers
National Association for the Advancement of Colored People (NAACP) Papers
Lawrence E. Spivak Papers
Curtis LeMay Papers

Lyndon Baines Johnson Library, Austin, Texas (LBJ)

Drew Pearson Papers
LBJ Papers

Maxwell Air Force Research Studies Institute Archives, Montgomery, Alabama (MAFRI)

Records of Air Combat Operations, 8th Air Force, 58th wing, January 1–August 14,
    1945.

Minnesota Historical Society, Minneapolis, Minnesota (MHS)

Hubert H. Humphrey Papers

Reynolds Library, University of Alabama–Birmingham (UAB)

Arthur Bremer Diary, March 2–April 7, 1972

Richard Nixon Presidential Materials, National Archives, II College Park, Maryland (RN)

Dwight Chapin Files
Charles W. Colson Files
Harry Dent Files
John Ehrlichman Files
H. R. Haldeman Files
Kenneth Khachigian Files
President's Office Files

President's "Personal" Files
White House Special Files,
    Central Files (WHSFCF)
White House Special Files,
    Administrative Files (WHSFAF)
White House Subject Files (WHSF)

Trevor Arnett Library, Atlanta University, Atlanta, Georgia (AU)

Southern Regional Council Papers

United States Archives, Washington, D.C. (USA)

Democratic National Committee Papers

University of South Alabama Library, Mobile, Alabama (USA)

Wilmer Hall Records

William Stanley Hoole Special Collections Library, the University of Alabama, Tuscaloosa, Alabama (UAL)

Gladys Burns Papers
James Hare Papers
Lister Hill Papers
John Sparkman Papers

LETTERS

Robert Bushouse, June 19, 1993; June 8, 1994
Art Feiner, February 8, 1993; June 1, 1993; May 28, 1994
Edward R. Fields, July 26, 1963
George F. Leahy, February 18, 1993; June 19, 1993
Jack Ray, August 6, 1993; June 1, 1994
Pierre Salinger, January 21, 1991
Starr Smith, June 1, 1994

ORAL HISTORY MATERIALS

Author's Interviews

Note: Interviews that were taped and transcribed are indicated with an asterisk. All my tapes and transcripts, as well as notes of untaped conversations, are available for review by scholars in the Special Collections of the Emory University Library, Atlanta, Georgia.

Robert Alton, November 28, 1988
Harry Ashmore, May 12, 1989
Joe Azbell, February 14, 1989
Bill Baxley, November 13, 1988
Winton (Red) Blount, November 1, 1988
Albert P. Brewer, July 29, 1988*
Robert Bushouse, February 21, 1993
John Cashin, September 12, 1988
Douglas Cater, September 25, 1990
Ira DeMent, October 13, 1988
Harry Dent, July 20, 1988*

The Reverend Fred Dickerson, February 8, 1994
Dan Dowe, August 14, 1993
John Ehrlichman, October 4, 1993
Annie Laurie Gunter, January 27, 1988
John Herbers, August 1, 1993
Anthony Heffernan, May 25, 1994 (telephone)
Mrs. Lister Hill, March 17, 1989
James Edwin Horton, Jr., May 27, 1992
William Bradford Huie, March 24, 1985
Irwin T. Hyatt, November 4, 1988
Bob Ingram, July 15, 1988
Ray Jenkins, April 12, 1994
    April 24, 1994
Hawk Johnson, October 15, 1990
Ruth Johnson, January 26, 1994
Peggy Sue (Wallace) Kennedy, February 22, 1991
Bill Jones, August 3, 1990
George LeMaistre, July 24, 1991
McDowell Lee, January 21, 1987
Jyles Machen, May 14, 1991
Charles Morgan, July 11, 1994
Earl Morgan, February 24, 1989
Jack Nelson, November 21, 1993
Brendan P. O'Regan, August 8, 1988
Lucille Prince, February 1, 1991
Frank Rose, June 19, 1998
Harrison Salisbury, July 28, 1991
Broward Segrest, January 11, 1989
    February 16, 1994
Jack Shows, January 19, 1989
Claude Sitton, August 1, 1993
Starr Smith, June 10, 1988
Phillip Sullivan, June 10, 1993
The Reverend Walter Telfer, June 22, 1989
Seymore Trammell, November 28, 1988*
    January 11, 1989*
    February 14, 1989*
    August 15, 1989*
Judith Turnipseed, July 21, 1988
Tom Turnipseed, July 7, 1988
    July 21, 1988*
    March 3, 1994
Cornelia Wallace, October 14, 1988
Judge Will Wilson, April 19, 1993
Macon Weaver, August 4, 1993
Robert Zellner, November 12, 1993
Richard Zind, April 4, 1993

Alabama Public Television Interviews

These interviews were conducted by APT in 1985 for a two-hour documentary on Governor George Wallace. The unedited video interviews may be viewed in the University of Alabama's William Stanley Hoole Special Collections Library.

Mabel Amos
Brandy Ayers
Mel Bailey
William Barnard
Jeff Bennett
Glen Curlee
Johnny Ford
Jimmy Faulkner
Al Fox
Fred Gray
Ernest (Sonny) Hornsby
Bob Ingram
Bob Inman
Bill Jones
Ray Jenkins

John Lewis
Hugh Maddox
Jim Martin
Bertie Parrish
Alan Parker
John Patterson
Joe Reed
Vaughn Hill Robinson
Anita Smith
Joe Smitherman
Elvin Stanton
Bob Vance
Macon Weaver
George Wallace, Jr.
Don Wassoon

John F. Kennedy Library Interviews

Ross Barnett*
Earl Blaik*
Paul Dixon*
Theodore Hesburgh*
Nicholas Katzenbach*
Robert F. Kennedy*
Martin Luther King, Jr.*

Burke Marshall*
John Patterson*
George C. Wallace*
Lee White*
Harris Wofford*
Seymore Wolfbein*

Lyndon Baines Johnson Library Interviews

Nicholas Katzenbach*
Burke Marshall*
Juanita Roberts*
Jack Valenti*

Walter DeVries–Jack Bass Interviews

(On deposit in the Southern Historical Collection, Chapel Hill, N.C.).

Richard Arrington*
Bill Baxley*
Jere Beasley*
Winton (Red) Blount*

Johnny Ford*
Charles Comillion*
Ray Jenkins*
Frank Johnson*

Alan Parker*
John Patterson*
Pierre Pelham*
Joe Reed*

Arthur Shore*
Robert Vance*
George Wallace*

Other Interviews

Schuyler A. Baker, by Elena Vorbovia, November 10, 1988*
Charles W. Colson, by Frederick J. Graboske, June 15, September 21, 1988* (Nixon Presidential Materials Project)
Virginia Durr, by Paul Stekler, January 2, 1994*
Ed Ewing, by Elena Vorbovia, November 10, 1988*
Richard Nixon, by Herbert Parmet, November 16, 1988*
Arthur Shores, by William A. Elwood, May 11, 1987*
George Wallace, Jr., by Elena Vorbovia, November 10, 1988*

ACKNOWLEDGMENTS

THE LATE ALABAMA novelist William Bradford Huie once suggested to me (as he had to others) that I should write a study of George Wallace and his impact on American politics. I asked him why, if it was such a good idea, hadn't he taken on the project.

"Well," he said, "the people who love Wallace don't buy books and the people who hate him sure as hell don't want to read about him."

I think he was wrong on both counts; I am sure that my editor, Alice Mayhew, feels the same. She responded to this project with enthusiasm when it was first presented to her in the summer of 1990 and she continued to support it even when it fell behind schedule. Simon & Schuster associate editor Elizabeth Stein has dealt with all my requests with unfailing cheerfulness and Lydia Buechler and Jolanta Benal have been the copy editors every writer would like to have. Jennifer Weidman meticulously read the manuscript and, with great diplomacy, made helpful suggestions.

Since I began research on this book in the early winter of 1988, I have come to depend upon the advice and help of many individuals. Unlike Will Rogers, I cannot claim that I never met a man (or a woman) I didn't like. But I can honestly say that, in six and a half years of research, I never met a librarian who wasn't unfailingly helpful. And I know that I tested the patience of half the staff at Emory's Woodruff Library at one time or another, particularly Marie Nitschke, who always responded no matter how outlandish the request. I could not begin to name all the individuals who assisted me, but I would be amiss if I did not single out Ed Bridges, the director of the Alabama Department of Archives and History, and all of his staff. When George Wallace used to claim that the people of Alabama were just as "cultured and refined and gracious" (and helpful, he might have added) as "anyone else in America," he must have had this department in mind.

I am also grateful to the Archives and Manuscript Division of the Birmingham Public Library; the University of Alabama's William Stanley Hoole Special Collections Library; the Manuscript Division of the Library of Congress; the United States Archives; the Research Library of the Federal Bureau of Investigation; the Maxwell Air Force Research Studies Institute Archives; the Minnesota Historical Society; the Reynolds Library of the University of Alabama, Birmingham; the University of South Alabama Library; the Trevor Arnett Library of Atlanta University; the Southern Collection of the University of North Carolina; the Special Collections of Emory University's Woodruff Library; and the staffs of the John F. Kennedy, Lyndon Johnson, and Jimmy Carter Presidential Libraries. Joe Terry and Camille Elebash of Alabama Public Television gave me access to their extensive unedited interviews (over sixty hours) filmed as part of their documentary on George Wallace. And I am particularly grateful to the personnel of the Nixon Presidential Materials Project who, under difficult circumstances, dealt with my requests with unfailing professionalism and good humor.

Although I was able to examine the uncatalogued papers of Governor Wallace when they were stored at the University of Alabama, Birmingham, these documents—originally donated to the Alabama State Department of Archives and History—have been reclaimed by Governor Wallace and placed under the control of the George Wallace Foundation. I hope that the Foundation will make these materials available without restriction to future scholars as soon as possible.

My Montgomery friends—Virginia Durr, Dorothy Moore, John and Judy Wagnon, Elizabeth and Richard Deibert, Earl and Kay Martin and Wayne Greenhaw—gave me food, lodging, and congenial companionship as this project has evolved. Greenhaw, author of a perceptive Wallace biography, was particularly generous in offering his assistance.

Ronald Goldfarb began as my agent; by the end of the writing of this book, he was my friend. At times he must have felt he was as much therapist as literary agent/attorney, but he always performed such ancillary duties with grace and good humor. Alicia Carter, Bill Wieland, Virginia Shadron, Ruth and Tony Badger, Jim Roark, Jack Bass, and Phyllis Schwartz gave me their support and encouragement. So did my friend and sister, Shirley Whitehead, who has always been there when I needed her.

There were others. My friend Bill Leuchtenberg kept sending me useful material he uncovered in his own research on recent American history. Susan McGrath, Chris Lambert, Steve Goodson, Elena Vorbovia, Amy Scott and Christine Lutz furnished invaluable research assistance. At a critical moment, Carolyn Sung of the Library of Congress bailed me out with some emergency research assistance. Jerry Shiverdecker furnished important research materials and helped me locate some of the photographs in this book. Pat Austin made usable copies of many of the illustrations.

And then there were those who made the ultimate sacrifice. Paul Stekler, Ray Jenkins, Steve Goodson, and Andy Doyle read the manuscript, gave me advice on matters great and small, and remained friends. Jeff Norrell and my son, David, performed the even more heroic task of reading the manuscript in its original 1,100-page version and suggesting where I might begin the arduous process of reducing it to a less epic or (depending upon one's

perspective) less bloated length. In return, I release them from all responsibility for my errors of judgment and fact.

More than fifty individuals took the time to submit to interviews with me
over the years and I owe them all my thanks. Seymore Trammell, George
Wallace's most influential political adviser and state cabinet officer in the
1960s, generously spent several days with me sharing his memories and his
knowledge of those years. Life has not always dealt kindly with him, but he
has emerged with a remarkably upbeat outlook and he was often as candid
in assessing his own shortcomings as those of his old boss, George Wallace.
We did not always agree on our politics and I was aware that he spoke as a
partisan. But in all our extensive interviews, I never found an instance in
which he misled me. He has his own fascinating story and I hope he will
eventually have a chance to tell it.

Nixon aides John Ehrlichman and Harry Dent were candid and cooperative in discussing their views on the relationship between Wallace and their
former boss. Other Nixon aides were neither accessible nor candid. (Charles
Colson, the born-again former White House counsel, had the most compel-
ling excuse. Mr. Colson would like to cooperate, explained his assistant, but
he was "too busy doing the Lord's work.")

Alabama journalist Starr Smith and Governor Wallace's press secretary Bill
Jones were also particularly helpful in answering repeated follow-up questions. Marie Jemison sent me a steady flow of research materials records she
had collected on the Wallace years. Five members of Wallace's World War II
B-29 crew—George Bushouse, George Leahy, Art Feiner, Jack Ray, and
Richard Zind—shared with me their engrossing accounts of wartime service
with George Wallace. I only wish I could have done their story justice.

I am particularly indebted to Dr. James Pittman, former dean of the University of Alabama School of Medicine and a longtime student of the connections between mental illness and political assassinations. In 1984, Dr.
Pittman learned that a Wisconsin construction worker had found the buried
first half of the secret journal of the man who gunned down George Wallace
in 1972, Arthur Bremer. (The second half of the diary had been found by FBI
agents in 1972 and published the following year by *Harper's* Magazine Press
as *The Diary of an Assassin.*) Dr. Pittman eventually was able to verify the
authenticity of the document and purchase it. In 1993, he was kind enough
to furnish me a copy of this missing portion of the diary which he has now
placed in the Reynolds Library of the University of Alabama, Birmingham.

The National Endowment for the Humanities made it possible for me to
spend an invaluable year at the National Humanities Center in the middle
stages of my research on this project. I would like to thank the Louisiana
State University Department of History and the Louisiana State University
Press for allowing me to incorporate portions of my 1992 Fleming lectures
into this book. Emory University has generously supported my research on

this project with research assistance and release time; members of my department were equally supportive by refraining from asking me when the book would be finished. In my own department, Rosalyn Page and Becky Herring rescued me from disasters great and small. Without Patsy Stockbridge, who prepared several versions of this manuscript, *The Politics of Rage* would still be unfinished.

AND then there is my wife, Jane. Given the sensitive nature of the "man-woman thing" (as George Bush might have said), there is peril for any male author who describes too enthusiastically the contribution of his spouse. (Exploitation is the word that leaps to most of our minds.) But I am bound to tell the truth. She encouraged and supported me at each step of this project. She read and edited every line, rescuing me from my worst stylistic barbarities. And when I despaired of reducing my original manuscript to a manageable size, she gave me the heart to carry on. Most of all, she made the journey worthwhile. To her, this book is dedicated with love and gratitude.

INDEX

NOTE: GW refers to George C. Wallace; JFK refers to John F. Kennedy; LBJ refers to Lyndon B. Johnson; RFK refers to Robert F. Kennedy.

Aaron, Edward, 230
Abernathy, Ralph, 246, 260, 375, 461
abortion, 361, 456, 457
Abrams, Creighton, 144, 150
Adams, Ralph, 51, 202–3, 277, 365
AFL-CIO. *See* organized labor
Agnew, Spiro, 330–31, 332
Alabama: bars civil rights demonstrations, 163–64; constitution of (1901), 40, 262–63; "outsiders" in, 35, 239; prison conditions in, 457; recruitment of industry in, 77–78; self-insurance system in, 268; state employees as source of manpower for GW, 300; succession provision in, 263, 264, 265–272, 292, 456; survey of political climate of, 261–62; tax issues in, 381–382. *See also specific person or department of government*
Alabama Attorney General's Office, 68–69, 232
Alabama Department of Public Safety. *See* Alabama State Troopers; Lingo, Albert
Alabama Journal, 282–83
Alabama Legislative Commission to Preserve the Peace, 231–32, 233–34, 239, 246
Alabama legislature: and civil rights activists, 244–45; GW denounces civil rights activists to, 255–56; GW as freshman in, 76–78; and GW as "most promising young legislator," 78; GW as page in, 30–31; KKK investigation by, 234; and succession

provision, 265–72; and tax issues, 381–82
Alabama press. *See specific person, newspaper, or event*
Alabama Progressive Baptist State Convention, 461
Alabama Project (IRS), 400–409
Alabama Sovereignty Commission, 232–233, 234, 239, 260–61
Alabama State Troopers: antisubversive squad of, 227–35; as bodyguards, 314, 340; and civil rights activists, 119, 125–27, 227–35, 242, 243, 244; complaints about, 238–39, 244–45; and election of 1966, 281; and election of 1968, 342; GW's changes to, 230; image of, 262; and KKK, 259; in Marion, 242, 243, 244; and Selma-to-Montgomery march, 246, 247–48, 259, 260. *See also* Lingo, Albert J.
Alabama State University, 461
Albany, Georgia, 117, 229
Allen, Ben, 125–26, 131–32, 147, 230
Allen, James, 271, 272
Alsop, Joseph, 341
Alsop, Stewart, 383
Alton, Robert, 408
American Independent Party, 300, 370. *See also* election of 1968
American Nazi Party, 366
American University, JFK commencement address at, 142, 155
Americans for Constitutional Action, 201, 296

Americans for Democratic Action, 217, 373

Anderson, Jack, 390, 391, 400

anti-intellectualism, 379, 425, 466

anti-Semitism, 296, 297, 336, 342

Ashmore, Harry, 86

Askew, Reubin, 414

assassination of GW: and Bremer's shooting of GW, 437–38; and Bremer's stalking of GW, 434–37; and Brewer's trial/sentence, 444; as communist-inspired, 452; and FBI, 439–40, 441, 443, 444; and GW's political future, 446; Nixon's reaction to, 438–45; as White House-directed conspiracy, 452–55

Auburn University, 382

Austin, "Big Ruby" Folsom, 415

autobiography, of GW, 464

Ayers, Brandt, 249, 385

Azbell, Joe, 304

Bacon, Roger, 390

Baker, Howard, 444

Baker, Robert, 209

Baker, Stanley, 394

Baker, Wilson, 241

Bakker, Jim and Tammy, 298

Baltimore, Maryland, 331

Bankhead, John, 46

Barbour County, Alabama: economy of, 37; and election of 1966, 291–92; and GW's politicking while in military, 63, 75; history of, 32–41; populism in, 37–41; race relations in, 35–36; Republican Party in, 35, 37; violence in, 36–37; voting in, 36–37; voting rights investigation in, 97, 98–104; White Citizens' Council in, 85; white supremacy in, 36–37. *See also specific town*

Barkan, Al, 352

Barnett, Ross: and election of 1964, 201; and election of 1968, 295; GW compared with, 156; and July Fourth "Patriots' Rally Against Tyranny," 216; limited mental faculties of, 196; and Senate Commerce Committee hearings, 158; tape recording of conversations with, 120; and University of Alabama integration, 154; and University of Mississippi integration, 110–11, 113, 120

Bartlett, Charles, 209

Bearden, Redge, 242

Beckwith, Byron de la, 153–54

Bennett, Bruce, 160

Bennett, Jeff, 112, 114, 146, 238

Benson, Ezra Taft, 354, 356

Benston, Jim, 249

Bergbauer, Irvin, 47

Bergholz, Richard, 316

Bernstein, Carl, 452

Berry, Abner W., 158–59

Bible reading, 162

Bickel, Alexander, 380–81

Bilbo, Theodore, 69

Birmingham, Alabama: blame for events in, 115, 124, 128; bombings in, 115, 116, 126, 127, 258; and children's crusade, 124; civil rights demonstrations in, 114–17, 119, 124–28; GW's strategy concerning, 127; Klansman in, 167; and labor movement, 229; NAACP in, 116; school integration in, 162, 167; state troopers in, 119, 125–27; violence in, 164–67

Black, Hugo, 46, 71, 293

"Black Power," 302–3, 306

black separatism, 303

blacks: alliance with whites as threat to Democrats, 39; and black capitalism, 374; as children, 62; and election of 1966, 276, 285, 286; excluded from grand juries, 84; fear of, 379; Folsom's appeals to, 73; and "good niggers" vs. troublemakers, 230–31; GW's views about, 237–38; inferiority of, 62, 237–38, 372; insubordination of, 35, 36–37; and Jeffersonian Democrats, 39; and Lurleen Wallace vote, 292; migration of, 24–25, 301; Nixon's views about, 372; poverty of, 372–74; support for GW by, 456; and voting, 36–37; and whites' historical memory, 35. *See also specific person*

Blease, Coley, 69

Blough, Robert M., 129

Blount, Winton (Red), 129, 145, 146, 385–86, 387, 388, 392, 407, 410, 414

Bolden, Willie, 241–42, 243

bombings, 238. *See also specific person, city or event*

Borawski, Elinor, 261, 262
Boutwell, Albert, 117, 127, 162
Braaten, David, 340
Bremer, Arthur: arrest of, 437–38; attempted assassination of GW, 437–38; in Canada, 429–431; childhood/youth of, 419–20; as Democratic party volunteer, 419, 428–29; disinformation operation involving, 441–444; GW stalked by, 427, 433–37; GW wants to know about, 452; Nixon stalked by, 419, 429–31, 433, 443; Nixon's strategy concerning, 440–44; and Pemrich situation, 421–422; personality of, 419–21, 440; search of apartment of, 440, 443, 452; trial/sentence of, 444; as a White House-directed assassinator, 452–55
Brewer, Albert: as an administrator, 385; and election of 1970, 383, 384–385, 386–89, 391–95; on GW's style, 381, 382; GW's talk with on death of Lurleen, 322, 323; and Lurleen Wallace's health, 279; Nixon helps, 384–385, 387–89, 392; and succession bill, 272
Brewer, Martha, 272, 393
Brewster, Daniel, 212–15
Brewster, Kingman, 200
Brikates, Richard, 46
Broder, David, 209
Brooke, Edward W., 237
Brown, Cecil, 96
Brown, H. Rap, 331
Brown, Pat, 304, 324
Brown University, 198
Brown v. *Board of Education*, 82, 86, 87, 99, 129, 197, 335, 350
Brownell, Herbert, 97
Bryant, Anita, 456
Bryant, Bear, 111
Bryce State Hospital, 321–22
Buchanan, Patrick, 396, 433, 466
Buckley, James, 426
Buckley, William F., 296
Bullock County, Alabama, 97
Bundy, Edgar, 295
Bundy, McGeorge, 133
Burns, Cecil (brother-in-law), 52
Burns, Henry (father-in-law), 52, 68, 320
Burns, Janie Estelle (mother-in-law), 52, 79, 309, 320

Burns, Lurleen. *See* Wallace, Lurleen Burns
Bushouse, Robert, 55, 58, 61, 62, 63–64
busing: and Democratic Party, 448; and election of 1972, 424, 426, 427, 432, 445, 448; and GW's legacy, 466; GW's views about, 418, 432, 434; and liberalism, 426; Nixon's views about, 423, 425–26; polls about, 375
Byrd, Harry, 237

Cahaba River Group (KKK), 140
California, 307–8, 310–16, 342, 343
Calley, William, 386
Cambridge, Maryland, 213–14
Camp, Billy Joe, 426, 427, 435, 446
Campaign Reform Act of 1970, 387
Campus Crusade for Christ, 336
Canada: Bremer stalks Nixon in, 429–31
Carmichael, Stokely, 303, 306, 331
Carswell, G. Harrold, 397–98
Carter, Asa: as anti-Semite, 296; and election of 1962, 106–7; and election of 1966, 277; and election of 1968, 276, 295, 297; and election of 1970, 391, 393; and IRS investigation, 402; as Klansman, 107, 139, 210; mentioned, 109; personality of, 295; and RFK's visit to Alabama, 120; salary of, 300; as speechwriter, 106–7, 139, 149, 196, 216, 294, 300; and University of Alabama integration, 149
Carter, Jimmy, 457, 458
Carto, Willis, 295, 296–97
Cashin, John, 393
Celler, Emanuel, 89–90
Central Intelligence Agency (CIA), 455
Champion, Leo, 206, 207
Chandler, A. B. (Happy), 354–56
Chaney, James, 222–23
Chestnut, J. L., Jr., 236, 245
children's crusade (Birmingham, Alabama), 124
Chisholm, Shirley, 452
Chotiner, Murray, 390
Chris, Nicholas, 298
Christian Anti-Communist Crusade, 295, 296, 299
Christian Coalition, 466
Christian Nationalist Crusade, 342
Christian, Sam, 131
Church League of America, 295, 296

circuit judge, GW as, 78–79, 236
civil rights: Alabama law bars dem-
    onstrations about, 163–64; and elec-
    tion of 1964, 205; and election of
    1968, 329; GW's speeches about, 205;
    LBJ's congressional address about,
    254–55; Nixon's views about, 327,
    329, 371–372; Senate Commerce
    Committee hearings about, 157–60;
    and television, 376–77. *See also* civil
    rights activists; school desegregation;
    specific person or act
Civil Rights Act (1957), 89–90, 96–97
Civil Rights Act (1964): as communist-
    inspired, 217; Connor as father of,
    262; Dirksen's support for, 151, 214–
    215; and election of 1964, 205, 211–
    212, 213, 224, 225; and Goldwater,
    218; GW's views about, 217; and
    House of Representatives, 202; and in-
    troduction of bill, 151–53, 155; and
    Nixon, 327; signing of, 215
civil rights activists: and Alabama legis-
    lature, 244–25; and Alabama State
    Troopers, 227–35, 242, 243, 244; as
    communist-inspired, 124, 158–60,
    161, 228, 229, 231, 232, 233–34, 244,
    253, 254, 255–56, 260–61, 305–6; and
    GW's college speaking tours, 200;
    and liberalism, 230–31; Mississippi
    arrests of, 223; and voting rights,
    241–42; in White House, 251; wire-
    tapping of, 229. *See also specific per-
    son, organization, or town/city*
Civil Rights Commission, 97, 98–104
Civil War, 42–44
Clark, Jim: and Birmingham violence,
    126; and election of 1968, 295; and
    KKK, 343; and Pettus Bridge confron-
    tation, 240, 241, 242, 245, 247, 248–
    249, 251, 255; and Selma-to-
    Montgomery march, 258, 259
Clark, Kenneth, 197
Clayton, Preston C., 78–79
Clayton, Alabama, 34, 42, 79
Clio, Alabama, 17–18, 23–25, 34, 42
Cloud, John, 248, 249
Cochran, John, 461
Cohen, Richard, 339–40, 341
Cohn, Bob, 106
Cohn, Roy, 410
Coleman, Tom, 257–58

college speaking tours, of GW, 195–99,
    200
Colorado, 307
Colson, Charles (Chuck), 405, 412, 413,
    414, 426, 439, 442, 448, 452, 453,
    454, 455; and break-in of Bremer's
    apartment, 440-41
Comer, Braxton Bragg, 36, 37
Comer, Wallace, 36–37
Committee for Political Action (COPE),
    352
communism: Alabama State Troopers
    combat, 229; and attempted assassi-
    nation of GW, 452; and Birmingham
    demonstrations, 115, 124; and civil
    rights activists, 115, 124, 158–60, 161,
    228, 229, 231, 232, 233–34, 244, 253,
    254, 255–56, 260–61, 305–6; and
    election of 1958, 92, 94, 95; and elec-
    tion of 1964, 207; and election of
    1966, 281, 282, 289; and election of
    1968, 295–96, 297, 298, 310–11, 313,
    328–29, 339, 358, 366; and election
    of 1972, 449; and GW as demagogue,
    345; and GW's 1963 inaugural
    speech, 108–9; and July Fourth "Pa-
    triots' Rally Against Tyranny," 216,
    217; and KKK, 94; and NAACP, 95;
    as post-World War II issue, 69, 73;
    and race riots, 304, 305–6; and Uni-
    versity of Alabama integration, 130
Connally, John, 438, 449–50
Connally, Nellie, 449
Connor, Eugene (Bull), 115–17, 124,
    126, 139, 165, 166, 229, 262
Conservative Society of America, 295
Cook, Drexel, 392
Cook, Elmer, 250–51
Cooper, Bill, 230
corporations, 70, 73, 74
Corrupt Campaign Practices Act (1925),
    407
corruption: in Alabama, 401–3; in Dem-
    ocratic Party, 37; and election of
    1892, 39; and election of 1954,
    401–2; in Folsom administration, 81,
    107, 401–2; in GW administration,
    226, 228, 268, 269, 342; and GW's
    finances in 1968 election, 369–70;
    and succession provision, 268, 269.
    See also Internal Revenue Service
Cotillion Club, 49–50

Cotton, Norris, 160
Council on Equal Opportunity, 251–52
Cox, Harold, 118
Craig, Calvin, 216
crime, 375, 378, 426, 456
Cronkite, Walter, 209, 367
Cuban missile crisis, 111
Cumming, Joe, 209
Curlee, Glen, 47, 48, 89, 100, 309, 462
Curtis, Carl, 218

Daggett, A. S., 36
Daley, Richard, 303
Dallas County, Alabama, 240. *See also*
    Selma, Alabama
Daniels, Jonathan, 257–58
Dartmouth College, 198
Davis, John W. III, 459
Davis, Lou, 53
Davis, Neal, 106
Death of a Salesman (Miller), 465
DeCarlo, John, 419–22
"Declaration of Good Faith," 261
deGraffenried, Ryan, 108–9, 267, 268,
    276, 279–80
DeMent, Ira, 401, 406, 411
Democratic National Committee, 426–27
Democratic Party: and busing, 418, 448;
    communist influence on, 233; con-
    ventions of, 87–89, 224, 331–32, 447–
    48, 449; and election of 1968, 331–
    332, 351; and election of 1972, 426,
    447–448, 449; erosion of, 379; FDR
    and Southern, 71; GW announces
    candidacy in, 412; GW as corrosive
    influence on, 396; GW as powerful
    force in, 428; liberalism in, 398; and
    organized labor, 449; pro-black
    stance of, 378, 418; Scammon et al.'s
    criticisms of, 376–77; splintering of,
    411; voter anger at, 426. *See also* Dix-
    iecrats; *specific person*
Democratic Party (Alabama), 89–90,
    224, 396; class alliance of blacks and
    whites as threat to, 39; corruption in,
    37
Dent, Harry: and election of 1968, 328,
    347, 350, 363; and election of 1972,
    379, 396, 433, 447, 448; and GW as
    threat to Nixon, 383, 384, 385, 396;
    and GW-Nixon meeting, 414; men-
    tioned, 453

Denton, Tommy, 28
Dickerson, Robert M., 461
Dickinson, Bill, 260, 261
Dirksen, Everett, 151, 214–15, 218
Dixiecrats, 87, 236, 369
Dixon, Frank, 69
Doar, John, 241
Dobynes, James, 242
"dolls" experiment (Kenneth Clark), 197
Dorman, Michael, 142, 413
Dothard, E. C., 290, 340, 437
Douglas, Paul, 97
Douglas, William O., 400
Drew, Robert, 143–44, 151
DuBois, Gordon O. II, 197
Durr, Virginia, 291, 322, 464–65

Eagleton, Thomas, 450, 452
Earlham College: GW's speech at, 211
Eastland, James, 118, 159, 160, 223,
    306–7
Eastview Klavern (KKK), 140
Eckl, Louis, 109
economy: and black capitalism, 374;
    and black poverty, 372–74; and civil
    rights legislation, 348; and election of
    1968, 347–48, 352; and election of
    1972, 374, 426; and Family Assistance
    Plan, 374; GW's views about, 352,
    381–82; in 1920s and 1930s, 23–25;
    Nixon's views about, 374; and popu-
    lism, 38; and white resistance to seg-
    regation, 261; after World War II, 69.
    See also taxes; *specific county or
    town*
education, 76, 83, 382. *See also* school
    desegregation; University of Ala-
    bama; University of Alabama integra-
    tion; University of Mississippi
Ehrlich, Harold, 228
Ehrlichman, John: and civil rights, 371–
    372; and election of 1970, 387; and
    election of 1972, 423; and FBI-Secret
    Service conflicts, 440; and GW's as-
    sassination, 444; mentioned, 351; on
    Moynihan's poverty program, 374; on
    Nixon and domestic affairs, 371; and
    Nixon's political enemies, 439
Eisenhower, David, 414
Eisenhower, Dwight D., 96–97, 99, 100,
    296, 326, 335
election of 1876, 37

election of 1892, 38–39
election of 1936, 48
election of 1942, 50, 51
election of 1946, 69–75
election of 1948, 87–88, 236, 369
election of 1950, 78
election of 1952, 78–79, 98
election of 1954, 81–82, 401–2
election of 1956, 86, 87, 88–89
election of 1958, 90–96, 98, 236, 274
election of 1960, 296
election of 1962, 100–101, 104–9, 274–275, 288, 299
election of 1964: anti-Johnson pamphlets in, 297; Democratic convention for, 224; and Goldwater, 218–22, 224–25, 325, 361; and GW as Goldwater's vice president, 219–21; GW hints about aspirations in, 201; GW withdraws from, 221–22, 224; GW's "brain trust" for, 201–2; and GW's finances, 299; issues in, 262, 362; and LBJ, 201–2, 203, 210, 211, 212, 222, 224–25; polls during, 224; primaries in, 202–15, 280, 343; and race riots, 307; and Republican convention, 219–22; Republican Party in, 288; results of, 224–25; and Rockefeller divorce, 416; and third party efforts, 220, 221, 224; and ultra right, 343; and white backlash dream, 225
election of 1966, 265–69, 274–77, 281–289, 306–7, 313, 325
election of 1968: and California, 307–8, 310–16, 331, 342; and Democratic convention, 331–32; election night in, 367–69; events influencing, 301–7; and gender issues, 362; getting on primary ballot for, 307–8; GW plans to run in, 266; GW as threat to Nixon in, 350–51, 352; GW's campaign headquarters for, 341–42; GW's conditions for abandoning race in, 339; GW's finances for, 295–301, 311–12, 317, 334, 335–38, 353, 364–65, 369–370; GW's staff for, 341–43, 364; GW's strategy for, 295–30, 338–43, 365; GW's style in, 345–47, 362–63; issues in, 295–96, 297, 327, 334–35, 345, 347–51, 352, 357–61, 366, 369; logistics for, 339–40; and Lurleen's illness/death, 317–23; and Madison Square Garden rally, 365–67; Nixon's finances for, 331, 334; Nixon's strategy for, 326–31, 332–33, 347, 363–64; Nixon's style in, 363; Nixon's views of issues in, 345, 348–49, 350, 363–364; and photo opportunities, 334; polls during, 338, 343, 351, 352, 363, 364, 368; and press, 334, 339–41, 368; and Republican convention, 329–30, 375; results of, 368–69, 375; and television, 332–33, 345–47; and third-party effort, 328, 339, 343, 369; turning point in, 351; typical GW campaign day in, 337; and ultra-right, 295–301, 356, 366; vice-presidential candidates in, 330–31, 332, 354–62, 384; and Wisconsin, 427–29; and Woodley conference, 295–96. *See also* Humphrey, Hubert—and election of 1968; *specific person*
election of 1970, 370, 376–77, 383, 384–85, 386–89, 391–99
election of 1972: collapse of Democratic presidential efforts in, 450; and Democratic National Committee, 426–27; and Democratic National Convention, 447–48, 449; and Eagleton matter, 450, 452; election of 1970's influence on, 395–99; Florida primary in, 412, 418, 423–24, 426; GW announces Democratic candidacy in, 412, 422; GW backs away from running in, 410–11; and GW as threat to Nixon, 380, 381, 383, 384, 385, 395–99, 400–409, 433, 445–46, 447, 448–50, 453; and GW-Nixon cooperation, 432–33, 447, 448–50; and GW-Nixon meeting, 410, 412–14; GW's advisors for, 424–25; GW's finances for, 382, 448; GW's plans to run in, 370; GW's strategy for, 382, 399–400, 427; GW's style for, 424; GW's tacit endorsement of Republicans in, 449–50; issues in, 379–80, 396–97, 398–99, 418, 422–23, 425–26, 427–28, 432, 445, 447–48; and liberalism, 397, 398; McGovern nominated in, 448; and Maryland, 435–38, 445; and Michigan, 427, 431–432, 433–35, 445; Nixon's strategy for, 374, 379–80, 381, 383–85, 395–99, 409–10, 426, 432–33, 447;

and political realignments in 1970s, 379–80; polls about, 409, 423–24, 427, 433, 435, 445, 447; potential candidates for, 383–84; and primary filing dates, 446; Republicans gain South in, 450; and third-party effort, 381, 396, 407–8, 410, 411, 412, 414, 433, 446, 447, 448, 449, 450; and Wisconsin primary, 419–22, 427, 431

election of 1974, 456

election of 1976, 455, 456–58

election of 1982, 462–63

election of 1986, 463

Elliott, Carl: and blacks, 286; and election of 1964, 288; and election of 1966, 274, 285–86, 287; and election of 1968, 275; family background of, 274; GW meets, 50; and GW's ambitions, 78; GW's relationship with, 274–75; as liberal, 71; as University of Alabama alumni, 46

Elliott, Jane, 50

Ellis, Handy, 73

Ellsberg, Daniel, 442

The Emerging Republican Majority (Phillips), 379

"enemies list," 390, 413, 439

Engle, Clair, 160

English, John, 428

environmental issues, 360–61

Epps, Joseph, 131

Equal Rights Amendment, 457

Eufaula, Alabama, 33–34, 36–37, 44

evangelicalism, 298–300, 456, 466. *See also* religion; televangelism

Evans, Rowland, 387–88, 410, 413

Evers, Medgar, 153–54

Ewing, Ed, 300, 311, 312, 316, 358, 360, 370

Face the Nation (television), 195, 221–222, 254

Falwell, Jerry, 298, 459–60

Family Assistance Plan, 374, 398–99

Farrah, Albert J., 46

Farrow, Thomas, 440

Faubus, Orval, 113, 163

Faulkner, Jimmy, 90, 93, 94, 300

Federal Bureau of Investigation (FBI): and black exclusion from grand juries, 84; and Freedom Summer Project, 223; and GW's assassination,

439–40, 441, 443, 444, 453, 454; illegal burglaries by, 438–39

Feiner, Art, 56, 57, 60, 62, 67

Feingold, Stanley, 306

Felt, W. Mark, 438–39, 441, 443

Ferguson, James, 272–73

Ferguson, Miriam (Ma), 272–73

Ferrell, C. Halford, 235

Fields, Edward R., 139, 164, 165–67. *See also* National States' Rights Party

Finch, Robert, 371, 397, 445

Fine, Joe, 311

Fite, Rankin, 405

Florence State College, 270

Florida, 231, 369, 412, 418, 423–24, 426, 457

Flowers, Richmond: and blacks, 285, 286; and election of 1966, 275–76, 285, 287; as go-between with federal government, 118; and Sixteenth Street Baptist Church bombing, 275–276; as "soft" on integration, 232; and University of Alabama integration, 147, 275

Flowers, Walter, 454, 455

Folsom, Ed, 251

Folsom, Jim: and Adam Clayton Powell, 84–85, 107; and Alabama State Troopers, 230; appeals to blacks, 73; Cornelia Wallace as niece of, 415; corruption in administration of, 81, 107, 401–2; and election of 1942, 51; and election of 1946, 69–75; and election of 1950, 78; and election of 1954, 81–82; and election of 1962, 107–8; and election of 1966, 284; finished as politician, 87; as governor, 75–76; GW's relationship with, 69, 81, 84, 85–86, 87, 107; on GW's womanizing, 104; and interposition doctrine, 86–87; issues for, 72–73; and "n" word, 237; physicial appearance of, 70; rules for politics of, 81; and school desegregation, 82, 83; as Southern politician, 70; style of, 71–72, 74; and succession provision, 267; "Tweety Bird" speech of, 107; vulnerability of, 81; and White Citizens' Council, 87

Ford, Gerald, 250, 400–401, 457

Foreman, Clark, 293

Forster, Adolph, 53

Fowler, Wally, 314

Fox, Al, 300
Frady, Marshall, 42, 52, 96*n*, 106, 291, 299, 376
France, Bill, 448
Frankfurter, Felix, 380
Franklin, Aaron, 29
Franklin, Ben, 252
Fraternal Order of the Police, GW's speech to, 305
"freedom of choice" plan, 350, 363
Freedom Riders (1961), 166, 289
Freedom Summer (1964), 222–23, 306

Gaston Motel (Birmingham, Alabama), bombing of, 126, 127
Gettysburg, Pennsylvania: commemoration of battle of, 157
Gibson, Fred, 30
Gilchrist, Robert, 267, 270, 284
Gilmore, M. W., 239
Gilpatric, Roswell, 357
Gingrich, Newt, 466–67
Goldwater, Barry: and election of 1964, 218–22, 224–25, 325, 361; and election of 1968, 326–27; and GW, 224; and Nixon, 325; platform of, 218; as right wing, 288; Southern Strategy of, 326–27
Gonzales, Henry, 411
Goodman, Andrew, murder of, 222–23
Gore, Eunice, 285
Graham, Billy, 298, 389–90, 449
Graham, Henry V., 150
Graham, Wally, 268–69
grand juries, black exclusion from, 84
Grand Ole Opry, 315–16
Gray, Henry, 269
Gray, James, 201
Gray, L. Patrick, 438, 439, 444
Greenberg, Jack, 256
Greenhaw, Wayne, 29, 82, 103, 104, 135, 217, 281
Griffin, Marvin, 85, 354
Gruber, Bronko, 139, 151, 206–7
Guthman, Edwin, 119, 122

Haig, Alexander, 445, 454–55
Haldeman, H. R.: and election of 1962, 325; and election of 1968, 332, 333; and election of 1970, 387, 388, 392; and election of 1972, 423, 433, 449; and GW as threat to Nixon, 453; and

GW-Nixon meeting, 414; and GW's assassination, 438, 441; and IRS investigation, 389, 390, 414; mentioned, 351, 381, 395, 397, 398, 426, 445; and Nixon's political enemies, 439; and political realignments in 1970s, 380; and Stroud story, 413
Hall, Grover, Jr., 83, 94, 96, 135–36, 138, 143, 269, 383
Hall, Grover, Sr., 135
Hall, Joan, 443
Halstead, Juanita, 277, 278
Hamblen, Stuart, 363
Hamill, Pete, 376
Hammond, Kenneth, 271
Hanes, Arthur, 117, 127
Harbinson, George, 57
Hardin, Taylor, 150, 391, 427, 454–55
Hardwick, Elizabeth, 377
Hargis, Billy James, 295, 298–99
Harlow, Bryce, 397–98
Harper, Oscar, 91, 96, 106, 202–3, 284, 300, 402–3, 417
Harris, Roy, 201
Harris, T. O., 242
Hart, Gary, 427
Harvard University, GW speech at, 196–99
Harwood, David, 317, 318
Hawkins, John, 231, 232, 233
Haynsworth, Clement, 397
Heffernan, Tony, 237, 392
Heflin, Howell, 107
Heflin, Thomas (Tom-Tom), 69–70
Henley, Wallace, 433
Herbers, John, 242
Herbert, Kevin, 60
Herbstreith, Dolores and Lloyd, 203, 204
Higby, Lawrence, 392
Higginbotham, Frank, 243
Highlander Folk School, 158–59, 160
Hill, Lister: and civil rights activists, 251; and election of 1962, 288; GW's relationship with, 87; and JFK's tour of TVA, 128; as liberal, 71; response to blacks by, 238; and RFK-GW talks, 118; and "Southern Manifesto," 86; as University of Alabama alumni, 46; and University of Alabama integration, 139
Hillman, Sidney, 73
Hilyer, Meady, 317

Hines, Jack, 238–39
Hodges, Grey, 422, 428
Hodgson, Godfrey, 334
Hodl, Mary, 280
Hofstadter, Richard, 344
Hogan, Lawrence, 454
Holland, E. L., 199
Hollings, Ernest (Fritz), 113
homosexuality, 231, 456
Hood, James, 130, 131–32, 138, 141, 147, 149, 151, 238
Hoover, J. Edgar, 159, 354, 438
Horton, James Edwin, Jr., 266–67, 269–70
Horton, James Edwin, Sr., 267
Horton, Myles, 158
Hoskins, Bob, 279–80
House, Jack, 300–301, 338, 339, 361
housing, 205, 207, 349, 423
Huie, William Bradford, 198, 285, 290
Human Events, 296
Humphrey, Hubert: and busing, 418; and Council on Equal Opportunity, 251–52; as Democratic Party leader, 426; and election of 1972, 428, 431, 432, 433, 446, visits GW, 452
Humphrey, Hubert—and election of 1968: and campaign organization, 339; as Democratic nominee, 331, 332; and economic issues, 347; and finances, 335; and GW's views about Humphrey, 358; and LeMay as vice-president candidate, 360; prime television time speech of, 351; and school desegregation, 363; support for, 343, 350–51, 352, 364; and turning point of campaign, 351; and Vietnam, 345, 351
Hunt, Bunker, 336–37, 356, 358, 369–370, 410
Hunt, E. Howard, 441–42, 443, 452
Hunt, H. L., 273, 295, 335–36, 392, 410
Huntingdon College, 227–28
Huntsville, Alabama, 162, 200
Hurley, Ruby, 92–93
Huston, Tom, 390
Hutchinson, H. H., 320
Hyatt, Irwin, 198

immigrants, 379
impeachment issue, 454–55
Indiana, 209–12, 433

industrial bonds, 77–78
Ingram, Bob, 85, 107, 146, 256, 269, 272, 279, 322, 388–89, 392
integration: GW's strategy to delay, 92–93. *See also* school desegregation; University of Alabama integration
Internal Revenue Service (IRS): and "enemies list," 390; investigation of Wallace administration by, 389–91, 400–409, 410, 411–14
interposition doctrine, 86–87, 163

Jackson, Cecil: and election of 1964, 219; and election of 1966, 277; and election of 1968, 300, 311, 312, 336, 342, 356, 358, 361, 364–65, 368, 369; and election of 1970, 391; as lawyer, 370; and school integration, 167; as speechwriter, 145; and University of Alabama integration, 114, 141
Jackson, Jimmie Lee, 243–44, 245–46, 251
Jackson, Shelly (J.S.), 20, 30
Jackson, Viola, 243
Jackson, Mississippi, 223, 335
Janeway, Eliot, 349
Jeffersonian Democrats, 38–39
Jemison, Lloyd, 315
Jenkins, Herbert, 165
Jenkins, Ray, 226, 237, 249, 282–83, 289–90, 381, 449, 458
Jews, 296, 297. *See also* anti-Semitism
John Birch Society, 158, 275, 295, 296, 305, 314, 336, 343, 356
Johnson, Frank: and election of 1970, 386; as federal district attorney, 99, 100; and forgiveness of GW, 461–462; and Freedom Rider case, 289; GW's relationship with, 47–48, 51, 100, 103–4; and Montgomery bus boycott, 99; and prison conditions, 457; and race issues, 48–49; as Republican, 48; reputation of, 99; RFK's note to, 123; and ROTC, 51; and school desegregation, 462; and Selma-to-Montgomery march, 247n, 255–56, 289; as traitor, 99; and University of Alabama integration, 119–120; and voting rights investigation, 98–104
Johnson, Hawk, 62–63
Johnson, John, 120

Johnson, Johnny, 462
Johnson, Lyndon: and civil rights legislation, 96–97, 134, 151, 215; communist influence on, 233; and election of 1964, 201–2, 203, 205, 210, 211, 212, 222, 224–25; and election of 1968, 325–26, 351; and Ferguson succession, 272–73; GW meeting with, 251–54; and "n" word, 237; popularity of, 201–2, 205; Southern support for, 211; and Vietnam, 325–26, 327, 351; and violence in Alabama, 251
Johnson, Paul, 223
Johnson, R. B. and Bertha, 21
Johnson, Ruth, 47–48, 51, 100, 461–62
Johnson, Tom, 273
Johnston, Olin D., 86
Jones, Bill: in advertising business, 370; and civil rights activists, 244; and civil rights legislation, 96*n*; defense of troopers and police by, 244; and election of 1958, 96; and election of 1964, 206, 213, 214, 222, 224; and election of 1968, 300, 311, 336, 352, 353, 354, 358, 359, 360, 364, 365, 369; and election of 1970, 391; and Elliott, 275; and GW-Johnson meeting, 252; and GW's college tour, 198; and Hunt money, 370; and Lurleen's gubernatorial candidacy, 281; on rewarding friends, 403; and Selma-to-Montgomery march, 246–47, 249, 258, 261; and succession provision, 265–66; and University of Alabama integration, 114, 122, 139, 143, 147; and Wallace's womanizing, 353, 354
Jones, Bob, 128
Jones, Don, 154–55
Jones, Thomas, 39
Jones, W. R., 234
Jones, Walter, 92, 93
Jordan, Clarence, 234
Jordan, James, 223
judge, GW as circuit, 78–79, 236. *See also specific person*
July Fourth "Patriots' Rally Against Tyranny" (Atlanta, Georgia), 216–18
Justice Department, U.S.: civil rights division of, 97. *See also specific person*

Kaiser, Robert Blair, 434
Kalmbach, Herbert, 387, 388, 392

Kapuściński, Ryszard, 467–68
Katzenbach, Nicholas: and election of 1966, 287; and University of Alabama integration, 111, 141, 142–43, 144, 145, 146, 147, 148–49, 151
Kefauver, Estes, 89
Kelley, Clarence, 454
Kempton, Murray, 212
Kennedy, Edward, 383–84, 438, 439, 441, 442, 455
Kennedy, Ethel, 452
Kennedy, John F.: American University speech of, 142, 155; assassination of, 199; birthday of, 133; and civil rights legislation, 133–35, 151–53, 155; communist influence on, 233; and election of 1946, 69; and election of 1960, 206; erosion of support for, 154; and foreign policy, 142, 155; GW's admiration for, 199; GW's talk with, 128–29; GW's views of, 346; and Hunt forgeries, 442; and industrial bonds, 77–78; and IRS investigations, 389; and LeMay, 357; mentioned, 119, 120; style of, 346; and television, 333; and TVA tour, 128–29; and University of Alabama integration, 144
Kennedy, Joseph, 333
Kennedy, Robert F.: assassination of, 331, 434; and Birmingham civil rights demonstrations, 127; and civil rights legislation, 134, 151, 152; and election of 1968, 331; and Flowers, 275; GW's attacks on, 283; political ambitions of, 283; and University of Alabama integration, 112, 117–23, 140, 141, 143, 144, 145, 146, 150; and University of Mississippi integration, 110–11; Wallace's views of, 118; wiretapping by, 160
Kenyatta, Jomo, 237
Kiels, Elias and Willie, 35–37, 44
Kihss, Peter, 298
Kiker, Douglas, 344
Kilpatrick, James J., 86, 136, 280, 293
King, Carleton J., 250
King, Coretta Scott, 461
King, Martin Luther, Jr.: arrests of, 119, 241; assassination of, 331; and Birmingham civil rights demonstrations, 124, 126, 127; and "Black Power,"

303; and Civil Rights Act, 215; communist influence on, 157–58, 159, 161, 232, 233–34, 304; and election of 1966, 285–86; GW's views about, 123, 128, 156, 157–58, 159, 161, 240; as historical model, 466; and JFK, 151; and March on Washington, 257; and Montgomery bus boycott, 83, 99; as most dangerous individual in American society, 304; and Selma-to-Montgomery march, 246–250, 256, 257, 258; sexual misdeeds of, 260; as speech giver, 156; threats to life of, 126, 246; and University of Alabama integration, 123; wiretaps on, 160. *See also* Southern Christian Leadership Conference (SCLC)

Klein, Herbert, 325

Klein, Joe, 460

Kleindienst, Richard, 401, 410, 411, 413, 414

Kohn, John: and election of 1966, 277; and election of 1970, 395; on GW's political ambitions, 265; and IRS investigation, 406; as speechwriter, 149, 196, 197; and University of Alabama integration, 141, 145, 146, 147, 149

Kolb, Reuben, 37–39, 44

Ku Klux Klan: and Aaron case, 230; Alabama legislature investigates, 234; and Alabama State Troopers, 229, 259; and Birmingham violence, 115, 116, 126, 166; and bombing Johnson family, 462; and communism, 94; and election of 1958, 94; and election of 1964, 210; and election of 1966, 276; and election of 1968, 356, 366; and Evers murder, 153–54; and Freedom Rider case, 289; and Freedom Summer Project, 222–23; GW as anti-, 236; GW's relationship with, 276; Hall's attacks on, 135; in Indiana, 210; and National States' Rights Party, 139–40; New York State prosecutes, 92; and school integration, 162; and Selma-to-Montgomery march, 257, 259; and threats on King's life, 246; and University of Alabama integration, 139–41; violence by, 262. *See also specific person*

labor. *See* organized labor

Lane, Marvin, 258–59

Lanham, John S., 334

Lardner, George, Jr., 412, 418, 424

LaRue, Fred, 363

law and order, 348–49, 366, 378, 418, 456

law practice, of GW, 51, 68–69, 76, 79, 104

Lawrence, William, 209

lawyers, black, 236

Leahy, George, 57, 58, 66–67

Lee, Cager, 242

Lee, McDowell, 75, 77, 90

legislative page, GW as a, 30–31

LeMaistre, George, 129–30

LeMay, Curtis, 59, 60, 61, 64, 354, 357–362, 366, 368

Lesher, Stephan, 96n, 238n, 418, 464

Lewis, Anthony, 134, 135, 137, 138

Lewis, Arthur, 261

Lewis, John (SNCC activist), 245, 247–248, 460–62

Lewis, Muriel, 261

liberalism: and busing, 426; and civil rights activists, 230–31; in Democratic Party, 398; and election of 1966, 283; and election of 1968, 295, 296, 347; and election of 1972, 397, 398; Goldwater's views about, 221; and July Fourth "Patriots' Rally Against Tyranny," 217; "new," 373; and Nixon's impeachment, 455; Nixon's views about, 374; purged from Nixon administration, 397; and school desegregation, 397; and "Silent Majority," 377; and succession provision, 266; Wallace administration attacks on, 228, 239; and working class, 377

Liberty Amendment, 203

Liberty Lobby, 296, 297, 314

Liberty Road Baptist Church (Lynchburg, Virginia), 459–60

Liddy, G. Gordon, 454

Life Line Foundation, 295

Life magazine, 343, 442

Lincoln, Abraham, 155

Lingo, Albert J.: and antisubversive unit, 234; and Birmingham violence, 125–27, 166–67; and changes to Alabama State Troopers, 230; and civil rights activists, 227–28; and Freedom

Lingo, Albert J. (*cont.*)
  Summer Project, 223; and reinstate-
    ment of revoked driver's licenses,
    382; reprimand of, 249; and school
    integration, 167; and Selma-to-
    Montgomery march, 247, 247*n*, 249,
    255, 259; and University of Alabama
    integration, 131–32, 139
Little Rock (Arkansas) crisis, 160
Liuo, Viola, 257, 258–59, 272
Loftis, W. U. (Bill), 243, 244
Loh, Jules, 136, 211
Long, Huey, 69, 344, 345, 400, 403
Lowe, Julian, 268–69, 271
Lowndes County, Alabama, 247
Lubell, Samuel, 287, 349, 350
Lucy, Autherine, 83–84, 93, 107, 111,
  130
Lukash, William, 446
Lynne, Seybourn H., 138–39

MacArthur, Douglas, 336
McCarthy, Eugene, 331
McCarthy, Joseph, 209, 295, 344
McConnell, John, 130
McDermott, John, 346
McDowell, A. M., 31
McEachern, William (great uncle), 25
McGee, Frank, 135, 137, 209
McGinniss, Joe, 333, 378–79
McGovern, George: blamed for GW's
  assassination, 441–44, 452; Bremer
  considers shooting, 443; and busing,
  418; as Democratic Party leader, 426;
  and GW's legacy, 465; visits GW, 452
McGovern, George—and election of
  1972: and communism, 449; and
  Democratic National Committee, 427;
  end of efforts of, 450; GW's feelings
  about, 449, 450; and Michigan primary, 431, 432; Nixon's feelings
  about, 384, 447; Nixon's strategy concerning, 441–44; nomination for
  president of, 448; support for, 445;
  and Wisconsin primary, 428, 431
McIntire, Carl, 295, 298
McLuhan, Marshall, 345
MacNeil, Robert, 212
McQueen, Billy, 68
Maddox, Lester, 216, 306
Madison Square Garden, GW rally at,
  365–67

Magnuson, Warren, 160
Magruder, Jeb, 412
Malone, Vivian, 130, 131–32, 138, 141,
  147, 149–50, 151, 238, 238*n*
Mangum, George, 341
Manion, Dean Clarence, 295
Manion Forum, 295, 336
Mann, Floyd, 227, 228
Mann, James, 454
March on Washington (1963), 163, 234,
  257
Margold, Jane, 286
Marion, Alabama, 241–46
Marshall, Burke: and Birmingham civil
  rights demonstrations, 114, 125, 127,
  129; and civil rights legislation, 134,
  151, 152; and University of Alabama
  integration, 110, 111, 112, 114, 117,
  118, 119, 120, 123, 144, 145, 147
Marshall, Thomas, 330
Marshall, Thurgood, 118
Martin, Harold, 269, 394, 407, 457–58
Martin, James, 219–21, 288–92
Martin, Ramona, 237
Martin, Wynn, 102
Maryland, 212–15, 280, 435–38, 445
Matthews, Sam, 115
Mayall, Alvin, 315, 342
Mayhall, Roy, 293
media: Alabama State Troopers attack
  on, 242–44; and GW's assassination,
  443; GW's relations with, 244, 254;
  and Selma-to-Montgomery march,
  248, 249–50. *See also specific person,
  newspaper, or event*
Meet the Press (television), 135–38, 339
mental hospitals, 321–22
Meredith, James, 110–11, 302–3
Meriwether, Charles, 94, 95, 96
Metcalf, Neil, 271
Methodist Christian Advocate, 235
Michigan, 427, 431–32, 433–35, 445
migration: of blacks, 24–25, 301; of
  whites, 25
Mikell, Robert, 259
Miller, Arthur, 465
Miller, Orloff, 250
Milliken, Roger, 221, 363
Minutemen of America, 366
Mitchell, John: and election of 1968,
  329, 330, 332, 333, 334, 347; and
  election of 1972, 446, 447; and GW's

assassination, 453; and IRS investigation, 400, 401, 405, 410, 411, 412, 414; and political realignments in 1970s, 379
Mitchell, Martha, 453
Mizell, Wallace (Buck), 23, 41
mob rule, 163
Mobile, Alabama, 162
Mohr, Clarence, 361
Mollenhoff, Clark, 389, 390
Montgomery, Charles, 292–93
Montgomery, Alabama, 75, 83, 99, 224, 291
Montgomery Advertiser, 289
Moore, Jamie, 126–27
Moore, Russell, 201
Moorer, Otto, 247
Moral Majority movement, 459–60
Morgan, Charles, 228
Morgan, Earl: and election of 1968, 311, 353, 354, 356, 358, 359, 360, 364–65; on GW's feelings of JFK's assassination, 199; and school integration, 167; and the Selma-to-Montgomery march, 252; and University of Alabama integration, 145, 146
Moynihan, Daniel Patrick, 372–74, 398
Muskie, Edmund, 384, 398, 409, 418, 428, 431, 432

Nachman, Martha, 273
National Association for the Advancement of Colored People (NAACP), 83, 92–93, 95, 116, 121, 162, 197
National Council of Churches, 233
National Defense Education Act (1958), 274
National Guard: federalization of, 113, 147, 150, 154, 256; in Kentucky, 355; and Maryland primary (1964), 214; and race riots, 301–2; and school integration, 355; and Selma-to-Montgomery march, 256; and University of Alabama integration, 113, 147, 150, 154
National Press Club, 417
National States' Rights Party, 139–40, 164, 165–67, 229. *See also* Fields, Edward R.
National Welfare Rights Organization, 374
National Youth Administration, 159

Nelson, Jack, 157, 286, 298, 340, 359, 454
New York Times, 250. *See also specific reporter*
Newsweek magazine, 343, 351, 369, 375, 424
Nixon, E. D., 291, 461
Nixon, Richard M.: and Billy Graham, 298; Bremer stalks, 419, 429–31, 433, 443; campaign chest of, 387; and civil rights legislation, 97; and domestic affairs, 371; and election of 1946, 69, 73; and election of 1960, 324; and election of 1962, 324–25; and election of 1964, 325; and election of 1970, 384–85, 387–89, 392; and foreign policy, 325, 327, 422–23, 429–31, 465; and Goldwater, 325; and GW's assassination, 438–45; GW's cooperation with, 432–33, 447, 448–50; and GW's legacy, 465; and GW's meeting with, 410, 412–14; and impeachment issue, 454–455; and Moynihan, 373–74; and press, 324–25, 332–33, 334; Rather's questioning of, 412–13; style of, 363; and Thurmond, 328–29, 330, 332; turning point in political recovery of, 325; visits GW in hospital, 445–46. *See also* election of 1968; election of 1972; *specific issue*
North Carolina, 457
Norville, Peyton, 148
Notre Dame University, GW's speech at, 211
Novak, Michael, 314, 428
Novak, Robert, 387–88, 410, 413
nuclear weapons, 359–60, 362
Nunn, Louis, 414

O'Brien, Larry, 426
Ohio, 307
The Old Time Gospel Hour (television), 459–60
Ole Miss. *See* University of Mississippi
Olsen, Clark, 250
organized labor, 70, 73–74, 229, 285–286, 351–52, 432, 449
outside interference, 35, 239

Painter, Willie, 131, 227–28
Panetta, Leon, 397
Parks, Rosa, 158, 291, 460

566   *Index*

Parmet, Herbert, 326, 331, 465
Partlow State School, 321–22
Patrick Henry Press, 201–2
Patterson, John: and antisubversive
    squad, 229–30; on educational ap-
    propriations, 382; and election of
    1958, 90, 91–92, 93–96, 98; and elec-
    tion of 1966, 274, 284; and election
    of 1968, 337; and integration, 113,
    114; and succession provision, 267,
    268; and Trammell, 98; wiretapping
    by, 229–30
Peabody, Endicott, 198
Pearl, Minnie, 90, 105
Pearson, Drew, 113
Pearson, Ed, 299
Pelfrey, Virgil, 29
Pemberton, John, 406
Pemrich, Joan, 421–22
Pentagon Papers, 442
Perez, Leander, 201, 295, 296
Perry County, Alabama, 241–45
Perry, Joe, 277, 279
Persons, Gordon, 77, 78
Persons, Maida, 416
Petroff, Johnny, 57
Pettus Bridge confrontation, 248–50,
    255, 262
Philadelphia Plan, 374
Phillips, Kevin, 378–80, 399
Pierce, Laurens, 436
Pincus, Walter, 340
Plessy v. *Ferguson* (1896), 40
politics: and corporations, 70; dissent-
    ing tradition in Alabama, 70; domi-
    nant interests in Alabama, 40–41;
    GW as key to understanding reshap-
    ing of American, 465; and GW as
    volunteer in Alabama, 50; GW's early
    interest in, 29–31; ideology in Ala-
    bama, 51; in 1920s and 1930s, 40–41;
    as struggle between good and evil,
    466–68. *See also* populism; *specific
    party, county, town, or person*
politics of hate, 379
Polk, James K., 411
populism, 37–41, 344–45, 379, 415,
    425, 467
poverty, 372–74. *See also* Family Assis-
    tance Plan
Powell, Adam Clayton, 84–85, 107
Powell, Sherman, 285

Presley, Elvis, 452
press: and election of 1968, 334, 339–
    341, 368; and Nixon, 324–25, 334.
    See also specific person
Price, Cecil, 222–23
Price, Raymond, 332, 398
Pritchett, Laurie, 126, 229
Pruitt, C. A. (Hardboy), 162

Quayle, Oliver, 387

race discussions, between GW and
    friends, 48–49, 62
race relations: in Barbour County, Ala-
    bama, 35–36; and GW as moderate,
    236; GW's obsession with, 237; and
    "n" word, 236–37; national attitudes
    on, 349–50; Nixon's views on, 379–
    380; and populism, 39–40; and reli-
    gion, 235. *See also specific person,
    organization, or event*
race riots, 301–7, 331, 349, 372
racial amalgamation: GW's views of,
    196, 238
Radcliffe College, 196–99
Rainach, Willie, 201
Raine, Frances, 392
Rather, Dan, 156, 412–13
Ray, Jack, 57–58, 59, 60, 61, 63, 64, 65
Rayburn, Sam, 89
Reagan, Ronald, 313, 329, 330, 349,
    439, 466
The Real Majority (Scammon, Watten-
    berg), 377–78
Reeb, James, 250–51
Reed, Ralph, 466
Reeves, Herbert E. (Gene), 140
Reid, Edward, 78, 118–19, 120
religion: and GW as born-again Chris-
    tian, 459–60; GW's views about, 29;
    and racial issues, 235; and religious
    fundamentalism, 466, 467. *See also*
    evangelicalism; televangelists
Republican Party: abandons blacks, 40;
    in Barbour County, Alabama, 35, 37;
    conventions of the, 219–22, 329–30,
    375; and election of 1962, 288; and
    election of 1966, 287–92; "populist"
    faction of, 379; and profile of south-
    ern Republicans, 219; and realign-
    ments of 1970s, 379; rebuilding the,
    369; in South, 35, 225, 450

Reserve Officer Training programs, 51
Reuther, Walter, 233
Reynolds, John, 203–9
Richardson, Elliot, 423
Richardson, Gloria, 214
Rickey, Branch, 355
right wing, 295–301, 343. *See also*
    specific person or organization
Riley, Jason, 58, 63
Rives, Richard, 86, 99
Roberts, Oral, 298
Roberts, Roscoe, 270
Robertson, Pat, 298
Robinson, Jackie, 355, 356
Robinson, Vaughn Hill, 232
Rockefeller, Nelson, 329, 416
Roe v. *Wade*, 457
Roosevelt, Franklin Delano, 30, 48, 71,
    274, 389
Rose, Alfred, 405
Rose, Frank, 110, 111–12, 114, 131, 140,
    145, 148, 150
Rosenfeld, H., 102
Ross, Burt, 198
Ross, Nellie Taylor, 273
Roton, Ralph R., 234, 258
Rovere, Richard, 209, 396
Rowe, Gary, 140, 141, 258
Rowe, James, 96–97
Rowley, James, 440, 444
Royster, Vermont, 135, 137–38
Russell, Richard, 87, 211
Rustin, Bayard, 234

Salinger, Pierre, 128, 133
Salisbury, Harrison, 114–15, 229
Sanders, Colonel, 354
Sanders, Wynnie ("Mom"), 53
Scammon, Richard, 369, 377–78
Schanno, Joseph, 452
school desegregation: Bickel's article
    about, 380–81; and election of 1966,
    288–89; and election of 1968, 349,
    350; and election of 1970, 383, 384;
    and election of 1972, 396–97; and
    "freedom of choice" plan, 350, 363;
    GW changes views about, 417; GW
    urges parents to ignore orders about,
    383, 384; GW's strategy about, 82–84,
    161, 163; in Kentucky, 355; and liber-
    alism, 397; and National Guard, 355;
    Nixon's views about, 350, 363–64,

371–72, 380–81, 396–97, 409, 423; in
    north, 349; polls about, 375; and vio-
    lence, 166–67. *See also Brown* v.
    Board of Education; busing; *specific
    town/city*
School District of Abington Township v.
    Schempp, 162
school prayer, 162, 207, 424, 460
schools: for retarded, 321–22. *See also
    Brown* v. *Board of Education*; school
    desegregation
Schrag, Peter, 377
Schwarz, Fred, 295, 298
Scottsboro trials, 267
Secret Service, 440, 441, 444
segregation, 73, 226. *See also* civil rights
    activists; school desegregation; Uni-
    versity of Alabama integration;
    specific court decision or legislation
Segrest, Broward, 226, 370, 401, 405,
    406, 408, 409, 411
self-insurance system (Alabama), 268
Selma, Alabama: as an American trag-
    edy, 254; civil rights activists in, 240–
    241, 245, 250–51, 304; as civil rights
    rallying cry, 254–55; and election of
    1966, 285, 287; growth of, 240; as
    mockery of GW's claims, 262; reac-
    tion to violence in, 261; and "The
    Story of Selma" (film), 260; White
    Citizens' Council in, 240
The Selma to Montgomery March
    (film), 260–61
Selma-to-Montgomery march (1965),
    246–50, 255–61, 287, 289. *See also*
    Pettus Bridge confrontation
Senate Commerce Committee, GW ap-
    pears before, 157–60
separate but equal, 40, 73, 137, 138,
    144–45
Sessions, William, 401, 408, 411
sexual culture, 259–61
Shearer, Robert, 307–8, 311
Sheats, Charles, 48
Shelton, Robert (Bobby): on Asa Carter,
    107; and election of 1958, 94, 95; and
    election of 1966, 281; and election of
    1968, 342; as Klansman, 94, 139, 234,
    281; salary for, 300; and Selma-to-
    Montgomery march, 259; and Univer-
    sity of Alabama integration, 140–41.
    See also Ku Klux Klan

Sherrill, Robert, 196, 304
Shores, Arthur, 236
Shorter, John, 33
Shroder, R. I., 444
Shuttlesworth, Fred, 107, 116, 124, 128, 158, 159, 165
"Silent Majority," 375–80, 465
Silverman, David, 402
Simmons, William, 295, 307
Sirhan, Sirhan, 434
Sitton, Claude, 141, 148, 234
Sixteenth Amendment, 203
Sixteenth Street Baptist Church bombing, 275–76
Smith, Anita, 318, 319
Smith College, 198
Smith, Dick, 335, 367–68, 370
Smith, Ellison (Cotton Ed), 69
Smith, Farley, 201
Smith, Gladys (aunt), 19
Smith, Kate (grandmother), 18
Smith, Moreland, 235
Smith, Mozelle. *See* Wallace, Mozelle Smith
Smith, Obediah Howard (grandfather), 18
Smith, Starr, 96, 96*n*
Smith, Wilford Thomas (uncle), 19
Smitherman, Joseph, 241
Snider, Charles, 426, 427, 431, 448, 455, 456
Snively, Cornelia. *See* Wallace, Cornelia Snively (wife)
social class, 78. *See also* working class
social disorder, 348–49
Social Issues, 378, 396, 418
Solomon, James R. (Jim Bob), 392
Sorensen, Ted, 151
South Carolina Broadcasters Association, 161
South Union State Junior College, 268–69
Southern Christian Leadership Conference (SCLC), 117, 240–42, 303
Southern Conference Educational Fund, 158
Southern Conference for Human Welfare, 230–31
"Southern Manifesto," 86
Southern politicians: image of, 69–70

Southern Strategy: of Goldwater, 326–327; of GW, 338–43; of Nixon, 326–331, 332–33, 347, 383, 409–10
"Southern Woman," 322
Soviet Union, last days of, 467–68
Sparkman, John, 46, 71, 86, 89, 118, 261–62, 264–65
Sparks, Chauncey, 31, 50, 51, 68, 69, 79
Sparrow, Hugh, 291
speaking tour: college, 195–99, 200; and election of 1972, 399–400; in South in 1965, 160–62
Speigle, Ross, 437
Spivak, Lawrence E., 135, 339
"Stand Up for America: The Story of George C. Wallace" (pamphlet), 297
Stans, Maurice, 332
states' rights, 84, 86, 335, 392. *See also* University of Alabama integration
statewide militia, formation of a, 113
Steineker, Catherine, 80, 308, 317, 318
Stephens, Elton, 32
Stevenson, Adlai, 86, 89
Stoner, J. B., 164–65
Story, Ellis, 84
"The Story of Selma" (film), 260
Strachan, Gordon, 433
Strickland, Ed, 233, 235
Stroud, Kandy, 413
Strout, Richard, 367
Student Nonviolent Coordinating Committee (SNCC), 227, 240–41, 245
Students for a Democratic Society, 366
succession provision, 263, 264, 265–72, 292, 456
Supreme Court: Fields calls for execution of members of, 165; GW's views about, 162, 313, 339, 367; mob rule decisions of, 163; NAACP appeals to, 93; Nixon's appointments to, 397–98; Thurmond's views of, 328. *See also specific decision*
Sussex, James, 131
Swaggart, Jimmy, 298
Symer, Sid, 125
Synon, John, 295

Taft, Robert, 69
Talmadge, Eugene, 69, 165
tax revolt, 427–28

taxes: and GW.views as freshman legislator, 76, 77
Taylor, James, 437, 463
Taylor, Lisa. *See* Wallace, Lisa Taylor
(wife)
televangelism, 298–99, 459–60
television, 248, 257, 332–33, 345–47,
376–77. *See also specific reporter or
program*
Tennessee Valley Authority, JFK tour
of, 128–29
terHorst, Gerald, 442–43
theory of proportionality, 255
third-party effort: and election of 1968,
328, 339, 343, 369; and election of
1972, 381, 396, 407–8, 410, 411, 412,
414, 433, 446, 447, 448, 449, 450; GW
renounces, 411, 412, 413, 414; and
IRS investigation, 410, 411, 412, 413,
414
Thomas, Rex, 84, 146
Thompson, Hunter, 346
Thornton, Ray, 454
Thrower, Randolph, 400
Thurmond, J. Strom, 86, 87, 156, 328–
329, 330, 332, 336, 392
Time magazine, 343, 424
Timmerman, George Bell, 89
Timmons, Bill, 454
Today (television), 258
Todd, A. W. (Tod), 285
Todd, Jesse, 342
Tower, John, 330
Trammell, Seymore: and bypassing attorney general's office, 232; and civil
rights legislation, 96*n*; as district attorney, 97, 98; and election of 1952,
98; and election of 1958, 98; and
election of 1962, 98, 106; and election of 1966, 277; and election of
1968, 300, 307, 308, 311–12, 316, 336,
338, 342, 352, 353, 354, 356, 357,
358, 360, 361, 364–65, 369; and election of 1970, 391, 407; on Gerald
Wallace, 405, 408; and the GW-
Johnson meeting, 253, 254; GW's
clash with, 407; and Hunt money,
369–70; indictment/conviction of,
411–12; and IRS investigation, 407–8,
411, 413; as lawyer, 370; loans
money to GW campaign, 311–12;
and Lurleen Wallace's gubernatorial

candidacy, 277; on NAACP, 123; per-
sonal/professional background of,
97–98; reputation of, 98; RFK's views
of, 123; and school integration, 167;
and succession provision, 268–69;
and University of Alabama integration, 114, 122, 123, 146, 148; and voting rights investigation, 101, 102
Treleaven, Harry, 333, 363
tuberculosis hospitals, 77
Turner, Albert, 241, 243, 245, 246
Turnipseed, Tom: and election of 1968,
301, 310, 342, 356, 365; and election
of 1970, 392, 393–94; and election
of 1972, 433, 448; and IRS investigation,
408–9; mentioned, 453; and race-
baiting, 392; resignation of, 417; style
of, 362
Tuscaloosa, Alabama, 162
Tuskegee, Alabama, 162, 167
Tuskegee Institute: GW as trustee for,
76, 236
Twentieth Century Reformation, 295,
296

ultra-right: and election of 1968, 295,
296, 356, 366. *See also specific person
or organization*
Un-American Activities Committee, U.S.
House, 231
United Daughters of the Confederacy,
43
United Klans of America, 94, 139–40,
234
University of Alabama: appropriations
for, 382; and election of 1970, 386–
387; football at, 45, 46, 111; GW as
student at, 45–51; GW's speeches at,
386; as training ground for aspiring
politicians, 46; Wallace attends,
41–42
University of Alabama integration: and
Autherine Lucy case, 83–84, 93, 107,
111, 130; and communism, 130; and
corporate task force, 129–30; and
federal government, 110, 111–14,
117–23, 139, 141; filming of, 143–46,
151; and GW injunction against appearing on campus, 138–39, 145; GW
strategy concerning, 139; and GW's
Meet the Press interview, 137; GW's
stand at door of, 142–51; Hood and

University of Alabama integration (*cont*)
Malone applications to, 130, 131–32,
138, 141, 147, 149–50, 151, 238; and
KKK, 139–41; leaks about, 142; Lingo's
investigation of applications to, 131–
132; and National Guard, 113, 147, 150,
154; reaction to, 154–55; and RFK-
Wallace talks, 118–23; trustees of, 112–
113, 130, 145; and violence, 113–14, 143,
146; Wallace strategy in, 112–14
University of Alabama Medical School,
460
University of Mississippi integration,
110–11, 120, 123, 129, 134, 141, 147,
235, 288
university system, in California, 313
urban race riots, 301–7, 331, 349
urbanization, 25, 70

Valenti, Jack, 253
Valeriani, Richard, 242–43, 244, 249,
258
Vance, Robert, 385–86
Vardaman, James K., 69
Ventress, Mary Jo, 80–81, 274, 309, 310
vice presidency, 330
Vickers, John, 321
victimization, 255, 398
Vidal, Gore, 453
Vietnam: and breakdown in American
society, 372; Carmichael's views
about, 306; and election of 1968,
325–26, 327, 345, 347, 351, 357–60,
362; and election of 1970, 386;
and election of 1972, 423, 432, 445,
447; FBI activities concerning, 438–
439; Humphrey's views about, 345,
351; and Hunt forgeries, 442;
Nixon's views about, 326, 327, 345,
351; polls about, 326; and "Tet" offensive, 326
Viguerie, Richard, 455–56
violence: in Barbour County, Alabama,
36–37, 44; and election of 1968, 348–
349; Kennedys as responsible for,
163; and school integration, 166–67;
and Selma-to-Montgomery march,
247, 248–49; and University of Alabama integration, 146. *See also* Ku
Klux Klan; *specific city or event*
Vivian, C. T., 241–42, 245
Voorhis, Jerry, 73

voter registration, 222–23, 285, 287
voting, 36–37, 40. *See also* voter registration; voting rights; *specific legislation, town, or county*
voting rights: and civil rights activists,
241–42; Civil Rights Commission investigation of, 97, 98–104
Voting Rights Act (1965), 250, 262, 327

Walker, Anne Kendrick, 32–33, 34–35,
42
The Wall Street Journal, 283. *See also
specific reporter*
Wallace, Bobbi Jo (daughter), 55, 56,
58, 65, 80, 309, 368
Wallace, Cornelia Snively (wife): and
blame for assassination, 452; and
Bremer's stalking/assassination of
GW, 434, 435, 437; divorce of, 459;
early career/first marriage of, 415–
416; and GW's cooperation with
Nixon, 448, 449; and GW's political
future after assassination, 446, 451;
influence on GW of, 416–17, 427;
marital relations of, 452, 458–59;
mentioned, 456; and Michigan primary, 431; and Nixon's hospital visit
to GW, 445–46; Wallace marriage of,
416–17; youth of, 415–16
Wallace, Edwin (uncle), 23
Wallace family: finances of, 32, 41, 79,
80; and political life, 104–5; relationships in, 41–42
Wallace, George C.: abuse of power
by, 227–35; as an athlete, 26–29, 46;
birth of, 21; as born-again Christian,
459–60; childhood/youth of, 23, 25–
28, 459; college years of, 41–42; contradictory behavior of, 236–40; as
demagogue, 109, 344–47, 367; drinking of, 104; early jobs of, 32; as family man/father, 42, 79–80, 104–5, 321,
323, 464; as "humane segregationist,"
48; image of, 417; legacy of, 465–68;
as loser, 50, 96, 468; and Lurleen's
illness/death, 308–10, 317–20; medical condition of, 451; mental health
of, 66–67, 106, 142–43, 353, 448, 450,
451–52; northern perceptions of, 156;
official inauguration biography of,
87; as "paternalistic segregationist,"
48, 76; physical appearance of, 415;

political ambitions of, 56–57, 62, 78, 262, 265, 293, 370, 455, 458; public opinion about, 262; as risk taker, 78; seeks forgiveness, 460–62; self-deception of, 344; as speech giver, 156; spinal meningitis of, 53, 54; and women, 29, 49, 51, 104, 352–54, 416, 458–59

Wallace, George C.—style of: and civil rights topics, 160–61; as demagogue, 345–47; and election of 1946, 74–75; and election of 1962, 424, 425; and election of 1968, 313–15, 345–47, 362–63; and Folsom governorship, 76; and Folsom as mentor, 81–82; and GW's intellectual abilities, 381–388; and GW's political ambitions, 381–88; as legislative page, 31; and *Meet the Press* interview, 135, 136; moderation of, 417; with press, 340–341; and religion, 424; and segregation, 226; and support for GW, 226; and White Citizens' Council speeches, 161

Wallace, George C., Jr. (son): birth of, 79; childhood/youth of, 80, 105; and election of 1986, 463; and Lurleen's gubernatorial candidacy, 281; and Lurleen's illness/death, 309, 319, 320, 321; and University of Alabama integration, 146

Wallace, George Corley (father), 17, 19–24, 25, 26, 29–30, 41

Wallace, George Oscar (grandfather), 19–20, 21, 26, 30, 41

Wallace, Gerald (brother): birth of, 21; childhood/youth of, 28, 41; education of, 404; and election of 1968, 311, 312, 364–65, 370; and election of 1970, 392; and election of 1972, 417; and election of 1976, 456–57; and election of 1986, 463; on family matters, 21, 22, 23, 28; financial affairs of, 364–65, 370, 404; and GW-Cornelia Snively marriage, 416, 417, 458; GW's relationship with, 405; health of, 76–77, 404; and IRS investigation, 390–91, 400–409, 411–14; as lawyer, 79, 104, 404; personality of, 404; Trammell's views about, 405, 408; Turnipseed's differences with, 417

Wallace, Jack (brother), 21, 29, 31, 41, 277, 365, 404

Wallace, Janie Lee (daughter), 105, 144, 146, 277, 281, 309, 368

Wallace, Lisa Taylor (wife), 416, 462–63

Wallace, Lurleen Burns (wife): black votes for, 292; cancer of, 277–79, 308–10, 312; courtship/marriage of, 52, 53–54; death of, 317–20; and election of 1946, 74; and election of 1968, 312, 313; friends of, 80–81; funeral of, 320–21; gubernatorial race of, 272–74, 277, 279, 280–81, 290–92; GW meets, 51, 52; inauguration of, 294–95; jobs of, 81; marital relations of, 59, 79–80, 104–5, 265, 278, 309, 312, 319; mentioned, 103; as mother, 55; personality of, 56; reactions to political life by, 79–80, 104–5; Sanders as mother to, 53; as "Southern Woman," 322; and University of Alabama integration, 146; and working class, 274; and World War II, 55–57, 58, 59, 65; youth of, 52–53

Wallace, Marianne (sister), 21, 41, 53, 80, 404

Wallace, Mary Elizabeth McEachern (grandmother), 20, 25

Wallace, Mozelle Smith (mother): childhood of, 18–19; community activities of, 21–22; courtship/marriage of, 17, 20, 21; family background of, 18–19; finances of, 41, 404; and GW's marriage, 53; GW's views of, 25–26; jobs of, 41; marital relations of, 22; as mother, 21, 25–26, 28, 42; music of, 17, 19, 22

Wallace, Nora Mae Wyatt (step-grandmother), 26, 145

Wallace, Peggy Sue (daughter): birth of, 79; childhood/youth of, 105; and GW as father, 42; GW's relationship with, 321; and Lurleen's gubernatorial candidacy, 281; and Lurleen's illness/death, 309, 319, 320, 321; mentioned, 435; and University of Alabama integration, 146

The Wallace Story (TV film), 338

Wallace-Cater Act (1951), 77–78

Warner, James, 166–67

Warren, Earl, 335

Washington Post, 424–25. *See also specific reporter*
Watergate, 444–45, 452, 453–54
Watson, Billy, 106
Wattenberg, Ben, 369, 377–78
Watts riot (Los Angeles, California), 301–2, 305
Wayne, John, 335, 389–90
Weaver, Macon, 148
Weeks, Barney, 285–86
Welch, Ja-Neen, 352–54
Welch, Joseph, 295
Welch, Robert, 296, 343
welfare system, 372–74, 378, 398–99, 426
Wendland, Michael, 434
West, C. L. (Bill), 342–43
white backlash, 349, 418, 466
White, Byron, 229–30
White Citizens' Council: in Barbour County, 85; and *Brown* decision, 82–83; California ties of, 308; centers of, 240; and election of 1958, 95; and election of 1964, 343; and election of 1968, 308, 335, 343, 356; and Elliott-GW relationship, 275; and Folsom, 87; GW's speeches to, 161; and Lewises, 261; membership of, 84; and Montgomery bus boycott, 99; and school integration, 162; and University of Alabama integration, 154
white folks' myths, 42–43
white supremacy: and Alabama Democratic Party, 89–90; in Barbour County, Alabama, 36–37; and Birmingham civil rights demonstrations, 115; and election of 1958, 92, 95; GW's support of, 235; and Jeffersonian Democrats, 39; King's speech about, 257; triumph of, 85–86; and U.S. House hearings about civil rights legislation, 89–90; and whites' historical memory, 35
White, Theodore H., 18, 340–41, 384, 415, 417
white unity, 227–35

Wicker, Tom, 236, 340
Wilkins, Collie Leroy, 272
Wilkins, Roy, 303
Williams, Aubrey, 158–59, 160
Williams, Harn, Jr., 285
Williams, Hosea, 246, 247–48, 256
Williams, J. Sterling, 78
Williams, John Bell, 414
Williams, T. Harry, 69
Williams v. *Wallace*, 247*n*
Wills, Chill, 314–15
Wills, Garry, 302, 341, 379, 413–14
Wilmer Hall (orphanage), 19
Wilson, Richard, 381
Wilson, Will, 400–401, 408, 411, 413, 414
Winston County, Alabama, 48
wiretapping, 229–30, 312
Wisconsin, 419–22, 427–29, 431
Women for Constitutional Government, 120
Women for Wallace, 393
Wood, Robert, 375–76
Woodley conference, 295–96
Woods, Charles, 284–85
Woods, Evelyn, 151
Woodward, Robert, 452
Wooten, Jim, 236–37
working class, 274, 313–16, 375–76, 377, 379
World War II: and GW's discharged from military, 66; and GW's health, 53, 54, 66–67; GW's military activities during, 53, 54–65; and GW's refusal to take part in training, 65–66; and ROTC, 50–51

Yale University, LeMay speech at, 360–61
Yancey, William Lowndes, 144
Young, Andrew, 246

Zarvos, Nick, 437
Zellner, Robert, 227–28, 291
Ziegler, Ron, 425
Zind, Richard, 55, 57, 61, 62, 63, 65